# Sculptures from Punjab

Iconography and Style

# Sculptures from Punjab

## Iconography and Style

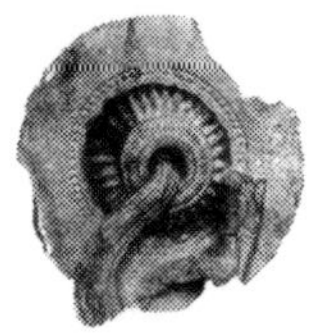

By

Devendra Handa

Aryan Books International

New Delhi

SCULPTURES FROM PUNJAB
Iconography and Style

ISBN: 978-81-7305-414-3



Published in **2011** by
**ARYAN BOOKS INTERNATIONAL**
Pooja Apartments, 4B, Ansari Road, Darya Ganj, New Delhi-110 002 (India)
Tel.: 23287589, 23255799; Fax: 91-11-23270385
E-mail: aryanbooks@gmail.com
**www.aryanbooks.co.in**

Printed in India at Mudrak, Delhi-110091

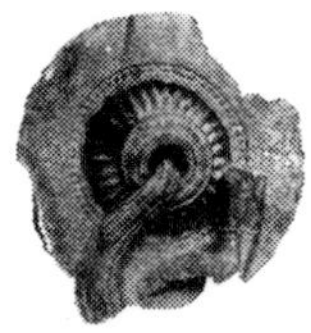

Dedicated to

**Padma Bhushan Dr. B.N. Goswamy**
(Professor Emeritus of Art History, Panjab University, Chandigarh)

whose passion for study and interpretation of miniature paintings has won world acclaim,
whose expositions carry the conviction of logic and appeal,
who has perfected the art of presentation
and
made immense contribution to knowledge

# Preface

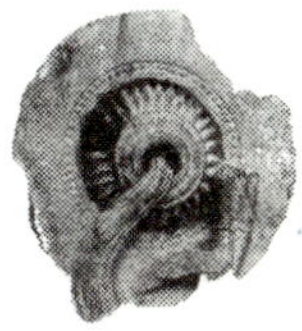

Punjab in this work has been used for the present-day state of Punjab in India which is only a fraction of what it was before the partition of the country in 1947. Its strategic geographical location made it serve as India's window towards the west and also as the portal for many an alien invasion in ancient and medieval times. As such, Punjab has been a state progressive in its outlook to receive foreign occupants, their ideas and influences on the one hand and to bear the brunt of all inroads and suffer the devastating blows of the iconoclastic hordes in the medieval period in particular on the other. Islamic fundamentalism resulted in desecrating, damaging and wiping out standing temples and the establishment of Islamic rule and continuing iconoclasm wrought further blows erasing all surviving fanes in the region. There is not even a single old temple left in the state now and sculptures have been a great rarity. Urbanization and flourishing agricultural activities in the post-partition days have also been instrumental in wiping out large number of ancient sites. Punjab has almost been a terra incognita with regard to sculptural art before the spectacular discovery of Kushāṇa railing pillars at Sanghol in 1982. Stray discoveries of sculptures made by some officials of the State Department of Archaeology and Museums or reported by some enlightened citizens too have remained generally confined to departmental archives, brochures or newspapers. Sculptural and architectural remains are therefore sill a great rarity in the state and the standing joke that 'the culture of Punjab is agriculture' continues to amuse most of the people.

There is an old Sanskrit saying that '*Nirasta-pādape deśe eraṇḍo'pi drumāyate*', i.e., even a castor-oil plant (a small plant with a scanty number of leaves) is regarded as a tree in a tree-less region. So, all sculptural and architectural relics, irrespective of their aesthetic and iconographic merit, are regarded as significant here. Sustained interest in the archaeological heritage of Punjab for the last more than four decades has enabled me to pick up the shreds and put them together to obtain a coherent picture. The complete picture, however, is still a desired dream but we have some good flashes of light here and there which enlighten our path. I have availed of all the discoveries made till now by others and by my own self. During this long period of the last forty-five years some sculptures have even been stolen and lost.

Many officials and individuals who helped me in my explorations and endeavors have shifted to other ranks and places and some have even left this world. There are, however, still many names which are quite fresh in my memory owing my gratitude for the help and succor they offered. The Directors and officials of the State Department of Archaeology and Museums have always been kind and helpful. The respective officials and care-takers of the site museums at Dholbaha, Hoshiarpur, Sanghol and Ropar provided all possible facilities and help. My old friend Late Sd. Piara Singh, who served the department in various capacities during his career, used to bring almost everything to my notice during our long association and also provided the photographs of numerous objects some of which have been utilized here. Sd. Kuldip Singh, Gurdev Singh, and of course all their colleagues, rendered help from time to time. Shri G.B. Sharma too has been kind enough to discuss certain things and furnish bits of information. The Director-General, National Museum, New Delhi kindly supplied the photographs of Sanghol pillars and Dr. S.K. Pathak of the same museum was quite helpful in obtaining them in time. Director, Government Museum & Art Gallery, Chandigarh provided the scans of some Sanghol pillars now displayed in the Museum. Mr. Surinder Dhami helped me not only in refining some of the scans but also preparing scans from some of my very old negatives. Mrs. Poonam Khanna and the library staff too provided information and necessary help. Dr. Subhash Parihar of Faridkot, a well-known scholar of Mughal architecture, obliged me not only by sending some of his rare reference books but also some photographs and information about the location of certain villages and sites. My Late friend Dr. Suraj Bhan had put his album of the art remains of the region at my disposal. Prof. Ashvini Agrawal has ever been available to me for scholarly discussions, library help and has also provided me the photograph of the rare and unpublished terracotta figure of Kārttikeya from Sanghol. We have been visiting various sites together during our long association. Dr. Lalman too has accompanied us on most of the occasions and also provided bits of information and help. I don't find adequate words to appreciate the help of Prof. Manmohan Kumar (MD University, Rohtak) who put the whole collection of his photographs of sculptures from the region at my disposal. My friend Mrs. Anne Shankar helped me by photographing the sculptural and other remains in the Hoshiarpur museum and state government holdings. My old class-fellow Shri Om Prakash Sud provided information and sent photographs of sculptures in the Panjpipla Śivālā at Bahdurpur, Hoshiarpur. Prof. S.P. Shukla of Kurukshetra allowed me to utilize not only the sketches of some Sanghol sculptures from his published articles but also prepared many others at my request. Shri Rameshwar Dass of Sunam brought to my notice all what was discovered from Sunam from time to time and also accompanied me to various sites and provided photographs of stone and metal sculptures and other remains from the site. Some illustrations have been copied from the publications of the Archaeological Survey of India, the National Museum, state brochures and others and I express my thankfulness to all the concerned authorities.

The sources of the various photographs that have been used are given below:

| | |
|---|---|
| ASI, New Delhi/IAR | 1-2, 8, 52 |
| Ashvini Agrawal | 169 |
| Dept. of AIHCA, PU, Chandigarh | 3, 13, 15-16, 18, 37, 50, 68, 73-74, 92, 120, 150 |
| Dept. of Arch. & Mus., Pb. | 4, 6, 54, 98, 218, 334 |
| D.R. Gehlot | 294, 297 |
| G.B. Sharma & M. Kumar | 70, 130, 192 |
| Govt. Museum, Chandigarh | 227-28, 230, 236, 249, 254, 259 |

| | |
|---|---|
| Manmohan Kumar | 19, 21, 26, 60, 67, 75, 77, 86, 94-95, 108-09, 114, 121, 139-40, 155, 160, 168, 171, 174, 195, 197, 200-201, 203, 215, 269, 275, 277, 291-92, 294-95 |
| National Museum, New Delhi | 190-91, 193, 221, 225-26, 229, 232-35, 237-41, 243-48, 251, 253, 255-58, 260-61 |
| Piara Singh | 62, 65, 93, 96, 103-05, 125-29, 137-38, 162-64, 270, 282, 288, 298-300, 335-38 |
| Rameshwar Dass | 39-41, 48, 53, 84-85, 91, 107, 122, 142, 146-48, 157-58, 184-86, 307-32 |
| Subhash Parihar | 76, 281 |

I am thankful to the Indian Council of Historical Research, New Delhi for giving me Senior Academic Fellowship which enabled me to prepare the draft of this work. The ICHR, however, is in no way responsible for the opinions expressed in this book.

I am grateful to Dr. N.P. Joshi and Shri R.C. Agrawala, the well-known authorities on art and iconography, for their encouragements. Prof. B.N. Goswamy has been very gracious to accept the dedication of this book as a token of my respect and appreciation of his erudition, interpretations, expositions and the art of presentation which he has taken to newer heights. He is a source of inspiration to others.

To thank my wife Avinash who has shouldered all domestic duties to leave me free for my academic pursuits and my son Tushar Handa for the technical help on the computer rendered from time to time will be mere formality.

The word Punjab has been spelled with a variant of Panjab also. The latter spellings were generally used before the partition and the former form has been adopted by the state government now. The university at Chandigarh, however, is following the spellings of the pre-partition days. As such, both Punjab and Panjab have been used in this work. The names of numerous towns and cities are also written with alternatives, e.g. Majhoor and Majhur, Nalas and Nolas, Roopnagar and Rupnagar, Samooran and Samuran, etc. The computer effect may also be seen in some of the spellings. Though care has been taken to present the text as accurately as possible yet some errors of omission and commission may have crept in for which I seek the forgiveness of the readers. Let me hope that together with 'Sculptures From Haryana: Iconography and Style' published earlier in 2006 this work will give a fair idea of the sculptural art of the region to the readers.

# 1401, PUSHPAC Complex,
Sector 49 B, Chandigarh – 160 047

**Devendra Handa**

# Contents

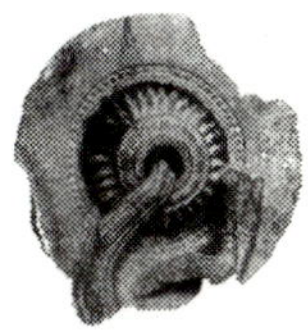

# Transliteration Table

| | | | | |
|---|---|---|---|---|
| अ A, a | आ Ā, ā | इ I, i | ई Ī, ī | उ U, u |
| ऊ Ū, ū | ऋ Ṛi, ṛi | ऌ Ḷ, ḷ | ए E, e | ऐ Ai, ai |
| ओ O, o | औ Au, au | अँ Aṃ, aṃ | अः Aḥ, aḥ | |
| क् K, k | ख् Kh, kh | ग् G, g | घ् Gh, gh | ङ् Ṅ, ṅ |
| च् Ch, ch | छ् Chh, chh | ज् J, j | झ् Jh, jh | ञ् Ñ, ñ |
| ट् Ṭ, ṭ | ठ् Ṭh, ṭh | ड् Ḍ, ḍ | ढ् Ḍh, ḍh | ण् Ṇ, ṇ |
| त् T, t | थ् Th, th | द् D, d | ध् Dh, dh | न् N, n |
| प् P, p | फ् Ph, ph | ब् B, b | भ् Bh, bh | म् M, m |
| य् Y, y | र् R, r | ल् L, l | व् V, v | श् Ś, ś |
| ष् Sh, sh | स् S, s | ह् H, h | क्ष् Ksh, ksh | त्र् Tr, tr |
| ज्ञ् Jñ, jñ | | | | |

Jihvāmūlīya X    Upadhamānīya ≍    Avagraha

Common words and modern names are usually written without diacriticals.
In the original titles and quotations, Ṛ/ṛ, C/c, Ṣ/ṣ have also been used for ऋ, च्, ष्, etc.

# Abbreviations

| | |
|---|---|
| *AI* | *Ancient India*, Bulletin of the Archaeological Survey of India |
| AIHCA | Department of Ancient Indian History, Culture and Archaeology |
| *Ait. Br.* | *Aitareya Brāhmaṇa* |
| *ARASI* | *Annual Report, Archaeological Survey of India* |
| *AV* | Atharvaveda |
| BCE | Before Common/Current Era |
| *Bhāg. P.* | Bhāgavata Purāṇa |
| *BMCAI* | *Coins of Ancient India (in the British Museum)* by John Allan |
| BORI | Bhandarkar Oriental Research Institute |
| *c.* | *circa* |
| *CAGI* | Cunningham's *Geography of Ancient India* |
| *CASR* | Cunningham's *Archaeological Survey Report* |
| CE | Common/Current Era |
| Ch/ch. | Chapter/s |
| *CII* | *Corpus Inscriptionum Indicarum* |
| *DHI* | *Development of Hindu Iconography* by J.N. Banerjea |
| *EHI* | *Elements of Hindu Iconography* by T.A.G. Rao |
| *EI* | *Epigraphia Indica* |
| GOS | Gaekwad Oriental Series |
| *HV* | *Harivaṃśa Purāṇa* |
| *IAR* | *Indian Archaeology – A Review* |
| *IGI* | *Imperial Gazetteer of India* |
| *JAA* | *Jaina Art and Architecture*, edited by A. Ghosh |
| *JNSI* | *Journal of the Numismatic Society of India* |
| *JOI* | *Journal of the Oriental Institute*, Vadodara |
| *Mbh.* | *Mahābhārata* |
| *P.* | *Purāṇa* |

| | |
|---|---|
| *PDG* | *Panjab District Gazetteer* |
| *PURBA* | *Panjab University Research Bulletin (Arts)*, Chandigarh |
| *Rām.* | *Rāmāyaṇa* |
| *Rodgers' Report* | *Report of the Panjab Circle of the Archaeological Survey for 1888-89* by Charles Jas. Rodgers |
| *RTA* | *Rajasthan Through the Ages* (Gen. Ed. Dasharatha Sharma) |
| *RV* | *Ṛigveda* |
| *SAIS* | *Studies in Ancient Indian Seals* by K.K. Thaplyal |
| *Śat. Br.* | *Śatapatha Brāhmaṇa* |
| *Tait. Ār.* | *Taittirīya Āraṇyaka* |
| *Tait. Br.* | *Taittirīya Brāhmaṇa* |
| *VIJ* | *Vishveshvaranand Indological Journal*, Hoshiarpur |
| *VSMRS* | *Vaiṣṇavism, Śaivism and Minor Religious Systems* by R.G. Bhandarkar |
| vv. | verses |

# List of Illustrations

FIGURES

PLATES

243. Yaksharohī, Sanghol.
244. Same, closer view.
245. Prasādhikā, Sanghol.
246. Aśoka-dohada, Sanghol.
247. *Śālabhañjikā*, Sanghol.
248. *Śālabhañjikā*, Sanghol.
249. *Śālabhañjikā*, Chandigarh Museum.
250. *Śālabhañjikā*, Chandigarh Museum.
251. Upāsikā, Sanghol.
252. Another female devotee, Sanghol.
253. *Yakshī* holding lotus flowers, Sanghol.
254. *Yakshī* holding flowers, Chandigarh Museum.
255. *Yakshī* holding wine-jar and flute, Sanghol.
256. Languorous lady, Sanghol.
257. Damsel playing harmonica, Sanghol.
258. Śṛiṅgāra-rachanā, Sanghol.
259. Śṛiṅgāra-rachanā, Chandigarh Museum.
260. Devotee with flowers, Sanghol.
261. Devotee holding a garland, Sanghol.
262. Devotee holding a bunch of flowers, Sanghol.
263. Fly-whisker, Sanghol.
264. Śaka devotee, Karhali.
265. Architrave showing meditating male, female passing on a babe to another and a royal female being fanned by a maid, Sanghol.
266. Other side of the architrave showing elephant, horse and three human figures holding flower bunches, Sanghol.
267. Buddha in *dharmachakra-pravartana-mudrā*, Zahura.
268. Headless marble Buddha in *bhūmisparśa-mudrā*, Kharar.
269. Sarvatobhadra, Dholbaha.
270. Sarvatobhadra, Bhalur.
271. Neminātha from Khizrabad.
272. Seated Jina, Mard Khera.
273. Meditative Jina, Mard Khera.
274. Jina in *khaḍgāsana*, architectural piece, Mard Khera.
275. Broken Jina figure in *padmāsana*, Dholbaha.
276. Architectural piece showing a Jina, Dholbaha.
277. Fragmentary piece, Dholbaha.
278. Fragmentary *nāgara-kūṭa*, Kharar.
279. Fragmentary *nāgara-kūṭa*, Kharar.
280. Fragmentary *nāgara-kūṭa*, Sanghol.
281. Fragment of a Jina figure, Rupalon.
282. Meditative Jina figure, Majhur.
283. Jaina Tīrthaṅkara Śreyāṃsanātha, Sunam.
284. Pedestal of an image of Neminātha, Sunam.
285. Same, inscription on the pedestal.
286. Architectural piece of the wall of a Jaina temple, Sunam.
287. Fragment of the socle of a Jaina temple, Sunam.

# 1

# Introduction: Historical Backdrop and Sites

## INTRODUCTION

Punjab of the pre-partition days was a very large state, extending from Attock on the Indus in the northwest to Puh touching the border of Tibet and China in the northeast, and from Kilar on the Chenab just south of the border of Jammu and Kashmir in the north to Hodal, nearly 90 km south of Delhi, and about 50 km north of Mathura in the south (Fig.1). From the Indus to the Yamuna, it was a vast territory, bigger than many of the modern day countries, lying between the rivers Kubhā (Kabul) and Yamunā and watered by the seven rivers – Sarasvatī, Satluj (Śatadru), Beas (Vipāśā), Ravi (Irāvatī, Purushṇī), Chenab (Asiknī, Chandrabhāgā), Jhelum (Marudvṛidhā, Vitastā) and Sindh, i.e., Indus (Sindhu), corresponding to Sapta-Sindhu region of the Vedic times.[1] The spread of the so-called Indus or Harappan or Sarasvatī culture and the existence of numerous cities, many of which exist in the Punjab, Haryana, Rajasthan and Gujarat, indicate that it was well connected with other regions through a network of various trade and other routes. It was here that the Aryans were settled mostly and performed their sacrifices on the river banks. The term Sapta-Sindhu is comparable to the Hapta-hendu of the *Venidad* (I.73).[2] After the desiccation of the Sarasvatī, which was the river par excellence in the Ṛigvedic period, some time during the first half of the second millennium BCE, the region came to be designated as Pañcha-nada, literally meaning 'five rivers or waters', i.e., the country of the five rivers – Śatadru, Vipāśā, Irāvatī, Chandrabhāgā and Vitastā.[3] This land served as India's window towards the northwest. The names and designations of various characters and places mentioned in the *Mahābhārata* and the *Rāmāyaṇa* bear witness to this, for example, Gāndhārī, Gandhāra-nareśa, Śakuni, Mādrī, Kaikeyī, etc. The word Pañcha-nada remained in use till Vikrama Samvat 1890 (CE 1833), as we find its mention quite a few times in the Jaina Paṭṭāvalīs.[4] The modern term Punjab (*Pañja-āba* – 'five waters') is derived from the Sanskrit word Pañchāpa (*Pañcha+apaḥ* 'five waters'), which too has remained in use till recent times.[5]

The partition of the country in 1947 resulted in the division of Punjab between India and Pakistan. The international border which formed the boundary between Indian and Pakistani Punjab extended from about Phangota in district Pathankot on the Ravi, south of the border of

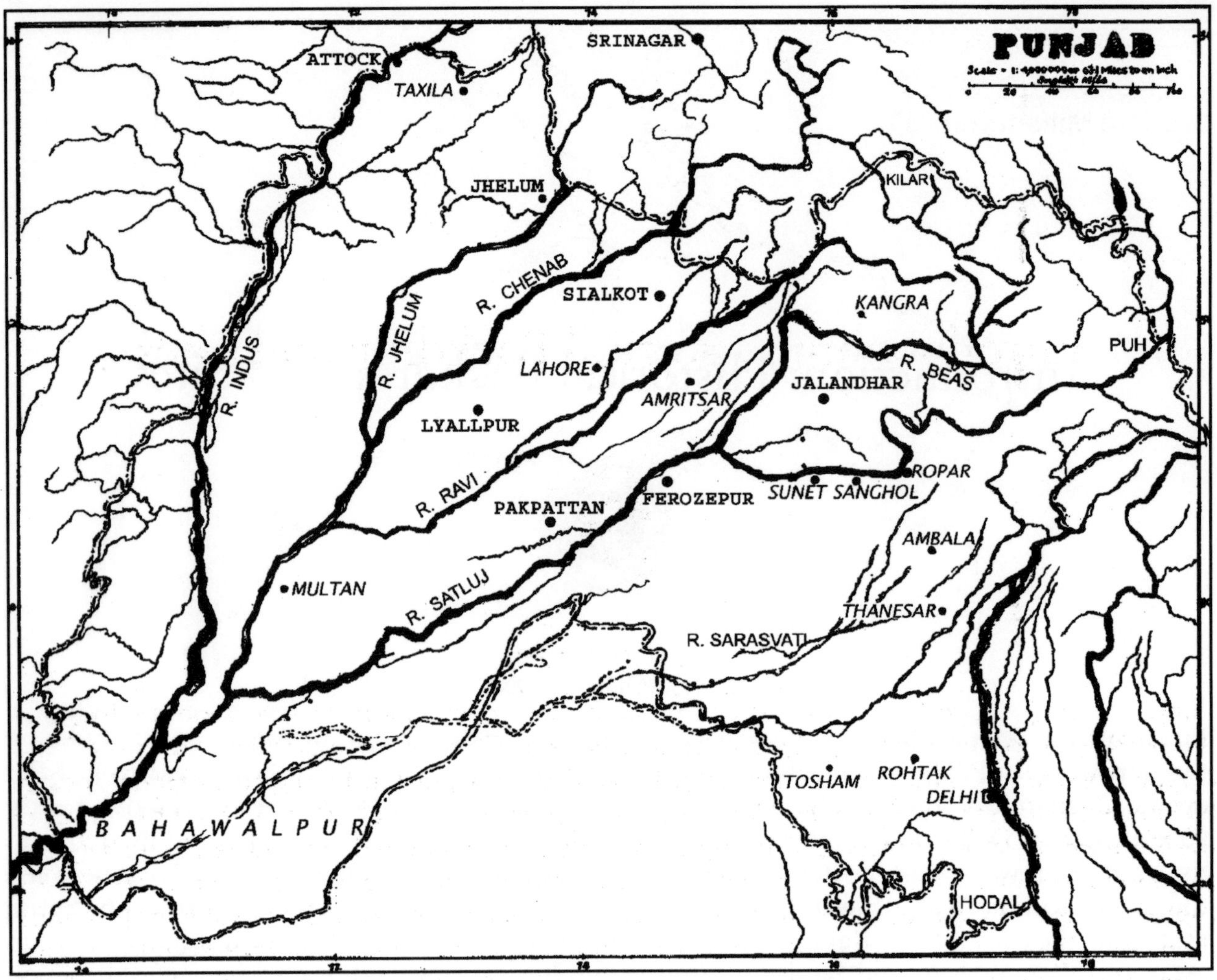


**Fig. 1.** Map of old Punjab before the partition.

Jammu to Dera Baba Nanak and then further southwest roughly along the southern side of the Ravi to Kakkar, nearly 15 km northwest of Attari, taking a southward turn to Hussainiwala on the southern bank of the Satluj near Ferozepur proceeding to Fazilka in the southwest along the Satluj from where it turned southwards to Ganganagar in Rajasthan. Thus, a larger part of the state went to the share of Pakistan. When India gained Independence, the collective Punjab hill states were integrated into a single, centrally-administered unit under the charge of a chief commissioner.

A name was given to this unit – Himachal Pradesh. In 1954, Bilaspur was added, and in 1966, the rest of what we now know as Himachal Pradesh was merged into 'The Mountain State'. The Indian Punjab was further divided and its southern portion, extending roughly south of the river Ghaggar from near Kalka to Sirsa and thence to Ganganagar, was carved out as the Haryana State on November 1, 1966. The hilly portion which roughly extends east of a line drawn from Paonta Sahib near the right or north bank of the Yamuna River to Pathankot on the southern bank of the Ravi forms part of Himachal Pradesh. In 1971, it was granted statehood. The present state of Punjab thus shares its border with Jammu and Kashmir on its north, Himachal on the northeast, Pakistan on the west, Rajasthan on the southwest and Haryana

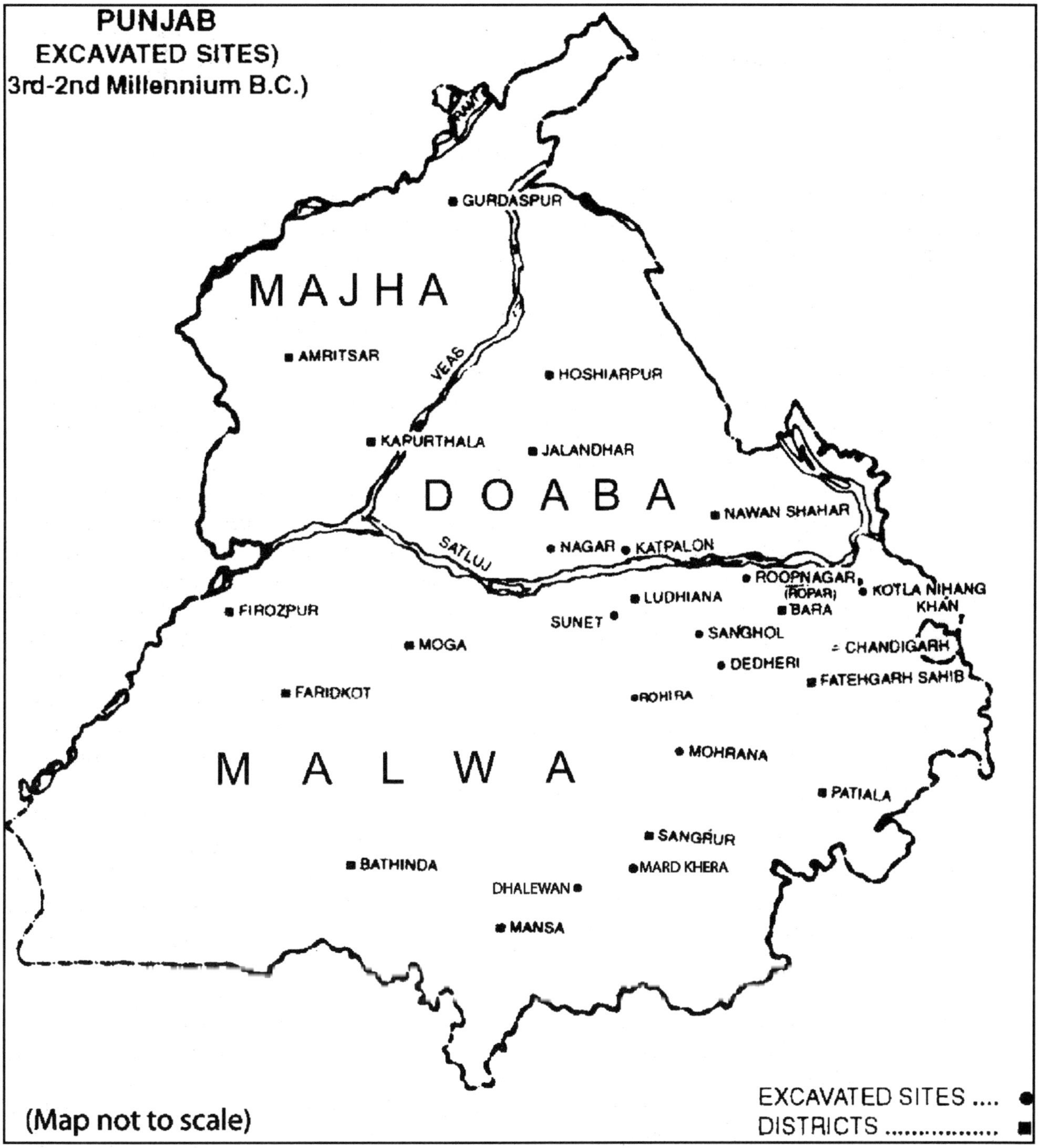


**Fig. 2.** Punjab: Topographical divisions and excavated sites.

on the south and southeast. It has twenty districts at present and covers an area of 50,362 square km, with a population of nearly twenty-five million people. Chandigarh, the Union Territory, is the capital of both Punjab and Haryana. Topographically, Punjab is divided into three regions by its rivers – the Majha (< Skt. *Madhya*, i.e., the middle portion as it was before the partition) north of the river Beas with Amritsar as its main city, the Doaba (< do+āba = two rivers) sandwiched between the rivers Beas and Satluj with Jalandhar as the main city, and the

Malwa (Mālavā), south of the Satluj River with Bathinda, Ludhiana and Patiala as the main cities. Some of the excavated sites throw light on the proto-historic and early historic cultures of the region (Fig. 2).

## HISTORICAL BACKGROUND

During the time of Buddha (sixth-fifth century BCE), there were sixteen major states (*soḷasa Mahājanapada*) and numerous other smaller or tribal states (*Janapadas*) of which Mālavas (Malloi of the Greek historians) and Kshudrakas (Oxydrakai) were located between the Jhelum and Ravi. Darius I of Persia invaded parts of northwest India in the sixth century BCE and made Indus one of his satrapies. He "hired mercenary troops from India, namely the Hydrakes (Oxydrakai = Kshudrakas)."[6] The Mālavas and the Kshudrakas had joined a military confederation which was known to Pāṇini (IV.2, 45) in *circa* 400 BCE. The *Mahābhārata* (Vana Parva, 52, 15), too, alludes to their association. There were other tribal states like the Śibis, Madras, Śālvas, Kekayas, Yaudheyas and others in the Punjab at that time. During 327-26 BCE, some of these tribes fought against Alexander who could penetrate into India up to the river Beas where his troops revolted and refused to advance any further. Chandragupta Maurya succeeded in subjugating various tribal states after Alexander and ultimately conquered Pāṭaliputra and thus held sway over a large part of the Indian sub-continent during 321-298 BCE. Seleucus, who succeeded to the eastern part of Alexander's vast empire, attacked India but was defeated by Chandragupta and ceded Khotan, Kashgar, Yarkand, etc. and also gave his daughter in marriage. This resulted in trade, traffic and political relationship between the two regimes. Throughout the ages, Punjab has remained a crucible of cultures as numerous people have been coming to this region invading it and also settling here often as we shall see in the sequel. An unending amalgamation and movement of communities and confluence of cultures resulted in a pragmatic, experimental and utilitarian outlook on life and a robust common-sense view which debilitated the root of all sorts of dogmas, conventions and conservatism.

Chandragupta was succeeded by his son Bindusāra, who posted his son prince Aśoka as the governor of Takshaśilā (Taxila) which probably exposed Aśoka to western ideas and arts. Aśoka became the emperor succeeding his father and subsequent to his war against Kaliṅga, he inclined towards Buddhism and spread the faith to distant lands. According to Buddhist texts, ten *stūpas* 'sepulchral mounds' were erected at different places following Buddha's *parinibbāna* 'Complete Emancipation': eight over the parts of the body-relics of Buddha, one over the urn in which the relics were collected and divided, and one over the charcoal collected from the funeral pyre at Kuśīnagara.[7] Aśoka is said to have collected relics from seven of these *śārīrika-stūpas.*[8] Later, some of these *stūpas* were renovated and railings & gateways adorned with beautiful sculptures were added to them. The Chinese pilgrim Xuan Zang has referred to Aśokan *stūpas* at Takshaśilā (Taxila), She-to-tu-lu (Śatadru) and elsewhere as we shall see subsequently. It is from Aśokan times that we start getting stone pillars surmounted by figures and sculptures. The typical Mauryan polish witnessed on Chunar sandstone pillars is also seen on stone sculptures. Terracotta hand-modelled figures belonging to this period have also been discovered from some excavated and explored sites. The early female figurines, generally designated as Mother Goddess, show punched and applied decorations. Their collar, necklace and girdle too are quite often appliqué, though we also see incised cross design in some cases.

The excavations at Ropar in Punjab yielded from the earliest historical level (Period III: *circa* 600-200 BCE) a polished ringstone betraying fine workmanship minutely carved with figures and motifs associated with the cult of the Goddess of Fertility (Pl. 1).[9] The frontal posture of the

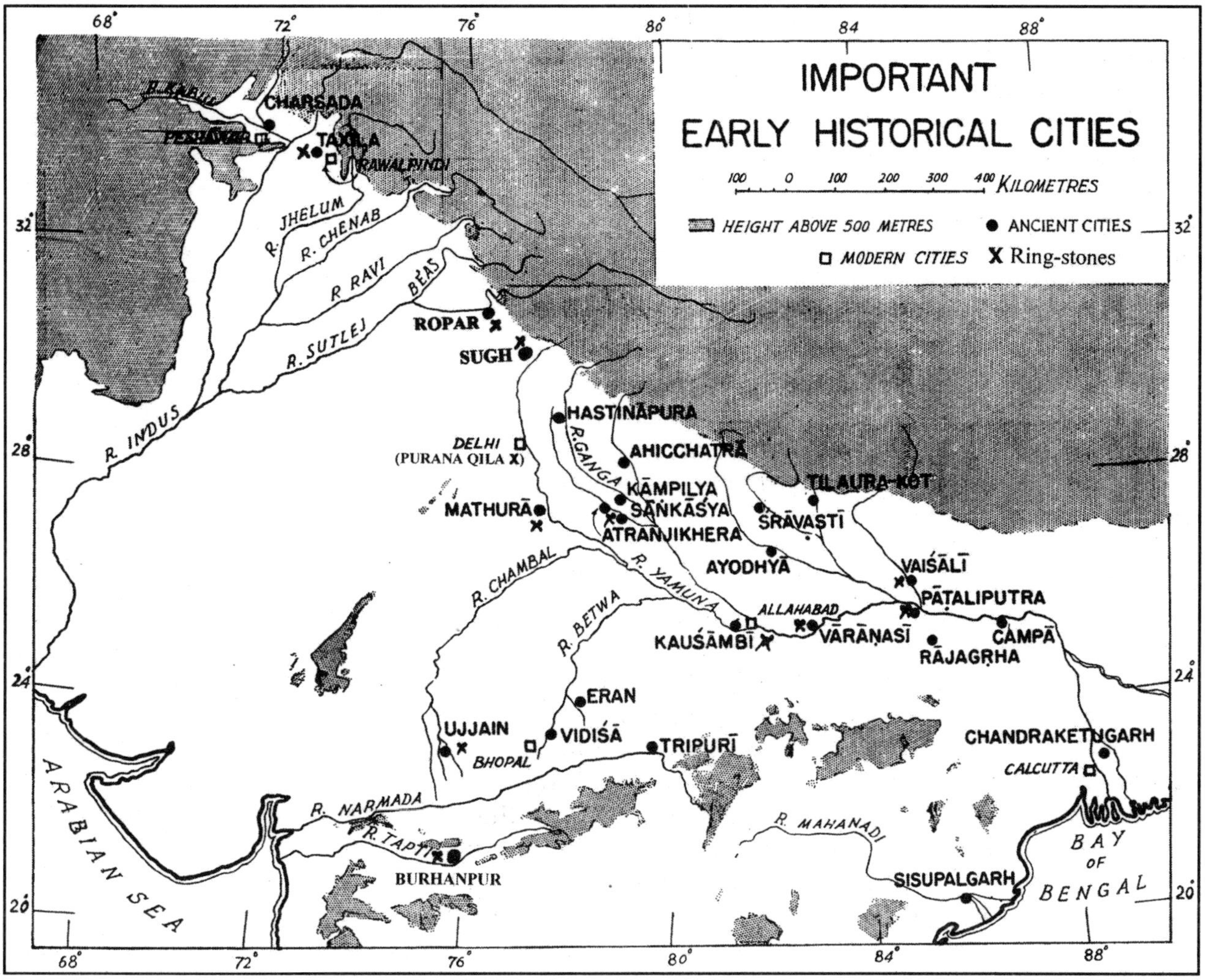


**Fig. 3.** Map showing the distribution of ringstones (after A. Ghosh).

nude female figure with wide pelvis, splayed feet and slantingly suspended arms remind us of the figure of the Earth Goddess on a small repousseé gold plaque belonging to the seventh or eighth century BCE and excavated from the Vedic burial-mound at Lauriya Nandangarh.[10] The disc also shows a sage sitting near his hut giving a round object to a female devotee standing in profile towards him with folded hands. Discs of this type have been discovered from various early historic sites like Taxila, Mathura, Sankisa, Kauśāmbī, Varanasi, Vaiśālī, Pāṭaliputra, Ujjain, etc. (Fig. 3), which seem to have been important cities connected with trade, culture and religion.[11]

The last Mauryan emperor Bṛihadratha was assassinated by his Commander-in-Chief Pushyamitra Śuṅga in about 185 BCE. He ruled till about 148 BCE, during which period he fought against the Bactrian Greeks, the successors of Seleucus, who were casting greedy eyes to annex Indian territories. It were probably Apollodotus and Menander under Demetrius who invaded India and besieged Sāketa (Ayodhyā) and Mādhyamikā (Nagari near Chittore) as referred to by Patañjali in his *Mahābhāshya* (II.2, 111) – *Aruṇadyavanaḥ Sāketam, aruṇadyavano Mādhyamikām.* Kālidāsa's Sanskrit drama *Mālavikāgnimitram* also refers to the fight between Pushyamitra's grandson and the Yavanas (i.e., Ionians, the Greeks) on the banks of the river Sindhu. Pushyamitra is portrayed as an anti-Buddhist ruler in Buddhist texts[12] though we find that the great *stūpa* of

Sanchi, originally built by Aśoka, was encased and a railing was added to it. The Bharhut *stūpa* was also bedecked with a massive and beautiful railing during the second century BCE.

In the Śuṅga period, the use of moulds on a large scale distinguishes the clay figurines from the Mauryan repertoire and augurs the inception of a truly native and indigenous physiognomy and idiom. The Mother Goddess makes way for exquisitely executed *Yaksha* and *Yakshī* figurines, some of them shown nude, the latter having a broad pelvis with mount of Venus indicated prominently, which seems to connect them with fertility and fecundity. These figures are proportionate and betray modelling in bold relief and are generally treated with a red slip. They show complete control of contours, linear rhythm, sensitive treatment, elegance, sophisticated expressions, elaborate coiffures, diaphanous drapery, profuse ornamentation, multiplicity of poses and attitudes. Figure sculptures and terracotta figurines, particularly the *yakshī* and allied figures, were richly decorated and a new style evolved. The use of moulds became more popular for creating terracotta figurines. Śuṅga terracottas showing a couple, beautiful *yakshī* and *yaksha* figures with cherubic expression from Ropar (Pl. 2), compare very well with their parallels discovered from other sites like Mathura,[13] Ahichhatrā,[14] Kauśāmbī,[15] etc. A well-draped and ornamented *yakshī* from Sunet (Pl. 3) with face worn out and bent acutely on her right shoulder must have been a magnificent figure originally. With elaborate headgear, large circular earrings, broad torque, nether garment secured by a pearl-stringed girdle and long garland forming a loop on the knees exudes uncanny grace. The pleats of the *dhotī* are indicated by parallel engraved lines on the legs. The suspended right hand probably supports the free end of the *uttarīya* 'upper garment' but the object held in the left hand, at the level of the waist, is not clear. The figure betrays characteristic Śuṅga qualities and reminds us of the stone *yakshī* found from near the Qutb Minar in Mehrauli in 1912 carved on a railing pillar and now housed in the National Museum, New Delhi.[16] Of course the moulded Śuṅga terracottas of Punjab, Haryana and the Gangetic plains show a general likeness and indicate the uniformity of style[17] which prevailed over the large territory of northern India during the reign of Pushyamitra Śuṅga.

The issuance of coinage by the Audumbaras with Pathankot (ancient Pratishṭhāna) as the capital and by the Mitras between the Beas and the Ghaggar, by the Agras around Hisar, Ārjunāyanas to their west, the Yaudheyas at Rohtak, Mitras and others at Mathura, and by various other monarchies at Ayodhya, Kauśāmbī, etc.[18] indicates that Pushyamitra's successors could not retain their sway in this part of the country. The migration of tribes like the Mālavas, Śibis, etc. from their original homes speaks of the pressure of the Greeks like Apollodotus, Menander and their successors in this region. The Bactrian rulers, however, do not seem to have been religious bigots and we know of Agathocles depicting Vāsudeva and Saṃkarshaṇa on his coins (Figs. 4-5).[19]

The Garuḍa-dhvaja Pillar Inscription of Vidiśā[20] is a well known example of Heliodoros, son of Diya (Dion), a resident of Taxila and Greek ambassador to King Bhāga-bhadra of Vidiśā, adopting Vaishṇavism in the second century BCE. Coins of Menander (165-135 BCE), who ruled from Śākala (modern Sialkot, now in Pakistan), and other Indo-Greek rulers have been found from various sites in Punjab – Ghuram, Hathur, Ropar, Machhiwara, etc. – including coin moulds of Menander and Apollodotus II from Ghuram and Ropar respectively. Menander was favourably inclined towards Buddhism.[21] It was perhaps because of this tolerant attitude that while an indigenous school of art developed at Mathura, another school incorporating western (Graeco-Roman) impact evolved in the Gandhāra region. There was interaction between the Mathura and Gandhāra schools of art and they influenced each other.[22] The impact of the Gandhāra school is very clearly seen on the art of Sanghol as we shall see consequently.

The Śaka conquest of Punjab is variously attributed by scholars to Maues (c. 85-60 BCE),[23] Azes (c. 60-20 BCE)[24] and Rājuvula (c. 25 BCE-c. 5 CE).[25] The Greeks were definitely expelled from

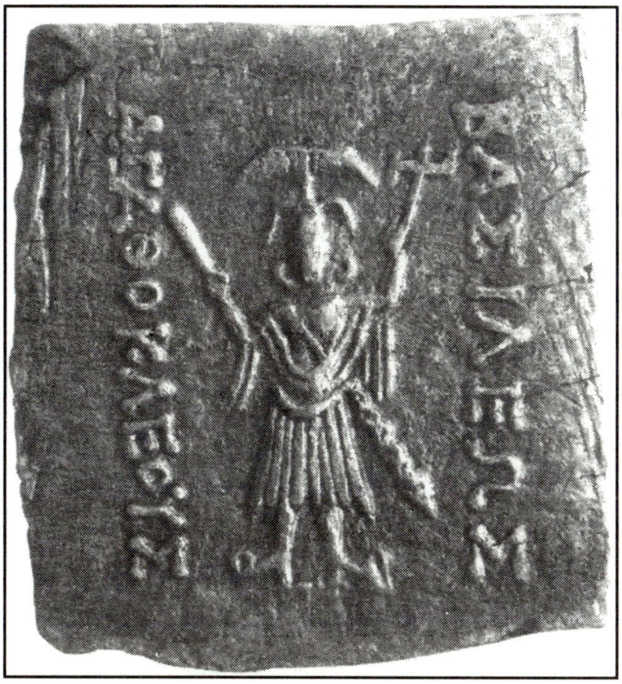

**Fig. 4.** Saṃkarshaṇa on the coins of Agathocles.

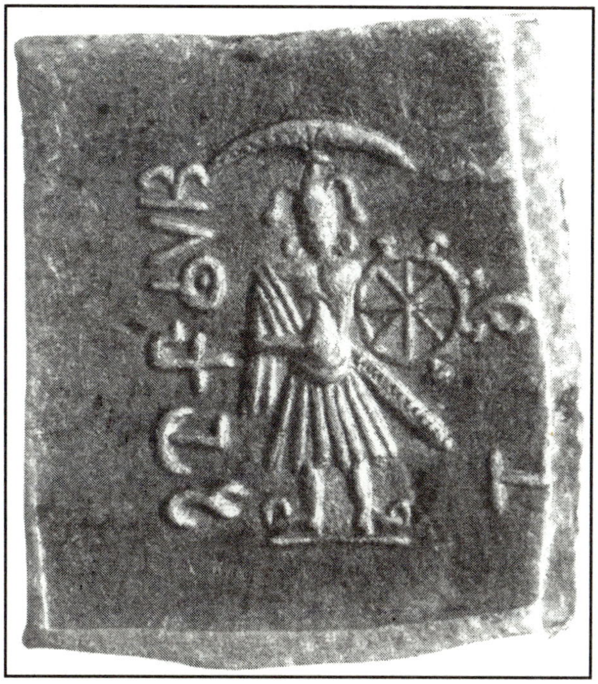

**Fig. 5.** Vāsudeva on the coins of Agathocles.

Taxila and Punjab region in about 55 BCE when Azes dethroned Hippostratos, the last Greek king to rule over Taxila and western Punjab. The Śakas subsequently extended their sway to the Mathura region. Coins of Azes[26] have been found from Amritsar and Kaithal[27] and his satrap Rājuvula from Sunet near Ludhiana, Sultanpur Lodhi and Nurmahal in the Jalandhar Doab, and from Mathura and some other sites in western Uttar Pradesh.[28] Rājuvula used the Greek, Kharoshṭhī and Brāhmī scripts in his coin-legends. The first two indicate that he hailed from the northwestern area of the Indian subcontinent. Coins of Gondophares have been discovered from a large number of sites in Punjab: Ajaḍāma in district Hoshiarpur, Pathankot in district Gurdaspur, Nurpur in district Jalandhar, Brass in district Patiala, Rohira in district Sangrur, Sunet and Kheri Naudh Singh in district Ludhiana, and Sanghol in district Fatehgarh Sahib.[29]

The religious attitude of the Śaka-Parthian potentates is very well reflected in their coins and inscriptions. Śiva figures on the coins of the Parthian king Gondophares,[30] while Azes,[31] Azilises[32] and Rājuvula[33] adopted the Indian motif of Lakshmī or *abhisheka* (anointment of) Lakshmī on their coins. The famous lion capital found at Mathura bears inscriptions perpetuating *inter alia* a religious donation in the Cave Monastery (Guhā-vihāra), which included or was perhaps given in addition to the establishment of the relic of Lord Buddha by the chief queen (/consort) of *Mahākshatrapa* Rajula.[34] The Mathura lion-capital inscription refers to Śoḍāsa as the son of Rājuvula and a *Kshatrapa* during the reign of his father. He is referred to as a *Mahākshatrapa* in a Mathura inscription of the year 72 (= CE 15?). His coins have, however, not been found from Punjab and their absence indicates the rise of the Parthian power.

The Kuṇindas performed Vedic sacrifices, as evidenced by the fire altars at Sanghol. These continued even in the times of Gondophares and the Kushāṇas.[35] The sacrificial priests may have looked like the nearly 12.5 cm high bronze figure of the *Yājñika* Brāhmaṇa (sacrificial priest) found from Ropar (Pl. 4) in excavations from the levels of Period IV (*circa* 200 BCE-CE 600) along with Kuṇinda and Śaka-Kushāṇa coins.[36] Overlying the Kuṇinda strata at Sanghol is the cultural deposit which yielded Parthian coins belonging to Gondophares (c. 50-5 BCE).

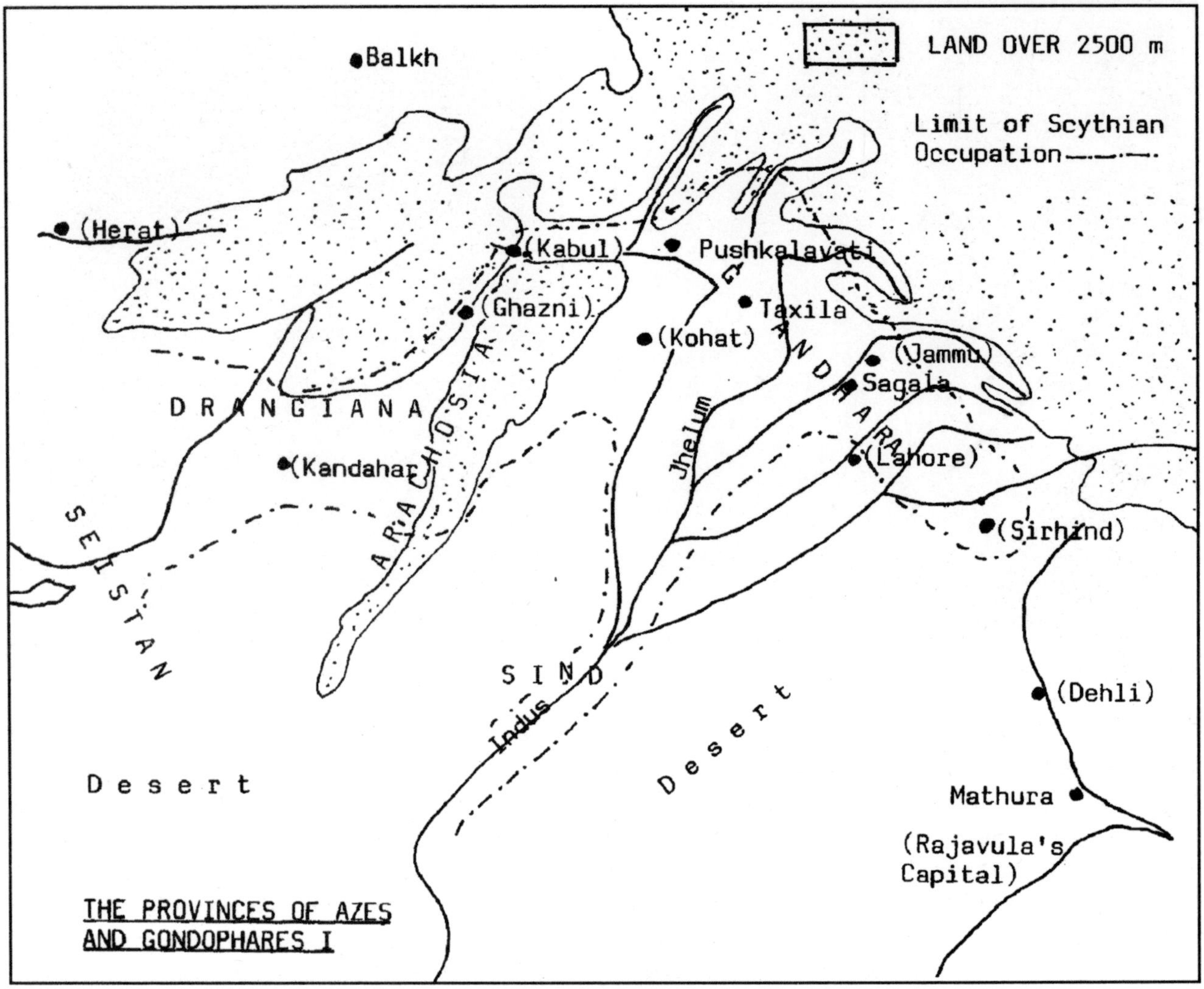


**Fig. 6.** Scytho-Parthian dominions (after Robert Senior).

R.C. Senior[37] has concluded that Azes was succeeded by Gondophares and his nephew Abdagases immediately in some areas and before his death in others, and that there were several kings who used the name or title Gondophares. Numerous coins of Gondophares have been found from Sanghol besides one of his circular clay sealing showing a crude figure of Pallas holding a shield in her outstretched right hand and a thunderbolt in the left with marginal Kharoshṭhī legend *rajadirajasa tratarasa Gudupharasa* resembling the reverse device of his coins.

According to Robert Senior, the Scythian-Parthian dominions extended from Sirhind to Kabul and Herat in the west (Fig. 6). Being a part of the Scytho-Parthian dominions which extended from Gandhāra, Arachosia, Drangiana and Seistan to Punjab, the people here may not have remained unaffected by the alien impact. Foreigners depicted in clay found from Sunam, Sunet, Shambhu, Hathur, and elsewhere in Punjab and adjoining Haryana (Pl. 5) bear witness to it. The Śaka-type pointed hat worn by some of the figures indicates the presence of foreigners in the towns of Punjab and Haryana in substantial numbers. The alien physiognomy of some others corroborates it. The royal devotee or personage from Karhali (Pl. 247) and various figures in clay, stucco or stone obtained from Sanghol, the couple seated on a throne as depicted on a Sanghol terracotta (Pl. 193) and the *yakshī* taking wine (Madhupāna) from a glass (Pl. 226) bear unmistakable Parthian impact as we shall see subsequently. Sanghol must have enjoyed the benefit of being the eastern outpost of the empire, particularly during the rule of Gondophares.

There is no evidence of the rule of the successors of Gondophares from Sanghol or even anywhere else from this region. Kujula Kadphises may have been contemporary of Gondophares' successors. But for one of his copper coin procured by Rodgers at Amritsar during 1888-89, none other has been found so far. The earliest Kushāṇa occupation in the Punjab seems to have taken place as a result of the campaigns of Soter Megas (*c.* CE 25 -55). His true identity is still a matter of debate but it is evident that he paved the way for the reign of Wema (Wima) Kadphises (c. CE 55-78). The Rabatak inscription records the name of Kujula Kadphises' son as Vema Taktu whom Joe Cribb proposed to identify with 'Soter Megas' of the coins.[38] Though some scholars raised certain objections against this hypothesis, Bopearachchi has pointed out the differences between the coinages of the Kushāṇas and of Soter Megas. He has cited literary and numismatic data to prove that Soter Megas was the general to whom Yangaozhen (Vema Taktu) confided India according to Hou Hanshu, and who later usurped the throne of the Kushāṇa Empire and struck coins using his epithet of Soter Megas.[39]

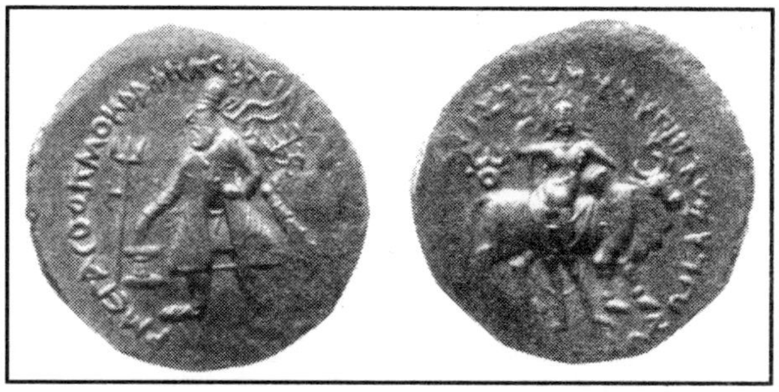

**Fig. 7.** Śiva with Nandī on the reverse of Wema Kadphises' coin (Lingen collection).

Wema Kadphises, whose coins have been found from a number of sites in the Punjab, ushered in a new era of the proliferation of cultural, religious, artistic and political developments. He himself was a *Māheśvara*, a devotee of Śiva, as evidenced by his coins which carry on the reverse the Kharoshṭhī legend *Maharajasa rajadirajasa sarvaloga ishvarasa mahishvarasa himakapishasa tradata* with Śiva standing by his bull and holding a trident[40] (Fig. 7).

Recently, another of his coin-type struck in the memory of his father, discovered some time back from Peshawar,[41] shows tri-cephalic Śiva also (Fig. 8) indicating the popularity of this form and Wema's propensity towards Maheśvara.

Kanishka, the son and successor of Wema Kadphises, is well known in history as a great protagonist of Buddhism. He held sway over a very vast area with Purushapura (Peshawar) as his capital. Mathura developed as a great centre of art and religion. Unprecedented development took place during his reign. He was the first king to depict Buddha on his coins.[42] His successor Huvishka is known for depicting Greek, Roman, Iranian and Indian deities including Śiva, Skanda Kumara, Viśākha and Mahāsena[43] and Buddha.[44] The Kushāṇas seem to have got completely Indianized by now as the next ruler Vāsudeva got not only an Indian name but also issued a coin-type in gold depicting four-armed Vāsudeva, i.e., Vishṇu, supporting the Vaishṇava attributes.[45]

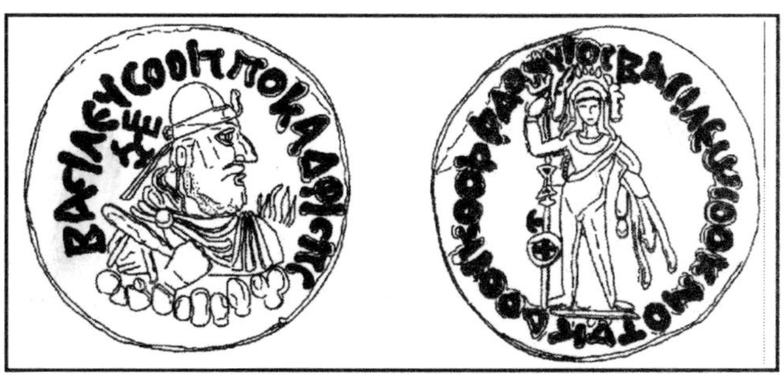

**Fig. 8.** Tri-cephalous Śiva on a coin of Wema Kadphises (after Osmund Bopearachchi).

The weakening of the Kushāṇa power seems to have provided an opportunity to the Yaudheyas to extend their sway to the plains of Punjab and Haryana. Their coins, coin-moulds, seals and sealings indicate that Sunet, Rohtak, Naurangabad near Bhiwani and Agroha were their strongholds.[46] The Prayāga (Allahabad) Praśasti of

Samudragupta tells us that the tribe was subjugated by Samudragupta and rendered as tax-paying but was otherwise left as autonomous.[47] There is no evidence of direct rule of the Guptas in the Punjab though the art of the area seems to have followed the general trends and characteristics of northern India prevailing during their rule. The terracotta figurine of a seated lady playing on the *vīṇā* 'lyre' found from Ropar (Pl. 6) reminds us of the Lyrist Type coins of Samudragupta. Terracotta human head from Zahura (Pl. 7) and Mahishamardinī figure from Sanghol (Pl. 107) conform to the Gupta style which was prevailing throughout North India at that time. The bronze disc from Ropar showing a winged griffin (Pl. 209) gives us an idea of the metal craft of the Gupta period. The persistence of the traits of Gupta idiom is witnessed in the subsequent period, as we shall see in the sequel.

The Hūṇas started their attacks from northwest in the last decade of the fifth century during the reign of Kumāragupta and though thwarted once by the brave resistance of Skandagupta, they ultimately succeeded in defeating the Guptas and of course their feudatory Yaudheyas in the Punjab and penetrated as deep as the Malwa in Central India. The depredation wrought by them in the region is indicated by a conflagration as seen in a post-Gupta layer running in most part of the cultural deposits of the mound at Ajaḍāma and also by the devastation of the Buddhist *stūpa* at Sanghol. Though the coins of an early Hūṇa potentate Khiṅgila carry the Vaishṇavite attributes of conch and disc as we shall see subsequently, his successor Toramāṇa adopted a solar symbol and his successor Mihirakula a bull with the legend 'Jayatu Vṛishaḥ' indicating his Śaivite inclination. Some Jaina texts, however, refer to them as inclined towards Jainism also as we shall see subsequently. A large number of their coins have been recovered from Sanghol. The Hūṇas seem to have continued their rule over the region for some generations, as evidenced by the coins recovered from Sanghol. They wielded their authority over the region till the Pushpabhūtis gained ascendancy during the second half of the sixth century CE. During the first half of the seventh century CE, the region was under the hegemony of Harsha and his feudatory at Jālandhara was King Udita or Udito under whose patronage the Chinese pilgrim Xuan Zang spent four months in the Nagaradhana Vihāra studying Buddhist texts with Chandravarman.[48]

The history of the region after Harsha is shrouded in mystery as no definite evidence is available. It is suggested that Harshavardhana's cousin (maternal uncle's son) Bhaṇḍi established himself over the Thanesar region and his family continued to rule till the ascendancy of the Pratīhāras.[49] We do not know the extant of his empire in the north but it is not unlikely that his dominions extended into Punjab. The Bhaṇḍis may have remained subservient to the Kanauj throne. Vākpatirāja refers to the march of Yaśovarman's army through Marudeśa, Śrīkaṇṭha, Kurukshetra, etc. to check the menace of the Pārasīka invasion in the northern region.[50] Yaśovarman (*circa* CE 690-740) was accompanied by his Pratīhāra feudatory Nāgabhaṭṭa I (*circa* CE 725-56) in his march.[51] Kalhaṇa tells us that Yaśovarman was defeated at the hands of the Kashmir ruler Lalitāditya Muktāpīḍa (*circa* CE 695-732).[52] This political event seems to have paved the way for the influence of Kashmirian traits to be adopted in Punjab and Himachal Pradesh. The successors of the Bhaṇḍi family, however, seem to have retained their hold over some regions, which was subsequently wrested by the Tomaras who served as feudatories of the Pratīhāras. Vatsarāja (*circa* CE 775-95), the grandson of Nāgabhaṭṭa I,[53] is also credited with victories against the rulers of Karṇāṭa and Lāṭa (Gujarat), Jayāpīḍa of Kashmir, the lord of Gauḍa (Dharmapāla), the Mlechchhas (Muslim) and Kīra (Kangra).[54] Pratīhāra inscriptions of Bhoja (CE 836-90) and Mahendrapāla (CE 890-910) from Pehowa[55] and the popularity of the Pratīhāra style indicate the strong impact of the Pratīhāra hold which extended to Punjab and may have even reached the confines of Kashmir. Coins of Bhoja Ādivarāha found from Sultanpur

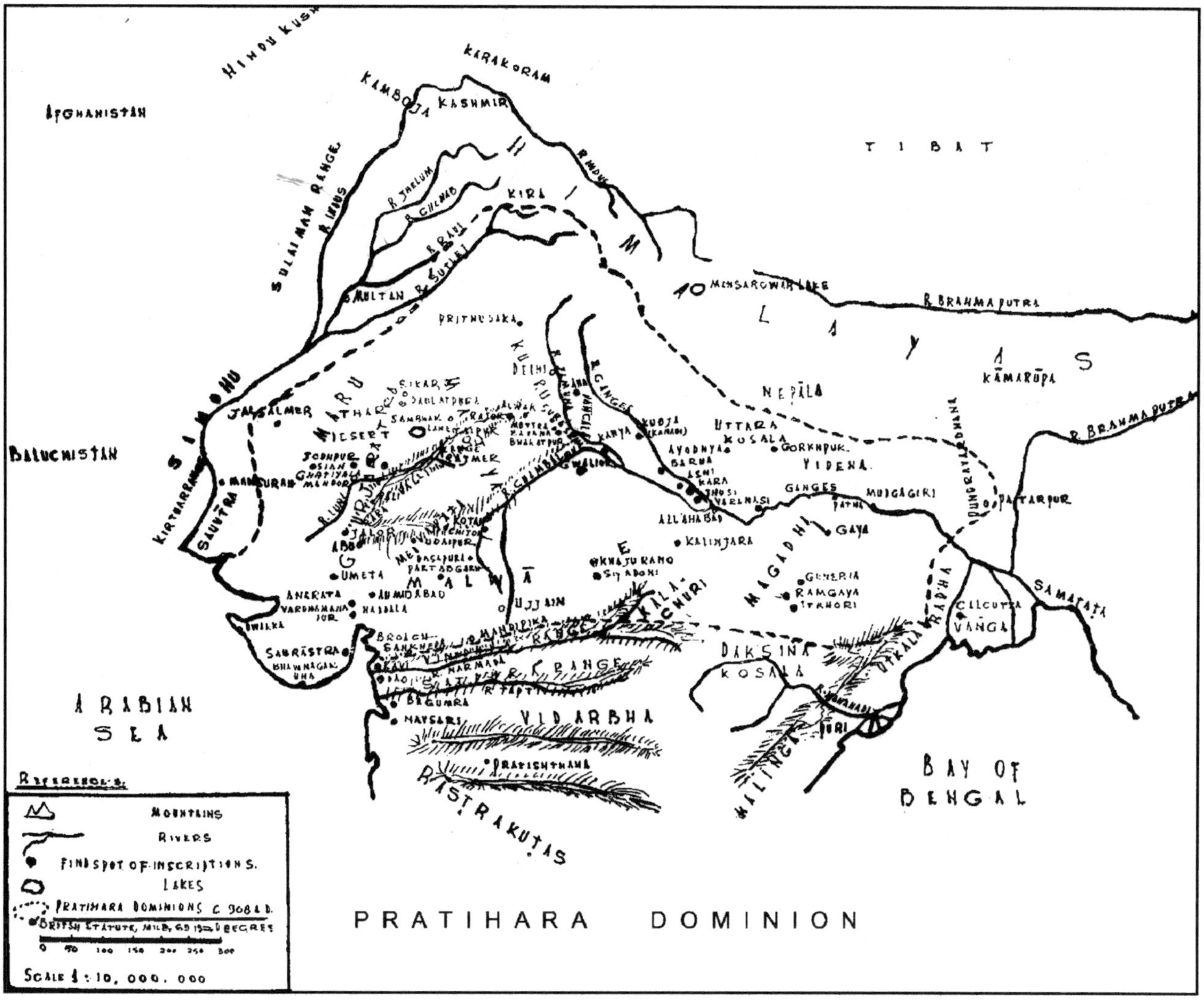


**Fig. 9.** Map showing Pratīhāra dominion (after Dasharatha Sharma).

Lodhi[56] and Jalandhar[57] also confirm the Pratīhāra sway over Punjab. The vast dominions of the Pratīhāras, flourishing of trade, development of trade routes and patronage provided to art activities opened the avenues of influences coming from Rajasthan, Central India, western Uttar Pradesh and the hills of Uttarakhand on Punjab sculptures as we shall see in the sequel. The Pratīhāra dominions included the whole of present day Punjab (Fig. 9).[58] Mahendrapāla's son was Mahīpāla (known dates are 914, 917 and 922), who is referred to by Rājaśekhara as the pearl-jewel of the Raghu family and the *Mahārājādhirāja* of Āryavarta.[59] He is said to have conquered the Kulūtas (people of Kullu), who was like a battle-axe to the Kuntalas and had taken away by force the fortunes of the Ramaṭhas.[60] Even the Shāhis of Kabul acknowledged his sovereignty.[61] We do not have any evidence of the continuation of Pratīhāras after Mahīpāla. His son was Devapāla (CE 948).

Bathinda stone inscription of the reign of *Mahārāja* Śatrughnadeva,[62] palaeographically dated to the tenth century, contains the word *Sāmanta* in line 15, indicating that at the weakening of the Pratīhāra power independent rulers like Śatrughnadeva occupied some territories in the Punjab. We do not know exactly as to which dynasty he belonged, what were his exact dates and what exactly was the extent of his dominions. The inscription is very much fragmentary and was engraved probably at the consecration of a Vishṇu temple. The site has, however, not yielded any such remains though two Jaina images were accidentally discovered here. Rājaśekhara refers to Pṛithūdaka (Pehowa) on the river Sarasvatī as the northern outpost of Madhyadeśa beyond which lay the Uttarāpatha with numerous dynasties and tribes like the Śakas, Kekayas, Vokkāṇas, Hūṇas, Kambojas, Vāhlīkas, Vahlavas (Pahlavas?), Limpākas, Kulūtas, Kīras, Taṅgaṇas, Tushāras, Turushkas, etc.[63] As of now, the Sarasvatī River seems to have thus served as the boundary between Madhyadeśa and Uttarāpatha during the tenth century CE. The dominions of Śatrughnadeva may have extended southward to this river. Probably, soon the Hindu Shāhi rulers of Udbhāṇḍapura (Ohind) exerted themselves at least in some parts of Punjab if not all. Bull/Horseman type coins bearing the name/title of Sāmantadeva found from Bhudan and Sunam (in kilograms) in district Sangrur, Chak Gujran (50 coins) in district Hoshiarpur, Dina Nagar in district Gurdaspur, Hathur and Tihar in district Ludhiana, Janer in district Moga, Kubaheri in district Ropar, Nandgarh in district Bathinda, Sarai Naga in district Faridkot, Sultanpur Lodhi in district Kapurthala, and various other places[64] bear ample evidence to their influence in the area. The invasions and depredations of the Muslims also started during this period. The reign of Jayapāla Shāhi ended in a tragedy. In CE 1001, Mahmud of Ghazni invaded the Shāhi dominion and in spite of putting up a heroic fight Jayapāla lost the battle. The victorious Muslim army relentlessly plundered the wealth of the Shāhis and carried out a terrible slaughter of people. Unable to bear the ignominy, Jayapāla burnt himself to death.[65] It is difficult to reconstruct the history of the region for about half a century when probably every dynasty and tribe named above had a free hand to establish its hegemony.

Muslim invasions on India had started in CE 712 when Muhammad bin Qasim attacked Sind. Thereafter, we find Yaśovarman, Nāgabhaṭṭa I, Vatsarāja and others trying to stem their tide but in the eleventh century, the repeated depredations of Mahmud Ghaznavi and his successor Masud paved the way for the events to come. The former raided and ravished the region in CE 1011 and took away the life-size idol of Chakrasvāmī from Thanesar and placed it in the hippodrome of Ghazna to be desecrated further by the people there.[66] Mahmud added a greater part of Punjab to the Ghaznavide empire and the aggressive policy followed by him was continued by his successors with a fair amount of success. During the reign of Masud, Ahmad Nialtigin led his troops to Banaras and looted it for twelve hours. Masud himself besieged Hansi in December 1036 and stormed it in January 1037. Masud's son Majdud governed the whole region from the Indus to Hansi but when his brother Maudud ascended the throne of Ghazni, he refused allegiance to him. Maudud wanted to punish him but died at Lahore under mysterious circumstances, perhaps due to poisoning, in CE 1040. The internal dissensions of the Ghaznavids, however, provided an opportunity to the confederacy of the Chauhan, Paramāra and Kalachuri potentates to recapture Hansi, Thanesar and Punjab up to Lahore.[67] After a brief respite, the Muslim aggression started again and Masud's grandson Mahmud (son of Ibrahim), who was then governor of Punjab, led an expedition to Ujjain in CE 1075.[68] Taking advantage of the disturbed conditions, the Lohara kings of Kashmir, Ananta and his son Kalaśa, led an expedition to Kanauj.[69] Their sway over the Punjab-Haryana region, however, was cut short by the Tomaras who reasserted their authority.[70] Tomara ruler Rudra was slain by Chauhan Chandanarāja (II) whose grandson Siṃharāja (CE 956) subdued Salavaṇa (Tomara). The Harsha inscription of Vigraharāja II (CE 973) mentions, besides the above two, the names of two more Tomara rulers Tantrapāla and Kshmāpāla also.[71] Muslim attacks remained unabated and internal dissensions, internecine wars and *mātsya-nyāya* (law of the fish) became the common features of the age and everyone was on a look-out for opportunities to accomplish selfish motives. The Āmoda plates of the Haihaya ruler Pṛithvīdeva dated Chedi Saṃvat 831 = CE 1080 make a reference to distant

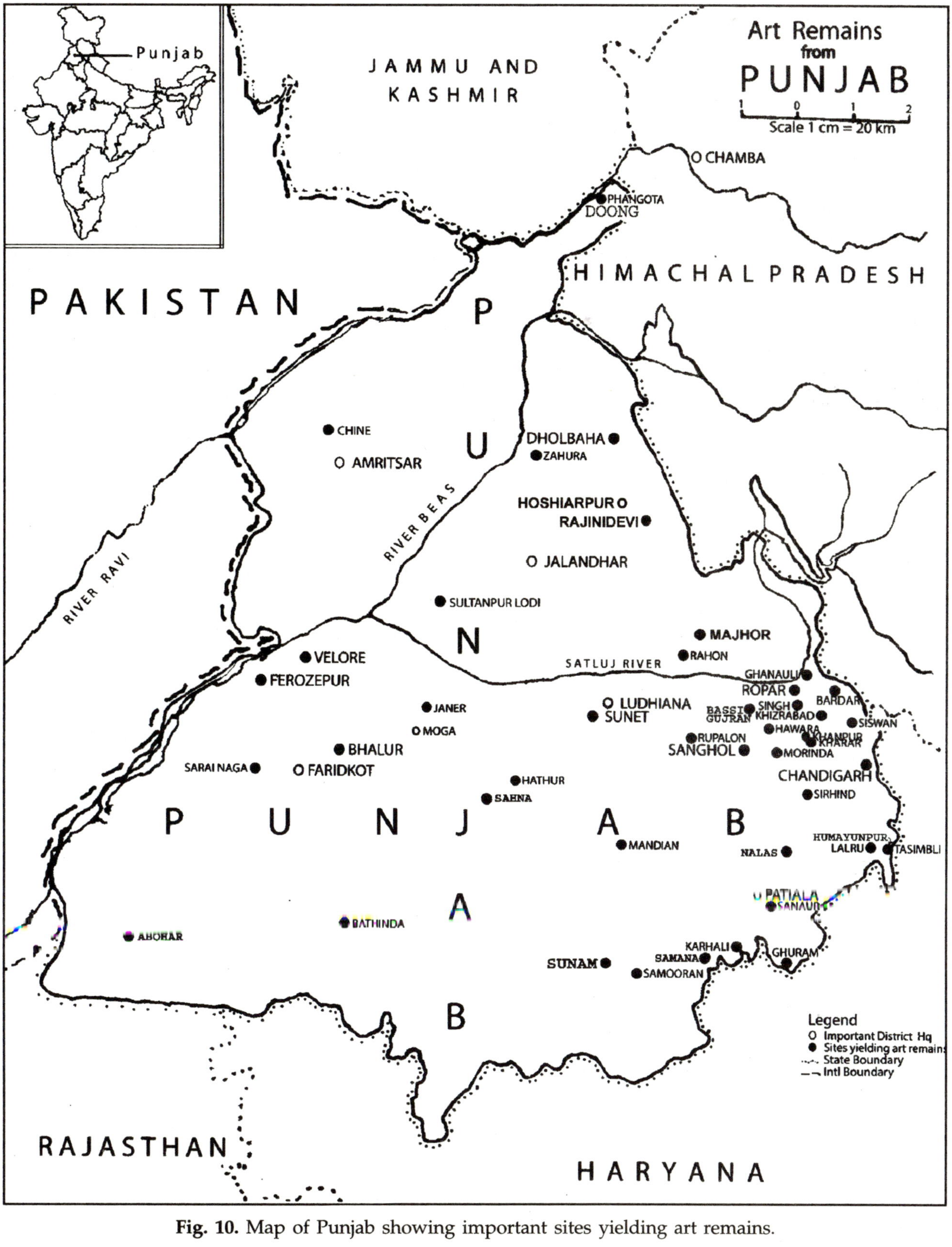


**Fig. 10.** Map of Punjab showing important sites yielding art remains.

Turushkas who happened to be in occupation of a part of the Punjab when this inscription was incised.[72]

Nicknamed as Anna and Ānāka, the Chauhan ruler Arṇorāja, son of Ajayarāja and Somaladevī, was a young man when he was put on the throne a little before VS 1190 (CE 1133) by his father who retired to the forest adjoining the lake Pushkar. Anna probably ruled for about two decades and is credited with defeating Naravarman of Malwa, slaughtering the Turushkas near Ajmer, leading an expedition into the Haritānaka country (Haryana) and carrying arms up to the Sindhu and the Sarasvatī.[73] The route of this expedition was through Pallu and Nohar in Rajasthan to Sirsa in Haryana and probably beyond in Punjab, as indicated by the discovery of coins of Somaladevī at these and other places including Sunam and Samana in district Sangrur, Punjab. Hemachandra, a contemporary writer, hints at the help he received from the rulers of eastern Madra and the towns of Vāhlīkadeśa and calls him as Udīchyapati (lord of the north).[74] Arṇorāja's son Vigraharāja IV had defeated the Bhādānakas and the Tomaras. His Siwalik (also known as Delhi-Topra) Pillar Inscription of VS 1220 (CE 1163) indicates that he held sway from the Himalayas to the Vindhyas.[75] Hansi Stone Slab Inscription of the reign of Pṛithvīrāja III dated Saṃvat 1224 (now in the Royal Scottish Museum, Edinburgh) describes Pṛithvīrāja II as Rāma (*Pṛithvīrājo mahārājo Rāmo[']sau saṃśayaṃ vinā*) and tells us that his maternal uncle Kilhaṇa was entrusted with the protection of the strong fort of Hansi from the Muslims and while chasing the foe he burnt Pañchapura, i.e., Pinjaur (near Chandigarh).[76] Pṛithvīrāja II was succeeded by Someśvara (CE 1169-77) who was followed by Pṛithvīrāja III (CE 1177-91), the famous Pṛithvīrāja Chauhan. His dominions included parts of Punjab up to Bathinda at least in the north.[77] The eventful overlordship of the Chauhans had brought Punjab closer to Rajasthan and people, particularly the Jaina monks, moved freely to Punjab and marble and metal images started to be imported in Punjab as we shall see in the sequel. His unfortunate defeat at the hands of Muhammad Ghori, however, changed the course of history and opened the portal of Muslim rule in India during which religious bigotry saw its zenith and all Hindu temples in Punjab were demolished and images desecrated. The only respite perhaps was during the reign of Akbar but his successors reverted to the same old policy. There is no ancient standing temple which has survived in the Punjab and old sculptures are a rarity. Some chance discoveries, excavations at Sanghol, occasional explorations, etc., however, have brought to light sculptures of which nearly half of the Sanghol images have been studied properly and published exquisitely.[78] Some others have also been noticed[79] but a large number of them are still awaiting proper treatment. During almost the last four decades of our interest, we have listed the following 50 ancient sites in the present day state of Punjab which have yielded evidence of temple remains or sculptures (Fig. 10).

## SITES YIELDING ART REMAINS

### 1. Abohar

Situated in 30° 9' N & 74° 16' E, Abohar is an important ancient town in the Fazilka tehsil of Ferozepur district. Tradition ascribes its foundation to Jaura, a grandson of the legendary Bhatti king, Rājā Rasālu. It was the capital of Bhattiana. It was named Uboh-har or the 'pool of Uboh', after Jaura's wife. There is a large mound covered by modern buildings in its northern part. The remains of a mud fort here have been now under protection of the Archaeology department of the State. Abohar must be a very old place as Cunningham recovered Yaudheya coins from here.[80] It lay on the ancient high road from Multan to Delhi and was visited by Ibn Batuta in CE 1332. It is mentioned as A(/Ā)bhora in the *Kharatara-Gachchha-Bṛihad-Gurvāvali* as an important centre of Jainism where Āchārya Jina-chandra lived with eighty-four resident disciples.[81] The Government Museum and Art Gallery, Chandigarh houses two twelfth century fragmentary sandstone pieces measuring 51 X 28 X 17.5 cm (Acc. No. 3805) and 55 X 29 X 15 cm respectively showing a female and a male on either side of a pilaster, their positions being transversed in the two pieces. The site needs a thorough probe and is sure to yield old sculptures and temple remains.

## 2. Ajadam

The village of Ajadam (Ajaḍāma) is situated about 10 km southwest of Hoshiarpur as the crow flies. A link road connects it with a bridge on the Nasrala Nala on Hoshiarpur-Jalandhar road. It may also be approached from Hoshiarpur-Phagwara road which lies about 3 km south of the village. The extensive old mound of Ajadam becomes visible from a distance of about 3 km. In ancient times, it must have been a very large town as its ruins extend all around the village covering approximately an area of more than one km square. The highest point of the mound rises to about 10 meters. The mound, however, has been cut into several parts by the roads and tracks constructed by the villagers. Expanding population and urbanization has covered large parts of the mound and if the modern tendency of leveling it for a constructional purpose continues, there will be no part left uncovered within a few coming years.

The site is particularly rich in Kushāṇa ceramics, Gupta-stamped pottery and medieval wares. Śuṅga red ware bowls and sherds of black-slipped and grey wares, assignable to the second half of the first millennium BCE, were also picked up from the site when I first visited it on 6 June 1970. Bricks measuring 10.75 x 10.75 and 10.75 x 21.5 inches were also noticed besides the wedge-shaped ones measuring 13 x 10 x 6.5 inches. The peripheral portions yield late Harappan potsherds also. The exposed sections which have resulted from the cutting of the mound for the construction of roads and tracks reveal two distinct ashy layers with the remains of the Gupta period sandwiched between them. It is likely that the site may have been invaded once by the aliens before the Gupta period and by the Hūṇas towards the close of the Gupta period in the end of the fifth or the beginning of the sixth century CE. The mound yields beads, coins (Indo-Greek, Gondophernes, Kushāṇa and Mitra), bricks, terracotta figurines and other old relics besides pottery. A local tradition connects it with Sahasrabāhu. Since the Haihaya king Kārttavīrya Arjuna Sahasrabāhu is better known, the name of Kekaya king Sahasrachitya (*Mbh*, Āśramavāsika Parva, 20.6-9) seems to have been confused with him. Linguistically, however, the present name of the village may be derived from Aja-grāma (a village founded by King Aja) or Ūjaṛa-grāma (a deserted village).[82] Coins of Zoilus, Hermaeus, Gondophares, Ayamita and a terracotta mould of Durgā are important finds from this place.[83]

## 3. Amritsar

Amritsar is a well known city of India famous for its Golden Temple. Rodgers and Allan have referred to the coins of Hermaeus, Azes, Azes and Aspavarman, Kujula Kadphises and Samudragupta procured from here.[84] An image of Vaikuṇṭha has been registered at this place. Amritsar has remained a stronghold of the Jainas also in the late medieval period.

## 4. Baghraul

Baghraul is located on the Sangrur-Patran road close to the border with Patiala. There is an old mound between Baghraul and the village Kapial which yielded, about three decades back, a beautiful stone *tri-tīrthikā*, about 50 cm in height, which was taken by the wife of a high official of the district. The site has also yielded some very badly mutilated buff-coloured sandstone Jina images.

### 5. Bardar

This is a small hamlet situated in the Siwaliks, about 20 km east of Rupnagar on the old Siswan-Ropar road. It contains ruins of an ancient city. A number of stone images and copper utensils were discovered in a field in 1874. These included an image of Durgā and other minor Hindu deities indicating the existence of a temple at the spot. The city may have been destroyed in some sudden convulsion like an earthquake. Later, Jats and Gujars came to inhabit it and there are remains of a Rajput stronghold. Old wells have come to light at various times. Images have been frequently unearthed from here, some of which were deposited in a Śivālā at Ropar.[85] Mostly these images are not traceable anywhere now.

### 6. Bassi Gujaran

Situated about 4 km west-southwest of Chamkaur Sahib, south of the Sirhind Canal, and nearly 20 km northeast of Samrala in district Rupnagar near its border with district Fatehgarh Sahib, Bassi Gujaran has a large mound extending from near the canal for about a km southwards and rising to nearly ten meters at places which yields archaeological relics consisting of red ware sherds, sometimes bearing paintings in black pigment, revealing late Harappan affinity, grey ware, large bricks of Kushāṇa period and medieval red pottery, brickbats, etc. A small sandstone plaque depicting seated Sūrya has been recovered from here. The mound is fast disappearing due to the villagers' attempts at leveling it for agricultural activities.[86]

### 7. Bathinda

Bathinda (formerly spelled as Bhatinda), a district headquarters of Punjab, is located on the Delhi-Ferozepur section of the Northern Railway, about 240 km northwest of Delhi and 125 km south-southeast of Ferozepur. It is well-connected by road with all important cities of Punjab as well as with Jind and Sirsa in Haryana, Hanumangarh and Bikaner in Rajasthan. Two Jaina marble images of Naminātha and Neminātha, the latter inscribed and with a *parikara,* were discovered accidentally while a brick-kiln owner was supervising farm operation in his agricultural fields near the milk plant on Dabwali road, near Bathinda in October, 1979.[87]

### 8. Bhalur

Bhalur is a small village in Moga district of Punjab, situated 18 km east of Faridkot and about 25 km southwest of the district headquarter. It was an important Jaina centre during the medieval period and has yielded a Jaina Sarvatobhadra of the Pratihāra period. Some time back, a hoard of 56 silver coins of Shah Alam II and Maharaja Ranjit Singh was found while digging the foundations of a Gurdwara at this place.

### 9. Bhudan

Bhudan in tehsil Malerkotla of district Sangrur has a mound which yielded Painted Grey Ware and medieval relics including late Kushāṇa and Shāhi coins of Sāmantadeva.[88] Some relics of art have also been obtained from this site. In the Thakurdwara at this place is preserved a bronze image of Jaina *yakshī* Ajitabalā.

### 10. Burail/Chandigarh

Chandigarh is a well known ultra modern city of India planned by the French architect Le Corbusier in the early fifties of the last century. Chandigarh is the capital of Punjab and Haryana and is a Union Territory. The 121 square km area of the city includes 21 villages. Village Burail, located on an ancient mound, now forms part of the Sector 45, Chandigarh. It is situated about 6 km northwest of the main Bus Stand (ISBT, Sector 17). Originally, the village was located on the left bank of a small rivulet or *nullah* which passed through Sectors 6-7, 19-20 and 33 and 45 but has subsequently been filled up as a result of urbanization. The mound yielded Harappan, Painted Grey, Śuṅga-Kushāṇa, early medieval and medieval pottery. Muslim coins of silver and copper have also been reported to have been found from the site. During the laying down of the foundations for a Śiva temple in the west of the village near the Government High School in Sector 45, the labourers dug out the remains of an old temple which included a 9th-century Śiva-liṅga of grey sandstone which is now installed in the present temple and also an image of Gaṇeśa now fixed in the wall. Some sculptures were removed to another temple called Khera Mandir for worship and included worn-out images of Vishṇu, a fly-whisker, a Vaishṇava acolyte wearing a long garland, a *vyāla* and a stele showing Brahmā.[89] Expansion and renovation at the Khera temple in 2007 further led to the discovery of many more sculptures, mostly Jaina, belonging to tenth century CE. The Jaina sculptures have been removed to and preserved in the Government Museum and Art Gallery at Chandigarh.

### 11. CHINE/CHINNA

Now spelled as Chhina and Harsha Chhina (Alexander Cunningham spelled it as Chine), the place is located about 15 km northwest of Amritsar on the road to Ajnala near the well known Raja Sansi International Airport (31° 45' 06" N and 74° 45' 74" E) having a very large ancient mound associated with Alexander. The mound is spread over more than 50 acres and is

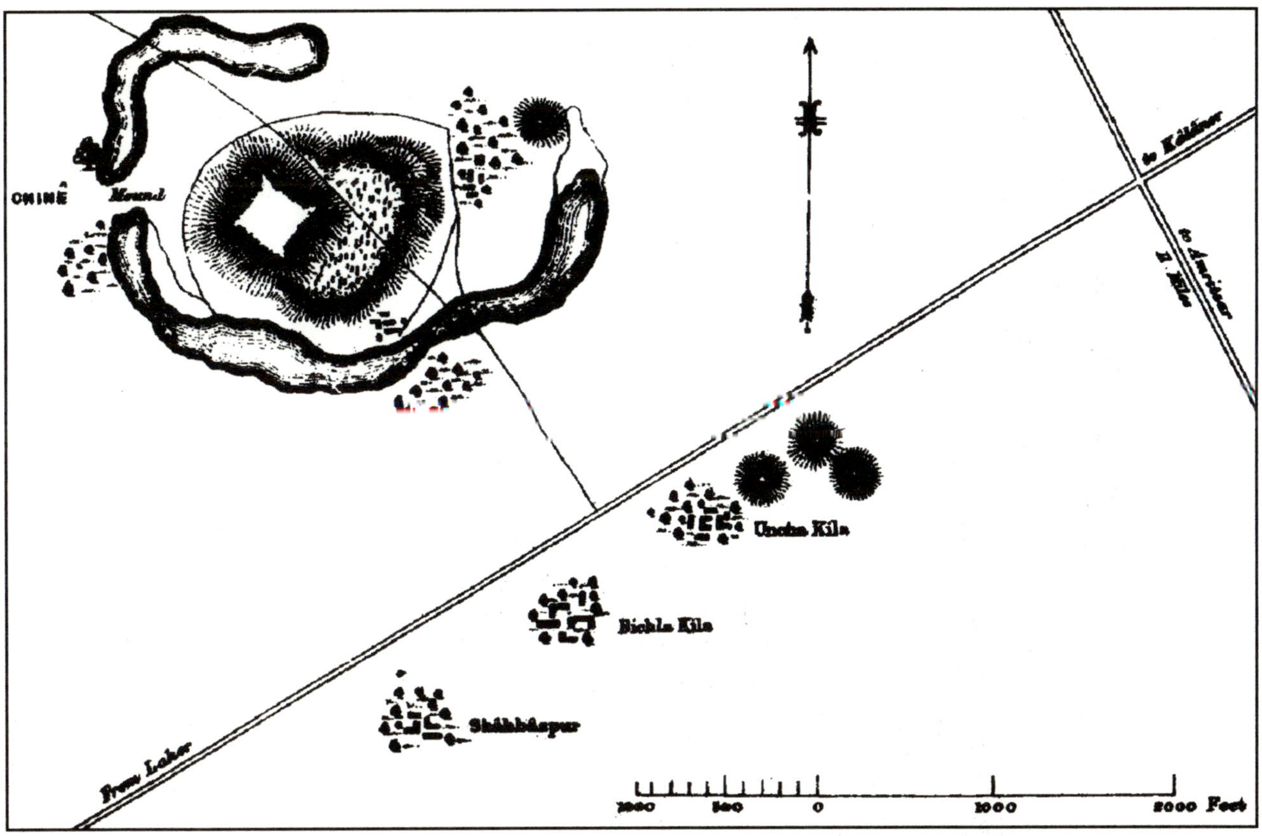


**Fig. 11.** The mound at Chinna (after Alexander Cunningham).

approximately 10 metres high with vertical sections at places. Sherds of late Harappan, painted grey and grey, black-slipped, plain red wares and medieval pottery may be picked up from the mound.[90] Cunningham identified it with the capital of Chīnabhukti of the Chinese pilgrim Xuan Zang's times, where Kanishka had lodged the sons of an outlying vassal of China sent to him as hostages who introduced pears and peaches in India. The mound yielded late Harappan pottery, Painted Grey Ware, Grey Ware and Black-slipped ware besides the early historic red ware and medieval pottery indicating a very long life-span. The site deserves to be excavated. The Chinese pilgrim spent fourteen months in a monastery here studying *Abhidharma* treatises with a Buddhist monk Vinītaprabha. Cunningham found the mound (Fig. 11) thickly covered with large bricks of 31.5 X 21.5 X 6.5 cm size and also referred to a Vishṇu image.[91] Nothing, however, is known of it now.

The mound is very rich in antiquities even now but unfortunately, it has not been explored properly. A local resident of Amritsar and some amateur historians have collected some antiquities from this site.

### 12. Dholbaha

Dholbaha is situated in a picturesque valley at the foot of the Siwalik Hills on the bank of a rivulet about 30 km north of Hoshiarpur. It is connected with Hoshiarpur by a road via Hariana on Hoshiarpur-Tanda road. The name of the town seems to have been derived from Dhavala-vaha 'white rivulet', the murmuring stream with crystalline water on the bank of which it is located. Gifted with natural amenities, the place was the playground of man during the Pleistocene period as evidenced by the discovery of chopper-chopping tools, hand-axes, cores and flakes. A Neolithic celt indicates the presence here of Neolithic man also. In about seventh century CE, it started flourishing as a mart for the hilly region of Himachal Pradesh on a trade route which connected the plains with the hills. While digging the foundations of a *thana* here, old Hindu and Jaina sculptures were found. Many of these sculptures were collected and placed in the temple at Dholbaha but many were left in situ. An inscription (never deciphered, apparently) was reproduced in Colonel Abbott's Memorandum on the first eight years of British rule in Hoshiarpur. It was probably a Sati monument. Parts of the image are also reproduced on page 379 of the Memorandum.[92] Pottery, sculptures and architectural remains scattered over an area of nearly 6.5 km indicate how fast the town developed and attracted affluent iconolatry with the Hindus and the Jainas erecting their edifices, thereby establishing art ateliers on the site as evidenced by some unfinished sculptures. Potsherds picked up from the site belong to the Kushāṇa, Gupta, early and late medieval periods.[93] No sculptures of the Kushāṇa and Gupta periods have, however, been found from Dholbaha, indicating that the real efflorescence took place in the early medieval period only. The art activity was perhaps at its acme during the Pratihāra period. Ultimately, however, it seems to have fallen to the iconoclastic hordes like most other sites of the area. The fort of Malot, which was erected during the reign of Bahlol Lodhi (CE 1451-89), is only 9 km southeast of Dholbaha.[94] I also saw old bricks measuring 32 x 24 cm during my first visit to the site on June 11, 1970.

The State Department of Archaeology undertook scientific clearance on two hill-tops (DLB-1 and 2) during 1990-92 for two seasons. These hill-tops were the sites of dilapidated temples. DLB-1 revealed the foundations of a temple only up to the floor level made of sandstone blocks set in dry masonry. Square on plan with entrance on all the four sides, it probably had a covered circumambulatory path. Presence of two types of pillars in the circumambulatory passage allowed free sunlight in it. The outer wall of the main shrine was 3.73 m high and 2.29 m wide. The inner side of the wall was built of gravels and rough sandstone cut into blocks. The foundation was built of three courses of quartzite pebbles, gravels and roughly hewn stones while the uppermost course consisted of fine gravels and pebbles. The total thickness of the terrace from base to floor was 3.20 m. The superstructure probably consisted of huge stone blocks kept in position by sheer weight and balance without any use of mortar or binding material. Potsherd comprising mostly sharp-edged rim and bases of bowls were recovered mainly from the place where heavy weight was to be put. This may have been done to protect the structure from the shocks of tremors during an earthquake. DLB-2, consisting of rectangular sanctum of 4.08 x 2.26 m up to the plinth level with entrance on the eastern side, showed the pedestal for the main image and a *praṇāla* (water channel) attached to the sanctum opening towards the south, indicating it to be a Śaiva temple. The two temples were tentatively dated to 14th and 16th century, respectively.[95]

### 13. Doong (Mukesar/Mukleshwar Caves)

Mukesar/Mukleshwar (now popularly called Mukteśvara) caves are located about 10 km up the Ravi from Shahpur Kandi on the left bank of the river near village Doong (also approachable from village Phongota), tehsil Pathankot of district Gurdaspur. There are four cave-temples of the Gupta period attributed to the Pāṇḍavas. The caves are artificial and seem to have remained in use up to the medieval period when the doorways were worked. On the facade of one of the caves were carved two female figures and on the left side of the cave was engraved an inscription in four lines in the late Gupta characters. Soft sandstone sculptures in the caves have decayed almost beyond recognition and an inscription on one of the doorjambs has become undecipherable. However, from the traces of letters, it seems to have belonged to *circa* 11th century CE.[96]

### 14. Ferozepur

Ferozepur is the district headquarters and an important city occupying a strategic position. It lies a few km south of the Satluj near India's border with Pakistan. In ancient times, it seems to have stood on the route which connected the Gaṅgā Valley with the northwest. In the medieval period, it connected the Doaba regions and the Himachal hills with Rajasthan. James Prinsep referred to the Standard Type coins of Samudragupta obtained from Ferozepur.[97] During the British regime, it was an important cantonment. The Jaina temple here contains medieval bronzes.

### 15. Ghanauli

Village Ghanauli is situated about 10 km northeast of Rupnagar on the way to Nangal. The village is located on an ancient mound which has yielded Painted Grey Ware and a beautiful greyish sandstone image of Umā-Maheśvara belonging to the Pratihāra period. The site has almost entirely been dug away for constructing the Bhakra canal which flows close by. Occupational layers of old habitation were exposed on the northern boundary of the village along the embankment of the canal.[98]

### 16. Ghuram

Also known as Kuhram/Kohram and Ramgarh, Ghuram (30° 7' N and 76° 33' E) is situated about 40 km south of Rajpura and 35 km south-southeast of Patiala on the road to Pehowa in district Patiala just on the Punjab-Haryana border. Located on the flood plain of the Ghaggar, it is about 10 km northwest of Pehowa. A very large mound covering about 100 acres and nearly 30 metres in height exists here but is being encroached now. At some period of time, a fortification must have existed here as is indicated by a mass of burnt bricks seen in some areas. According to local traditions, it was the abode of the maternal grandfather of Rāma, son of King Daśaratha of Ayodhyā. Extensive ruins mark its former greatness.[99] Excavations undertaken by the Department of Cultural Affairs, Archaeology and Museums, Punjab indicate that it was first inhabited by the Painted Grey Ware people around 1000 BCE and continued to flourish to the early historic period when people used Northern Black Polished Ware, black slipped ware and red wares, sometimes stamped with designs. Coins of the Mitra rulers have been found here in regular strata. Coins and a coin mould of Menander were also discovered.[100] Amongst other remains, worth mentioning is a terracotta piece bearing Brāhmī inscription in the characters of *circa* 5th century CE. It was fortified during the Gurjara-Pratihāra period and some beautiful sculptures including doorjambs, carved pillars, architectural pieces and an image of Śeshaśāyī Vishṇu have also been collected from here. In the medieval period, Kuhram is first mentioned as surrendering to Muhammad Ghori in 1192 CE. It remained a fief of Delhi during the early period of Muhammadan empire but later fell into decay. It was attacked by Banda Bahadur in 1710 CE.[101]

### 17. Hathur

Located about 55 km southwest of Ludhiana and about 15 km southwest of Raikot on Ludhiana-Moga border in tehsil Jagraon, Hathur is an ancient site from which antiquities, including coins and sculptures, have been discovered quite often. The present name is believed to have been derived from Arhatpura.[102] Lord Mahāvīra is said to have spent a Chaumāsā (*chaturmāsa*, i.e., four months of rainy season) here during the time of Kanakh Khetu Rājā. It was then known as Aichata Nagari.[103] No Jaina images have, however, been found from this place as yet and the site needs a thorough probe. An unidentified stone image of a male measuring 30 X 18 cm lies in the personal collection of Dr. Subhash Parihar of Faridkot. Some terracotta figurines and a mould of Mahishamardinī have also been recovered from the site.

### 18. Hawara

Hawara is a mound between Kurali and Sanghol in district Rupnagar. It has yielded medieval relics.[104] Fragments of medieval Hindu images, a terracotta figurine and a mould of Mahishamardinī have been obtained from this site.

### 19. Humayunpur-Tasimbali

The twin villages of Humayunpur-Tasimbali are located on the border of Punjab and Haryana on Lalru-Sidhpur road in tehsil Dera Bassi, district Mohali. According to a local tradition, it is the site of Rāmasara *tīrtha*. The Narasiṃha temple in Humayunpur has late medieval Daśāvatāra panels, a 20 X 20 cm worn out bust and head of Śiva, a 20 X 13 cm *makara-toraṇa* with Śiva on stele and Gaṇeśa on frieze and a 38 X 18 cm fragment of a pillar showing a *kīrtimukha, bharaṇī,* abacus, etc. while the Śiva-Durgā temple in Tisambali preserves a medieval pillar, part of a *nāgara-kūṭa* and late medieval Gaṇeśa and Nandī. These sculptures were recovered from the village pond where they may have been concealed intentionally to save them from desecration by the iconoclastic invaders or may have been immersed after having been destroyed by the invaders. According to the villagers, many of the broken sculptures were taken to Haridwar for immersion many years back by a *sādhu*.

### 20. Janer

Situated in 30° 54' N and 75° 09' E, Janer is a small village perched atop a large mound measuring about 7000 feet square and nearly 15 metres in height. It is situated about 10 km north of Moga on the road to Dharamkot close to the old bed of the Satluj.[105] The great mound represents the remains of an ancient town on Lahore-Meerut highway of yore referred to as Jajner[106] and Janid.[107] It has yielded antiquities and coins from the Indo-Scythian to the Muhammadan times.[108] During my first visit to this site in 1968, I had recovered copper coins of Kanishka and Raziya Sultana from here and noticed two images of Vishṇu, one complete and the other broken below the bust, exhumed by the villagers from this mound besides a large storage jar, beads of various shapes made of agate, opal, ruby, onyx, jasper, quartz, carnelian and lapis lazuli collected by a local inhabitant. The larger Vishṇu image was stolen but was recovered later and has now been set up in a specially built temple. Clay figurines of winged horse, elephant with rider, Varāha incarnation of Vishṇu, etc. have also been recovered from this site.

Cunningham has mentioned Jagner as one of its old names. A local tradition connects it with King Janaka. The present name may be derived from Janaka-nagara. Cunningham has recorded a story of its destruction which may have resulted from a famine. The mound deserves to be excavated before it is completely covered by housing and levelled for ploughing.[109]

### 21. Kalyan

Located about 7 km from Patiala on the road to Nabha, Kalyan (also called Panj Kalyan) has yielded lower part of an image of Ādinātha and a complete Tīrthaṅkara image of about 11th-12th century CE.[110] A terracotta mould of a goddess has also been picked up from here. The medieval Jaina temple at this place may have contained the depiction of the five scenes of the life of the Jinas (pre-birth, birth, consecration, perfection and emancipation) called *Kalyāṇaka* or *Pañcha-Kalyāṇa* in Jaina iconography and the place seems to have got its name from those scenes. The Hindu temple here contains two late medieval wooden sculptures of Gaṇeśa and some white marble images of Śiva-Pārvatī, Brahmā, Sūrya, etc. The site requires a deeper study and probe to reveal the remains of the temple which may have existed here.

### 22. Karhali

Situated about 25 km south-southwest of Patiala on the Guhla road, Karhali is the last village in Punjab on its border with Haryana on the said road. Old sherds and other remains are often recovered while ploughing. A buff sandstone portrait statue of the Kushāṇa period has also been recovered from this site.[111] The site needs a thorough probe and is likely to yield more important remains.

### 23. Khanpur

Khanpur is located opposite to Kharar on the right bank of the Patiala ki Rao in district Mohali, at the junction of the Ludhiana-Chandigarh and Rupnagar (Ropar)-Chandigarh roads, nearly 18 km from Chandigarh to its west and 25 km south of Rupnagar. A low mound, almost wiped out now for industrial units and urbanizing, yielded sherds of Painted Grey Ware, black-slipped and medieval wares.[112] In the mid-sixties of the last century, quite a few sculptures from this site were taken to and are now preserved in the Museum of the Department of Ancient Indian History, Culture and Archaeology, Panjab University, Chandigarh. A very rich collection of manuscripts existed here before the partition but, unfortunately, it was destroyed in a conflagration.

### 24. Kharar

It is located about 17 km northwest of Chandigarh on the left bank of the Patiala ki Rao on Chandigarh-Ludhiana/Rupnagar highway. Now almost defunct, a very large tank known as

Aja Sarovar after Aja, father of King Daśaratha, existed to the southeast of the present town. It has yielded pottery of Harappan affiliation with pre-Harappan impact.[113] Numerous old sculptures have been recovered from this tank, indicating the existence of numerous Hindu and Jaina temples during the medieval period. Large bricks of about 33 X 22 X 5 cm, probably belonging to the Kushāṇa period, were noticed here by Rodgers during 1888-89. Khanpur, on the other side of the rivulet, and Mundi Kharar or Churon ki Majri towards Chandigarh may have been parts of this town in olden times. Some sculptures from Mundi Kharar were removed to Central Museum, Lahore also and some were acquired by the Shimla Museum. A Vaikuṇṭha image is still under worship in Dera Baba Dhyan Dass, also known as Moriwala Mandir. Many sculptured fragments from this place acquired by Prof. Suraj Bhan and later by me are now housed in the Department of Ancient Indian History, Culture and Archaeology, Panjab University, Chandigarh. Many pieces from the site have also been lost.[114]

### 25. Khizrabad

It is located about 10 km east of Kurali in district Ropar and has yielded a beautiful Pratihāra image of Neminātha and a worn out figure of a goddess. Sherds of Painted Grey Ware have also been picked up from here.[115]

### 26. Lalru

Lalru is located on the Chandigarh-Ambala road and railway line, about 33 km south of Chandigarh and 12 km north of Ambala in tehsil Rajpura of district Patiala. Two medieval images of Vaikuṇṭha-Lakshmī and Yogāsana Vishṇu are fixed in the outer wall of a temple called Chaudhariom̤ kā Śivālā. According to some people, a local contractor brought them from Pinjaur and got them fixed here.

### 27. Majhur

Majhur (also spelled as Majhoor) is located about 14 km east of Nawanshahr, nearly 4 km south of the Chandigarh-Nawanshahr road, in district Nawanshahr. It can be approached from Balachaur via Charan on road to Rahon and is also linked with Jadla on Ropar-Nawanshahr road from where it is about 5 km southwest. The Satluj flows about one-and-a-half km south of it now. It must have been an important religious place as it has yielded quite a good number of medieval images of different deities and architectural pieces.

### 28. Mandian

Located in the Amloh tehsil of district Fatehgarh Sahib (formerly Patiala), Mandian has yielded a beautiful medieval Vishṇu image, pedestal of another Vishṇu image and some other remains. We, however, do not know whether the pedestal referred to above is the same 'fragment of sculpture' said to have been found from here which was referred to in the 'Annual Progress Report' of the Punjab Circle in 1908 or a different one.[116]

### 29. Mard Khera

Mard Khera is located on the Bhawanigarh-Sunam road, about 6 km east-southeast of Sunam. The old mound here yielded late Harappan and medieval pottery. It was excavated by the Chandigarh Circle of the Archaeological Survey of India.[117] An elegant image of Sūrya was found here in 1980 but was stolen later and has not been recovered yet. Some more medieval fragmentary pieces of Kshemaṇkarī, a beautiful female head probably of Pārvatī, Jaina Sarasvatī and Jina figures have been found from this site.

### 30. Morinda

Also known as Bāghāṃwālā due to the presence of green gardens in abundance, Morinda is located on the Chandigarh-Ludhiana highway about 32 km west of the former. Rodgers has described three old sculptured pillars and other remains from here: "They are 4 feet ½ inch high and are about 1 foot broad and 7½ inches thick. They are sculptured after the fashion of pillars in old Hindu temples. The tradition is that they were brought from the hills. They are now in a small temple north of the town. Two are used as door posts, and one stands up alone against the temple wall."[118] With the proliferation of urbanization, all old vestiges are being wiped out by and by.

### 31. Nolas

Located in tehsil Rajpura, district Patiala Nolas (also spelled as Nalas sometimes) has yielded a fragment of a medieval Vishṇu image and a stele showing Kubera. More remains may be lying buried here.

### 32. Rahon

Located on 31° 4' N and 76° 8' E, nearly 10 km south of Nawanshahr on the northern bank of the Satluj, Rahon is said to have been founded before the Christian era by one Rājā Rāghab, who gave it the name of Raghupura, which is still used by Hindu scholars. It was captured by Ghorewāha Rajputs in the time of Muhammad of Ghori whose leader renamed it Rāhon after a lady called Rāho.[119] Coins of Gondophares are also said to have been found from Rahon besides Late Harappan, early historic and medieval pottery.[120]

### 33. Rājinīdevī

Rājinīdevī is located about 12 km southeast of Hoshiarpur on the bank of an ephemeral runnel known after the present village on the Chandigarh-Hoshiarpur road. The present name may be derived from Rājanyā Devī, who may have been the tutelary deity of the Rājanya tribe which was located in this area and whose coins are reported to have been recovered from the Manaswal plateau of Hoshiarpur. There can be little doubt to the antiquity of the place as it is partially located on an old and extensive mound which measures about 500 X 200 meters and is approximately 7 meters in height. The mound is surrounded by Bhulewal village on the east, Bassi on the west, Chhoti Lehli on the southwest and Singhpur on the south. The oldest relics discovered from this mound during my first visit to the site on 8 June 1970 included grey ware sherds datable to the latter half of the first millennium BCE. Early historic plain red and black painted red wares indicated the continuity of the habitation in the centuries ensuing the beginning of the current era. Old coins are often found by the villagers while ploughing their fields. A fragment of the medieval image of dancing Gaṇeśa was found from this place. Some other fragments of sculptures seen in 1970 are no more present now. With the expansion of the village and expanding agricultural activity, the old mound is shrinking in size for being leveled every now and then. A modern temple dedicated to Rājinīdevī exists on the mound but people narrate different stories about her.[121]

### 34. Ropar (Rupnagar)

Ropar (30° 58' N Lat. and 76° 32' E Long.), now rechristened as Rupnagar, is a well known archaeological site on the southern bank of the river Satluj about 40 km northwest of Chandigarh. The old mound here is quite extensive and a part of it is covered by the modern town. A large block measuring about 1320 X 330 X 50-55 feet lying very close to the Government College was excavated by Dr. Y.D. Sharma during 1953-55 and an almost continuous sequence of occupations, six in number beginning with the Harappan, superimposed one over the other with some gaps of course, was revealed by the excavations. A Maurya ringstone (Pl. 1), beautiful Śuṅga and Gupta terracottas (Pls. 2 & 6), a bronze figure of a *Yājñika* Brāhmaṇa of Śaka-Kushāṇa period (Pl. 4), a late Kushāṇa carved bronze disc showing a winged griffin (Pl. 209), a Gupta brass mask of Śiva (Pl. 71), pedestal of a stone image of Ādinātha (Pl. 271) and numerous Jaina bronzes (Pls. 284-89) are known from this place.[122]

### 35. Rupalon

Rupalon (Lat. 31° 47' N and Long. 76° 7' E) is a small village situated some 3 km off the Samrala-Chawa road, in tehsil Samrala, district Ludhiana. The old mound measuring 400 X 200 m shows a deposit of about 3 m containing Harappan and early medieval material, including terracotta objects.[123] It seems to have contained an elegant Jaina temple in the tenth century, a fragment of which is now in the possession of Dr. Subhash Parihar of Faridkot.

### 36. Samana

Samana (30° 9' N & 76° 15' E) is the tehsil headquarters in district Patiala, located about 30 km southwest of the latter on the road to Patran and Tohana. It is a place of considerable antiquity. Tradition ascribes its foundation to the fugitives of Samanid dynasty of Persia on the site of a still older Naranjan Khera or Ratangarh.[124] It has yielded, amongst others, an architectural piece with Garuḍa belonging to about the 10th century CE.

### 37. Samuran

Located about 20 km east-southeast of Sunam, Samuran (also spelled as Samooran) was probably an important religious centre during the medieval period and has yielded Pratihāra images of Sūrya, Mahishamardinī and Jaina Tīrthaṅkaras. Many images found from here are said to have made their way to private collections also. The Chandigarh Circle of the Archaeological Survey of India also collected some fragmentary sandstone Jaina images from here.

### 38. Sanaur

Sanaur is located about 5 km southeast of Patiala and has yielded a typical Pratihāra stele carrying an image of Kubera.

### 39. Sahna

Sahna is located on the Barnala-Bhadaur road, about 15 km west-southwest of Barnala in district Sangrur. It has yielded a terracotta mould of Mahishamardinī.

### 40. Sanghol

Locally called Uchchā Piṇḍa (village on elevated level), Sanghol (30° 47' N and 76° 23' 30" E), now in district Fatehgarh Sahib, is one of the most well known and important archaeological sites of the Punjab which shot into international fame with the discovery of a Buddhist *stūpa* and the biggest-ever hoard of 117 Kushāṇa railing pillars of Mathura art in February 1985.[125] The village lies about a km south of the Chandigarh-Ludhiana highway, about 42 km west of the former and can also be approached from Morinda Railway Station on Sirhind-Nangal section or from Sirhind Railway junction itself being 9 and 16 km respectively from these places and connected with them by roads (Fig. 12). The river Satluj flows about 10 km north of Sanghol now but in ancient times, it may have been closer to the site as indicated by a dried-up old channel.

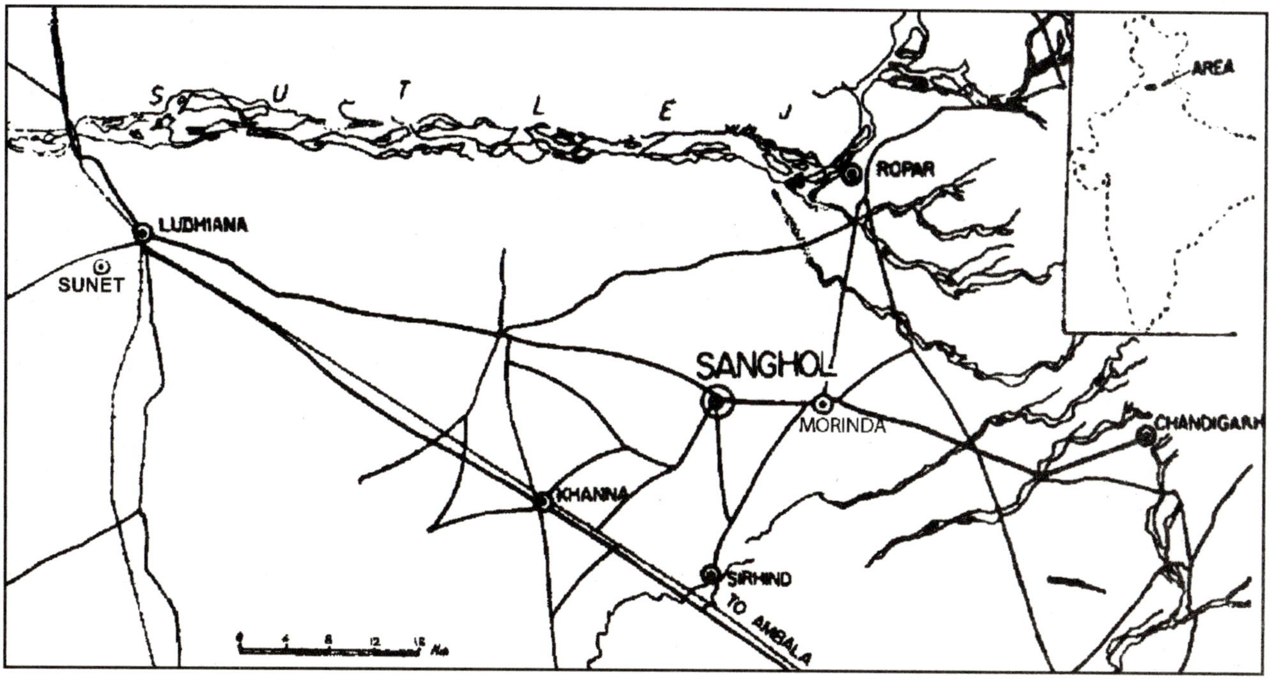


**Fig. 12.** Location of Sanghol (after G.B. Sharma).

According to local traditions, Sanghol was formerly known as 'Sāṃgala-dvīpa' and the folk tale of Rup Basant was associated with it like Ropar. The present name may be derived from Saṃgha-pura, a name which may have been given to it for its being a stronghold of the Buddhist congregation or Saṃgha. A beautiful clay sealing of the Gupta period carrying the Brāhmī legend *Nandipurasya* with a bull to right above is, however, regarded by some scholars to suggest its name as Nandipura during that period.

The present village is partially located on an old mound which covers an area of 200 X 220 m and touches a height of 24 m. There are some other low-lying mounds of which the Hathiwara to the northwest of the present habitation is the most important and has yielded significant archaeological remains. Excavations were undertaken here by Shri R.S. Bisht (1969-73), then by Shri G.B. Sharma from 1978-83 and ultimately from 1986 to 1990 when the Excavation Branch of the Archaeological Survey of India joined the State Department of Cultural Affairs, Archaeology and Museums, Punjab.[126] The excavations have revealed a cultural sequence of the following periods.

Period I – Chalcolithic or Bara Culture (*circa* 1900-1300 BCE)
Period II – Painted Grey Ware (*circa* 1100-700 BCE)
Period III – Black Slipped Ware (*circa* 600-200 BCE)
Period IV – Pre-Kushāṇa and later (100 BCE-CE 300)
Period V – Medieval and modern (from CE 1000)

It seems that the population was restricted to a much smaller part of the old town after the Kushāṇas. Some Gupta terracottas and seals/sealings, too, have been recovered, mostly from the surface. A considerable number of seals bearing the legend 'Śrī Mahārāja Kapila (saṃ)niyuktasyādhikaraṇasya' written in Gupta Brahmī characters of 4th-5th century indicate that Sanghol was the seat of a provincial or feudatory ruler during that period. A large number of seals and sealings bearing figures or symbols of various gods like Vishṇu and Śiva, and some terracotta figurines of Mahishamardinī have also been found from the site. From the area of the dispensary, many Hūṇa coins have been found.

Most spectacular, however, was the discovery of 117 Kushāṇa railing pillars, cross-bars and coping stones of Mathura idiom from near the main *stūpa*. Many other smaller and votive *stūpas*, Kushāṇa images of red sandstone, Gupta terracottas, stucco and seals and sealings were also exhumed or found from the surface. The city seems to have suffered depredations at the hands of the Hūṇas in their vigorous attacks during the last quarter of the fifth century. A large number of coins of Toramāna and Mihirakula, and a copper seal of the latter, have been recovered from the site. The glory and prestige of the town, however, seems to have dwindled considerably when the Chinese pilgrim visited this part of the country in the 7th century. The continued occupation of the site, however, is indicated by coins of Kota type, of the Hindu Shahi kings Spalapatideva and Sāmantadeva, and of Balban, etc.

### 41. Sarai Naga

Sarai Naga in the Faridkot tehsil and district has one of the very important old mounds which yielded relics from the early historic and medieval periods. Coins of Vāsudeva Kushāṇa, Sāmantadeva and later ones as well as some fragmentary sculptures have been found from this mound.[127]

### 42. Shahpur

Shahpur in tehsil Kharar, district Rupnagar has yielded some fragments of medieval Vaishṇava images.

### 43. Singh-Bhagwantpur

The twin village of Singh-Bhagwantpur is located on the Chandigarh-Ropar highway about 9 km north-northwest of Kurali and equidistant south-southeast of Rupnagar. A part of the village is located on an old mound which yielded Painted Grey Ware, black-slipped pottery and Kushāṇa and medieval remains. It was excavated by the Department of Ancient Indian History, Culture and Archaeology, Panjab University, Chandigarh during 1981-82.[128] A small image each of Vishṇu and Sūrya were obtained from this site.

### 44. Sirhind

Sirhind is a well known town of Punjab located about 70 km southeast of Ludhiana and 50 km northwest of Ambala on Ambala-Ludhiana section of the Northern Railway and the Sher Shah Suri Marg (National Highway No. 1). It was a mint town of the Mughals and Sikhs and figures prominently in the history of that period. Ballast for miles of railway lines for Patiala and Bathinda was obtained from the ruins of this city,[129] as a consequence of which no important remains except a few Mughal and Sikh monuments are left there.

The present site of the town, however, is not the place originally occupied by the historic Sirhind which was situated near the present Gurudwara Fatehgarh Saheb, some 4 km north of the present town. The site of the Gurudwara was originally occupied by a medieval fort. The remains of the historic town are scattered in 6 km radius of the Gurudwara. The nearby villages of Mir Miran, Talanian, Shaikhupura, Jandiali, Mahadian, etc., all formed parts of the historic Sirhind.

Cunningham visited this town in 1863-64 and alluded to its having been founded by the Sairindhras or 'the people of Sairindhra' referred to by the sixth century astronomer Varāhamihira in his treatise *Bṛihat Saṃhitā* (XIV.29-30). Since Varāhamihira himself has copied his account from that of the earlier astronomer, Parāśara, believed to have lived not later than the first century after Christ, the antiquity of the town may be taken to go back to that period and is confirmed by one coin of the Kushāṇa king Kanishka and a few specimens of the later Indo-Scythians found here by Cunningham.[130] Cunningham has also referred to a local tradition of its foundation by Sikander – Alexander and not Sikander Lodhi as done by some later writers.[131] During a visit to the Aam-Khas Bagh, a Mughal garden, I picked up some bricks of the Pratihāra period. Pratihāra pillars and images have also been obtained from this place.

### 45. Siswan

Situated at the entrance to the Siwaliks on the old Kurali-Shimla road, on the northern bank of the Siswan Nadi, it can be approached from Chandigarh also via a link road. In olden times, a road connected it with Ropar. Now reduced only to a small village, it was long the centre of an extensive trade with the Shimla states and Yarkand, and in spite of its out of the way location there was a thriving settlement of merchants there down to quite recent years. The route was given up after the opening of the Ambala-Kalka railway line in 1892. There is a temple dedicated to Bhairon (Bhairava, the gate-keeper of Śiva) which has been renovated from time to time utilizing old material.[132] Architectural pieces, including the doorjambs and fragments of sculptures on the top of a nearby hill, indicate the existence of a temple here during the tenth-eleventh centuries CE. With the development of the town old relics are vanishing from the site now. A dam has been constructed here to harness the Siswan choe which used to cause havoc during the rainy season earlier. Being close to Chandigarh, it is developing at a great pace now.

### 46. Sultanpur Lodi

Sultanpur Lodi is situated on the left bank of the Kali-Veni River, about 40 km west-southwest of Jalandhar. Cunningham identified it as the site of Tamasāvana described by the Chinese pilgrim Xuan Zang with numerous Buddhist *stūpas*, including one of King Aśoka containing the body relics of the Buddha, and monasteries. The site (Fig. 13) has yielded old coins ranging from cast copper ones to those of the Mughals.

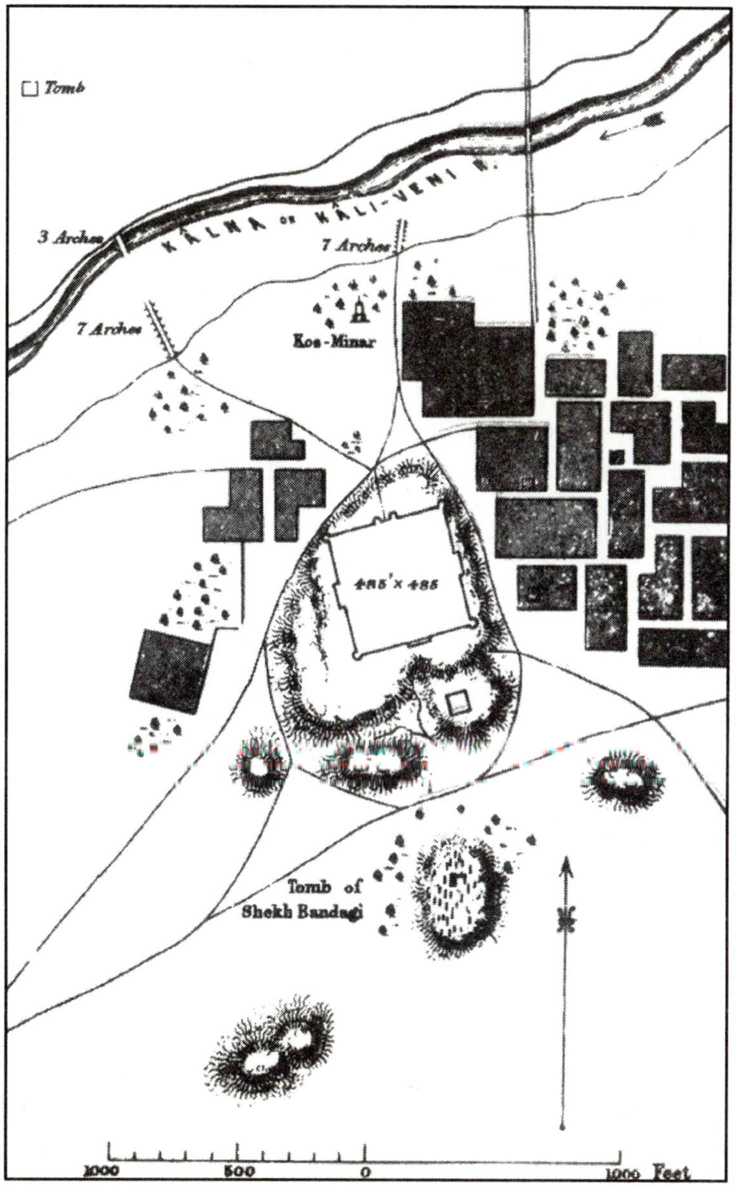


**Fig. 13.** The mound at Sultanpur Lodi (after Cunningham).

Daulat Khan Lodi made use of millions of old bricks measuring 28.75 x 20 x 5 cm in rebuilding the town and numerous others were perhaps utilized in the construction of the Jahangir serai. Cunningham also saw a brick of 11.5 X 8 X 2 inches including a carved one, a female figure in stone broken at the waist and a mould for making terracotta figurines of Gaṇeśa.[133] A *Mukha-liṅga* has also been recovered from the site.

### 47. Sunam

Situated about 18 km south of Sangrur on Ludhiana-Hisar section of the Northern Railway and well connected by road with Patiala, Bathinda, Ludhiana and Jakhal, Sunam is a well known town of Punjab. In ancient times, a palaeo-channel flowed from near the town which is partially inhabited on an old mound. Sherds of early and mature Harappan and Painted Grey Ware have been picked up from the mound. It is said that it was named Sunam during the time of Muhammad Ghori as it resembled the hump of a camel called 'Sunām' in Persian. The name may also be derived from the Sanskrit word 'Sunāma'. The site is also traditionally connected with the hermitage of Vālmīki, and a big tank called Sītā Sara is pointed out to be the pool where Sītā used to take bath. That it continued to flourish during the later half of the first millennium BCE is indicated by the discovery of plain Grey Ware from the site. Big hoards of Kushāṇa coins and terracottas found from here furnish evidence of its flourishing state at that time. In the absence of thorough investigations, it is difficult to say as to what happened during the subsequent half a millennium but the discovery of a hoard of 2½ kg silver coins of Sāmantadeva indicate that Sunam was an important town during the early medieval period. The town was wrested from the Hindu rulers by Muhammad Ghori during the last quarter of the 12th century. The earliest historical reference to the town, however, goes back to the time of Mahmud Ghaznavi as it finds mention in Alberuni's *Kitab-ul-Hind*.

During the 11th-12th centuries, Sunam was at the height of its glory. It formed part of the dominions of Iltutmish as an *iqta*. It was made the provincial headquarters during the reign of the Turk ruler Nasir-ud-Din Mahmud (AH 644-64 = CE 1246-65). It was captured by Balban. Coins of the Khalji, Tughlaq, Lodi rulers and the Mughals have been found from here. Quite a good number of medieval Hindu and Jaina images and architectural pieces indicate the existence here of numerous temples, which must have been destroyed during the Muslim rule.[134] The Jaina temple at Sunam was a great store-house of Jaina manuscripts, sculptures and bronzes at one time but many things have been donated and are fast disappearing now. Sculptures and architectural remains, old coins and other relics are now preserved in some temples and private collections. Sunam was famous for its carved wooden doorways, most of which have been sold out or disintegrated. It remained an important place during the Mughal period also and a Persian inscription of AH 987 (CE 1579) of the reign of Akbar has also been found from here.

### 48. Sunet

Sunet, once a small village situated in Long. 30° 55' North and Lat. 75° 51' East, about 5 km west of Ludhiana, a short distance south of the Ludhiana-Ferozepur road, has now been usurped by the Ludhiana city as a result of the growing urbanization and many modern colonies of the name of Aggarnagar, Bhai Randhir Singh Nagar, Satguru Nagar, etc. have come up on a substantial part of the old village. Locally, the village is called Uchchāpiṇḍa (village on a high plain) for being located on an elevated mound. When Alexander Cunningham visited the site in 1878-79, the mound measured 1750 feet in length and 1200 feet in breadth. He recorded that "Large bricks, 13 by 8 by 2¼ inches, are found in such a quantity that the Railway contractor obtained ballast sufficient for 18 miles of the Railway from the Satlej to Dorâha sarai. The fort of

Ludiana is said to have been built with them, and at the time of my visit I saw several cart-loads being taken to Ludiana."[135] Even the ballast for Ludhiana-Ferozepur railway line was taken from Sunet. Cunningham also saw two fragments of sculpture in sandstone, one being the body of a male figure, the other the knee of a squatted figure and states that, "At Sunit I obtained upwards of one thousand coins of which I was able to recognize 576. Amongst them was 1 coin of the Greek King Hermeus, 269 coins of the earlier Indo-Scythians, 132 of the later Indo-Scythians, 1 Gupta coin, and 126 of the Indo-Sassanian period. With them there were 2 old Hindu coins of Amogha-bhuti, 1 of Uttama-datta, and 17 of Vyâghra. Of Samanta Deva, about AD 900, there were no less than 20 specimens, but strange to say there was only one Muhammadan coin, an Ala-ud-din Muhammad of Delhi, amongst the 576 specimens."[136] From the total absence of coins of the Tomara kings of Delhi and the different Muhammadan dynasties, Cunningham concluded that "Sunit must have been destroyed during one of the invasions of Mahmud of Ghazni and afterwards remained unoccupied for many centuries."[137] About the destruction of Sunet, Tolbort and Cunningham have recorded the local legends.

During his tour of the Punjab in 1888-89, Charles J. Rodgers also surveyed Sunet 'very carefully on several successive days' and found that "The north end of the mound is occupied by the village of Sunet, but the highest part and many small mounds still exist, not built upon, towards the south and south-east of the village. It is from these that the antiquities of Sunet are now obtained by the villagers. These antiquities consist of seals in stone or metal, impressions of seals and coins on baked clay, coins, beads, carved bricks, images, old large bricks and dice."[138]

Carr-Stephens, too, had collected a large number of antiquities from Sunet, a bulk of which consisted of the coin moulds of the Yaudheya tribe bearing the Brāhmī legend *Yaudheya-gaṇasya jaya(ḥ)* and a clay sealing bearing the legend *Yaudheyānāṃ Jayamaṃtradharānāṃ* which he passed on to Dr. A.F.R. Hoernle.[139]

The present name Sunet has been derived by Prof. V.S. Agrawala[1409] from Saunetra mentioned by Pāṇini. According to the grammatical rules, the city founded by Sunetra would be known as Saunetra (*Sunetreṇa nirvṛittaṃ nagaraṃ Saunetram*), but the modern name is philologically more akin to Sunetra than Saunetra. There are numerous instances of the ancient cities named after their founders. Sunetra is mentioned in the *Mahābhārata*[141] as one of the sons of an earlier Dhṛitarāshṭra, son of Janamejaya. He seems to have been remembered as the eponymous founder of the ancient city. A small scale excavation of the site by G.B. Sharma[142] has, however, revealed the occupation of the site during the following periods:

| Period | | | |
|---|---|---|---|
| Period I: | Late Harappan | *circa* | 1800-1400 BCE |
| II: | Painted Grey Ware | | 1000-800 BCE |
| III: | Black Slipped & Grey Ware | | 600-200 BCE |
| IV: | Śuṅga-Kushāṇa | | 200 BCE-CE 300 |
| V: | Gupta | | CE 300-600 |
| VI: | Early Medieval | | CE 600-800 |

## 49. Velore

Velore is located about 9 km northeast of Ferozepur on the road to Zira and has yielded an almost complete image of Vishṇu. An image of Harihara was also discovered from this place.[143]

## 50. Zahura

Zahura (31° 37' 43" N and 75° 36' 08" E) is situated about 5 km southwest of Tanda Urmur in district Hoshiarpur just on its border with Jalndhar and Kapurthala. The old mound here lies just to the west and northwest of the village, measures about 1 km square and is nearly 30 metres in height. According to a local tradition, it was here that Janamejaya Pārīkshit, grandson of Abhimanyu, performed his *nāga-yajña* 'serpent sacrifice'. The sacred fire-altar of the sacrifice is pointed out in a temple built of *lakhauri* or Nanakshahi bricks to the north of the village. Those bitten by snakes are brought to the place and bathed in a nearby well as it is popularly believed that such an act neutralizes the snake venom. The mound has yielded Painted Grey Ware, black slipped, black painted red, plain red and red polished wares of the early historic period besides medieval and Muslim glazed wares. A large number of old bricks measuring 33-34 X 23-25 X 7-8 cm and square bricks of 25 X 25 cm have been found in the mound and used by the villagers in their tenements. Besides the central elevated portion which represents a medieval fort with a moat around assigned by the village elders to the Sikh period and destroyed by the British in the 19th century, the whole of the mound was under cultivation when I first visited the site about thirtyseven years back. While ploughing their fields on the mound, the villagers found old relics which were generally thrown away or even destroyed. A Gupta terracotta head with a beautiful coiffure was recovered but, unfortunately, its head was accidentally broken. A red sandstone bust of Buddha in *dharmachakrapravartana-mudrā* and two badly mutilated but interesting course-grained sandstone Mahishamardinī images obtained while ploughing the fields were, however, placed by the villagers in the above-mentioned temple.[144]

## NOTES AND REFERENCES

1. *Ṛigveda*, I.32, xii; 35, viii; 71.vii; 102, ii; II.12, vii; VIII.41, ix; 54. iv; 69, xiii; 96, i; IX.9, iv; 66, vi; X.43, iii; *Atharvaveda*, VI.61, iii; VII.57, ii; XX.17, iii; 34, xiii; 91, xii; 92, ix; etc.
2. Nundo Lal Dey, *The Geographical Dictionary of Ancient and Mediæval India*, Third edition, Delhi, 1971, pp. 180-81. Pañchanada was the name of a pilgrim place also in the Kurukshetra region (*Mbh.*, Vana Parva, 82, 83; 83, 16-17).
3. *Mahābhārata*, Sabhā Parva, 32, 11: *Tataḥ Pañchanadaṃ chaiva kṛitsnaṃ cha Kuru-jāṁgalam / Tathā Rohitakāraṇyaṃ maru-bhūmiścha kevalā //*. See also Karṇa Parva, 45; *Agni Purāṇa*, chapter 109.
4. *Śrī-Paṭṭāvalī-Samuchchaya*, compiled and edited by Muni Darshan Vijay, Viramgam, 1933: (*Śrī-Buddhi-vijaya-gaṇiḥ*) *Pañchanade saṃvegamata-dyotakeshu prathamaḥ* (p. 114); *Muni-Śrī-Vṛiddhi-chandraḥ/Yasya Pañchanade Rāmanagare navtyadhike ashṭādaśavarshe Osavaṃśe janma* (p. 115); *Tapasvī Śrī-Kāṃti-vijayaḥ Pañchanadīyaḥ* (p. 116); etc.
5. *Ibid.*, p. 115: *Śrī-Vijayānaṃda-Sūriḥ Pañchāpe Jainadharma-sthāpakaḥ. . . .*
6. R.C. Majumdar (Ed.), *The Age of Imperial Unity*, 4th ed., Bombay, 1968, p. 40. Curtius has referred to the Kshudrakas as Sudracae (J.W. McCrindle, *The Invasion of India by Alexander the Great as described by Arrian, Q. Curtius, Diodoros, Plutarch and Justin*, New Ed., Westminster, 1896, p. 238).
7. To resolve the controversy that arose following the demise of Buddha over his relics, a Brāhmaṇa named Droṇa, is said to have divided them into eight equal parts which were given to King Ajātaśatru of Magadha, the Lichchhavīs of Vaiśālī, the Śākyas of Kapilavastu, the Bulis of Allakappa, the Mallas of Kuśinagara, the Mallas of Pāvā, the Koliyas of Rāmagrāma and a Brāhmaṇa of Vethadvīpa for erecting *stūpas* over the corporeal relics. The Moriyas of Pipphalīvana who reached after the distribution took charcoal from the funeral pyre for erecting a *stūpa* at their capital and Droṇa himself, too, erected a *stūpa* over the urn in which the body relics were collected and divided.
8. He could not reopen the *stūpa* of Rāmagrāma because of the opposition of the Koliyas. There is, however, another tradition that Aśoka obtained the corporeal relics of Buddha from an underground chamber of Rājagṛiha where Ajātaśatru had secretly deposited the relics of seven of the original *śārīrika stūpas*.
9. Y.D. Sharma, "Exploration of Historical Sites", in *Ancient India*, Bulletin of the Archaeological Survey of India, No. 9, 1953, Special Jubilee Number, p. 123, Pl. XLVIII B; "Past Pattern in Living as Unfolded by Excavation at Ropar", *Lalit Kala*, Nos. 1-2 (April 1955-March 1956), p. 125, fig. 13; "Remains of Early Historical Cities", in *Archaeological Remains, Monuments and Museums*, Part I, Archaeological Survey of India, New Delhi, 1961, p. 48, Pl. XVI B. A small bronze statuette showing a similar mother goddess with elaborate head-dress, attenuated waist and broad rounded hips as depicted on the ringstone was also

found in excavation but it was unfortunately so much corroded that it concealed most of the details (*Lalit Kalā*, Nos. 1-2, p. 125, fig. 14).

10. Ananda K. Coomaraswamy, *History of Indian and Indonesian Art*, New York, 1927, p. 10, fig. 105. See also Prithvi K. Agrawala, *Early Indian Bronzes*, Varanasi, 1977, pp. 48-49, Illustration 70.
11. Coomaraswamy, *op. cit.*, p. 20; P.K. Agrawala, *Ancient Indian Mother-Goddess Votive Discs*, Varanasi, 1993; etc.
12. Cf. P.L. Vaidya (Ed.), *Divyāvadāna*, Darbhanga, 1959, Aśokāvadāna, p. 282: . . . .*Yāvadrājā Pushyamitraśchaturaṅgabalakāyaṃ saṃnāhayitvā-bhagavach-chhāsanaṃ vināśayishyāmīti Kukkuṭārāmaṃ nirgatataḥ/Dvāre cha siṃhanādo muktaḥ/Yāvatsa rājā bhītaḥ Pāṭaliputraṃ pravishṭaḥ/ Sa yāvachchhākalamanuprāptaḥ/Tenābhihitam – yo me śramaṇaśiro dāsyati, tasyāhaṃ dīnāraśataṃ dāsyāmi/.*
13. V.S. Agrawala, "Mathura Terracottas", *Journal of the U.P. Historical Society*, IX (11), pp. 6 ff; M.C. Joshi and C. Margabandhu, "Some Terracottas from Excavations at Mathura – A Study", *Journal of the Indian Society of Oriental Art*, No. 8 (1976-77), pp. 16-32.
14. V.S. Agrawala, *op. cit.*, p. 26 and "The Terracottas of Ahichchhatrā", *Ancient India*, No. 4, pp. 109 ff.
15. S.C. Kala, *Terracottas in the Allahabad Museum*, New Delhi, 1980, pp. 10 ff.
16. V.S Agrawala, "A New Yakshī Image from Mehrauli", *Journal of the U.P. Historical Society*, Vols. XXIV-XXV (1951-52), pp. 191-92 and plate (Reprinted in V.S. Agrawala, *Studies in Indian Art*, Varanasi, 1965, pp. 102-03).
17. Naman P. Ahuja, "Moulded Terracottas from the Indo-Gangetic Divide with Special Reference to Sugh" in P. Pal (ed.), *Indian Terracotta Sculpture – The Early Period, Marg*, Vol. 54, no. 1 (September 2002).
18. John Allan, *Catalogue of the Coins of Ancient India*, London, 1936 (*BMCAI*); Devendra Handa, *Tribal Coins of Ancient India*, New Delhi, 2007.
19. A.K. Narain, "The Two Hindu Divinities on the Coins of Agathocles from Ai-Khanum", *Journal of the Numismatic Society of India*, Vol. XXXV (1973), pp. 73-77, Pl. VII.
20. D.C. Sircar, *Select Inscriptions*, Vol. I, Calcutta, 1965, pp. 88-89.
21. Osmund Bopearachchi, "Was Sagala Menander's Capital?", *South Asian Archaeology 1989*, Monographs in World Archaeology, No. 14 (edited by Catherine Jarrige), Paris, 1989, pp. 327-37; Osmund Bopearachchi, "King Milinda's conversion to Buddhism, fact or fiction?" *Ancient Ceylon, Journal of the Archaeological Survey Department of Sri Lanka*, No. 7, 1990, pp. 1-15; T.W. Rhys Davids, *The Questions of King Milinda*, Sacred Books of the East Series, Vols. 35-36.
22. R.C. Sharma, "Interaction Between Mathura and Gandhara", *National Museum Bulletin*, Nos. 7-8 (1993), pp. 7-17.
23. H.C. Raychaudhuri, *Political History of Ancient India*, Calcutta, 1953, p. 437.
24. Osmund Bopearachchi, "Some Observations on the Chronology of the Early Kushans", Des Indo-Grecs aux Sassanides: donnees pour l'histoire et la geographie historique, *Res Orientales*, Vol. XVII (1997), p. 56.
25. S. Chattopadhyaya, *Early History of North India*, Calcutta, 1958, p. 62.
26. R.C. Senior ['Gondophares-Sases, St. Thomas and Era of Kanishka', in Manmohan Kumar (ed.), *Numismatic Studies*, Vol. 6, New Delhi, 2001, p. 88] refers to a hoard of coins which surfaced with a dealer in Delhi who had acquired a few tetradrachms from another dealer from Ambala. It contained a tetradrachm of Maues (enthroned deity type), two of Apollodotus II, one of Artemidoros and a Hippostratos tetradrachm while a second dealer in Delhi had drachms of Maues and Vonones. The coins of this hoard later appeared in London and in a subsequent visit, Senior saw more coins of this hoard in Srinagar. From personal information I know that the Ambala dealer had acquired a part of the big hoard found originally in Kashmir or Pakistan.
27. Charles Jas. Rodgers, *Report of the Panjab Circle of the Archaeological Survey for 1888-89*, Lahore, 1890, List of Coins, p. 2.
28. Allan, *op. cit.*, p. cxv.
29. G.B. Sharma and Manmohan Kumar, *Coins Seals and Sealings from Sanghol*, Chandigarh, 1986, pp. 44-50.
30. R.B. Whitehead, *Catalogue of Coins in the Punjab Museum*, Lahore, Vol. I, Oxford, 1914 (*PMC*, I), Pl. XV, no. 43. The nude male figure holding a scepter on the coins of Soter Megas (nameless king) [*Ibid.*, p. 163, Pl. XVI, no. 113] has also been identified as Śiva by some scholars.
31. *Ibid.*, Pl. XII, no. 308.

32. *Ibid.*, Pl. XIII, no. 332.
33. Alexander Cunningham, *Coins of Ancient India*, London, 1896, p. 85; Allan (1936), *op. cit.*, pp. cxv and 187.
34. S. Konow, Corpus Inscriptionum Indicarum, Vol. II, Part I, *Kharoshṭhī Inscriptions with the Exception of those of Aśoka*, Calcutta, 1929, p. 48.
35. C. Margabandhu, "Excavations at Sanghol, District Ludhiana, Punjab: 1985-90 – A Note on the Settlement Pattern and Cultural Sequence", in Jagat Pati Joshi (Chief Editor), *Facets of Indian Civilization: Recent Perspectives, Essays in Honour of Prof. B.B. Lal*, 3 vols., New Delhi, 1997, Vol. II, p. 378, Pl. 41.9.
36. Y.D. Sharma, "Past Pattern in Living as Unfolded by Excavation at Ropar", *Lalit Kala*, Nos. 1-2 (April 1955-March 1956), p. 126.
37. R.C. Senior, More Gondophares, Less Azes and Just Who Met St Thomas? *Oriental Numismatic Society Occasional Paper No. 25*. London: Oriental Numismatic Society, June 1991, pp. 1-12.
38. Joe Cribb, "A New Bactrian inscription of Kanishka the Great", *Silk Road Art & Archaeology*, Vol. 4 (1995-96), pp. 97-142.
39. Bopearachchi (2007), *op. cit.*, pp. 41-53.
40. Percy Gardner, *The Coins of the Greek and Scythic Kings of Bactria and India in the British Museum*, Chicago, 1976, pp. 124-28, Pl. XXV.6-12.
41. Bopearachchi (2007), *loc. cit.*
42. Gardner, *op. cit.*, pp. 129-35, Pls. XXVI-XXVII.1-7.
43. *Ibid.*, pp. 136-58, Pls. XXVII.8-XXIX.7.
44. Devendra Handa, "Huvishka's Buddha Image Gold Coin", *Numismatic Digest*, Vols. 29 (2005-2006), pp. 53-58.
45. Craig Alden Burns, "1984 Yields Two Unique Kushan Coins", *Ibid.*, Vol. IX (1985), pp. 52-53.
46. Devendra Handa, *Tribal Coins of Ancient India*, New Delhi, 2007, pp. 149-217.
47. John Faithful Fleet, Corpus Inscriptionum Indicarum, Vol. III; *The Inscriptions of the Early Gupta Kings and their successors*, Calcutta, 1888, p. 8: *Samataṭa-Ḍavāka-Kāmarūpa-Nepāla-Kartṛipur=ādi pratyanta-nṛipatibhir-Mālav=Ārjunāyana-Yaudheya-Madrak=Ābhīra-Prārjuna-Sanakānīka-Kāka-Kharparik=ādibhiścha sarvva-kara-dān=ājñā-karaṇa praṇām=āgamanena.*
48. Watters, pp. 296-97.
49. B.N. Puri, *History of the Gurjara Pratiharas*, Bombay, 1967, pp. 39 ff.
50. *Gauḍavaho*, edited by S.P. Pandit, Bombay, 1887, verse 484.
51. H.A. Phadke, *Haryana: Ancient and Medieval*, New Delhi, 1990, pp. 79-80.
52. *Rājataraṅgiṇī*, English translation by K.S. Pandit, New Delhi, 1977, IV.133-45.
53. *EI*, XVIII, p. 99, verse 7.
54. *Ibid.*, XLI, pp. 552 and 56, verses 5-7.
55. These inscriptions have been edited many times. For the latest re-edition, see Devendra Handa, *An Epic Pilgrimage: History and Antiquity of Pehowa: The Ancient Pṛithūdaka – A Mahābhārata Site on the Sarasvatī*, New Delhi, 2004, pp. 84-96.
56. Alexander Cunningham, *Archaeological Survey Report*, XIV, p. 67.
57. K.K. Maheshwari, *Imitations in Continuity: Tracking the Silver Coinage of Early Medieval India*, IIRNS, Mumbai, 2010, p. 262.
58. Dasharatha Sharma (Gen. Ed.), *Rajasthan Through the Ages*, Vol. I, Bikaner, 1966 (*RTA*), map facing p. 480.
59. *Raghuvaṃśa-muktā-maṇinā Āryavarta-mahārājādhirājena Śrī-Nirbhaya-narendra-nandanena* . . . . (*Bālabhārata*).
60. Rājaśekhara's *Bālabhārata*, verse 17: *Namita-Murala-maulīḥ pākalo Mekalānāṃ raṇa-kalita-Kaliṅgaḥ Keli-tat Keralendoḥ / Ajani jita-Kulūtāḥ Kuntalānāṃ kuṭhāro haṭha-hṛita-Ramaṭha-śrīḥ Śrī-Mahīpāladevaḥ //.*
61. *RTA*, p. 185.
62. Jagannath Agrawal, *Inscriptions of Haryana, Punjab, Himachal & Kashmir*, ICHR, New Delhi, 1991, pp. 144-46.
63. *Kāvyamīmāṃsā* of Rājaśekhara, edited by C.D. Dalal and R.A. Sastry, GOS, Baroda, 1934, p. 94: *Pṛithūdakāt-parata Uttarāpathaḥ yatra Śaka-Kekaya-Vokkāṇa-Hūṇa-Vāṇ=āyuja-Kamboja-Vāhlīka-Vahlava-Limpāka-Kulūta-Kīra-Taṅgaṇa-Tushāra-Turushka-barbara-Harahūra-Vahuhuka-Sahuḍa-Haṃsamārga-Ramaṭha-Karakaṇṭha-prabhṛitayo janapadāḥ //.*

64. G.B. Sharma and Manmohan Kumar (1986), *op. cit.*, pp. 44-50.
65. Jagannath Agrawal (1991), *op. cit.*, p. 25.
66. C.V. Vaidya, *History of Medieval Hindu India*, Pune, 1921-26, III, pp. 71 ff; Wolseley Haig, *Cambridge History of India* (Reprint, Delhi, 1958), III, pp. 18 ff; R.C. Majumdar (Ed.), *The Struggle for Empire*, Bombay, 1955, pp. 10-11. For original sources, see *Al-Beruni's India* (Ed. Edward Sachau, Delhi, 1989, reprint), Part I, p. 117 and Part II, p. 103; Al-Utbi's *Kitab-i-Yamini* (Eng. Tr. by James Reynolds), *Memoirs of Mahmud of Ghazni*, London, 1858, pp. 393 ff; Islami's *Fatuh-us-Salatin* (Ed. Agha Mahdi Hussain), Agra, 1938, I, p. 123; *Tarikh-i-Farishta* (Eng. Tr.) by John Briggs, *The Rise of the Mohammadan Power in India*, Calcutta, 1966, I, pp. 29-31; etc.
67. Vaidya, *loc. cit.*, pp. 70-71; *The Struggle for Empire*, pp. 94 ff.
68. *Ibid.*
69. Buddha Prakash, "Kashmir and Haryana in Eleventh Century", *Journal of Haryana Studies*, Kurukshetra, Vol. II (1970), pp. 13-17.
70. *RTA*, pp. 169 ff.
71. *Ibid.*, p. 553.
72. *Ibid.*, p. 172.
73. Dasharatha Sharma, *Early Chauhān Dynasties*, 2nd revised edition, Delhi, 1975, pp. 48-49 and 203-204.
74. Devendra Handa, "Anna's Northern Expedition", in D.W. Macdowal, Savita Sharma and Sanjay Garg (Eds.), *Indian Numismatics, History, Art & Culture: Essays in Honour of Dr. Parameshwari Lal Gupta*, 2 vols., Delhi, 1992, II, pp. 297-99.
75. F. Kielhorn, "Delhi Siwalik Pillar Inscription of Vīsaladeva, the Vikrama Year 1220", *Indian Antiquary*, XIX (1890), pp. 210-19, Third Inscription.
76. Jagannath Agrawal (1991), *op. cit.*, pp. 112-17.
77. *RTA*, map facing page 290.
78. S.P. Gupta (Ed.), *Kushāṇa Sculptures From Sanghol (1st-2nd Century AD): A Recent Discovery*, National Museum, New Delhi, 1985.
79. Y.D. Sharma (1953, 1955-56 & 1961), *loc. cit.*; *Indian Archaeology – A Reviw*, 1964-65, p. 75, Pl. LII.A; 1975-76, p. 73; 1977-78, p. 45; 1978-79, p. 19; 1987-88, pp. 95-99, Pls. XXXII-XL; 1988-89, pp. 69-73, Pls. XXIX-XL; 1989-90, pp. 88-94, Pls. XXV-XXX; Devendra Handa, "Some Sculptures from Punjab and Haryana", *Research Bulletin (Arts), Panjab University*, Chandigarh, Vol. VII, No. 1 (April, 1976), pp. 94-95, Figs. 4-5; "Sculptures from Punjab", Vol. XII (1981), *Ibid.*, p. 69, Figs. 6-7. "Trimūrti Mahishāsuramardinī", *East and West*, New Series, Vol. 29, Nos. 1-4 (December 1979), pp. 153-56, Figs. 1-2; "Medieval Brahmanical Sculptures From Punjab", *Roopa-Lekha*, Vol. LIV, No. 142 (March 1983), p. 32, Fig. 14; (1987), pp. 308-10; "Archaeological Remains from Sunam", *Panjab University Research Bulletin (Arts)*, Chandigarh, Vol. XVIII, No. 2 (October 1987), pp. 105-19, Pls. I-XXVIII; Manmohan Kumar, "Some Brahmanical Sculptures from Dholbaha", *Roopa-Lekha*, Vol. L (1981), pp. 49-51; V.C. Ohri, *Sculpture of the Western Himalayas (History and Stylistic Development)*, Delhi, 1991; Sanjeev P. Srivastava and R.P. Srivastava, *Studies in Punjab Sculpture*, New Delhi, 2001; brochures of the Department of Archaeology, Museums and Tourism, Punjab and of the National Museum, New Delhi; etc.
80. *BMCAI*, p. cli, fn. 8.
81. *Imperial Gazetteer of India*, Vol. I, pp. 450-51; *Kharatara-Gachchha-Bṛihad-Gurvāvali* of Jinapāla Upādhyāya and others, collected and edited by Jina Vijaya Muni, Bombay, 1956, p. 1. The Paṭṭāvalī refers to Jinachandrāchārya of Abohar, the guru of Vardhamāna Sūri, who had taken to the ease and comforts of living in the *chaitya*, dismayed by which Vardhamāna moved to Ḍhillī (Delhi) and was later ordinated by Uddyotanācharya there: *Abhora-deśe Jinachandrāchāryā deva-gṛiha-vāsinaśchaturaśīti-sthāvalaka-nāyakā āsan / Teshāṃ Vardhamāna-nāmā śishyaḥ/. . . Tasya mano na ramate chaityagṛihavāse sthātum / Tato guroḥ sammatyā nirgatya katichin-muni-sameto Ḍhillī-Vādalī-prabhṛiti-deśeshu samāyātaḥ / Tasmin prastāve tatraivoddyotanāchārya-sūri-vara āsīt/Tasya pārīve samagāgama-tattvaṃ buddhvā upasampadaṃ gṛihītavān/*
82. *IAR*, 1975-76, p. 73; Devendra Handa, "Some Ancient Cities and Towns of Punjab", in *Indological Studies (Essays in Memory of Shri S.P. Singhal)*, edited by Devendra Handa, Delhi, 1987, pp. 304-06.
83. G.B. Sharma and Manmohan Kumar (1986), *op. cit.*, p. 44; Sadhu Ram, "A Unique Terracotta Mould of Durgā from Panjab", *Vishveshvaranand Indological Journal*, Hoshiarpur, Vol. IX, pp. 137-38. See also *IAR*,

1975-76. p. 73 where a Kuṇinda coin is also reported to have been discovered along with the coins of the Indo-Greeks and of Gondophares.

84. *Rodgers' Report*, List of Coins, p. 2; *BMCAI*, p. 91, no. 210.
85. *Annual Report, Archaeological Survey of India*, Punjab Circle, 1910-11, pp. 18-20; *Panjab District Gazetteers*, Vol. VII, Part A: *Ambala District 1923-24*, Lahore, 1925, pp. 135-36.
86. *IAR*, 1977-78, p. 45; 1978-79, p. 19; Devendra Handa, "Medieval Brahmanical Sculptures from Punjab", *Roopa-Lekha*, Vol. LIV, No. 142 (March 1983), p. 32, Fig. 14; (1987), pp. 308-10.
87. *The Tribune*, dated 13.10.1979; *IAR*, 1979-80, p. 105.
88. G.B. Sharma and Manmohan Kumar (1986), *loc. cit.*; Suraj Bhan, *Excavation at Mitathal (1968) and Other Explorations in the Sutlej-Yamuna Divide*, Kurukshetra, 1975, p. 122.
89. Lalman, "Sculptural Remains from Burail (Chandigarh)", *Panjab University Research Bulletin (Arts)*, Vol. XX, No. 2 (October 1989), pp. 177-79, Figs. 1-5.
90. *IAR*, 1976-77, p. 41; Dilip K. Chakrabarti and Sukhdev Saini, *The Problem of the Sarasvati River and Notes on the Archaeological Geography of Haryana and Indian Panjab*, New Delhi, 2009, p. 243.
91. Alexander Cunningham, *Archaeological Survey Report (CASR)*, Vols. XIV, pp. 53-54 and XXI, p. 134; *IAR*, 1976-77, p. 41.
92. *Punjab District Gazetteers – Hoshiarpur District 1904* (Lahore, 1906), p. 14.
93. *IAR*, 1991-92, p. 91.
94. *Rodgers' Report*, p. 37.
95. *IAR*, 1990-91, p. 58; 1991-92, pp. 91-92.
96. *Ibid.*, 1975-76, p. 77; 1981-82, p. 98; *IGI*, II, pp. 59-61.
97. James Prinsep, *Essays in Indian Antiquities*, edited by Edward Thomas, London, 1858, p. 58.
98. *The Tribune*, dated July 17, 1984; *IAR*, 1983-84, p. 169, Pl. 82.
99. *Imperial Gazetteer of India*, Vol. II, p. 305.
100. G.B. Sharma and Manmohan Kumar, *op. cit.*, p. 45; *IAR*, 1975-76, p. 73; 1976-77, pp. 44-45, Pls. XXXI-XXXIV.
101. G.B. Sharma, "A Summary of Archaeological Excavations in Punjab", *Archaeology & Sculpture Exhibition*, Chandigarh, (no date), p. 13; *The Hindustan Times* dated 7.7.1976.
102. *Rodgers' Report*, p. 47. Coins of Menander, Vāsudeva, Kota and Gadhaiya types, Spalapatideva and Sāmantadeva are reported from here (G.B. Sharma and Manmohan Kumar, *op. cit.*, pp. 45-46).
103. *PDG – Vol. XV A: Ludhiana District and Malerkotla State 1904* (Lahore, 1907), pp. 227-28.
104. Suraj Bhan, *loc. cit.*
105. *CASR*, XIV, pp. 67-69; C.J. Rodgers, *A Revised List of Objects of Archaeological Interest in the Punjab*, Lahore, 1891, p. 32; Handa (1987), *op. cit.*, pp. 316-18.
106. Edward Sachau, *Alberuni's India*, New Delhi, 1964, p. 206.
107. *Ain-i-Akbari*, Eng. Tr. by Gladwin, Vol. 2, p. 343.
108. Cunningham, *loc. cit.*; Rodgers, *loc. cit.*
109. Handa (1987), *op. cit.*, pp. 316-18.
110. *IAR*, 1978-79, p. 55, p. 55, Pl. LIII.A. Shri G.B. Sharma has informed me (personal communication on 11. 07. 2010) that the stone *nāgarakūṭa* with a Jina, now in the Sanghol museum, was also obtained from this site.
111. Handa (1987), *op. cit.*, pp. 318-20.
112. *IAR*, 1964-65, p. 33; 1998-99, p. 135; Devendra Handa, "Relics of Art from Khanpur (Punjab)", in Shankar Goyal (Ed.), *Śrīrāmābhinandanam Reconstructing Indian History for S.R. Goyal*, Vol. II, Jaipur, 2003, pp. 507-12, Figs. 16.
113. *Kalyāṇa* (Tīrthāṅka), Gita Press, Gorakhpur, Jan. 1957, p. 67; *IAR*, 1962-63, p. 17; Suraj Bhan (1968), *op. cit.*, p. 123.
114. Handa (1987), *op. cit.*, pp. 320-22. G.B. Sharma and Manmohan Kumar (*op. cit.*, p. 46) have referred to the discovery of Vāsudeva type late Kushāṇa coins from Mundi Kharar.
115. *IAR*, 1998-99, p. 133.
116. *Annual Progress Report, Panjab Circle, 1908*, p. 44.
117. *Indian Archaeology – A Review*, 1981-82, p. 99.
118. *Rodgers' List*, p. 53.

119. *IGI*, I, p. 424.
120. G.B. Sharma and Manmohan Kumar, *op. cit.*, p. 47; *IAR*, 1976-77, p. 41.
121. Devendra Handa (1987), pp. 325-27.
122. B.B. Lal, "The Painted Grey Ware of the Upper Gangetic Basin", *Journal of the Royal Asiatic Society (Letters)*, Vol. XVI (1950), pp. 89 ff; "Excavation at Hastināpura and Other Explorations in the Upper Gaṅgā and Sutlej Basins (1950-52)", *Ancient India*, Nos. 10-11 (1954-55), p. 141; *Indian Archaeology – A Review*, 1953-54, pp. 6-7, Pls. II-IV; 1954-55, pp. 9-11, Pls. VI-IX; Y.D. Sharma, *Ancient India*, No. 9 (1953), pp. 125 ff; "Past Patterns in Living as Unfolded by Excavation at Ropar", *Lalit Kala*, Nos. 1-2 (April 1955-March 1956), pp. 122 ff; "Early Historic Cities", in A. Ghosh (Ed.), *Archaeological Remains, Monuments and Museums*, Part I, New Delhi, 1964, p. 8, Pl. II.A.
123. *IAR*, 1981-82, p. 55.
124. *IGI*, II, pp. 308-09.
125. S.P. Gupta (Ed.), *Kushāṇa Sculptures from Sanghol (1st-2nd Century AD): A Recent Discovery*, Vol. I, National Museum, New Delhi, May 1985.
126. *Indian Archaeology – A Review* (*IAR*) 1968-69, pp. 25-26; 1969-70, pp. 31-32; 1971-72, pp. 39-41; 1972-73, pp. 28 and 57; 1975-76, p. 73; 1977-78, pp. 43-44; 1978-79, p. 91; 1984-85, pp. 62-66 & 151, Pls. 35-36; 1985-86, pp. 67-69; 1986-87, pp. 69-71; 1987-88, pp. 95-99, Pls. XXXII-XL; 1988-89, pp. 69-73, Pls. XXIX-XL; 1989-90, pp. 88-94, Pls. XXV-XXX; "Some Further Evidence from Sanghol Excavations: 1986-87", in J.S. Ahluwalia (Ed.), *Historico-Archaeological Linkages of Punjabiat*, Department of Cultural Affairs, Archaeology, Archives and Museums, Punjab, Chandigarh, 1987, pp. 3-9, Pls. I-XVI; "Excavations at Sanghol, District Ludhiana, Punjab: 1985-90 – A Note on the Settlement Pattern and Cultural Sequence", in Jagat Pati Joshi (Chief Ed.), *Facets of Indian Civilization Recent Perspectives Essays in Honour of Prof. B.B. Lal*, 3 vols., New Delhi, 1997, Vol. II, pp. 373-81, Pls. 41.1-13; C. Margabandhu and G.S. Gaur, "Some Fresh Evidence from Sanghol Excavations, 1986", *Purātattva*, No. 16 (1985-86), pp. 73-78; "Sanghol Excavations, 1987, Some New Evidence", *Ibid.*, No. 17 (1986-87), pp. 1-4; "Excavations at Sanghol, Dist. Ludhiana, Punjab, 1985-90; Some New Evidence on the Cultural Sequence", in B.U. Nayak and N.C. Ghosh, *New Trends in Indian Art and Archaeology*, New Delhi, 1992, pp. 183-92; G.B. Sharma and Manmohan Kumar, *Coins, Seal and Sealings from Sanghol*, Chandigarh, 1986; etc.
127. *PDG: Ferozepur District*, Lahore, 1916, pp. 19-20; Sharma and Manmohan Kumar, *op. cit.*, p. 48.
128. *Indian Archaeology – A Review*, 1980-81, pp. 49-54. Harappan pottery was also reported from here later (*IAR*, 1998-99, p. 133).
129. *CASR*, II, p. 210; *Rodgers' Report*, pp. 1-8.
130. *CASR*, II, p. 212.
131. For details regarding its history, nomenclature, etc., see Subhash Parihar, *History and Architectural Remains of Sirhind – The Great Mughal City on Delhi-Lahore Highway*, New Delhi, 2006.
132. *Panjab District Gazetteers*, Vol. VII, Part A: Ambala District 1923-24, Lahore, 1925, pp. 25 & 135.
133. *CASR*, XIV, 54-58; Thomas Watters, *On Yuan Chwang's Travels in India*, 1st Indian Edition, Delhi, 1961, pp. 294-96.
134. Devendra Handa (October 1987), *op. cit.*, pp. 105-19, Pls. I-XXVIII. See also *IAR*, 1981-82, p. 99.
135. *CASR*, XIV, pp. 65-66. See also *Punjab District Gazetteer: Ludhiana District, 1888-89*, pp. 19-20; *Imperial Gazetteer of India*, Vol. I, p. 437; *IAR*, 1983-84, pp. 67-70.
136. *Ibid.*
137. *Ibid.*
138. *Rodgers' Report*, p. 34.
139. A.F.R. Húrnle, "Impressions of Clay Seals from Sunet", *Proceedings of the Asiatic Society of Bengal*, III, September 1884, pp. 137-40.
140. *Journal of the Numismatic Society of India*, Vol. IV (1942), p. 47 and *India as Known to Pāṇini*, Varanasi, 1963, p. 74.
141. *Mahābhārata*, Ādi Parva, 94.61.
142. *IAR*, 1971-72, p. 70; 1972-73, P. 57; G.B. Sharma, "A Summary of Archaeological Excavations in Punjab", *Archaeology & Sculpture Exhibition*, Cultural Affairs, Arch. Museum, and State Archives, Punjab, Chandigarh (no date), pp. 20-28.
143. *IAR*, 1964-65, p. 75, Pl. LII.A.
144. Handa (April, 1976), pp. 94-95, Figs. 4-5; (1981), p. 69, Figs. 6-7; (December 1979), pp. 153-56, Figs. 1-2.

# 2

# Vishṇu

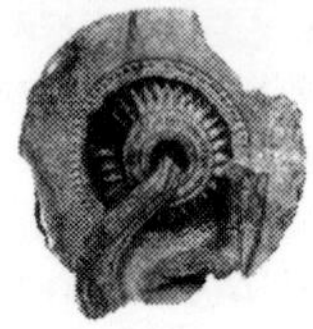

Yasmādvishṭamidaṃ viśvaṃ tasya śaktyā mahātmanaḥ /
Tasmātsā prochyate Vishṇurviśerdhātoḥ praveśanāt //

(*Vishṇu Purāṇa* III.1, 45)

Vishṇu has been invoked in five complete hymns and partially in another in the *Ṛigveda*.[1] His epithets *urukrama, vikrama* and *urugāya,* meaning wide going and wide traversing, led Macdonell,[2] Keith[3] and others[4] to ascribe him the solar origin. Gonda[5] has, however, tried to prove that Vishṇu also represented a fertility and vegetation god. In the *Brāhmaṇas,* Vishṇu is identified with sacrifice (*yajño vai Vishṇuḥ*) and since sacrifice was the highest form of religious expression, he gained ascendancy and achieved a higher status.[6] With the development of the concept of devotion during the Upanishadic period, a cult seems to have developed round the five Vṛishṇi heroes *(Vṛishṇi-pañchavīrāḥ),* of which Vāsudeva-Vishṇu was the main figure besides Saṃkarshaṇa, Pradyumna, Aniruddha and Sāmba.[7] According to the *Mahābhārata,* Vāsudeva is the Supreme Creator and Saṃkarshaṇa, representing all living beings, is only a form of Vāsudeva. From Saṃkarshaṇa sprang Pradyumna (mind) and from him came forth Aniruddha (self-consciousness). Vāsudeva describes the other four as his own *mūrtis* 'forms' produced from one another.[8] These four forms *(vyūhas)* are sometimes combined together and we get *chaturvyūhamūrtis* of Vishṇu, also called Vaikuṇṭha-*Chaturmūrti.*[9] Later, the number of *vyūhas* increased to twenty-four under the *Pāñcharātra* impact and the only difference amongst the twenty-four forms *(Chaturviṃśatimūrtis)* [10] of Vishṇu was the order of attributes in their hands. It is interesting to note that the number of Jaina Tīrthaṅkaras is also twenty-four and this number may have influenced the *vyūha* forms.

Bhandarkar has adduced sufficient evidence to establish that a religious cult centering on Vāsudeva had come into existence as early as the fourth-third century BCE.[11] The image of Herakles installed in front of the army of Porus on the bank of the river Vitastā, as referred to by the Greek historian Curtius, is identified as that of Vāsudeva-Kṛishṇa by some scholars and indicates his worship in the fourth century BCE.[12] Ptolemy also refers to the people around Vitastā as the worshippers of Vāsudeva.[13] The Garuḍa-dhvaja Pillar Inscription of Vidiśā[14] tells us that

Heliodoros, a Greek ambassador, who was the son of Diya (Dion), a resident of Taxila, installed the Garuḍa standard in honor of Vāsudeva at Vidiśā. Evidently, Vaishṇavism had spread to and was very popular in the Taxila region during the second century BCE. Square copper coins of Agathocles (171-160 BCE) found from Ai Khanoum in Afghanistan,[15] depicting Vāsudeva and Saṃkarshaṇa (Figs. 4-5), bear evidence to Vishṇu worship at an early date as noted above.

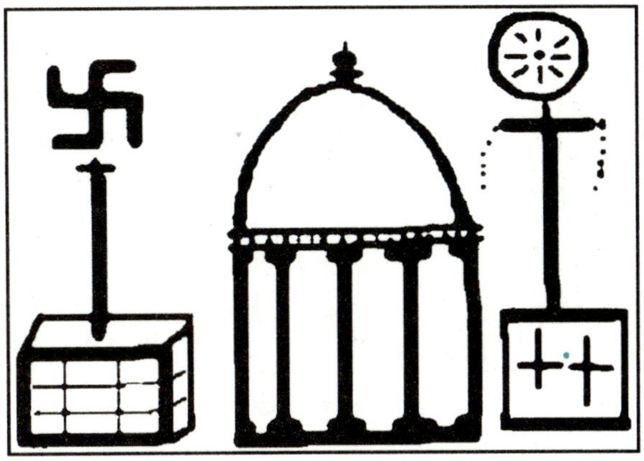

**Fig. 14.** Vaishṇava temple depicted on an Audumbara coin.

*Vibhavavāda* 'incarnation theory' as well as some folk cults may have further contributed to the evolution of Vishṇu cult. Vishṇu worship seems to have flourished in the Gupta age and got further popularity in the early medieval period. Ultimately, the cult of Vishṇu gained ascendancy over others and became the most important of the Brahmanical cults.

Punjab had its early association with Vāsudeva-Vishṇu. A square unattributed Audumbara coin shows a Vaishṇava temple along with *svastika* and *charka-dhvaja* flanking it (Fig. 14) providing evidence of the existence of such temples in the Pathankot region. A unique Vṛishṇi silver coin bearing Sudarśana *chakra* on the obverse and the typical Vṛishṇi emblem of half-lion and half-elephant on post on the reverse (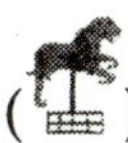)[16], sealings bearing the typical Vṛishṇi emblem of half-lion and half-elephant and discus on post in railing with or without the legend *Jaya Pachalaya*,[17] numerous seals and sealings with Brāhmī legends or typical Vṛishṇi emblems[18] and the copper coins of Vṛishṇi rulers found from Sunet and elsewhere[19] acquaint us of the relevance of Vaishṇavism in the Punjab during the first century BCE to third century CE. The Indianization of the Kushāṇas and the name Vāsudeva of Huvishka's successor also points to the popularity of Vaishṇavism in North India during the early centuries of the current era.[20]

Quite a good number of third-fourth century sealings from Sunet bear the legend *Jitaṃ Bhagavatā* with some Vṛishṇi devices on some of them, leaving absolutely no doubt that the deity invoked and worshipped was Vāsudeva-Vishṇu/Kṛishṇa. Similarly, the sealing with the legend *Jaya-Svāmi* must have belonged to the same deity as indicated by mace, discus and conch on it. Further corroboration comes from seals and sealings bearing the legend *Śrī Jitaṃ Bhagavatā Svāmi-Nārāyaṇena*, Vaishṇava emblems like conch and discus, containing individual names like Vishṇubhadra, Vishṇudāsa, Vishṇudatta, Vishṇusiṃha, Vishṇutrāta, Haridāsa, Harigupta, Hariśarmma, Śrī Nārāyaṇa, Śrī Nārāyaṇadeva, etc. Numerous clay sealings bearing the Brāhmī legend *Śaṅkara-Nārāyaṇābhyāṃ* must have been used in votive offerings to a temple dedicated to Hari-Hara. All these little clay documents[21] provide evidence of popularity of the Vaishṇava cult in this region during the Kushāṇa-Gupta period. The *Mahābhārata* refers to a holy place named Vishṇupada-tīrtha on the bank of the river Beas.[22]

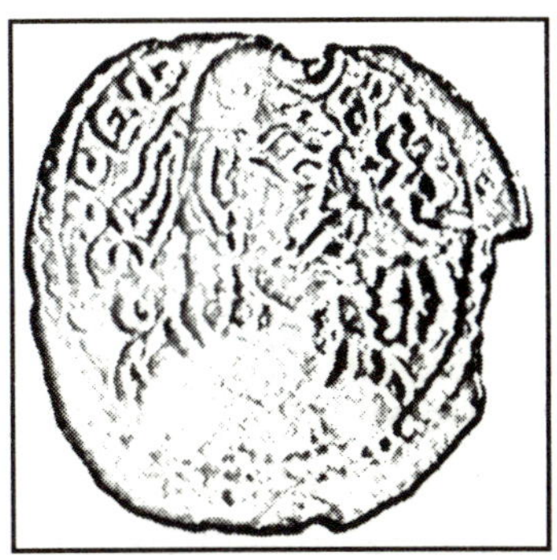

**Fig. 15.** Hūṇa coin of Khiṅgila with Brāhmī legend and disc (after K.K. Maheshwari).

While Kālidāsa's description of the exploits of Raghu in his *Raghuvaṃśa* indicates that the Hūṇas were settled in the northwestern frontiers of India at that time and had not penetrated into the country, the Bhitari Pillar Inscription[23] indicates that they

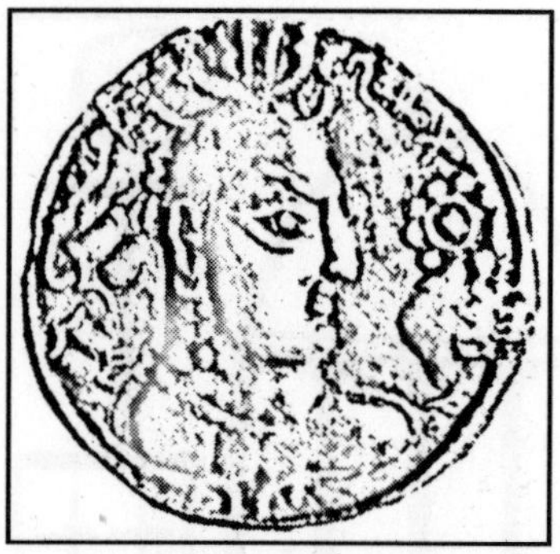

**Fig. 16.** Hūṇa coin of Khiṅgila with Brāhmī legend and Vaishṇava emblems of conch and wheel (after Maheshwari).

invaded India sometime during the reign of the Gupta king Skandagupta (CE 456-68), soon after his accession perhaps as the Bayana Hoard of Gupta gold coins contained only one coin of Skandagupta. At the time of the Hūṇa attack in about CE 456-57, Khiṅgila (*circa* CE 440-90), father of Toramāṇa, was ruling over the Kabul-Kapiśā region. Khiṅgila's early coins follow the pattern of the earlier Hūṇa issues of the region but the succeeding ones show the increasing evidence of Indian influence (Fig. 15-16).[24] On one of his coin series, we have the Brāhmī legend Devashāhi Khiṅgila and on another the Hindu influence is reflected by the introduction of Vishṇu's conch and discus before the bust to right. Though thwarted, Khiṅgila's contact with India and having been influenced by her religion and culture is indicated by these coins which also furnish evidence of the popularity of Vaishṇavism in the region extending at least up to Kapiśā-Gandhāra in the northwest.

Though Skandagupta's Junagarh Rock Inscription[25] dated GE 136 (=CE 458) records the victory of Skandagupta over the *mlechchhas*, i.e., the Hūṇas, Skandagupta's weakling successors provided an opportunity to the invaders to strike again. Budhagupta could not hold the Empire intact and Toramāṇa's Kura[26] and the Boar Inscription of Eran[27] indicate that he penetrated as far as eastern Malwa where Dhanyavishṇu, a younger brother of *Mahārāja* Mātṛivishṇu who was a feudatory of Budhagupta, had now to shift his allegiance to Toramāṇa.[28] The latter, too, has issued coins with a discus betraying his belief in Vaishṇavism though later he seems to have got inclined towards Śaivism, as revealed by the depiction of the bull and the legend 'Jayatu Vṛisha(ḥ)' on his coins.

The foregoing evidence indicates great popularity of Vaishṇavism in Punjab in ancient times. Curiously enough, however, the hitherto found images are not commensurate with literary and numismatic data. Ravages of time, clime and man seem to have wiped off and mutilated much of what existed here in ancient times. The paucity perhaps may be explained in the historic-geographical background of the region that has borne the brunt of repeated attacks of aliens and has been the venue of many a battle. The iconoclastic zeal of the foreign invaders resulted in the spoliation of ancient monuments and disappearance of images.[29] There are no standing temples existing in Punjab. We, however, feel that improper explorations and lack of proper documentation and publication are also partially responsible for the meagerness of the known material. Vaishṇava reliefs and their fragments as well as architectural pieces containing sculptural representations obtained so far from the state all belong to the medieval period. A majority of them are the standing images, and only a few are seated and reclining ones. They are described below.

## STANDING IMAGES (*STHĀNAKA-MŪRTIS*)

The only independent complete icon of Vishṇu comes from Velore, situated about 9 km east of Ferozepur on the road to Zira.[30] It is a beautiful sandstone image about one meter in height (Pl. 8). It shows the god standing in *samapāda-sthānaka-mudrā* on a *padma-pīṭha* placed on the central offset of the *saptaratha* pedestal. The back slab has been given an architectural setting with the upper part disposed in an imposing lotiform aureole. The quadrumanous god holds a mace and a disc in the rear right and left hands respectively, a conch in the natural left while the normal right hand with a rosary is disposed in *abhaya-mudrā* 'fear allaying posture'. The arrangement of the attributes thus conforms to the *Trivikrama* form of Vishṇu. The mode of

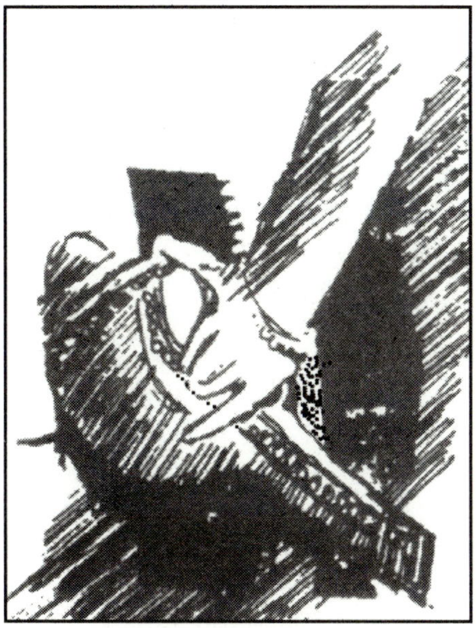

**Fig. 17.** Style of holding the conch in Vaishṇva sculptures.

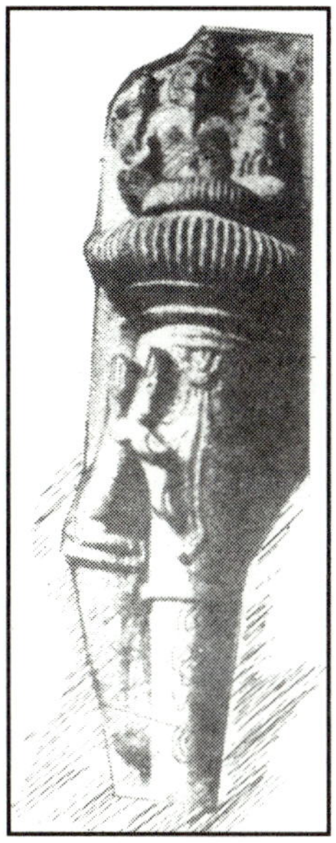

**Fig. 18.** Style of holding the mace.

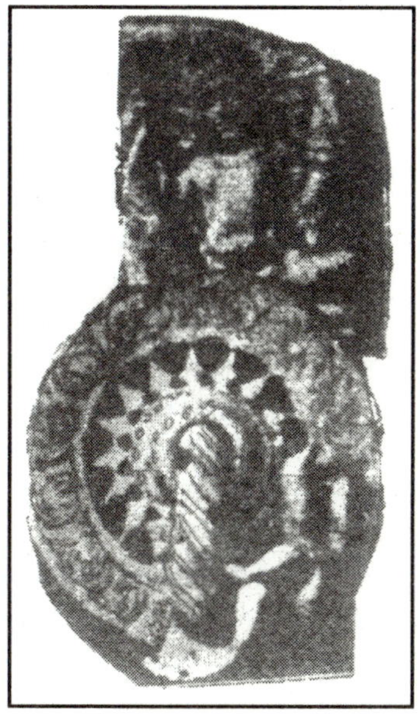

**Fig. 19.** Style of holding the wheel.

holding the conch by inserting the middle three fingers in its groove and gripping it by placing the little finger on its globular part and the thumb on its spiral head (Fig. 17) has continued from the Gupta period onwards, as may be seen in a Harihara image of fifth century from Mandasor now preserved in the State Museum at Bhopal.[31] It continued in the medieval period in Rajasthan[32] and Haryana.[33] The mode of holding the mace (Fig. 6) and the discus (Fig. 7), too, has been typical and popular in this region. The god wears a *kirīṭa-mukuṭa* adorned with jewels and pearls, ear ornaments, *graiveyaka, yajñopavīta, keyūras, kaṅkaṇas, kaṭi-sūtra* with a *kīrtimukha* in the centre as if vomiting a wreath which forms loops around the thighs with free ends dangling down to the knees partly covered by a sash across the thighs, *nūpuras,* finger rings and *Vaijayantīmālā*. There are three figures on either side of the feet of the god occupying each of the receding *rathas* of the pedestal. On the proper right stand Śaṅkha-purusha, Śrī and Balarāma while the corresponding other side shows Chakra-purusha, Sarasvatī and a male figure holding a sinuous object which may be a snake or a bow. If it is a snake, then the figure may be identified as that of Garuḍa. In case of the other possibility, the figure would represent Rāma. Garuḍa is generally represented with *karaṇḍa-mukuṭa* like the *āyudha-purushas,* but the crown here is of the *kirīṭa* variety and resembles that of Balarāma. So, if Rāma is represented here, as it seems more likely because we find the figure wearing even the long garland like Vishṇu and Balarāma, it is a unique feature for this Vishṇu image in Punjab.[34] Representation of Krishṇa and Balarāma as attendants of Vishṇu is a feature met with in a few sculptures in Rajasthan.[35] The *āyudha-purushas* bear *karaṇḍa* type of coiffeur while the spouses of the Lord bear *dhammilla* type, somewhat unusually high in proportion. The former carry the attributes they represent in their two hands near their chests bending slightly awkwardly towards Vishṇu, while the female figures are shown as holding lotus flowers by their stalks in their hands towards the main figure and support the dangling scarves in their yonder *pralamba* hands. The outer bands of the back slab in the middle show *gaja-śārdūla* figures capped by *makara-mukhas,* while the inner bands bear vine decorations. In the stele on either side of the crown are depicted four-armed Brahmā and Śiva seated in *lalitāsana* on the proper right and left. Brahmā is tri-cephalous with all juvenile faces and holds ladle and manuscript in the additional pair of hands, while the normal right is held in *abhaya* and left is concealed by the top of the club but probably supported a water pot. Śiva is uni-cephalic and holds a trident in his upper right hand and a snake in the corresponding left, while the natural hands are like that of Brahmā. Stylistically, the image under consideration may be placed in the eleventh century CE. Exquisite workmanship, minute care devoted even to the accessory figures, moderate ornamentation, plastic modelling of the contours and the elaborate iconographic formulation, however, bestow the sculpture an individuality of its own. The main figure standing in contraposto is characterized by some stiffness, the expression on the face too is formal and one misses the serene expression of the face, poise, grace and softness which were so characteristic of the Gupta art tradition.

An almost similar image was noticed and photographed in the early seventh decade of the last century by Dr. Suraj Bhan (of Panjab University, Chandigarh at that time) in a house in the village Khanpur on the right bank of the Patiala ki Rao opposite Kharar but is not traceable now.[36] Conceived on the pattern of the Velore image described above, it showed the god standing in a frontal pose on a lotus seat placed in the centre of a *sapta-ratha* pedestal (Pl. 9). All the hands, except the upper left which supports the disc, are broken. A part of the shaft of the mace that has survived, however, indicates that it was held vertically in the rear right hand of the god. The disposition of the surviving principal right arm reveals that the hand was held in protection affording pose. The lower left hand probably held a conch. The order of the emblems thus indicates that it was a form of Vishṇu similar to that of the Velore image, conforming to the *Trivikrama* form of *Rūpa-maṇḍana* or Nārāyaṇa of the *Padma Purāṇa*.[37] The god bears a high cylindrical crown bedecked with *kīrtimukhas*, jewels and pearl strings. They are placed over the combed hair. The halo behind the head shows lotus petals in the inner circle and *ardha-ratnas* in the outer ring. The god wears ear ornaments, pearl necklets, torque and a pearl necklace, doubly beaded *yajñopavīta*, beaded multi-stringed long garland having jewel and flower spacers between the legs and on the arms, *keyūras, valayas, aṅgulikās*, waist band with pendant strings falling on the thighs and a sash wound around the thighs. The *dhotī* may be guessed from the pleats visible between the legs. The feet of the god are slightly splayed out. The god has long eyes with bow-like eyebrows, long nose (slightly mutilated), thick lips and plump cheeks. The steles on the two sides of the head carry Brahmā and Śiva. The former on the proper right hand side is seated in *sukhāsana*, holding ladle in the back right hand, book and water pot in the rear and natural left hands with the normal right disposed in *abhaya*. The god is tri-cephalous with the central face bearded. Śiva, on the other side, is seated in *lalitāsana* on his mount Nandī with the principal right hand held in fear-allaying posture and others holding trident, snake and water pot in the *pradakshiṇā* order. The subsidiary figures flanking the god on the receding recesses of the pedestal are in exact conformity to the preceding example (Pl. 10). All the figures are complete. Śaṅkha-purusha and Chakra-purusha as well as Balarāma bear *karaṇḍa-mukuṭas* on their heads. Garuḍa has raised locks of hair and the two female figures bear *dhammilla* coiffures. The *gaja-śārdūla* motifs on the middle portions of the extreme slabs are intact and so is the upper part of the back slab showing the *makaras* and the divine musicians and garland bearers on the top rounded part of the *prabhāvali*. We thus see that in conception and composition, this image corresponds to the Velore Vishṇu but for only minor differences of details and may belong to almost the same date. The face, however, shows softness and body contours are sharper and in higher relief than the latter though the plain inner middle part of the back slab is somewhat irksome. When complete, it must have been a masterpiece of the Pratihāra art of Punjab.

Mandian in district Ludhiana has also yielded an image of Vishṇu which is quite similar to the Khanpur example but has suffered mutilation of its back slab as a result of which the halo, the upper left hand of the god and the stela have been lost (Pl. 11). Of the four hands, only the rear right holding the mace vertically has survived. The attributes of the four hands, the acolyte figures – three each on the right and left – of the god occupying the receding recesses of the pedestal, the carvings of the back slab, etc. may have been similar to the Khanpur image. More elaborate jewellery and elongation of the subsidiary figures of the Mandian image suggest a slightly later date.

A fragment of a Vishṇu image from Nalas in tehsil Rajpura of district Patiala (Pl. 12)[38] indicates that the Vishṇu image here must have been similar to the Khanpur example. The extant fragment shows the wheel held in Vishṇu's upper left hand, of which only three fingers are now visible. These fingers are placed exactly in the same way as in the Velore and Khanpur images though the tassel coming out of the hub of the wheel shows a graceful bend and some development over the previous examples. Tri-cephalous Brahmā with bearded central face seated in *sukhāsana* holding ladle, book and water pot in his hands with the natural right held in *abhaya* is also carved more carefully. The *vyāla* and the celestial dancer above as well as the *vidyādhara* figures on the circular arch along the halo are unfortunately badly mutilated. But what survives is enough to indicate its similarity with the Khanpur image to which it seems to be only slightly later. A badly mutilated part of a Vishṇu image from Kharar also shows the *chakra* held with similarly placed fingers with a stele above depicting four-handed Śiva and some other mutilated figures (Pl. 13) and corroborates the view that this was the popular mode of presenting the attributes in Vishṇu's hands in the ninth-tenth centuries CE in this part of the country.

Khanpur has yielded some other fragmentary sculptures,[39] thereby indicating the popularity of Vishṇu worship from about the ninth-tenth century CE. Two fragments, which fit perfectly well to form a pedestal of an image of Vishṇu, show the feet of the god on a lotus seat placed in the centre of the *sapta-ratha* pedestal (Pl. 14). The maximum height of the preserved portions of the pedestal is 82 cm. The main image must have been almost human size if not more. The disposition of the feet bearing anklets indicates that the god stood to front in *sama-pāda-sthānaka-mudrā*, flanked by Śaṅkha-purusha, Śrīdevī and Balarāma on the receding projections on the proper right and by Chakra-purusha, Sarasvatī and Garuḍa on the corresponding left side. A part of Vishṇu's *vanamālā* has survived by the sides of both the *āyudha-purushas*. An elephant to right may be seen above Garuḍa. All the attendant figures are beautifully attired and bedecked with usual dress and ornaments. Garuḍa stands in *gopālāsana* holding a snake in the left hand with right raised in salutation over the head. The head of Balarāma is broken but he may be identified by the shaft of the plough held across the body in both of his hands and also by the *vanamālā* he wears. Both the spouses of Vishṇu have been provided with small round halos behind their heads. Each wears a necklace whose pendant string falls gracefully on the belly from between the breasts. The lower garment is secured by the girdle as usual. The free end of the scarf is held by a *pralamba-hasta* on the outer side. Both bear *dhammilla* hair coiffures bedecked with *chūḍāmaṇis*. Śaṅkha-purusha bears *karaṇḍa-mukuṭa* and the coiffure of Chakra-purusha has chipped off in front. The ribbed lower end of the shaft of the mace in Vishṇu's (upper) right hand may be seen above the head of Śaṅkha-purusha. The minute care bestowed to these attendant figures is a noteworthy feature of the relief which may stylistically be related to the Pratihāra art idiom and placed in the tenth century CE. Another fragment procured from the site showing exquisitely carved *vidyādhara* couple wearing beautiful *dhammilla* coiffure, earrings, *aṅgadas*, *valayas*, etc. depicted in flying posture seems stylistically to belong to this pedestal.

A red sandstone *prabhāvali* with stele bears a great stylistic similarity to the image described above. The *prabhāvali* measures 47 X 50 cm and shows a beautiful eight-petal lotiform circle enclosed within two more circles having stepped pyramidal and half diamond decorations, the outermost circle having a beaded border. On a stele on the right are depicted Umā and Maheśvara on Nandī.[40] The pedestal of the stele on the right shows inverted lotus petal decorations. Nandī is seated to left with face to front and is caparisoned. Śiva is seated on its back in *lalitāsana* with Umā on his left leg. The right foot of the god is splayed outwards and wears an anklet. An elaborate *jaṭā-mukuṭa* with *chūḍāmaṇi* may be seen on his head. The god also wears earrings, *ekāvali*, sacred thread, armlets, wristlets, a scarf and a nether garment secured by the waist band. He holds a lotus in his normal right hand near the chest and the trident in his rear right. The upper part of the attribute, held vertically, is damaged. The principal left hand touches the left breast of Umā from behind her back. The upper left hand holds a snake. The right hand of Umā is placed on the right shoulder of Śiva and the left one touches her own left foot placed on the right thigh. She bears a massive *dhammilla* coiffure on her head and wears *karṇa-kuṇḍalas, hāra, keyūras, valayas* and an *adhovastra*. The facial expressions of the couple betray quietude. Just below this stele may be seen the elephantine proboscis of a *makara* holding a blossomed lily in the snout. On this flower stands cross-legged a female figure holding perhaps a fly-whisk in her hands. She bears a beautiful coiffure and is very exquisitely attired. Her quasi-closed eyes and a smile on her face betray her beatific and inner pleasure. On the upper fringe of the back slab are carved *vidyādhara* couples holding garlands or playing on musical instruments. Two *vidyādharas* are shown as supporting cylindrical crown at the apex, indicating that the main deity of the relief was either Vishṇu or Sūrya, more probably the former, as may be judged from some other relics found from this site. Another fragment of an aureole with *vidyādhara* figures on its outer periphery and a male figure inside was also procured from the site and is preserved in the museum of the Department of Ancient Indian History, Culture and Archeology of the Panjab University, Chandigarh.

Another badly damaged part of the *prabhāvali* (30 X 12 cm) of an image shows four mutilated figures of alternating male and female *vidyādharas* on the outer fringe of the surviving part of the *śiraśchakra*, which consists of four rows of beaded strings with lined divisions, spaced by full blown lotus flowers. The *vidyādhara* figures are depicted in flying postures with forward moving left leg folded and the right one stretched backwards. What is, however, interesting is the depiction of a male figure holding some unidentifiable objects in his hands, in a dancing pose, on the inner side of the aureole. This is a rare occurrence (Pl. 15). Stylistically, the piece seems to belong to a tenth century image, probably of Vishṇu.

A small sandstone fragment of 12 X 7.5 cm showing a horizontally placed conch over the head of an *āyudha-purusha* held in Vishṇu's lower left hand from Khanpur (Pl. 16)[41] is significant to indicate the popularity of the tradition of depicting the conch horizontally in the natural left hand of the god, as also seen in the Velore image and also probably the Vishṇu image from Khanpur described above. A ring can also be noticed on the thumb and the pointing finger of this hand and a *kaṅkaṇa* on his wrist. The *kanishṭhikā* is slightly damaged, *anāmikā* and *madhyamā* are inserted in the groove, *tarjanī* is placed on its body and the *aṅgushṭha* grips the spiral head of the conch. Majhur has yielded the figure of Śaṅkha-purusha who holds the sash on the right thigh in a similar fashion with his left hand supporting the vertical conch (Pl. 17).[42] The head and the feet of this figure are unfortunately broken but the accentuation of the hip to his left indicates his position on the proper right of the god.

Vishṇu's disc, having a diameter of 16 cm with a tassel issuing forth from its hub and with two fingers placed over it, also recovered from Khanpur, too, may have belonged to the Vishṇu image described above. A head bearing cylindrical crown measuring 31 X 19 cm in its extant form, being quite worn out, cannot be identified with certitude as belonging to the same image. Another small piece which is a part of the proper right hand side of the pedestal of an image of

Vishṇu shows a beautiful *kaṭi-hasta* female figure holding an unidentifiable object in the left hand near the shoulder. She stands slightly turned to her left and bears an exquisitely carved hair coiffure, multi-ringed ear ornament and a pearl necklace whose string falls from between her breasts and touches the girdle. She also wears bracelets. A sash of the lower garment crossing her thighs forms a knot on the right thigh. A hand wearing a beaded bracelet is placed on her head. Evidently, it is Vishṇu's hand and the female figure with massive rotund breasts represents Gadādevī. Just behind her is a male figure but it is very much mutilated and cannot be identified properly. The figure in front is completely destroyed. The excellent carving and sparing use of jewellery render it a piece of tenth century CE.

Kharar and Mundi Kharar have yielded dozens of fragmentary sculptures. About two dozen pieces were acquired by me for the Department of Ancient Indian History, Culture and Archaeology, Punjab University, Chandigarh in 1980. A sandstone piece (22 X 19 cm) from Mundi Kharar represents the feet of a deity, probably Vishṇu, wearing anklets, standing on a lotus seat borne by a female figure (Pṛithvī or sea-nymph) in *vīrāsana* flanked by anthropomorphic *nāgas* (Pl. 18). A fragment picked up from Kharar shows a badly damaged headless *āyudha-purusha*, probably Śaṅkha-purusha, standing holding the mutilated attribute in his left hand near the chest and resting the right on the thigh with waist accentuated to his proper left (towards the main deity) followed by another figure on the next receding recess of the pedestal. The *āyudha-purusha* wears a pearl necklace, sacred thread, wristlet and nether garment covering only the portion above the knees with a knot of the garment in front. It is the proper right hand side fragment of the pedestal of a tenth century Vishṇu image. Another exquisitely carved piece forms part of the *toraṇa* of a Vishṇu image. It shows the *vidyādharas* with a female figure standing gracefully in *tribhaṅga* on a lotus coming out of the mouth of a *makara* on the extreme right. Attached to it is a stele showing Brahmā holding a ladle and a book in the rear right and left hands, the natural right is placed on the knee and the proper left broken. The deity wears *jaṭā-mukuṭa*, ear ornaments, *ekāvali*, sacred thread, *vanamālā* and lower garment and is seated in *sukhāsana*. The aureole behind the head is broken. Left hand side parts of pedestals of Vishṇu images are known from Sanghol and Hawara also. The former shows a mutilated Chakra-purusha, a female with a beautiful *dhammilla* coiffure (Sarasvatī) in the middle and acephalic anthropomorphic Garuḍa holding a serpent in the left hand. The right hand was probably held over the head in salutation, but is completely gone now. Stylistically, it may be assigned to *circa* ninth century CE. The piece from Hawara is slightly later in date. A sandstone bust of Vishṇu (15 X 11 cm) from Shahpur in Kharar tehsil has a three-stringed necklace and a sacred thread. A lozenge-shaped *Śrīvatsa* symbol is also visible on the chest.[43]

Janer, situated about 10 km northwest of Moga on the road to Dharamkot, has yielded a fragmentary and a complete image of Vishṇu.[44] The bigger piece is almost complete. It is made of blackish stone and measures 90 X 50 cm (Pls. 19-20). It was discovered when the villagers were digging a part of the rain-gully to construct a *pucca* brick drain. The deity is standing in *sama-pāda-sthānaka* pose on a central lotus, at the base of which is a female figure, probably Pṛithvī, flanked on either side by a male figure in *añjali-mudrā,* perhaps the *nāgas* to judge from their slanting postures. The four-armed Vishṇu wears a high cylindrical crown, necklet, necklace, bracelets, wristlets, anklets, *Vaijayantī* flowing from over the arms to the knees, beautiful *maṇibandha* and ornamented under garment with fine *kaṭi-mekhalā* having beautiful pendants hanging on the thighs. *Śrīvatsa* is visible on the chest. In his additional right hand, the god is shown as holding the fluted mace with the thicker end upwards. The natural right hand is broken. In the extra left hand, he holds a wheel having sixteen spokes with a fillet issuing from its hub and supports a conch in the normal left. The style of holding the conch is similar to what we have seen earlier in case of a fragment from Khanpur (Pl. 16), i.e., by inserting the middle fingers into the groove of the conch and placing the little and pointing fingers on its globular body and thumb gripping the spiral head. The order of attributes in the four hands thus seems to be similar to the images described above, corresponding to the *Trivikrama* form (Nārāyaṇa according to *Padma Purāṇa*). On either side of the god near his feet are three figures almost in symmetrical postures. The male figures on the right and left of the god are the personified *āyudha-purushas* holding respectively a lotus and a conch in their left and right hands resting the other on the corresponding thighs. The female figure in the middle on the proper right holds a lotus by its stalk in her left hand and the *pralamba* right hand rests on the thigh. A very interesting feature is the depiction of the mace-end on her head suggesting her identification with Gadādevī. The central male figure on Vishṇu's left holding a round object may thus be identified as Chakra-purusha with some certainty. We thus see the depiction of all the four attributes in their personified form also. This is a very rare feature of Vishṇu images. Both the figures on the extreme recesses are male ones. The one on the extreme left is holding the shaft of some attribute. It is possible that these figures represent Balarāma and Garuḍa, as noted in some preceding images, but it is certainly very difficult to say so affirmatively. At the feet of Padma-purusha and Śaṅkha-purusha flanking the god on his right and left are shown two diminutive figures in *añjali-mudrā* looking upwards towards the god seated in profile with extended legs. They are perhaps the donor couple. The subsidiary figures bear very fine *piṅgalorddha* coiffures, wear *ekāvalis* or necklaces, ear ornaments, armlets, wristlets, etc. and are standing in very graceful postures. Two bearded sages, one on either side, sitting in *sukhāsana*, having a *kamaṇḍalu* in their left hands with right hands disposed in *abhaya-mudrā* fill the gap between the upper and lower hands of the deity.

Brahmā-Sarasvatī and Umā-Maheśvara adorn the steles on the right and left sides of the god. Both the steles are topped by flying *vidyādharas* holding wreaths of flowers. The extreme projections of the back slab are decorated with elephantine and leonine *vyāla* carvings surmounted by *makara-mukhas* and celestial male dancers. The beautiful eight-petalled effulgent halo is capped by a stele showing two *vidyādharas* in flying postures holding long-stalked lotuses in their right and left hands respectively and perhaps a crown looking like a jewel-box in the other in the centre. Also depicted on this stele are a tortoise on the right and a fish on the left, probably reminiscent of the Kūrma and Matsya incarnations of Vishṇu.

The conventional stiffness, rigidity and lifeless repetitiveness, meticulous details, over-elaboration, heavy ornamentation and drapery, crowded composition and languorous movement of this rather squat figure render it to be a work of the twelfth century CE. It shows some affinity with the sculptures from Rajasthan and Central India, particularly with the Vishṇu image from Baghera (district Ajmer, Rajasthan)[45] and Vishṇu from Khajuraho in the Allahabad Museum.[46] The features enumerated above are not visible in their totality in the above-mentioned images and seem to be the result of the regional development, which is also corroborated by the similar figure from Velore, not far from Janer, as described above. The mechanical grace, elegance and perfection, however, are quite obvious and it is one of the finest and most interesting medieval sculptures of the region found so far.

A beautiful bust of the god comes from the village Majhur in district Nawanshahr (Pl. 21).[47] The crown shows some similarity with that of Vishṇu from Janer but is more elegant. Unfortunately, all the hands are broken but the lozenge-shaped *śrīvatsa* mark on the chest, a part of the *vaijayantīmālā* on the shoulders and the cylindrical crown are enough to identify the deity with certitude. Besides the crown which is adorned with jewels, pearls and other precious stones placed on the head above the curls of the forehead, the god wears ear ornaments, a torque and a necklace having a round pendent with crocodile faces on the sides devouring or emitting the beaded strings. A double-beaded string with square spacers forms the sacred thread. There is a *tilaka* on the forehead. The inward looking eyes, long eyebrows, sturdy nose, prominent chin, plump cheeks, double fold on the neck resembling the spirals of a conch making the figure as *kambu-grīva*, broad shoulders and thin waist endow a pleasing look to the figure which may be dated to *circa* tenth century CE.

A very badly mutilated and worn-out figure broken below the waist measuring 11 X 9 cm comes from the village Burail, now forming part of Sector 45 of the Union Territory of Chandigarh. It was recovered while laying down the foundations of a Śiva temple near the Government High School and was removed to the Khera Mandir of Burail for worship.[48] The god stands to front resting the left hand on waist and the right disposed in *abhaya*. The left hand may have supported a conch or an attribute looking like a water flask. Since the hand is only partially visible and the relief is broken below the waist of the deity, it is difficult to determine the exact attribute. Since the god wears a foliated crown as seen in the late Kushāṇa images of Vishṇu found from Mathura,[49] it is likely that the attribute was a conch resembling a nectar flask, just like those images. All details of the face are lost and it difficult even to determine whether the deity bore four hands like them or possessed only two hands. Faint traces of the ear ornaments, necklace and what looks like the upper part of a mace held in the rear right hand of the god may be discerned. On the proper left hand is a part of the scarf or perhaps the long garland. The rear left hand may have carried the discus but is irretrievably lost. Of the other images of Vishṇu or fragments thereof found so far from Punjab, the earliest bust of an image of the god comes from Dholbaha near the foothills in district Hoshiarpur, which may have been an important caravan and market town on an old trade route connecting the plains of Punjab with Himachal Pradesh towards Baijnath in Kangra district and onwards to Kullu and the regions beyond. Carved in the Gupta art idiom of North-Central India, it shows the depression at the sides of the lips and emphasizes the roundness of the form though modelling is quite simple (Pl. 22). The serene expression with the eyes gently directed downwards and locks of hair falling over the shoulders lends a contemplative look to the face. The god wears an *ekāvali* of pearl beads, simple armlets and *karṇa-kuṇḍalas* and a part of the long garland has survived on his left arm. The cylindrical crown is also quite simple, bearing an array of semi-circular engravings which have almost worn out. Ohri dates it to the late seventh century CE.[50] A similar bust has unfortunately been worn out so much that it has lost all details. Still another bust datable to the late eighth or early ninth century betrays soft and sensitive modelling with fleshy round face having gently lowered eyes bearing a meditative expression: "The heavy outer necklace with a central spacer in the shape of *mukru* (sic., *mukuru*), heads decorated with a roundel over the joints, adds to the majestic bearing of the figure, and also heightens the inner strength of the well modelled chest. The delicately rendered ringlets of hair seen over the forehead and the crown with skillfully carved minute details, enhance the beauty of the work."[51] Another bust from this place is so worn out that no feature may be made out except the stunted flat crown and a part of the long garland on the shoulders (Pl. 23), which, however, are the sure evidence of the figure being that of Vishṇu. A head of Vishṇu from Dholbaha (Pl. 24), ascribable to *circa* tenth century, shows horizontally elongated eyes with well-marked eyebrows, well-modelled small mouth and nose and different physiognomic traits from the usual ethnic groups of the area. The crown depicts decorative patterns and motifs which betray meticulous care provided to them. It shows a *kīrtimukha* against half-diamond pattern spewing pearl garlands, which form lovely loops on the lower half of the crown all around. Well-combed curls and precisely and fairly finished hair add to the beauty of the face. The crown, combed hair and curls are comparable to the one seen on the head of Vishṇu image from Khanpur (Pl. 9). The smooth appearance of the surface enhances its grace. This image carved at Dholbaha betrays influences from different directions.[52]

Two more heads of Vishṇu from Dholbaha deserve mention. One of these shows similarly combed hair with curls on the sides but the crown is slightly different and depicts long-necked and beaked swans in profile picking the pearls from the pearl strings and garlands which adorn the crown (Pl. 25). The almond-shaped quasi-closed eyes with drooping lids and bow-like eyebrows, round plump cheeks, sturdy nose, thick lower lip and a beatific smile are the other notable features of the round face. Stylistically, it is a Pratihāra piece of the tenth century CE. The other head shows the god wearing a crown having criss-cross pattern and adorned with an *ardha-ratna* and pearl strings and garlands placed over the curls (Pl. 26). The forehead bears a *tilaka* mark. Facial features are more pronounced but lack the serenity and grace noticed in the foregoing examples. Stylistically, it may be assigned to *circa* eleventh century CE.

That Dholbaha developed as a great centre of art is indicated by some unfinished sculptures found at the site. One broken unfinished image of Vishṇu has also been recovered from this place (Pl. 27). Belonging to about the tenth century, it shows the figure of the god with head, feet and two hands gone, bearing chisel marks all over. An *āyudha-purusha* has survived up to the legs on the god's right. The mace in the upper right and horizontally held conch in the lower left hand indicate that the artists of Punjab stuck to the tradition of carving *Trivikrama* form of Vishṇu only (with wheel in the additional left hand), as noted in the images from Velore, Khanpur, Janer, etc.

Though no independent and complete image of Vishṇu has come down to us from Dholbaha, yet there is enough evidence to show the existence of temples dedicated to the god. An eleventh century architectural piece shows Vishṇu standing to front in a pillared niche flanked by female attendants and wearing the usual dress and ornaments (Pl. 28). The figure has suffered some diminution. The nose and both the lower hands have been damaged. In spite of this mutilation, we can be sure that the attributes in the hands of the god were in the same order as noted above in some of the complete and incomplete figures and also the style of holding them was similar to them (Pl. 29). Ohri has observed that

> The slender tall figures, particularly those of the female attendants, are paralleled by the tall and slim round columns of the niches. Makra (sic., *makara*) heads are carved at the sides in a highly stylized manner and the other figures shown besides them appear only as decorative motifs. . . . This style evolved in Rajasthan under the Paramaras and the presence of this type of work at Dholbaha shows a different source of influence. Similar type of work is also seen at Pinjore situated to the southeast of Dholbaha.[53]

Many other fragments from Dholbaha preserved at the site museum or displayed in the Government Museum in the Vishveshvaranand Vedic Research Institute, Sadhu Ashram at Hoshiarpur belong to the images of Vishṇu. A part of the pedestal exhibited here shows the feet of Vishṇu wearing anklets placed on a lotus *pīṭha* on the central offset of a *pañcha-ratha* pedestal with an *āyudha-purusha* and Garuḍa on the proper left on the respective receding recesses (Pl. 30). The attribute in the right hand of the *āyudha-purusha* is not visible and defies proper identification but the extreme figure with raised tufts of hair in horrification, holding a snake in the left hand and holding the right in salutation above the head, render its identification with Garuḍa as certain. The *kullah*-type conical cap on the head of the *āyudha-purusha*, the simple dress and *ekāvali* worn by both these acolytes indicate that it may have been a fragment of a ninth century image. Another part of the pedestal in the same museum (Pl. 31) shows an exquisitely carved, elongated figure of Vishṇu's spouse holding the lotus by its stalk in her right hand and holding the dangling scarf with the *pralamba* left hand, standing very gracefully slightly turned to her left. The *āyudha-purusha* preceding her is completely mutilated but the one following her on the extreme recess is depicted with his right hand disposed in *abhaya* and left placed on the respective thigh. He wears a *karaṇḍa-mukuṭa* on the head. The right hand in fear-allaying posture indicates his exalted status and the ploughshare placed on the ground near his left leg helps us to identify the figure as that of Balarāma. Unfortunately, the faces of both these figures are damaged but the softness of contours and the elegance of postures renders this piece of the pedestal to be a remarkable piece of *circa* eleventh century CE. A third fragment at the same place with similar figures but with a part of the *vanamālā* visible on the top left corner also surely belongs to some contemporary Vishṇu image (Pl. 32). Another fragment of the pedestal of a Vishṇu image from Dholbaha shows a badly mutilated Chakra-purusha holding the discus near the chest with head and legs broken (Pl. 33). The female figure depicted behind on the receding recess, however, presents a beautiful model of female form, though slightly elongated. The supple face betrays the softness of chiselwork and the *dhammilla* coiffure adds to the grace of the figure, which is further enhanced by the pendant string of the *ekāvali* falling vertically to the *netra-sūtra* from between the breasts. She is followed by a headless male figure who may have been anthropomorphic Garuḍa. Another fragment from the same site, though badly damaged, preserves the female bust with a pendant string of ringlets falling similarly from between the breasts to the girdle, with the *āyudha-purusha* preceding her and bearing a *karaṇḍa-mukuṭa, ekāvali, karṇa-kuṇḍalas*, sacred thread, etc. (Pl. 34). Both these pieces may be dated to *circa* ninth century CE. Two fragments in the store at the site museum, one showing the headless bust up to the thighs (Pl. 35) and the other from waist to knees (Pl. 36), also belong to the medieval images of Vishṇu.

A small portable headless figure of Vishṇu with all arms and feet broken was recovered during the excavations at Singh-Bhagwantpur, about 9 km north of Kurali on Chandigarh-Rupnagar highway in district Rupnagar (Pl. 37).[54] Folds on the neck, *ekāvali* and pearl necklace, double-stringed sacred thread, simple waist-band to secure the *dhotī* with linear folds serving as a sash on the thighs and the free end falling between the legs makes it an interesting piece datable to *circa* eighth century CE. This may have been one of the earliest images of Vishṇu found from anywhere in the Punjab. A small dagger tucked to the waist belt on the proper right makes it more interesting as having been influenced by Kashmiri art. Fragmentary Pratihāra reliefs of a fly-whisker and an attendant figure, both wearing long garlands, a stele with Brahmā and a *vyāla* found from Burail (Sector 45), Chandigarh also indicate the existence there of a Vaishṇava temple in the tenth century CE.[55]

The prevalence of the worship of Vishṇu at various other places is evidenced by small fragments of Vishṇu images. A badly mutilated small piece measuring 23 X 15 cm from Sarai Naga in district Faridkot forms part of the pedestal of a Vishṇu image. It shows an *āyudha-purusha* and Garuḍa standing on the receding recesses of the pedestal. The latter is recognizable from the snake it holds in the left hand with right raised to the head in salutation.[56] Left hand side part of the pedestal of another Vishṇu image from Sanghol is preserved in the museum of the Department of Ancient Indian History, Culture and Archaeology, Panjab University, Chandigarh. A similar piece is known from Hawara near Kurali in district Rupnagar. The most beautiful part of the pedestal of an image of Vishṇu, however, comes from Mandian near Dhuri in district Sangrur and is now displayed in the VVRI Museum at Hoshiarpur (Pl. 38).[57] It is almost similar to the pedestal from Dholbaha described above (Pl. 31), but is much better preserved. Chakra-purusha, Sarasvatī and Garuḍa are shown as standing slightly turned to their right on the three successive receding recesses of the proper left hand side of Vishṇu who may have stood on the central projection of the of the *sapta-ratha* pedestal. The head, left hand and legs of Chakra-purusha are irretrievably lost. He holds the disc with his right hand near the chest. Sarasvatī in the middle stands with her left knee bent slightly forward and supports a lotus in her right hand raised to the level of the shoulder and the hanging left hand, which may have held the scarf, is also lost. She wears ear ornaments, necklace with a strand falling from between the rotund breasts, *valayas*, *nūpuras* and the nether garment secured by the girdle. She has a high bun on her head, which is provided with a plain round halo behind. Anthropomorphic Garuḍa is also bedecked with similar jewellery and wears a sacred thread and *Vaijayantī* also. His left leg is also bent outwardly. He holds the snake in his right hand while the right is raised in salutation above the head. All the figures are elongated. The original image must have been a masterpiece of the Pratihāra art of Punjab.

Sunam in Sangrur district must have been a place of great importance in the medieval period containing some Hindu and Jaina temples.[58] Proper left hand side part of the *sapta-ratha* pedestal of a Vishṇu image, with the three figures of Chakra-purusha, Sarasvatī and Garuḍa on the receding recesses, quite similar to those noticed on the Mandian piece, has been found from this site indicating worship of the god (Pl. 39). It measures 46 X 24 cm in its extant state and indicates the Vishṇu image, of which it was a part, must have been almost life-size. The dresses, ornaments and even stances of the three figures are the same but the elongation of the Mandian example is lacking. This image belonging to the same period may have preceded the Mandian image by a few years. Another fragment of probably the same image, as indicated by the style, represents the stele showing Śiva seated on the Nandī in *sukhāsana* with Umā on his left thigh, a female figure standing on a lotus with left leg bent slightly outward holding a long shaft across her body on the extreme part of the back slab and *Gandharva* and *vidyādhara* couples above (Pl. 40). There is a beautiful halo behind the heads of Umā-Maheśvara. Minute care has been given to depicting all the figures reminiscent of the developed Pratihāra art. An elegantly cared *chakra* having a diameter of 12 cm with a tassel flowing from out of its hub (Pl. 41) found from the same place at Sunam may also have belonged to the same image. The fingers of Vishṇu which held it are unfortunately damaged but their remnants indicate the same fashion of holding the disc as seen in Velore, Khanpur, Nalas, Kharar and other examples. Another discus having a diameter of 14 cm with intact fingers found from Sunam (Pl. 42) not only confirms this tradition but also is an evidence of the existence of another image of Vishṇu here.

## BRASS IMAGE

Only one metal image of Vāsudeva Vishṇu, probably of brass (the exact metal can only be determined by metallographic examination) has come to our notice. It is now preserved in a temple at Sītā Sara in Sunam (Pl. 43). Vāsudeva, wearing usual dress and ornaments including the *Vaijayantīmālā*, *yajñopavīta* and broad lozenge-shaped *śrīvatsa*, is shown standing to front in *samapāda* on a cushion placed on an octagonal pedestal, holding the mace and disc in the rear right and left hands and conch with spiral end downwards in the normal left while the natural right is disposed in *varada* pose with a diamond on the palm. This is altogether an unnoticed feature. The holding of the conch with spiral end downwards, though witnessed in the Vishṇu images from Berikhera (district Jind) and Beri (district Rohtak) in Haryana,[59] is rare. The attributes of the four hands are similar to the Berikhera and Beri images and correspond to the Nārāyaṇa form of Vishṇu according to the *Padma Purāṇa* and 'Trivikrama' of the *Rūpa-maṇḍana*.[60] The inscription at the back of the image, however, refers to the god as Vāsudeva. The round face has almost closed eyes, sturdy nose, plump cheeks, smile on the lips and a strong chin. The long hair seems to be combed backwards with a flat-based cylindrical crown having triangular projections in front and on the sides. A male figure stands on his right and a female one on his left near the feet. The latter holding a lotus by its stalk in her raised right hand and *pralamba* left hand touching the knee may be identified as the spouse of the Lord. The object in the left hand of the male figure is not clear and it is difficult to identify him with certainty. He may be an *āyudha-purusha* or Garuḍa. A *parikara* with engraved decorations has been provided around with the apex ending as slightly projecting as the *chhattra* capped by *kalaśa* and round *āmalaka*-like finials. On the two sides just above the head are very small figures probably of Brahmā and Śiva, seated in *lalitāsana*. While the main image seems to have been cast, the *parikara* has been prepared from the metal sheet and has been engraved. There is an inscription in the Siddhamātṛikā script at the back on the *parikara* (Pl. 44), which reads as following:

*Saṃvata 1349 varshe Phāguṇa sudi 1 Ravau mahaṃ[ta*] Jayata Sīha śreyorthaṃ Śrī-Vāsudeva-mūrtti/ Mahaṃ Maṃḍalikena bheṭāvitā//*

[(This) image of Vāsudeva was gifted for the religious merit of Mahaṃta Jayata Siṃha on Sunday, the 1st of the bright fortnight of Phāguṇa in the year 1349 of the (Vikrama) Saṃvat by Mahaṃta Maṃḍalika.]

It is difficult to determine whether this metal image was cast at Sunam itself or brought from elsewhere but the fact that Sunam has traditionally been a place of metal vessels and that the Garuḍavāhī Vishṇu image on the lintel in the Śiva temple in the Malka Mohalla of this place described below also shows the same arrangement of attributes, including the conch with spiral end downwards in the normal left hand (Pl. 48), leads to the possibility of its having been created at Sunam. Its importance also lies in the fact that this is the only metal and the only inscribed image of Vishṇu discovered from the Punjab so far. It also acquaints us as to how the art of sculpting deteriorated after the advent of the iconoclastic Muslims in the twelfth century, when all existing temples in the region were destroyed and no new ones could be erected. The date of the present image (CE 1292) falls during the reign of Jalāl-ud-Dīn Fīroz (II) Khalji whose copper coin too has been found from Sunam. It may be pointed out that Sunam formed part of the dominions of Itutmish who appointed Saifuddīn Aibak, a Turkish slave he had purchased from Jamāluddīn, to the *iqta* of Sunam. During the thirteenth century, the town was at the height of its glory when it was made the provincial headquarters during the reign of the Turk ruler Nāsir-ud-Dīn Maḥmūd (AH 644-64 = CE 1246-65).[61] For personal worship, people seem to have resorted only to small portable images.

## SEATED IMAGES (*ĀSANA-MŪRTIS*)

As already noted above, the seated images of Vishṇu from Punjab are very few. A small sculpture of pinkish sandstone in possession of a local inhabitant at Janer is less than a foot in height and shows the god as wearing a *kirīṭa-mukuṭa*, ear ornaments, wristlets and a necklet (Pl. 45). The figure being worn out, details of the face, which is almost completely roundish, ornaments and the *śrīvatsa* mark are not visible. The four-armed deity holds in his upper right hand the mace with its thicker end upwards and a wheel having spokes and with a fillet issuing from its hub in the upper left hand. The lower left hand probably held a conch, which is only partially visible as the figure is broken below the bust. *Vaijayantī* is also slightly visible on the left arm. The lower right hand may have held a lotus or may have been disposed in *abhaya*. The figure is broken below the bust but the angle at which the lower left arm turns outward indicates that the deity was sitting. It is, however, difficult to ascertain whether the god was seated on Garuḍa or not. Stylistically, it may be dated to *circa* ninth century CE.

In the premises of the site museum at Dholbaha, some sculptured pieces may be seen embedded in a wall (Pl. 46). A figure of Vishṇu seated in *lalitāsana* in a *nāgara-kūṭa* may be seen amongst these. The figure is too small to discern the details properly but the three-peaked crown bespeaks of the influence from the hilly region of Himachal as also noticed on sculptures at the Siwalik foothills, particularly at Pinjore, Chandimandir, etc.[62] Another notable feature even of this small panel is the arrangement of attributes as noted in the foregoing examples. Another architectural piece having a socket hole on its top left for fitting the tenon of the slab to be placed above shows Vishṇu seated similarly with Śiva on his left (Pl. 47). It is carved in shallow relief for decorating the wall of some temple but maintains the tradition of positing the attributes in the same fashion.

A worn-out lintel, now preserved in the Śiva temple in Malka Mohalla at Sunam, shows Garuḍavāhī Vishṇu holding mace and discus in the rear pair of hands with natural right held in *abhaya* and the normal left supporting a conch with spiral end downwards (Pl. 48). The god wearing a long cylindrical crown, earrings, necklace, bracelets, etc. is seated in *sukhāsana* on anthropomorphic Garuḍa depicted in a flying posture. Because of the indifferent state of preservation, the details are not clear but it is the only example of the Garuḍavāhī Vishṇu known so far from the Punjab. Stylistically, it may be assigned to *circa* eleventh century CE.

## YOGA-NĀRĀYAṆA

A very interesting image of seated Vishṇu comes from Lalru, about 30 km south-southwest of Chandigarh on the road to Ambala in district Patiala. The image, measuring 60 X 27.5 cm, is now studded in the outer wall of Chaudhariāṃ Da Shiv Mandir (Pl. 49). It shows the god seated in *yogāsana* on a lotus seat with legs folded and the palms of the normal hands placed one over the other (*śvetapadme samāsīnamūrdhvasthitadakshiṇapādamadhassthavāmapādam aṅkavinyastavāma-karam*), wearing *kirīṭa-mukuṭa*, ear ornaments, necklet, necklace, sacred thread, armlets, bracelets, anklets and *vanamālā* (*kuṇḍalāgadahārādyābharaṇa-bhūshitam*). *Śrīvatsa* can be seen on the chest. The upper left hand holds the conch vertically with its spiral top pointing upwards. The corresponding right hand seems to hold perhaps a *chakra*, now badly damaged.[63] The image bears chisel marks all over it and seems to have been left unfinished. Local people inform that this image, along with the Vaikuṇṭha-Lakshmī image studded in the same wall beside it, was brought here from elsewhere, probably from Pinjore which once formed part of the Patiala State. The placid face with long, half-closed eyes bears beatific expression. Stylistically, it seems to belong to *circa* tenth century CE.

Images of Yogāsana Vishṇu are quite rare in the northern region and we know of only one example from Sirsa belonging to the eleventh century CE.[64] Some scholars regard Yoga-Nārāyaṇa images to be the representation of the Buddha incarnation of Vishṇu[65] but the *Bṛihatsaṃhitā* describes him as *nīchakeśaḥ*, i.e., with hair falling (on the shoulders) and the *Agnipurāṇa*, *Vishṇudharmottarapurāṇa* and *Rūpamaṇḍana* describe him only as two-handed,[66] so I don't think that four-handed images showing the god wearing a *kirīṭa-mukuṭa* should be regarded as such.

## RECLINING IMAGES (*ŚAYANA-MŪRTIS*)

### ŚESHAŚĀYĪ VISHṆU

Vishṇu, the god without any beginning and end (*Anādi & Ananta*), being eternal, naturally came to be associated with Ananta 'the Endless', a name of Śeshanāga, who has his abode in the primordial waters. The primitive Nāga worship seems to have played a pivotal role in the development of the concept, evolution and iconography of Vishṇu. Water being the essential requirement of life with air symbolizes life, fecundity and creation. So the concept of the creation of the universe is associated with Vishṇu as Nārāyaṇa 'the Lord of waters', as enunciated in the *Mahābhārata* which describes him as reclining on the primordial waters on the serpent-bed (*Śesha-śaiyyā*) and creating a lotus from his navel of his own wish, from which was born Brahmā who created the *viśva* (universe).[67] The depiction of Ādimūrti, Vishṇu lying on the coils of the serpent before the first creation, became a popular theme in the realm of plastic art from the Gupta period onwards.

Though seated and standing images of Vishṇu under the canopy of the great serpent have also been found,[68] yet the images of Vishṇu sleeping on the coils of the Śesha far outnumber those and have remained popular with the artists. The Tīrthayātrāparva of the *Mahābhārata* exhorts the pilgrims to worship Padmanābha-Nārāyaṇa at one of the *tīrthas* of Kurukshetra[69] but no early images of the god have come down to us and all the images of Śeshaśāyī discovered so far from Haryana[70] and Punjab belong only to the medieval period.

A badly mutilated, coarse-grained sandstone figure of Śeshaśāyī Vishṇu broken below the waist portion of the god and measuring 26.5 X 22 cm in its extant form once existed at Khanpur in the sixties of the last century but nothing is known about it now. The photograph of the worn-out relief taken then (Pl. 50) shows Vishṇu reclining on the coils of the five-hooded snake whose substantially mutilated hoods serve as a canopy for the god wearing *kirīṭa-mukuṭa, karṇa-kuṇḍalas, graiveyaka, agadas, yajñopavīta* and the *Vaijayantīmālā*. The mace lies horizontally with the thicker end towards the head of the god. A much mutilated female fly-whisker is seated behind the head of the deity. Vishṇu's right hand holding the lotus or *santānamañjarī* is held near the chest. The left arm is broken below the elbow. It may have held a conch. The extra right hand supporting the head and the additional left holding the discus, as usually seen in Śeshaśāyī images, are not visible.[71] In the upper register have partly survived the lower parts of three figures seated in *lalitāsana*. This register seems to have carried originally the *navagraha* figures. The part of the relief showing Brahmā seated on the lotus emanating from Vishṇu's navel, Lakshmī shampooing the right foot of the lord, and other figures, if any, are completely lost. Stylistically, the relief could be dated to *circa* tenth century CE.

Another image of four-handed (*chaturbhujam*) Śeshaśāyī Vishṇu from Siswan, about 15 km northwest of Chandigarh, is equally badly mutilated (Pl. 51) but betrays the compositional framework of the relief. Vishṇu as usual lies on the coils of the great serpent spread on a couch with a beautiful lotiform halo behind the head and wearing the conventional ornaments (*sarvābharaṇabhūshitam*), including the *yajñopavīta* and *Vaijayantīmālā*. The mace is placed with its thicker end near the head as in the preceding example. There are only traces of the hoods which may have canopied the head of the god as also of the female figure behind the couch. The rear right arm supporting the head is gone but the normal right is held near the chest, probably holding a lotus. Traces of the left hands holding the conch and discus may be seen. Brahmā seated on the lotus emanating from Vishṇu's navel has also chipped off. Lakshmī shampooing the right leg may be visualized on the right. In the space between Lakshmī and Brahmā may be seen Śiva holding trident, snake and two fighting figures, Madhu and Kaiṭabha perhaps. Seated in a row in the upper register are *Navagrahas* identifiable by the bust and serpentine figures of Rāhu and Ketu. It is very difficult, rather impossible, to discern the details but what remains indicates it to be a Pratihāra image of the tenth century CE.[72]

A third figure from Ghuram on the Punjab-Haryana border, 35 km south-southeast of Patiala on the road to Pehowa, is also similar and equally mutilated (Pl. 52). It, however, lacks the halo behind Vishṇu's head and preserves the figure of Brahmā seated on the lotus issuing from the god's navel. The four hands holding the lotus or *santānamañjarī*, supporting the head, discus and conch are present. The figure of Lakshmī massaging the feet of her Lord has worn out almost completely but the demons Madhu and Kaiṭabha in the fighting posture are quite clear. The upper register as usual depicts the planetary divinities, with Rāhu represented only by his head and Ketu as anthropo-reptilian figure in *añjali-mudrā*, followed by a garland-bearing *vidyādhara* hovering in the sky. A female figure with hands raised as if supporting the couch with five diminutive hybrid *nāgas* in profile with folded hands on either side are depicted below the couch. The original figure must have been a Pratihāra masterpiece but, just like the preceding examples, is very badly mutilated.

These Jalaśayanamūrtis of Vishṇu show a general similarity with those from the neighbouring Haryana and other regions of North India but do not correspond exactly with the forms prescribed in the iconographic texts like the *Jayākhya Saṃhitā, Vishṇudharmottara, Aparājitapṛichchhā, Rūpa-maṇḍana, Devatāmūrtiprakaraṇa, Vaikhānasāgama*, etc.

## Garuḍa

Garuḍa, as noted above, has been depicted in Punjab sculptures only as a subsidiary and attendant anthropomorphic figure and no independent image of this celestial vehicle of Vishṇu has been discovered from anywhere as yet. Two instances of his architectural depiction have also been noticed. Near Sītā Sara at Sunam is lying a worn-out architectural piece representing the *kumbhaka* of the *pratishṭhāna* of a temple showing winged anthropomorphic Garuḍa to right in *vīrāsana* with hands folded in *añjali-mudrā* in a pedimented pillared niche having *vyāla* figures leaping out from the pillars (Pl. 53). A much better architectural piece with triangular *chaitya*-dormer above found from Samana, however, shows *vīrāsana* Garuḍa with right hand held above the head and holding a snake with the left, stylistically assignable to *circa* twelfth century CE (Pl. 54).[73]

## NOTES AND REFERENCES

1. A.A. Macdonell, *Vedic Mythology*, Varanasi, 1963, pp. 37-39.
2. *Ibid.*
3. A.B. Keith, *Indian Mythology*, New York, 1964, p. 29.
4. E.W. Hopkins, *The Religion of India*, Boston, 1895, p. 56.
5. J. Gonda, *Aspects of Early Viṣṇuism*, Utrecht, 1954, pp.1-11.
6. *Śatapatha Brāhmaṇa* XIV. 1, 1; *Aitareya Brāhmaṇa* I.1; etc.
7. These Vṛishṇi heroes were later deified and identified with *parama, mahat* or *jīva, manas* and *ahaṃkāra*—the first four creative principles of the Sāṅkhya system. The Purāṇas attach some allegorical meanings also to these names. For details, see R.G. Bhandarkar, *Vaiṣṇavism, Śaivism and Minor Religious Systems*, Poona, 1928 (*VSMRS*), pp. 4 ff; Kalpana S. Desai, *Iconography of Viṣṇu*, New Delhi, 1973, pp. 3 and 37 ff.; N.P. Joshi, *Iconography of Balarāma*, New Delhi, 1979, pp. 10-15; etc.
8. *VSMRS*, p. 5.
9. *Mahābhārata* XIII, Vishṇu-Sahasranāma Stotra, verse 28: *Chaturātmā chaturvyūhaśchaturdaṃshṭraśchaturbhujaḥ.*
10. Kalpana Desai, *loc. cit.*
11. *VSMRS*, p. 4.
12. *Ibid*, p. 26. Megasthenes in his *Indica* also refers to a class of people who worshipped god Herakles. See also Ajay Mitra Shastri, "Herakles in Front of the Infantry of Porus", *Journal of Indian History*, Vol. XLII, pp. 119-26.
13. As quoted by Kalpana Desai, *op. cit.*, p. 5.
14. Sircar, *loc. cit.* The discovery of some un-inscribed square copper coins of second century BCE from Taxila (John Allan, *Catalogue of the Coins of Ancient India*, London, 1936, p. 229) containing the representation of pillar surmounted by a fan-palm capital which symbolically represents Saṃkarshaṇa (J.N. Banerjea, *Development of Hindu Iconography*, 2nd ed., Calcutta, 1956, p. 385) also indicates the popularity of

Vaishṇavism in northwest India during the second century BCE. See for details Brajesh Krishna, "The Development of Vaishnavism in Ancient Punjab", *Proceedings, Punjab History Conference, 17th Session*, Patiala, 1983, pp. 48 ff.
15. *Journal of the Numismatic Society of India*, Vol. XXXV, pp. 73-75. The discovery of some un-inscribed square copper coins of second century BCE from Taxila (*BMC*, p. 229) containing the representation of pillar surmounted by a fan-palm capital which symbolically represents Saṃkarshaṇa (*DHI*, p. 385), also indicates the popularity of Vaishṇavism in the northwest India during the second century BCE.
16. Allan, *op. cit.*, p. 281, pl. XVI. 5.
17. Swami Omanand Sarasvati, *Ancient Seals of Haryana*, Jhajjar, V.S. 2031, No. 189; Virajānanda Daivakaraṇi, *Bhārata ke Prāchīna Mudrāṃka* (Hindi), Jhajjar, 2010, p. 26, nos. 101-03.
18. Sarasvati, *op. cit.*, nos. 187-94; *JNSI*, XXXV, pp. 95-97; etc.
19. Devendra Handa, "Vṛishni Copper Coins From Punjab", *Numismatic Digest*, Vol. VII, Parts I & II, 1983, pp. 11-21.
20. It is, however, notable that Vishṇu has been represented on a gold coin of Kushāṇa Vāsudeva I.
21. For details of all these seals/sealings, see Devendra Handa, *Studies in Indian Coins and Seals*, Delhi, 1985, pp. 93-138.
22. *Mbh*, III.83, 103-04; 130, 8-9. Arjuna is said to have seen this pilgrim place in his dream also while going to the god Śiva along with Kṛishṇa (*Mbh*, VII.80, 35-36). Some scholars identify it with the Vishṇupadagiri of the Mehrauli Iron Pillar inscription of King Chandra.
23. Fleet (reprint 1970), p. 56.
24. Michael Alaram, 'A hoard of copper drachms from the Kabul-Kapisa region', in *Silk Road Art and Archaeology*, 6, London, 1999-2000, pp. 129-50.
25. Fleet (CII, III, reprint, Varanasi, 1970), p. 62.
26. George Bühler, 'The New Inscription of Toramāṇa Shāha', *EI*, 1, No. 29 (reprint, New Delhi, 1971), pp. 238-41.
27. Fleet, No. 33, pp. 158-61.
28. Soon, however, Toramāṇa seems to have been ousted from the Eran region by Bhānugupta (Fleet, 1970, pp. 92-93) but the Sanjeli copper-plate (R.N. Mehta and A.M. Thakkar, 1978) shows that Toramāṇa held sway up to north Gujarat where *Mahārāja* Bhūta accepted his suzerainty. The empire of Toramāṇa extended from Gandhāra to Kauśāmbī (where two of his seals have been found in excavations – G.R. Sharma, *The Excavations at Kauśāmbī*, Allahabad, 1960, pp. 15-16) in the east and also covered the Malwa and Rajputana regions touching the northern parts of Gujarat. The Risthal inscription of CE 515-16, however, reveals that Toramāṇa was defeated by the Aulikara king Prakāśadharmā (K.V. Ramesh and S.P. Tiwari, 1971, pp. 96-103).
29. Brajesh Krishna, *op. cit.*, pp. 48 ff.
30. *Indian Archaeology – A Review*, 1964-65, p. 75, Pl. LII.A.
31. R. Nagaswamy, *Art and Religion of the Bhairavas*, Chennai, 2006, p. 122, Fig. 82.
32. Kalpana Desai, *op. cit.*, Figs. 47 & 50.
33. Devendra Handa, *Sculptures From Haryana: Iconography and Style*, Shimla-New Delhi, 2006, Pls. 31, 33, 34, 42, 60, etc.
34. Devendra Handa, "Medieval Brahmanical Stone Sculpture from Punjab", *Roopa-Lekha*, Vol. LIV, Nos. 1-2 (March 1983), p. 21, Fig. 2.
35. R.C. Agrawala, "Krishna-Balarāma as Attendant Figures", *The Indian Historical Quarterly*, Calcutta, Vol. 38, No. 1 (March, 1962), pp. 86-87.
36. Devendra Handa, "Relics of Art from Khanpur (Punjab)", in Shankar Goyal (Ed.), *Śrīrāmābhinandanam: Reconstructing Indian History for S.R. Goyal, Vol. II – India's Ancient Past*, Jaipur, 2003, pp. 510-12, Fig. 6.
37. Kalpana Desai, *op. cit.*, p. 151.
38. Devendra Handa, "Sculptures from Punjab", *Punjab University Research Bulletin (Arts)*, Chandigarh, Vol. XII, Nos. 1-2, April-October, 1981, p. 71; Fig. 22.
39. Handa (2003), *op. cit.*, pp. 507-10, Figs. 1-5.
40. *Ibid.*, pp. 509-10, Fig. 4.
41. Handa (1983), *op. cit.*, p. 24, Fig. 4.

42. Sanjeev P. Srivastava and R.P. Srivastava (*Studies in Panjab Sculpture*, New Delhi, 2001, p. xv, Fig. 3) wrongly identify this image of Śaṅkha-purusha as that of Vishṇu.
43. Handa (1981), *op. cit.*, pp. 71-72.
44. Devendra Handa, "A Vishṇu Sculpture from Janer", *Panjab University Research Bulletin (Arts)*, Vol. V, No. 2 (October 1974), pp. 149-50, Fig. 1; Handa (1981), *op. cit.*, Figs. 9-10; (1983), pp. 21-23, Fig. 2; "Two Vishṇu Sculptures from Janer", *The Researcher*, Jaipur, Vols. XIV-XV (1984-85), pp. 51-53 and plates.
45. U.C. Bhattacharya, *Catalogue & Guide to Rajputana Museum, Ajmer, Rajasthan*, Part I, Sculptures, Jaipur, 1960-61, p. 11 and Pl. XV.
46. Pramod Chandra, *Stone Sculpture in the Allahabad Museum*, American Institute of Indian Studies, Publication No. 2, p. 147, No. 419, Pl. CXXXVII.
47. Handa (1981), *op. cit.*, p. 71, Fig. 17; Ohri (V.C. Ohri, *Sculpture of the Western Himalayas (History and Stylistic Development)*, Delhi, 1991, Pl. 6.5) wrongly mentions its provenance as Dholbaha.
48. Lalman, "Sculptural Remains From Burail (Chandigarh)", *Panjab University Research Bulletin (Arts)*, Vol. XX, No. 2 (October 1989), pp. 177-79, Fig. 1.
49. Kalpana Desai, *op. cit.*, p. 8, Figs. 1-3.
50. Ohri, *op. cit.*, p. 122.
51. *Ibid.*, p. 123.
52. *Ibid.*, pp. 123-24. See also Manmohan Kumar, "Some Brahmanical Sculptures from Dholbaha", *Roopa-Lekha*, Vol. L (1981), pp. 49-51.
53. Ohri, *op. cit.*, p. 126.
54. *Indian Archaeology 1980-81, A Review*, pp. 49-54.
55. Lalman (October 1989), *op. cit.*, pp. 177-79, Figs. 2-5.
56. Handa (1983), *op. cit.*, pp. 24-25 & 32, Fig. 17.
57. Ohri (*op. cit.*, Pl. 6.9) wrongly mentions its provenance as Dholbaha.
58. Devendra Handa, "Archaeological Remains from Sunam", *Panjab University Research Bulletin (Arts)*, XVIII (2), Dec. 1987, pp. 1-30 and figs.
59. Devendra Handa, *Sculptures From Haryana: Iconography & Style*, Shimla-New Delhi, 2006, pp. 53 and 56, Pls. 55 & 62 respectively.
60. Kalpana Desai, *op. cit.*, p. 151.
61. Handa (1987), p. 106.
62. Handa (2006), *op. cit.*, pp. 41 ff, Pls. 30, 35, 84, 214, etc.
63. Earlier, I thought the attribute to be a mace (*Ibid.*, p. 60, Pl. 69) but a careful scrutiny indicates it to be a discus.
64. *Ibid.*, pp. 59-60, Pl. 68.
65. Kalpana Desai, *op. cit.*, p. 141.
66. T.A. Gopinatha Rao, *Elements of Hindu Iconography* (Reprint, Indological Book House, Delhi, 1971), Vol. I, Part II, Appendix C (Pratimālakshaṇam), pp. 48-49.
67. *Mahābhārata*, Vana Parva, 194, 8-15; Śānti Parva, 47-48; etc.
68. Kalpana Desai, *op. cit.*, Figs. 19-20.
69. *Mbh*, Vana Parva, 81, 150.
70. Handa (2006), *op. cit.*, pp. 60-63, Pls. 70-73.
71. *Ibid.*; Kalpana Desai, *op. cit.*, Figs. 24-25.
72. My old colleague and friend Dr. Lalman has told me that the well known anthropologist Dr. S.R.K. Chopra of the Department of Anthropology (now retired), Punjab University, Chandigarh too had collected a Śeshaśāyī image of about two-foot size from Siswan.
73. Srivastava and Srivastava (*op. cit.*, p. xvii, Fig, 71) identify it as flying *Gandharva*.

# 3

# Vaishṇava Incarnations, Vaikuṇṭha and Composite Forms

A unique feature of Hindu mythology is the assumption of various forms by the Supreme Deity or Deities to accomplish certain objectives.[1] Though the earliest exposition of the theory of incarnation (*avatāra-vāda* or *vibhāva-vāda*) occurs in the *Bhagavadgītā*,[2] the origins of the concept of divine multiform, metamorphosis, transformation and reincarnation may be traced to the time of the *Ṛigveda* and later Vedic literature where we find the pre-figuration of several later stories particularly pertaining to the Vāmana 'Dwarf',[3] Matsya 'Fish',[4] Kūrma 'Tortoise',[5] and Varāha 'Boar'[6] forms, the last three being originally connected with Prajāpati. The great epic, however, attributes the functions of the Fish, Tortoise and Boar forms to Vishṇu and contains different lists with varying numbers of the *avatāras*. Of the varied lists,[7] however, the one occurring in the Nārāyaṇīya section gives for the first time the total number of incarnations as ten mentioning Haṃsa, Kūrma, Matsya, Varāha, Narasiṃha, Vāmana, Bhārgava Rāma, Dāśarathī Rāma, Sāttvata (i.e., Vasudeva/Balarama), and Kalkin.[8] The *Vāyu Purāṇa*[9] also mentions the ten incarnations of Vishṇu: Yajña, Narasiṃha, Vāmana, Dattatreya, unnamed fifth belonging to Tretā-yuga, Jāmadagnya Rāma, Dāśarathī Rāma, Vedavyāsa, Vāsudeva-Kṛishṇa and Kalkin, the future incarnation. We thus see that Buddha does not find place even in this list and Matsya, Kūrma and Varāha are replaced by Yajña, Dattātreya and Vedavyāsa. The first three *avatāras* (Yajña, Narasiṃha and Vāmana) are considered as celestial, and the rest are human incarnations. *Vibhāva-vāda* seems to have undergone several stages of evolution and the Buddhist conception of the former Buddhas may have influenced the development of the conception.[10] So Buddha, too, was included in the list soon. The *Matsya Purāṇa* enumerates the ten *avatāras* as the three divine incarnations of Nārāyaṇa, Narasiṃha and Vāmana, besides the seven human incarnations of Dattātreya, Māndhātṛi, Rāma Jāmadagnya, Rāma Dāśarathī, Vedavyāsa, Buddha and Kalki.[11] The *Bhāgavata Purāṇa* refers to innumerable incarnations of Vishṇu[12] but mentions twenty-two, twenty-three and sixteen at different places.[13] The *Sāttvata Saṃhitā*, an early Pāñcharātra work of *circa* eighth century CE, enumerates thirty-nine incarnations of Vishṇu[14] and this list has been copied almost verbatim in the *Ahirbudhnya Saṃhitā*.[15] The *Garuḍa Purāṇa* refers to twenty-two *avatāras* at one place[16] but accepts the following order of the ten incarnations elsewhere[17]:

*Matsyaḥ Kūrmo Varāhaścha Nṛisiṃho'tha Vāmanaḥ /*
*Rāmau Rāmaścha Kṛishṇaścha Buddhaḥ Kalki tathaiva cha //*

(Fish, Tortoise, Boar, Man-Lion, Dwarf, Paraśurāma/Dāśarathi Rāma, Balarāma, Kṛishṇa, Buddha and Kalki).

The *Agni Purāṇa*,[18] while stating that the past and future incarnations of Vishṇu are really innumerable, also describes the ten *avatāras* including Buddha and Kalki. *Varāha Purāṇa*, too, gives the stereotyped list of the ten incarnations as mentioned by the *Garuḍa Purāṇa*, and elsewhere in the following order: (1) Matsya, (2) Kūrma, (3) Varāha, (4) Narasiṃha, (5) Vāmana, (6) Paraśurāma, (7) Dāśarathī Rāma, (8) Sāttvata, i.e., Vāsudeva/Balarāma, (9) Buddha and (10) Kalki.[19] This order of incarnatory forms has been accepted by Pusalkar[20] and Hopkins[21] also. That this order had come to be generally accepted in about the seventh century CE is also proved by the Pallava Grantha inscription of the Ādivarāha Cave Temple, Māmallapuram.[22]

We thus see that though individual incarnations find mention in early literature, yet, collectively the generally accepted list may not have been finalized before the seventh century CE. It is also notable that though individually some incarnatory forms find representation in Indian art from about the Kushāṇa period, yet, collectively the ten *avatāras* do not seem to have been represented anywhere before CE 1000. Huntington has tried to show that the *avatāra* theory assumed an evolutionary pattern. She states that the first three *avatāras*, viz., Fish, Tortoise and Boar, are concerned with rescuing Manu, the Vedas, and the Earth from the waters and symbolize the emergence of life. The theri-anthropomorphic Narasiṃha is symbolic of nascent humanity. Vāmana, the dwarf, is a physically underdeveloped man while Paraśurāma, Dāśarathī Rāma, Kṛishṇa-Balarāma and Buddha represent the full potential of human qualities. Kalki, the future incarnation, may represent purity and plenitude.[23] It has, however, been rightly observed that this "pattern of evolution is purely interpretational and neither historical nor chronological in its association with Vishṇu".[24]

A sealing of Balabhadra from Sanghol and that of *Mahāsenāpati* Balabhadra from Sunet, of Śrī-Rāmachandra, Kṛishṇadatta and Kṛishṇaghosha from the latter site, show the popularity of these names after the gods during the Kushāṇa-Gupta period in the Punjab[25] but unfortunately Punjab has not yielded any early and independent images of most of the incarnations of Vishṇu. The standing Vishṇu image from Janer (Pls. 19-20) shows the depiction of Matsya and Kūrma on the top of the back slab. Vaikuṇṭha image under worship in the Moriwala Mandir at Kharar, however, carries the Daśāvatāra panels on its back slab and shows Matsya, Kūrma, Varāha and Vāmana on the proper right hand side from bottom upwards and Narasiṃha, Rāma, etc. on the corresponding left with Buddha and Kalki in *nāgara-kūṭas* on proper right and left. A *nāgara-kūṭa* of about tenth-eleventh century, measuring 30 X 26 cm, showing an indistinct figure of Kalki on horseback holding a sword in one hand raised above the head also indicates the existence of a Vishṇu image with the depiction of the different incarnations of the god at Kharar. A worn-out sandstone piece measuring 35 X 14 cm obtained from Mundi Kharar shows a figure turned to his left wearing a necklace, an *ardhoruk* and the long garland with right leg placed slantingly on the earth and right hand raised above, probably holding some weapon (Pl. 55). The head is broken but the remnants of a part of the conical crown at the back, the stance of *pratyālīḍhāsana* and the long garland indicate it to have been a part of a hybrid Nṛivarāha image originally having the face of a boar. A badly mutilated face of Varāha with exquisitely carved *karaṇḍa-mukuṭa* lies in the store of the site museum at Dholbaha. A sun-baked clay figurine from Janer (Pl. 56) also represents the four-handed theriomorphic god standing in *pratyālīḍha* supporting the earth goddess with one of his left hands. The earth goddess has also suffered mutilation but may be seen partially in the extant figurine. The other left hand is not visible and the attributes in the two right hands are also difficult to be determined properly. A prominent snake coming from behind and raising its head after forming a loop between the legs of the god attracts attention as representative of the waters from which the god rescued the earth goddess. The figure is not well proportioned and seems to belong to *circa* eighth century CE. The representation of the Varāha incarnation in clay, however, indicates as to how the different forms of the incarnations of Vishṇu had become popular for the common folk in the early medieval period.

A broken piece of a rectangular slab in a private collection recovered from some site in the Punjab depicts Narasiṃha form (Pl. 57). Only the lion face placed on a human bust has survived. Manes, wide open eyes and the lolling out tongue indicate the ferocity of the god. A small conical crown, pearl necklace, armlets and *vanamālā* are visible in the extant relief but the hands are broken. Originally, it must have been a beautiful Pratihāra image of ninth century CE.[26]

A much worn out image of Narasiṃha from Dholbaha emerging out of a column and tearing open the entrails of Hiraṇyakaśipu with his principal hands is displayed in the VVRI Museum at Hoshiarpur (Pl. 58). The back hands are raised upwards. The right leg is planted slantingly but firmly on the threshold with foot splayed out and the left leg is folded as in *pratyālīḍha* pose but the god is shown to front holding the demon on his knees. The round face seems to be somewhat heavy and disproportionate to the body. The piece may have adorned the wall of some tenth century Vaishṇava temple at Dholbaha.[27]

Studded in the wall of the approach way of the site museum at Dholbaha is a *chaitya* arch with four-armed hybrid Narasiṃha in the *chaitya-gavāksha* having a diameter of 24 cm showing the god seated to front in *godohana* posture holding the thinner end of the mace placed vertically on the ground in his two natural hands while the back hands hold unidentifiable objects, probably the disc and the conch (Pl. 59). The details are not very clear. The figure seems to have bedecked the *śukanāsa* of an eighth century temple at Dholbaha. The Manasādevī temple at Dholbaha contains a small figure of Rāma holding an arrow in the right hand and a bow in the left.

Amongst the numerous sculpted and architectural pieces collected in the site museum at Dholbaha is a very much worn out and badly mutilated frieze (Pl. 60, Fig. 20) which has hitherto remained neglected. It shows three human figures with the faces chopped off. The central figure is carved as holding some object looking like a necklace in his left hand near the belly and picking up some other object with his right hand from a roundish basket held by the extreme left figure in his left hand. The extreme right figure also has some object in his left hand. All the figures have suffered so much diminution that almost all details of their physical features, habiliments and ornamentation are lost irretrievably except that folds of the *dhotī* may be seen clearly on their thighs secured by beaded rope-like waistband. It would have certainly been impossible to identify the figures had a portion of the face of the extreme left figure not survived the iconoclastic blow. What remains is a monkey-like face and that provides the clue to the identification of

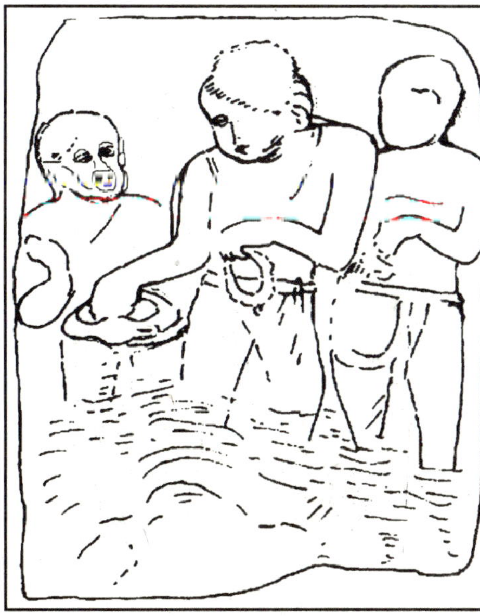

**Fig. 20.** Sugrīva showing Sītā's ornaments to Rāma and Lakshmaṇa.

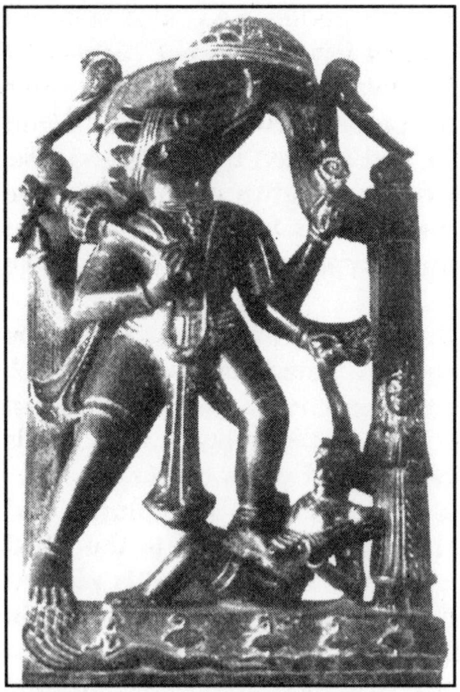

**Fig. 21.** Nṛi-Varāha, Punjab, nineteenth century.

the figures in the frieze. I think that this mutilated and worn-out relief represents monkey-faced Sugrīva showing Rāma and Lakshmaṇa the ornaments. The episode of the abduction of Sītā from the hermitage in Pañchavaṭī by Rāvaṇa during the period of the exile of Rāma has been depicted popularly in Indian sculptures.[28] According to the story as given in Vālmīki's *Rāmāyaṇa*, while Rāvaṇa was abducting Sītā on his aerial chariot, finding no help from anywhere Sītā saw five noble monkeys sitting on the peak of a mountain and threw her scarf and some of her ornaments on the ground so that they could tell Rāma of her.[29] Sugrīva tells Rāma that Sītā did so when he was sitting on the Ṛishyamūka mountain along with Hanumān, Nala, Nīla and Tāra. And then he showed that scarf and the ornaments to Rāma.[30]

It perhaps depicts that famous scene when Rāma passes on some ornaments to Lakshmaṇa for identification and he states –

*Nāhaṃ jānāmi keyūre nāhaṃ jānāmi kuṇḍale //*
*Nūpure tvabhijānāmi nityaṃ pādābhivandanāt /*
(Kishkindhā-kāṇḍa, VI.22-23)

[I.e., I do not know (=recognize) the armlets nor do I know the earrings, (but) I know the anklets because of bowing (to her feet) everyday.]

This is the only piece from the state to show a *Rāmāyaṇa* scene. The faces of Rāma, Lakshmaṇa and Sugrīva seem to have been damaged intentionally by some iconoclastic zealot. It is broken lamentably and perhaps used indiscriminately later, as a result of which it got worn out so badly that its lower portion has lost all features. This frieze, however, indicates that there existed a Pratihāra temple at Dholbaha which was garnished with epic scenes.

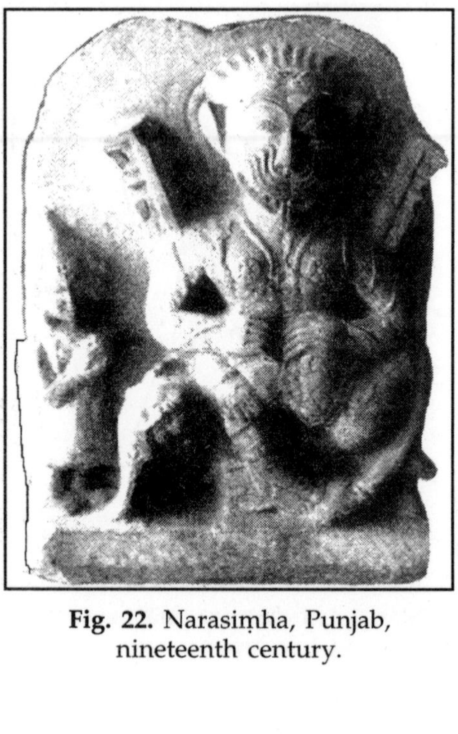

**Fig. 22.** Narasiṃha, Punjab, nineteenth century.

The tradition of the worship of Vishṇu in his different incarnations continued to the late medieval period as indicated by the standing images of the nine out of ten forms in Narasiṃha temple at Humayunpur, Dera Bassi tehsil in district Mohali just on the Punjab-Haryana border. The figures of Matsya and Kūrma are broken but the remaining ones represent Varāha, Nṛisiṃha, Vāmana, Rāma, Paraśurāma, Balarāma, Buddha and Kalki, each measuring 97 X 36 cm (Pl. 61). The village is located on an ancient mound and this frieze was recovered from the village pond. It must have been immersed in the pond to save it from being desecrated by the iconoclasts during the time of an attack. The villagers inform that many other images were obtained from the village pond but being damaged, they were taken by a *sādhu* to Haridwar and immersed in the Gaṅgā. One piece recovered from the pond – an architectural piece with a female figure – may still be seen in the Śiva-Durgā temple at Tasimbli adjoining Humayunpur. Nineteenth century Nṛi-Varāha (Fig. 21) and Narasiṃha (Fig. 22) images in the Department of Cultural Affairs, Archaeology and Museums, Punjab[31] betraying impact of folk art bring the tradition nearer to the present times.

## VAIKUṆṬHA-CHATURMŪRTIS

Vaikuṇṭha is one of the thousand names of Vishṇu according to the *Mahābhārata*[32] and the Purāṇas.[33] In the realm of plastic art, Vaikuṇṭha is a unitary multiple image which symbolically represents Vaikuṇṭha (i.e., Vāsudeva Vishṇu) as the Highest Being along with his three emanations[34] – Saṃkarshaṇa, Pradyumna, and Aniruddha – or incarnations, i. e., Nṛisiṃha, Varāha and Kapila.[35] The *Mahābhārata* refers to this esoteric form of Vishṇu as *Mūrtichatushṭaya*[36] but does not give any details. The first iconographical description of the Vaikuṇṭha image occurs in a *dhyāna* 'meditation' of the Pāñcharātra text *Jayākhya Saṃhitā* of the late or post-Gupta period where it has been described as having four faces of Vaikuṇṭha, Nṛisiṃha, Varāha and Kapila and four arms holding a conch, a discus, a mace, a lotus, and mounted on a white Garuḍa.[37] The *Vishṇudharmottara Purāṇa*, another text of the late Gupta period, states that the joint image of Vāsudeva (human), Saṃkarshaṇa (lion), Pradyumna (boar) and Aniruddha (terrific face) is called Vaikuṇṭha which should be quadric-cephalous (*Chaturmukha, Chaturmūrti*), having the main eastern face as placid representing strength (*bala*), southern leonine face representing knowledge (*jñāna*), northern boar face representing affluence (*aiśvarya*), and western terrific (*raudra*) face as representing energy (*śakti*).[38] Elsewhere, this very text lays down that it should have placid, Nṛisiṃha, Kapila, and Varāha faces on the east, south, west, and north sides respectively.[39] The octomanous deity should hold an arrow, a rosary, a pestle, etc. in the right hands and a shield, a plough, a bow, and a discus in the left ones.[40] Also, the god should ride the mount Garuḍa (*Garuḍa-sthitam*). Later texts like the *Aparājitapṛichchhā*,[41] *Rūpamaṇḍana*[42] and *Devatāmūrtiprakaraṇa*[43] also describe Vaikuṇṭhamūrti similarly as four-faced, eight-handed and riding the mount Garuḍa. The attributes, according to these texts, should be a mace, a sword, a discus and an arrow in the right hands[44] and a conch, a shield, a bow and a lotus in the left ones. Some scholars hold that the multi-headed (*bhūyishṭhavaktra*) images of Vishṇu were the central object of worship by the followers of the Tantrāntara sub-sect, which was popular during the medieval period with other Vaishṇava sub-sects like the Mantra, Āgama and Tantra.[45] The *Pādma*[46] and *Paushkara*[47] *saṃhitās* also describe Vishṇu, the chief deity of the Tantrāntara sub-sect, as having the placid, leonine and other faces.

Yaśovarmadeva's Khajuraho inscription of VS 1011 (=CE 954) tells us a very interesting story about the four-faced Vaikuṇṭha form of Vishṇu. It states that Kapila and two other demons had obtained a boon from Brahmā that they should be killed only by one who would assume their forms. In order to kill the demons, Vishṇu assumed the syncretistic form of Vaikuṇṭha with the faces of lion, boar and Kapila.[48] This mythological story, however, is not met with anywhere else.[49]

Very few temples of Vaikuṇṭha have survived the vicissitudes of nature and human vandalism. Yaśovarman had installed the four-faced Vaikuṇṭha image in the Lakshmaṇa temple at Khajuraho, which he constructed for this very purpose. This image was brought from the Kailāśa region by Bhoṭanātha and presented to the Sāhi king of Kīra (Kangra region) as a token of friendship. Herambapāla took this image forcibly from the Sāhi ruler and the Chandella king Yaśovarman took this image from Herambapāla's son Hayapati Devapāla. The *bhadra* (cardinal, main) niches of the sanctum of this temple contain images of Varāha, Narasiṃha and Hayagrīva, indicating the association with and importance of these incarnatory forms for Vaikuṇṭha. The present image of the Lakshmaṇa temple, however, is about 150 years later.[50] The other Vaikuṇṭha temple known to us is the larger Sās (of the Sās-Bahu) temple at Gwalior built in CE 1093 by the Kachchhapaghāta king Mahīpāla.

Four-faced Vaikuṇṭha images, which were popularly worshipped by the followers of the Pāñcharātra of the Kāśmīrāgama, also called Tantrāntara Siddhānta, are characteristic of the Kashmir region.[51] This sect worshipped the multi-headed (*bhūyishṭha-mukha*) Vishṇu. Numerous images of Vaikuṇṭha were installed in Kashmir from eighth century onwards. Queen Diddā, wife of Kshemagupta and grand-daughter of the Sāhi king Bhīma, installed Vaikuṇṭha images and founded Diddāsvāmin shrine in CE 972[52] and Queen Ratnādevī constructed a Vaikuṇṭha-maṭha in mid-twelfth century CE.[53]

A unique four-faced *Yaksha* image from Bhita, now exhibited in the State Museum, Lucknow,[54] showing small figures of lion and boar below the badly mutilated side faces at the waist level, is regarded by some scholars to represent the earliest attempt at carving the Vaikuṇṭha form in the second century BCE.[55] The existence of the Vaikuṇṭha form at such an early age, however, seems to be historically impossible as the earliest Vaikuṇṭha images showing the lion and boar heads may be traced to only the Gupta period.[56] Most of the scholars, however, regard Vaikuṇṭha image of the Kushāṇa period from Mathura which shows three busts attached to it, one on the top and two near the shoulders, as the earliest representation of this deity.[57] Vaikuṇṭha images showing lion and boar faces, however, seem to have come into existence during the Gupta period.[58] It is difficult to prove that they were inspired by three-headed Maheśa-mūrtis or were an attempt to bring together the worshippers of Vishṇu and his Varāha and Narasiṃha forms, which too were quite popular during the Gupta period. During the early medieval period, Vaikuṇṭha worship had grown quite popular in the hill region of Kashmir and Himachal Pradesh. Vaikuṇṭha-mūrtis continued to be carved during this period from Kashmir to Madhya Pradesh and from Uttar Pradesh to Gujarat.[59] The Vaikuṇṭha form seems to have travelled from the north even to Karnataka as indicated by an inscribed medieval *makara-toraṇa* from Huli in district Belgaum, which shows the four armed Vaikuṇṭha, seated on a *padma-pīṭha* in *mahārājalīlāsana*. The only independent sculptural representation of Vaikuṇṭha, assignable to *circa* twelfth-thirteenth century, however, comes from Banashankari temple, Basavakalyāṇa, district Bijapur, Karnataka. It is a relief sculpture executed on a rectangular sandstone slab, depicting Lakshmī-Vaikuṇṭha seated on Garuḍa in *ardhapadmāsana*, holding discus and mace in the upper hands, lotus in the normal right hand and embracing the goddess Lakshmī with the lower left hand. Gadā is shown in a minuscule fashion on the extreme left. Garuḍa has fluttering wings and holds *amṛita-kalaśa* in his two hands.[60] There is evidence that Vaikuṇṭha worship was prevalent in the Gandhāra region also.[61]

The early Brahmanical Vaikuṇṭha figures may be regarded the visual images of the cosmogonic theory. Their anthropomorphic figures are emanatory; they issue from a central figure and represent, not a group of figures, but a process of cosmic becoming in its continuity. The assemblage of emerging anthropomorphic figures emanating from one central body betrays the sculptural rendering of a process, representing an ongoing progression in its three-dimensional form. The multiple sculptural form presents the virtual correspondence to a theological thought-structure created in the Pāñcharātra system to celebrate Vishṇu as the universe.[62]

In Bhāgavata theology,[63] the principal cult-figures were the five Vṛishṇi heroes.[64] The Pāñcharātra system transformed four of them (except Sāmba) into symbols of the stages in a new formulation of the cosmogonic process. Sāmba, the fifth member and the other son of Kṛishṇa besides Pradyumna, was left out for having disgraced himself for he had dressed as a woman and taunted the sages who cursed him to give birth to an iron club from which came the swords which destroyed the Yādavas, Kṛishṇa's clan in Dvārikā.[65] The unitary multiple image gradually lost its inherent emanatory, cosmogonic character and the full-bodied figures issuing laterally and apically from their source, became reduced to their heads only, inaugurating the subsequent multi-headed images of gods.[66]

The *Jayākhya Saṃhitā* (VI. 73) describes Vaikuṇṭha as *anādinidhana,* without beginning and end, and *jagatsrashṭā īśvara,* God who created the Universe. According to the *Bhāgavata Purāṇa* (X.6, 26), Vaikuṇṭha is beseeched for the protection of children from various evil spirits.

During the course of our investigations, we have come across some interesting specimens from the Punjab.[67] They are described in the following lines.

A standing quadrumanous Vaikuṇṭha image exists at Chandpur Rahon in district Nawanshahr. Measuring 62.5 x 35 cm, it shows the god standing in *samapāda-sthānaka* pose on a lotus *pīṭha* placed on the central projection of a *pañcharatha* pedestal (Pl. 62). Besides the central placid human face, there are lion and boar faces on the proper right and left sides. An eight-petalled aureole is partially visible behind the head. On the top corners are carved garland-bearing *vidyādharas*, one on either side. The god holds mace and disc in the rear right and left hands and a conch in the normal left. The principal right hand is mutilated but it seems to have held a lotus. The arrangement of attributes conforms to the 'Trivikrama' form of Vishṇu. The god wears a flat crown on the head, ear ornaments, bracelets, *dhotī, śrīvatsa* on the chest and the *vanamālā*. On either side of the feet are two attendant figures. They may have been Śrī, Sarasvatī, Garuḍa and an *āyudha-purusha*. Since the image has been badly besmeared with oil and vermillion and is in a very indifferent state of preservation, the details are not clear and nothing certain can be stated about the subsidiary figures. The identification proposed here is only circumstantial and provisional. Lotus-petalled gloriole, not too high crown and sparse jewellery indicate that the image may have belonged to *circa* ninth century CE.

More than three decades ago, Prof. Sadhu Ram had published a fragmentary relief from Kharar (Pl. 63), which he wrongly identified as Narasiṃha.[68] The beautiful head with a high cylindrical crown bedecked with pearl garlands and festoons and a *kīrtimukha* in the centre placed on the placid human face with an eight-petalled halo behind and the lion and boar faces attached to it on the proper right and left certainly belong to what must have once been a very elegant image of Vaikuṇṭha belonging to *circa* tenth century CE.

Another Vaikuṇṭha image (Pl. 64) measuring 104 X 65 cm is still under worship in Ḍerā Bābā Dhyāna Dāsa (also known as Morīwālā or Śiva Mandira) at Kharar. The god stands in *ābhaṅga* on a *pañcharatha* pedestal accompanied on either side by two attendant figures on the receding recesses. The god wears a high cylindrical crown over the central human face to which are appended in profile a lion face on the proper right and a boar face on the left. Usual ornaments, including the *Vaijayantīmālā,* may be seen on the person of the deity. The normal left hand holds a conch vertically and the back left hand is placed on the head of the Chakra-purusha (now damaged). The principal right hand seems to have been held in the gesture of reassurance while the rear right is placed on the head of a female figure which may be identified as Gadādevī. Behind her is a male figure in *gopālāsana* holding the shaft of what may have been a plough. As such, the figure may be identified with Balarāma. On the corresponding other side is perhaps Garuḍa in a symmetrical posture. The back slab shows Daśāvatāra panels on the two sides, surmounted by *nāgara-kūṭas*. Matsya, Kūrma, Varāha and Vāmana may be seen on the right hand side from bottom upwards and Nṛisiṃha, Rāma, etc. on the other. *Gaja-śārdūlas* and *makara-mukhas* may also be discerned on the extreme recesses. Since the image is still under worship, it has been marred by oil, dust and vermillion. The small dingy cell in which it is enshrined also obscures some of the details. The image may be dated to *circa* eleventh century on stylistic grounds.[69]

## TRAILOKYA-MOHANA

A Vaikuṇṭha image is known from Amritsar region (Pl. 65). It depicts the deity standing in contraposto and having the usual lion and boar heads on the right and left of the central human face bedecked with a *kirīṭa-mukuṭa, ekāvali* and necklaces, beaded strings going to the back from under the arms, sacred thread, armlets, wristlets, anklets, lower garment held in position by an elaborate girdle and the long garland. The lion and boar faces are in three-fourth profile. The god has sixteen hands. The sixteen-handed form of Vaikuṇṭha is known as Trailokya-Mohana. Most of the arms, however, are broken. Three of the surviving right hands hold a sword, arrows and a club while in the extant left hands may be seen discus, shield, bow, staff (ploughshare?), etc. There is an ornamental arch above the head of the god over which is carved Sūrya, seated cross-legged, holding lotuses in his two hands and flanked by garland bearing *vidyādharas*. On the proper right hand side stele is depicted bearded tri-cephalous Brahmā in *lalitāsana* holding rosary, ladle, book and water pot in his four hands. Śiva occupies the left stele in a similar posture but holding trident and snake in the rear pair of hands. Four attendant figures appear near the feet, two on each side. On the proper right may be seen Śaṅkha-purusha and Śrī, while on the left appear Chakra-purusha and Garuḍa. They wear beautiful dresses and ornaments.

The whole composition seems to be crowded and the faces of the figures lack expressions. Tendency towards elaboration and over-ornamentation is evident. As such, the relief may be ascribed to *circa* twelfth century CE.

## VAIKUṆṬHA-LAKSHMĪ

Studded in the wall of the Śiva temple (known as Chaudhariyoṃ kā Śivālā also) at Lalru, about 33 km southwest of Chandigarh on the main road to Ambala, in district Mohali (Punjab), is a unique image of Vaikuṇṭha-Lakshmī (Pl. 66). It measures 72.5 X 40 cm. Badly encrusted with whitewash, oil, dust and vermillion like the preceding image, it is not in a good state of preservation. Being, however, a unique sculpture, it deserves attention and must be treated chemically and preserved properly. The god is shown as standing to front holding a lotus and a mace in the principal and extra right hands, and a conch and disc in the corresponding left hands respectively. He wears a high *kirīṭa-mukuṭa* on the central human face. Lion and boar faces appear as usual on the right and left sides. The former is slightly damaged. The god wears earrings, necklet, necklace, sacred thread, wristlets, anklets and *vaijayantīmālā*. The nether garment is secured by an elaborate waistband. On the proper left of the god stands Lakshmī slightly turned towards him. She holds a lotus in her right hand near the right shoulder and a *kuṇḍikā* (nectar flask) in the suspended left hand. Earrings, necklet with a belt-like pendant falling from between her breasts, armlets, bracelets, nether garment held in position by a girdle and a long garland resembling the one worn by her spouse may be seen on her person. Between the feet of Vaikuṇṭha and Lakshmī is carved a small figure of four-handed avian-anthropomorphic Garuḍa turned to his proper right, i.e., Vaikuṇṭha. Wearing usual ornaments, Garuḍa stands folding his proper pair of hands near the chest in salutation of his Lord. In the back left hand, he holds a snake. The attribute in his rear right hand is not clear. The lower half of Garuḍa seems to be avian. On the proper right of Vaikuṇṭha stands Chakra-purusha holding the weapon he personifies in his left hand, while the other hand rests on the respective thigh.

From nowhere in India has any image of standing quadrumanous Vaikuṇṭha accompanied by Lakshmī and attended by four-armed hybrid Garuḍa and Chakra-purusha been found. This, thus, is a unique image in the whole realm of plastic art in India. Stylistically, it seems to belong to *circa* tenth century CE.[70]

We thus see that Punjab has yielded Trailokya-Mohana and Vaikuṇṭha-Lakshmī types of Vaikuṇṭha images. They are all carved in relief and none in the round. The god is invariably shown as standing, wearing *kirīṭa-mukuṭa* and *Vaijayantīmālā*, and is accompanied by Garuḍa as an attendant. Standing Vaikuṇṭha with Lakshmī attended by four-handed avian-anthropomorphic Garuḍa is an innovation made by the artist.

## SYNCRETISTIC IMAGES

The Vedic concept of *'sa esha eka eva vṛideka eva'* (He is One and the only One God)[71] and *'Ekaṃ sad viprā bahudhā vadanti'* (The wise call that One by various names), [72] etc.[73] reflect the way of thinking of the Hindus who, though divided later in a good number of sects, each having its own set of religious beliefs and observances, did not feel any religious acrimony amongst them and have emphasized through the ages the sentiment of the one eternally existing principle in different ways.[74] The Upanishads,[75] the *Bhagavadgītā*[76] and the Purāṇas[77] show the persistence of this sentiment and the influence it exercised on the people.

Though blatant examples of morbid sectarianism are not rare in the field of plastic art, particularly during the medieval period, yet attempts of reconciliation and rapprochement between rival sects and creeds outnumber the former. The Purāṇas, wherein we find the development, growth and expansion of Hindu mythology, show a general tenor and tendency of broad toleration between the various sects of Hinduism.[78] The process of synthesis seems to have been at work from a fairly early date and the mental attitude of the early foreign immigrants like the Śakas, the Pahlavas and the Kushāṇas may also have been an important contributory factor to the growth of cult-syncretism.[79] The Kushāṇa example of Harihara[80] and Ardhanārīśvara[81] indicate that Vaishṇavism, Śaivism and Śāktism were the great cults of that period. The Hindu concept of Trinity and the Smṛiti injunctions strengthened the concept of unity, and the process of synthesis culminated in the *pañchopāsanā* that is well-represented by the Pañchāyatana worship of the *smārtas* and by the *pañchāyatana* 'quincunx' temples; *Chaturmukha* Śiva-*liṅgas* depicting Gaṇapati, Vishṇu, Pārvatī and Sūrya on the four sides of the central Śaiva emblem and the Hariharahiraṇyagarbha (Sūrya-Hari-Hara-Pitāmaha) images during the early medieval period, combining almost all the prominent contemporary cults. Sometimes, even the Buddhist and Jaina influence is also discernible on Hindu composite icons. The syncretistic tendency seems to have been fairly popular during the medieval period and is interestingly illustrated by a large number of images of that period.[82] In the Punjab, however, like most other cultic sculptures, composite images are a rarity but numerous seals/sealings from Sunet bearing the Brāhmī legend *Śaṅkara-Nārāyaṇābhyāṃ* in third-fourth century characters do indicate the popularity of Harihara temples and images. Incidentally, Harihara is the only syncretistic form of composite images found from the Punjab.

### HARIHARA

The earliest literary reference to the composite form of Vishṇu and Śiva occurs in the *Mahābhārata*[83] wherein we find Arjuna addressing a hymn to Hari-Rudra after the completion of his penance. The *Vishṇu Purāṇa* also refers to the identity of Śiva and Vishṇu (*Śaṅkaro bhagavāñchhauriḥ).*[84] Elsewhere in the same text, Kṛishṇa, an incarnation or form of Hari (Vishṇu), talks of his identity with Śaṅkara.[85]

The composite image of Vishṇu and Śiva has been called variously as Harihara, Haryardha, Śiva-Nārāyaṇa, Śaṅkara-Nārāyaṇa, etc. in the epigraphs and iconographical texts. The *Matsya Purāṇa* prescribes that the left side of the image of Śiva-Nārāyaṇa should be occupied by *Mādhava*

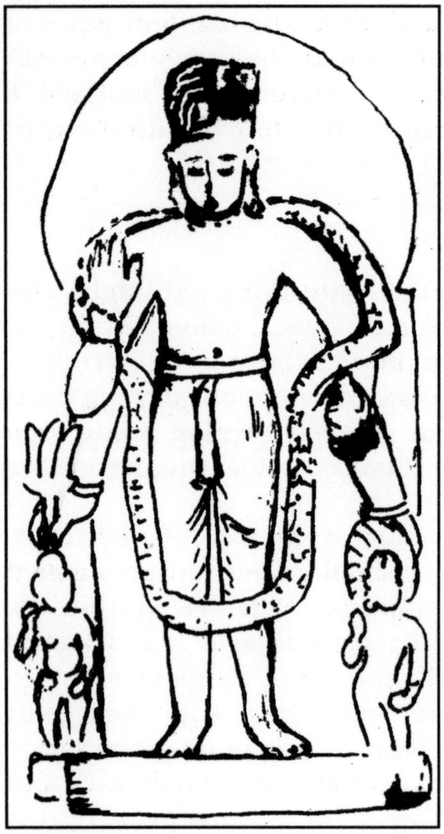

**Fig. 23.** Harihara, Dholbaha.

(Kṛishṇa = Vishṇu) and the right side by Śiva. Both the (left) arms of Kṛishṇa should be adorned with bejewelled bracelets and should hold conch shell and discus or mace. Kṛishṇa should have a calm expression; yellow garment and a bejewelled foot; (the right half representing Śiva) should wear necklets, sacred thread, and the serpents and show the right arm in *varada-mudrā*. He should wear the lower garment of skin and have the foot adorned with jewels and serpents.[86]

The *Vishṇudharmottara Purāṇa* also suggests the right half to belong to Śiva and the other half to Hṛishīkeśa but prescribes *vara*, trident, *chakra* and lotus in the four hands with bull (Nandī) on the right side and Garuḍa on the left.[87] The *Devatāmūrtiprakaraṇa* repeats this description[88] as also of Śiva-Nārāyaṇa as found in the *Matsya Purāṇa* detailed above.[89] It also describes the image of Kṛishṇa-Śaṅkara, which differs only in having a rosary instead of *varada-mudrā* in one of the hands of Śiva.[90]

The *Suprabhedāgama* says that Vishṇu should be shown with a *kirīṭa-mukuṭa* and Śaṅkara with matted locks.[91] The *Śilparatna*[92] and the *Pūrvakāraṇāgama*[93] not only prescribe similar treatment of the head but also mention crescent on Śiva's locks.

Though both Vaishṇavism[94] and Śaivism[95] were the prominent and popular cults in Punjab-Haryana region from quite early times, yet no image of Harihara belonging to the Kushāṇa or Gupta period has been found from the region so far. That Śiva and Vishṇu were worshipped together during this period is evidenced by seals/sealings from Sunet which show trident-discus combined, trident and discus together, and those bearing the legend *Śaṅkara-Nārāyaṇābhyāṃ*.[96] It is not surprising that like many other parts of India, syncretistic tendency gained ascendancy here from the early medieval period.

Punjab has yielded four Harihara images so far. The earliest of these, belonging to *circa* sixth century, once existed at Dholbaha (Pl. 67, Fig. 23) but was stolen subsequently. The four-handed god stood in contraposto flanked by small acolyte figures of Chakra-purusha on the left and probably Triśūla-purusha on the right, both standing in *dvibhaṅga* resting the left arm on the respective hip and right one raised in *abhaya*. The main figure of Harihara shows the vertical division of the cylindrical crown and matted locks on the head which helps us to identify the figure with certainty. The face has suffered mutilation. The god wears ear ornaments, armlets, wristlets and the long garland besides the *dhotī* held in position by a girdle. The image being in an indifferent state of preservation, other features are not quite clear. The locks of hair falling on the shoulders on Vishṇu's side, the bifurcation of the hands at the elbows, the depiction of the *āyudha-purushas* and the facial expression and delineation of the Triśūla-purusha betray the Gupta traits. The god holds conch in the front left hand and the suspended additional left holds a discus placed on the back of the head of the acolyte figure. The front right hand is disposed in *abhaya-mudrā* while the suspended back hand holds the trident with its shaft placed on the head of the *āyudha-purusha*. The style of holding the trident with a small shaft in the suspended hand is noteworthy and provides this image distinctiveness of its own. Another Harihara image belonging to eighth-ninth century was seen at Velore in district Ferozepur in the sixties of the last century but nothing is known of its whereabouts now. Another image, made of greyish sandstone and measuring 24 X 17 cm, is an exquisite piece and was recovered from Khanpur. It is now preserved in the museum of the Department of AIHCA, Panjab Univesity, Chandigarh (Pl. 68).[97] It represents the head and bust of Harihara with semi-circular top of the back slab. The matted locks on the proper right hand side and the cylindrical crown bedecked with pearl strings and central crest jewel on the other half are clear enough to reveal the identity of the deity. The god bears hair combed backwards and wears *karṇa-kuṇḍalas*, *ekāvali* and *yajñopavīta*. The long garland may be seen on the shoulders and a part of the extant left arm which seems to have borne a *keyūra*. That the god was four-handed is clear from the broken part of the upper left arm. The right arms, in fact all the arms are, however, completely lost. The spikes of the trident and the looped body of the serpent to the proper right of the deity are the still surviving parts of Śiva's attributes. The disposition of the broken part of the floral stele on the proper left of the head indicates that the upper left hand of the god held a discus. The attributes of the normal left hand is a matter of guess only. The god has elongated eyes, thick lips and pointed chin. The nose is damaged. The expression is that of a beatific smile. Stylistically, the image may be assigned to *circa* tenth century CE.

Another image of Harihara from Dholbaha is now exhibited in the VVRI Museum at Hoshiarpur (Pl. 69). It is quite worn out and it is rather difficult to discern all details. All hands, except the upper right which holds a trident, are broken. The feet are also lost. The vertical division of the crown into *jaṭā* and *kirīṭa*, however, helps us to identify the figure as that of Harihara.[98] It is also a tenth century relief.

## NOTES AND REFERENCES

1. *DHI*, p. 388.
2. *Bhagavadgītā*, IV.7-8.
3. *RV*, I.154, 1-2; *Ś. Br.* I.2, 5.
4. *Ś.Br.* I.8, 1, 1-6.
5. *Taittirīya Saṃhitā*, VII.1, 5; *Tait. Br.* I.1, 3.
6. *Ś. Br.*, XIV.1, 2, 11; *Tait. Ār.* VI.3, 5, 8; and X.1, 6.
7. *Mbh*, XII.349, 37; 389, 77-90, etc. The *HV* (I.41) quotes a list of ten incarnations, which omits Matsya, Kūrma, one Rāma and includes Paushkaraka, Datta, Keśava, and Vyāsa. Cf. *Brahma P.*, ch. 213.
8. *Mbh*, XII.389, 104.
9. Ch. 98, vv. 71 ff.
10. D.C. Sircar, *Studies in the Religious Life of Ancient and Medieval India*, Delhi, 1971, p. 42
11. *Matsya P.* LVII.237-48.
12. *Bhāg. P.* I.3, 26:

    *Avatārā hyasaṃkhyeyā Hareḥ sattvanidherdvijāḥ /*
    *Yathāvidāsinaḥ kulyāḥ sarasaḥ syuḥ sahasraśaḥ //*
13. *Ibid.*, I.3, 6-22; II.7, 1 ff and XI.4, 3ff respectively.
14. As quoted by Banerjea, *DHI*, pp. 391-92.
15. Otto E. Schrader, *Introduction to the Pañcarātra and the Ahirbudhnya Saṃhitā*, Madras, 1916, pp. 42 ff.
16. *Garuḍa P.* I.1, 13-15.
17. *Ibid.* II.20, 31.
18. *Agni P.* Chs. 2-16. Cf. *Varāha P.* chs. 39-48.
19. *Varāha P.* IV.2.
20. A.D. Pusalkar, *Studies in the Epics and Puranas*, Bombay, 1955, p. 10.
21. E.W. Hopkins, *Epic Mythology*, p. 217.
22. See R. Champakalakshmi, *Vaiṣṇava Iconography in the Tamil Country*, New Delhi, 1981, p. 81.

23. Ronald M. Huntington, "Avatāras and Yugas: An Essay in Puranic Cosmology", *Purāṇam*, Vol. VI, No. 1 (Jan. 1964), pp. 33-37.
24. Champakalakshmi, *op. cit.*, p. 28.
25. Handa (1985), *op. cit.*, pp. 96 ff.
26. Handa (1983), *op. cit.*, pp. 25-26, Fig. 10.
27. A beautifully executed stone image of two-handed Narasiṃha holding the mace vertically between his legs with realistic lion face and manes belonging to the eighth century is known from Verinag in Kashmir and a similar late eighth century brass image is under worship at Brahmaur, while a ninth century four-handed image seated in an identical pose to our example but wearing a crown is under worship at Swai, Himagiri in Chamba (Ohri, *op. cit.*, Pls. 4.20, 66 & 55, respectively).
28. Jayantika Kala, *Epic Secenes in Indian Plastic Art*, New Delhi, 1988, pp. 28-29.
29. *Vālmīki Rāmāyaṇa*, Araṇya-kāṇḍa, LIV.1-3: *Hṛiyamāṇā tu Vaidehī kaṃchchinnāthamapaśyantī / Dadarśa giri-śṛiṅgasthān pañcha vānara-puṅgavān // Teshāṃ madhye viśālākshī kauśeyaṃ kanaka-prabham / Uttarīyaṃ varārohā śubhāṇyābharaṇāni cha // Mumocha yadi Rāmāya śaṃsayuriti bhāminī / Vastramutsṛijya tanmadhye nikshiptaṃ saha-bhūshaṇam //*
30. Kishkindhā-kāṇḍa, VI.15: *Uttarīyaṃ gṛihītvā tu sa tānyābharaṇāni cha / Idaṃ paśyeti Rāmāya darśayāmāsa vānaraḥ //*
31. *Punjab Government Museum, Hoshiarpur*, Chandigarh (no date).
32. *Mahābhārata* (Gita Press edition) VI. 775, 15.
33. *Bhāgavata Purāṇa* III. 16, 6 and VIII. 5, 4; *Vishṇu Purāṇa* III.1, 41.
34. The concept of devotion perhaps owes its origin to the practice of hero worship. Vāsudeva, Saṃkarshaṇa, Aniruddha, Pradyumna and Sāmba were the five heroes of the Vṛishṇi clan whose rule in Punjab is evidenced by their coins, seals and sealings (See for details, John Allan, *BMC*, pp. clv-clvii and 281, Pl. XVI.5; Swami Omanand Sarasvati, *Ancient Seals of Haryana*, Jhajjar, vs 2031, Nos. 187 ff; Devendra Handa, *Studies in Indian Coins and Seals*, Delhi, 1985, pp. 66-74, etc.). Later on, the Vṛishṇi heroes were deified and incorporated in the cosmological speculations of the Sāṅkhya system. The *Mbh.* (BORI ed. XII. 326, 38-39) tells us that "The principal heroes of the cult were identified with the four creative principles of the Sāṅkhya system – *parama*, *mahat* or *jīva*, *manas* and *ahaṃkāra*. Vāsudeva is the highest *nirguṇātmaka*; from him emanates Saṃkarshaṇa in the form of *jīva* or individual soul; from him emanates Pradyumna in the form of *manas* and lastly comes Aniruddha identified as *ahaṃkāra*" (Vide Kalpana Desai, *op. cit.*, p. 3).
35. Regarding various incarnatory forms of Vishṇu mentioned in different texts, see *DHI*, pp. 388-92. The *Mahābhārata* identifies Kapila with Sūrya (III.3, 181), Agni and the founder of the Sāṅkhya philosophy (III, 211, 21: *Agni sa Kapilo Sāṅkhyayoga-pravartakaḥ*) and as a form of Vāsudeva (III, 106, 2). The *Bhāgavata Purāṇa* (I. 3, 10) and the *Rāmāyaṇa* (Ed. G.H. Bhatt, Oriental Institute, Baroda, I.39, 26-28) regard Kapila to be an incarnation of Vishṇu. See also and Cf. S.N. Chaturvedi, "The Vaikuṇṭha Images and the Khajuraho Inscription of Yaśovarmmadeva", *Journal of the Indian Society of Oriental Art*, New Series, Calcutta, Vol. XIV (1984-85), pp. 47 ff.
36. *Mbh*, XIII.326, 43.
37. *Jayākhya Saṃhitā* (GOS, Baroda, 1931) VI. 73-76:

    *Anādinidhanaṃ devaṃ jagatsrashṭāramīśvaram /*
    *Dhyāyechchaturbhujaṃ vipre śaṅkhachakragadādharam //*
    *Chaturvaktraṃ sunayanaṃ sukāntaṃ padmapāṇinam /*
    *Vaikuṇṭhaṃ Narasiṃhāsyaṃ Vārāhaṃ Kapilānanam //*
    *Śuklaṃ khageśvarārūḍhaṃ sarvābharaṇabhūshitam /*
    *Sarvalakshaṇasampannaṃ mālyāmbaradharaṃ vibhum //*
    *Kirīṭakaustubhadharaṃ karpūrāliptavigraham /*
    *Sūryāyutasahasrābhaṃ sarvadevanamaskṛitam //*

38. *Vishṇudharmottara Purāṇa* (GOS, Baroda, 1958) III. 44, 43-45:

    *Ekamūrtidharaḥ kāryā[o] Vaikuṇṭhetyābhiśabditaḥ /*
    *Chaturmukhaḥ saḥ karttavyaḥ prāguktavadānanaḥ prabhuḥ //*
    *Chaturmūrtiḥ sa bhavati kṛite mukhachatushṭaye /*
    *Pūrvaṃ saumyamukhaṃ kāryaṃ yattu mukhyatamaṃ viduḥ //*

*Karttavyaṃ siṃhavaktrābhaṃ tu dakshiṇam /*
    *Paśchimaṃ vadanaṃ raudraṃ yattadaiśvaryamuchyate //*

39. *Ibid.*, III. 44, 11-12:
*Saumyaṃ tu vadanaṃ pūrvaṃ Nārasiṃhaṃtu dakshiṇam /*
    *Kāpilaṃ paśchimaṃ vaktraṃ tahtā Vārāhamuttaram //*
40. *Ibid.*, III. 44, 12-13 as suggested by Kalpana Desai, *op. cit.*, p. 39, and fn. 21.
41. *Aparājitapṛichchhā*, 219, vv. 25-27:
*Pravachmyatha Vaikuṇṭhaṃ so'ashṭabāhurmahābalaḥ /*
    *Garuḍasthaśchaturvaktraḥ karttavyaḥ śāntimichchhitā //*
*Gadākhaḍgau bāṇachakre dakshiṇe'strachatushṭayam /*
    *Śaṅkhaṃ kheṭo dhanuḥ padmaṃ vāme chāstra chatushṭayam //*
*Pūrvataḥ purushākāro Narasiṃhaścha dakshiṇe /*
    *Apare Śrīmukhākāro Vārāhāsyastathottare //*
42. *Rūpamaṇḍana*, III. 52-54:
*Vaikuṇṭhaṃ cha pravakshyāmi so'shṭabāhurmahābalaḥ /*
    *Tārkshyāsanaśchaturvaktraḥ karttavyaḥ śāntimichchhitā //*
*Gadāṃ khaḍgaṃ śaraṃ chakraṃ dakshiṇe syāchchatushṭayam /*
    *Śaṅkhaṃ kheṭaṃ dhanuḥ padmaṃ vāme dadyāchchatushṭayam //*
*Agrataḥ pururshākāraṃ Nārasiṃhaṃ cha dakshiṇe /*
    *Aparaṃ strīmukhākāraṃ Vārāhasya tathottare //*
43. *Devatāmūrtiprakaraṇa*, V. 91-93.
44. *Vāṇachakre* of the *Aparājitapṛichchhā* has been changed to *'śaraṃ chakraṃ'* in the *Rūpamaṇḍana*. Also *'śrīmukhaṃ'* of the former becomes *'strīmukhaṃ'* in the latter.
45. Pratapaditya Pal, *Vaiṣṇava Iconology In Nepal – A Study in Art and Religion*, Calcutta, 1985, p. 108.
46. *Saumyasiṃhādibhūyishṭhavaktrabhṛidaiśchaturmukha /*
    *Dvitrimukhabhedā vā mūrtirekaiva pūjyate //*
*Samvṛitā parivāraiḥ svairvinā vā sarvakāmadā /*
    *Yatra tantrāntaraṃ tatsyāchchaturtha chaturānana //*

(As quoted by Pal, *loc. cit.*, p. 176)

47. *Mukhyānuvṛittibhedena yatra siṃhādayastu vai /*
    *Chatustridvayādkenaiva yogenābhyarchite tu vai (natu) //*
*Saṃvṛitāḥ parivāreṇa svena svenonvi(sthi)tāstu vā /*
    *Yachchhaktyārādhitaṃ sarvaṃ viddhi tantrāntarṃ tu tat //*

(*Paushkarasaṃhitā*, 38, 300-02)

48. *Epigraphia Indica*, Vol. I, p. 124:
*Dadhānānekāṃ yaḥ kiripurushasiṃhobhayajusham /*
    *Tadākārochchhedyāṃ tanumasuramukhyānajavarāt //*
*Jaghana trinugran jagati Kapiladinavatu vaḥ /*
    *Sa Vaikuṇṭhaḥ kaṇṭhadhvanichakitaniḥśeshabhuvanaḥ //*

Dr. L.K. Tripathi has rightly amended the last compound word of the first line to *'Kiripurushasiṃhānanajushaṃ'* ("Restoration of the First Verse of the Yaśovarman Stone Inscription," *Bhāratī*, Varanasi, No. 4, 1960-61, pp. 115ff). This has further been amended to *'Kiripurushasiṃhāravajusham'* recently (For details see, Devangana Desai, *The Religious Imagery of Khajuraho*, Mumbai, 1996, Appendix B, p. 212).
49. V.S. Pathak, "Vaikuṇṭha at Khajuraho and Kāśmīrāgama School", *Journal of the Madhya Pradesh Itihāsa Parishad*, Bhopal, No. 2, 1960, pp. 9ff and "Vaikuṇṭha kā Vikāsa", in *Rāshṭrakavi Maithilīśaraṇa Gupta Abhinandana Grantha*, Calcutta, 1959, pp. 532ff.
50. Devangana Desai, *op. cit.*, pp. 211-17.
51. *Ibid.*, p. 53. Pathak, *op. cit.*, p. 11; H. Daniel Smith, *A Descriptive Bibliography of the Pāñcharātrāgama*, 2 Vols., GOS Nos. 25 and 168, Baroda, 1975 & 1980 respectively.
52. *Rājataraṅgiṇī* of Kalhaṇa, Eng. tr. by R.S. Pandit, Sahitya Academi, New Delhi, 1977 (reprint), VI, 300, 305.

53. *Ibid.*, VIII, 2433.
54. N.P. Joshi, *Catalogue of the Brahmanical Sculptures in the State Museum, Lucknow*, Part I, Lucknow, 1972, pp. 116-16. Also see *East and West*, New Series, Vol. 22, Nos. 1-2 (March-June 1972), pp. 41-43, Figs. 1-4; Debala Mitra, "Vishṇu Chaturmūrti Images in Hari Rai Temple at Chamba", in *Arts of Himachal Pradesh* (Ed. V.C. Ohri), State Museum, Simla, 1975, pp. 2-3. She, however, assigns the image to 1st century BCE. See also Chaturvedi, *op. cit.*, pp. 48-49.
55. T.S. Maxwell, *Viśvarūpa*, Delhi (OUP), 1988, pp. 125ff.
56. N.P. Joshi, *Mathurā kī Mūrtikalā* (Hindi), Mathura, 1965, Pl. 38. There are examples even of *Chaturvyūha Śakti* (Kushāṇa, Mathurā), Śiva (Kushāṇa, Musanagar, U.P.) and other deities showing emanatory busts coming out of the shoulders. For details and illustrations, see T.S. Maxwell, *op. cit.*
57. Kalpana Desai, *op. cit.*, pp. 40- 41.
58. *Ibid.*, pp. 40-47.
59. Maxwell, *op. cit.*, p. 31.
60. K.P. Poonacha, M.V. Visweswara and T.M. Kesava, "An Interesting Inscribed Makara Torana From Huli, District Belgaum", in *Facets of Indian Civilization: Recent Perspectives – Essays in Honour of Prof. B.B. Lal* (Chief Editor Jagat Pati Joshi) Vol. II, Aryan Books International, New Delhi, 1997, pp. 448-53 and Pls. 55.9 & 10.
61. Information from Dr. Deen Bandhu Pandey, BHU, Varanasi.
62. If the main central figure with a club, *vanamālā* and *kirīṭa-mukuṭa* may be identified with Vāsudeva-Kṛishṇa and the figure emanating from his right shoulder holding a wine-cup in his left hand and probably also a canopy of serpent hoods as Saṃkarshaṇa, then the identification of the complete original image as a plastic representation of the Pāñcharātra *chatur-vyūha* cosmogonic metaphor seems to be quite certain.
63. R.G. Bhandarkar, *op. cit.*, pp. 1-41.
64. Mora Well Inscription of Śoḍāsa refers to the five Vṛishṇi heroes – *Bhagavatāṃ Vṛishṇīnāṃ pañchavīrānāṃ pratimāḥ...* (*Epigraphia Indica*, Vol. XXIV, pp. 194ff). Some Vṛishṇi seals/sealings and copper coins have also been discovered from Sunet near Ludhiana in Punjab (Swami Omanand Sarasvati, *Ancient Seals of Haryana*, Jhajjar, vs 2031, No. 189; *Journal of the Numismatic Society of India*, XI, pp. 87-91; Devendra Handa, *Studies in Indian Coins and Seals*, Delhi, 1985, pp. 66-74 and 99ff). So far, only one sculptural representation of the five Vṛishṇi heroes has been known from Kondamotu in Andhra Pradesh. For details, see Abdul Wahid Khan, *An Early Sculpture of Nṛsiṃha*, Hyderabad, 1964, Pl. I.
65. The connection between the Bhāgavata and Pāñcharātra systems has been discussed by various scholars. See *DHI*, pp. 386-87; Kalpana Desai, *op. cit.*, pp. 2-4; W.E. Begley, *Viṣṇu's Flaming Wheel: The Iconography of the Sudarśana Cakra*, New York, 1973, pp. 17-18, 37-40, etc.
66. Maxwell, *op. cit.*, pp. x-xi.
67. Devendra Handa, "Vaikuṇṭha Images from Punjab", *Ajaya-Śrī: Recent Studies in Indology (Prof. Ajay Mitra Shastri Felicitation Volume)*, Vol. 2, Delhi, 1989, pp. 499-504, Pls. 153-57.
68. Sadhu Ram, "Two Unpublished Sculptures: Hari Hara and Narasiṃha", *Vishveshvaranand Indological Journal*, Hoshiarpur, Vol. XV, Part I (March, 1977), pp. 123-24, Pl. I.
69. Devendra Handa (1983), *op. cit.*, pp. 27-28, Fig. 12.
70. Handa (1983), *op. cit.*, pp. 26-27.
71. *Atharvaveda*, XIII.4, 20.
72. *Ṛigveda*, I.164, 46.
73. *Ibid.*, II.1, 3-4; III.54, 17; VIII.I, 27, 58, 2; 114, 5; *Atharvaveda*, XIII.4; *Vājasaneyī-Saṃhitā* XXXII.1; etc.
74. B.N. Sharma, "Puranic Message of Religious Tolerance and its Limitations", *Purāṇa*, Varanasi, Vol. XIII, No. 1 (Jan. 1971), p. 4.
75. *Aitareya Upanishad* X. 114, 5; *Nṛisiṃhatāpan Upanishad* I. 3, 9; etc.
76. VIII.9; IX.23, etc.
77. *Agni Purāṇa*, 1.1; *Vishṇu Purāṇa*, I.2, 66; *Śiva Purāṇa*, IX, 55-56; *Skanda Purāṇa* XXIII. 41; *Padma Purāṇa*, Sṛishṭi Khaṇḍa XXIII.60; Pātāla Khaṇḍa XVIII; *Harivaṃśa*, II.125, 26ff; etc.
78. Sharma, *op. cit.*, pp. 4-25.
79. *DHI*, pp. 241-42.

80. D.B. Diskalkar, "Some Brahmanical Sculptures in the Mathura Museum", *Journal of the U. P. Historical Society*, Lucknow, Vol. V, Part-I (Jan. 1932), p. 44, Pl. 18; *DHI*, pp. 123-24.
81. *DHI*, pp. 181- 82.
82. *Ibid.*, p. 544. See also Shanti Lal Nagar, *Composite Deities in Indian Art and Literature*, New Delhi, 1989. The following combinations seem to have remained popular:
    i) Vishṇu and Śiva – Harihara, Haryardha, Śiva-Nārāyaṇa or Śaṅkara-Nārāyaṇa.
    ii) Vishṇu and Sūrya – Vishṇu-Nārāyaṇa.
    iii) Vishṇu and Kārttikeya – Brahmaṇyadeva-Vishṇu,
    iv) Vishṇu and Buddha – Yoga-Nārāyaṇa, Yogeśvara-Vishṇu, Vishṇu-Lokeśvara.
    v) Vishṇu, Śiva and Brahmā – Hariharapitāmaha.
    vi) Vishṇu, Śiva, Brahmā and Sūrya – Hariharahiraṇyagarbha or Sūrya-Hari-Hara-Pitāmaha.
    vii) Vishṇu, Śiva, Sūrya and Buddha – Hari-Hara-Sūrya-Buddha.
    viii) Śiva and Buddha – Śiva-Lokeśvara.
    ix) Śiva and Pārvatī – Ardhanārīśvara.
    x) Śiva and Sūrya – Mārttaṇḍa-Bhairava or Śiva-Bhāskara.
    xi) Sūrya and Brahmā.
83. *Mahābhārata* (BORI, Poona), III.40, 57.
84. *Vishṇu Purāṇa* (Gītā Press Ed.), I.8, 23.
85. *Ibid.*, V. 33, 47-49.

    *Tvayā yadabhayaṃ dattaṃ taddattamakhilaṃ mayā /*
    *matto' vibhinnamātmānaṃ drashṭumarhasi Śaṅkara / /*
    *Yo' haṃ sa tvaṃ jagachchedaṃ sadevāsuramānusham /*
    *matto nānyadaśeshaṃ yattattvaṃ jñātumihārhasi //*
    *Āvidyāmohitātmanaḥ purushā bhinnadarśinaḥ /*
    *vadanti bhedaṃ paśyanti chāvayorantaraṃ Hara / /*

86. *Matsya Purāṇa*, (Ānandāśrama Sanskrit Series, Poona, 1907) 260, vv. 22-27:

    *Vāmārdhe mādhavaṃ vidyāddakshiṇe Śūlapāṇinam /*
    *Bāhudvayañcha Kṛishṇasya maṇikeyūrabhūshitam //* .
    *Śaṅkhachakradharaṃ śāntamāraktāṅguliviprabham /*
    *chakrasthāne gadāṃ vāpi pāṇau dadyād gadābhṛitaḥ / /*
    *Śaṅkhañchaivetare dadyāt kaṭyardhaḥ bhūshaṇojjvalam /*
    *pītavastraparidhānaṃ charaṇaṃ maṇibhūshitam //*
    *Bhujagahāravalayaṃ varadaṃ dakshiṇam karam /*
    *vyālopavītasaṃyuktaṃ kaṭyardhaṃ kṛittivāsasam //*
    *Maṇiratnaiścha saṃyuktaṃ pādaṃ nāgavibhūshitam /*
    *Śivanārāyaṇasyaiva kalpayedrūpamuttamam //*

87. *Vishṇudharmottara Purāṇa* (GOS, Baroda, 1958) III.

    *Kāryaṃ Hariharasyāpi dakshiṇārdhaṃ sadāśivaḥ /*
    *vāmamardhaṃ Hṛishīkeśaśśvetanīlākṛitiḥ kramāt //*
    *Varatriśūlachakrābjadhāriṇo bāhvaḥ kramāt /*
    *dakshiṇe vṛishabhaḥ pārśve vāmabhāge vihagarāṭ //*

88. *Devatāmūrtiprakaraṇa* (Calcutta, 1936), VI.56-57.
89. *Ibid.*, VI.35-41.
90. *Ibid.*, VI.33-34.
91. *Vishṇuṃ kirīṭasaṃyuktaṃ Śaṅkaraṃ tu jaṭānvitam.*
    For complete description, see the text as given by T.A.G. Rao (*EHI*, Vol. II, Part II, Appendix B, p. 168).
92. *Ibid.*, pp. 170-71.
93. *Ibid.*
94. Handa (1985), *op. cit.*, pp. 119ff.
95. *Ibid.*
96. *Ibid.*
97. Handa (1983), *op. cit.*, p. 28 and (2003), *op. cit.*, p. 508, Fig. 1.
98. Sanjeev P. Srivastava and R.P. Srivastava (*op. cit.*, p. xv, Fig. 5) wrongly identify it as 'Standing Vishnu'.

# 4

# Śiva

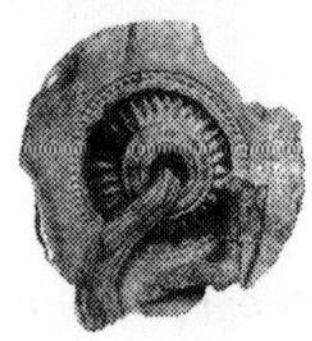

## ŚAIVA IMAGES

Śiva is an important deity of the Hindu Trinity (Brahmā-Vishṇu-Maheśa). As Paśupati, he is regarded as a proto-historic deity.[1] The terrific god Rudra associated with hills and animals in the *Ṛigveda*[2] came to be looked upon as the lord of all creatures (Paśupati) and a Mahāyogī, an originator and exponent of various arts and accomplishments like music, dancing, etc., thus becoming Śiva 'the auspicious.'[3] The *Atharvaveda* presupposes his ascendancy to the supreme position[4] and assigns him various epithets such as Bhava, Śarva, Paśupati, Ugra, Mahādeva and Īśāna, to which the *Śatapatha* (IV.1, 3, 7) and the *Kauśītaki Brāhmaṇa* (VI.1, 9) added Aśani and typified his terrific and peaceful aspects – *ghora* and *saumya,* respectively.[5] It is, however, of interest that in the *Ṛigveda* (II.33, 6-8), one of Rudra's epithets is Vṛishabha and in the *Taittirīya Saṃhitā* of the *Yajurveda* (I.8, 6), he is associated with Ambikā as his sister. The *Mahābhārata* (VII.74, 56) describes Śiva as the creator, omnipresent and omniscient, and the *Rāmāyaṇa* (I.36, 9-10) accords him the rank and status of the highest god. The latter also mentions Nandī (VII.16, 8). The sectarian Purāṇas accord Śiva the supreme status.

Though there is ample literary evidence regarding the continuation and development of the cult of Rudra-Śiva from the Ṛigvedic to the early historic and later times, yet there is an utter lack of archaeological data from the decline of the Harappan civilization to about third-second century BCE.[6] Patañjali's reference to Śiva-Bhāgavatas[7] proves beyond cavil the existence of a Pāśupata sect in India during the second century BCE. Bull, the vehicle of Śiva, also regarded as the zoomorphic representation of Śiva, is depicted on punch-marked, local and tribal coinages.[8] Punch-marked coins are generally believed to have appeared in about the fifth century BCE.[9] Ajay Mitra Shastri considered the figure on Kāḍa coins to be the earliest anthropomorphic representation of Śiva.[10] These coins are datable to *circa* third-second century BCE and the largest number of definitely known provenance of these coins suggests their circulation at and around Sugh near Jagadhari in Haryana.[11] The Audumbara coins of Śivadāsa, Rudradāsa and Dharaghosha, datable to second-first century BCE and found from Pathankot in Punjab and the neighbouring area of Himachal Pradesh, however, furnish clinching evidence of the prevalence

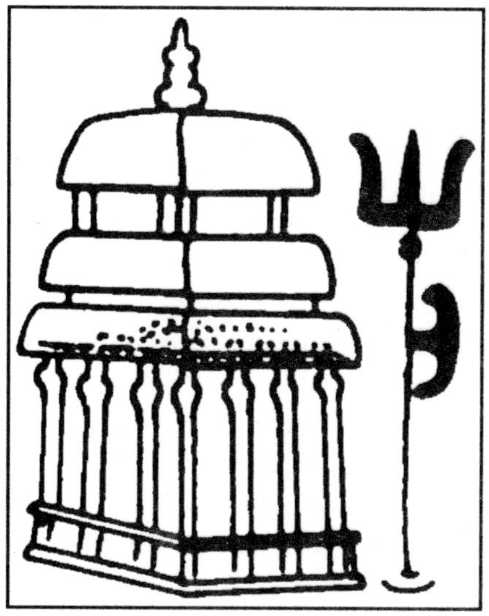

Fig. 24. Śiva temple on Audumbara coins.

of Śaivism in the region. Not only the names of the rulers are Śaivite, the coins also depict a Śiva temple with trident-battleaxe by its side (Fig. 24). Irrefragable evidence of the anthropomorphic representation of Śiva on coins, however, is presented by the coins of Wema Kadphises (Figs. 7-8) and Gondophernes, which have also been found from various sites in the Punjab and belong to the first century BCE/CE.[12] The Gudimallam Liṅgodbhavamūrti[13] and the Bhita *Pañchamukha* Śiva-*liṅga*,[14] dated by some scholars to *circa* third-second century BCE, are not considered to be much later.[15] A mutilated terracotta plaque of late Śuṅga period, now in the Bharat Kala Bhawan, Banaras, is regarded by Biswas to represent Śiva riding on his mount Nandī.[16] But the absence of any definite Śaiva emblems in the hands of or on the person of the rider renders the identification to be quite doubtful. There is, however, no denying the fact that the images of Śiva, both in stone and clay, began to be created popularly during the Kushāṇa period. From then onwards, we see an ascendancy and profusion of the iconic forms and representation of not only Śiva, but also of other deities. Early images of Śiva are rare in Punjab but his worship seems to have remained quite popular in the *Liṅga* form through the centuries, as is evidenced from some specimens found from different places.

Seals and sealings from Punjab, mostly of the Kushāṇa-Gupta periods, portray Śiva in iconic, aniconic and theriomorphic forms. A sealing from Sunet shows a trident-axe above the legend Maheśvara. Another one has the legend *Rudraśarma* with a trident above. One seal depicts a beautiful *śālabhañjikā* and has the legend *Śrī-Bhavadevasya*. It is notable that some pieces show a similar device and have the legend *Śrī-Rudrasya*.[17] Bhava and Rudra are the well-known names of Śiva. Thaplyal[18] has offered an ingenious explanation of the device and legend. He says that the tree may represent Śiva and the exquisite female figure, Pārvatī. In epigraphs and literature also, Pārvatī has been likened to *śālabhañjikā* and Śiva to the pillar. One of Śiva's names is Sthāṇu, which means a tree-trunk. A sealing with the legend *Śrī-Sthāṇusya* has also been found from Sunet. Even if Rudra and Bhavadeva of the above-mentioned seal and sealing be taken to be the names of their owners, they seem to have chosen the Śaiva device suitable to their names.[19]

Names ending in *Īśvara* are regarded as typically characteristic of the names of Śaiva shrines.[20] We have seals/sealings bearing the legend *Śrī-Gomīśvarasya* and *Śrī-Vyaumīśvarasya* from Sunet. These indicate that there existed various Śaiva shrines at the place during the Gupta period. Sealings bearing the name of Gaṅgabhadra with a trident and snake above, Śrī-Nandiśiri, Śrī-Īśānabhadra, etc. betray the popularity of Śaivism in the Punjab in *circa* third-fourth centuries. We feel that the sealings bearing the legends Śrī-Atimuttaka with Nandī to right above and *Śrī-Atimutakasa* with a trident above and Nandī seated to left on the back should also be associated with Śaivism. Probably, the indifferent state of preservation of the pieces has resulted in the erroneous reading of 'ta' for 'va' and 'ta/tta' for 'kta'. The original legends may have been *Śrī-Avimuktaka* and *Śrīr=Avimuktakasya*. Seals/sealings with comparable readings have been found from elsewhere also and they are all Śaivite.[21] Avimukta has been explained as a place or shrine never deserted by Śiva or free from sin in the *Skanda*[22] and *Liṅga Purāṇa*,[23] respectively. The *Mahābhārata* speaks very highly of the sanctity of Avimukta where one could free oneself from even the most heinous sins.[24] Numerous other seals/sealings from Sunet show recumbent, standing or trotting bull, trident, snake, etc. They are all evidently Śaivite in nature.[25] That Śiva and Vishṇu were worshipped together is evidenced by seals/sealings from Sunet, which show trident-discus combined, trident and discus together, and those bearing the legend *Śaṅkara-Nārāyaṇābhyāṃ*.[26]

Anthropomorphic representation of Śiva is to be found on some sealings from Sanghol. Three of these seem to be the impressions of a single seal and depict two-armed Śiva slightly turned to his right holding a long shaft, probably of a trident, with his right hand and an indistinct object in the left, perhaps animal skin. Two others depict artistically modelled quadrumanous Śiva as standing slightly turned to his left. He wears a *dhotī* with sides crossing each other between the legs and bears a top knot and also perhaps beard. The arms emanate directly from the shoulders. The god holds a sword[27] in the rear (lower) right hand, trident with a very long shaft in the normal (upper) right hand, thunderbolt in the back (upper) left and antelope skin in the proper left hand (Pl. 70). The sealing may be attributed to the Kushāṇa period. Iconographically, these sigils present interesting features and are the earliest representations of the deity from the region.

## BRASS MASK

A unique inscribed bronze mask of Śiva deposited in the Laṭūriyā Mahādeva Mandir at Ropar shows the god wearing large *karṇa-kuṇḍalas*, a tubular *graiveyaka* with a jewel in the centre and three rings on either side, beaded turbinated headgear with a frontal belt of large beads on the forehead and a circular hairdo above having wide open eyes, sturdy nose, moustached upper lip, thick lower lip, strong chin and plump cheeks. The lower part of the mask bears a Sanskrit inscription in two lines in northern characters of the Brāhmī script, datable to the fifth century on palaeographic grounds. It reads: *Śri(ī)-Kuvilasya Mitrāvasu-putrasya devadharma*. The 16 letters of the epigraph measure ¼ to ⅝ inch in height. The mask has been permanently fixed in the small cell of the temple with cement, and the inscribed portion lies buried and is not at all visible now (Pl. 71).[28] A photograph of this mask was taken by the Survey during 1910-11 and is deposited in the Photo-Library of the Archaeological Survey of India in its Ropar Album. A copy of the original photograph lies in the Ropar Museum also. Also photographed at that time were some loose sculptures in Sandhūriyāṃ dā Śivālā: door-jamb, a bracket and an image of Durgā riding a lion in the Assistant Commissioner's bungalow at Ropar and the old sites of Bardar, some 20 km east of Ropar on the old Ropar-Siswan road, from where some marble statues and copper utensils were found about 1874 but nothing is known of them now.[29] The District Gazetteer records that some of the stone images, including that of Durgā on lion unearthed at Bardar, were deposited in a Shivala at Ropar. So, it is quite likely that the said brass mask too was recovered from Bardar and made its way to the Śiva temple at Ropar.[30]

## ICONIC REPRESENTATIONS

Independent iconic representations of Śiva are very rare in Punjab. A black stone badly mutilated head of Gupta idiom in the site museum at Sanghol shows a horizontal third eye on the forehead (Pl. 72). It is an iconographically indeterminate figure as it shows spiral locks on the head instead of the locks as usually seen on Śiva's head. The horizontally placed third eye on the forehead, however, suggests that it may have belonged to an image of Śiva originally. Clay sealings from Sanghol noted above (Pl. 70) do suggest the popularity of Śaiva worship at this place in the early period. We know that Toramāṇa, who attacked India, and his successor Mihirakula, whose coins have been recovered from Sanghol, issued amongst others coins bearing the figure of bull and the legend 'Jayatu Vṛishaḥ'.

A much worn out, coarse-grained stone bust broken below the waist bearing matted locks and wearing a broad featureless torque, holding a round object (*bījapuraka*?) in his right hand near the chest (Pl. 73) from Dholbaha may have originally been that of Śiva but one cannot be very certain about it as all the other three hands are broken and the attributes thereof are difficult to make out. The placid expression, drooping eyelids, depressions on both the sides of the mouth and soft contours, however, remind us of the lingering traits of Gupta idiom and the piece may be dated to *circa* seventh century on stylistic grounds. Another head from the same site with strands of horizontal, vertical and drooping matted locks, half-open eyes with arch-like eyebrows, sturdy nose, thick lips and oval face (Pl. 74), too, may have belonged to the same deity, though not surely. Stylistically, however, it may have been carved in the ninth century. Another head from Dholbaha having an unusually high *jaṭā-jūṭa* with meditative face (Pl. 75), datable to the ensuing century, may also have belonged to Śiva but one cannot be very sure of it. Certainly, however, it is not that of Vishṇu as believed by Srivastava and Srivastava.[31] Sculptural and architectural fragments fixed on the wall of the approach way of the site museum at Dholbaha contain a piece of probably the lintel of a Śiva temple measuring 26 X 30 cm showing four-handed Śiva sitting in *sukhāsana* with normal right hand disposed in the posture of reassurance and holding trident, snake and water pot in the other hands in order of *pradakshiṇā* (Pl. 45). An architectural piece from Dholbaha shows Śiva seated in a pillared niche next to that of Vishṇu (Pl. 46). Unfortunately, the piece is broken leaving us without the proper left hand side of Śiva completely visible. Seated in *lalitāsana,* the god bears *jaṭā-mukuṭa, graiveyaka, yajñopavīta, kaṅkaṇas, nūpuras,* etc. and holds the trident and perhaps a *bījapuraka* in the additional and natural right hands, the left ones being broken. A socket on the top left of the piece for fixing the tenon of the block to be placed above it clearly indicates it to have been a piece of the wall of a tenth century temple. Another very badly mutilated panel from Dholbaha in a private collection, datable to the Pratihāra period, shows the left folded foot of Śiva seated on Nandī to left, holding in his suspended left hand a water pot (Pl. 76). A bracelet and part of the long garland on the extant arm may also be seen. The rear left hand rising upwards is broken from the elbow but it may be presumed to have held the snake. The complete image must have been a good specimen of the art of the region but is unfortunately badly broken. Dholbaha has yielded yet another figure of the god seated in *lalitāsana* in a pedimented *rathikā* between ribbed pillars holding trident in the additional right hand and the snake in the upper left (Pl. 77). The natural right hand seems to be disposed in fear-allaying pose, while the corresponding left is mutilated. Matted locks on the head, ear ornaments, pearly necklace and long garland over the forearms are gracefully executed as also the sitting posture. The face is slightly damaged, yet the serenity of expression may be made out. The figure shows slight elongation but the modelling is immaculate. The niche is placed between *makara-mukhas*. The image may be dated to *circa* ninth century on stylistic grounds.

An image with broken head has been recovered from Kharar. The extant bust is shown as wearing pearl necklet and necklace with a *śrīvatsa* between them, armlet on the (extant) proper left arm, and the sacred thread. Behind the head was carved an eight-petal halo. The steles on the right and left show Brahmā and Vishṇu. Bearded Brahmā is shown as seated on a lotus seat in *padmāsana* with the proper right hand in *abhaya* and left holding the water pot whereas the rear pair of hands supports the *sruk* and the book. Vishṇu wearing a *kirīṭa-mukuṭa* sits similarly holding mace and discus in the rear right and left hands with proper hands disposed as those of Brahmā. Three *mālyadhara vidyādhara* figures in flying postures are carved along the circular edge of the halo and connect the two steles. Since there is no coat of mail on the chest, the figure may have belonged to Śiva. Stylistically, the image belongs to tenth century CE.

An architectural piece detached from the *adhishṭhāna* of a temple shows two figures of four-handed Śiva seated on his mount Nandī in *lalitāsana,* holding the trident and snake in the rear right and left hands, the normal left hand suspended near the corresponding knee and perhaps holding a water pot; the natural right hand in the two examples differs in their stances. One figure shows it holding a *nīlotpala* and in the other, it seems to be in *varada* pose (Pl. 78). The difference of the posture of the natural right hands indicates that perhaps different forms of the god were intended as is suggested by the visible folded right leg of the god on the right side where the piece has broken. It is possible though not sure that the *adhishṭhāna* carried the figures of Ekādaśa-Rudras. All details are lost because of the easily weathering nature of the local shale stone. Carved above is a frieze of beautiful *kīrtimukhas.* The piece may have belonged to a tenth century Śiva temple. Another architectural piece from the place is preserved in the site museum and shows a frieze of standing figures of the god, of which three have survived leaving us only to guess their exact number (Pl. 79). The rear hands hold the trident and multi-hooded snake as in the preceding figures, and the natural right is suspended in *varada* with a rosary but the attributes in the other are not clearly visible. Very interesting, however, is the depiction of goose to right as the vehicle of the central figure near the right foot. The vehicle depicted with the figure on viewer's right is damaged but it certainly was neither a goose nor a bull. Could it be that of Garuḍa? Whether Garuḍa or some other mount, the presence of the goose with a figure of Śiva seems to indicate that the artist intended to show the identity of Śiva with Brahmā and perhaps also with Vishṇu, and may be with some other deities. We do not know exactly whether the temple to which this frieze originally belonged was dedicated to Śiva or Vishṇu. The *Vishṇu Purāṇa* (V.19, 50-58),[32] however, clearly states that the Supreme Being is called as Brahmā, Vishṇu, Śiva, etc. only by imagination of the worshipper (*Brahmā-vishṇu-śivādyābhiḥ kalpanābhiḥ udīritaḥ*) and establishes the identity of the Supreme Being with Vishṇu, Brahmā, Paśupati (Śiva) and other gods –

*Tvaṃ brahmā paśupatiḥ aryamā vidhātā*
*Tvaṃ vishṇuḥ triadśa-patiḥ samīrṇo agniḥ*
*Toyeśo dhanapatiḥ antakaḥ bhavān*
*Sṛijati pāti gabhasti rūpaḥ*
*Viśvaṃ cha te guṇamayaḥ ayam aja prapañchaḥ*
*Rūpaṃ paraṃ saditi vāchakamaksharaṃ yat*
*Jñānātmne sadāste praṇato'smi nityam*

The identity of Śiva with various other deities is referred to in the *Kūrma Purāṇa* (Uttarārdham, XXXV.66-72) also, where Śiva says –

*Eko'haṃ bhagavān kālah hynādiḥ antakṛit vibhuḥ /*
*Samāsthāya paraṃ bhāvaṃ prokto rudro manīshibhiḥ //*
*Mamiva sā parā-śaktiḥ devī vidyeti viśrutā /*
*Dṛishṭo hi bhagavān nūnaṃ vidyādehaḥ svayaṃ tataḥ //*
*Evaṃ etāni tattvāni pradhānapurusheśvaraḥ /*
*Vishṇu brahmā cha bhagavān rudraḥ kāla iti śrutiḥ //*
*Trayaṃ etadanādyantaṃ brahmaṇyeva vyavasthitaṃ /*
*Tadātmakaṃ tadavyaktaṃ tadaksharamit śrutiḥ //*

The *Brahmavaivarta-purāṇa* (Śrī-Kṛishṇa-janma-khaṇḍa, XXXVIII, 65-78) contains the Śiva-*stotra* of Himālaya, which too describes the unity of Śiva with Brahmā, Vishṇu, Sūrya and other gods –

*Tvaṃ brahmā sṛishṭikartā cha tvaṃ vishṇuścha paripālakaḥ /*
*Tvaṃ Śivaḥ śivadā'nantaḥ sarva-saṃhāra-kārakaḥ //*
*Tvamīśvaro guṇātīto jyotīrūpaḥ sanātanaḥ //*
*Prakṛitiḥ prakṛitīścha prākṛitaḥ prakṛiteḥ paraḥ //*
*Nānārūpavidhātā tvaṃ bhaktānāṃ dhyāna-hetave /*
*Yeshu rūpeshu yatprītistadrūpaṃ vibharshi cha //*
*Sūryastvaṃ sṛishṭi-janaka ādhāraḥ sarvatejasām /*
*Somastvaṃśasya pātā cha satataṃ śītaraśminā //*

The Śākta tradition also confirms the identity of Śiva, Vishṇu, Brahmā and Sūrya: "God indeed is the maker of the creation and dissolution of these collective worlds. He is Viṣṇu. He is Śiva. He is Brahmā. He is Sūrya and Soma. All in everyway has determined him alone."[33] An attempt seems to have been made here to show the identity of Śiva with Brahmā, Vishṇu and probably other gods also.

Another badly damaged frieze from Dholbaha, which may have contained a row of such images but has preserved only one of those, depicts the god with similar dress and ornaments including the long garland standing in an analogous pose and holding the same attributes with water pot in the suspended normal left hand clearly visible and shows the goose near the left foot of the god (Pl. 80). It may have been part of the same temple to which the preceding piece belonged. We are not aware of any other example/s of this type from other sites in Punjab or even other states. These reliefs belonging to a temple of the tenth century, however, present an interesting feature.

## MAHEŚA-MŪRTI

We have already referred to a terracotta sealing from Sunet bearing a trident-axe above the legend Maheśvara. The people of Punjab thus seem to have been well-acquainted with the god under this name during the Kushāṇa-Gupta period. The depiction of three-faced Maheśvara on Kushāṇa gold coins also shows the popularity of this form in the region. Quite interesting is a sculpture from Dholbaha displayed in the museum at Hoshiarpur, showing the bust of the three-faced god (Pl. 81). The image has worn out badly, concealing most of the details. The god seems to wear floral *karṇābhūshaṇas* and a double-stringed sacred thread, and the two hands hold some round objects at the level of the chest, perhaps a *bījapuraka* and a water pot. The central face bears a high bun of matted locks kept in position by a fillet tied around in the middle. The face may have been placid but details are lost. The face on his proper right seems to be that of Umā whose locks of hair combed upwards have been tied with a pearl string to support the bun above. The face on the proper left has wide open round eyes and a grinning expression and may belong to Aghora. Here, thus, we have the Trimūrti or Maheśa-mūrti, which is the only example of its type in the whole of the northern region including Haryana, Punjab, Himachal Pradesh and Kashmir. It may be dated to about ninth century on stylistic grounds.

Three-faced Śiva may be seen in a broken *bhadramukha* from Dholbaha in the same museum (Pl. 82). The faces as usual are quite worn out but still show individual features. There is one more *chaitya* window at the site which is better preserved and shows, like the preceding one, a skillfully carved *pūrṇa-kalaśa* motif on it (Pl. 83) showing the three faces in the *gavāksha*, the central one of which has a three-peaked crown betraying impact from the hills. The material being locally available stone which weathered easily, the figures have lost many of the details but still reveal the controlled chisel work of the artists in the tenth century. At least two more *bhadramukhas* from Dholbaha preserved in the site museum show the three faces but they are in a very badly mutilated and worn-out condition.

## NAṬARĀJA

Images of dancing Śiva, popularly known as Naṭarāja (literally 'King of dancers'), are known from various parts of India from the Gupta period onwards.[34] The complex symbolism and the philosophic implications of Śiva's dance have been discussed and explained by various scholars.[35] Naṭarāja images were perhaps not popular in the region north of Mathura as in its south and east.[36] Kashmir has been one of the greatest seats of Śiva worship but has yielded only one Naṭarāja image.[37] No images have been found from Himachal Pradesh. Naṭarāja images were not known even from Haryana till recently when this author brought to light a few pieces.[38] This extreme scarcity in the northern region lends importance to any new discoveries even though the examples may not be artistically superb or unique. Our survey of the relics of art in the state of Punjab has resulted in the discovery of an image of Naṭarāja and a fragment thereof, which are described below.

A beautifully carved image of Naṭarāja was recovered from Bathinda some years ago (Pl. 84). The god is depicted as bearing an exquisite *dhammilla*-type coiffure with curled locks of hair falling gracefully on the shoulders. He wears ear ornaments, an *ekāvali* and a broad *graiveyaka*, sacred thread, lozenge-shaped *śrīvatsa* on the chest, elaborate armlets, bracelets, scarf and lower garment secured by a waistband. The upper right hand in *chatura* dance pose also holds a circular *akshamālā* and the left hand holds the snake, the normal ones support the shaft of a trident or *vīṇā* (broken at the top) and a *kuṇḍikā*. The legs are broken below the knees but the extant portions are clearly disposed in the act of dancing. The face exudes serenity. The eyes seem to have been closed in the exhilaration of the dance. The *chatura-hasta* and the stance of the legs very well convey the movements of the dance pose. The figure is balanced perfectly. We are yet to discover a similar relief showing this particular arrangement of attributes. The image is thus an interesting piece iconographically as well as artistically. The sparse jewellery, the rectangular back slab, simple composition, softness of contours, and controlled chisel work indicate it to be a work of the seventh century.

A fragment measuring 16 X 21 cm in the Satya-Nārāyaṇa temple at Sunam (Pl. 85) showing the proper left hand top side of an image with a hand holding a snake going along the beaded circular fringe of the halo and a hovering garland-bearing *vidyādhara* on the stele, is certainly a part of the image of Umā-Maheśvara or perhaps Naṭarāja. The beaded rim of the stele, *ekāvali* of the *vidyādhara*, beaded rim of the aureole of the extant piece, too, belong to eighth century.

## UMĀ- MAHEŚVARA

The earliest representation of Umā-Maheśvara from Punjab comes again from Dholbaha and is datable to *circa* eighth century CE. Displayed in the VVRI Museum at Hoshiarpur, the image shows the divine couple standing in a relaxed posture in *dvibhaṅga* almost asymmetrically with Nandī to left behind (Pl. 86). Śiva's left foot bears the burden of the body and the right foot is splayed outward more than the former. The matted locks of Śiva have been tied in the middle with a bun above. He wears *karṇābhūshaṇa, ekāvali, yajñopavīta, kaṅkaṇas* and loin-cloth.[39] The normal right hand of the god is raised to the level of the shoulder in *abhaya,* while the natural left is suspended and holding the water pot. The additional right hand which comes from behind the shoulder is placed on the hump of the Nandī standing behind. The extra left hand is not visible. The figure emphasizes the ascetic nature of Śiva. Umā stands gracefully bending her left knee forward and bearing the main load of the body on her right foot. The right hand, though slightly damaged, seems to have been disposed in the posture of reassurance like that of Śiva and the object in her left hand is not clear. Her diaphanous nether garment forms a sash on her thighs coming winding from behind the right thigh and rising to the left side with its free end suspended from the left waist. Her hair is beautifully braided. She wears *karṇa-kuṇḍalas* and an *ekāvali,* a string whereof falls on her belly from between her breasts. There is a big round plain aureole behind the couple. Nandī standing behind Śiva has his head to front. A feeling of grace permeates from the figures of the divine couple in spite of the weathering of the relief. The modelling is soft and delicate though the plastic mass is not full. Ohri observes that "A stylistic prototype of this sculpture is seen at Lakha-mandal, but some affinities in the use of motifs, with Kashmir or the northwestern region are also noticed. . . ."[40] He also finds some difference in the arrangement of the attributes in the hands of the couple and remarks that "This sculpture, in spite of some northwestern connection, exhibits the stylistic traits and norms of North India. The figure of Shiva and Parvati are not ornamented in the manner as one sees in case of images of these deities from Kashmir."[41]

Another much weathered image of the couple broken below the bellies from Dholbaha has been exhibited in the same museum (Pl. 87). Śiva bears matted locks over combed hair and wears earrings and pearl necklace and perhaps a sacred thread also. With his natural left hand wound from the back of Umā, he is touching her left breast and the additional left hand holds the snake that goes from behind the heads of the couple to Śiva's right but its head is broken. Both the right hands of the god are gone. The tenuous waist of Śiva is accentuated towards Umā, perhaps for a closer embrace. Umā too is depicted embracing her Lord with her right hand which is placed on Śiva's right shoulder. Her left hand is broken below the elbow. She bears a big bun over combed hair and wears ornaments analogous to those of Śiva. The finer details of the figures have been lost by weathering but the softness of modelling, fullness of the plastic mass of the supple bodies and balance of composition are sufficiently evident. The image may be stylistically assigned to the ninth century CE.

The Government Museum at Hoshiarpur has another broken and unfinished image of a slightly later date from Dholbaha, betraying the continuing popularity of depicting Umā-Maheśvara in this manner (Pl. 88). Here, Śiva's natural and additional right hands, though mutilated slightly, seem to be holding the head of a small snake and holding the shaft of the trident while the left hands are similar to those of the preceding figure. Bracelets may also be seen on his forearms. Diamond-shaped *śrīvatsa* exists on the chest. In spite of the figure being left unfinished, the placidity of Śiva's face is quite clear. His matted locks are adorned with a jewel in front and he wears a multiple-stringed necklace. Umā is seated on Śiva's folded left leg slightly turned towards him. Her right hand rests on Śiva's right shoulder and her left hand rests on her right thigh but the object held in the hand is not clear. She wears *karṇa-kuṇḍalas,* necklace, armlets, bracelets and nether garment secured by a pearl waistband with its free end falling on the thighs. This and the other unfinished images from Dholbaha indicate some sudden attack or interruption in art activity at the site in the tenth century. A stylistic change after this interruption may also be noticed to have taken place at Dholbaha, as indicated by another sculpture showing Śiva and Pārvatī seated on a lotus placed on the back of a caparisoned Nandī to left with head facing to front (Pl. 89). The heads of both the figures are irretrievably lost as also their legs and some other limbs. The only extant natural left hand of Śiva is shown as coming from Uma's back and touching her left breast as in the preceding examples. The disposition of the remaining hands may just be assumed to have been similar. Umā too seems to have been shown similarly putting her right hand on Śiva's right shoulder. Her left hand is broken. Notable, however, are the elongated and tenuous figures of the couple and their dress and ornamentation. Śiva wears a multi-stringed pearl necklace, sacred thread, *dhotī* secured by a girdle, a long garland coming from behind the right waist and going back from around the right knee and an embroidered scarf forming a circular loop from around the back and thighs. Umā's necklace is unique in having its pendent string falling to the right of her waist from between her breasts as having additional decorative flowers or jewels appended to it. While her bust is inclined towards Śiva, the body below the middle is turning away to her left. The facile Nandī has also been bedecked with appropriate trappings and has its face turned to front with downcast eyes. Ohri has observed that "The ornaments seen on the figures of Shiva-Parvati are treated in a manner different from the ornaments in fashion in the case of Kashmir works and are obviously of the North Indian types. Stylistic change affecting the work at this centre and not showing the traits which are associated with the northwest region inform us about the political changes or turmoils witnessed by this region and consequently different cultural trends started influencing this area."[42] He finds a clear stylistic affinity with the sculptures of north-central India and dates it to the twelfth century or to a slightly later period.[43] It is difficult to agree with it. We feel inclined to date this image to the eleventh century CE.[44]

An architectural piece, which seems to be the part of the lintel of a temple dedicated to Śiva or Umā-Maheśvara, also shows a similar figure as the *lalāṭa-bimba* with *gandharva* and *vidyādhara* figures on the right and a loving couple in the left panel (Pl. 90). An almost complete small panel of 22.5 X 14 cm from Sunam showing Umā-Maheśvara seated similarly on couchant Nandī to right on a fully blossomed lotus reveals that this style of depiction was popular in other parts of Punjab also during the Pratihāra period (Pl. 91). Here, Śiva is seated on Nandī in *lalitāsana* with Umā on his left lap as usual and in the fashion noted in the foregoing examples. The trident in Śiva's rear right hand is placed on his bent knee and the normal right hand holds a *nīlotpala* near the chest. The left hands embrace Umā and hold the snake. The tapering matted locks with a frontal beaded band, vertical third eye on the forehead, arch-like eye-brows, ear ornaments, *ekāvali*, beaded bracelets, simple *yajñopavīta*, *dhotī* covering the legs almost entirely with its free end falling gracefully in front and held in position with a pearl girdle show the continuity of the mature Pratihāra traits while the elongation of the figures, somewhat queer expressions and postures betray decline which had set in in the art tradition of the late tenth and eleventh centuries. This small panel may have originally been the stele of perhaps a Vishṇu image but it also shows the stylistic trends and the popularity of the fashioning of Umā-Maheśvara images in this particular way. Another stele of a Vishṇu image from Kharar, though very badly mutilated, substantiates this (Pl. 92) though the snake held in the rear left hand of Śiva behind Umā's head gives the impression of the figure being that of Gaṅgā.

A splendid piece representing the bust of Umā with Śiva's hand clasping her waist below the left breast has been obtained from Majhur in Nawanshahr district (Pl. 93). A *kīrtimukha* in her *dhammilla* coiffure, long quasi-closed eyes, circular ear ornaments, *ekāvali* and a necklace with a pendant falling from between the breasts and touching the girdle, beaded armlet on the extant left arm, embroidered scarf simulating a long garland and a ring on Śiva's thumb are noteworthy. Quietude of expression, soft modelling, roundness of form, fullness of plastic mass, pleasing curves and contours and exquisite chisel work indicate that when complete, the image must have been a masterpiece of the Pratihāra art of late tenth century CE.[45] A broken image from Dholbaha showing the bust of Umā with her right arm rising to go around Śiva's neck (Pl. 94) may too have belonged to a similar image.

The development of the Pratihāra style, however, is evidenced by Umā-Maheśvara image from Ghanauli near Rupnagar, now displayed in the museum at Hoshiarpur (Pl. 95). It was discovered by one Ramesh Chand, a Panch of the village, from a local pond in 1984. Like some other examples, the image seems to have been immersed by the devotees to save it from being broken and/or polluted by the iconoclastic invaders. Carved on a rectangular fine-grained grey sandstone measuring 127 X 70 cm in its extant form, it shows the space divided horizontally and vertically into several registers with the figures of Umā-Maheśvara seated on caparisoned and well-bedecked Nandī to left occupying its major central part prominently. The (viewer's) lower left portion of the rectangular slab, including the pedestal of the image, is broken from its middle. A lotiform circular halo is shown behind their heads. There is an elaborate *jaṭā-mukuṭa* adorned with jewels and pearl strings on Śiva's head. Traces of a vertical third eye are faintly visible on the forehead (not visible in the illustration). The god wears *śaṅkhapatra-kuṇḍalas*, double-stringed pearl necklet and single-stringed *muktāhāra* with lozenge-shaped *śrīvatsa* on the chest in the loop of the necklace. Sacred thread and *valayas* may also be seen on his person. Śiva is seated in *lalitāsana* on the bull but the right leg is destroyed in the relief. The four-handed god is turned slightly towards Umā seated on his folded left leg. The latter, too, is sitting slightly turned towards her spouse with body below the waist taking outward twist. Faces of both the figures are shown in three-fourth profile. Umā also bears elaborate hair coiffure with a massive *dhammilla*. She wears similar ear ornaments and *valayas* but the necklace as usual has a string falling on her belly through her breasts. The proper right hand of the god holds the *nīlotpala* and the back one which supported the trident is lost. The god embraces his spouse with his left hand which touches her right breast from behind her back as usual and the rear left holds the snake whose tail comes winding from behind the heads of the couple to Śiva's right. The stele on the two sides of the halo show Brahmā-Sarasvatī and Vishṇu-Lakshmī seated like Umā-Maheśvara. The register above depicts seven garland-bearing *vidyādharas* in a row while at the top are shown bull-headed Ashṭāvasus. The extreme *śākhās* below them carry the figures of females with outwardly carved *makara-mukhas* below. Nandī is also adorned with jewel strings on the head and a garland in the neck. At the back of Nandī seems to have been carved Kārttikeya but the figure of Gaṇeśa, which may have existed on the corresponding left side, is lost because of the breaking of the slab. Upper part of an emaciated figure of Bhṛiṅgī, however, has survived on the front left leg of the bull. Though the modelling is still soft, the absence of expressive serenity and overcrowding of figures indicates the trend which had set in during the period of eleventh century to which this image may be assigned stylistically.[46]

A small stele showing Umā-Maheśvara on Nandī in a private collection with still higher coiffures and disproportionate bodies (Pl. 96) augurs the decline which had set in during the subsequent century in the region.

An exquisitely carved head of Nandī with decorative chain on the head and around the neck has been recovered from Siswan (Pl. 97), but we have no means to determine whether it carried only Śiva or Umā-Maheśvara or some other form of Śiva. The complete original image, however, must have remained a good example of the Pratihāra art of *circa* tenth century CE.

## ŚIVA-LIṄGAS

The worship of Śiva in the form of a *Liṅga*[47] 'Phallus', the pillar supporting the universe, has been practiced in India since ancient times.[48] The *Rāmāyaṇa* refers to Rāma worshipping Śiva in the form of a sand *Liṅga* at Rāmeśvaram before the construction of the bridge to Laṅkā (*setu-bandha*).[49] The *Mahābhārata*, too, contains numerous references to the worship of Śiva-*liṅga*. Arjuna is described to have worshipped Śiva by making a clay image of the great god.[50] The early Śiva-*liṅgas* may, thus, have been made of perishable materials and have, therefore, not survived. The earliest known examples, generally believed to go back to the second century BCE, are from Gudimallam[51] and Bhita.[52]

The *Liṅga Purāṇa* (99.8) refers to the eternal creative power of the *Liṅga* by stating that all beings merge in it at the time of the great Destruction and emerge from it at the time of the Creation of the universe –

*Layaṃ gachchhanti bhūtāni saṃhāre nikhilaṃ yataḥ /*
*Sṛishṭikāle punaḥ sṛishṭastasmālliṅgamudāhṛitam //*

Daily worship of the *Liṅga* was enjoined upon all the people and it is said that failing this the *dvijas* 'twice-born' will become *chaṇḍālas* 'low-born depraved' and a *śūdra* 'low-born' will be born as a boar in his next life.[53] The *Śiva Purāṇa* gives details of various types of Śiva-*liṅgas* and the religious ceremonies associated with their installation and worship.[54] The *Agni* (LIV.33-34), *Matsya* (262.10-11), and *Vishṇudharmottara Purāṇa* (III.74), *Samarāṅgaṇa-sūtradhāra* (ch. 70), *Rūpa-Maṇḍana* (IV.37-84), *Aparājitapṛichchhā* (chs. 197-203), and various other texts[55] describe different types of Śiva-*liṅgas* and their parts. Broadly speaking, the Śiva-*liṅgas* may be grouped under two broad categories: (1) *Nishkala* (*Sthāṇu*) or plain, and (2) *Sakala* or those which bear human faces or full iconic representations of Śiva or even other deities.

*Liṅgas* bearing one or more faces are known as *Mukha-liṅgas*.[56] A *mukha-liṅga* with turbaned base in the Bharatpur Museum[57] and another with curls in the Philadelphia Museum are regarded to be the earliest *mukha-liṅgas* belonging to *circa* second century BCE. It was, however, in the Kushāṇa period that the *mukha-liṅgas*, particularly the *eka-mukha liṅgas*, became quite popular. Many of them are preserved in various museums and even *in situ*.

## MUKHA-LIṄGA

Though the neighbouring state of Haryana has yielded quite a few *mukha-liṅgas* from the Kushāṇa period onwards,[58] it is strange that no early *mukha-liṅga* has come down to us in the Punjab. The only *mukha-liṅga* known from this state comes from Sultanpur Lodhi in district Kapurthala and belongs to the tenth century CE (Pl. 98). The square Brahma-bhāga is fixed in the square socket of a round *pīṭha* (without the water channel for the flow of the lustral water) decorated with a design of inverted lotus leaves with two receding circular rings on the top. The octagonal Vishṇu-bhāga is plain and the *mukha* is carved on the round Rudra-bhāga, which has a rounded top. The serene face with quasi-closed eyes and *chāpākāra* eyebrows, slightly damaged sturdy nose, small thick lips, plump cheeks and stout chin gives a beatific expression. There is a vertical third eye on the forehead. The face is fleshy and well-modelled and the plastic surface is smooth and sensitive. The execution of the whole figure shows skillful chisel work. The three-peaked crown adorned with pearl strings and a crescent on the central facet placed on hair combed upwards with decorative ringlets on the forehead, lotus over the ears, earrings and multiple-stringed beaded necklace reminds us of images of Śiva from the hills of Kashmir and Himachal Pradesh which started to be profusely ornamented from the ninth century onwards like those of Vishṇu, who is quite often depicted as wearing a similar crown. This *mukha-liṅga,* thus, betrays some stylistic affinity with Kashmir sculptures. Ohri observes that "In this sculpture the head of Shiva is shown crowned and the design of the crown also follows the type in vogue in the northwest. At its centre a crescent is shown and thus the god is known by the name of *Chandrashekhara*, the moon-crowned one. The motif of crescent was again more popular in Central Asia and the Kashmir region."[59]

## PLAIN *LIṄGAS*

As noted above, *Liṅgas* are of two types: *sakala* and *nishkala*; the former having parts or divisions and the latter without parts or indivisible. *Liṅgas* have been, and still continue to be, popular in

Śiva temples. They are generally equally divided into three parts – the lowest square part called Brahma-bhāga, the middle octagonal part known as Vishṇu-bhāga and the uppermost round part called Rudra-bhāga. They were set up in circular or oval *yoni-pīṭhas* having a protruding water channel appended to it. Some old *liṅgas* are found detached from the *yoni-pīṭhas*. Subsequently, there grew the tendency of setting up only the rounded part conforming to the Rudra-bhāga in the *pīṭhas*.

Numerous plain *liṅgas* have been found from Dholbaha, which indicate the popularity of the worship of Śiva and the existence of Śaiva temples at the place. One such piece in the site museum seems to have been set up in an earlier *yoni-pīṭha* (Pl. 99) which shows the lowermost part decorated with inverted lotus leaf design followed by an *antaḥ-patra*, a round *bharaṇī*, a smaller *antaḥ-patra* and two rings of diminishing sizes with a square socket for fixing the Brahma-bhāga into it. The Śiva-*liṅga* fixed in it, however, has got only the rounded Rudra-bhāga. Another similar example may also be seen at the same place (Pl. 100) but it is badly weathered and does not show the inverted leaf decoration and has also suffered a vertical crack. A third piece at the site, however, shows the weathered and undecorated *yoni-pīṭha* with square Brahma-bhāga fixed in it with the octagonal Vishṇu-bhāga and rounded Rudra-bhāga visible above (Pl. 101). There are quite a few detached *liṅgas* also in the site museum showing the tripartite divisions or simply the plain ones. A plain Śiva-liṅga of *circa* ninth century was recovered while laying down the foundations of a Śiva temple in village Burail (Chandigarh) and was installed in the old Śiva temple of the village for worship.[60]

Reference may also be made to the cave temples at Mukesar, about 10 km from Shahpur up the Ravi on its left bank near Parhankot in district Gurdaspur, where there are four artificial caves cut out of the solid rock on the south side of the soft sandstone cliff which projects into the river attributed to the Pāṇḍavas. They have medieval doorways with Śiva-*liṅgas* inside still worshipped by the adventurous visitors who take the trouble of reaching there bearing the hazards of the approach. There are some worn out unidentifiable sculptures on the pillars inside and traces of a medieval inscription have also been noticed on one of the doorways. The inscription is so worn out like the sculptures that it is impossible to decipher it but judging from the character of the few visible letters, it may be dated approximately to the eleventh century CE.[61]

## NANDĪ

Śiva seems to have been worshipped in his theriomorphic form of a bull which has been depicted on punch-marked, tribal and many other dynastic coins from about the middle of the first millennium BCE.[62] Vṛishabha was originally an epithet of Rudra. The *Mbh* (XIII.225, 25) refers to Nandikeśvara as the mount of Śiva. Several other texts like the *Rāmāyaṇa, Liṅga Purāṇa, Bhāgavata Purāṇa*, etc. also narrate stories of his origin.[63]

In plastic art, Nandī is represented in anthropomorphic form as a duplicate of Śiva, in theriomorphic form as a bull and therianthropomorphic form as bull-faced human. The bull form, however, has remained quite popular through the periods. A beautifully carved medieval humped bull seated to left with legs folded but unfortunately with its head lost is now preserved at the site museum at Dholbaha (Pl. 102). It acquaints us of the vigour of the animal commensurate with the power and prowess of Rudra-Śiva who is well known in Hindu mythology as the god of destruction (Mahākāla). It may have stood before an image or *Liṅga* of Śiva in a temple of *circa* tenth century CE at Dholbaha. Another Nandī of about the same date has been put up at the beginning of the stairs of the site museum.

The foregoing account indicates that though literary, archaeological and numismatic evidence shows the prevalence of Śiva worship in early times, yet no early images or *Liṅgas* have come down to us and the earliest evidence is provided by the brass mask of Bardar now fixed in a temple at Rupnagar. Śiva's worship may have been popular in the medieval times but no independent icon of the god has come to light as yet. Remains from Dholbaha at the foothills in Hoshiarpur district reveal it to be a stronghold of Śaiva worship where many temples of the god may have existed from eighth through twelfth centuries. The most popular form, however, was Umā-Maheśvara, many specimens of which come from this site including an unfinished one though the best piece has been recovered from Ghanauli near Rupnagar. Sunam in district Sangrur was probably the other important place of Śaiva worship. Naṭarāja form was popular in the Bathinda region which has yielded the only but interesting image. The sole evidence of the *Mukha-liṅga* worship comes from Sultanpur Lodhi in district Kapurthala.

## NOTES AND REFERENCES

1. Sir John Marshall, *Mohenjodaro and the Indus Civilization*, Vol. I, London, 1931, pp. 48 ff and Pls. VII-XII.
2. Macdonell, *op. cit.*, pp. 74ff.
3. *DHI*, pp. 446-47.
4. *VSMRS*, pp. 145ff.
5. *DHI*, p. 448; *VSMRS*, pp. 145ff.
6. T.A. Gopinath Rao, *Elements of Hindu Iconography* (Reprint, Delhi 1971), Vol. II, Pt.1, pp. 39ff; *VSMRS*, pp. 145ff; V.S. Agrawala, *Śiva-Mahādeva*, Varanasi, 1966; Pranabanand Jash, *History of Śaivism*, Calcutta, 1974; R.K. Siddhantashastree, *Śaivism Through the Ages*, Delhi, 1975; Mahadev Chakravarti, *The Concept of Rudra-Śiva Through the Ages*, Delhi, 1986; etc.
7. Commenting on Pāṇini's *sūtra* V.2, 76. Also see Bhandarkar, *op. cit.*, p. 165.
8. John Allan, *Catalogue of the Coins of Ancient India in the British Museum*, London, 1936.
9. P.L. Gupta and T.R. Hardaker, *Ancient Indian Silver Punchmarked Coins of the Magadha-Maurya Karshapana Series*, Anjaneri, 1985, p. 1ff.
10. Ajay Mitra Shastri, "Symbols on Tribal Coins: An Interpretative Study" in *Seminar Papers on Tribal Coins of Ancient India (C.200 BC to 400 AD)*, edited by Jai Prakash Singh and Nisar Ahmad, Varanasi, 1977, pp. 88-89.
11. Allan, *op. cit.*, pp. xciii and 145; Devendra Handa, "Kada Coins From Sugh", *Numismatic Digest*, Vol. 20 (1996), pp. 25-32.
12. Percy Gardner, *The Coins of the Greek and Scythic Kings of Bactria and India in the British Museum*, Chicago, 1966, pp. 104 (Gondophernes) and 124-128 (Kadphises II).
13. I.K. Sarma, *The Development of Early Saiva Art and Architecture (with special reference to Andhra Pradesh)*, Delhi, 1982, pp. 61-62 has suggested a date of third second century BCE while D.R. Bhandarkar (*Carmichael Lectures on Ancient Indian Numismatics*, Calcutta 1921, pp. 19-20) assigns it to the fourth century CE. For a discussion of these and various other views, see H. Sarkar, 'Beginnings of Śaivism in South India with Special Reference to Date of Gudimallam Liṅga' in *Rupanjali in memory of O.C. Gangoly* (Ed. By K.K. Ganguli and S.S. Biswas), Calcutta, 1986, pp. 115ff.
14. The Bhita Pañchamukha Śiva-*liṅga* has been assigned to *circa* third-second century BCE by Marshall (*Annual Report of the Archaeological Survey of India*, 1911-12, p. 49, pl. XI.8) and N.P. Joshi (*Catalogue of the Brahmanical Sculpture in the State Museum, Lucknow*, Part I, Lucknow, 1972, pp. 99-101, Figs. 24-27). Rao (*op. cit.*, pp. 63-65) considered it to be of the pre-Christian period and J.N. Banerjea (*DHI*, pp.464-65) dates it to the first century BCE. D.R. Bhandarkar (*loc. cit.*) has suggested for it a date in the Kushāṇa period. For a detailed discussion, see Sarkar (*loc. cit*).
15. Sarkar, *loc. cit*.
16. T.K. Biswas, "Early Śaivite Terracottas in Bharat Kala Bhavan", in *Dimensions of Indian Art (Pupul Jayakar Seventy)*, edited by Lokesh Chandra and Jyotindra Jain, Delhi, 1986, Vol. I (Text), p. 45, Vol. II (plates), p. 10, Fig. 1.

17. For a detailed account of seals and sealings from Punjab, see Handa (1985), *op. cit.*, pp. 93-138. See also Virajānanda Daivakaraṇi (2010), *op. cit.*, p. 27, nos. 106, 108 and 116 for the sealings of Rudraśarma, Rudravarma and Bhava respectively.
18. K.K. Thaplyal, *Studies in Ancient Indian Seals*, Lucknow, 1971, p. 217.
19. *Ibid.*, p. 205.
20. *Ibid.*, pp. 139-44.
21. *Ibid.*
22. *Skanda Purāṇa*, Kāśī Khaṇḍa, XXVI.27.
23. *Liṅga Purāṇa*, Pūrvabhāga, 92.143.
24. *Mbh* (Gita Press ed.), Vana Parva, 84.78-79.
25. Handa (1985), *loc. cit.*
26. *Ibid.*
27. Not a mace as described by Shastri and Sharma in *JNSI*, XXXVII, p. 207.
28. *Annual Report, Archaeological Survey of India*, Punjab Circle, 1910-11, pp. 18-19.
29. *Ibid.*, p. 20.
30. *Panjab District Gazetteers*, Vol. VII, Part A: Ambala District 1923-24, Lahore, 1925, pp. 135-36.
31. Srivastava and Srivastava, *loc. cit.*, Fig. 16. The extra-high *jaṭā-jūṭa* is comparable to some figures of central India (A.L. Srivastava, *Umā-Maheśvara: An Iconographic Study of the Divine Couple*, Kasganj, 2004, Figs. 17, 20, 21, 28, etc.).
32. As quoted by R. Nagaswamy, *Foundations of Indian Art*, Chennai, 2002, p. 25, fn. 32 but not seen by me in the Gita Press edition of the *Vishṇupurāṇa*.
33. *Tripurā Rahasyam*, with English Translation by Maharishi Ramana Samvid, Bangalore, 2000, ch. 7 as quoted by Nagaswamy, *op. cit.*, p. 18. The *Vishṇupurāṇa* (Gita Press edn, I.22, 58) also refers to Brahmā, Vishṇu and Śiva as the three main energies of the Supreme Being: *Brahmā-Vishṇu-Śivā brahmanpradhānā Brahma-śaktayaḥ* / which he assumes for the generation, sustenance and destruction of the world (I.2, 66): *Sṛishṭisthityantakaraṇīṃ brahma-vishṇu-śivātmikām / Sa saṃjñāṃ yāti bhagavāneka eva janārdanaḥ //*. Kālidāsa in his *Kumārasambhava* (VII.44) echoes the same concept by stating that Brahmā, Vishṇu and Maheśa are the three different aspects of one and the same form: *ekaiva mūrtirvibhide tridhā sa*. The *Nāradapurāṇa* (Pūrva-bhāga, LXXXI.107) too refers to this concept (*Sa Brahmā sa Śivo vipra sa Hariḥ saiva Devarāṭ*) and it has been repeated elsewhere also.
34. C. Sivaramamurti, *Naṭarāja in Art, Thought and Literature*, New Delhi, 1975; A-M Gaston, *Śiva in Dance, Myth and Iconography*, Delhi, 1982.
35. A.K. Coomaraswamy, *The Dance of Siva*, Bombay, 1948; Jose Pereira, "The Naṭarāja Theme, a new interpretation", *Journal of the Royal Asiatic Society of Bombay*, vol. XXX (1), 1955, pp. 71-86; J.M. Somasudaram Pillai, *Śiva Naṭarāja – The Cosmic Dancer in Cidambaram*, Chidambaram, 1970; Sivaramamurti, *op. cit.*, pp. 23-41; etc.
36. Gaston, *op. cit.*, p. 213 (map).
37. Sivaramamurti, *op. cit.*, p. 306, fig. 184.
38. Handa (2006), *op. cit.*, pp. 135-36, Pls. 154-56.
39. Manmohan Kumar (1981, *op. cit.*, p. 51) mentions *sarpa-hāra* also but it is not clear.
40. Ohri, *op. cit.*, p. 122.
41. *Ibid.*, p. 123.
42. *Ibid.*, p. 125.
43. *Ibid.*
44. Cf. Manmohan Kumar (1981, *op. cit.*, p. 51) who holds that "This sculpture is a fine specimen of the Gurjara Pratihāra times with artistic, plastic conception".
45. Handa (1983), *op. cit.*, p. 30 & Fig. 6 on p. 22.
46. Cf. Ohri (*op. cit.*, p. 126) who dates it to 12th century CE.
47. *Liṅga* is a Sanskrit word meaning a sign, symbol, mark, or even an image.
48. Westropp and C. S. Wake, *Symbol Worship: Influence of the Phallic Ideas in the Religions of Antiquity*, New Delhi, 1979.
49. *Rāmāyaṇa*, Yuddha-kāṇḍa, 123.20.

50. *Mahābhārata* III.39, 65:

*Sa ramyaṃ śaraṇaṃ gatvā bhagavantaṃ Pinākinam/*
*Mṛinmayaṃ sthaṇḍilaṃ kṛitvā mālyenāpūjayad Bhavam//*

51. A.K. Coomaraswamy, *Introduction to Indian Art*, Delhi, 1969, Fig. 16.
52. R.D. Banerji, "Three Sculptures in the Lucknow Museum", *ARASI, 1909-10*, pp. 147-48, Pl. LIV, Figs. C, D and E.
53. *Liṅgārchanatantra* and *Prāṇatoshṇītantra* as quoted by R.K. Bhattacharyya, "Popularity of Śiva Worship in India", *VIJ*, X (I-ii), p. 82.
54. *Śiva Purāṇa*, Prathama Vidyeśvara Saṃhitā, ch. XI; *Vāyu Saṃhitā*, Uttara Bhāga, ch. XXIV, etc.
55. *EHI*, II, Appedix B.
56. *Rūpa-Maṇḍana* describes *mukha-liṅgas* with one, three and four faces –

*Mukha-liṅgaṃ trivaktraṃ syādekavaktraṃ chaturmukhaṃ /*
*Shaṇmukhaṃ chaikavaktraṃ syāt trivaktre pṛishṭhake na hi //*

57. *Catalogue & Guide To State Museum, Bharatpur (Rajasthan)*, Jaipur, 1960- 61, p. 9, Pl. II.
58. Handa (2006), *op. cit.*, pp. 129-33, Pls. 143-51.
59. Ohri, *op. cit.*, p. 124. Similar figures of sixth-seventh and eighth-ninth century *Ekamukha-Liṅgas* carved on the round Rudra-bhāga of the phallus in the State Museum, Bhopal have been identified with Tatpurusha Mahādeva (For details see R. Nagaswamy, *The Art and Religion of the Bhairavas*, Chennai, 2006, pp. 112-13, Fig. 46 and 19, respectively).
60. Lalman (1989), *loc cit.*
61. Charles J. Rodgers, *Revised List of Objects of Archaeological Interest in the Punjab*, Lahore, 1891, p. 33; *Imperial Gazetteer of India*, Vol. II, District Gurdaspur, pp. 59-61.
62. John Allan, *loc. cit.*
63. *EHI*, II, pp. 455-59.

# 5

# Śakti

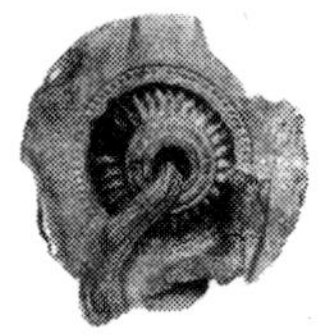

## FEMALE DEITIES

Over-awed perhaps by the destructive and creative powers of the natural phenomena, floral and faunal world around him, Man has ever been a worshipper of Śakti – the universal energy. Śakti worship can be traced back in India, as in many other parts of the world, to a very remote past. The prehistoric rock paintings and terracotta mother-goddess figurines, the Vedic invocation to Vāk and other female deities, their identification with primeval energy and depiction as the creator of universe, the mothers of gods, the spouses of supreme deities, and the various names and epithets like Umā-Haimavatī, Rudrānī, Bhavānī, Īśānī, Ambikā, Āryā, Durgā, Kālī, Kauśikī, Kātyāyaṇī, Aparṇā, Nārāyaṇī, Śivā, Jagadambā, etc. in literary works down the Ṛigvedic period are not only indicative of her continued worship but also of different Aryan, non-Aryan and other multifarious strands which contributed to the formation of the concept of her composite character. The culmination is reached in the Devī-Māhātmya of the *Mārkaṇḍeya Purāṇa* which characterizes Devī as symbolizing supreme energy, highest knowledge and absolute truth.[1] Representative of the three *guṇas* ('qualities', *sattva, rajas* and *tamas*) and the malign and benign aspects, Śakti has been conceived of in various forms – as the inherent energy of different deities and as the primeval, supreme, universal energy itself. As such, we find her represented as the counterpart of the various gods or assuming different forms to redress the gods and men of their woes and miseries and punish the wicked.[2] Though mother-goddess figurines have been discovered from some excavated sites in the Punjab, yet like other deities their plastic representations of the early period are a great rarity. Even in the medieval period, we find the images of only a few forms of the female divinities. We will describe below the deities whose images have come down to us.

### Pārvatī

Pārvatī,[3] the daughter of the great snow-clad mountain Himavān and Menā, occupies an important place in the galaxy of female divinities described in literature and *śilpa* texts and represented in art. Symbolizing primordial power, she is the source of various *Śaktis* 'energies'[4] and is known by multiple names such as Umā, Aparṇā, Gaurī, etc. In order to obtain Śiva, who was absorbed in meditation, as her spouse, she prepared to undertake penance. Seeing her tender age, Menā discouraged her to do so by the words *'U mā'* 'oh, no'. She thus came to be known as Umā.[5] During her austerities, she discarded even the fallen leaves of trees and plants for subsistence and became Aparṇā, i.e., one (living) without leaves.[6] The austerity of penance continued and ultimately she observed *pañchāgnitapas* placing herself in the middle of the four fires with sun as the fifth source of heat. It is this incidence, which has popularly been depicted in sculptures from the Kushāṇa period onwards[7] in different parts on India. As yet no such image belonging to the Gupta period is known but copious literary references, the depiction of *pañchatapas* Pārvatī in the sixth century Cave No. 1 at Badami[8] and Cave No. 21 at Ellora datable to *circa* CE 600[9] indicate the continuity of the tradition. Four-armed Pārvatī holding *varada* 'boon giving pose', rosary, *kuśa* 'grass' and water flask in her hands, with lion and deer at the feet from Muṇḍeśvarī (Bihar), assignable to seventh century CE, [10] is another important early image. In the Pratihāra period, the popularity of this form seems to have increased much and a large number of images of *tapasvinī* Pārvatī have been found from Uttar Pradesh, Madhya Pradesh and Rajasthan.[11] Images datable to the eighth and ninth centuries CE are very simple in nature and direct in appeal. They show the goddess as seated or standing amidst four fires flanked by lion and deer near her feet.[12] During the following two centuries, the goddess is invariably depicted as standing on a *godhā* 'alligator' accompanied by a number of attendants. These images are lavishly ornamented.[13] Madhya Pradesh, Uttar Pradesh and Rajasthan remained the nucleus zone of *pañchatapas* Pārvatī images and four-handed form was the most popular, rather the invariable type. The popularity of this form, however, seems to have waned considerably after the eleventh-twelfth centuries.

Though Śakti worship has remained popular, and still continues to be so, in the whole of northern India from very early times, and a few images of the goddess have recently been published from the neighbouring region of Haryana[14] yet it is strange that no image of *tapasvinī* Pārvatī is known from the region comprising the present day states of Punjab, Himachal Pradesh, and Jammu & Kashmir.

A four-handed Pratihāra image of standing Pārvatī with Kārttikeya near her left foot found from the Aja Sarovara at Kharar was set up under a pipal tree in the Gurukula by the side of the tank. I had seen it in 1980 but unfortunately did not have the camera and pen and paper to photograph and take notes of it. When I visited the site a few weeks later, it had been stolen and was never recovered. No other complete or near complete image of Pārvatī has come to my notice from anywhere in the Punjab. There are, however, some fragmentary pieces which probably, but not certainly, may be regarded as belonging to the images of Pārvatī.

A head from Sarai Naga in district Muktsar shows a plump, placid face with eyes almost closed in ecstasy bearing an exquisitely carved *dhammilla* coiffure adorned with jewels and pearl strings with a *kīrtimukha* clasp in the centre and wearing *karṇa-kuṇḍalas* (Pl. 103). The nose is damaged but the face still seems to be quite graceful. The original image must have remained an elegant piece of the Pratihāra art during the 10th century CE. Another head from this place shows hair combed skillfully, forming curls on both sides of the parting of hair and having an elaborate coiffure held in position with pearl strings and adorned with floral decorations (Pls. 104-105). There is an auspicious *tilaka* mark on the forehead, the ecstatic eyes are half closed and bear arched eyebrows. The cheeks are fleshy, nose is slightly mutilated, lips are thick and the chin is sturdy giving the face a beatific expression. Behind this head is a subsidiary figure bearing a crown on the head, wearing earrings and an *ekāvali* and holding some unidentifiable object in left hand. The right hand touching the right knee and holding some attribute going over the right shoulder is broken. It is difficult to identify this male figure with certitude but he may have been Kārttikeya holding the lance or *śakti* in his left hand.

Another very elegantly carved detached head has been found from Mard Khera, bearing an exquisite *dhammilla* with an exquisite *lalāṭikā* showing a circular pod in front from which comes out a beaded tassel hung over the forehead bearing a *tripuṇḍa*. The hair is held tightly in position by pearl strings going around the head (Pl. 106). The *lalāṭikā* on the forehead is a vertical eye-shaped *tilaka* mark. The eyebrows look like a bow, the eyes with drooping eyelids give an impression of introversion, the sturdy nose characterizes her inner strength and the lips bear beatific smile. Locks of loose hair fall on her right shoulder. How wonderful the original complete image would have been can only be guessed. The auspicious mark on the forehead and the frontal *tripuṇḍa* and *liṅga*-like decorations suggest it to have been the face of Pārvatī though we do not have any means to ascertain this. Stylistically, it seems to belong to late tenth century CE.

A grey sandstone head from Sunam, which may have belonged to a tenth century image of Pārvatī originally, is plumper with fleshy cheeks, drooping eyelids and bow-like eyebrows (Pl. 107).[15] The hair has been combed sideways from the parting line and tied with a rope-like beaded string having a *chūḍāmaṇi* in the centre and arranged in *dhammilla*-type coiffure above.

In the site museum at Dholbaha is preserved a badly mutilated architectural piece showing the bust of a female figure in an arched *rathikā* (Pl. 108). Remnants of the arch with *ardha-ratna* decoration flanked by *nāgara-kūṭas* surmounting the side pillars indicate it to have belonged to an elegant medieval temple of *circa* tenth century CE. The female figure standing under the arch is broken below the waist and all the features, except the exquisite *dhammilla* coiffure decorated with a central jewel, have chipped off. A lotus stalk rising from the left side of the arm and going around the head with fully blossomed flower at the drooping end adds additional grace to this otherwise featureless figure. Her hanging right arm is broken below the elbow and the left rising to the shoulder from the elbow is damaged to render it impossible to determine the attribute held in it. The accentuation of the hip to her left indicates that she stood in a graceful posture. There is absolutely no clue to the identity of this female figure who may have been Pārvatī or any other female divinity.

Another badly mutilated Pratihāra image from Sirhind, showing the female bust with front left hand in dancing pose and the back one holding a flower (?) and having a part of the lotus halo behind the head and stele with headless deity seated in *sukhāsana*, may doubtfully be identified as that of Pārvatī (Pl. 109).

## Durgā

Scholars believe that a number of deities worshipped by hill tribes are traceable in Durgā.[16] As a synonym of Ambikā, who is described in the *Vājasaneyi Saṃhitā* (III.57) and the *Taittirīya Brāhmaṇa* (I.6, 10, 4-5) as Rudra's sister, the name of Durgā Vairochanī appears along with Kātyāyanī and Kanyā-Kumārī for the first time in the *Taittirīya Āraṇyaka* (X.1, 7) as Rudra's consort. The Āgamas and the Purāṇas refer to her nine manifestations (Nava Durgā) and describe her iconographic features in details.[17]

Rao has described different forms of Durgā as having four, eight or more hands, three eyes, beautiful look with a well-developed bust, stout thighs and big hips, clad in garments, adorned with *karaṇḍa-mukuṭa* and wearing various ornaments.[18] Standing in *samabhaṅga*, *dvibhaṅga* or *tribhaṅga* upon a lotus, head of a buffalo or a lion, she should carry a trident and noose, or a parrot or mirror and a blue lily[19] if two-handed; a noose and a goad with the other two hands disposed in *abhaya* and *varada* poses in four-handed variety or carrying, in addition, a conch, discus, bow, arrows, sword, shield, etc. if multi-handed.

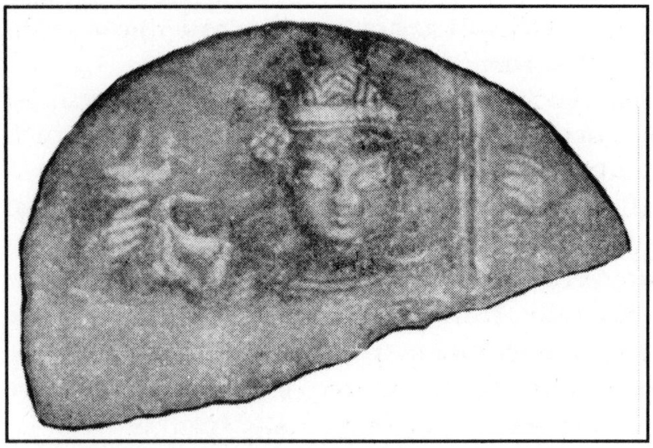

**Fig. 25.** Terracotta mould from Ajadam (after Sadhu Ram).

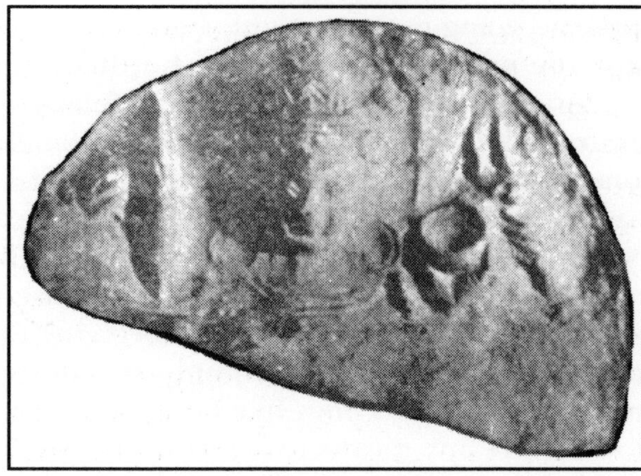

**Fig. 26.** Plaster cast of the mould from Ajadam.

The popularity of the worship of Durgā amongst the common folk is known from a terracotta mould representing the goddess discovered from village Ajaḍāma, about 15 km southwest of Hoshiarpur. The mould was found complete but was unfortunately broken by the village urchins who, ignorant of its religious significance and historical value, played with it and dashed it to the ground. In its extant form, it measures 13 X 7 cm. The goddess carried a drinking bowl and a trident in her left hands and the right ones supported a vertically held sword and a bell (Figs. 25-26). The goddess bears a three-peaked tiara bedecked with flowers on the sides and wears large circular rings in the ears, a double-stringed necklace and bracelets. The third eye has been carved vertically on the forehead. The facial expression betrays benign and compassionate look. The mould seems to bear the influence of folk art as well as the impact of the hills and may be assigned to *circa* ninth century CE on stylistic grounds.[20]

An oval-shaped terracotta moulded female figure with a leaf-like double-lined bandolin showing prominent dots or serrations between the lines seated cross-legged and having a tiara marked with three vertical strokes simulating a triple-peaked crown with the three prongs of the trident above found from Hawara near Kurali (Pl. 110) may be regarded as the representation of Durgā or Mahishamardinī in medieval folk idiom. The figure is slightly damaged below the legs and the attributes in (four?) hands are also not clear. But it betrays the popularity of the worship of the goddess by common folk.

A very crudely executed and worn-out bust of Durgā, broken below the breasts, obtained from Dholbaha is displayed in the VVRI Museum at Hoshiarpur (Pl. 111). It shows the goddess bearing a three-tiered crown with looped curls on both sides of the head which give the impression of animal heads on the sides. Such looped curls appear in Himachal sculptures at quite an early period of *circa* eighth century CE and may be seen in an image of Durgā from Hat Koti in the Shimla Museum.[21] She wears circular earrings, necklace with a big pendant falling on the breasts, an *uttarīya* and bracelets and holds a cup and a sword in the right hands and a noose in the back left hand. The natural left hand is broken. The figure has been carved on a coarse-grained rectangular slab with upper corners and top slightly rounded. The wearing out has destroyed all details. The extant figure seems to be somewhat disproportionate with a massive head but shorter bust. The crown betrays Pahari impact. The image may have been created in twelfth or thirteenth century CE.

Another fragmentary specimen of the depiction of Durgā in the Punjab also comes from Dholbaha, where it has been put up in the area adjoining the site museum with people still continuing to disfigure it by applying oil and vermilion to it and offering grains and other such things (Pl. 112). The fragment represents only the portion below the waist and the pedestal below showing the face of a lion on the left below the folded right leg of the goddess. The left leg too is folded likewise forming an unusual posture for the deity. Both the feet are placed on a lotus, which is flanked by very crudely carved human figures. A broad band probably marking the girdle and a part of the long garland covering it is visible on the waist. The lion indicates that the image may have been that of Durgā belonging to about twelfth century CE.

## Kshemaṅarī

Kshemaṅkarī is one of the nine forms of Durgā.[22] In the *Devī Purāṇa* (39.121 ff), she is identified with primeval energy. She is called Kshemaṅkarī as she always protects the gods and the worshippers.[23] In art, she is generally recognized by two lions depicted on her pedestal or as her vehicles. The existence of an image of Kshemaṅkarī Durgā is evidenced by a pedestal recovered from Mard Khera near Sunam, which shows a lotus placed in the centre of the pedestal with outward moving, facing lions flanking it (Pl. 113). Fingers of only the right foot placed on the lotus indicate that the deity was depicted as seated in *lalitāsana* with the left leg folded. A diminutive kneeling figure in profile and another standing to front behind that with left hand hanging down and the right one touching the chin or mouth have survived on the proper left (viewer's right) hand side of the relief which is badly encrusted with oil, vermilion and dust, indicating that the image remained under worship for a long period. On the front facet of the pedestal were perhaps carved the figures of the donor couple in *añjali-mudrā* seated in profile with folded legs but only one of these have survived and the other has left traces of its breakage. Though Mahishamardinī and Lakshmī too are sometimes depicted with two lions, yet the absence of the buffalo definitely rules out the possibility of its being the former. Evidence of the worship of Kshemaṅkarī Durgā from the neighbouring Haryana depicted with two lions on the pedestal[24] renders it more probable that the present pedestal also belonged to Durgā Kshemaṅkarī. The image may be dated to *circa* twelfth century on stylistic grounds.

## Mahishāsuramardinī

Of all the female deities, the worship of Mahishāsuramardinī seems to have remained most popular. Mahishāsuramardinī, literally meaning 'the crusher of the buffalo demon', is one of the earliest and most important manifestations of Durgā in her ferocious form. The *Vāmana Purāṇa* (chs. 17-20) gives a detailed account of the destruction of Mahishāsura[25] at the hands of Devī. Gods, having been defeated by the demon Mahisha, approached Vishṇu under the leadership of Brahmā, for protection. Śaṅkara was also present there. On hearing the grievances of the gods, Vishṇu, and at his command Brahmā, Śiva and all other gods, emitted flames of anger from their eyes and faces as a result of which a mountain of effulgence was formed. From this mountain came forth profusely resplendent eighteen-armed goddess Kātyāyanī whom Śiva gave a trident, Vishṇu a disc, Varuṇa a conch, Agni a dart, Yama an iron rod, Vāyu a bow, Sūrya a quiver and arrows, Indra a thunderbolt, Kubera a mace, Brahmā a rosary and a water-pot, Kāla sword and a shield, Viśvakarma a battle-axe and other weapons, Himavān a lion, etc. Other gods also gave her various weapons and ornaments. Kātyāyanī then proceeded to the Vindhya mountain where Chaṇḍa and Muṇḍa saw her and reported about her beauty to their king Mahishāsura. Having heard high encomiums of her splendid and beautiful form, the demon-king was determined to obtain her and marched with his army to the vicinity of the mountain from where he sent Dundubhi, his grandson, as messenger. Devī told him that she would marry the demon Mahisha if he vanquished her in combat. A severe battle ensued in which the whole army was routed and killed but the demon-king, because of a boon granted by Śiva, had been rendered invulnerable. Seeing that the army had been destroyed, the demon advanced for a personal combat.[26] Ultimately, during the terrible duel, Durgā dismounted from her lion and jumped upon the back of Mahisha and pierced his neck with the trident by the right hand while trampling on his back with her right leg.[27] It is this incident of the combat which is very popular in Indian art.[28] Her victory over the demon Mahisha is regarded as symbolic of the triumph of virtue over evil.[29] Rao thinks that the story indicates the substitution of the buffalo totem worship by a form of Devī worship among some early primitive tribes in the country.[30] The *Mahābhārata* and several Purāṇas, especially the *Mārkaṇḍeya*, also narrate the exploits of Devī.[31]

Though the antiquity of her images has been traced back to the pre-Kushāṇa times,[32] yet her cult seems to have become popular in North India during the Kushāṇa period, as evidenced by quite a few terracotta and stone plaques and statuettes found from the Mathura region.[33] It is interesting to note that in the earliest reliefs, the goddess has only two or four hands and is shown as subduing the buffalo demon by sheer physical force – by compressing the throat of the animal or pulling out its tongue by one hand and pressing its back by the other. Stunted spear or trident is her principal weapon, which she holds in one or two of her additional hands.[34] Six or more handed varieties of the Kushāṇa images of Mahishamardinī are also known.[35] Lion as the vehicle of the goddess, though absent initially, makes its appearance in the late Kushāṇa period[36] but does not become an essential adjunct of her images till the early medieval period. If present, it was depicted as a docile animal. During the Gupta period, the goddess is generally shown as pressing the back of the buffalo with her right or left foot and piercing it with a long-handled spear or trident held in her principal right hand. The next stage of development of the Mahishāsuramardinī images in northern India is beautifully described in the Devī-Māhātmya of the *Mārkaṇḍeya Purāṇa*[37] assignable to the seventh century CE if not earlier[38] –

*Evamuktvā samutapatya sārūḍhā taṃ mahāsuram /*
*Pādenākramya kaṇṭhe cha śūlenainamatāḍayat //*

*Tataḥ so'pi pādākrāntastayā nijamukhāttataḥ /*
*Arddhanishkrānta eveti devyā vīryyena saṃvṛitaḥ //*

*Arddhanishkrānta evāsau yudhyamāno mahāsuraḥ /*
*Tayā mahāsinā devyā śiraśchhittvā nipātitaḥ //*

When the demon emerged in anthropomorphic form out of the severed neck of the buffalo, the goddess slew him with her sword. This form of the goddess has been very popular with the artists from *circa* eighth century CE onwards.[39]

As noted above, the worship of Mahishāsuramardinī seems to have become popular in and around Mathura, including Haryana,[40] but we are yet to discover such an early evidence from the Punjab. A terracotta figurine from Sanghol, now preserved and displayed in the site museum, however, shows that the goddess was quite popular in the Gupta period when it started to be delineated in common man's art also (Pl. 114). The figure has suffered some damage but has preserved enough to reveal the combat of the four-handed goddess with the buffalo demon. The surviving portion shows the goddess bearing *chhattrākāra* curled hair falling on both the shoulders in typical Gupta style, as witnessed in some terracotta figurines from Rajghat and Ahichchhatrā.[41] The round face bears thick eyebrows, eyes with drooping eyelids, sturdy nose with what looks like a ring in the nostrils, plump fleshy cheeks and a beatific smile on the lips. There is a *graiveyaka* with threaded roundels in the neck and perhaps also a necklace, multiple bangles on the arms and almost the whole of the body is covered by garment marked by embossed linear folds. A part of the garment twisted like a rope serves as the girdle. The lower portion of

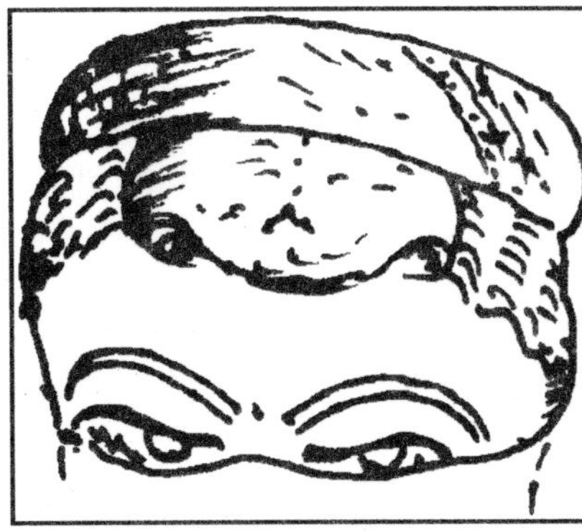

**Fig. 27.** Fragmentary head, probably of Mahishāsuramardinī, from Sanghol.

the plaque is missing but the stance of the goddess indicates that she stood in *pratyālīḍha,* planting her left foot firmly on the ground and pressing the back of the buffalo with her right foot. She is thrusting the long-handled trident into the body of the demon with her back right hand (now broken) while the normal one seems to be placed on the respective knee to betray the effortlessness with which she killed the demon. The helplessness and ferocity of the buffalo are indicated by its upraised mouth and swollen nostrils but the front left hand pressing the mouth and the back one holding it from the neck to strangulate it betray the energy the goddess possesses to accomplish the job. Since the plaque is broken below, we have no evidence regarding the appearance and role of the lion. The terracotta may be dated to fifth century on stylistic grounds.

A very fragmentary red sandstone head found from Sanghol broken below the eyes shows the broad forehead ornament having hair combed beautifully in tresses and tied in a bun with a twisted pearl string but the surviving part of the wide open eyes in a real frighteneing posture (Pl. 115, Fig. 27). Stylistically belonging to the late Gupta period, it may have originally been a head of Mahishāsuramardinī.

A well-modelled seventh century image of four-armed Mahishāsuramardinī measuring 150 X 59.5 cm from Doghi in district Una, which formed part of Hoshiarpur district in Punjab earlier but lies in Himachal now, must have been a cult icon to judge from its size. Standing in *pratyālīḍha* posture, the goddess is trampling the buffalo demon lifting it by the tail with her natural left hand and piercing his neck with the trident held in her normal right hand.[42] The additional right hand supports a sword while the corresponding left holds a circular shield. The mount lion which is usually seen in the images of Mahishāsuramardinī is absent. Near-contemporary four-handed images of the goddess of this type in Himachal Pradesh generally show a bell in the upper left hand but it is replaced here by the shield which shows its affinity to the images of the Punjab plains. It may be mentioned here that Doghi is not far from Dholbaha.

The next evidence of her worship comes from Dholbaha. The image is now displayed in the Hoshiarpur museum (Pl. 116). The eight-handed goddess stands with waist accentuated to her right and bearing the weight of the body on her right foot. The left foot is placed on the back of the buffalo from whose severed head comes out the demon in human form, trying to take out a sword with his right hand from the sheath held in his left hand to strike at the goddess who is rendering him helpless by twisting his neck with her proper left hand. Another left hand seems to be placed on the respective thigh, the third one is irretrievably lost and the uppermost left holds a shield above the head. The uppermost right hand, likewise, is raised above the head holding a *chakra,* the next is placed on the head of an attendant, the third holds a sword vertically and the normal right supports a cup near the right shoulder. The goddess bears matted locks adorned with a jewel and pearl strings, ear ornaments, pearl necklace whose loose strings fall on the belly from between the breasts and turn sideways on the waist, armlets, beaded bracelets and *dhotī* secured by a girdle. The general demeanour of the goddess seems to be one of little concern and effortlessness, which is endorsed by an expression of quietude and serenity on her face. The absence of lion is notable. There is a big plain halo behind the head. Tense curves and angular disposition of the limbs makes the figure look quite powerful. The modelling of this figure shows similarity with the image of Śiva-Pārvatī from Dholbaha described above (Pl. 86) and is stylistically different from the sculptures of Kashmir. Following contemporary practice in northern India, the roundness of modelling is emphasized. Ohri has observed that "The sword shown in the goddess' (sic.) right hand is of an uncommon type; its rounded form with a rim, shown just above the hilt, appears almost identical to the rounded part of the spear seen in the right hand of the image of Sakti in a temple at Chhatrahi."[43] Stylistically, the image may be dated to eighth century CE.[44]

A ten-handed complete image of Mahishamardinī or Kāyāyanī is still under worship in a dark dungy cell of a small temple near the site museum at Dholbaha (Pl. 117). One simply wonders as to how it escaped the iconoclastic hands of the invaders. It is probable that this image was set up in the present temple which was got constructed by Diwan Dina Nath, a minister in the court of Maharaja Ranjit Singh (CE 1799-1839), who revived the site and got constructed here a sarai and a rest-house also. In construction of these buildings, material of earlier temples was freely utilized. Beautiful early medieval sculptured friezes may be seen implanted in the plinth of the Bhatanwali temple. Having been fixed rather carelessly in the niche of this tenement and being under worship for quite some time, it has badly been besmeared by sandal paste, oil and vermilion which have concealed most of the details. Wearing usual dress and ornaments and standing in *pratyālīḍha,* Mahishāsuramardinī has placed her right foot on a lotus cushion posited on the back of the caparisoned buffalo who is being attacked at the back by the pouncing lion. The goddess is thrusting the trident held in her natural right hand into the neck of the buffalo from which is emerging the demon in human form whose tuft of locks is held by the former in her normal left hand. The extra right hands are shown as holding the handle of probably a mace, dart, sword and iron rod (?), while the additional left hands support a bell, bow, wheel (?) and shield (from bottom upwards). The fullness of the plastic mass, round modelling, soft curves and angles of this otherwise complicated composition make it a masterpiece of the Pratihāra art of Punjab during the late tenth century CE. A fragment preserved in the store of the site museum at Dholbaha shows only the buffalo being attacked by the lion from behind (Pl. 118) and indicates the popularity of Mahishāsuramardinī at this place during the tenth-eleventh centuries. The buffalo is bedecked with a decorative chain around the neck and also at the hind portion. On its back is placed the right foot of the goddess trampling it. The lion holds the tail of the buffalo in its mouth. The utter agony of the demon is indicated by its forelegs folded upwards with hoof touching its belly.

A fragmentary slab from Samuran near Sunam also shows Mahishāsuramardinī holding a sword horizontally at the back of her head in her upper right hand and thrusting the long-handled trident held in both the natural hands into the body of the buffalo, which is only to be presumed as the piece is broken below the waist of the goddess (Pl. 119). That the extra left hand was raised above to support some attribute is indicated by the extant part. There is a big round aureole with lotus leaves behind the head and a garland-bearing *vidyādhara* on the top left corner indicates the existence of a similar figure on the corresponding top right corner also. The *dhammilla* coiffure has a round clasp in the centre and is held in position by pearl strings. Bearing a beatific smile, the goddess has arched eyebrows. She wears ear ornaments, a double-stringed pearl necklace with free-ends falling to her left waist from between the breasts, beaded bracelets, a garland-like scarf, *dhotī*, etc. The pendent string of the necklace indicates the movement of the upper body to right betraying the *pratyālīḍha* posture of the goddess. Since the relief is broken below the waist, the rest has to be presumed. Stylistically, the image may be dated to *circa* tenth century CE. A small bust measuring 31.5 X 13.0 cm found from Kharar (Pl. 120), showing only the breasts with a double-stringed necklace with a round pendent from which flows down the free end from between the breasts, having a scarf over the shoulders, bearing more than two hands as suggested by breakage, may too have belonged in all probability to a tenth century image of the goddess. That Mahishāsuramardinī was worshipped at Kharar during the 10th century is indicated by a highly worn-out and mutilated piece broken into two pieces showing the body of the buffalo being pierced by a trident and anthropomorphic demon emerging from the severed head of the animal. Sirhind too has yielded a very badly damaged image of a goddess holding a noose in the uppermost right hand and probably the shaft of a trident or sword in the normal right hand and a bow in one of the extant left hand (Pl. 121). The face is broken but the plain round aureole behind with two *gandharva* and *vidyādhara* figures on the top left corner of the rectangular frieze have survived. The surviving portions of the arms on the left side indicate the figure to have been ten-handed. The image may thus have been that of Kātyāyanī or ten-handed Mahishāsuramrdinī belonging to *circa* ninth century CE, as suggested by the style of carving and ornamentation.

Another fragment of coarse-grained sandstone measuring 23 X 18.5 cm showing the proper left hand side and lower portion of the image below the broken breast comes from Sunam and depicts the four right hands of the goddess as holding the hilt of the trident, cup, sword and taking out an arrow from the quiver at the back of the right shoulder (Pl. 122).[45] A beautiful Pratihāra image of Mahishāsuramardinī, now worshipped in a Thakurdwara at Tandwal in district Ambala, said to have originally been brought there from Kaithal, shows exactly similar attributes in her right hands. The attributes in the left hands are shield, bell, bow with natural left strangulating the anthropomorphic demon emerging from the severed head of the buffalo.[46] The original image may be presumed to have been depicted similarly as standing in *pratyālīḍha* combating the buffalo demon. The goddess wears circular ear ornaments and a broad beaded *graiveyaka* with pendant string falling down as noticed in the foregoing examples. Armlets and bracelets may also be seen on the arms. Notable, however, is the triple peaked crown adorned with an almond-shaped jewel in the centre and beaded loops and strings telling us of its affinity with the examples from the hilly regions. The image may be dated to late tenth or early eleventh century CE.

Nearly forty years back, I came across two interesting images of Mahishāsuramardinī obtained by villagers while ploughing their fields on the old mound at Zahura, about 5 km southwest of Tanda Urmur in district Hoshiarpur.[47] The smaller of the two figures (Pl. 123) which measures 48 X 34 cm has been enshrined in the central niche of a temple said to have been built on the spot of the fire-altar of Janamejaya Pārīkshit's serpent sacrifice to the north of the village and is worshipped by the local people. Here, the six-armed goddess is shown thrusting the trident into the body of the buffalo from whose decapitated head the demon emerges in anthropomorphic form. The trident is held in the middle right hand while the other two hold a sword and some indistinct object, probably an arrow. The goddess is trampling on the back of the demon with her right foot. There is a long-beaked bird (līlā-śuka as seen in a sculpture in the Ambikā temple at Jagat in Rajasthan) on her upper left hand; the middle left is holding a bow while the lowest one is placed on the head of a dwarfish figure, perhaps an associate of the demon. The lion is pouncing upon the demon on the proper right. The whole image is very badly worn out and mutilated, and all details have been lost. Interesting, however, is the fact that the goddess having the central human face seems to have an elephantine proboscis on her left indicating the existence of another face on the right also, but that is totally gone.

The second image measures 73 X 43 cm and is also badly damaged. Here the ten-handed goddess, standing as usual in the *pratyālīḍha* posture trampling the back of the buffalo demon with her right foot, is shown holding in her four visible right hands a sword, a cup and the trident and perhaps taking out an arrow from the quiver while the extra left hands hold a *muṇḍa*, a bow, a shield and the severed buffalo-head (Pl. 124). With her natural left hand she is twisting the neck of the anthropomorphic demon emerging from the severed head of the slain buffalo. There are only traces of the docile lion at the back of the buffalo watching the scene quietly. Furrow marks have damaged the image badly. The goddess is wearing earrings, necklace with pendent string falling vertically and a turreted crown over the head of the female face. A very interesting feature of the image, however, is the appearance of what looks like a lion face on her right and a boar face on the left as seen in the Vaikuṇṭha images.

A three-faced goddess with central face of a horse and the side ones of a lion and a boar is known from Bijolian, in district Bhilwara or Rajasthan.[48] A two-faced Vārāhī image having a central human face and the face of a boar on the left belonging to eighth-ninth century CE has also come to light from Jogeśvarī in district Almora, Uttarakhand.[49] But nowhere in India have we come across any sculpture of Mahishāsuramardinī with three faces. Here, in the first sculpture, we see the elephant face (the third face on the proper right being lost irretrievably), combining the Vaināyikī aspect with Mahishamardinī, and in the latter, the Nārasiṃhī and Vārāhī aspects. These sculptures were perhaps inspired by the Vishṇu-Chaturmūrtis, having central human face, lion and boar faces on the right and left sides (and a fourth one, the demoniacal invisible face on the back). Three-headed Vaikuṇṭhī actually occurs at Masrur.[50] According to the *Vishṇudharmottara* (III.47, 2-17; III.85), this type of composite figure combining three or four aspects of the god is known as Vaikuṇṭha as we have already seen. This type was very popular in the early medieval period in Kashmir[51] and Himachal Pradesh,[52] from where it descended to the hills and plains of Punjab and Haryana.[53] The depiction of a bird seems to have been Rajasthani influence for we know of an image of Mahishāsuramardinī with a parrot from Ambikā Mātā temple at Jagat near Chittoregarh in Rajasthan.[54] Punjab thus seems to have remained the meeting place of different artistic traditions in the medieval period.

The holding of the *muṇḍa* and the severed buffalo head in the hands are also unique features. The number of arms, the weapons and other objects held in the hands, different attitudes of the lion mount, etc. point to some chronological difference between the two sculptures but the analogous execution of the theme points to their being the products of a common artistic tradition. These sculptures may, therefore, be ascribed to *circa* late ninth and early tenth centuries CE. Though both the sculptures are deplorably damaged, yet they show much animation and must have been beautiful specimens of the medieval art of Punjab. Even in their mutilated condition, they are extremely important examples of Indian plastic art.

The popularity of the worship of Mahishamardinī even during the Muslim period is evidenced by two small bronzes in private possessions at Kharar. One of these shows the eight-armed goddess wearing triple-peaked crown with a ribbed finial-like top-knot wearing the usual dress and ornaments standing in *pratyālīḍha* resting her right foot on the back of the lion holding the top tuft of the anthropomorphic demon by her natural left hand and thrusting the trident into its neck with her normal right hand (Pl. 125). It is difficult to identify the attribute in her lowermost extra right hand but the next two carry an arrow and dagger. The additional left hands show from the topmost shield and bow, while the next one seems to hold an iron rod (?). The severed head of the buffalo lies below indicating the sequence of events. A warrior in a charging posture on the bottom right corner of the pedestal seems to be the demon's associate while another human figure on the corresponding left side holding the weapons in the two hands stands unconcerned. The complicated but still balanced figure seems to have been solid cast and belongs to the sixteenth century CE.

The second figure is smaller and simpler in format and shows the goddess killing the buffalo by piercing its head with long-handled trident held in her normal right hand and holding the anthropomorphic demon emerging from the severed neck from the tuft at the top of the head with her normal left like the preceding image (Pl. 126). The demon is depicted as holding a sword in his right hand and shield in the left. The extra left hand of the goddess is holding a mace and the right one some unidentifiable weapon. The lion near her right foot is jumping as if to attack the demon. The goddess wears a tapering crown and usual dress and ornaments. Noteworthy, however, is the depiction of crescent and sun on either side of her head indicative of the eternity of the victory of the great divine energy over sin and wickedness. These lunar and solar symbols remind us of the Kushāṇa Mahishamardinī figures holding round objects representing sun and moon in her hands.[55] An oval ribbed plate with pointed oval decorations on the fringe and tapering finial serves the dual purpose of a back slab and aureole. The goddess is shown standing to front in an awkward posture indicating that artist was not conversant with the *pratyālīḍha* and did not have any grounding in classical works. The image betrays folk impact and may be dated to *circa* sixteenth-seventeenth century CE. The continuity of the popularity of the goddess in the late medieval period is further shown by a crudely modelled moulded clay figure found from Hathur (Pl. 127). We have already referred to above to a clay mould from Hawara (Pl. 103), which may have been that of Mahishāsuramardinī. A similar mould comes from Sahna in district Sangrur, which shows the goddess killing the demon with a trident (Pl. 128).

We thus see that the worship of Mahishāsuramardinī, though popular in Haryana during the Kushāṇa period, reached Punjab in the Gupta period as per our present evidence and all the early images depict her using her hands also to uplift, contain or strangulate the buffalo demon. In the early medieval period of seventh and eighth centuries, we see her carrying various weapons including the sword which is invariably held vertically. From the close of the eighth century we see the sword held horizontally behind or above the head, which probably was a Pratihāra innovation under Vatsarāja. During the eleventh and twelfth centuries, the images grow more elaborate and complicated. During the Sultanate period, stone sculptures of Hindu divinities almost ceased to be carved in this region. The liberal religious policy during Akbar's rule provided some respite but no fillip and only personal and portable metal images were cast without much care for the iconographic descriptions and prescriptions in the Śilpa texts. These images also bore folk impact.

## Kālī

A form of Kālī seems to have been depicted in a terracotta mould from Hawara showing the goddess as standing in *ālīḍha* probably on a corpse (*śavārūḍhā*) holding a sword horizontally at the back of her head in her uppermost right hand while the lowermost right hand is drawing out an arrow from a quiver placed near her right foot. The second and third right hands are holding a long shaft and a long handled trident. The normal left hand is placed on the head of a mutilated human figure and additional left hands seem to hold a bow, a skull and probably a shield (Pl. 129). The goddess wears a three-peaked crown, earrings, necklace, a broad girdle to secure the *dhotī* and a long garland. The figure is enclosed in a double-lined frame with dots between on the two sides and above. Stylistically, it seems to belong to *circa* tenth century CE.

## Lakshmī

In Indian mythology, Lakshmī is famous as the goddess of wealth. She symbolizes luck and good fortune. As such, she has come to be respected and worshipped alike by the Hindus, Buddhists and Jainas.[56] The antiquity of the concept of Lakshmī has been traced to the Chalcolithic times.[57] Probably folk elements were instrumental in shaping her ideology and form. Even though the word Śrī, which later became a synonym of Lakshmī, occurs in the *Ṛigveda* (I.87, 6) yet the concrete concept about her person can only be traced from the later Vedic period onwards. In the epic and Paurāṇic period, she came to be recognized as the Śakti of Vāsudeva Vishṇu.[58] As the goddess of wealth, she became naturally associated with Kubera, also the god of wealth.[59] Still later, she formed a triad with Kubera and Gaṇeśa. Lakshmī has been represented on seals and coins from about the second century BCE.[60] In Indian art, Śrī-Lakshmī is associated with lotus flowers – she stands on a lotus, amid lotuses and even herself holding lotus/lotuses. Another popular form of her depiction is the Gaja-Lakshmī (or Abhisheka-Lakshmī) showing the deity being anointed by elephants inverting pitchers of water over her.[61]

Lakshmī has always been worshipped by all communities irrespective of their religious leanings. The adoption of the honorific *Śrī* is indicative of the popularity of the goddess indirectly. This prefix is almost ubiquitous on seals and sealings of Punjab. As far as the anthropomorphic representation of the goddess is concerned, a clay sealing from Sunet shows two-armed Lakshmī holding a flower in the right hand with left placed on the knee, seated on a lion to right and anointed by elephants, stylistically belonging to about the first century BCE.[62] Another sealing from the same site bearing the legend *Śrī-Sthānasya* is taken to suggest "that a temple dedicated to *Śrī-Lakshmī* probably existed there".[63] There are, however, numerous seals and sealings from Sunet which represent the goddess symbolically in the form of *Śrīvatsa*.[64] A terracotta sealing from Sanghol (Pl. 130) shows the goddess stading on a lotus, wearing necklace and earrings, holding a flower in her right hand raised to the level of the shoulder. Her left hand is hanging down and holding some indistinct object. There are traces of Brāhmī legend on the right margin but the legend remains un-deciphered. The sealing has been dated to *circa* first century CE on artistic consideration.[65] An inscribed terracotta seal of the Gupta period obtained during the scientific clearance of the mound at Ropar (Rupnagar) some time back shows the nimbate goddess seated in *lalitāsana* holding lotus flowers by their long stalks in her hands flanked by a discus of sixteen spokes with beaded rim on her right and a *Śrīvatsa* on her left (Pl. 131).[66] These examples are sufficient evidence of the popularity of the worship of the goddess of wealth and welfare in the Punjab during the early period but unfortunately no sculptures of the period have come down to us.

A headless female image from Dholbaha broken below the knees and on the sides, also displayed in the Hoshiarpur Museum, shows lotus flowers in two of the four hands of the goddess and may thus be identified with Lakshmī (Pl. 132). The normal right arm of the goddess is suspended and may have been disposed in *varada-mudrā*. The extant part of the image indicates that the goddess stood in graceful *dvi-bhaṅga* pose wearing usual dress and ornaments, the details of which have been lost by the wearing out of the relief. The roundness and fullness of the mass, pleasing curves and contours indicate it to be a work of the tenth century CE.

### Gaja-Lakshmī

The Gaja-Lakshmī motif was quite popular in the early centuries of BCE/CE as evidenced by numerous representations on Bharhut and Sanchi and on early Indian coins. Coins of Sujyeshṭha of second century BCE circulating at Sugh in district Yamunanagar carry the earliest representation of Gaja-Lakshmī.[67] Thereafter, we find this motif on the coins of Azes and Ranjubula, which circulated in the whole of the region extending from the northwest to Mathura, carried this motif. So the worship of Gaja-Lakshmī seems to have remained quite popular in this region in the early period. A broken clay sealing depicting Gaja-Lakshmī belonging to *circa* first-second century CE from Sunet is housed in the Jhajjar Museum.[68] Unfortunately, however, no early stone images of this form are available now from this region.

Displayed in the Hoshiarpur Museum is an image of two-handed Gaja-Lakshmī from Dholbaha seated in *sukhāsana* on a cushion (or perhaps crudely depicted lion to right) holding lotus in the right hand and an unidentifiable round object (*bījapuraka*?) in the left hand (Pl. 133). The figure is stunted and the proportions have not been maintained properly. She bears a broad *dhammilla* coiffure decorated with almond-shaped jewel made of big beads, large earrings, necklace with a pendant string falling on the belly from between the breasts, armlets, bracelets, anklets and *dhotī* secured by a waistband. The back slab is rounded at the top showing two elephants inverting pitchers of water on her. Missing, however, is the fullness of mass and contours and sharpness of curves and chisel work. The image may have been carved in the late twelfth or early thirteenth century CE. The depiction of the deity with only two hands is notable.

### Sarasvatī

As the goddess of learning and fine arts, Sarasvatī commands equal respect from the Hindus, Buddhists and the Jainas. She is depicted in the plastic art as seated or standing and holding, amongst others, lotus and *vīṇā* as her distinctive attributes. The Jainas popularly depicted a book or manuscript in one of her hands and regarded her as Śrutadevī.

A small image of Sarasvatī may be seen in the central niche of an architectural piece, probably a part of the *adhishṭhāna* of a temple, from Dholbaha now preserved in the site museum (Pl. 134). Sarasvatī sits in *lalitāsana* holding manuscript in her rear right hand, *vīṇā* in the back left and water pot in the natural left hands with proper right disposed in *varada*. It is difficult to make out all details from this worn-out small frieze. On either side of the niche are depicted five dancers and musicians playing on the *mṛidaṅga*, *vīṇā*, flute, etc. The dancers and the musicians have been depicted in different poses. Below are shown *gandharva* and *vidyādhara* couples in pillared *rathikās*, all in different postures. The frieze belongs to some tenth century temple of Dholbaha.

A small image of Sarasvatī seated cross-legged in a pillared *rathikā* holding a lotus in her right hand and book in the left has been recovered from Mard Khera near Sunam (Pl. 135). The triple-ribbed pillars on the side suggest an eleventh or twelfth century date for this subsidiary image. Since the site has yielded evidence of the existence of both Hindu and Jaina temples, it is difficult to determine whether this image belongs to a Hindu or a Jaina fane.

## SAPTA-MĀTṚIKĀS

The concept of the Seven Mothers goes back perhaps to the Vedic times, yet it is strange that the Purāṇas vary in giving their numbers and names.[60] The usually accepted list, supported by iconographic data, however, comprises the names of Brahmāṇī, Māheśvarī, Kaumārī, Vaishṇavī, Vārāhī, Indrānī and Chāmuṇḍā. The *Bṛihatsaṃhitā*, *Vishṇudharmottara Purāṇa* (III.73), and some Āgamas state that the Mātṛikās should be sculptured in accordance with their respective gods and should have similar emblems. The *Agni Purāṇa* (XX.18-22), Āgamas, *Rūpa-Maṇḍana*, etc., however, detail out their iconographic features thus: four-faced fair complexioned Brahmāṇī should ride a swan and hold *kuṇḍa*, *akshapātra*, *akshamālā* and *sruk* in her four hands; Māheśvarī should be seated on a bull and carry a bow and arrow in her right hands and a discus in the left; Kaumārī should ride a peacock and wield a spear; seated on Garuḍa, Vaishṇavī should carry *śaṅkha*, *chakra*, *gadā*, and *padma*; Vārāhī seated on a buffalo should have a boar's face and hold a staff and bowl or plough and *śakti* or *ghaṇṭā*, *chāmara*, *gadā* and *chakra*. Indrānī should be seated on the elephant with a thunderbolt in her left hand; Chāmuṇḍā should ride a corpse, have three eyes, erect hair, emaciated body, wear tiger-skin and hold in her hands a bowl and trident with others in *abhaya* and *varada mudrā* or holding a goad, sword, shield, noose, bow, staff and hatchet.

The images of the Mātṛikās are carved in a group or individually, in the panels of the lintels of the doorways or on other architectural parts. Though the earliest evidence from the neighbouring state of Haryana comes from Gokarṇa-kā-Tālāb, Rohtak where five of the seven Mātṛikās of the Kushāṇa period have survived sitting in European style[70] on a loose piece,[71] yet there is great paucity of the Mātṛikā reliefs from Punjab. Only two images of Brahmāṇī and Māheśvarī have come to our notice.

### Brahmāṇī

The exact provenance of this sole example of the Brahmāṇī image is not known precisely but it is believably recovered from the Punjab. This beautiful image shows the Mātṛikā wearing *karaṇḍa-mukuṭa*, necklace, *vaikaksyaka*, *keyūras*, *karṇa-kuṇḍalas*, *aṅgadas*, *valayas*, and *nūpuras*, seated in *sukhāsana* with a goose carved on the seat, holding a rosary in the *varada* normal right hand, a lotus in the rear right and a leaf-like object in the normal let hand (Pl. 136). The back slab forming the aureole behind the head and the portion of the right leg are broken. Nevertheless, this is a beautiful image ascribable to *circa* tenth century CE.[72]

### Māheśvarī

The figure of Māheśvarī carved on an architectural piece belonging to a Śiva temple at Majhur is displayed in the VVRI Museum at Hoshiarpur (Pl. 137). She stands on a pedestal in *dvi-bhaṅga* wearing exquisitely bedecked *karaṇḍa-mukuṭa*, ear ornaments, armlets, bracelets, necklace with pendant string falling on her left waist from between her breasts, *dhotī* held in position by an elaborate girdle forming loops, tassels and sash on the thighs, *nūpuras* and a long garland. Her face has suffered damage. She holds trident and snake in her rear pair of hands, normal right is suspended and seems to be holding a cock perched on a plantain plant while the *pralamba* natural left holds a water vessel. If the natural right hand really holds a cock, it is interesting and provides this image uniqueness. The left foot of the goddess is slightly splayed outward. The figure is perfectly balanced and exhibits excellent chisel work. Stylistically, it may be assigned to twelfth century CE.

### Kaumārī

An architectural piece of about tenth century CE from Dholbaha shows a very mutilated niched figure of a four-handed female deity holding a lance in the proper rear hand and a diminutive bird, probably a peacock, near her right foot (Pl. 138). As such the deity may be identified with Kaumārī.

## RIVER GODDESSES

River goddesses Gaṅgā and Yamunā riding crocodile and tortoise respectively came to be invariably shown on the proper right and left of the doorframes from early medieval period. In the Gupta period they occupied the T-shaped frames on the top corners of the door-surrounds. Unfortunately we do not have any standing temples in the whole of Punjab but surely such figures must have existed at least on the temples of this region also from the early medieval period. A five-band doorjamb from Dholbaha shows Gaṅgā standing in *ābhaṅga* with her hip slightly accentuated towards her left under the canopy of a full blown lotus holding a blossomed lotus by its long stalk in her *pralamba* right hand and probably a water flask in the hanging left hand which has suffered some damage like her face (Pl. 139). Crocodile, the vehicle of the goddess, has been shown near her left foot with snout turned upwards as if looking towards her. The *dhammilla* coiffure, earrings, necklace, armlets, wristlets, nether garment secured by an elaborate girdle and long garland are discernible in spite of the indifferent state of preservation and damage suffered by the image which may have originally been a beautiful representation of the deity belonging to the eleventh century CE. Yamunā too has been found on an architectural piece from Dholbaha (Pl. 140). With face and body slightly turned towards her right, she is shown as standing on a lotus placed on the back of a tortoise to left. Both the hands are damaged but their stance indicates that the right hand supported a lotus raised to the level of the head and the *pralamba* left hand also held a lotus by its long stalk. She thus seems to have been equated with and representative of Lakshmī. Bearing a *karaṇḍa-mukuṭa* and usual dress and ornaments including a long garland, it must have originally been an elegant image of *circa* tenth century.

A *pedyā* from Kharar shows Yamunā standing in *dvi-bhaṅga* with hip accentuated towards her right supporting the water pot in her right hand and holding the free end of her *uttarīya* in the *pralamba* left hand accompanied by a male attendant holding in his right hand a lotus twig which branches out to serve as the canopies over their heads in the form of drooping full-blossomed lotus flowers (Pl. 141). His suspended left hand holds the sash. Both the figures are very exquisitely carved with usual items of drapery and ornamentation, which may be assigned to *circa* tenth century on stylistic grounds.

Another *pedyā* of a doorjamb showing the river goddess Yamunā attended by a female figure and accompanied by Padma-purusha is preserved in a modern temple at Sunam (Pl. 142). This must have originally been a part of a tenth century Vishṇu temple at Sunam. The river-goddess stands gracefully slightly turned to her right under the canopy of a full-blown lotus. She holds a water pot in her right hand held near the shoulder and the end of the upper garment in her suspended left hand. She bears a beautifully bedecked *dhammilla* hair-coiffure and wears large earrings, a double-stranded pearl necklace with one string suspended to the belly from between the round rotund breasts, armlets, beaded bracelets, anklets and lower garment secured by a waistband. Her attendant is also similarly dressed but stands in *gopālāsana* holding a lotus twig from which one branch rises straight with a full blown flower at the top and two other branches turn sideways to serve as canopies of drooping blossomed lotus flowers at their ends on the head of the river goddess and jointly over the heads of the female attendant and Padma-purusha standing behind her. Padma-purusha supports a lotus in his right hand near the chest with left akimbo. Padma-purusha also stands in *gopālāsana*. Just above the *pedyā* may be seen a *naga* with human body and serpentine tail in *añjali-mudrā* on the *antaśśākhā*, a couple (badly damaged) on the *rūpa-śākhā* and a leogryph on the *bāhya-śākhā*. The *nāga-śākhā* and Padma-purusha vouch for it to be the part of the door-surround of a Vishṇu temple.[73]

## NOTES AND REFERENCES

1. V.S. Agrawala, "The Devī-Māhātmya", *Journal of Indian History*, Vol. 43, No. 3 (1964), pp. 823-32.
2. Cf. *Mārkaṇḍeya Purāṇa* (Ed. Panchanan Tarkaratna, Calcutta, Śaka 1812), Nārāyaṇī-Stuti, Ch. 91, v. 51 –
   *Itthaṃ yadā yadā bādhā dānavotthā bhavishyati /*
   *Tadā tadāvatīryāhaṃ karishyamyarisaṃkshayam//*
3. '*Pārvatī parvatodbhavā*', *Aparājitapṛichchhā*, 222.9; *Rūpamaṇḍana*, V.3. Also *Kumārasambhava* I.26: *Pārvatītyabhijanena nāmnā.*
4. *Mārkaṇḍeya Purāṇa*, Ch. 85, v. 40: *Śarīrakoshādyattasyāḥ Pārvattya niḥsṛitāmbikā/Kauśikīti samasteshu tato gīyate//.*
5. *Kumārasambhava* I. 26; *Brahma Purāṇa* 34.86.

6. R.D. Trivedi, *Iconography of Pārvatī*, Delhi 1981, pp. 22-23. Cf. J.N. Banerjea (*DHI*, p. 492) who explains Aparṇā as 'nude'. See also *Brahma Purāṇa* 34, 85.
7. S.B. Singh, *Brahmanical Icons in Northern India*, New Delhi, 1977, p. 149.
8. R.D. Banerji, *Bas Reliefs of Badami*, Memoirs of the Archaeological Survey of India, No. 25, 1928, p. 10, PI. VI. a.
9. R. Sen Gupta, "The Panels of Kalyāṇasundaramūrti at Ellora", *Lalit Kala*, No. 7 (1960), p. 14.
10. K. Deva, "Iconography of Pārvatī as Tapasvinī", *Bharati*, Varanasi, N.S., No. 1, 1968, p. 2.
11. S.B. Singh, *op. cit.*, pp. 149-51; Trivedi, *op. cit.*, pp. 35ff.
12. Lion as the vehicle of Durgā (Pārvatī as the consort of Śiva) is well known. The myth of its creation from the wrath of Pārvatī against Śiva is given in details in the *Matsya* (Ch. 153, pp. 124ff) and *Padma Purāṇa* (Sṛishṭikhaṇḍa, 45.54-65, p. 423). It is interesting to note that deer is also depicted as her mount in some Pallava sculptures. See R. Nagaswami, *Tantric Cult of South India*, Delhi, 1982, Pls. 35 and 40. The depiction of both of animals, however, seems to suggest the sylvan environment in which Pārvatī performed the *pañchatapas*, as pointed out by Trivedi (*op. cit.*, pp. 37-39). The depiction of two deer in some of the images further supports this view.
13. Trivedi, *op. cit.*, p.60.
14. Handa (2006), *op. cit.*, pp. 153-57, Pls. 187-91. Thaplyal has identified the *Śālabhañjikā* depicted on two of Sunet sigils with Pārvatī (*SAIS*, pp. 175-76) which is only probable and not sure.
15. Handa (1978), *op. cit.*, Pl. XXII.
16. *DHI*, pp. 489ff.
17. *EHI*, I, pp. 356ff.
18. *Ibid.*, pp. 341-42.
19. S.B. Singh, *op. cit.*, p. 154.
20. Sadhu Ram, "A Unique Terracotta Mould of Durgā from Panjab", *VIJ*, IX, pp. 137-38.
21. Ohri, Pl. 6.40; Berkson, Ill. 169.
22. *EHI*, I, p. 342. For a recent analysis of the iconography of Kshemaṅkarī, see A.L. Srivastava, "Kṣemaṅkarī: A Riddle in her Identification," *Kalā: The Journal of Indian Art History Congress*, Vol. XVI (2010-2011), pp. 1-7.
23. *Padma Purāṇa*, V.30, 2ff.
24. Handa (2006), *op. cit.*, pp. 158-59, Pls. 198-201.
25. For an account of his birth and exploits, see *Agni Purāṇa*, chs. 17-20; *Brahmāṇḍa Purāṇa* II.19, 40-41; *Matsya Purāṇa* 122.59-60; *Vāyu Purāṇa* 49.37; *Vishṇu Purāṇa* II.4, 27; etc.
26. *EHI*, I, p. 366.
27. Cf. *Mārkaṇḍeya Purāṇa*, Devī-Māhātmya (III.37).
28. *DHI*, p. 498.
29. *East and West*, New Series, Vol. XIX, Nos. 3-4, p. 420; Cf. *Padma Purāṇa* I.35.
30. *EHI*, I, p. 354.
31. *Ibid.*, pp. 348ff.
32. R.C. Agrawala, "Some Sculptures of Durga Mahishasuramardini from Rajasthan", *Brahma Vidya*, New Series, Adyar, Vol.19, Nos. 1-2, pp. 37-46; "A Terracotta plaque of Mahishamardini from Nagar", *Lalit Kala*, Nos. 1-2, 1955-56, p. 73; "The Goddess Mahisasuramardini in Early Indian Art", *Artibus Asiae*, Vol. XXI, no. 2, pp. 124-27, Figs. 1-2; H. Hartel, "Some Results of the Excavation at Sonkh; A Preliminary Report", in *German Scholars on India*, Vol. II, Bombay, 1976, pp. 74-78 and 92, Figs. 10-36; Gourishankar De, "The Earliest Mahishamardini Image of India", paper presented at the 42nd Annual Session of the Indian History Congress, Bodh Gaya, 1981; B.N. Mukherjee, "Foreign Elements in Iconograph of Mahishasuramardini – The War Goddess of India", *Zeitschrift der Deutschen Morgenldndischen Gesellschaft*, Supplement VI, Vom 21, Bis 25, Marz 1983, pp. 406-08; etc.
33. J.Ph. Vogel, *Catalogue of the Archaeological Museum at Mathura*, Allahabad, 1910, p. 97; V.S. Agrawala, "Mathura Terracottas", *The Journal of the United Provinces Historical Society*, Lucknow, Vol. IX, Part II, pp. 32ff, Fig. 47 and 53; "A Catalogue of the Brahmanical Images in Mathura Art", *Ibid.*, Vol. XXII, 1949, p. 158; Odette Viennot, "The Goddess Mahishasuramardini in Kushana Art", *Artibus Asiae*, Vol. XIX, nos. 3-4, 1956, pp. 368-73, Fig. 1; R.C. Agrawala (1958), *op. cit.*, pp. 124-27; "Mahisamardini Plaque in the

Gurukul Museum at Jhajjar, Haryana", in *Ajaya-Śrī: Recent Studies in Indology (Prof. Ajay Mitra Shastri Felicitation Volume)*, Vol. II, Delhi, 1989, pp. 397-98, Pl. 52; Hartel (1956), *op. cit.*, p. 92, Fig. 36; Gritli Von Mitterwallner, "The Kusana Type of the Goddess Mahisasuramardini as Compared to the Gupta and Medieval Types", in *German Scholars on India*, Vol. II, Fig. 1-3; S. Czuma, *Kushana Sculpture – Images from Early India*, Cleveland, 1985, pp. 105-06; Mukherjee (1983), *op. cit.*, Figs. 3-9.

34. Hartel (1976), *op. cit.*, Fig. 36; Mitterwallner, *op. cit.*, Figs. 1-3; Mukherjee, *op. cit.*, p. 406, Figs. 3-7.
35. R. C. Agrawala (1958), *op. cit.*, p. 123; (1989), *op. cit.*, pp. 397-98, pl. 52; Mukherjee, *op. cit.*, Fig. 7.
36. Mitterwallner, *op. cit.*, p. 205.
37. *Mārkaṇḍeya Purāṇa*, Vaṅgavāsī Steam Press, Calcutta, Ch. 83, vv, 37-39.
38. Nileshvari Y. Desai, *Ancient Indian Society, Religion and Mythology as Depicted in the Markandeya Purana: A Critical Study*, Baroda, 1968, pp. 3-4.
39. M. Seshadri, "Mahishasuramardini", *Half-Yearly Journal of the Mysore University*, Mysore, Section A - Art, Vol. XXII, no. 2, pp. 1-28 & Pls. 1-43.
40. Handa (2008), *op. cit.*, pp. 159ff, Pls. 202-05.
41. V.S. Agrawala, *Gupta Art (A History of Indian Art in the Gupta Period 300-600 AD)*, compiled and edited by P.K. Agrawala, Varanasi, 1977, p. 53, Text fig. 26-27, Pl. III.42; P.K. Agrawala, *Gupta-kālīna Kalā evaṃ Vāstu*, Varanasi, 1994, pp. 59-60, Figs. 161 and 167; V.S. Agrawala, "Terracotta Figurines of Ahichchhatrā, District Bareilly, U.P.", *Ancient India*, Bulletin of the Archaeological Survey of India, New Delhi, No. 4 (1947-48), p. 111, Fig. 1.6-7.
42. Ohri (1991), *op. cit.*, p. 126; S.M. Sethi, *A Catalogue of Stone Sculptures in the Museums of Himachal Pradesh*, Shimla, 2002, p. 29, Fig. 15. Bearing Acc. No. 83.146. This image is now preserved in the State Museum, Shimla. Sethi spells the name of the site as Dhogi.
43. Ohri, *op. cit.*, p. 123.
44. Berkson (p. 363, Ill. 368) dates it to *circa* ninth century CE. Manmohan Kumar (*loc. cit.*, pp. 51-52) wrongly dates it to *c.* tenth-eleventh centuries.
45. Handa (1987), *op. cit.*, Pl. 11.
46. Handa (2006), *op. cit.*, p. 168, Pl. 217. Another very elegant Pratihāra figure from Sirsa also shows similar disposition of all the hands though the third right hand is shown as taking out the arrow from the quiver placed on the ground (*Ibid.*, pp. 167-68, Pl. 215).
47. Handa (1979), *loc. cit.*
48. *Lalit Kalā*, 12 (1962), Pl. XVI.8; *Bhāratīya Vidyā*, XX-XXI (1960-61), p. 304, Pl. IV.
49. *Ibid.*, p. 47, Pl. XXX.2.
50. Though the fourth demoniacal face of Kapila was also carved on the back in the hills of Himachal Pradesh and Kashmir, yet it was the three-headed figures which outnumber those with the Kapila head at the back. For the depiction of tri-cephalous Vaikuṇṭhī, see Michael W. Meister, "Mapping Masrur's Iconography", in Gerd J.R. Mevissen and Arundhati Banerji (eds.), *Prajñādhara: Essays on Asian Art History Epigraphy and Culture in Honour of Gouriswar Bhattacharya*, Vol. 1, New Delhi, 2009, pp. 89-94, Pl. 7.9. I have seen with my friend Prof. Ashvini Agrawal a beautiful scan of the Vaikuṇṭhī image of Masrur and it seems to belong stylistically to *circa* 8th century CE. It is notable that images of the Buddhist goddess of Light and Victory, Mārīchī, are also depicted with another human face on left and sow face on right [Claudine Bautze-Picron, "Between Śākyamuni and Vairocana: Mārīcī, Goddess of Light and Victory", *Silk Road Art and Archaeology*, Kamakura, Vol. 7 (2001), pp. 263-310] but since these images are known only from Bangladesh, West Bengal, Bihar and Orissa, they do not seem to have served as the model.
51. *DHI*, p. 408.
52. Ohri, *op. cit*.
53. Handa (2006), *op. cit.*, pp. 65-73, Pls. 77-87.
54. K.V. Soundara Rajan, "A Devī Cult Nucleus at Jagat, Rajasthan", *Vishveshvaranand Indological Journal*, Hoshiarpur, Vol. I, Part 1 (March 963), pp. 136-37; R.C. Agrawala, "Khajuraho of Rajasthan: The Temple of Ambikā at Jagat", *Artibus Asiae*, X (1964), pp. 43-65 and plates.
55. H. Haertel, *Indische Sculpturen*, 1, Berlin, 1960, p. 68, no. 28; B.N. Mukherjee, "Foreign Elements in Iconography of Mahishasuramardini – The War Goddess of India", *Zeitschrift der Deutschen*

*Morgenlandischen Gesellschaft*, Supplement VI, Vom. 21, Bis 25, Marz 1983, fig. 7; Handa (2006), *op. cit.*, Pl. 203.

56. *DHI*, P. 370. See also Rai Govinda Chandra, *Prāchīna Bhārata meṃ Lakshmī Pratimā – Eka Adhyayana*, Varanasi, 1964.
57. B. Chatterjee, "Antiquity of the Concept of Lakshṃī", in *Foreigners in Ancient India and Lakṣmī and Sarasvatī in Art and Literature* (Ed. D.C. Sircar), Calcutta, 1970, pp. 152-57.
58. *DHI*, p. 370.
59. Cf. *Mahābhārata* II.10, 19; III.168, 3; etc.
60. *DHI*, pp. 133ff; Sircar (1970), *op. cit.*, pp. 112-31.
61. Cf. *Padmasthā padmahastā cha gajotkshiptaghaṭaplutā /*
*Śrīḥ padmamālinī chaiva Kālikākṛitireva cha //*
62. Handa (1985), *op. cit.*, p. 123. See also Daivakaraṇi (2010), *op. cit.*, p. 27, no. 125.
63. *SAIS*, p. 102. Cf. Handa (1985), *loc. cit.*
64. Handa (1985), *loc. cit.*
65. Sharma and Kumar, *op. cit.*, p. 61, Pl. IV.1.
66. P.K. Mishra, "A Unique Sealing from Ropar", in Devendra Handa (Ed.), *Oriental Numismatic Studies*, Vol. 2, New Delhi, 1999, pp. 51-52, Pls. IV-V.
67. Devendra Handa, *Early Indian Coins from Sugh*, New Delhi, 2006, p. 86, Pl. XV.1.
68. Daivakarṇi, *loc. cit.*
69. *DHI*, p. 383.
70. Cf. J.C. Harle, *op. cit.*, Pl. 27.
71. Devendra Handa, "Gupta Reliefs from Haryana", *Bulletin of Museums and Archaeology, U.P.*, Lucknow, No. 35-36 (1985), p. 16, Fig. 2.
72. Handa (1983), *op. cit.*, p. 30, fig. 9 on p. 25.
73. Handa (1987), *op. cit.*, p. 113, Pl. XI.

# 6

# Sūrya

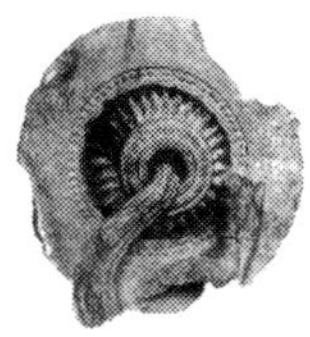

Sūrya, the brightest amongst the visible celestial luminous bodies and the 'one who animates or arouses (the world)', has been worshipped by mankind since time immemorial in an aniconic form initially and iconic form later on.[1] The world over there seems to have existed the tendency to deify natural phenomena. Described in the *Ṛigveda* (I.164, 46) as 'the beautiful-winged celestial bird Garutmān,' 'a little white brilliant steed brought by Ushas' (*RV* VII.73, 3) and 'moving on a car driven by one, several or seven fleet and ruddy steeds' (*RV* I.115, 3-4; VII.60, 3; 63, 2; etc.), he is shown later as riding on a one-wheeled (*eka-chakra*) chariot drawn by four, five or seven horses with Aruṇa, a brother of Garutmān, as his charioteer, attended on either side by arrow-shooting Ushā and Pratyushā personifying the different aspects of 'dawn' and signifying the driving away of darkness. Lotus, symbolic of the presence of sun in which it blossoms, became his attribute in both the hands to show ubiquity. Lotus also symbolizes the beauty of creation,[2] which can only be realized in the light provided by sun. His name Aryaman, Vivasvān and Mitra have their foreign parallels.[3] In the early centuries of the current era, the import of the Maga (Bhojaka)[4] priests from Iran gave a new turn to Sun worship in India. Scythian impact brought for Sūrya long boots, *avyanga*,[5] acolytes wearing typical northern dress (*udīchya-veśa*), and sometimes a dagger also, thus causing a reorientation in the creation of his images, in North India in particular, and the Paurāṇic mythology played its part in providing him wives and sons, which too are sometimes shown on his images. Described as 'the soul of the movable and the immovable things' in the *Ṛigveda* (I.115, 1), Sūrya did not take much time to become 'the lord of the gods' (*deveśvara* – *Mbh.* II.50, 16). The lord of light became the embodiment of the Hindu trinity in the Gupta period and various cults vied with each other in identifying their Supreme deities with Sūrya. 'Supreme Godhead' of Sūrya became established[6] and Sun worship spread far and wide, in every direction, like his rays.

Literary evidence furnishes evidence of the continuity of the worship of the Sun throughout from the period of the *Ṛigveda* onwards. The ubiquity of the sun symbol on the coins of the punch-marked series (except the latest examples), the coins issued by rulers with their names ending in Mitra found from various parts of the country, and Kushāṇa coins with the figure of

Miiro (Mihira = Sun), Helios, etc. show that Sun-worship has remained popular throughout the early centuries before and after the current era.[7]

We have a dynasty ruling over Punjab whose kings bore Mitra-ending names – Aja-Mitra, Mahi-Mitra, Mahābhūti-Mitra, Indra-Mitra and Bhānu-Mitra. Their copper coins bearing Brāhmī and Kharoshṭhī legends have been found from the Manaswal plateau of Hoshiarpur, Ropar, Sunet, Samana and Ghuram (District Patiala) and are datable to *circa* second-first centuries BCE.[8] Sometimes we find the aniconic representation of the sun as a wheel in art. Many seals/ sealings from Sunet show this device. Besides these, the copper seals of Mihira from Sanghol and Śrī-Mitrasoma from Sunet and terracotta sealings with the legend *Raveḥ, Śrī-Mitrasya, Mitra-devasya, Śrī-Sūryasya* with horse above, *Śrī-Sūryabhadrasya* and *Mantri-Mitraghosha* from the latter site do indicate the esteem with which the solar divinity was held.[9]

Numerous coins showing the depiction of fire-altar have been found from various parts of the country, including Punjab. The device is generally believed to have come on Indian coins as an impact of the Sassanians who were sun-worshippers and depicted the fire-altar on their coins. The depiction of fire-altar on a sealing of Ripu-śalya from Sunet may be taken to be the result of the Sassanian influence. The sealing of Śrī-Veṅṅa from the same site also shows this device.[10]

Places bearing the name like Surajpur and pools or tanks known as Suraj-kund are found practically over the whole of the country including Punjab. Sunam probably bore the name of Surajpur in the medieval period as indicated by its reference in Alberuni's *Kitab-ul-Hind*.[11] Archaeological relics of Sunam and the area around it also indicate the region to have been the centre of sun worship.

The most elegant and almost complete image of Sūrya was unearthed at Mard Khera to the southeast of Sunam on 19 September 1980 (Pl. 143) by a few village girls while digging earth from the old mound.[11] People from all over the region flocked to see it. People refer to the place of its discovery as the Suraj Kund and believe that there was a temple of the Sun god here. The image was immersed in the Suraj Kund to save it from iconoclastic invaders. Though the officials of the state and central governments of the departments of archaeology were informed of this discovery, yet in their anxiety of losing it to those departments, they started worshipping it by offering coins and other things. The villagers ultimately constructed a small octagonal enclosure and installed it inside.[12] Made of light buff coloured sandstone and measuring 122 X 86 cm, it shows the god standing in *samapāda-sthānaka-mudrā* on a lotus seat placed on the central projection of the *sapta-ratha* pedestal. The god wears a high cylindrical crown adorned with diamonds, jewels, rosettes and loops of pearl strings; ear ornaments; pearl necklaces; coat of mail called *avyaṅga*; undergarment secured by an elaborate girdle forming loops on the thighs with free ends falling straight on the shanks and touching the knees. Double-incised lines represent the folds of the nether garment. The god wears long boots reminiscent of the Scythian impact and characteristic of the North India Sun images. Rings around the thumb and other fingers may also be seen. There is an exquisitely carved lotiform halo behind the head. The scarf hanging from over the arms down to the lower part of the legs simulate the *vanamālā*. The hair of the god has been combed in curls. There is a *tilaka* mark on the forehead and a diamond-shaped *śrīvatsa* on the chest. The eyes are half-closed and the eyebrows look like a curved bow (*chāpākāra*). The tip of the nose is slightly damaged. The face is oval with plump cheeks. A beatific smile adds to the grace of the figure. In the two hands of the god are shown minutely carved full blown lotus flowers held by their stalks.

On the right and left of the feet are depicted well-dressed male and female figures probably representing the donor couple adoring the deity with folded hands. Just behind these figures stand Daṇḍa and Piṅgala, the two acolytes on the proper left and right of the god. Both wear typical northerners' dress, *udīchyaveśa* and pleasing ornaments. The Scythian *kullah*-type conical cap is noteworthy. Piṅgala is bearded, has moustaches and holds a stylus and leaf in his right and left hands. Daṇḍa supports a spear in his right hand and his left hand rests on the respective thigh. Both of them stand gracefully, slightly turned towards their Lord. They are followed on the receding *rathas* of the pedestal on either side by female fly-whiskers, probably Chhāyā and Suvarchā, the consorts of Sūrya, holding a lotus in the hand towards the god and *chowrie* in the other. They bear prominent *dhammilla* coiffures bedecked with almond-shaped jewels in front, pearl strings, clips and clasps. Circular discs in their ears, *ekāvalis* and pearl necklaces, armlets, bracelets, nether garments held in position by girdles and long scarves may also be seen on their persons. On the extreme recesses stand the sons of the god, each holding a nectar flask in the left hand with right disposed in *abhaya*, allaying fear of the worshippers. They bear *jaṭā-mukuṭa* and usual ornaments representing either Aśvinī-kumāras (who are generally shown as horse-headed) or the two Manus.

At the waist level of the god above the figures of Daṇḍa and Piṅgala stand partly concealed behind the hands of the god outward facing Ushā and Pratyushā, shooting arrows from the bows held in their hands. The extreme bands of the back slab at this level carry *aśva-vyāla* figures jumping outwards. On either side of the head of Sūrya are shown Brahmā and Vishṇu on his right and left, respectively. The juvenile tri-cephalous Brahmā is shown as seated in *sukhāsana* on a lotus seat holding *sruk* and book in the rear right and left hands, a water pot in the principal left with normal right in *abhaya*, holding a rosary. Vishṇu on the other side also sits in *sukhāsana* on the back of the anthropomorphic Garuḍa, who is depicted in a flying posture. The quadrumanous god holds mace and disc in the extra pair of hands, conch in the proper left with natural right hand in protection affording pose. There is a heart-shaped gloriole behind the heads of Brahmā and a round one behind Vishṇu's head. Just below the steles on either side are the stylized *makara-mukhas* holding in their elephant-trunk like snouts the stalks of lotuses on which stand female fly-whiskers. Just above these two deities are carved the garland-bearing *vidyādhara* couples in flying postures.

Though crowded by various figures, yet the image is distinctive by the minute care provided to each of them and the fineness of chisel work. Somewhat marred by the ignorant villagers by their touch and application of oil (Pl. 144), this twelfth century image was stolen some years back and never recovered.

A gigantic image of Sūrya, said to have been found from Sunam, is now preserved in the Department of Archaeology and Museums, Haryana at Panchkula (Index No. 1/101).[15] This more than a human size icon was so heavy that it could not be lifted without a crane and seems to have, therefore, been broken into parts of which the bust and the leg portions (Pl. 145) are the biggest. The middle portion perhaps was shattered into numerous pieces because of the impact of the stroke of the big hammer and since they could not be pieced together, they were not collected and preserved except the two pieces showing the hands holding the lotus flowers. The head shows *kirīṭa-mukuṭa* adorned with pearls and jewels and ears with bejewelled rings. The face is unfortunately mutilated but the almond-shaped eyes, plump cheeks and full lips may still be discerned on an oval face. The upper part of the back slab is elliptical and serves as the aureole behind the head of the god. It has a beaded edge. On either side of the head are depicted *vidyādhara* couples, the male in the flying posture holding a wreath in both of his hands and the female seated on his extended back leg in *añjali-mudrā*. Both wear pearl necklets, bracelets and beautiful earrings. Their coiffures too are quite pleasing. Below the steles carrying the *vidyādhara* couples may be seen the conventional *makara-mukhas*, the one on the proper left of the god being damaged. The lower portion of the image is better preserved and shows some interesting and characteristic features. The ends of the triple-folded scarf fall down gracefully from over the forearms. A square spacer with a lotus motif adorns the scarf between the legs at its lowest point. The golden chain which secured the *dhotī* falls straight on the legs touching the knees after forming a loop on each shank. The nether garment is quite heavy and almost clings to the legs showing the body lines. Boots on the feet of the god are also very clear. The god stands on the central projection of the *pañcha-ratha* pedestal flanked on either side with pursuivants, Daṇḍa on the left and Piṅgala on the right, both followed by female figures who may be identified with Chhāyā and Suvarchā. The grace of the posture of these subsidiary figures is worthy of note. Both Daṇḍa and Piṅgala, wearing typical Scythian conical helmets, stand with their waists bent towards the god but busts held across the waists. The female figures stand cross-legged in *gopālāsana* but have the upper parts of their bodies almost parallel to those of Daṇḍa and Piṅgala who wear a diamond-shaped *śrīvatsa* on their chests and wear beautiful dresses and ornaments. The female figures too have been carved with minute care and are very pleasing. The image may be assigned to *circa* tenth century on stylistic grounds.

There is more evidence of the existence of Sun temple/s at Sunam. A part of an architectural piece of about 10th century measuring 35 X 19 cm shows Sūrya in pedimented niches in standing and seated postures (Pl. 146). A small fragment recovered from Sunam shows the bearded Piṅgala holding pen and leaf in the two hands followed by a female figure, probably Sūrya's spouse, wearing a *dhammilla* coiffure. It seems to be a part of the Sun image of *circa* eighth-ninth century at Sunam. Two more fragments confirm and corroborate the evidence of the existence of Sun images and temples at Sunam during ninth-tenth centuries. Both these represent *vidyādhara* figures, measuring 12 X 10 and 12 X 8 cm respectively, and may have originally been parts of the different Sūrya images as prominent full-blossomed lotus flowers may still be seen below these figures. One of these which may have adorned the proper left hand side of the god (Pl. 147) hovers in the sky near the head of the god behind which was carved a lotiform halo still partially preserved in the extant relief. The semi-celestial bears a *dhammilla* coiffure and wears earrings, pearl necklace and bracelets and holds the garland which too shows beaded decoration. The other fragment depicts a more slender *vidyādhara* who holds a twisted garland (Pl. 148). But for earrings, other ornaments are not visible on his person. These figures betray slight stylistic differences and may be assigned to ninth and tenth centuries CE.[16]

Another fine image of Sūrya comes from Samuran in Sunam *tehsil*. Made of coarse-grained buff coloured sandstone, this independently carved image measures 46.5 X 28.5 cm and depicts the god in the same way as noticed above standing to front on the central offset of a *pañcha-ratha* pedestal accompanied by Piṅgala holding stylus and leaf followed by a female figure (Suvarchā or a fly-whisker) in *gopālāsana* on the successive recesses on his proper right and Daṇḍa carrying a long spear in his right hand with left resting on his bent left knee followed by Chhāyā or a fly-whisker in asymmetrical poses (Pl. 149). The heads of both the attendant figures on the proper right hand side are damaged. Sūrya as usual wears a long cylindrical crown, slightly broken on one side, and other items of drapery and ornaments and has a big *śiraśchakra* bearing lotus-leaf decorations with garland bearing *vidyādharas* on either side of his head partly covered by lotuses held in his hands. Notable, however, is the depiction of a diminutive figure of standing Pṛithvī at the feet of Sūrya. Similar depiction of the Earth Goddess Mahāśvetā at the feet of Sūrya may be seen in some images from Osian in Rajasthan.[17] This is a Pratihāra image of late tenth century CE.

While excavating at Singh-Bhagwantpur about 9 km south of Ropar on Chandigarh-Ropar highway during 1980, we had procured an image of Sūrya as the surface find showing the god standing to front holding as usual full-blossomed lotus flowers in the two hands, wearing the cylindrical crown and the coat of mail, accompanied by his acolytes Daṇḍa and Piṅgala wearing typical northerners' dress (Pl. 150). Sūrya also supports a scarf on his arms in simulation of

Vishṇu's *vanamālā*. The image is broken below the knees of the god. It is a late Pratihāra piece of *circa* eleventh century preserved in the museum of the Department of Ancient Indian History, Culture and Archaeology, Panjab University, Chandigarh.

A part of the pedestal of an image of Sūrya has also been noticed at Kharar. It shows the three attendant figures of Daṇḍa, Sūrya's consort and son Āśvin standing slightly turned to their right in beautiful *dvibhaṅga* poses on the receding recesses of the *sapta-ratha* pedestal. Daṇḍa holds a long sceptre in his right hand with left akimbo, Sūrya's spouse supports a lotus with her right hand and the left hangs down gracefully holding the scarf; the horse-headed Āśvin holds a water pot in his right hand and left one is *kaṭi-hasta*. All the figures are unfortunately quite worn out. The fragment may be dated to tenth century CE.[18]

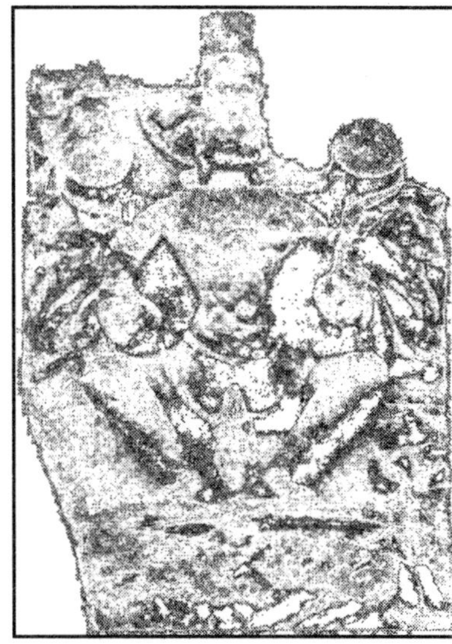

**Fig. 28.** Sūrya from Doghi.

Doghi near Una, now in Himachal Pradesh, was a part of district Hoshiarpur before the reorganization of the state of Punjab in 1966. An image of sandstone Sūrya datable to late tenth or early eleventh century CE was found from this site (Fig. 28). The god is depicted as squatting in the Kushāṇa style on a *tri-ratha* pedestal carved with seven prancing horses reined by the diminutive figure of the charioteer Aruṇa, who is wearing a conical cap and stands at his knees. The god Sūrya holds as usual lotuses in his two hands raised to the level of the shoulders. Between his feet is shown the diminutive figure of the Earth goddess Pṛithvī standing facing in *sama-pāda-sthānaka-mudrā*. On the right buttress of the pedestal stands Sūrya's acolyte Daṇḍa holding a sceptre in both his hands. The corresponding recess on the proper right, which may have carried the figure of Piṅgala, is broken. In the middle of the back slab at the waist level are shown Ushā and Pratyushā in warrior's posture shooting arrows. The lotiform aureole behind the head of Sūrya has survived only partially.[19] Ohri has observed that

> It is made in a style which had developed in this area by the amalgamation of the traits of the northwest and the North Indian sculptures. This image, though damaged is significant as a work of art. The figure is wrought over a stele in such a high relief that shadows appearing at its sides create the impression as if it is not attached to the slab. Tense muscles and geometric form of this image make it dynamic and convey a feeling as if the figure of Surya is moving forward. The torso of the figure is so modelled that with its slender waist and well-built shoulders and chest, it acquires a triangular shape which lends the figure an intense vitality.[20]

The tradition of Sun worship seems to have continued in Punjab up to the late medieval period also as is indicated by a small plaque recovered from the old mound of Bassi Gujaran near Chamkaur Sahib in district Rupnagar (Pl. 151). It shows the seated god wearing a crown, coat of mail and holding two lotus flowers in his hands. Under the figure is carved a lotus with two stylized horses on the sides representative of the chariot drawn by horses.

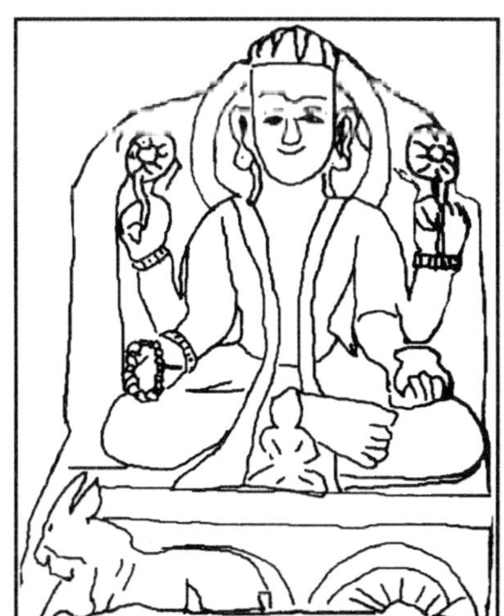

**Fig. 29.** Dhātṛi Sūrya from Panj Kalyan.

Still more interesting is a marble image at Panj Kalyan in district Patiala (Fig. 29) showing the god seated to front cross-legged on a chariot drawn by horses and holding the blossomed lotus flowers in the rear pair of hands while the normal right hold a rosary and the natural left a water pot. A broad long scarf is worn like a necklace with its free ends falling in front across the calves. Aruṇa, the charioteer, is seated to front with folded hands near the feet of the god. Sūrya wears all usual ornaments but is bare foot. This depiction conforms to the Dhātṛi form of Sūrya which is rather rare in this part of the country.[21]

## NOTES AND REFERENCES

1. Lalta Prasad Pandey, *Sun-Worship in Ancient India*, Delhi-Patna-Varanasi, 1971, pp. 1ff; V.C. Srivastava, *Sun-Worship in Ancient India*, Delhi, 1971, pp. 122-26.
2. Chamanlal Gautam, *Devavāda kā Vaijñānika Svarūpa* (Hindi) I, Vishṇu-Rahasya, Bareilly, 1967, pp. 375-404.
3. Surya Kanta, *Vaidika Devaśāstra* (Hindi), Delhi, 1961, pp. 98-103.
4. According to the *Bhavishya Purāṇa* (ch. 134), the Magas were brought from Śākadvīpa (Iran) to serve as the priests of a Sun temple erected on the bank of the river Chandrabhāgā by Sāmba, son of Kṛishṇa from Jāmbavatī.
5. It is the Indianised form of *Aiwiyaonghen*, the sacred waist-girdle of the Iranians. See *DHI*, p. 437.
6. H. Goetz, "Sūrya as the Supreme Godhead", in *Professor P.K. Gode Commemoration Volume*, Poona, 1960, pp. 113 ff and Fig.
7. For details see Shanti Lal Nagar, *Sūrya and Sun Cult*, New Delhi, 1995.
8. Devendra Handa, *Tribal Coins of Ancient India*, New Delhi, 2007, pp. 234-44, Pls. LXXVI-LXXVII.
9. Handa (1985), op. cit., p. 122.
10. *Ibid.*
11. Handa (1987), *op. cit.*, p. 112.
12. Handa (1983), *op. cit.*, pp. 31-32, Fig. 13.
13. *The Tribune*, Chandigarh, July 22, 1983.
14. Handa (1983), *op. cit.*, p. 31, Fig. 15.
15. Handa (1987), *op. cit.*, pp. 110-12, Pl. V a & b.
16. *Ibid.*
17. Devendra Handa, *Osian: History, Archaeology, Art and Architecture*, Delhi, 1984, pp. 96-97, Pl. 61 and p. 134, Pl. 96 (Sūryahariharahiraṇyagarbha).
18. Srivastava duo has illustrated a small figure of Sūrya holding lotus flowers in his hands and accompanied by one acolyte figure on either side from Dholbaha datable to *circa* tenth century CE (*op. cit*, Fig. 61). They have referred to another figure as 'standing Surya' which actually is a haloed head wearing a crown of three peaks and the foliage or branches of a tree (?) behind. There is no definite clue to identify the image with certainty.
19. Ohri, *op. cit.*, p. 127, Pl. 6.14; Sethi, *op. cit.*, pp. 58-59, Fig. 37.
20. Ohri, *loc. cit.*
21. Handa (1983), *op. cit.*, p. 32, Fig. 3 on p. 21.

# 7

# Gaṇesa

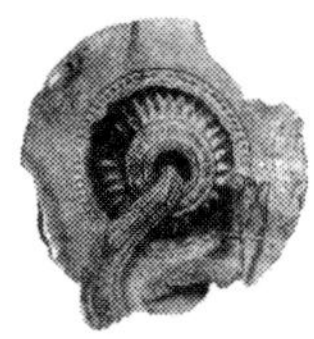

The elephant-headed god popularly known as Gaṇeśa is the god of wisdom and success. Like Vishṇu, Śiva and Lalitā who are endowed with a thousand names (*sahsra-nāma*), Gaṇeśa too possesses numerous names like Gajānana, Gajamukha, Guharāja, Ekadanta, Heramba, Lambodara, Vakratuṇḍa, Vināyaka, Vighneśa, Vighneśvara, Vighnapati, Guhyāgraja, etc., which bespeak of his physical, sociological, mental and qualitative characteristics. He is equated with Gaṇapati,[1] the lord of the Gaṇas of the Vedic times. Though the most popular deity from the medieval period onwards, yet his name is not found anywhere in the early literature.[2] It is in the *Baudhāyana Dharmasūtra*[3] (II.5, 6) that we get his first unmistakable reference. Probably initially, he was connected with *Yaksha* and Nāga cults of folk divinities.[4] Dr. Sampurnananda assigned him a non-Aryan origin.[5] His very name and epithets like Gaṇeśvara, Vināyaka, etc. suggest that he represented a group of divinities and stood at the head of that.[6] In the early phase of his worship, he was the deity who created obstacles (*vighnas*) but by a natural opposite corollary, he became the 'destroyer of obstacles' (*vighna-vināśana*) and the 'bestower of success' (*siddhi-dātā*).[7] In the *Mahābhārata* (Ādi Parva I.75-79), Gaṇeśa is described as the scribe of the epic. Gaṇapati's reputation for wisdom seems to originate from the term Gaṇapati used for Bṛihaspati in the *Ṛigveda* (II.23, 1). Bṛihaspati is the Vedic god of wisdom and is called the sage of the sages. Head is the repository of brain and wisdom. The big head of the elephant perhaps symbolizes the highest wisdom. In the *Yājñavalkya Saṃhitā* (I.271 ff) for the first time, Vināyaka is described as the son of Ambikā. Various Purāṇas narrate the stories of his birth and life,[8] and the *Gaṇeśa Purāṇa*[9] elevates him to the status of the Supreme God – the creator, protector and destroyer of the universe. A Kushāṇa coin bears the figure of Śiva with the legend 'Gaṇeśa', apparently for Śiva. A late Kushāṇa sealing from Sonkh near Mathura, however, depicts the elephant-headed god and provides evidence of his worship in the early centuries. The earliest epigraphic reference to Gaṇapati, the name of a Nāga ruler, is found in the Prayāga *Praśasti* of Samudragupta. A cult seems to have developed round Gaṇapati soon after, if not before or during the Gupta period,[10] and spread far and wide in the old world during the medieval period.[11] He is worshipped by all classes of the Hindus (except Śrī-Vaishṇavas) at the commencement of any religious ceremony. Though the *Amarakosha* gives *'ekadanta'* (having one tooth or tusk), *'gajamukha'* (elephant-faced) and *'lambodara'* (having long paunch or pot belly) as the synonyms of Gaṇapati, [12] which have their iconographic connotations and significance, yet the *Bṛihatsaṃhitā* (LVII.58) contains the first iconographic description of the deity.[13] It states that Gaṇeśa should have an elephant's face with a single tusk and a bulging belly and should carry a *kuṭhāra* (hatchet) and a *mūlakanda* (turnip of dark foliage root) in his hands. No such image has come to light as yet. Even otherwise also, it is believed by scholars that two-handed Gaṇeśa is a rarity.[14] The *Vighneśvara Pratishṭhā Vidhi* and the *Gaṇeśa Purāṇa*, which refer to two-handed Gaṇeśa, indicate that the two-handed images existed.[15] According to the *Gaṇeśa Purāṇa* (I.18, 21), Mahotkaṭa Gaṇapati has a lion as his *vāhana* (*siṃhārūḍhaḥ*) in the Kṛitayuga, Mayūragaṇapati has peacock as his *vāhana* in the Tretā, Gajānana in the Dvāpara has rat as his vehicle and Dhūmraketugaṇapati in the Kali has horse. This Purāṇa also explains in a legend the circumstances in which the rat became the vehicle of the god. The *Brahmavaivarta Purāṇa* (III.13, 12), however, tells us that Vasundharā, the goddess of earth, gave mouse to Gaṇeśa as a vehicle. The *Vishṇudharmottara Purāṇa* (III.71, 13-16) describes Gaṇeśa image as having an elephantine face with one tusk and a bulging belly, wearing tiger skin (*vyāghra-charma*) and serpentine sacred thread (*sarpa-yajñopavīta*), carrying trident and rosary in his right hands and *paraśu* (axe) and *modaka-pātra* (bowl of sweet-balls) in his left seated in *lalitāsana*. The *Matsya Purāṇa* prescribes that the image of Gaṇapati should have an elephantine face, large belly, large extended three eyes, big trunk, one tusk, strong arms, feet and shoulders, and should carry a tusk and a lotus flower in the right hands and battle-axe and pot of ambrosia in the left ones. He should also be accompanied by his consorts Ṛiddhi and Buddhi, and the mount Mūshaka, the rat.[16] The *Agni Purāṇa* (L.23-26), *Aparājitapṛichchhā* (12.35-37), *Rūpa-Maṇḍana*[17] and some Āgamas also describe four and more handed images of the god similarly or with slight differences.[18] Also, a variety of his images are described in various texts and found actually.[19] He is the most universally adorned of all the Hindu gods and his images are found practically in every part of India. His popularity transcended the borders and extended to Nepal, Tibet, China, Burma, Siam, Indo-China, Korea, Japan, Java, Bali, Borneo, Afghanistan and Central Asia.

No seals/sealings representing Gaṇeśa in any form – iconic or aniconic – have been found as yet from any site in Punjab. It is also significant that we do not have any plastic representation of the deity either from this state belonging to the Gupta or even late Gupta period. Cunningham had seen a mould for making terracotta figurines of Gaṇeśa at Sulṭanpur Lodi.[20] Unfortunately, however, he did not describe and illustrate it nor did he give any idea of its date. The medieval images of the god found so far from the State are not commensurate with his popularity and their number looks very insignificant when compared with the number of his images found from other parts of the country.

Independent images of Gaṇeśa in Punjab are a rarity, except for some broken and detached reliefs. What may have been the earliest images of the deity belonging to seventh century CE were found from Doghi, which formed part of district Hoshiarpur before 1966 but now lies in district Una of Himachal Pradesh. They are now preserved in the State Museum, Shimla.[21] The bigger of the two pieces (Acc. No. 83.147) measures 115.0 X 72.0 cm and shows the pot-bellied god seated on a cushioned seat on a *pañcha-ratha* pedestal in *sukhāsana* with left leg folded and right bent at the knee perpendicularly. The legs have suffered mutilation. A tiny figure of mouse, the vehicle of the god, is depicted on the left of the pedestal. The right tusk protrudes out slightly. The god is wearing the *sarpa-yajñopavīta*. The trunk twirling to the left picks up sweet-balls from a bowl held in the left hand while the right hand is disposed in *abhaya*. The temples are adorned with pearl strings and anklets on the feet may also be discerned. The second image (Acc. No. 83.148) measures 71.5 X 59 cm and is in a very indifferent state of preservation. The four-handed god seems to hold his tusk in the normal right hand and the upper right is broken. The additional left seems to support an axe and the natural left as usual the *modaka-pātra* from which the god takes the sweet-ball with its trunk. One piece from Dholbaha is now displayed in the VVRI Museum at Hoshiarpur and portrays the four-handed god as sitting in *sukhāsana* wearing a simple nether garment, a conical cover for the scalp, a sacred thread and bracelets (Pl. 152). The elephantine face (*gaja-mukha*) with ears simulating winnowing baskets looks quite natural. The stomach has not yet developed into pot-belly. The trunk twirls to the left hand to pick up a sweet-ball from the bowl held in the natural left hand. The back left hand seems to hold the stalk of a lotus flower. The god holds the broken tusk in his normal right hand and a *paraśu* in the back right. The vehicle of the god is missing. This naturalistic relief of the deity with simple dress and sparse ornamentation seems to belong to *circa* eighth century CE.

In the same museum and from the same site, an architectural piece shows the elephant-faced god seated similarly (Pl. 153). The indifferent state of preservation and breakage on the proper right side of the relief renders the determination of the attributes in the right hands only as assumption but they may have been the broken tusk or radish in the normal right and a lotus in the additional one. The left hands, however, may be made out fairly well as holding the bowl of sweet-balls and a *kuṭhāra*. The trunk takes a turn to his left to pick up a sweet-ball. Large ear flaps look like the winnowing baskets and the god seems to wear a flat tiara on the head. Details of drapery and jewellery are completely lost but the belly looks slightly developed yet certainly not like a pot yet. On stylistic grounds, it may be dated to late eighth or early ninth century CE.

A ninth century image of the god was recovered while excavating the foundations of a Śiva temple at Burail (Chandigarh) and was fixed in the wall for worship. Some details were lost by mutilation and others have been concealed by fixing the image in a wall and plastering cement on the figure.

Further development may be noticed in another figure of the god from Dholbaha and in the Hoshiarpur museum though the image has suffered greater mutilation (Pl. 154). Almost similar to the preceding piece in posture, drapery and ornamentation, the god has a snake around the waist and in front of the folded left leg. The rear left hand seems to hold a lotus. The tummy is developing into a pot belly now. The additional right hand is broken and the attribute in the normal hand, tusk by assumption, is not clear. The mount, too, is not visible. The image may belong to late ninth century.

A square sectioned pillar from Sirhind, datable to the late eighth or early ninth century CE, carries the figure of the elephant-headed god in a medallion having a beaded border (Pl. 155). Gaṇeśa is seated gracefully on a cushion with right leg folded and left foot placed on the earth with leg bent slightly inwards from the knee. The god bears a small tiara on the naturalistic head with large winnowing-basket like ears. The trunk is broken but its tip placed on the bowl of sweet-balls held in the lower left hand makes it clear that like all North Indian images of the god, it took a twirl to its left. The face too has suffered mutilation. The god is shown as wearing an *ekāvalī*, serpentine sacred thread with the head of the reptile placed on the slightly developed pot belly above the navel, armlets, anklets and an under garment. The normal right hand which may have held the broken tusk is mutilated and the additional right holds a lotus. The corresponding left supports a battle-axe.

A left hand side part of the lintel of a door-surround of a tenth century temple from Dholbaha in the Hoshiarpur museum reveals that Gaṇeśa was depicted popularly as the *lalāṭa-bimba* of the medieval temples in the region (Pl. 156). Unfortunately, the figure of Gaṇeśa and of course this *uttaraṅga* is broken from a part of the god's right side, leaving us only to guess that the depiction of the god was similar to the foregoing examples. To the left of Gaṇeśa are four more figures in niches with pediments above but it is difficult to recognize them because of their worn-out condition. Another door-surround preserved under a tree near Sītā Sara at Sunam shows Gaṇeśa as the central piece in a pedimented niche (Pl. 157). Seated in *sukhāsana,* the four-handed elephant-faced god is shown with tusk, axe, lotus and bowl of sweet-balls in his four hands in the *pardakshiṇā* order. On the extremities of this lintel are depicted *vyāla* figures, one above the other in two panels, the lower one facing inwards and the upper one turned outwards. On either side of the *lalāṭa-bimba* are two pedimented niches, each with garland-bearing *vidyādharas* in between. The niches show Sūrya, Brahmā, Vishṇu and Śiva. The lintel may have thus belonged either to a Gaṇeśa temple or more probably to a Devī (Pārvatī or Mahishāsuramardinī) temple. Just below the extreme niches are the panels with two dancing figures with another standing (perhaps dancing) figure towards the *lalāṭa-bimba*. The intermediary space is divided into two registers, the upper one showing four small panels depicting the upper half portions of *vidyādharas* bearing garlands and the lower one ornamental scrollwork. The door-jambs in all probability consisted of five bands. The fane, to which this *uttaraṅga* belonged, may have been in existence during the tenth century CE.[22] Another similar *uttaraṅga* of the same period at Sītā Sara also shows Gaṇeśa as the *lalāṭa-bimba* (Pl. 158).

## DANCING GAṆEŚA

Images of dancing Gaṇeśa seem to have remained more popular in the Punjab than his other forms. It was more than three decades back that I published the broken pedestal of a small image from Rajinidevi near Hoshiarpur.[23] This pedestal shows only the feet of the god bearing anklets, the right one held sideways (towards the proper right) with tow lifted slightly and heal touching the ground, the left foot splayed out with a mouse (viewer's right) and a dwarfish *gaṇa* figure playing on the drum on the receding recess of the pedestal (Pl. 159). The depiction of the small mouse helps us to identify the image with certainty to have belonged to Gaṇeśa in a dancing pose, as suggested by the placement and position of the two feet. I had seen some more fragments of sculptures in the village during my visit in the sixties of the last century but I could not locate them during subsequent visits many years after. Obviously, those fragments including the present broken pedestal belonged to a tenth century temple at the place.

A beautiful but broken figure of Gaṇeśa from Dholbaha (Pl. 160) wrongly identified by some official as reclining Gaṇeśa and described as such in the departmental brochures and website,[24] and also followed by Manmohan Kumar,[25] shows the elephant-headed god wearing a small tiara bearing rosette designs with large winnowing basket-like ears, swinging his head and body to his right holding some handled object[26] in his right hand with left disposed slantingly towards his right waist in dancing posture. The figure is broken below the belly. Since the image in its broken condition could not be held straight or vertically and was laid in a horizontal position, it was mistaken as reclining (Fig. 30). No such reclining images of Gaṇeśa have been prescribed in any of the iconographic texts though

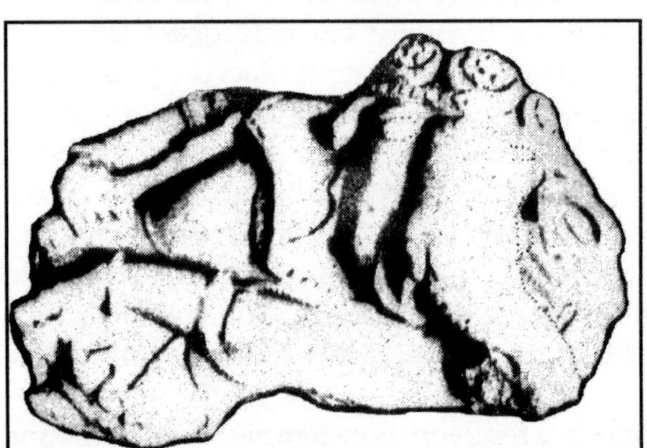

**Fig. 30.** Gaṇeśa from Dholbaha, lateral stance.

we get details of numerous other types of his images. If viewed properly, we can visualize its dancing stance with head turned to left and trunk swaying to right (Fig. 31).

It certainly is an image of the dancing Gaṇeśa, stylistically assignable to *circa* late eighth or early ninth century CE, and has rightly been described as such by Ohri.[27] Ohri has brought out its stylistic traits and importance properly:

> An image of Ganesa from Dholbaha though damaged and incomplete is quite important as an effective work of art for the mixed stylistic traits seen in it. The half closed eyes of this figure suggest that the god is engrossed in dancing which he is enjoying. A vigorous movement in dancing is suggested by the flexed figure of Ganesa and the trunk forcefully swung to the left while the left arm is turned with a visible effort towards the right for maintaining balance. Narrow forehead seen in this figure is though a characteristic of the images of Ganesa made in the early medieval period in this hilly area, this image appears to be a work of the ninth century as it lacks a robust plasticity associated with the works of the earlier period. The sculptor's emphasis in this image is on the plastic surface for making it more expressive and sensitive.[28]

Ohri dates this image to ninth century CE but the type of crown consisting of three crescents, each one of which holds a lotus, is commonly seen in Kashmir images starting from seventh century.[29] In the ninth century, it grows quite elaborate with details of lotus leaves.[30] We, therefore, feel inclined to concur with Berkson who has put it in the eighth century CE.[310] Another representation of dancing Gaṇeśa with both legs bent at knees and trunk turning to proper right may be seen on a *nāgara-kūṭa* of *circa* thirteenth century, preserved in the store of the site museum at Dholbaha (Pl. 161).

Akbar's reign seems to have provided some respite to the Hindus when they started building their temples again. Shivala Panjpipla at Bahadurpur, Hoshiarpur may have come into existence during Akbar's reign. It contains two small stone images of Gaṇeśa measuring 20 x 38 cm and 11 x 16 cm, Durgā (20 X 36 cm), Nandī (13 x 9 cm and 11 x 16 cm) and others belonging to the late sixteenth or early seventeenth century. They have not been carved as per the textual iconographic prescriptions and betray folk impact. There may be some other such examples also in the Punjab but the coercive measures of imposing *jaziya* and opposition to iconolatory soon after his death proved a dampener. We may refer here to an attempt in the post Mughal period when images of Gaṇeśa were attempted in wooden medium. One such icon exists in a temple at the village Rau ke Kalan in district Faridkot (Pl. 162). The *kulluh*-like crown clearly betrays Islamic impact and the trunk of the god twirling to the right to pick up a sweet-ball from the bowl held in the right hand indicates that the textual prescriptions and North Indian tradition had completely been forgotten by the artists by this time. Another wooden image in the Hindu temple at Panj Kalyan in district Patiala shows the trunk of the god suspended somewhat slantingly to pick up the sweet-ball from the bowl in the normal right hand (Pl. 163). The attributes in the other hands are not carved out properly. These images may have been created during the eighteenth-nineteenth centuries when the iconoclastic tyranny and Nadir Shah's depredations ended in Punjab and import of marble images from Rajasthan had not yet picked up.

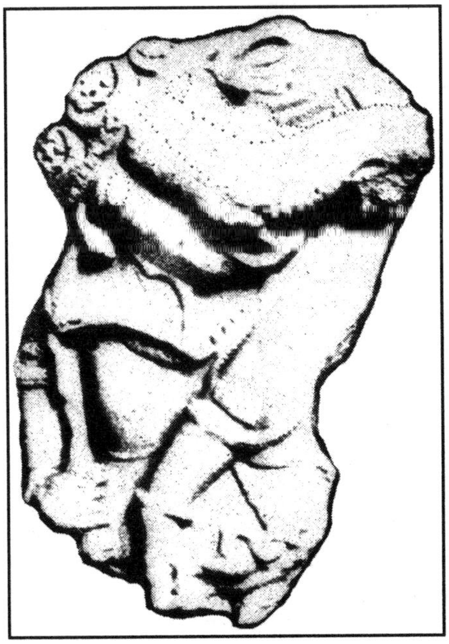

**Fig. 31.** Gaṇeśa from Dholbaha, vertical stance.

## NOTES AND REFERENCES

1. Cf. *Ṛigveda* II.23, 1: *Gaṇānāṃ tvā Gaṇpatiṃ havāmahe.*
2. *Vājasaneyī Saṃhitā* XIX.25; *Mādhyandina Saṃhitā* XVI.25; XXIII.19; *Aitareya Brāhmaṇa* I.21; *Taittirīya Āraṇyaka* IX.15; etc.
3. A.K. Coomaraswamy, *Yakṣas*, Part I, Delhi, 1971, pp. 7 and 42, Pl. XXIII.1.
4. Dr. Sampurnananda, *Hindu Deva Parivāra kā Vikāsa* (Hindi), Allahabad, 1964, p. 147.
5. *VSMRS*, p. 147. The *Yājñavalkya Smṛiti* refers to six Vināyakas such as Mita, Sammita, Śāla, Kaṭaṅkaṭa, Kūshmāṇḍa and Rājaputra.
6. *DHI*, p. 355.
7. I.271 ff.
8. See for details, *EHI*, Vol. I, pp. 33ff and Dr. Sampurnananda, *Gaṇeśa* (Hindi), Varanasi, vs 2001, pp. 6-10.
9. S.B. Singh, *Brahmanical Icons in Northern India*, New Delhi, 1977, p. 134.
10. Cf. R.G. Bhandarkar, *VSMRS*, pp. 149-50.
11. Alice Getty, *Gaṇeśa*, Oxford, 1936; M.K. Dhavalikar, "Gaṇeśa Beyond the Indian Frontiers," in *India's Contribution to World Thought and Culture*, Madras, 1970, pp. 1-16; P. Banerjee, "Hindu Deities in Central Asia", *Ibid.*, pp. 281-88; Amarendra Nath, "Gaṇeśa in Central Asian Art: An Identification", *Journal of the Indian Society of Oriental Art*, New Series, Calcutta, Vol. VI, 1974-75, pp. 1-4; etc.
12. *Amarakosha* I.1, 38: *Vināyaka-Vighnarāja-Dvaimātura-Gaṇādhipaḥ/ Apyekadanto-Heramba-Lambodara-Gajānanaḥ//*
13. *Pramathādhipo gajamukhaḥ pralambajaṭharaḥ kuṭhāradhārī syāt / Ekavishāṇo bibhranmūlakandaṃ sunīladalakamalam //* R.G. Bhandarkar (*loc. cit.*) had doubted the authenticity of this verse but Banerjea (*DHI*, p. 357) differs from him.
14. Cf. *EHI*, I, Appendix C, pp. 1-13; *VSMRS*, *loc. cit.*; *Bhāratīya Vidyā* XIII, pp. 29-50; XXXIX (i), pp. 14-19, Pls. I-II.
15. *Bhāratīya Vidyā* XXXIX (i), p. 18. See also S.B. Singh, *op. cit.*, pp. 138-40.
16. *Matsya Purāṇa* 260.52-55. The Āgamas refer to Bhāratī, Śrī, Siddhi, Vighneśvarī, Kshudhi, etc. also as his consorts.
17. See for details *EHI*, Vol. I, pp. 48ff and Appendix C.
18. D.N. Shukla, *Bhāratīya Vāstuśāstra* (*Pratimā Vijñāna*), Vol. IV, pp. 280-81. The *Śāradātilaka* describes fifty-one forms of Gaṇeśa, each with its own attributes. See for details H.K. Sashtry, *South Indian Images of Gods and Goddesses*, New Delhi, 1986 (reprint), p. 173.
19. *Bhāratīya Vidyā* XIII. 19-50; Getty, *op. cit.*
20. *CASR*, XIV, p. 58.
21. Ohri, *op. cit.*, p. 126, Pl. 6.13; Sethi, *op. cit.*, pp. 30-31, Fig. 17.
22. Handa (1987), *op. cit.*, p. 115, Pl. XVIII.
23. Devendra Handa, "Some Sculptures from Punjab and Haryana", *Panjab University Research Bulletin (Arts)*, Chandigarh, Vol. VII, No. 1 (April, 1976), p. 94, Fig. 3; (1981), p. 73, Fig. 14.
24. *Punjab Government Museum Hoshiarpur*, Chandigarh (no date), unnumbered last page; *Dholbaha: An Ancient Historic Site in Punjab, Department of Archaeology and Museums, Punjab* (place and date of publication not specified), p. 1; S.S. Talwar, *A Glimpse of Punjab Archaeology at Sanghol & Dholbaha*, Souvenir: Punjab History Conference (7th Session), Punjabi University, Patiala (no date), p. 17 & fig.
25. Manmohan Kumar (1981), *op. cit.*, pp. 50-52.
26. Manmohan Kumar (*loc. cit.*) identifies it as a sword.
27. Ohri, *op. cit.*, p. 125, Pl. 6.6.
28. *Ibid.*
29. Cf. Vishṇu with Chakra-purusha and Gadā-devī from Bijbehara in Sri Partap Singh Museum, Srinagar. See for details Bansi Lal Malla, *Sculptures of Kashmir (600-1200 AD)*, Delhi, 1990, Pl. 9.
30. *Ibid.*, Pls. 41-43.
31. Carmel Berkson, *The Life of Form in Indian Sculpture*, New Delhi, 2000, p. 11.

# 8

# Miscellaneous Icons and Decorative Sculptures

The Hindu pantheon went on growing with the passage of time, as a result of which the number of deities and their *parivāra* and *āvaraṇa-devatās* also grew substantially. Some of these gods had their own cults developed around them but others had limited following or even regional in character. As compared with most other states, images of the different deities are quite rare in the Punjab and we do not get many images of the minor gods. Important deities represented by their images in the state are, however, described below.

## BRAHMĀ

Born in a golden egg (Hiraṇyagarbha) and the first deity of the orthodox Brahmanical triad, Brahmā could not gather importance comparable to the other members of the Trinity, not even others like Sūrya, Devī and Gaṇapati. It was probably because the act of creation came to be associated with the followers of different cults with their own respective divinities.[1] Though his worship is enjoined upon all those who worship Vishnu or Śiva and he figures as one of the most important of the *parivava-devatas* of the first *prakaraṇa* of a temple dedicated to either of the above-mentioned deities,[2] yet there is no denying the fact that he enjoyed no success as a cult god and was reduced to the status of a titular deity only to find sometimes, not always as laid down in some scriptures, a niche here or there, in a Hindu shrine. Though even a late text like the *Rūpa-Maṇḍana* describes Brahmā's temple along with *parivāra-devatās*, *dvārapālas*, etc., yet there are very few temples dedicated to him.[3] However, we find only subsidiary images of the god in the Hindu temples.

The earliest iconographic description of Brahmā occurs in the *Bṛihatsaṃhitā*. It says that the four-handed god holds a ritual water-pot (*kamaṇḍalu*) in one of his hands and is seated on a lotus.[4] Evidently, his images in the early period were two-handed like those of other deities.[5] He is referred to as having four hands in all later texts. The *Āditya Purāṇa* refers to his four faces, lotus seat and Sāvitrī on his left lap.[6] The *Vishṇu Purāṇa* refers to Brahmā with eyes closed as in meditation and seated on a chariot drawn by seven swans (*Saptahaṃsarathasthitam*).[7]

By the time of the Āgamas, great elaboration had taken place in his iconic representations.[8] The *Aṃśumadbhedāgama* describes the four-handed god as having *jaṭā-mukuṭa*, wearing ornaments, *yajña-sūtra*, *kaṭi-sūtra*, rearing beard and holding water-vessel, ladle, etc. as also showing *abhaya* and *varada* poses. He may be seated or standing on a lotus seat and is also associated with Sarasvatī and Sāvitrī.[9] *Suprabhedāgama* refers to four-faced and four-armed Brahmā as wearing all ornaments, *jaṭā-mukuṭa*, holding *kamaṇḍalu* and *akshamālā* 'rosary' with Sāvitrī on his left.[10] The *Śilparatna* describes him as seated on a lotus seat (*kamalāsana*) or riding a swan (*haṃsārūḍham*), holding a ladle and *kamaṇḍalu*, with right hand in *varada* pose and the four Vedas in front. He should be flanked by Sarasvatī and Sāvitrī on his right and left.[11] The *Rūpa-Maṇḍana* prescribes a rosary, ladle or lotus, book and water-vessel in hands, a beard and lotus seat for him.[12]

We do not agree with Banerjea who held that "it is curious that in none of these elaborate accounts there is an explicit reference to his face or faces being bearded."[13] The *Aṃśumadbhedāgama* clearly states that Brahmā should bear *kūrcha* (*kūrchchaṃ chaiva tu dhārayet*).[14] Since *kūrcha*, which is also translated as 'a handful of *kuśa* grass'[15] is never depicted in Indian images, we would prefer its other meaning of 'beard'. Also, we do not subscribe to the view of the learned savant that "all the later images of Brahmā have bearded faces".[16] We shall see presently that facts go against this view.

No independent image of Brahmā has been discovered from anywhere in the Punjab as yet. We have already seen that Brahmā, sometimes with Sarasvatī also, has often been depicted on the steles of Vishṇu images. Some more such fragments have been described here.

The best-preserved fragment comes from Majhur and represents Brahmā-Sarasvatī seated in *sukhāsana* on the mount goose, on a full-blossomed *padma-pīṭha* (Pl. 164). Tri-cephalous Brahmā, with all juvenile faces, bears *jaṭā-mukuṭa* adorned with an almond-shaped jewel in the centre. He wears a *yajñopavīta*, a long beaded garland and the nether garment secured by a pearl girdle. His natural right hand is disposed in *abhaya-mudrā* and the rear right holds the ladle by its handle near the shoulder. The additional left holds the manuscript and his normal left comes from behind the back of Sarasvatī seated on his folded left leg to touch her left breast. Sarasvatī also embraces the god with her right hand put on his right shoulder. Her left hand is broken. She wears earrings and beaded necklace and girdle. The folds of the nether garment have been carved on the shanks. She is seated awkwardly with both of her legs folded sideways parallel to Brahmā's folded left leg. The back slab has been rounded at the top and its edge is beaded to serve as the aureole. Lotus petal decorations are also visible above it. The head of the goose is broken but a beaded necklet around its neck has survived. The right knee of Brahmā has also suffered some mutilation. Stylistically, it may be dated to *circa* tenth century CE.

Dholbaha has yielded quite a few fragments representing the steles of probably Vishṇu images. In the approach way to the museum, some carved pieces are fixed in a wall (Pl. 46). A piece representing a *nāgara-kūṭa* measuring 14 X 34 cm shows four-handed, three-faced Brahmā seated in *sukhāsana* with proper right hand disposed in *abhaya* and holding the ladle, book and water pot in the other hands in the *pradakshiṇā* order. His central face is bearded. The other fragment measuring 13 X 12 cm shows the similar figure but with juvenile faces and the vehicle swan is also shown near the left foot of the god. This latter fragment is more beautiful than the former. Two fragments are displayed in the Government Museum at Hoshiarpur. The bigger one of these shows Brahmā seated in *lalitāsana* on a *padma-pīṭha* bearing matted locks and wearing the usual simple ornaments and clothes with natural right hand disposed in *varada* with rosary, extra right holding the ladle, additional left holding the book and normal left, slightly damaged, probably holding the water pot (Pl. 165). The central face of Brahmā is bearded.

The back slab has been rounded and beaded at the top. Just above may be seen a garland-bearing *vidyādhara* partially covered by the top of the stele. On the extreme band of the back slab to the proper right of Brahmā is carved a *vyāla* figure with the face of a boar and above it is seated on a lotus a male figure with right hand in *abhaya*. It is difficult to identify this figure. On the proper left hand side of the god has survived a part of the gloriole with lotus petal decorations but the main deity is only a matter of guess. The carvings indicate it to have been a part of the tenth century image. The second fragment is made of black stone and is not in a good state of preservation (Pl. 166). The visible details indicate it to have been carved similar to the preceding one but for the juvenile faces of the god. The rounded part of the gloriole of the main image may be seen on the proper left of this stele. Stylistically, however, it seems to belong to the late tenth or early eleventh century CE.

Kharar has also yielded quite a few fragments broken from Vishṇu images and showing full or parts of steles carrying the figures of Brahmā. One in red sandstone measuring 13 X 18 cm shows a stele with three-faced Brahmā wearing *jaṭā-mukuṭa*, necklace, ear ornaments, armlets, wristlets and the scared thread. The god holds a ladle, a book and water vessel with one hand near the chest, probably in *abhaya-mudrā*. The deity is slightly pot-bellied. A circular curve on the proper left shows probably the aureole of the main figure. *Makara-mukha* on the left with lotus issuing forth from it and surmounted by a small damaged figure facing towards Brahmā is indicative of the minute care of the sculptor. Part of an aureole with a miniature figure of Brahmā on a lotus (12 X 9 cm), another mutilated three-faced figure of Brahmā with his vehicle on the pedestal (20 X 12 cm), etc. are some notable figures. That Brahmā used to be carved with central bearded face is indicated by another very badly mutilated fragment from Kharar showing the god seated in *sukhāsana* with *abhaya*, ladle, book and water pot as the attributes (Pl. 167). Another stele, probably of an image of Śiva from Kharar, also corroborates it as in spite of its badly broken state, it shows the long beard of the central face though the face itself has gone (Pl. 168). A juvenile face on the proper left side indicates a similar face on the corresponding right side also. The figure of Sarasvatī seated in Brahmā's left lap and embracing him has just some traces left. The existence of what looks like the serpent head over Sarasvatī's head indicates the original image to have been that of Śiva. The upper register shows five equally mutilated male figures with hips accentuated towards their left side. Probably an equal number of such figures existed on the corresponding other side also. The number ten would suggest the figures to represent the ten incarnatory forms of Vishṇu but it is rather difficult to say so with certainty as those forms are rarely represented in this way and with an image of Śiva. Dholbaha has also yielded similar figures on the jambs of a door-surround of a temple as we shall see subsequently. These fragments described above may be dated to *circa* tenth century CE.

A small fragment, 18 X 14 cm in size, recovered while excavating the foundations of a temple at Burail (Chandigarh) shows a stele depicting three-headed Brahmā seated in *sukhāsna* holding a ladle and a book in his rear right and left hands with principal right hand disposed in fear-allaying posture and the left holding a water vessel. The central face of the god is bearded. To the extreme right of the deity exists a subsidiary figure resting his right hand on the slightly bent right knee, very much mutilated now. Partly visible circular halo on the left of the god indicates that this figure was carved on the right hand side of an image of some deity, probably Vishṇu, the top part of the mace in whose upper right hand has partially survived under the water pot in Brahmā's lower left hand. Stylistically, it may be dated to *circa* ninth century CE.

We thus see that Brahmā was depicted as tri-cephalous in all medieval images with juvenile faces or with central bearded face with or without the vehicle and his spouse and holding rosary (sometimes in *varada* or *abhaya hasta* also), ladle, book and water pot as his favourite attributes in the Punjab as in Haryana.[17]

## KĀRTTIKEYA

The history and antiquity of *Kārttikeya,* known variously as Skanda, Kumāra, Guha, Viśākha, Mahāsena, Shaṇmukha, Shaḍānana, Brahmaṇyadeva, Subrahmaṇya, Muruga, Murugan, etc. are shrouded in mystery. Though the name Skanda or Kārttikeya does not occur in the *Ṛigveda,*[18] yet Kumāra has been mentioned several times.[19] Kumāra stands for a boy, a child, a youth, a son or a descendant but at one place it appears as an independent deity in the *Ṛigveda.*[20] Sukumar Sen regards Kumāra of the *Ṛigveda* as the prototype of Skanda-Kārttikeya.[21] The *Atharvaveda* mentions Kumāra as *agnibhūti.*[22] In the Vedic literature, Rudra has been called as Agni also[23] and the *Mahābhārata* mentions Dahana (Fire) as one of the names of the eleven Rudras.[24] Many of the epithets of Agni in the *Ṛigveda* have later been applied to Kumāra. The connection of Agni[25] and Rudra[26] with war seems to have stood at the root of the epic concept of Kumāra as the Generalissimo of the divine forces. The *Śatapatha Brāhmaṇa* presents an epitome of the various myths by referring to Kumāra as the son of Prajāpati, also named Rudra because he wept or cried (*rud*), Rudra being Agni and Kumāra being the ninth name of Agni (Rudra) and so on.[27]

The multiple aspects of Skanda have also been highlighted in the *Skanda-yāga,* also called *Dhūrta-Kalpa,* a *pariśishṭa* 'appendix' of the *Atharvaveda.*[28] It refers to his various names and associates him with peacock (*yaṃ vahanti mayūrāḥ*), lance or spear (*yasyāmoghā sadā śakti nityaṃ ghaṇṭā-patākinī*), mothers (*Yaścha mātṛigaṇairnityaṃ parivṛito yuvā*) and refers to his multiple parentage-

*Āgneyaṃ kṛittikāputramaindraṃ kechidadhīyate /*
*Kechit pāśupataṃ Raudraṃ yo'si so' si namo'stu te iti //*

In the Sūtra period (600-200 BCE), the status of Skanda seems to have been elevated to the level of the supreme gods. The *Hiraṇyakeśin Gṛihya Sūtra* (II.9, 19) mentions him along with Vishṇu, Rudra, etc. The *Baudhāyana Dharma Sūtra* identifies him with Sanatkumāra, Shaṇmukha, Viśākha, Mahāsena, etc.

The epics and the Purāṇas[29] deal in details with the stories of the birth and deeds of Kārttikeya. The Śalyaparvan gives us an idea of the various myths of his parentage which might have been floating in the society as the son of Pitāmaha, Brahman, Maheśvara, Agni, Umā, Kṛittikās (Pleiads), Gaṅgā.[30]

The Vanaparva (*Mbh.* III, 213-21) narrates the story of the birth of Skanda from Agni (*Mbh.* IX.43-465). It is said that having seen the wives of the Seven Sages (Saptarshi), Agni fell in love with them. Svāhā, the daughter of Daksha (Prajāpati), mated with Agni assuming successively forms of six of the wives of the seven Ṛishis. Agni deposited a part of his seed, each time and Svāhā cast the seed on the top of the of the *Śveta* (white) mountain in Śaravana (forest of reeds) where it developed into Skanda, with six heads. The Śalyaparvan (*Mbh.* XIII.83-84), however, tells us that when at the sight of Umā the vital seed of Śiva fell into the blazing fire (Agni) and developed into a fetus, Agni, unable to bear it, deposited the fiery fetus in the river Gaṅgā on Brahmā's advice. Gaṅgā, too, unable to sustain it, abandoned it in the Śaravana on the Himālayas where the embryo developed into a lustrous child. The divine child was seen by the six Kṛittikās, who, out of motherly tenderness, sucked him at their breasts. The child sucked all the six Kṛittikās assuming six mouths. And hence his name Kārttikeya. Bṛihaspati, the preceptor of the gods, then performed the consecration ceremony of his birth. Gathered at that occasion were, amongst others, his parents and sustainers, in order to please whom he divided himself into four forms – Skanda, Śākha, Viśākha and Naigameya, for the satisfaction of Rudra, Umā, Gaṅgā and Agni.

The *Mahābhārata* and the Purāṇas[31] acquaint us with the story of his appointment as the Generalissimo of the army of the gods. On that occasion, he was offered various gifts by different gods which included spear (*Śakti*) from Indra, large army from Śiva, *vaijayantī* from Vishṇu, peacock from Garuḍa, cock from Aruṇa (or Varuṇa or Agni), etc.[32] Skanda's consort is Devasenā, also called Shashṭhī. [33]

We have already noted the elevation of status and popularity of Skanda during the Sūtra period. Kauṭilya refers to the construction of shrines of various gods like Aparājitā, Apratihata, Jayanta, Vijayanta, Śiva, Vaiśravaṇa, Aśvins, Śrī and Madirā in various parts of the city – *Aparājitāpratihata-Jayanta-Vijayanta-koshṭhān Śiva-Vaiśravaṇāśvin Śrī-Madirā-gṛihaṃ cha.*[34] Commenting upon a *Sūtra* of Pāṇini, Patañjali refers to the images of Śiva, Skanda and Viśākha made for worship and the sale thereof by the Mauryas for making money: *Apaṇya ityuchyate tatredaṃ na sidhyati/ Śivaḥ Skandaḥ Viśākha iti/ Kiṃ kāraṇaṃ/ Mauryairhiraṇyārthibhirarchāḥ prakalpitāḥ.*[35]

These and numerous other references, however, indicate that Skanda, Viśākha, Mahāsena, Jayanta, Vaijayanta, etc. were not yet one but different deities. Huvishka's coin-type with three standing figures named as 'Skando Komaro Bizago Maaceno'[36] clearly demonstrates it. The *Vishṇudharmottara* (III.71, 3) also describes the four-fold images of Kārttikeya:

*Chaturmūrteḥ Kumārasya rūpaṃ te vachmi Yādava /*
*Kumāraścha tathā Skando Viśākhaścha Guhastathā //*

The amalgamation, however, seems to have taken place immediately after the Kushāṇa period as we find Kārttikeya, Skanda, Kumāra, Shaṇmukha, Brahmaṇyadeva used for the same deity in later literature.

Kārttikeya is closely associated with Haryana. There are various *tīrthas* in Kurukshetra sacred to him.[37] Pṛithūdaka is described to have been the venue of his consecration to the post of Generalissimo and has a temple dedicated to him.[38] Rohitaka is also described to be a city dear to him.[39] The *Mahāmāyūrī* also refers to his worship at Rohitaka.[40]

In the realm of art, the earliest depiction of Kārttikeya is believed to be on the coins – punch-marked,[41] Ujjayinī,[42] Kāḍa,[43] etc.

Numerous stone and bronze images of two-handed Kārttikeya holding a long spear in one of the hands found from the Mathura region[44] and the coins of Huvishka[45] indicate the popularity of the god in the region. The Yaudheyas, an *āyudha-jīvi saṅgha* mentioned by Pāṇini, worshipped Kārttikeya as their national god. The Shaḍānana-Shashṭhī type coins show the god and the goddess with the following arrangements of heads:[46]

| Kārttikeya | Shashṭhī |
|---|---|
| 1. Parallel rows of heads | Circular heads |
| 2. Circular arrangement of heads | Parallel heads |
| 3. Parallel rows of heads | Parallel heads |

Though the depictions of Kārttikeya in stone and his different aspects like Skando-Komaro, Bizago and Maaceno were popular in the Kushāṇa art of Mathura, yet the absence of any six-headed specimen indicates that it was the Yaudheya innovation. The parallel and circular arrangements of the heads of the deity and his consort, too, were devised indigenously. Neither the stone nor the numismatic representations, however, reveal the presence of peacock, the vehicle of the god, till this period. Kārttikeya-Devasenā type Yaudheya coins bearing the Brāhmī legend *Yaudheya-gaṇasya jaya(ḥ)*, however, depict the deity as uni-cephalous accompanied by the peacock as his vehicle.[47]

Kālidāsa's *Kumārasambhava* and the christening of the rulers of the Gupta dynasty as Kumāragupta (I and II) and Skandagupta, together with the depiction of the deity on the coins,[48] indicate the popularity of Kārttikeya during the Gupta period. It is, however, notable that during this period, the uni-cephalous form with peacock was more popular. That the tradition of six-headed form, too, may have continued, though no specimens belonging to the Gupta period have come down to us, is indicated by a unique bronze image of the god from the Punjab hills (now in Himachal Pradesh), showing six-headed Kārttikeya (with a circular arrangement of the heads) holding *Śakti-devī* in his left hand and the *mayūra-purusha* in the right. The image has been dated to sixth-seventh century CE.[49]

The literary and numismatic data cited above would indicate the great popularity of Kārttikeye in the region. Though quite a good number of his images have been found from Haryana,[50] yet there is a general paucity of his representations as far as the area of the present-day Punjab is concerned in spite of the fact that Achaleshwar near Batala is associated with an episode of his life. It is said that with reference to their vehicles, once there was a competition between Gaṇeśa and Kārttikeya as to who could go faster. Both were asked to go around the world to prove their speed. While Kārttikeya rode his peacock and went fast, Gaṇeśa circumambulated his parents and was declared victor. When Kārttikeya came back and learnt it, he fixed his abode at that place which is pointed out to be Achaleshwar and cursed that any woman who sees him will become barren.

Prof. Ashvini Agrawal possesses a very badly mutilated terracotta image from Sanghol which shows traces of a tri-cephalous figure seated in *bhadrāsana* holding a long lance (*yasyāmoghā sadā śakti*) in his right hand (Pl. 169). The figure is broken above the three heads but the available space would indicate that the other three heads were carved above those. Two mutilated female figures, each holding both the breasts with respective hands, with trace of a third figure above them may be seen on the left side of the main figure and three similar ones may be presumed to have existed on the corresponding other side. These six female figures holding their breasts as if to feed a babe may have been those of the six Kṛittikās associated with Kārttikeya as his mothers (*yaścha mātṛigaṇairnityaṃ parivṛito yuvā*). If our presumptions are correct, the relief may have originally represented multi-headed Kārttikeya with the six Kṛittikās. Though the figure is available only in traces, yet the carvings indicate it have belonged to the early third century CE in Kushāṇa idiom. It may be pointed out here that the motif of a goddess or female touching or pressing her breast was very common in the Kushāṇa period and we find it depicted in Mathura and Sanghol sculptures.[51] The beauty, art and importance of the image leave much to our imagination.

Dholbaha has yielded an independent life-size image of eight-handed Kārttikeya, which is now exhibited in the Government Museum at Hoshiarpur (Pl. 170). The uni-cephalous god is seated in *lalitāsana* on a couch with left leg folded and the right one suspended gracefully at an angle with foot splayed outward. The facial expression is that of quietude. He bears matted locks on the head and wears earrings, broad torque, armlets, bracelets, anklets, sacred thread, long garland and *dhotī* held in position by a simple beaded girdle. There is a *śrīvatsa* mark also on the chest. Traces indicate that he held a spear in his normal right hand. A sword held horizontally at the back of the head in the uppermost hand may, however, be seen clearly. One of the other two hands holds the hilt of some attribute and the other one, now almost completely lost, may have held an arrow. The natural left hand is placed on the folded left leg of the god and is broken. The uppermost extra left hand holds a shield; the next may have held a bow and the remaining one some other attribute now beyond recognition. On the central offset of the *tri-ratha* pedestal are traces of the peacock, the vehicle of the god, to left but it does not seem to have been carved with the care endowed to the main figure and bears chisel marks. These marks may be seen on the receding recess on (viewer's) right also. The back slab has been curved at the top but the halo has not been indicated clearly. The main figure, however, has been carved carefully showing a mastery of the chisel work. The composition is balanced, modelling simple and roundness of the form appears emphasised. Stylistically, it may be regarded as an elegant specimen of Pratihāra art assignable to *circa* ninth century CE.

Another figure of Kārttikeya is fixed in a 22 X 35 cm niche in the wall of the approach way to the site museum at Dholbaha (Pl. 171). The god is standing gracefully in a double flexion posture with waist slightly accentuated to his right holding a mace-like thick sceptre or a cudgel as generally held by Lakulīśa in his right hand. His left hand is placed on the neck of the peacock to right, whose long tail is spread behind the back and head of the god to form an aureole. A dwarfish male figure is shown on his right. Unfortunately, the image is quite worn out to discern the details of his face, coiffure, dress and ornaments. The god, as in the preceding example, is uni-face. The fullness of the plastic mass and simplicity of modelling characterize the figure as a fine specimen of about the same period. Another small pedimented *rathikā* fixed close to this image (Pl. 171) shows the god standing similarly with waist accentuated to his right holding the long spear across the body in his left hand and a lotus by its long stalk in the right hand. The tri-ribbed pillars of the *rathikā* indicate its date as the tenth century CE.

## DIKPĀLAS

Though the worship of Indra, Yama, Varuṇa and Kubera as *lokapālas* had been fairly well recognized by the first century BCE, as indicated clearly by the Naneghat inscription of Nāganikā, yet the development of the concept of the eight *dikpālas* seems to have taken place a few centuries later and we get the traditional number and nomenclature as Indra, Vahni (Agni), Pitṛipati (Yama), Nairṛita, Varuṇa, Marut, Kubera and Īśa (Īśāna), beginning from the east to the northeast for the first time in the *Amarakosha* (II.2, 6).[52] This conception of the eight *dikpālas* grew traditional in the medieval period when they became an invariable adjunct of the temples. Though there are no standing temples in Punjab and Haryana, stray pieces from the latter state[53] indicate the continuation of the practice followed in other parts of the country. One would expect the same to be the case in Punjab also but it is surprising that even a site like Dholbaha has not yielded any evidence to this effect.

An architectural piece at the site museum of Dholbaha shows a small niched four-handed male figure seated cross-legged on a lotus wearing a cylindrical crown and holding unidentifiable objects in the four hands with outward moving elephants in profile in the lower corners (Pl. 172). The *kirīṭa* and the elephants suggest the figure to be that of Indra, but one cannot be definite about it in the absence of *vajra*, the characteristic attribute of the god in his hand. Even if the figure be that of Indra, it is difficult to accept him as the *dikpala* Indra because of its small size and having been carved on the *adhishṭhāna* of a temple datable to *circa* tenth century CE. Similarly, it is difficult to accept the very small four-handed standing figure on an architectural piece as that of Īśāna though he seems to hold trident and snake in the rear pair of hands and has the normal hands hanging down, may be in *varada* pose and holding a water pot (Pl. 173). From Sanaur in district Patiala is known a beautiful ninth century stele showing young Kubera wearing an *ekāvali* seated in *sukhāsna* in a miniature pillared niche holding a cup in the right hand and mongoose in the left (Pl. 174). The *makara-mukha* partly visible on the left suggests it to be the right hand side stele of some bigger sculpture and not the *dikpāla* Kubera who occupies the northern niche of the temple wall. It is a typical Pratihāra piece.

Were the temples of Punjab different than other parts of North India not to show the *dikpāla* images on their walls? No definite answer can be given at this stage and more evidence is required to reach any definite conclusion in this regard.

Equally enigmatic is the absence of the figures of the *Navagrahas* from any site in Punjab.

## GANDHARVAS, VIDYĀDHARAS, KINNARAS AND APASARASES

"The *gandharva* minstrels and the *vidyādhara* angels, the *kinnara* bird-men and the *apasaras* maidens add, by their presence, material meaning to the spiritual content of a medieval Indian temple."[54] They are classed as demigods and occupy subsidiary rungs on the ladder of celestial hierarchy. They were never conceived to be objects of worship. It has, however, been aptly remarked that "in terms of plastic expression, they, all the same, rival and occasionally excel their superiors, the higher gods."[55]

*Vidyādharas*, *vidyādharīs* or couples are generally shown as garland-bearing semi-celestials on the upper corners of the images flanking the head of the deities or occupying the rounded tops, sometimes accompanying figures holding crowns, or even on some other parts of the temple walls or ceilings. *Gandharvas* playing on the musical instruments, sometimes accompanied by their spouses, are shown on the top corners of some images or pillars, or even panels decorating the basement mouldings or walls of the temples.[56] We have described above the *gandharvas* and *vidyādharas*, alone or couples, as the adjuncts of various images described above. Single *vidyādhara* figures bearing garlands in their hands and depicted in flying postures may also be seen fixed in the wall of the approach way of the site museum at Dholbaha (Pl. 39). Many fragmentary friezes in the site museum show these minstrels and angels singly or in couples (Pls. 175-76). One frieze shows a class of musicians practicing music and dance (Pl. 177). In the Government Museum at Hoshiarpur are also displayed fragments showing *gandharva* and *vidyādhara* figures detached from images (Pls. 178-80) or architectural pieces (Pls. 181-83). A *gandharva* couple has been shown on the abacus of a pillar belonging to a Jaina temple at Sunam (Pl. 184).

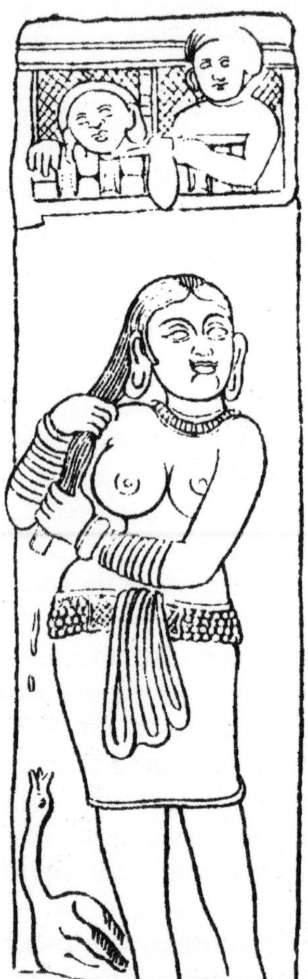

**Fig. 32.** Lady squeezing hair from Mathura.

*Kinnaras* were generally shown on the *udumbaras* of the temples and two good examples thereof exist at Sunam, one of which shows a fragment with a central *kīrttimukha* in a square panel with anthropo-avian *kinnara* (*udadhiputra*) holding a pot and moving inwards to his left followed by a mythical lion lolling out its tongue with fore part of the body raised (Pl. 185). The other piece is similar but not in a good state of preservation. It, however, shows another figure behind the lion (Pl. 186).

*Apasarases* are the personification of female beauty and sexual pleasure. They sing, dance, play on musical instruments, sport and seduce. The *Kshīrārṇava* of Viśvakarmā (CXX, 85-134) emphasizes repeatedly that *Devāṅganas* should be depicted in dancing acts and postures, and classifies them into 32 types on the basis of their acts and postures. They generally adorn the temple walls assuming various beauteous forms: slender, seductive, sensual; singing, dancing, coquetting, disrobing, revealing their physical charm, sporting with ball, yawning, pedicuring, binding anklets, bedecking themselves, rinsing water from the wet pleats of hair, removing thorn, fondling a baby, playing with pets, applying collyrium, etc. Unfortunately, we do not have many examples from the medieval temple remains at Dholbaha and other places in Punjab except two figures of fly-whiskers from the former which give us some idea of their portraiture. Both of them are exhibited in the Government Museum at Hoshiarpur now (Pls. 187-88). The depiction of female beauty in plastic art, however, goes back

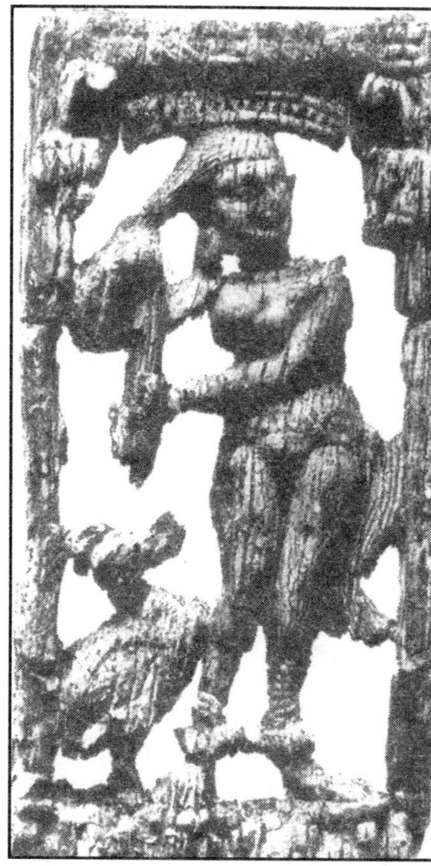

**Fig. 33.** Lady squeezing hair, ivory from Begram (after Bopearachchi).

to a much earlier period and we have the *yakshī* and *Śālabhañjikā* figures from Śuṅga period onwards depicted on the railing pillars and brackets of the *stūpas* and their gateways, on caves, on pillars, doorjambs, walls, lintels and even other places. Early Indian ivories, particularly from Amaravati, and terracottas from Ahichhatra and paintings at Ajanta also show such figures. Nearer home, reference has already been made to some terracotta sealings from Sunet depicting *Śālabhañjikā* motif. More examples of *Śālabhañjikās* on Kushāṇa railing pillars have come to light from Sanghol.[57] Two pieces illustrated here for the first time (Pl. 189-90) are beautiful examples of the Buddhist Kushāṇa art of the Mathura School. Another *yakshī* represents a *sadyaḥ-snātā* or Karpūramañjarī, a beautiful lady in the full bloom of her youth who is fresh from her bath and is wringing her wet tresses to squeeze out water and a swan or *chātaka* bird is depicted as trying to pick the water drops falling from the squeezed locks considering them as pearls (Pl. 191).[58] A terracotta figurine from Sunet also shows a *sadyassnātā* squeezing her hair (Pl. 192). This theme was very popular with the artists and finds depiction on a Mathura railing pillar also (Fig. 32)[59] as well as in Begram ivory (Fig. 33).[60] It continued down to the medieval period to be represented on the temple walls of the period.[61] Some more examples of beautiful *yakshīs* from Sanghol are *Paribhoga-darśinī* (*yakshī* with a mirror), *Naṭī* (acrobatic dancer), mother playing with a child, *Yakshārohī* (*yakshī* riding *vāma yaksha*), *Darpaṇa-dhāriṇī* (*yakshī* with a mirror), *Kamala-dhāriṇī* (lady holding lotus flowers), *Madhupāna* (lady taking a drink), mother and child playing with a rattle, *Prasādhikā* (lady's maid carrying a toilet tray), *Dugdha-dhāriṇī* (lady holding her right breast to suckle the babe), langorous lady pulling her limbs in lassitude, *Śṛigāriṇī* (lady putting on a necklace), lady playing harmonica, female with a flute and wine flask, etc.[62] The depiction of some of these forms seems to have continued. In the medieval period we find *Sura-sundarīs* or *Devāṅganas* playing with a ball or a pet, tying anklets or applying henna or taking out a thorn from the foot, holding a mirror, reading or writing a letter, applying collyrium, fondling a child, disrobing, coquetting, dancing, playing on different musical instruments, etc. became an essential feature of the decorative plan of the temples.[63]

## MITHUNA

The depiction of the *mithuna* 'a pair' essentially implying a duality of a male and a female is taken to form an exemplery model of creativity and fertility. The concept of duality has come down to us from the Vedic times and seems to have assumed symbolical meaning of fecundity, plenty and auspiciousness. The theme of the *Mithuna* or the depiction of couples was widely cherished by the Indian artists as an auspicious motif. The representation of the male and female figures or couples ranging from graceful to amorous with the passage of time was a universal practice in the whole of India from about the second century BCE and it transgressed all sectarian limits.[64] *Mithuna* or couple figures in superposed panels on the pilasters of Cave IV at Pitalkhora (second century BCE), superimposed one above the other flanking a Dharmachakra-pillar at Amaravati, on the doorframes of Cave III at Nasik (second centuy CE), and the standardized composition of Gupta temple doorframes showing superimposed *mithuna* panels (*mithuna-śākhās*) are interesting examples.[65] A terracotta sealing of Gupta idiom from Sanghol shows a *mithuna* representing the lady offering a drink to the male (Pl. 193). We have some examples of the *mithunas* on temple buildings from Dholbaha. The best preserved are the two doorjambs belonging to a temple at Dholbaha, now displayed in the Governement Museum, Hoshiarpur, which show the couple putting one arm around the back and shoulder of the partner in a very graceful manner (Pl. 194). The expressions of both the male and the female are those of peace and quietude and no intensity of feelings is reflected in the relief. Both wear simple dress and ornaments. Rectangular panels above show five standing figures turned slightly to their left, *kīrttimukha* and *gandharva* and *vidyādhara* couples respectively. The temple to which they belonged may have come into existence in the tenth or eleventh century CE. A panel on the site also depicts a couple standing gracefully slightly turned to each other (Pl. 195). Another broken panel in the same museum shows a warrior with a sword tucked to his waist belt in an apologetic posture trying to appease his spouse by touching her chin with his right hand (Pl. 196). The lady is extending her right arm across her partner's right arm and touching her right breast with her left hand. Both are slightly turned towards each other and the latter has poised her body on her right leg with left bent at the knee and its toe touching the ground with heel raised. The minute details of the faces are lost but their figures are quite attractive and graceful. The panel seems to be contemporary to the foregoing doorjambs. A third *mithuna* with heads of the couple damaged is preserved in the store of the site museum at Dholbaha. The female stands turned to her left and the man behind her is depicted again, as if appeasing her by holding her right arm (Pl. 197). An interesting feature of the panel is the pillar consisting of pots placed one over the other. This panel, too, belongs to the same period.

## GHAṬA-PALLAVA

*Ghaṭa-pallava* (vase and foliage) or *Pūrṇa-kalaśa* (full vase) is the symbol of plenty and prosperity, creativity and fullness. Its depiction is regarded very auspicious. Two good examples of the depiction of the *ghaṭa-pallava* motif, probably on *ruchaka* pillars, also come from Dholbaha (Pls. 198-99). The former is very detailed and elaborate and the latter shows a *kīrttimukha* beneath it. A pillar near Sirhind (Pl. 200) also shows the *ardha-padma* and *ghaṭa-pallava* motifs, indicating that the depiction of such motifs was quite popular in this region as elsewhere also. Another broken pillar nearby (Pl. 201) shows beautiful carivings but we are not sure whether it carried similar motifs or not.

## KĪRTTIMUKHA

*Kīrttimukha* or 'face of glory', which starts appearing as an architectural motif in the Gupta period, is the symbolic manifestation of the terrific aspect of Śiva used traditionally to wave off the evil effects of the obnoxious eyes.[66] A grotesque mask generally conventionalised as lion's face, it is used on the temple walls to relieve the monotony and filling blank spaces and came to be regarded as a sacred symbol. It is found in a myriad variety of forms on images and different parts of the temples. Some of the *kīrttimukhas* have been referred to above incidentally while describing the images and other temple remains, and some good examples are known from Sunam (Pls. 202). A characteristic feature of these *kīrttimukhas* is that they are generally shown as emiting garlands which are held by *vidyādharas,* who are depicted on the corners in flying postures or human figures are shown as running away from them.

## KĪCHAKA OR BHĀRAPUTRA

Architectural piece of a Jaina temple from Sunam illustrated above (Pl. 199.5) shows a *kīrttimukha* at the top and a *kīchaka* or *Bhāraputra* or *Bhāravāhaka* below. Another specimen of the Atlantis comes from Dholbaha. Two friezes are preserved in the site museum depicting a lion hunting scene, at the extreme end of which we find the four-armed *kīchaka* bearing the load of the superstructure on his upraised additional hands and balancing his body by sharing the load by normal hands put vertically on the respective knees (Pls. 203-204). The hunting scene has been depicted beautifully by showing the elephant winding its trunk on the neck of the attacking lion and an associate or soldier of the hunter-king attacking the lion by piercing the spear in its belly from below. The king or the hunter is charging with a long spear while sitting at the tail-end of the back of the elephant and another soldier with his weapon walks behind in protection. In the second frieze, the lion is fighting the elephant sitting on its hauches and the soldier is trying to pierce the mouth of the lion with his long spear (Pl. 204). Ohri has observed that

> Naturalistic rendering of the animal figures and taut muscles of the figure of attendant holding a spear in the Dholbaha fragment exhibit the skill of the artist. The type of rounded (as if lathe-turned) pillar seen at the left in this slab is associated with sculpture and architecture of the late Pratihara period. This slab, thus, appears to have been produced around the tenth-eleventh century. Linear quality of the work and the type of the modelling of the human figures seen in it also support the suggested period.[67]

## VYĀLA

*Vyālas* are fabulous 'grotesque' hybrid creatures seen abundantly in Indian temples and plastic art. They are generally of a decorative nature. The Purāṇas often mention Gajānana, Siṃhānana, Vyāghrānana, Aśvānana, Varāhasadṛiśānana, Mṛigendravadana, Kākamukha, Kharamukha, Gṛidhramukha, Haṃsavaktra, Kukkuṭavaktra, etc. Bhuvanadeva includes most of these in his list of sixteen griffins in his *Aparājitapṛichchhā*: *siṃha* (lion), *gaja* (elephant), *aśva* (horse), *nara* (human), *vṛisha* (bull), *mesha* (ram), *śuka* (parrot), *śūkara* (boar), *mahisha* (buffalo), *mūshaka* (mouse), *kīṭa* (insect or wretched elephant), *vānara* (monkey), *kukkuṭa* (cock), *mayūra* (peacock), *aja* (goat), and *sarpa* (snake) *vyālas*. Indian artists have translated most of these descriptive names into lively representations of fabulous composite figures in plastic art. Winged and fish-tailed animals like the lion, elephant, horse, stag, crocodile, centaurs, tritons, etc. are also quite common in Indian art. Their depiction on image slabs and temple walls was a popular artifice of the builders to provide contrast to human sculptures and avoid the monotony of repetition. Available hybrid figures show that they have been executed aesthetically and with perfection. As elsewhere, there are some good specimens of *vyāla* figures in Punjab sculptures also, showing purely mythical animals amongst which elephant and lion (*gaja-śārdūla*) are the common type.[68] Images of Vishṇu (Pls. 8-9 & 19) and Sūrya (Pls. 143-44) show the *vyāla* figures on their back slabs. A fragment showing Brahmā on a stele has the partially preserved face of a boar as the *vyāla* (Pl. 165). Another fragment from Dholbaha in the Hoshiarpur museum shows a composite form of horse and elephant with a rider (Pl. 205). An architectural fragment from Ghuram also shows a *vyāla* with a rider (Pl. 206).

Though not exactly a *vyāla* but an elephant with a rider or *mahāvata* 'elephant driver' (Pl. 207) from Janer in unbaked clay belonging to an early period, which seems to be a part of a larger architectural depiction of some palace or similar mansion, betrays the mastery of the craftsman to depict such motifs in a naturalistic way in the region.[69] Here, the elephant seems to be depicted in the act of sitting to receive the royal personage on its back. The folded hind leg, slantingly extended foreleg, back touching the ground and the stance of the *mahāvata* show the

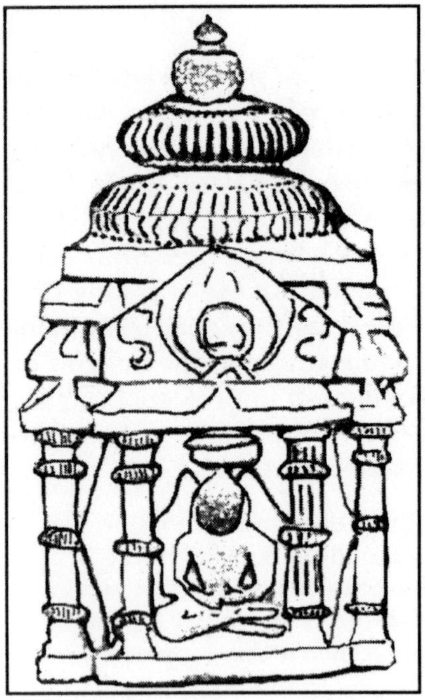

**Fig. 34.** *Nāgara-kūṭa* with a Jina from Kharar.

keen observation and efficiency of the artist, which is further substantiated by the figure of a fabulous unbaked winged lion having the feet of elephant in poor man's art from Janer (Pl. 208). The latter betrays some alien impact also and reminds us of the late Kushāṇa bronze plaque from Ropar, showing a winged griffin in a medallion (Pl. 209). The outer ring of this medallion is decorated with leaf motif all around.

A badly worn-out doorjamb from Majhur represents the *dvāraśākhā* of a fully developed medieval temple of twelfth century and shows the central *mithuna-śākhā* flanked by *gaṇa-śākhā* with a *vyāla* at its bottom and an unidentifiable female deity or attendant figure at the base in a pedimented and well-ornamented niche (Pl. 210). The other jambs are not clear but one of them may have certainly been the *patra-śākhā* with lotus-leaf design. A much mutilated and woefully worn-out fragment of a *pañcha-śākhā* doorjamb from Siswan shows the *Lahara-vallarī* design on the *antaśśākhā* and what looks like a *vyāla-śākhā* as the *bāhya-śākhā* (Pl. 211).

The temple style of the region, thus, may not have been different from that of the North Indian Nāgara style in general, as indicated by a *nāgara-kūṭa* (30 X 26 cm) found from Kharar (Pl. 212) and another one belonging to a Jaina temple from Sanghol (Fig. 34) but it is difficult to say if there were any regional characteristics or variations as there are no standing temples existing now.

## NOTES AND REFERENCES

1. *DHI*, p. 510.
2. *EHI*, II, pp. 502-03.
3. *Ibid.*, *DHI*, p. 515.
4. *Bṛihatsaṃhitā*, LVII.41: *Brahmā kamaṇḍalu-karaśchaturmukhaḥ paṅkajāsanasaṃsthitaścha.*
5. C. Sivaramamurti, "Geographical and Chronological Factors in Indian Iconography," *Ancient India*, No. 6, p. 21.
6. *EHI*, II, Appendix B, p. 245.
7. As quoted by Rao (*Ibid.*). Cf. *VDP* III.44, 6.
8. *DHI*, p. 516.
9. *EHI*, II, Appendix B, pp. 243-44.
10. *Ibid.*, p. 244.
11. *Ibid.*
12. *Rūpa-Maṇḍana* II.7.
13. *DHI*, p. 516.
14. *EHI*, II, p. 243.
15. V.S. Apte, *Sanskrit-English Dictionary*, Delhi-Varanasi-Patna, 1959, p. 157.
16. *DHI*, p. 517. Sivaramamurti (*AI*, No. 6, p. 35) also states that Brahmā in Rajasthan and Gujarat is represented with a beard like an old sage emphasizing the Pitāmaha (grandfather) aspect of the god. Cf. Devendra Handa, *Osian: History, Archaeology, Art & Architecture*, Delhi, 1984, pp. 134-37, Pls. 97-98.
17. Handa (2006), *op. cit.*, pp. 204-09, Pls. 273-80.
18. The word Skanda is derived from the root *Skandir*, which is used in words like *Chaskanda*, *Skanna*, etc., which occur in the *RV*. Nowhere, however, does the word Skanda occur in that text. It occurs for the first time in the *Chhāndogya Upanishad* (VII.26, 2). Kārttikeya occurs in the *Maitrāyaṇī Saṃhitā* for the first time.

19. Seventeen times. See for details P.K. Agrawala, *Skanda-Kārttikeya*, Varanasi, 1967, p. 1 and Kanchan Sinha, *Kārttikeya in Indian Art & Literature*, Delhi, 1979, p. 1.
20. *RV* X. 135. In the *RV* IV. 15,7-10 *Kumāra* seems to occur as a proper name.
21. Sukumar Sen, "Iranian Sorasha and Indian Skanda", *Indo-Iranica*, Vol. IV, No. 1 (July, 1950), p. 27.
22. *Atharva Veda* VI.67, 2.
23. For detailed references, see P.K. Agrawala (1967), *op. cit.*, pp. 1-11; Sinha, *op. cit.*, pp. 1-15; Asim Kumar Chatterjee, *The Cult of Skanda-Kārttikeya in Ancient India*, Calcutta, 1970, pp. 1-70; R. Navaratnam, *Kārttikeya – The Divine Child*, Bombay, 1973, pp. 1ff.
24. *Mahābhārata* I.103, 9.
25. *RV* VII.63, 1; X. 84, 2: *Kāṭhaka Saṃhitā* 36, 8; *Maitrāyaṇī Saṃhitā* I.10, 14; III.13, 14; *Śatapatha Brāhmaṇa* V, 3,1, 1.
26. *AV* XI.2, 31; 1; *Vājasaneyī Saṃhitā* XVI.17; *Śatapatha Brāhmaṇa* IX.1, 1, 18.
27. *Sacred Books of the East Series*, Vol. XLI (Pt. III, Eng. Tr. by Eggling), pp. 157ff.
28. For relevant portions and their English translation, see, P.K. Agrawala (1967), *op. cit.*, Appendix II, pp. 104-10.
29. *Bhavishya Purāṇa*, Brahmaparvan, Ch.39; *Brahma Purāṇa*, Ch.128; *Brahmāṇḍa Purāṇa* II.40; *Brahma-Vaivarta Purāṇa* III.1-2 & 14; *Liṅga* I.104, 105; *Matsya*, Chs. 108-60; *Padma* VI.38; *Saura*, Chs. 60-62; *Śiva* IX.19; *Skanda* I.1, 20-30; I.2, 20-32; VI.261; *Vāmana*, Ch. 25 & 52; *Vāyu* LII, 20-50; *Vishṇudharmottara* 1.228, etc.
30. P.K. Agrawala (1967), *op. cit.*, p. 24.
31. *Mbh.*, IX.44, 1-12; *Skanda*, VI.264, 6; etc.
32. *Mbh.* XII. 86, 15 ff; III.218, 32; IX.45, 41-47; 86, 15-25. *Tvashṭā* is also said to have presented Skanda a toy as *Kukkuṭa* and Vishṇu is said to have presented him a fowl and a peacock [P.K. Agrawala (1967), *op. cit.*, pp. 56-57].
33. *Mbh.* III.213, 16ff. Cf. *Mbh.* III. 218, 49. She is identified with Lakshmī also. For details see Hopkins, *op. cit.*, p. 229; J. Gonda, *Aspects of Early Viṣṇuism*, Utrecht, 1954, p.218. For the iconography of Shashṭhī see R.C. Agrawala, "Goddess Shasṭhī in Mathura Sculpture", *Bulletin of Museums & Archaeology in U.P.*, Lucknow, No. 4 (Dec. 1969), pp. 1-6 and N.P. Joshi, "Sasthi in Literature and Art", in *Ajaya-Śrī: Recent Studies in Indology (Prof. Ajay Mitra Shastri Felicitation Volume)*, ed. by Devendra Handa, Delhi, 1989, Vol. 2, pp. 391-95.
34. *Kauṭilīya Arthaśāstra* II.4, 17.
35. *Mahābhāshya* of Patañjali, ed. by F. Kielhorn, Vol. II, p. 429.
36. Percy Gardner, *The Coins of the Greek and Scythic Kings of Bactria and India in the British Museum*, London, 1886 (Reprint, New Delhi, 1967), Pl. XXVIII 22-24.
37. P.K. Agrawala (1967), *op. cit.*, p. 87; Chatterjee, *op. cit.*, pp. 82ff.
38. Devendra Handa, *An Epic Pilgrimage – History and Antiquity of Pehowa: Ancient Pṛithūdaka – A Mahābhārata Site on the Sarasvatī*, New Delhi, 2004, p.44.
39. *Mbh.*, Sabhāparva, 29.4:

    *Tato bahudhanaṃ ramyaṃ gavāḍhyaṃ dhanadhānyavat /*
    *Kārttikeyasya dayitaṃ Rohitakamupādravat //*

40. *Mahāmāyūrī* (ed. Sylvan Levi, *Journal Asiatique*, 1915) verse 21 – *Rohitake Kārttikeyaḥ Kumāro lokaviśrutaḥ.*
41. Allan, *op. cit.*, p. xxxvi. Cf. Alexander Cunningham, *Coins of Ancient India*, pp. 97-98; *DHI*, pp. 117, 141; Moti Chandra, "Presidential Address", *Journal of the Numismatic Society of India*, XVI, p. 8.
42. Allan, *op. cit.*, p. 245.
43. Devendra Handa, *Early Indian Coins from Sugh*, Delhi, 2006, pp. 72-85, Pls. XI-XIV; Ajay Mitra Shastri, "Symbols on Tribal Coins: An Interpretative Study", in *Seminar Papers on the Tribal Coins of Ancient India (C.200 BC to 400 AD)*, Eds. Jai Prakash Singh & Nisar Ahmad, Varanasi, 1977, p. 89.
44. P.K. Agrawala (1967), *op. cit.*, pp. 46-52, Pls. VII-XII; Chaterjee, *op. cit.*, pp. 114ff, Figs. 1-4; Sinha, *op. cit.*, pp. 109-17.
45. Gardner, *loc. cit.*
46. P.L. Gupta, Editorial Note, *Numismatic Digest*, Bombay, Vol. II, Pt. II, p. 22.
47. Allan, *op. cit.*, pp. cl-cli and 276-78, Pl. Xl.1-9.

48. John Allan, *Catalogue of the Coins of the Gupta Dynasties and of Śaśāṅka, King of Gauḍa*, London, 1914, pp. 84ff, Pl. XV.5-14; A.S. Altekar, *Coinage of the Gupta Empire*, Varanasi, 1957, pp. 165-275, Pl. XIII.11-14.
49. R.C. Agrawala, "A Rare Bronze of Skanda Kumāra from the Punjab Hills", *Vishveshvaranand Indological Journal*, Hoshiarpur, Vol. V, pp. 206-08.
50. Handa (2006), *op. cit.*, pp. 209-16, Pls. 281-88.
51. S.P. Gupta (Ed.), *Kushāṇa Sculptures from Sanghol (1st-2nd Century AD): A Recent Discovery*, National Museum, New Delhi, 1985, p. 30, Figs. 4.6-7, Pl. 10. A fifth century seated Vaishṇavī *mātṛikā* from Samalaji in the Baroda Museum is also shown as holding the nipple of her left breast and offering it to the child in her left lap. Carmel Berkson, *The Life of Form in Indian Sculpture*, New Delhi, 2000, p. 138, Ill. 130.
52. *Manusmṛiti* (V.4-7) refers to the eight *dikpālas* as Indra, Anila (Vāyu), Yama, Arka (Sūrya), Agni, Varuṇa, Chandra (Soma) and Vitteśa (Kubera).
53. Handa (2006), *op. cit.*, pp. 219-25, Pls. 294-306.
54. *Journal of Oriental Institute*, Baroda, Vol. XX, No. 2, p. 143.
55. *Ibid.*
56. Cf. R.S. Panchamukhi, *Gandharvas & Kinnaras in Indian Iconography*, Dharwar, 1951.
57. For those already published, see S.P. Gupta, *op. cit.*, cover page & pp. 60-61, Pl. 1; pp. 78-79, Pl. 16B and p. 81, Pl. 18 .
58. *Ibid.*, pp. 62-63, Pl. 3.
59. *Ibid.*, p. 26, fig. 4.1.
60. Osmund Bopearachchi, "Recent Archaeological Discoveries from Afghanistan and Pakistan", *Bulletin of Miho Museum*, Vol. V, March 2005, p. 23, Fig. 28.
61. *Marg*, XII (2), March 1959, p. 57, Fig. 12; Devendra Handa, *Osian: History, Archaeology, Art & Architecture*, Delhi, 1984, p. 163, Pl. 125.
62. Gupta, *op. cit.*, pp. 116ff.
63. Handa (1984), *loc. cit.*, Pls. 121-129. Various temples at Khajuraho and elsewhere show such figures in large numbers.
64. For a lengthy and fuller treatment of the scope, significance and treatment of the *mithuna* figures on temple walls, see R. Nath, *The Art of Khajuraho*, New Delhi, 1980.
65. P.K. Agrawala, *Mithuna, the Male-Female Symbol in Indian Art and Thought*, Delhi, 1983.
66. For details and historical development of the motif, see M.K. Dhavalikar, "Kirtimukha", in M.S. Nagaraja Rao (Ed.), *Kusumāñjali: New Interpretation of Indian Art & Culture – Sh. C. Sivaramamurti Commemoration Volume*, Vol. II, Delhi, 1987, pp. 349-54, Figs. 5.
67. Ohri, *op. cit.*, p. 125.
68. For a detailed discussion, see M.A. Dhaky, *The Vyāla Figures on the Medieval Temples of India*, Varanasi, 1965; Shanti Lal Nagar, *Composite Deities in Indian Art and Literature*, New Delhi, 1989, pp. 140-51.
69. Cf. Gupta terracotta figurine from Suratgarh in Rajasthan showing an elephant with a prone person on his back vide Urmila Sant, *Terracotta Art of Rajasthan*, New Delhi, 1997, p. 173, Pl. XLII.

# 9

# Buddhist Sculptures

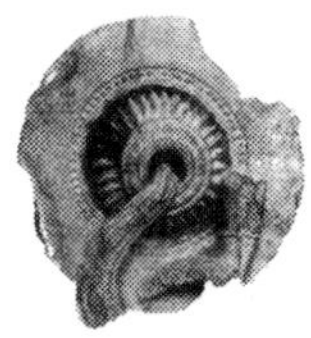

The *Vinaya* of the Mūlasarvāstivādins refers to Buddha's long journey along with Ānanda from Hastināpura to Rohitaka and from there to Gandhāra and Uḍḍiyāna and back with *Yaksha* Vajrapāṇi but Frauwallner regards the account of this journry to be a later interpolation.[1] During his lifetime, Buddha did not travel beyond Śrāvastī. The literary traditions of his travels to distant places are all later and cannot be relied upon. No evidence of the prevalence of Buddhism in Punjab is available before the time of the Mauryan Emperor Aśoka who is well known to have spread Buddhism far and wide. He is said to have collected relics from seven of the *Śārīrika-stūpas* (Buddhist sepulchral monuments or kinds of Topes for keeping the corporeal remains) and distributed them into 84,000 *stūpas,* which he built subsequently throughout the length and breadth of his empire. The Chinese pilgrim Yuang Chwang (Xuan Zang), however, makes a specific reference to Aśokan *stūpas* in the Hīnayāna monastery at Ta-mo-su-fa-na or Tāmasa-vana, the 'black forest',[2] and in the capital of the She-to-tu-lu country[3] which are generally believed to have been located in the Punjab. He also refers to Buddhist *stūpas,* monasteries and establishments at various other places.

Aśoka's patronage seems to have contributed a lot to spread Buddhism and take it to the grass roots that even aliens started adopting it. The well-known Indo-Greek ruler Menander (165-135 BCE) is believed by some scholars to have been converted to Buddhism by *Thera* Nāgasena and become a great champion of this faith.[4] Some scholars, however, doubt it that he was converted to Buddhism. It will not be irrelevant here to quote Plutarch who records that "When a certain man named Menander, who had been a good king of the Bactrians, died in camp, the cities celebrated his funeral as usual in other respects, but in respect of his remains they put forth rival claims and only with difficulty came to terms, agreeing that they should divide the ashes equally and go away and should erect monuments to him in all their cities."[5] This episode reminds us of the passage in the Mahāparinibbāna-sutta in the *Dīghanikāya,* describing the famous dispute that took place amongst some Indian monarchs and *Janapadas* 'tribal states' to share the ashes of the Buddha in order to deposit them in a series of *stūpas.*[6] There thus remains no doubt to Menander being a great benefactor of Buddhism even if he was not converted to

Buddhism. Some scholars take the depiction of the *chakra* on one of his coin-types as the *dharma-chakra* 'the wheel of Law' and interpret it as an extremely discreet allusion to his personal belief.[7] *Mahāvaṃsa*, the great chronicle of Ceylon, mentions that when the Sinhalese king Duttugamunu (161-137 BCE), a contemporary of Menander, invited foreign delegations at the time of the inauguration of the great *stūpa* Ruwanvali Dāgoba, there came from Alasandā, the Greek city (*yonanagarālasandā*) the *thera* Yonamahadammarakhita with thirty thousand *bhikkhus*.[8] Even if we take the number of the delegation to be an exaggeration, we cannot ignore the fact that Buddhism was quite popular in the Greek territory in the northwest at that time. Menander's coins have been found from Begram (near Kabul) to Mathura and even other far-flung territories.[9] He performed many acts of piety. It is likely that many Greeks followed Menander in adopting Buddhism, donating to the Buddhist establishments and spreading the faith. They were also responsible for evolving a new style of Buddhist art which flourished in northwest India, including the Gandhāra region.[10]

Xuan Zang tells us that at Sagala, generally identified with Śākala or modern Sialkot (now in Pakistan) and believed to be Menander's capital,[11] existed a Hīnayāna Buddhist monastery and a *stūpa* beside that where the Four Past Buddhas had preached and where there were their footprints. Vasubandhu had composed *Paramārtha-Satya-Śāstra*, now lost, at this place.[12] In Chi-na-p'uh-ti (Chīnabhukti), where Kanishka had arranged the stay of the Chinese hostages, there were ten Buddhist monasteries and nine Deva-Temples.[13] Its capital has been identified with Patti or Chhine in district Amritsar. In She-lan-ta-lo (Jālandhara), there existed 50 monasteries with more than 2000 Brethren who made special studies in the Great and Little Vehicles. In one of these monasteries, the Nagaradhana Vihāra, Xuan Zang found the learned Brother named Chandravarma, with whom he spent four months studying an Abhidharma work.[14]

Pushyamitra Śuṅga (185-148 BCE) has been described in the Buddhist accounts as a persecutor of the Buddhists. He is said to have chased the Buddhists up to Śākala and made a statement there that he will reward a hundred *dīnāras* to a person who would give him the head of a Buddhist monk.[15] But the Bharhut and Sanchi *stūpas*, the Karle caves and a large number of private donations recorded on the Buddhist monuments of the period indicate that popular support to Buddhism remained unabated and Buddhist art and architecture continued to flourish during the Śuṅga period.

Ta-mo-su-fa-na (Tāmasa-vana) of Xuan Zang has been identified by Cunningham with Sultanpur Lodi, situated on the left bank of the Kali-Veni River, nearly 40 km west-southwest of Jalandhar. He states, "When I first saw Sultânpur in November 1838, during the life-time of Ranjit Singh, I approached it from the west through a thick jungle of elephant grass, or *sarkanda*, from 10 to 15 feet in height. On my next visit, in March 1846, when the army was returning from Lahor, I discovered that the town was situated near the edge of a vast quagmire of black mud, which was only thinly covered with a crust of clayey soil."[16] The present name was given to the town founded by Daulat Khan Lodi when he was the Governor of Lahor during the reign of Ibrahim Lodi. Since a lot of change has taken place in the recent decades with the proliferation of agricultural and urban activity, we can't do better than quote Cunningham, though at some length, because he has corroborated what Xuan Zang had penned down centuries ago, to know what existed here more than a century and a half back. Cunningham observed that

> the great mound on which the Bâdshâhi serai now stands, and the numerous ancient coins found there, prove beyond all doubt that the site must have been occupied at a very early date [. . . .] I have a strong suspicion that [. . . .] the walls of the serai must have been built on the foundations of the old Buddhist monastery [. . .] Inside the great monastery there was a stūpa 200 feet in height with the

> thrones of the four Buddhas and a promenade. All these of course have disappeared when the fort was built by Daulat Khan Lodi; its ruins must have added considerably to the height of the mound, which is 30 feet above the road outside. There were hundreds and thousands of stūpas containing relics of Buddha, besides small stūpas without number. These monuments were so close together that their shadows mingled. But many of the stūpas must have been in ruins, as the pilgrim notes that 'the teeth and bones of former saints who had obtained Nirvâna were still found.' The monastery of Tâmasavana was famous as the place where Kâtyayana had composed the *Abhidharma-jñâna-prasthâva*.[17]

Cunningham was close to the truth to say that the countless *stūpas* seen by Xuan Zang must have been used up in the houses of the city when it was rebuilt by Daulat Khan and whatsoever may have been left by him, would have been carried off by the Mughal builders of Jehangir's serai. The antiquity of Sultanpur is vouched by the discovery of ancient coins – square copper piece with elephant and Kharoshṭhī legend on obverse and lion on reverse, 13 coins of Rajubula besides 5 Ādivarāha type silver, 2 of Sāmantadeva and 6 of Madanapāla Deva and other Hindu coins (34 in all) and 51 Muhammadan coins.[18]

During his itinerary between CE 629 and 645, the Chinese pilgrim visited Ku-lu-to and from there he proceeded to She-to-tu-lu. The former has been identified with Kullu in Himachal Pradesh and the latter has been equated with the kingdom of Śatadru (Satluj) and identified with Sirhind by Cunningham: 'the position of Śatadru will correspond almost exactly with the large city of Sirhind, which both history and tradition affirm to be the oldest place in this part of the country'.[19] Xuan Zang described the country of She-to-tu-lo thus:

> This was above 2000 *li* in circuit, bounded on the west by a large river (supposed to be the Sutlej), and its capital was 17 or 18 *li* in circuit. It was an agricultural and fruit-producing country, and yielded much gold, silver, and other precious substances. The inhabitants were in good circumstances and led moral lives, observing social distinctions and adhering devoutly to Buddhism. In and around the capital were ten monasteries, but they were desolate, and the Brethren were very few. About three *li* to the south-east of the capital was an Asoka tope above 200 feet high, and beside it were traces of spots on which the Four Past Buddhas had sat and walked up and down.[20]

S.S. Talwar, an Archaeological Officer of the Punjab State Department of Archaeology under whom the excavations were taken up at Sanghol for the first time, observed that "The name Sanghol might have been derived from Sanghālaya, a home of Sangh or Sanghpur meaning the town of Sangh for the reason that there were located some Buddhist monasteries. In all probability it may be the She-to-tu-lu of the Chinese pilgrim, Hieun Tsang who refers to the existence of ten monasteries in and around it."[21] The suggestion is quite logical and corresponds to the pilgrim's description. Even now Morinda is called Baghanwala (a town of mango groves) by the old people. The suggestion has been picked up by the subsequent writers on the subject[22] rightly perhaps. There is no doubt that Buddhism spread to northwest India and even beyond its boundaries during the reign of Aśoka, as is indicated by literary and epigraphic evidence and the Buddhist remains discovered from various places. The inclination of Menader towards Buddhism also indicates its popularity in the northwest including Punjab but no Buddhist relics belonging definitely to a period prior to first century BCE/CE have been found from anywhere yet from the present-day Indian Punjab. A Kharoshṭhī sealing belonging to Spikilaka (Fig. 35) has been found from Sanghol and has been dated to late first century BCE to early

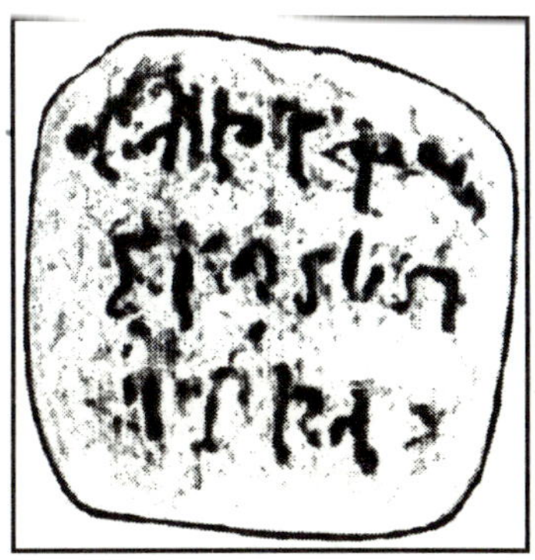

**Fig. 35.** Kharoshṭhī sealing of Spikilaka, Sanghol (after G.B. Sharma).

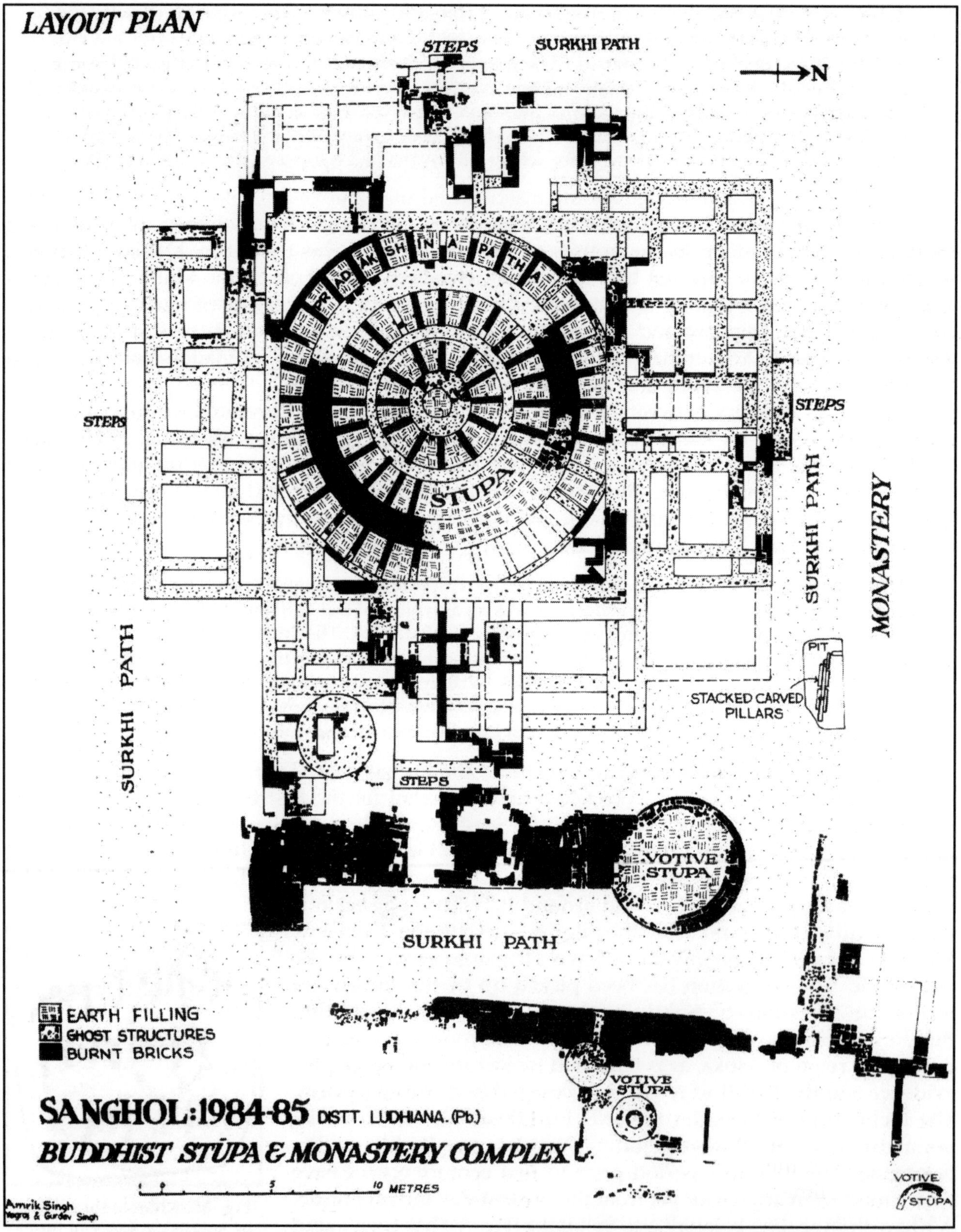


**Fig. 36.** Layout plan of the *stūpas* and monasteries at Sanghol (after G.B. Sharma).

first century CE, indicating clearly that it had become a Buddhist stronghold and many aliens professing Buddhist faith had settled here.

It is quite likely that the Buddhist *stūpa* at Sanghol was in existence during the first century BCE or early first century CE. The Parthian ruler Gondopheres, whose coins have also been obtained from Sanghol in substantial numbers,[23] and the Kushāṇa rulers Soter Megas and Wema Kadphises, who came after the Parthians,[24] are not known to have patronized Buddhism. There is a possibility of the *stūpa* having been disturbed during one of the raids of the Parthians or early Śaka-Kushāṇas as is indicated by the inscribed lid of a relic casket referred to below. The Kushāṇa emperor Kanishka, however, was another protagonist of Buddhism which took a great filip during his reign. The *stūpa* thus seems to have been constructed or reconstructed on a larger scale during the reign of this king or his successor: "In the Kushana period, 1st to 3rd century AD, the township was enlarged enormously and made a great centre of trade and traffic as well as religion and art."[25] It was during this period that a large citadel with internal and external moats was established to protect the interests of the people from outside attack as also to provide status and dignity to the settlement. Coins, seals and sealings discovered at the site in large numbers clearly indicate that Sanghol was one of the most prosperous towns during the Kushāṇa period.[26] We can't do better than quote the excavator regarding some details about the *stūpa* at Sanghol (Fig. 36):

> The most important monument of the Kushāṇa period excavated at Sanghol is a cylindrical stupa of 16 m diameter built over a raised platform. The monument is in ruins, only some basal courses of the brick masonry have been found preserved. The architectural plan of the stupa is like the dharmachakra or spoked wheel. It had three concentric rings of brick masonry with intervening spaces divided by radiating spokes of similar brick masonry at regular intervals. The brick sizes normally are 33x22x5 cm and 30x20x6 cm. The stupa lies at a distance of 60 m from the mud fortification which had surrounded the township. The core of the stupa consists of a thick circular wall of brick masonry filled with earth. Within the core was deposited a steatite relic casket whose remains have been found at two different places in the dig which establishes the fact that the stupa was completely ransacked at some point of time.[27]

The lid of the relic casket bears the Kharoshṭhī legend 'Upāsakasa Ayabhadrasa' in the characters of first century BCE/CE (Fig. 37):

A human tooth, some ashes and bones as also the lower part of the relic casket have been recovered from the core and other parts of the *stūpa* and it has been surmised that "This would indicate that the casket belonged to an upāsaka or lay disciple named Aryabhadra or Bhadra, the noble one. Apparently the casket and so also the stupa were the gifts of this person. The casket is supposed to have contained the relics of the Buddha although it is in no way certain."[28] The Dharmarājikā *stūpa* at Taxila, the Jaina stūpa at Kaṅkālī Ṭīlā in Mathura and the Ikshvāku *stūpas* at Nagarjunakonda in Andhra Pradesh have also been built on *dharmachakra* plan similar to the Sanghol *stūpa*.

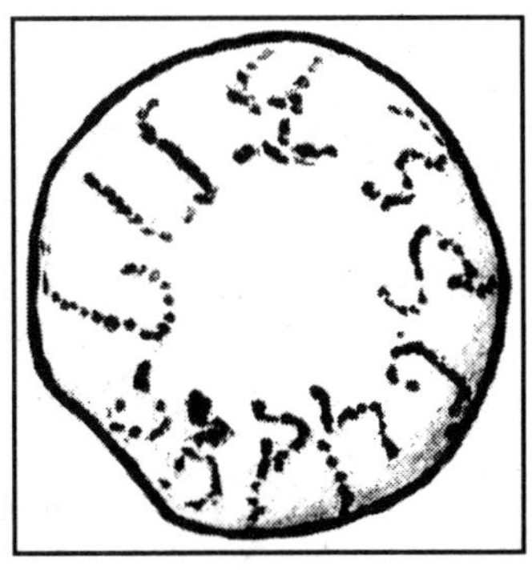

**Fig. 37.** Inscribed lid of the relic casket, Sanghol (after G.B. Sharma).

Another circular wall was built at a distance of 1.5 m to provide a *pradakshiṇā-patha*. The triangular spaces between this wall and the square platform were filled with earth and brick-bats to raise the level of the platform and steps were provided at the cardinal axes to approach the circumambulatory. The platform was neatly plastered with lime mortar from outside. A 5.34 m *surkhī* (red) or murram pathway surrounded the platform at the ground level. Subsequently, however, the lay worshippers seem to have erected

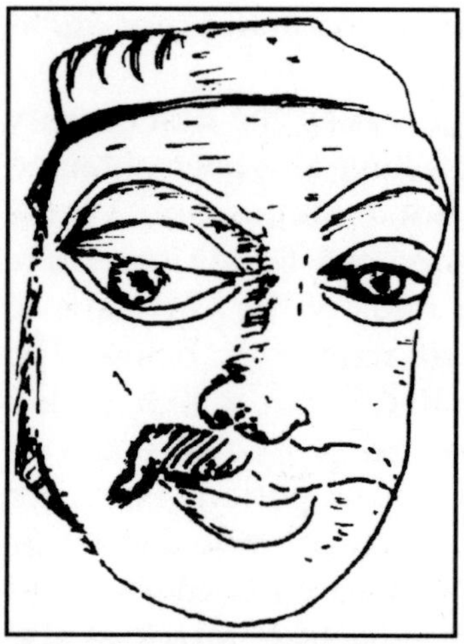

Fig. 38. Male head, Sanghol.

some votive *stūpas* of solid mud core on the eastern flank. Monastic buildings, not fully and properly excavated, came up on all the four sides of the *stūpa*.

Nagaraja Rao has pointed out that

> While on the evidence of Chinese pilgrim's account, we may surmise that Sanghol stupa was the work of Aśoka, on the basis of art evidence, the embellishment of the stupa may have taken place during late 2nd century AD or the first half of 3rd century. The stupa appears to have continued to be in worship till 5th century as is evident from the discovery of a stucco head which clealy belongs to the Gandhara workmanship. As is well known, stucco heads occur in Gandhara in the 4th and 5th century AD and hence the one from Sanghol may be placed in 4th century AD.[29]

This Buddha head in hard stucco (Pl. 213) showing wavy hair-locks is now preserved in the Patiala Museum.[30]

Another Buddha head in clay with quasi-closed eyes, wavy hair style and large bun-shaped top-knot or *ushṇīsha* and bearing a discrete smile painted red (Pl. 214) may also belong to the same period if not earlier.[31] Sandrine Gill obseves that "It must have belonged to the main cult image or one of the main cult images of the site."[32] Like many other sculptures from Sanghol, these images provide unmistakable evidence for the presence of the Gandhāra sculptures at this site during the post-Kushāṇa period. The presence of the aliens here is revealed by the Kharoshṭhī seals/sealings and a terracotta plaque depicting a couple in Hellenistic dress referred to above and is further substantiated by the head of a male in buff sandstone with large eyelids and bow-like eyebrows over almond-shaped eyes, straight sturdy nose with prominent central ridge and broad nostrils, thick drooping moustache and a hair-band or fillet on the head belonging to the second-third century CE (Pl. 215, Fig. 38) and another stone head showing foreign physiognomic features and drooping moustache, probably belonging to an alien trader and/or a Buddhist (Pl. 216). An architectural piece with a small figure of headless Buddha seated in *padmāsana* (Pl. 217) with both shoulders covered by a heavily pleated *saṃghāṭī* in Gandhāra style and a red sandstone image of Bodhisattva seated similarly, unfortunately again with its head and a part of the gloriole lost, with right hand raised in *abhaya* to the level of the shoulder and turned slightly inwards (Pl. 218, Fig. 29), furnish evidence of the type of images worshipped during the Kushāṇa period.

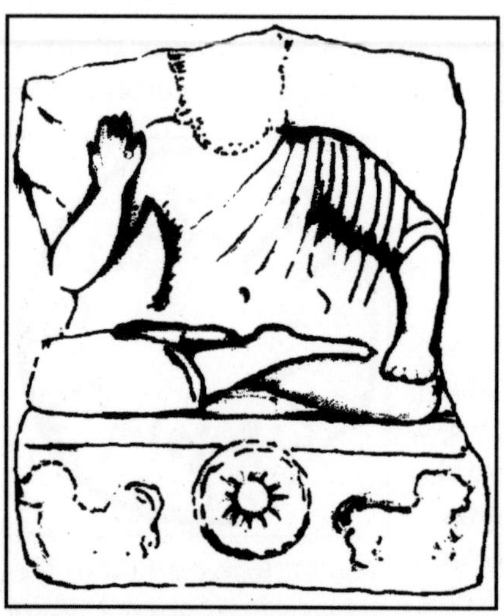

Fig. 39. Bodhisattva, Sanghol.

The most spectacular and epoch-making discovery at Sanghol, however, was made on 1 February 1985 when 117 sculptures of great artistic magnitude belonging to the Mathura School of art during the Kushāṇa period were discovered stacked at one place in a pit cut into the *surkhi* path of the circumambulatory in the northeast corner of the *stūpa*. The hoard consisted of 58 *vedikā-stambhas* (upright pillars), 7 double-sided pillars, 35 *sūchis* or cross-bars and 13 *ushṇīsha* or coping stones, all belonging to the railing which must have been meant for the square platform. The Dharmarājikā-stūpa plan, presence of foreigners like Spikilaka, use of Kharoshṭhī and the Mathura idiom of sculptures suggest that "there was a brisk movement of the people, trade and ideas all along the *uttarāpatha* or Northern Route on which the site of Sanghol was strategically located and that the peoples of Punjab and of the Ganga-Yamuna valley then shared one and the same religion and one and the same art idiom and art style as vehicle for their artistic activities and spiritual attainments".[33]

Commenting on the artistic accomplishment of the Sanghol sculptures, Nagaraja Rao seems to indicate that they were not imported from Mathura but created at Sanghol itself. He observes,

> All the figure sculptures appear to have been carved in a relatively low relief, as compared to the bold relief in which the typical Mathura sculpture of the Kushāṇa period is carved. Secondly, from the point of view of aesthetic delineation, the modelling of the Sanghol figures, appears to be coarser than that at Mathura. Moreover, the figures are not marked by that free movement which is characteristic of the Mathura school. In fact the failure of the artist is evident in those sculptures in which the female is shown from the back. This has resulted in flattening of the female form. All this, however, need not be taken as a blemish on the part of Sanghol artist but is perhaps the product of the provincial school of the metropolitan Mathura. It is nonetheless not unlikely that the Kushāṇa School which flowered at Mathura was probably on the decline in the beginning of the 3rd century, of the heydays of the Imperial Kushāṇas. In that case, Sanghol can be taken to represent the late facies of the Mathura School.[34]

Sandrine too feels that "The most plausible hypothesis is that stone-cutters and sculptors from Mathura workshops carried the stone from Mathura to Sanghol and carved the railing on the site."[35] D.C. Bhattacharryya also sounds a note of caution to this effect when he says that "The historicity of the socio-cultural mobility between Mathura and Punjab during the Kushana period and the feasibility of the sculptures being exported from Mathura region should be carefully examined before coming to an assertive conclusion."[36] It is, however, a well known fact that sculptures of the Kushāṇa art of the Mathura School have been found at distant places away from Mathura. Extensive excavations undertaken at Sanghol have yielded only some chips of the spotted Sikri red sandstone used for these sculptures and other components of the railing. No workshop or mass of waste material has, however, been recovered from the site. It was always easier in ancient times to obtain finished products rather than the raw material. So, while agreeing that the art displayed by Sanghol specimens represents a decadent phase, we do not subscribe to the view that they were created at Sanghol. Specimens of Gandhāra art have been found from various places in Punjab and Haryana but that does not mean that they were carved here in the local ateliers.

"The art of Sanghol is mainly the art of sālabhañjikās," observed S.P. Gupta.[37] The *yakshīs* carved on the railing pillars with their broad, plump and heavy hips to support a girdle, large deep navel, middle with three folds, round, rotund breasts are the paragons of female beauty and "reveal the perfection both technically and in the evocation of a gentle erotic mood and charm without being vulgar which provoke feelings of sensuality, difficult to find anywhere else in the world art".[38] A bewildering variety of lotus has been used for the back of the *vedikā-stambhas* (Pl. 219-220). The cross-bars and the coping stones too have been daintily carved with a variety of motifs, the most prominent being the lotus and rosettes on the former (Pl. 221-24, Fig. 40) and *chaitya* motifs on the latter, with different decorative patterns on each example.

The figure sculptures carved on the railing pillars are the most artistic and must have been the handiwork of the sculptors of Mathura. They depict women in full bloom of their youth scantily dressed with diaphanous lower garments held in position by a broad waist girdle consisting of multiple strands of pearls, standing in *tribhaṅga* in alluring postures, and sometimes engaged even in amorous pranks. The usual ornaments include torque or necklace consisting of multiple strings of beads woven into a twisted pattern, cylindrical ear ornaments with conical ends or spiral rings, multiple bangles, bracelets, double armlets, puffed anklets, etc. and hair combed stylistically into a single braid or in a looped knot at the top.

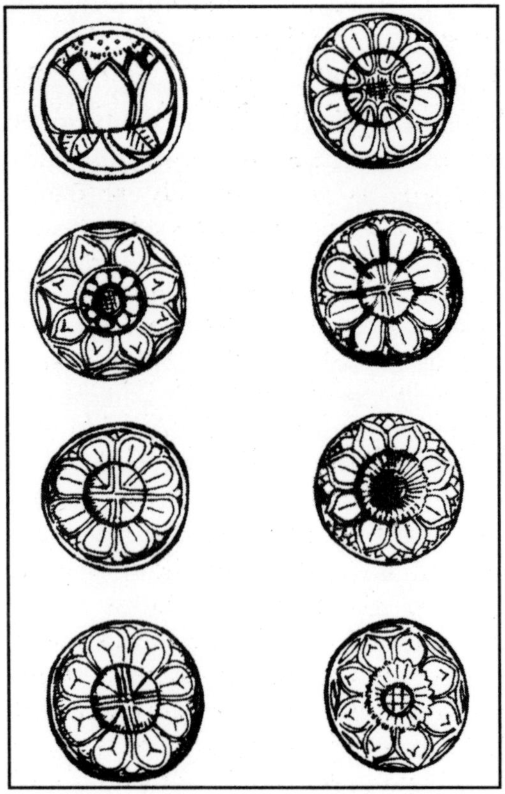

**Fig. 40.** Lotus medallions, Sanghol.

Of the 117 sculptures discovered at Sanghol, 64 were duly treated and displayed for some time in the National Museum, New Delhi in 1985 and published with copious notes, descriptions, details and beautiful plates. Of these, 33 are the cross-bars with lotus medallions and interestingly enough they all show a form different from others. Six of them are the coping stones which generally show semicircular niches within two arched mouldings resembling bent bamboos on both faces containing various symbols in the niches. The largest coping stone is 2.45 m in length, 18 cm high with a depth of 14 cm and has 16 niches depicting floral motif, front elevation of the railing and main gate to the *stūpa*, winged lions, a relic casket bedecked with garlands and having knobbed lid placed on a cushion, outward moving winged lions, floral motif, *śrīvatsa*, *svastika*, *triratna*, two different varieties of *nāgapushpa* or honey-suckle motif, and the front of a railing and gate of a *stūpa* with an inverted lotus dropping gems on the floor (Acc. No. 83).[39] Another piece (149 X 18X 13.5 cm, Acc. No. 15) depicts a window, façade of a *stūpa* with railing, garlands in a container made of leaves, *ushṇīsha* or turban of prince Siddhārtha and a floral motif on the front while the back niches carry different varieties of *nāgapushpa* or honey-suckle and a window. A third fragment of a coping stone (Acc. No. 2, 79 X 18.5 X 13 cm) depicts in the front niches the frontal view of the *stūpa* with an inverted lotus shedding gems on the ground and a profusely adorned lady wearing an *ekāvali* and *kaṅkaṇas* holding three or four lotus flowers in her right hand probably going for worship, while the back niches depict a young lady with a bouquet of flowers and *triratna* symbol. One fragment of an *ushṇīsha* shows devotees in *añjali-mudrā* paying obeisance to Buddha's alms bowl which is placed in the central niche on the front face while the back face contains niches depicting a male devotee carrying lotus stalks in his raised right hand, decorated *stūpa* with long cylindrical drum, hemispherical top capped by *harmikā* and a devotee with folded hands (Acc. No. 18, 88 X 18 X 11 cm). Other fragments show garlands in basket, honeysuckle (Acc. No. 5, 70 X 20 X 14 cm) and honeysuckle and floral motifs (Acc. No. 20, 98 X 19 X 15.5 cm). One corner pillar (Acc. No. 17, 100 X 16 X 14 cm) shows a *Dharmachakra* and a lion on the two facets (Pls. 225-26), while another (Acc. No. 38, 101 X 17 X 14 cm) shows a column emerging from a *pūrṇaghaṭa* base capped by an *āmalaka* with a sejant lion with an open mouth on the abacus on one facet recalling Aśoka's Vaiśālī pillar and carries the depiction of a *stūpa*, a devotee with a bouquet in the *chaitya-gṛiha* and another devotee with a garland in three sections from top to bottom on the other facet.[40] From amongst the unpublished corner stones, one (Acc. No. 8) deserves special mention. It is on loan to the Government Museum and Art Gallery at Chandigarh and shows on its front face a multi-storied Buddhist shrine with a female figure giving alms to a Buddhist mendicant at the base (Pl. 227). The tiara on the head of the female and her dress indicate that the scene may have been that of Yaśodharā giving alms to Buddha but the smallness of the panel and the absence of Rāhula are the deterrents to make any definitive identification. The tower-like shrine, however, brings to our mind similar depictions from Mathura and elsewhere.[41] Equally noteworthy is its back side for its exquisitely carved meandering creeper emanating from the mouth of a crocodile with semi-circular gaps of the meanders beautifully bedecked with leaves and fruits of the plant (Pl. 228), which reminds us of similar devices at Sanchi, Amaravati, Bharhut, Mathura, Amin, etc. coming out of the mouth of the *makara* or a seated *yaksha*.[42] 25 *Vedikā-stambhas* (railing pillars) described and illustrated in the National Museum publication are, however, the most exquisite pieces and depict beautiful young damsels commonly known as *Śālabhañjikās* or *Yakshīs* or Vṛikshikās portrayed in slender proportions and in the most evocative and charming postures with fullness of flesh mirroring contemporary urbane elements and enjoyment of life. They are generally shown in very graceful postures standing on somewhat ugly, smiling or morose, dwarfish and crouching human or animal or hybrid (man-buffalo or man-ram) figures. These beautifully chiselled damsels surpass all other contemporary figures in lyrical expression and sensuous charm, as if the first poems of love were written softly in the vibrant and pulsating layers of the soft and smooth sandstone. These *sura-sundarīs* are often clad in diaphanous *dhotīs* encircling the navel and dangling down at many points and various levels, generally exhibiting nudity, with bare bosoms bursting forth with youthfulness. They wear multiple bangles, broad torque, ear and head ornaments but the five-stringed girdles are the loveliest. Varieties of coiffures, captivating smile, bashful countenance, coyish eyes and luring stances enhance their charm further. Some of these *yakshīs* or beautiful maids deserve to be revisited here.

## PARIBHOGA-DARŚINĪ

*Yakshī* standing gracefully over a crouching dwarf *yaksha* holding a mirror in her bent left hand and pointing to a small crescent-like nail mark (*nakha-kshata*) on her right cheek with the pointing finger of her right hand (Paribhoga-darśinī, Acc. No. 25) is a real voluptuous and exhilarating beauty (Pl. 229) which captivates the onlooker with her curving broad hips billowing towards massive rotund breasts bursting with uncontrollable passion. The figure manages to 'conjure up visions of undisguised exaltation of physical desire, although the nudity is marked by a subtle sense of restraint'.[43] She is elegantly attired in a flowing diaphanous robe with looped tail-end and folds visible on the sides of the shanks and puffed anklets with four-stringed *mekhalā* emphasizing her beauty and charm. The gemmed strings and round clasp of the waistband, pearl bracelets, multiple bangles, broad studded torque and drum-shaped ear ornaments betray the affluence of the elite society and its cultivated taste. The ugly dwarf below underlines the progenerative symbolism and provides a contrast. On the top are carved two youthful figures behind the railing in balcony. The back of the railing pillar is adorned as usual with lotus medallions. The still unpublished railing pillars also contain an example of similar Paribhoga-darśinī (Acc. No. 14, Pl. 230, Fig. 41) standing slightly turned to her right with a mild bend in her right leg looking into a rectangular mirror in her left hand and pointing out to the *nakha-kshata* with her right pointing finger. She wears a broad *mekhalā* studded with gems and pearl strings, and the diaphanous *dhotī* or perhaps the sash coming from over the left waist is knotted and looped on her right hip. Under the pedestal is carved a crocodile to left with tail twirled like that of a fish. The *yakshī* stands under a railed balcony having a door flanked by windows with slightly opened panels. The Punjab government has loaned some of the duplicate figures (Acc. Nos. 8, 14, 47, 84, 114 and 115) to the Government Museum and Art Gallery of Chandigarh and this being one of them is now on display there. A third piece with this

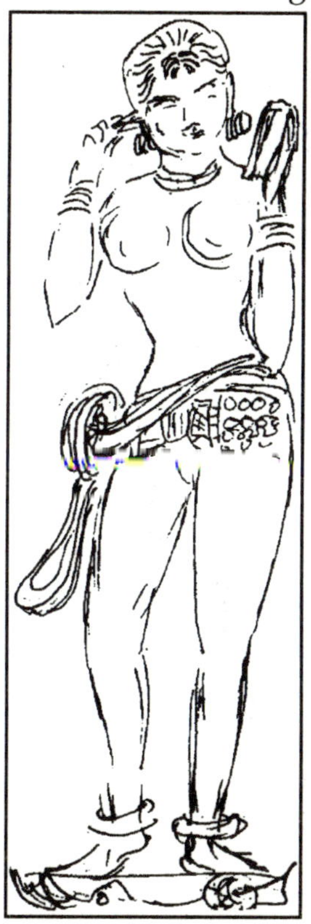

**Fig. 41.** Paribhogadar-śinī (Acc. No. 14), Sanghol.

theme is not in a good state of preservation and shows the damsel oozing with youthfulness standing under a balcony and pointing out the nail-mark with her pointing finger of the right hand (Pl. 231). Her left hand is broken.

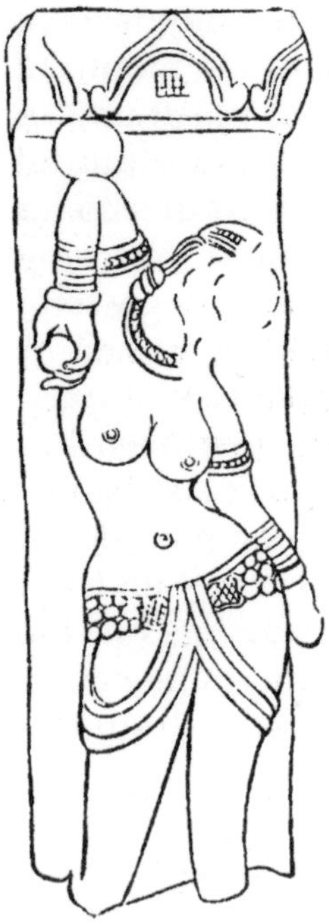

**Fig. 42.** Naṭī from Mathura.

## NAṬĪ (ACROBATIC DANCER)

The depiction of the acrobatic dancer or Naṭī (Acc. No. 81, Pl. 232) balancing a pot on the elbow of her raised and bent left arm is just like a snapshot of a critical fleeting moment of her performance and reminds us of a Naṭī on a railing pillar from Mathura balancing a ball on the elbow of her right arm while holding another in the right hand (Fig. 42).[44]

The uplifted bent left arm is perfectly balanced by a tilt in the head, twist at the waist and the bend of the free right hand. A stylistic characteristic of contemporary hair-styling as seen in many other figures is indicated by a flower-like decoration by cutting some hair above the centre of the forehead and combing others backward and allowing them to fall gracefully at the back. The broad torque, ear-plugs, multiple bangles, the upper garment rolled and suspended from the waistband to form loops and cover the personal part, the loose undergarment to allow the freedom of quick movements and the puffed anklets matching many other figures in the repertoire acquaint us of the contemporary dress and ornamentation. It is to be noted that the habiliments and ornaments not only represent the fast actions of the acrobat but also enhance their effectiveness. The strong shanks supporting the broad hips present a perfect match to the rotund round breasts but the alacrity of danseuse is shown by the artist by the bends, stances and contours of the limbs. Just above the danseuse is a railed balcony with two square windows from which a male and a female are peeping at the performance of the acrobatic dancer with keen interest. The crocodile with wide open mouth and twirled tail is depicted on the platform over which the danseuse is giving her performance. The back of the pillar is decorated as usual with lotus medallions.

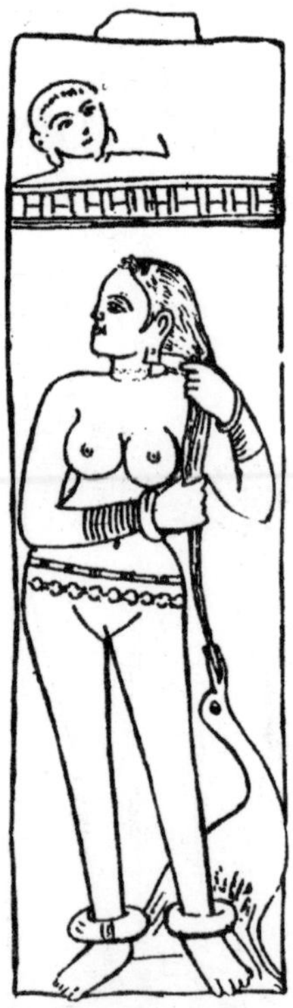

**Fig. 43.** Lady wringing her tresses (Acc. No. 103), Sanghol (after S.P. Shukla).

## SADYAḤ-SNĀTĀ

As noted earlier, the depiction of Sadyaḥ-snātā has remained quite popular in India with the poets and artists who have been very susceptible to the beauties and charms of the ladies in the full bloom of their youth and portraying them exquisitely. The theme of a lady fresh from her bath and wringing her wet tresses to squeeze out water drops from them not only crossed geographical boundaries but also transcended different plastic media like stone, ivory and clay (Pl. 192 and Figs. 32-33). The railing pillar from Sanghol (Acc. No. 103, Pl. 191)[45] depicts the damsel brimming with her full blossomed youthfulness having just finished her bath and wringing out her hair to squeeze out water drops but a swan or *chātaka* bird coming stealthily from behind her left leg, and perhaps unnoticed by her, mistaking the water drops to be pearls falling from the tresses has taken the tip of wet tress in its beak so as not to allow even a single drop fall on the floor (Fig. 43). With head turned to her right and the long tress held in her hands, the lady is shown frontally wearing ear ornaments, multiple bangles, puffed anklets and a diaphanous *dhotī* secured by the *mekhalā*. On the balcony above a young lady and perhaps her spouse (now mutilated) are shown looking at her. The platform below the *keśagumphinī* 'lady arranging her hair' shows a fabulous crouching winged lion.

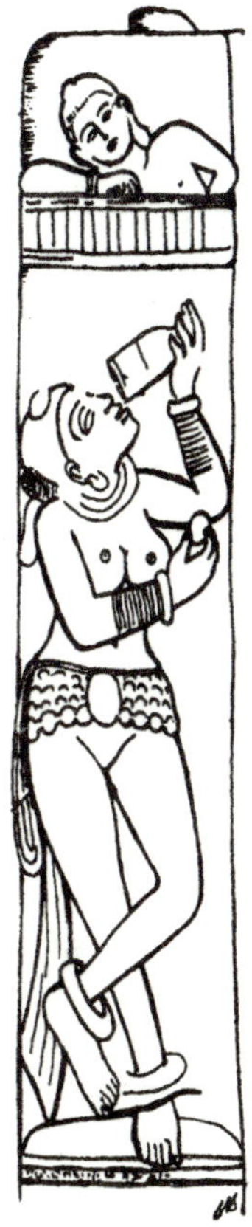

Fig. 44. Madhupāna (Acc. No. 6), Sanghol (after Shukla).

## MADHUPĀNA (LADY TAKING WINE)

A semi-nude damsel exuding youth, vitality and sensuality standing and drinking wine from a tilted goblet held in her left hand firmly from its base (Acc. No. 6, Pl. 233)[46] is a charming figure. Standing with shoulders and posteriors touching the wall-surface and right foot of the slanting leg firmly planted on a cushion, the left leg bent at the knee to cross the right one and touching the cushion by its toe with heel held up, wearing a transparent *dhotī* secured by a multi-strand *mekhalā* with a circular central clasp covering only the upper part of the pubic region and the upper end of the *dhotī* falling in the form of a loop on the side of the right shank, the bust turned to her left with head tilted, eyes inebriated and closed, face held upwards to take even the last drop of the drink add to the grace of the figure and betray the ingenuity of the artist (Pl. 234). Her right hand is bent at the elbow, holding what looks like a sweat ball to be taken along with the drink. With elaborate coiffure showing hair combed beautifully and knotted at the nape of the neck to allow the looped end-tress fall from it, earrings, and double-banded broad torque, *kaṅkaṇas* and *keyūras* covering most part of the forearms, the lady represents the elite, fashionable and opulent stratum of the society. Her lover is watching her in anticipation of the obvious enjoyment from the balcony with his head resting on the right arm (Fig. 44). The back of the railing pillar is decorated as usual with lotus medallions.

## DARPAṆA-DHĀRIṆĪ (YAKSHĪ WITH A MIRROR)

A beautiful *yakshī* standing on an ugly, burly and short crouching *yaksha* is shown as wearing a new necklace and looking in a mirror held in her left hand to adjust and see how it sets off her beauty (Acc. No. 101, Pl. 235).[47] The *kadamba* (*Strephegyne parviflora*) tree under which she stands is in full bloom to match her resplendence and full array of her ornaments like the anklets, the jewel-studded waistband, usual bejewelled wristlets and multiple bangles, heavy pully-like earrings, and the weighty necklace which she holds and adjusts with her right hand. She bears an elaborate coiffure showing the hair combed and gathered in the forepart of the head in the form of a pointed crest bedecked with rings of flowers. The lower garment as usual is hardly perceptible and is wrapped round her lower half with the inner end-folds suspended over the right thigh and gathered into folds behind her back.

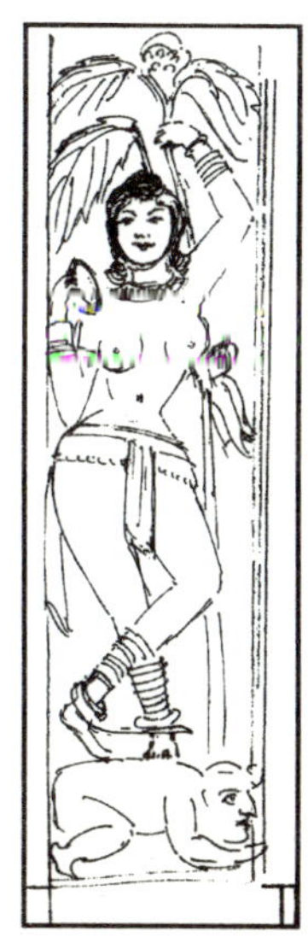

Fig. 45. *Yakshī* holding mirror (Acc. No. 114), Sanghol.

The theme of lady with a mirror seems to have remained quite popular at Sanghol. Another example now on display in the Chandigarh museum (Acc. No. 114, Pl. 236) is of a śālabhañjikā standing cross-legged on a similar ugly, burly crouching *yaksha* holding the branch of the tree with her left hand above her head and supporting what looks like a circular mirror in her right hand (Fig. 45). Wearing usual ornaments, she is shown with the free ends of her lower garment falling gracefully in front and on the back of her right leg. The beautiful *yakshī* stands cross-legged on the burly dwarf *yaksha* with her right foot firmly planted on his back. The dwarf *yaksha* is shown bearing the full weight of the lady on his shoulders with a sagging belly and is resting his chin on his palms squarely placed on the floor to counteract the weight. Another unpublished śālabhañjikā (Acc. No. 28, Fig. 46) is shown standing gracefully in a posture similar to the Paribhogadarśinī (Acc. No. 25) described above with the difference that she pulls the bough of the tree with her upraised left hand above the head and holds a flower-like object in her right hand raised to the level of the corresponding shoulder. The coiffure, too, betrays some difference. There is a tripartite division of locks on the forehead with a central flower-like form and the side locks combed sideways. The hair is tied with a tassel above and the locks form a bun resembling the hoods of a serpent. Jewellery is very sparse. She is elegantly attired and the multi-stringed waistband with a central circular clasp is used to secure the transparent *dhotī*. The flowing robe is looped on her right loin and the tail-end dangles along her left thigh.

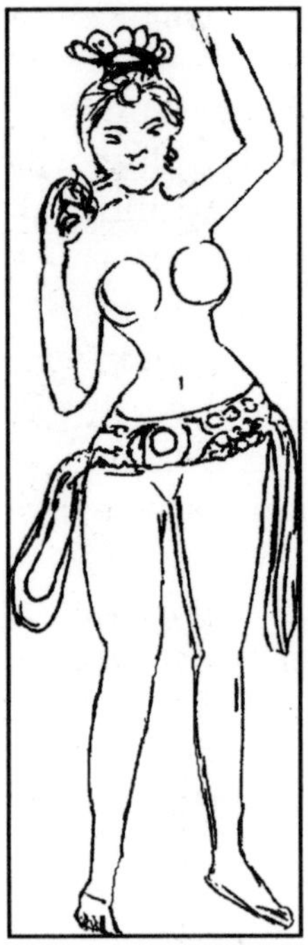

**Fig. 46.** *Śālabhañjikā* with a flower (Acc. No. 28), Sanghol.

## MOTHER AND CHILD

The figure on a railing pillar (Acc. No. 41, Pl. 237) has been given the title 'Mother and Child' (Fig. 47). It has been described thus:

> A young mother with her astridal grown up child is seen ascending a steep hill, probably to offer worship at the stupa; for her beaming face betrays eagerness and anticipation. She is also suitably dressed for the occasion. Her diaphanous *dhotī* can be spotted partly between her legs and partly below her navel. Her coiffure with its eye-catching tilt, receding tiers of plaits capped by a bun and the large flower-like cap of hair on the forehead is arresting. No less so is the way she has adorned herself with ornaments – three types of anklets, tight-fitting ones, loose hollow jingling ones and loose thin tinkling one; five stringed *mekhalā*; two types of bangles, tight-fitting rings and loose pelvis one dangling over the wrist; two types of necklaces, one *ekāvali* and one pearl; and drum-like *kuṇḍalas*. Only the armlet is missing. The child is adorned with a pearl necklace, armlet and bangles.[48]

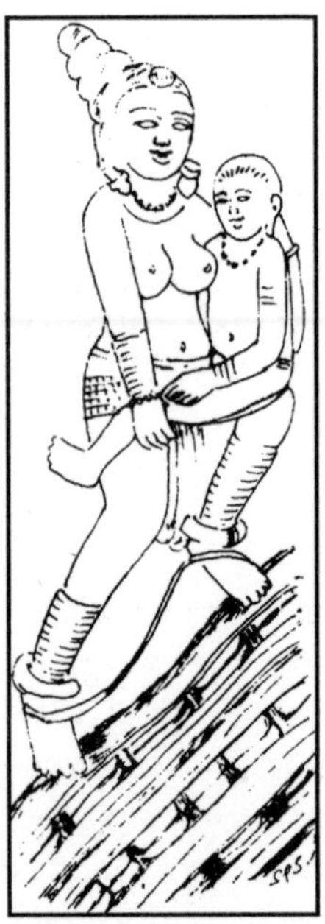

**Fig. 47.** Mother and child (Acc. No. 41), Sanghol (after Shukla).

P. Banerjee has identified the depiction of the female carrying the male with the seduction of Ṛishyaśṛiṅga.[49] The story of Ṛishyaśṛiṅga occurs in the epics[50] and the *Jātakas* and was also known outside India. Ṛishyaśṛiṅga was the son of Sage Vibhāṇḍaka who was devoted to penance and Vedic studies. Once, while washing his mouth, Vibhāṇḍaka saw nymph Urvaśī flying in the sky. He was so infatuated by her charm that he could not control his emotions and had seminal emission which was lapped up by a doe (actually a *deva-kanyā* 'divine girl' transformed into a doe due to a curse and was to be relieved of the curse after giving birth to a son) while taking water in the stream. Consequently, she gave birth to a child who had a human body with a horn on the forehead and thus came to be known as Ṛishyaśṛiṅga. The boy was brought up by Vibhāṇḍaka in his woodland hermitage in solitude as severely self-controlled and made perfect in studies and penance. Thinking him to be his future competitor, Indra devised various means to deviate him from the path of *brahmacharya* (celibacy). As per the *Alambushā Jātaka* (No.

523), Indra sent the beautiful nymph Alambushā to seduce the boy when his father was away. She lured the young sage and the inevitable happened. The story is given with some variations in the *Nalinikā Jātaka* (No. 526) and the *Rāmāyaṇa* and the *Mahābhārata* also. The sage boy was brought to the capital of King Romapada across the Gaṅgā to the land of Aṅga by the pleasure-giving ladies where he was ultimately married to Śāntā, daughter of King Daśaratha but adopted by childless Romapada. Ṛishyaśṛiṅga officiated as a priest at the time of the *Putreshṭi-yajña* (sacrifice performed with the desire of obtaining son/s) of Daśaratha, as a result of which four sons were born to him. According to the *Mahābhārata*, he was brought to the Aṅga country by courtesans where the ultimate took place. A railing pillar from Bhūteśvara preserved in the Archaeological Museum at Mathura shows the seduction of Ṛishyaśṛiṅga in three scenes: (i) four courtesans of Aṅga going to the hermitage of the sage in a boat, (ii) Ṛishyaśṛiṅga with the seductress, and (iii) the seductress clasping Ṛishyaśṛiṅga.[51]

Since Ṛishyaśṛiṅga is represented in the Bhūteśvara and another Mathura pillar with a horn on the head, the absence of this feature makes it difficult to accept the representation of the Sanghol pillar with the story of the seduction of Ṛishyaśṛiṅga.[52] The boy too does not seem to be young enough to cohabit with the lady.

The top of the panel shows two women in the balcony observing the mother and child with smiles of fondness. The incline of the hill and its layered structure have been delineated with ingenuity by the artist through a series of parallel folds of the stone.

## MOTHER CARRYING CHILD

The depiction of the mother and child seems to have been quite a favourite theme with the Kushāṇa artists. An upright depicts a young mother feeling the joy of feeding her child held astride her waist on her left hip and supported by her left cupped palm (Acc. No. 19, Pl. 238). With her bent right arm and cupped palm she is supporting her left breast to offer it to the kid. 'The ample sphere of her bosom reveals plenitude. This is highlighted by her slender waist and deep, small navel.'[53] The usual ornaments include the puffed anklets, bejewelled wristlets, spiralled bangles, four-stringed gemmed waistband, armlets, double necklace and earrings. Diaphanous *dhotī* covers her lower parts and the upper inner edge of the *dhotī* is folded in the shape of a fan and suspended from the waistband in front to conceal her private part. The outer upper edge of the *dhotī* hangs over her left hip in the form of a loop. Her hair is combed in short tresses gathering the ends into a knot on the forehead. 'Her face, with sharp nose, curved well-rounded lower lip, arched eye brows and narrow pupils reveal the joy a mother feels when feeding her child'.[54] The child fondly touches the breast of his mother with his left hand.

## DUGDHADHĀRIṆĪ

The theme of Dugdhadhāriṇī (Acc. No. 52 A, Pl. 239), a charming *yakshī* standing on a crouching dwarfish *yaksha* holding her rotund left breast with her right hand and lightly pressing the nipple with the thumb, seems to have been inspired from Mathura. Aesthetically adorned with the usual ornaments like the puffed beaded anklets, waist band, beaded wristlets and multiple bangles, armlets, broad necklace and ear plugs, she holds stylistically the frontally rolled part of the transparent *dhotī* with folds represented as parallel lines in her left hand at the respective thigh, leaving its knotted free end fall gracefully on the side. The thin slightly bent waist, neck and head add a unique grace to the figure which reminds us of Śrī-Lakshmī in Mathura sculptures with similar spherical bosoms 'like golden jars full of milk' and the posture of holding the bosom in this fashion.[55] In another case (Acc. No. 63, Pl. 240), a young mother is seen dangling a rattle

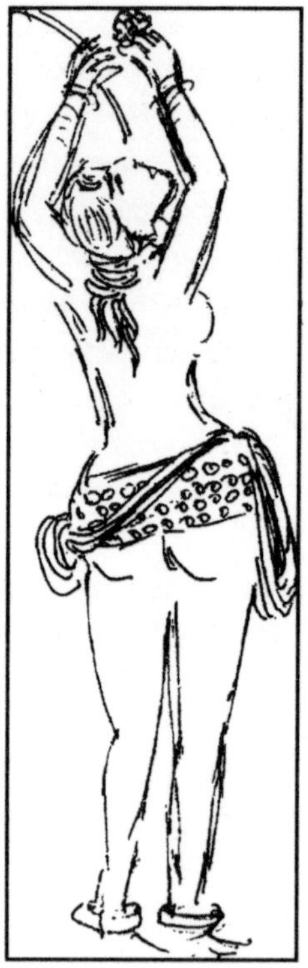

**Fig. 48.** *Yakshī* plucking flower (Acc. No. 49), Sanghol.

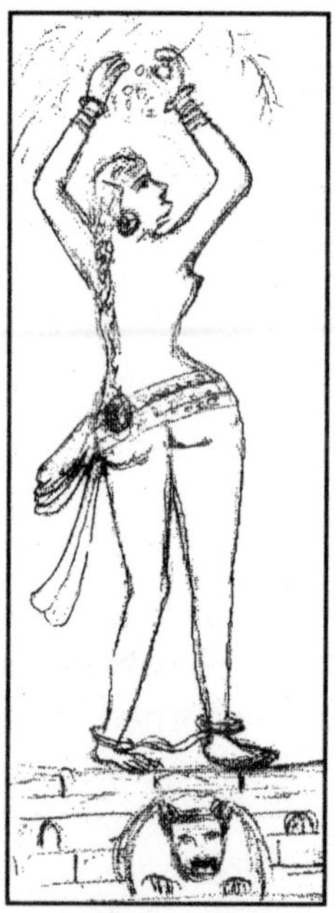

**Fig. 49.** *Yakshī* plucking fruits or flowers (Acc. No. 27), Sanghol.

in front of her child who may have obviously been amazed at the sound coming out of the rattle with two jingling balls. In an expression of astonishment at the sounds of the rattle, the child is shown as touching his chin with his right hand.[56] In yet another example (Acc. No. 48, Pl. 241), 'the artist has captured the joyous moment when the mother is holding a son aloft and both are laughing in exhilaration. The young mother and her child are seen under a blossoming tree, full with delicate long leaves and fully round flowers. The mother's back and upturned face and the child are seen realistically depicted. The mother has rolled the top portion of the sari and wound it round her waist and hips so as to allow the arm free movement. In her total absorption in the paly, she is not aware that her left leg is on the very verge of the slab on which she is standing. The mother has plaited her hair and suspended the braid, the end of which is secured with ball-like suspenders three in number. She is wearing the usual ornaments like *nūpura*, four-tiered *mekhalā*, *valaya* and *kaṅkaṇa* (bangles). Her ear ornament is in the form of a spiral. The child is also adorned with bangles and waist band. This is a simple everyday domestic scene. In the hands of the sculptor, this fleeting incident has become immortal'.[57]

Amongst the lesser known *vedikā* pillars, there are three more depicting the damsels in similar postures. One of them (Acc. No. 49, Fig. 48)[58] seems to have been the work of the same artist who created the mother and child described just above. The *yakshī* here is shown wearing almost similar dress and ornaments with the only difference that the hair is combed backwards and looped at the nape of the neck to let free ends of the tresses fall on the back. Instead of holding the child aloft, the *yakshī* here is plucking a blossomed flower from the twig of the tree with her two hands held above and bent at the elbows. Her head, however, seems to be bent excessively downwards. Standing in an analogous posture on a pedestal of horizontally laid slabs, the other *yakshī* (Acc. No. 27, Pl. 242, Fig. 49)[59] is depicted in the act of plucking fruits or holding the blossomed flowers in her hands. The lower portion of the body shows a slight inward bend of the left knee and the bust is turned more to her right than the foregoing examples, as is indicated by the long braid falling on the left side of her back. The braid has a ball-like suspender which touches the left hip of the lady. The hardly perceptible lower garment is wrapped around the waist and the hips with the inner end-folds looped and suspended on the left. Her right leg is planted firmly on the ground and the left one shows a slight inward bend to provide the required support to the bust to bend backwards. The face is not upturned like the preceding examples but is shown in three-fourth profile with head turned slightly backwards. The nose, lips and chin have suffered some mutilation. A crack runs from chin to right ear. The calf is also mutilated. There are calcareous accretions all over the sculpture. On the pedestal is depicted the frontal face of the moustached *yaksha* with animal-like ears (lion?) peeping out of a dormer window. The figure bears heavy calcareous accretion all over. Another example of a lady seen from the back picking a flower from a tree bears more expressive face, clearly modelled fingers, stunted bust and voluminous hip (Acc. No. 43)[60] indicating the individuality and stylistic differences in the artistic accomplishments of different artists while executing similar themes.

### YAKSHĀROHĪ (YAKSHĪ RIDING VĀMA YAKSHA)

One pillar (Acc. No. 22, Pl. 243, Fig. 50) shows an interesting and rather unusual scene of a *yakshī* being borne by a *yaksha* under a *sāla* tree (*shorea robusta*). Seated astride on his back, the radiant youthful *yakshī*, sumptuously bejewelled with anklets, wristlets, multiple bangles, armlets, richly decorated five-strand waistband, pearl necklet, broad torque, ear ornaments and wearing a diaphanous *dhotī*, bears a subtle smile on her plump face as if enjoying the ride to its full, which is also reflected by her joyous eyes. Her hair has been combed backward stylistically and then wound at the back in a long conical knot. The obese ageing *yaksha*, however, seems to be unable to bear the burden and tries to keep his body balanced with the support of his arms, with his left hand placed on the knee. His age is indicated by his bald head and his agony is reflected by his dour mien and grinning face (Pl. 244). The full blossomed tree with wafting branches, falling leaves and bent stem provides a parallel to the beauty and the 'beast'.[61]

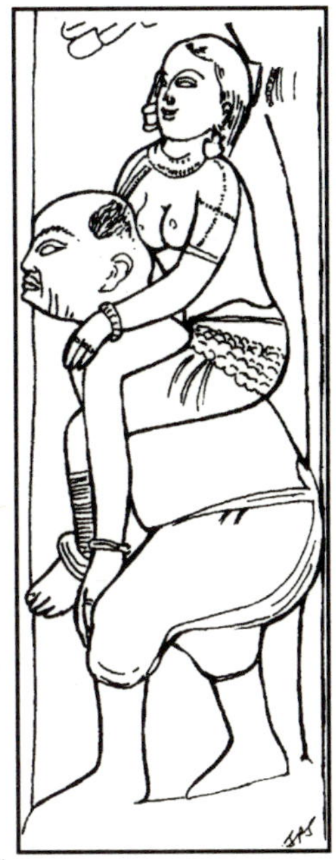

**Fig. 50.** Yaksharohī (Acc. No. 22), Sanghol (after Shukla).

Radha Banerjee regards this depiction as the representation of the story of *Mahāummaga Jātaka,* which brings out the extraordinary intelligence and presence of mind of the Bodhisattava in one of his births as Mahaushadha. The portion of the *Mahāummaga Jātaka* relevant for our purpose, as given by Radha Banerjee, is as follows:

> During the time when the Bodhisattva was born as Mahaushadha, there was a person called Golakāla, who was black and dwarfish or short-sized. His wife was called Dīrghatāla (i.e. a tall lady). Once Golakāla wanted to meet his parents and told his wife to prepare some cakes. Dīrghatāla at first refused to oblige her husband saying that it was no use seeing the parents. After persistent entreaty by Golakāla, she prepared some cakes. Thereafter, Golakāla and his wife carried food for the parents and started on their journey. In course of time, they reached the bank of a stream, which was not very deep but they were afraid of the rushing water and did not dare to cross it. While they stood on the bank they saw a man in a miserable state, Dīrghapṛishṭha by name (whose back was very broad) passing by that side. Golakāla and his wife wanted to know from him whether the river was deep or shallow. Understanding their fear of water, Dīrghapṛishṭha told them that the river was very deep with many kinds of voracious fish in it. Then, Golakāla asked him to tell them how to cross the river. In reply he told them that he had struck up a friendship with the crocodiles and monsters inhabiting this river and they would not be able to harm him. Thus assured, Golakāla requested him to help them cross the river. Dīrghapṛishṭha readily agreed to do so. The couple was pleased with him and gave him food to eat.
>
> Having finished his meal, he asked who was to be carried first. Golakāla asked him to take his wife first. So requested Dīrghapṛishṭha placed the wife on his back and went down to the river. When Dīrghapṛishṭha had gone a little, he crouched down and waded along in a bent posture to give the impression that the water was very deep and he was to proceed very cautiously. When Dīrghapṛishṭha reached the middle of the stream, he proposed his love to Dīrghatāla and offered to marry her. Dīrghatāla also fell in love with Dīrghapṛishṭha and readily agreed to his proposal. Thus conversing in a happy mood they reached the other side of the river and began to amuse themselves which aroused jealousy in the mind of Golakāla. In excitement he jumped into the river and crossed it easily as it was in reality very shallow. Golakāla caught hold of Dīrghapṛishṭha and brought him and his own wife to Mahaushadha who was known for his justice. When

> Mahaushadha cross-examined Dīrghapṛishṭha, he could not get satisfactory answers to his questions. The guilt of Dīrghapṛishṭha was easily established and Mahaushadha handed over Dīrghatāla to her real husband, Golakāla.[62]

Radha Banerjee thinks that the panel presents only the first part of the story, i.e. Dīrghapṛishṭha carrying Dīrghatāla and going down to the river and the physical features of Dīrghapṛishṭha and his couching movements answer to the description given of him in the *Mahāummagga Jātaka*.[63] S.P. Gupta feels that "this identification is also somewhat doubtful since the panel nowhere includes the Bodhisattva Mahausadha".[64] S.P. Shukla too has expressed his doubts about this identification and states that "In this scene the man carrying maiden on his back is old and appears not performing his duty gladly. The scene, in question, may be interpreted in the light of wine-drinking themes of Sanghol. The lady, in intoxicated condition, is either being carried to her lover's home or being taken to her own residence by an old hired man."[65]

## PRASĀDHIKĀ OR ANNAPŪRṆĀ (LADY CARRYING A TRAY)

The depiction of a lady carrying a tray on a railing pillar (Acc. No. 112, Pl. 245) has been identified as Prasādhikā by Sharma *et al* as they think that the female shown here is a lady's maid

> holding a circular basket with a conical cap in her bent left hand and probably a light water vessel in her right hand. The maid's ornaments are in low relief. Her *mekhalā* (girdle) appears to be made of four rows of coins, each row suspended over the one below it. She is wearing a thin lower garment, the upper half of which is rolled and secured in the *mekhalā* and hung loosely from it . . . The anklets are, however, large and heavy for her slender feet. Her feet, the right one at right angle to the left, suggest movement. This is further reinforced by the slightly bent upper part of her body and the two concave curves at her waist. The effect of the maid's movement can be noticed on the folded cushion beneath her feet; below her left foot which is placed firmly, the compression is more; below her right foot which is placed lightly on the cushion the compression is less. Another maid is watching the maid from the balcony with curiosity and admiration. The back is decorated with lotus medallions.[66]

The exquisite and heavy ornamentation, however, does not indicate the lady to be a maid. The water vessel in her suspended right hand would indicate that she is carrying food in the tray held over her left shoulder with her left hand.

## AŚOKA-DOHADA

The theme of Aśoka-dohada is equally celebrated in literature and art. It was the poetic belief in ancient India that an Aśoka tree (*Saraca indica*) blooms when an inebriated young unmarried maiden touches or kicks its stem with the sole of her anklet-adorned foot. A railing pillar from Sanghol (Acc. No. 102, Pl. 223, second pillar from left) delineates this theme beautifully by showing a young lady leaning against an Aśoka tree with the sole of her right foot touching the base of the tree-trunk. She is holding a goblet full of wine in her left hand while the right holds a ball of sweetmeat. As usual, she is exquisitely adorned with bejewelled ornaments. Hair parted into a semicircle in leaf-like forms at the centre and combed backwards before being rolled in conical tiers leaving the pony-tail hang down loosely indicates *kokila keśapāśa* hair-style which is eye-catching. The maiden wears pully-like earrings, beaded necklace, wristlets and multiple bangles, five-stringed waistband with circular central clasps, anklets and a diaphanous *dhotī*. A graceful poise and compositional equilibrium has been maintained by the artist.

Another example of Aśoka-dohada (Acc. No. 113, Pl. 223, first pillar from left) shows the young lady as resting against the Aśoka tree with the sole of her right foot touching the trunk of the tree. Even in this case, "Her coiffure is interesting. A semicircular gap is made in the hair on the forehead. It is parted in the centre and combed in the form of two leaves. The rest of the hair is combed and allowed to hang freely on the back; fillet holds the loose hair on the head while three thick circular clips on the loose hanging hair keep it in place."[67] A prominent *tilaka* mark is visible in the semicircular gap on the forehead. With folds mildly visible on the left shoulder, she has rolled the upper portion of the transparent *sārī* and thrown it across a branch of the tree and is pulling it, as indicated by the bent trunk behind her. She is wearing the usual ornaments. The rectangular pedestal bears a border and is decorated with two four-petalled flowers and the back is bedecked with lotus medallions as in other cases (Pl. 246). It has been observed that "The delineation is somewhat unconventional. The soft acute angle formed by the bent right leg goes perfectly well with the obtuse angle formed by the bent right arm which is almost parallel to the pedestal on which she is standing. This is the perfect pose for exerting maximum pull. The tree is also tall, slender and curving like the body of the *Śālabhañjikā*."[68] The damsel on a railing pillar displayed in the Sanghol museum (Acc. No. 40)[69] stands turned to her left poised on her left leg with the right bent obtusely at the knee and foot pressing the trunk of the tree behind her. The heel of the right foot almost touches the buttock. The figure shows slight elongation and betrays individual stylistic difference from others of this genre.

## ŚĀLABHAÑJIKĀS

As pointed out above, 'the art of Sanghol is mainly the art of śālabhañjikās'. There are some beautiful depictions of *yakshīs* seen pulling a branch of a flowering tree. Amongst the published specimens, one piece (Acc. No. 52 B, Pl. 247) shows the *yakshī* standing on a crouching vāma *yaksha*, wearing an exquisite four-stringed *mekhalā* studded with gems held in place by two rings and a third one serving as the clasp in the middle. Large gem-studded arm-band covering the fore part of her upper arms, multiple bangles covering the fore arms, broad gemmed torque, pulley-shaped ear ornaments, massive breasts, plump face, broad hip accentuated towards her right, stylish coiffure and ecstatic expression are the features which attract our attention. "The drooping branches, the uplifted left arm, the akimbo right arm and the transparent garment bring out in relief the beautiful features of the lady. The ugly dwarf with his sagging belly serves to emphasize her beauty further."[70] Standing on a vāma *yaksha,* another śālabhañjikā attired in diaphanous *dhotī* and displaying her alluring charms wearing usual ornaments and attractive coiffure is pulling a branch of a tree with her left arm raised above the head and the right one, suspended along the corresponding side of the waist with a flower held in the hand, presents a picture of perfect balance of corporeal contours, angles, alignments, human life and vegetation (Acc. No. 108, Pl. 248).[71]

A much better preserved śālabhañjikā standing parallel to the bends of the stem of a tree in an analogous pose on a vāma *yaksha* to right under her feet is displayed in the Chandigarh museum (Acc. No. 89, Pl. 249). Wearing multiple bangles and *kaṅkaṇas*, pulley-shaped ear ornaments, a broad torque, studded waistband having a circular clasp covering the upper part of the pubic region and puffed anklets, she has an utterly attenuated waist and extra wide hips somewhat balanced by her round rotund breasts. Her slanting right leg bears the weight of the body with foot placed firmly near the neck of the crouching dwarf while the left leg bent at the knee goes to the back of the *yaksha* and touches it with its toe with heel held upwards. The loose end of the diaphanous *dhotī* is looped on the right of her side and falls down stylishly to touch the ground. The expression is that of joy and satisfaction with a subtle smile on the face. Another

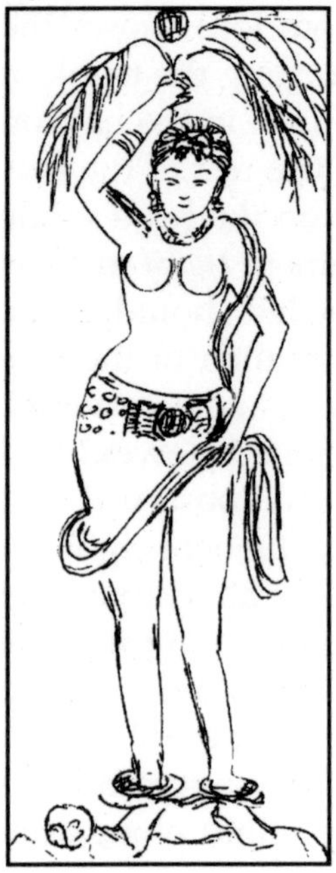

**Fig. 51.** *Śālabhañjikā* (Acc. No. 110), Sanghol.

śālabhañjikā in the same museum (Acc. No. 47, Pl. 250) has a more balanced body and stands on a cushion to front in *ābhaṅga* with middle portion slightly accentuated to her left. The broad hips bear a four-stranded *mekhalā* having a square frame for the circular clasp. The navel is marked with a deep groove.

Another *vedikā-stambha* now displayed in the Sanghol Museum shows the youthful *yakshī* standing gracefully in an analogous posture, pulling the bough of the blossoming tree on a bordered rectangular pedestal divided into two parts which are decorated with four-petalled flowers (Pl. 190). Her hair is combed backwards forming small curls in front. The drum-shaped ear ornaments and the broad torque are quite similar to the preceding example but the elaborate armlet has been done away with. The forearms are covered by a studded bracelet and multiple bangles. The four-strand girdle having a central round clasp studded with precious stones is used to secure the nether garment whose pleats may be seen in minutely carved slanting lines covering the private part and the right thigh. The sculpture thus betrays the astuteness of the artist who has covered the nudity with diaphanous *dhotī*. The *yakshī* wears triple-strand tinkling anklets to generate a pleasing musical sound with her movements. Her right foot is planted firmy on the pedestal and the left one touches the ground with its toe while the heel is held vertically upwards as the leg is bent at the knee and crosses the right one. Attired elegantly in flowing robes with looped folds on the side and tail-ends dangling down gracefully towards the corner of the pedestal, this exhilarating beauty conjures up a vision of perfect balance of body contours, rhythmic movements and subtle expressions.

Another śālabhañjikā figure displayed in the same museum (Pl. 189) shares many of its features with the known examples. The *yakshī* here stands in almost frontal posture with a slight bend (*ābhaṅga*) of the body pulling a branch of the flowering tree with her left hand above her head. Delicate treatment in carving the undulations of the long leaves and bones and bulbous flowers at different planes with rippling effect resulting from the breeze is witnessed here just as in other cases. The hair of the *yakshī* is arranged in the form of large flower-like cap on the forehead and curled locks at the back like the fan-tail of a peacock. The drum-shaped ear ornaments, broad studded necklace, multiple bangles on the forearms, *mekhalā* with circular central clasp, rolled and twisted anklets recall similar ornaments worn by diverse *yakshīs*. Nudity is conspicuous in spite of the *dhotī* which is diaphanous. The object held by her in her right hand looks like a flower but one can't be sure of it. The flowing robes form pleated loops on both sides of the waist and the free end dangles down along the left leg. The rectangular bordered pedestal below her feet shows two four-petalled flowers frontally.

A third śālabhañjikā (Acc. No. 110, Fig. 51) is a good example of the sparse use of drapery and jewellery. It shows the voluptuous beauty pulling the branch of the tree by her right hand above her head and holding the rolled and looped end of the flowing robe in her left near the corresponding hip. The upper part of her *sārī* is rolled and taken from the left hip across the upper arm to the left shoulder from where it descends diagonally to the right knee and then takes an upward turn to the left thigh where it is held by the left hand. The tail end of the *sārī* is looped and suspended to the level of the left knee. As usual she wears earrings, broad torque, bangles, *mekhalā* with different strands having circular central clasp and puffed anklets. She stands on a prostrate *yaksha* to left. The figure exudes elegance despite being simple.

## UPĀSIKĀ (FEMALE DEVOTEE)

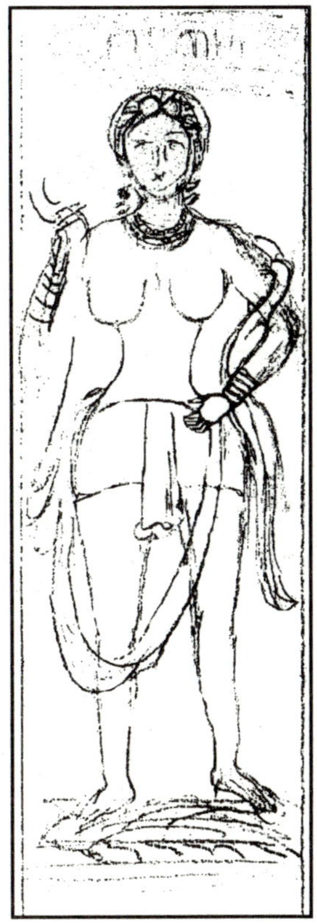

**Fig. 52.** Female devotee (Acc. No. 99), Sanghol.

A *yakshī* wearing *kuṇḍalas, valayas, mekhalā, nūpuras,* etc. holding a garland in her right hand and rolled part of the *sārī* in the left standing under a blossoming tree on a prostrate dwarf *yaksha* has been identified as an Upāsikā 'Female devotee' (Acc. No. 69, Pl. 251).[72] Another female devotee is amongst the exhibited lot now in the museum at Sanghol (Pl. 252). With a slight bend of the waist, she stands on a cushion placed on a stone platform on the front face of which is shown a crouching fabulous winged lion resembling the one as seen on the pedestal of the Sadyaḥ-snātā or Karpūramañjarī described above (Pl. 191).[73] The legs below the hips are depicted as slanting but the feet are almost in *sama* 'even, straight' posture. Behind and above her head are the branches of a tree with long leaves with conspicuous bones. The *yakshī* wears the usual ornaments – earrings, torque, armlets, *kaṅkaṇas* and multiple bangles, waistband and anklets. Her coiffure, however, consists of receding tiers of plaits with a bun atop and large flower-like cap of hair on the forehead, resembling very much the coiffure of the figure identified as the mother ascending a hill with child or the seductress of the sage Ṛishyaśṛinga as discussed above (Pl. 241, Fig. 47). The upper garment wound from behind the back appears from under the left arm and hip, and rolled and tied with a knot on the right hip. The *dhotī* which she wears can be guessed from the pleats engraved on her left thigh with free end visible between her legs but the thin transparent garment has helped only in setting off the beauty, tenderness and smoothness of her limbs. The multi-stringed garland goes well with the curve of the left arm of the Upāsikā.

Comparable to this Upāsikā is another unpublished figure (Acc. No. 99, Fig. 52) who stands frontally with slightly splayed-out feet on a dwarf wearing double-stringed necklace, ear ornaments, and multiple bangles with upper part of the *sārī* rolled and taken from her left hip across the upper arm to the left shoulder from where it descends diagonally to the right side of the waist and then looping down to the knee to ascend to the left where it is supported by the left hand to let the free end fall parallel to the the left knee. The top inner edge of the *sārī* is folded in the shape of a fan and suspended in front from the *nīvī* or navel. The pillar being not in a good state of preservation, the folds of the rolled *sārī* are mutilated at places. There is an empty balcony above and its lower edges too have suffered damage. The stone is much weathered and friable at places, particularly on the ventral side of the dwarf. The lips and nose of the damsel are also damaged and the image is thickly covered by calcarious accretions. As usual the back side of the pillar carries the lotus motif and the sides show mortise holes.

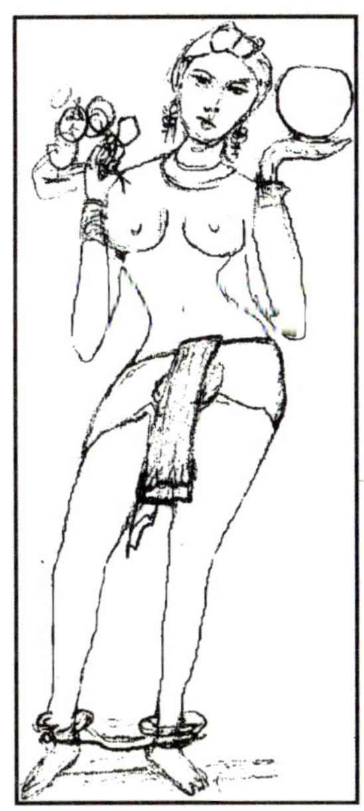

**Fig. 53.** *Yakshī* holding flowers (Acc. No. 50), Sanghol.

## YAKSHĪ HOLDING LOTUS FLOWERS AND WINE JAR

An unpublished railing pillar (Acc. No. 50, Fig. 53) depicts a damsel standing under a tree wearing broad torque, ear ornaments, bangles and anklets with *ardhoruk* type nether garment showing the top inner edge

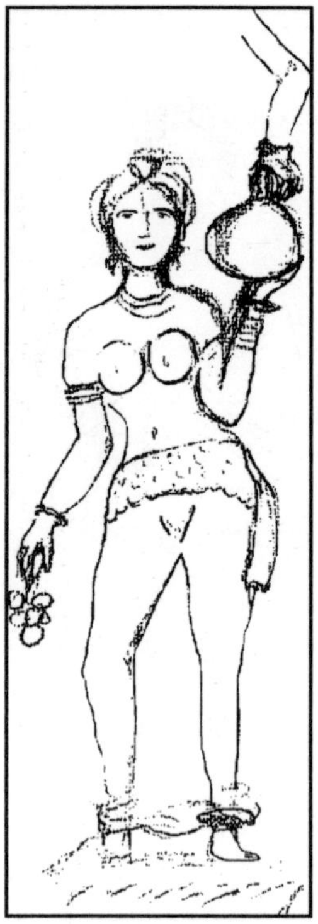

**Fig. 54.** *Yakshī* carrying flowers and wine jar (Acc. No. 82), Sanghol.

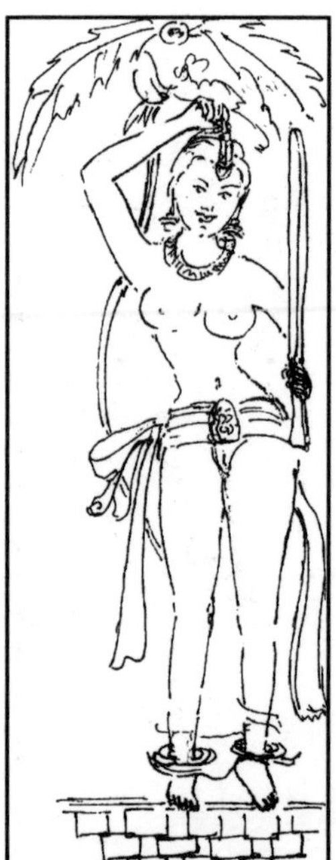

**Fig. 55.** Khaḍga-dhāriṇī (Acc. No. 21), Sanghol.

flared in front like a fan from the *nīvi* below the navel, holding a bunch of lotus flowers in her right hand raised to her right shoulder and carrying in her similarly raised left hand what looks like a big round fruit or globular wine jar, more probably the latter as shown in a similar and complete red sandstone railing pillar found from Bhuteshwar and displayed in the Mathura museum.[74] The back shows two lotus flowers with *ardha-padma* or half lotus figures at the top and bottom. The relief has suffered mutilation here and there. Bearing an exquisite coiffure, rotund breasts, attenuated waist and broad hips, the *yakshī* may well be compared with one already known from the lot (Acc. No. 46, Pl. 253) who carries a bouquet of three or four flowers by their stalk in her right hand almost parallel to her face.[75] She is dressed in a thin lower garment, which has been secured by a sash knotted below the navel with one end suspended between the legs concealing her nudity. Her left arm is held akimbo. Two girls in the balcony above are looking at her. Very similar is another beautiful *yakshī* holding three flowers by their stalks sharing most of the features of the preceding example (Acc. No. 29, Pl. 254) with the difference that her upper garment is rolled and suspended from her *mekhalā* to form loops and cover her personal part and that instead of two girls looking at her from the balcony, we have a lady peeping at her from behind a curtain on the top. Another pillar also shows a similar *yakshī* carrying a bunch of lotus flowers in her suspended right hand and a similar globular wine jar in her left hand near the shoulder (Acc. No. 82, Fig. 54). She stands to front with left hip accentuated outward and right leg bent slightly. Her nose and upper lip have suffered mutilation. Interestingly, an arm of a human figure in the balcony above comes down to take the wine jar held in her left hand but the figure in the balcony is, unfortunately, completely lost. The image is heavily patinated and has also suffered damage at places. Both the figures described above are comparable in beauty and charm to the beautiful females carrying wine flask (Acc. No. 85) and flute (Acc. No. 42, Pl. 255), and the *yakshī* holding lotus flowers known earlier from Sanghol.

## KHAḌGA-DHĀRIṆĪ (YAKSHĪ WITH A SWORD)

Still awaiting publication is the exquisitely carved and very pleasing image of a young and beautiful woman standing on a rock under a tree adjusting the chained head-locket on her forehead with her right hand and holding a sword vertically in her left hand (Acc. No. 21, Fig. 55), which may be compared favourably with the ladies putting on a necklace (Acc. Nos. 88 B and 33 A). An almost identical *yakshī* is depicted on a railing pillar from Kankali Tila, Mathura also.[76] Since the sword does not match well with the act of makeup, the object which looks like the sword may even be a long looking glass held by a handle at its lower end. Resplendent in her array of ornaments like the *nūpuras*, the jewel-studded *mekhalā*, the pair of heavy earrings and the gemmed necklace, her imperceptible *sārī* is wrapped around her lower half with the inner end-folds suspended over her right thigh, gathered into folds and thrown behind the back from where the loose ends fall gracefully on the two sides of the legs. With perfect female anatomy, proportions of limbs, balanced body, magnetic contours and slenderness as well as voluptuousness, the figure exudes unparalleled grace and is one of the finest specimens of the art of Sanghol. Together with the languorous lady (Acc. No. 88 A, Pl. 256), the damsel playing harmonica (Acc. No. 33 B, Pl. 257), etc., this is a unique figure which betrays the ingenuity of the craftsmen despite the fact that all these belong to the same genre to which other *yakshī* figures belong.

## ALASA-KANYĀ (LANGUOROUS DAMSEL)

One pillar shows a resplendently draped damsel in a diaphanous robe stretching and pulling her limbs in lassitude by lifting her left arm behind her head and pulling it with the right one (Pl. 256). She bears well-combed hair dressed in four buns and is bejewelled appropriately. The grace of her figure is enhanced by the effortlessly rolled and tied upper garment or perhaps one end of the *dhotī*.

> The parabolic curve formed on her right by her chest, waist and hips because of the tension generated by the pull of her hands and the almost imperceptible bend at her knee convey the languor of her body, which compress on the back of the dwarf over whom the *yakshī* is standing.[77]

Another similar figure but with the arms transversed also exists in the lot and shows the popularity of this motif.[78]

## ŚṚIṄGĀRA-RACHANĀ (LADY PUTTING ON A NECKLACE)

We know from the published sculptures of Sanghol of a voluptuous and well-adorned *yakshī* standing on a kneeling vāma *yaksha* adjusting a necklace around her neck (Acc. No. 88 B, Pl. 258).[79] There are three more examples of this type and the *yakshī* has been shown with right and left hands akimbo, adjusting the necklace with the other hand.[80] One of these is now on display in the Chandigarh museum (Acc. No. 104, Pl. 259) showing the *yakshī* standing cross-legged on a supine dwarfish *yaksha* under a balcony.

## COUPLE

Very rare is a depiction on a *vedikā-stambha* (Acc. No. 1, Pl. 224, Fig. 56) of a couple in a grove indicated by a blossomed tree above. A standing male seems to support a kneeling woman by her shoulder. The lady is shown with both her legs bent and reminds us of the so-called Bacchanalian scene from Maholi (Mathura), now in the National Museum, New Delhi, depicting the similar posture of an intoxicated lady held by her right shoulder by a standing man and supported on the other side by another male figure of smaller size and assisted by a lady in the back.[81] Sandrine Gill observes, "It would not be surprising to find such a theme in Sanghol, where wine drinking and carrying of wine vessels is depicted several times."[82]

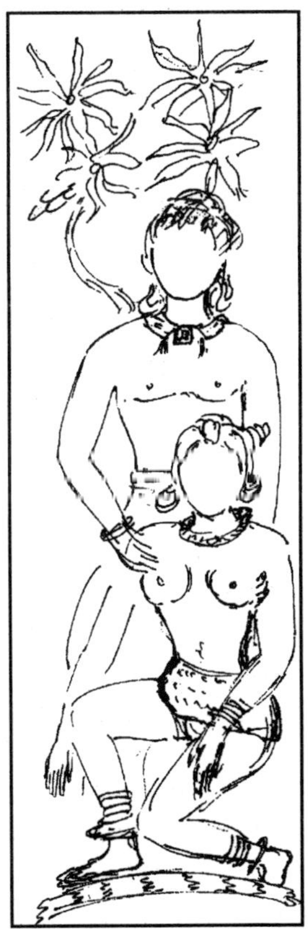

**Fig. 56.** A couple (Acc. No. 1), Sanghol.

## MALE FIGURES

The depiction of male figures on the *vedikā-stambhas* is comparatively rare. 'Kushāṇa Sculptures from Sanghol' illustrates only two devotees

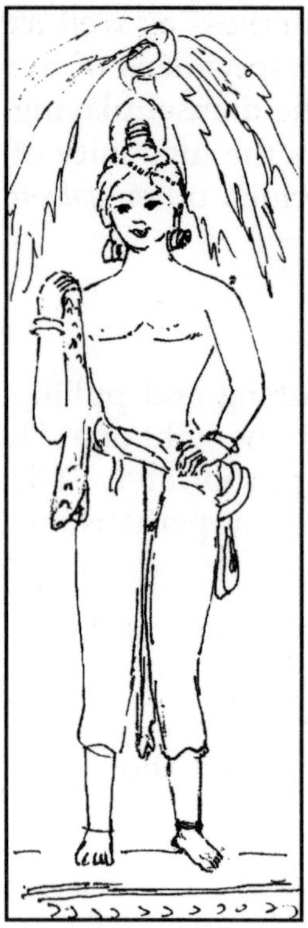

**Fig. 57.** A male devotee (Acc. No. 67), Sanghol.

(Upāsaka), one of them being royal (Pl. 224, second pillar from left). The latter (Acc. No. 105, Pl. 260) is shown as wearing a gem-studded diadem with its crown set with flowers which focus attention on his royal bearing. He has a broad chest and stands akimbo holding a long twisted beaded garland in his right hand. His placid face and broad forehead reveal his inner feelings and devotion. He wears a diaphanous *dhotī* secured by beaded tassels falling on his thighs with free ends falling to the ground between his legs, and a scarf with usual folds which goes winding from over his left shoulder to the back and appears on his right hip from where it falls to the knee and then ascends to the left groin to get the support of his left hand before finally falling down along the left leg. Ornaments like *kaṅkaṇa*, *keyūra*, *kaṇṭhā*, *kuṇḍalas*, etc. may be discerned on his person. The pedestal shows a winged lion and the bipartite railed balcony above has curtained colonnade. Almost similar royal devotee standing on a cushion under a tree (Pl. 224, third pillar from left) also exists and has been used in the restructured railing in the Sanghol museum. Standing on a prostrate dwarf, the lay devotee (Acc. No. 30, Pl 261) holds the long twisted garland in his right hand with the left resting on the hip. A thin and transparent *chīvara* or shawl with deep rippling lines and curves marking the pleats covers a part of his bust and goes over the shoulder. With hair done in the style of Buddha or Buddhist monks, he wears in his elongated ears ear-plugs and no other ornaments. A young lady in the balcony above is gazing at this young monk.

An unpublished railing pillar (Acc. No. 67, Fig. 57) shows another lay devotee standing facing under a tree holding a similar long garland of flowers in his right hand with the left hand placed on the hip. His hair is done with a top-knot and adorned with a pearl string; he wears ear-plugs, *kaṅkaṇas* and tight-fitting *dhotī* with the upper end twisted to form the waistband and coiled and looped on the left waist. The pleated free or loose end of the nether garment falls down between his legs. Another corner pillar depicts a male figure standing to front with a slight bend (*ābhaṅga*) in the body and feet slightly splayed out holding a bunch of flowers in his right hand near the shoulder and resting the left on the respective thigh (Acc. No. 68 A, Pl. 262). He has the coiffure of a mendicant but is shown as wearing pulley-shaped ear-plugs, a broad gilded necklace, multiple bracelets and probably the anklets also. The transparent *dhotī* can be made out from the free end falling between the thighs but thick rolled sash comes slantingly from the right groin to the left thigh where it is knotted forming a big loop with the loose end falling along the left leg and the upper end falling vertically on the right thigh. Encrustation has covered some of the details, particularly near the left leg. A round full-blossomed lotus-like object appears from behind the left shoulder and goes to the level of the head. The railed balcony above shows a couple. The man on viewer's left is resting his head on the right palm and reclining, while the female on his left seems to be looking at the devotee below. The other side of this pillar shows a fly-whisker devotee holding the *chāmara* in his right hand and resting the left on the waist (Pl. 263).

Mention may be made here to a buff Sikri sandstone portrait image of a Śaka devotee (Pl. 264) obtained from the ancient mound of village Karhali situated about 25 km south-southwest of Patiala on road to Guhla just on the border of Punjab with Haryana.[83] It was obtained by a farmer while ploughing his field. This free-standing statue measuring 28.7 X 7.5 cm seems to have remained exposed to the elements of nature for long and is in a very indifferent state of preservation. Since the whole surface of the pedestal, as also of the lower portion of the image,

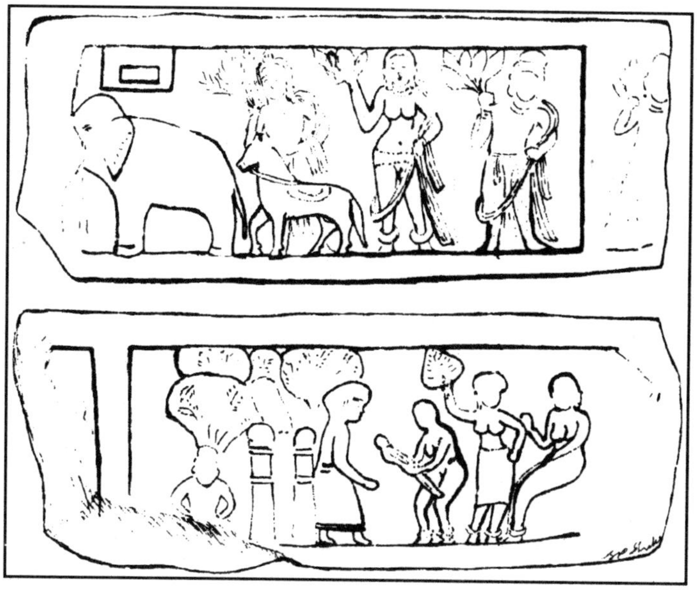

**Fig. 58.** Scenes depicted on the two sides of the architrave, Sanghol (after Shukla).

has chipped off badly, it is difficult to ascertain whether it was inscribed or not. However, the heavy, tailored and sewn Indo-Scythian costume of early Kushāṇa royal statuary is wanting here. We do not see the triangular tunic, wide waist belt, sturdy and padded shoes but the high conical Indo-Scythian helmet is quite conspicuous. The loose ends of a scarf which covered his back seem to have been knotted at his chest.[84] There are traces of earrings, torque and bracelets but the possibility of the latter two being the collar and cuffs of a tight-fitting jacket cannot be ruled out. This, together with the close-fitting undergarment, resembles the dress of a donor or a devotee on a *vedikā* pillar of Mathura.[85] Traces of a long garland or the stems of lotus flowers in his right hand raised to the level of the shoulder, as noticed in the hands of the two devotee figures of Sanghol described above, bring him closer to this class of figures. The figure seems to have been bare-footed. The left hand is akimbo but it is not clear if it held any object also. The right foot is flat and points straight while the left foot is slightly splayed outwards; the body shows a slight flexion at the waist. The bust seems to be somewhat leaning forward. The face has got some sort of a personal identity in being oval and bearing a broad nose, thick lips, unfocussed and languid eyes. The figure thus seems to combine the features of a royal portrait with that of a donor or a devotee. Its size matches well with the Kushāṇa princely portrait statues of Mathura. Frontality, hieratic symmetry, typical costume and head-gear, splayed feet, sturdy shoes, etc. are some of the dominant stylistic traits of early Kushāṇa portrait statues which represent potentates, princes, nobles and state functionaries. Most of the Kushāṇa portrait statues known so far in India come from Mathura, the major political centre of the Kushāṇa empire, and its surrounding regions.[86] The image under discussion, however, lacks the vitality which is visible in most of the Mathura statues. A compromise seems to have been affected between the exotic cultural and aesthetic principals and the indigenous practice of carving. It is not certain whether it was an import from the Mathura region as indicated by the typical buff sandstone of the area or a local creation. Stylistically, however, it betrays a marked decline in the art of portraiture of the mature Kushāṇa period and may be dated to the early third century CE. Since the piece is torn out of context, its religious affiliation cannot be determined with certainty.

Reverting again to Sanghol, we may refer to a double-sided red sandstone architrave of a gateway (Pls. 265-66 & Fig. 58) recovered in the open from Stūpa No. 2 area and now displayed in the local museum.[87] One side of the architrave shows in a palatial setting a crowned figure meditating under an Aśoka tree on left, two females in the middle – one on the right handing over a babe to the other and a royal female seated on a wicker stool holding a cup in her right hand being fanned by a maid on the right. The other side depicts an elephant followed by a caparisoned horse walking to left and a female flanked on either side by a male figure standing to front holding bunches of flowers in their upraised right hands, each supporting the free end of the scarf with their left hand at the respective hip. A part of the broken panel on the right indicates that similar flower-holding figures were depicted there. It is notable that the style of supporting the free end of the scarf with the lef hand at waist shown in the human figures here very much resembles that of the royal and the female devotee described above. G.B. Sharma[88] refers to its discovery from a monastic cell and observes that it depicted Jātaka stories. Shashi Asthana also followed this view.[89] S.P. Gupta felt that "The architrave depicts on one side devotees and on the other side some scenes of some popular story, perhaps the Nanda-Sundari."[90] S.P. Shukla thinks that the architrave "depicts on one side the birth scene of Gautama (the Buddha) and on the other side the elephant and horse, symbolic of the white elephant (which his mother saw in her dream) and the great departure (*mahābhinishkramaṇa*) of the Buddha".[91] These observations, however, do not explain the presence of the different figures in the scenes and it must be admitted that the depictions have defied proper identification till now.[92]

We thus see that Sanghol was an important centre of culture, religion, trade and polity and a meeting place of the Mathura and Gandhāra Schools of art. The railing pillars and other stray sculptures found from here present a very significant chapter of the Buddhist art of Kushāṇa and early Gupta period in Punjab.

The name of Huvishka's successor Vāsudeva is indicative of the change that was taking place in the religious beliefs of the Kushāṇas. With the subsequent decline of Kushāṇa power in India, particularly the present-day Punjab state of the country, Buddhist activities of establishing *stūpas*, monasteries and images too seem to have declined considerably though some people settled at sites like Sanghol still continued to profess the faith as is vouched by Gandhāra Buddhist stucco, clay and stone figures. Probably, it continued to follow a downward trend and suffered a blow with the inroads of the Hūṇas. The overall picture at the time of Xuan Zang's visit was that of decline and desolation of Buddhist establishments. There is, however, no denying the fact that people here and there continued to profess the religion. The Buddhist relics found so far from the area also corroborate the same.

Zahura near Tanda Urmur in Hoshiarpur district has yielded an image of Buddha (Pl. 267) measuring 27 X 21 cm. It is broken below the bust and is quite worn out. In this coarse-grained sandstone icon, Buddha has been depicted in *vyākhyāna-mudrā*, i.e., the posture of explaining the essential doctrines of Dhamma. There is a plain oval aureole behind the figure. Long hanging ear-lobes, a sign of greatness (*mahāpurusha-lakshaṇa*), are very clear. The face is oval and the hair is curly betraying Gupta idiom. But the typical serene Gupta expression is missing. The figure may be ascribed to the seventh century CE.[93] It may be recalled that Zahura may have formed part of the kingdom of She-lan-ta-lo (Jālandhara) of Xuan Zang's time. King Udito or Udita had treated the pilgrim courteously during his visit to the capital where he stayed for four months studying with the learned Brother Chandravarma.[94]

The only other image of Buddha recovered so far from the state is a small headless marble figure measuring 15 X 12 cm from Kharar near Chandigarh, showing Buddha seated cross-legged on a rock represented by criss-cross lines on the face of the seat (Pl. 268).[95] He is wearing a *dhotī* and the upper garment (*saṃghāṭī*) which comes from under his right armpit and covers the chest and left shoulder. The folds of both these clothes are marked by engraved lines which may be seen even on the back side. Buddha's left hand is placed on his lap and he touches the earth with his right hand as prescribed in the iconographic texts for *bhūmisparśa-mudrā*. The piece was recovered along with some other Brahmanical images from a Śiva temple on the ghat of Aja Sarovara at Kharar. The stone used is marble, indicating import from Rajasthan as even at present. Execution is very rough indicating a date as late as the sixteenth century CE when during the rule of Akbar, there was some religious relaxation. The small size indicates portability and personal use. It may be recalled that Kharar has yielded numerous Brahmanical and Jaina images also and seems to have remained an important religious centre during the medieval and late medieval periods where people professing different beliefs lived amiably.

## NOTES AND REFERENCES

1. E. Frauwallner, *The Earliest Vinaya and the Beginnings of Buddhist Literature*, Rome, 1956, pp. 31ff.
2. Thomas Watters, *On Yuan Chwang's Travels in India*, First Indian Edition, Delhi, 1961, p. 294.
3. *Ibid.*, pp. 299-300.
4. T.W. Rhys Davids, *The Questions of King Milinda*, Sacred Books of the East Series, Vols. 35-36. Kshemendra's *Avadānakalpalatā* also corroborates it (*Ibid.*, Vol. 36, p. XVII).
5. *Moralia*, 821, Eng. Tr. by H.N. Fowler, Oxford, 1936, p. 278.
6. T.W. Rhys Davids, "Mahā-parinibbāna-Suttanta", in *Buddhist Sūtras*, Oxford, 1881, pp. 130ff and in *Dīghanikāya*, Vol. III, Oxford, 1890, pp. 186-91.
7. A.K. Narain, *The Indo-Greeks*, Oxford, 1957, pp. 97-98; Osmund Bopearachchi, "King Milinda's conversion to Buddhism, fact or fiction?" *Ancient Ceylon, Journal of the Archaeological Survey Department of Sri Lanka*, No. 7, 1990, pp. 1-15.
8. W. Geiger, *The Mahāvaṃsa or The Great Chronicle of Ceylon*, London, 1912, p. 194.
9. W.W. Tarn, *The Greeks in Bactria and India*, Cambridge, 1951, pp. 227ff; J.N. Banerjea in *A Comprehensive History of India*, Vol. II, Delhi, 1957, p. 74.
10. P.C. Bagchi in P.V. Bapat (Ed.), *2500 Years of Buddhism*, Delhi, 1964, pp. 54-55.
11. Osmund Bopearachchi, "Was Sagala Menander's Capital?", *South Asian Archaeology 1989*, Monographs in World Archaeology, No. 14 (edited by Catherine Jarrige), Paris, 1989, pp. 327-37.
12. *Watters*, *op. cit.*, p. 291.
13. *Ibid.*
14. *Ibid.*, p. 296. R.K. Mookerji, *Ancient Indian Education*, Delhi, 1960, p. 512. Jālandhara is believed to be the venue of the Fourth Buddhist Council held during the reign of Kanishka, while others regard Kashmir as its venue (Bapat, *op. cit.*, p. 42; B.C. Law, *Indological Studies*, Part III, Allahabad, 1954, pp. 175-76).
15. *Yāvat-Pushyamitro yāvat saṃghārāmaṃ bhikshūṃścha praghātayan prasthitaḥ/ Sa yāvatchhākalamanuprāptaḥ/ Tenābhihitam - 'Yo me śramaṇa—śiraṃ dāsyati tasyāhaṃ dīnāra-śataṃ dāsyāmi'* (Aśokāvadāna). P.L. Vaidya (Ed), *Divyāvadāna*, Mithila Institute, Darbhanga, 1959, p. 282.
16. *CASR*, XIV, p. 55.
17. *Ibid.*, pp. 54-57. Aśoka had invited Brethren from this monastery to his Council (Mookerji, *op. cit.*, pp. 511-12).
18. *Ibid.*, pp. 57-58.
19. Alexander Cunningham, *The Ancient Geography of India*, Reprint, Varanasi, 1963, pp. 191-22.
20. Watters, *op. cit*, pp. 299-300.
21. Talwar, *op. cit.*, pp. 5-6.
22. G.B. Sharma, "A Summary of Archaeological Excavations in Punjab", *Archaeology and Sculpture Exhibition*, Chandigarh, no date, pp. 3-4; M.S. Nagaraja Rao, "The Stupa at Sanghol" in S.P. Gupta, *op. cit.*, pp. 21-22; etc. Rao also accepts the main *stūpa* at Sanghol to have been built by Aśoka but there is hardly any archaeological evidence to support this view.
23. G.B. Sharma and Manmohan Kumar, *Coins Seals and Sealings from Sanghol*, Chandigarh, 1986, pp. 15-17.
24. *Ibid.*, pp. 17-19.
25. G.B. Sharma (1985), p. 17.
26. *Ibid.*
27. *Ibid.*, p. 18.
28. *Ibid.*, p. 19. S.P. Shukla, however, thinks that this relic casket belonged not to the main but to one of the minor *stūpas* which may have been set up in the memory of lay-disciple Āryabhadra. See for details S.P. Shukla, "Sanghol: Kushāṇa Buddhist Stupa and Sculptures" in *Buddhist Art and Thought* (edited by Kewal Krishan Mittal and Ashvini Agrawal), New Delhi, 1993, pp. 131-36.
29. Rao, *op. cit.*, p. 24.
30. S.P. Gupta (2003), p. 19, Pl. VI.
31. *Ibid.*, Pl. V.

32. Sandrine Gill, "Celestial Women in a Ring around the Buddhist Stupa: The Case of Sanghol" in Himanshu Prabha Ray (ed.), *Sanghol and the Archaeology of Punjab*, New Delhi, 2010, p. 148, Fig. 7.4. On the evidence of the site attendant Sandrine refers to it as the stucco head found in the course of the 1984-85 excavation on the east side of the *stūpa* and feels that a date earlier than 4th century for this image is not impossible. Cf. 4th century Gandhāra Buddha stucco heads in the Chandigarh Museum vide D.C. Bhattacharya (ed.), *Gandhāra Sculpture in the Government Museum and Art Gallery, Chandigarh (in the light of the International Colloquium held in 1998 at Chandigarh)*, Chandigarh, 2002, pp. 88, 159, acc. Nos. 162, 164, 168, etc.
33. G.B. Sharma, *loc. cit*, See also Shashi Asthana, "The Kushana Art of Sanghol", *Lalit Kala*, Vol. 24 (1990), pp. 9-13. See also Archana Rani, *Saṃghola evaṃ Mathurā kī Kalā* (Hindi), Delhi, 2007 which contains the line-drawings and half-tone illustrations of the most number of figures on the railing pillars so far.
34. Rao, *op. cit.*, p. 23.
35. Sandrine Gill, *op. cit.*, p. 150.
36. D.C. Bhattacharyya, "The Glory That Was Sanghol" in J.S. Ahluwalia (Ed.), *Historico-Archaeological Linkages of Punjabiat*, Department of Cultural Affairs, Archaeology, Archives and Museums, Punjab, Chandigarh, 1987, p. 14.
37. S.P. Gupta, *op. cit.*, p. 6.
38. Laxmi P. Sihare, "Director's Foreword", *Ibid.*, p. 13. S.P. Shukla thinks that "the *Kāmuka* female figures on the railing pillars of the Buddhist stūpas at Mathura and Sanghol were the creations of the artist-craftsmen of Mathura school of art. These were not the portraits of divinities. Their presence indicated a complete change in Buddhist outlook towards women-folk, whom they earlier thought as a barrier in self-control and *nirvāṇa*. The sensuous figures reflected the idiosyncracy of the Kushāṇas, the rich and affluent class of the society, who allowed freedom of all kind to women." [S.P. Shukla, "Kāmuka Female Figures in the Kushana Art and their bearing on the Buddhist Ideology", *National Museum Bulletin*, New Delhi, Nos. 7 & 8 (1993), pp. 19-28].
39. S.P. Gupta, *op. cit.*, p. 134, no. 26. What has been referred to as a relic casket may be the coffin representing the *Mahāparinirvāṇa*.
40. *Ibid.*, pp. 129 (no. 15 a-b) 133 (no. 25 a-b) respectively.
41. Ananda K. Coomaraswamy, *History of Indian and Indonesian Art*, New York, 1927, Pl. XIX, Figs. 69-69A.
42. O. Viennot, "Typologie du Makara et essai de chronologie", *Arts Asiatiques*, Paris, I (3), 1954, pp. 191-93, pls. I and III.2; V.A. Smith, *Jaina Stupa of Mathura*, Allahabad, 1901, pl. XXVI, back view; A. Coomaraswamy, *La Sculpture de Bharhut*, Paris, 1956, Pl. XXXV.101; V.S. Agrawala, *Indian Art*, I, Varanasi, 1965, Pl. XXV, fig. 676; R.C. Agrawala, "Śuṅga Pillars from Amin, near Kurukshetra", *Lalit Kalā*, No. 14 (1969), pp. 50-52, Pl. XVII, Figs. 4 and 8.
43. S.P. Gupta, p. 124; Archana Rani, *op. cit.*, Pl. 39.
44. *Ibid.*, pp. 124-25, Pl. 2 and p. 40.
45. *Ibid.*, p. 125, Pl. 3; B.N. Goswamy, *Essence of Indian Art*, p. 63, Pl. 31; Archana Rani, *op. cit.*, Pl. 94.
46. *Ibid.*, p. 128, Pl. 12; Archana Rani, *op. cit.*, Pl. 25.
47. *Ibid.*, p. 126, Pl. 8; Archana Rani, *op. cit.*, Pl. 19.
48. *Ibid.*, p. 127, Pl. 10; Archana Rani, *op. cit.*, Pl. 17.
49. P. Banerjee, "The Story of Rishyasringa as depicted in the Art of Sanghol, Punjab", in Devendra Handa and Ashvini Agrawal (eds.), *Ratna-Chandrikā: Panorama of Oriental Studies (Shri R.C. Agrawala Festschrift)*, New Delhi, 1989, pp. 125-29, Pls. 15.1-3.
50. *Rām*, Bālakāṇḍa, chs. IX-X; *Mbh*, (Sabhā Parva, XI.23; Vana Parva, CX.37-39; CXI.13, CXII; CXIII.8-11; Śānti Parva, CCXXXIV.34).
51. V.S. Agrawala, *Indian Art*, Varanasi, 1965, Fig. 138a. A relief from the Bharhut railing of 2nd century BCE preserved in the Indian Museum, Kolkata depicts the scene of the birth of Ṛishyaśṛiṅga from the doe in a hermitage. For details see P. Banerjee, *Rama in Indian Literature, Art and Thought*, Delhi, 1986.
52. Cf. S.P. Shukla in *Buddhist Art and Thought*, pp. 132-33.
53. G.B. Sharma *et al* in S.P. Gupta (2001), *op. cit.*, p. 127.
54. *Ibid.*
55. *Ibid.*, p. 129, Pl. 16a.
56. *Ibid.*, pp. 128-29, Pl. 13.
57. *Ibid.*, p. 126, Pl. 6; Archana Rani, *op. cit.*, Pl. 84; Sandrine Gill, *op. cit.*, p. 158, Fig. 7.21.

58. It has recently been partially illustrated by Sandrine Gill (*Ibid.*, Fig. 7.19).
59. *Ibid.*, Fig. 7.20.
60. Sandrine Gill, *op. cit.*, p. 158, Fig. 7.18.
61. G.B. Sharma *et al* in S.P. Gupta, Pl. 7; B.N. Goswamy, *Essence of Indian Art*, p. 114, Pl. 77.
62. R. Banerjee, "The Mahaummaga Jataka in Kushan Sculpture from Sanghol", *Roopa-Lekha*, Vol. LIX, no. 1 & 2 (April 1987), pp. 90-92.
63. *Ibid.*
64. S.P. Gupta (2001), *op. cit.*, p. 22, fn. 6. Gupta, however, mentions the author erroneously as P. Banerjee.
65. S.P. Shukla, *loc. cit.*, p. 133.
66. Sharma *et al* in S.P. Gupta, *op. cit.*, p. 129, Pl. 14.
67. *Ibid.*, p. 130, Pl. 17.
68. *Ibid.*
69. Sandrine Gill, *op. cit.*, p. 151, Fig. 7.6.
70. Sharma *et al* in S.P. Gupta, *op. cit.*, p. 130, Pl. 16 B.
71. *Ibid.*, pp. 130-31, Pl. 18.
72. *Ibid.*, pp. 132-33, Pl. 23.
73. Winged lion is depicted on the pedestal of the royal devotte also (*Ibid.*, p. 77, Pl. 9).
74. Acc. No. 11.151.4. For illustration see Jitendra Kumar, *Masterpieces of Mathura Museum*, Mathura, 1989, p. 62, Pls. 25-26.
75. Sharma *et al* in S.P. Gupta, p. 131, Pl. 20.
76. Pratapaditya Pal, *The Peaceful Liberators: Jaina Art from India*, Los Angeles & London, 1996, p. 105, Catalogue No. 3. See also B.N. Goswamy, *op. cit.*, p. 65, Pl. 33.
77. *Sanghol Sculptures*, p. 131, Pl. 19a.
78. Archana Rani, *op. cit.*, Pl. 111.
79. *Sanghol Sculptures*, p. 111, Pl. 19b.
80. Archana Rani, *op. cit.*, Pls. 106-09.
81. Shashi Asthana, "The Kushāṇa Art of Mathura", in S.P. Gupta, p. 41, Fig. 4.11; J.C. Harle, *The Art and Architecture of the Indian Subcontinent*, London, 1986, p. 68, fig. 49.
82. Sandrine Gill, *op. cit.*, p. 153, Fig. 7.11. Cf. *yakshārohī* lady (Acc. No. 22) described above.
83. Devendra Handa, "A Kuṣāṇa Portrait Statue from Punjab", *Bulletin of Museums & Archaeology in UP*, Lucknow, N. 37 (June 1986), pp. 1-2 & Pl.
84. Scarf coming from the back over the shoulders and knotted at the chest is comparable to a torso from Morā near Mathura. For details see J.M. Rosenfield, *The Dynastic Arts of the Kushans*, Berkeley, 1967, Pl. 51.
85. *Ibid.*, Pl. 27.
86. F.S. Growse, *Mathura, a district memoir*, Allahabad, 1883 (3rd edn.); J. Ph. Vogel, *Catalogue of the Archaeological Museum of Mathura*, Allahabad, 1910 & *La Sculptre de Mathura*, Paris and Bruxelles, 1930; V.S. Agrawala, *Handbook of the Sculptures in the Curzon Museum of Archaeology in Muthra*, Allahabad, 1933; Rosenfield, *op. cit.*, pp. 138-53.
87. G.B. Sharma, "A Summary of Archaeological Excavations in Punjab", Archaeology & Sculpture Exhibition, Cultural Affairs, Arch., Museums, and State Archives, Punjab, Chandigarh, no date, p. 9; S.P. Gupta (2001), *op. cit.*, pp. 20-22, Pl. IX; Sandrine Gill, *op. cit.*, p. 147, Figs. 7.3a-b.
88. G.B. Sharma, *ibid.*, p. 3.
89. Shashi Asthana, "The Kuṣāṇa Art of Sanghol", *Lalit Kala*, no. 24, p. 10.
90. S.P. Gupta (2001), *op. cit.*, p. 20.
91. S.P. Shukla in *Buddhist Art and Thought*, p. 132.
92. Sandrine Gill (*op. cit.*, p. 147) refers to the possibility of the scenes being connected with Buddha and Aśoka but admits the difficulty of their proper identification in the absence of a broader iconographical context or epigraphic evidence.
93. Devendra Handa, "Some Sculptures from Punjab and Haryana", *Panjab University Research Bulletin (Arts)*, Vol. VII, No. 1 (April 1976), p. 95, Fig. 4.
94. Watters, *op. cit.*, pp. 296-97; *CAGI*, pp. 115-19.
95. Handa (1976), *op. cit.*, Fig. 2.

# 10

# Jaina Sculptures

## JAINA IMAGES

The Jainas believe their religion to be eternal, having been revealed repeatedly by twenty-four Tīrthaṅkaras 'path makers', of which the last two are certainly historical figures. Pārśva, the penultimate pontiff, lived between 877-777 BCE, and the last Tīrthaṅkara Mahāvīra died two hundred and fifty years later, i.e., in 527 BCE.[1]

The first Jaina Tīrthaṅkara Ṛishabha or Ādinātha, generally regarded as a mythological person and dated to millions of years back, is said to have turned the wheel of faith at Takshaśilā and also visited the Yavana country (i.e., Ionia). He divided his kingdom before renouncing the world amongst his eldest two sons Bharata and Bāhubalī, with Ayodhya and Takshaśilā as their capitals. When Bāhubalī was ruling over Takshaśilā, his ascetic father Ṛishabha visited his kingdom. On hearing the news of his father's visit, Bāhubalī prepared for a grand reception for the great saint but the latter returned from Siṃhapura (near Katas or Punja Sahib, the famous Sikh place of pilgrimage in district Jhelum of Pakistan) without reaching his son's capital. As a memorial to his father's visit, however, Bāhubalī built a *stūpa* on the spot from which Ṛishabha had returned.[2] Takshaśilā had not come into existence before the sixth century BCE and the Ionian kingdom was not established before the eighth-seventh century BCE, so the facts stated above are not compatible with historical and archaeological evidence.[3] Since the construction of Temples F and G at Sirkap, which were regarded as Buddhist earlier, differed from those found at Taxila and resembled closely to those represented on the *Āyāgapaṭṭas* associated with the Jaina *stūpa* excavated at the Kaṅkālī Ṭīlā at Mathura, John Marshall and some other scholars who follow him regard them as of Jaina affiliation[4] but A. Ghosh does not find any justification for Marshall's doubtful supposition.[5]

The westernmost cities visited by Pārśva include Kauśāmbī, Ahichchhatrā and Hastināpura which have all been excavated and were in existence during his time. Though the Jaina tradition associates Supārśvanātha (seventh Tīrthaṅkara), Neminātha (twenty-first Tīrthaṅkara), Arishṭanemi (twenty-second Tīrthaṅkara) and Mahāvīra (twenty-fourth Tīrthaṅkara) with Mathura, yet there is hardly any evidence to substantiate that Jainism got any firm footing at

Mathura before the second century BCE. It is, however, Mahāvīra about whom we get some authentic details. Born at Kuṇḍagrāma, a suburb of Vaiśālī (Basarh in northern Bihar), he was an elder contemporary of Buddha. He organized and spread Jainism to parts of Uttar Pradesh, Bihar and West Bengal. The *Uttarādhyayana Sūtra* records that Mahāvīra had advised the Jaina monks not to roam beyond Thūṇā which is situated on the western boundary of Āryadeśa, later called Madhyadeśa, perhaps because Jainism had not penetrated beyond this place by that time.[6] Thūṇā is generally identified with Thanesar (ancient Sthāṇvīśvara, modern Thanesar and Kurukshetra).[7] So, no Tīrthaṅkara seems to have ever visited Punjab and Jainism had not reached here till the time of the last Tīrthaṅkara. According to tradition, King Bimbisāra and his son Ajātaśatru of Magadha were devotees of Mahāvīra. Ajātaśatru shifted his capital from Rājagṛiha to Pāṭaliputra where his son Udāyī is said to have built a Jaina temple, but there is no archaeological evidence to corroborate it. The succeeding Nandas and Chandragupta Maurya too seem to have been favourably inclined towards Jainism. Megasthenes mentions Sarmanes (*Śramaṇa*) in his court[8] and a tradition states that when a Jaina pontiff Bhadrabāhu predicted a famine of twelve long years in Magadha, Chandragupta himself migrated to South India and died there by practicing a fast unto death (*sallekhanā*).[9] Aśoka's spirit of toleration and broadmindedness is reflected in his instructions that the Brāhmaṇas, Śramaṇas, Nirgranthas and Ājīvikās should be given due honour and care.[10] Since the *Nirgranthas* ('knotless', generally regarded to be Jaina ascetics) have been mentioned only in the Seventh Pillar Edict engraved on the Delhi-Topra pillar, which was brought to Firoz Shah Kotla, Delhi by Sultan Firoz Tughlaq from the village Topra near Jagadhari in district Yamunanagar, A.K. Roy thinks that by the time of Aśoka, the Jaina religion had spread as far north as this place[11] but it must be admitted that there is no definite evidence to support it.

The Jaina texts are, however, eloquent about Aśoka's son Kuṇāla. His son Samprati contributed greatly to the spread of Jainism.[12] Roy refers to the founding of the Uddeha-gaṇa by Rohaṇa, a disciple of the Jaina monk Suhastin who was a contemporary of Samprati.[13] Uddeha-gaṇa was divided into four branches, one of which was Udambarika or Udaṃbarijjiyā connected with the Udumbaras, whose capital was Pratishṭhāna, i.e., Pathankot. Jaina *śramaṇas* are said to have been active there.[14] Audumbara coinage, however, does not show any impact of Jainism nor is there any other evidence to prove the identity of the Udumbarika branch of the Jaina Uddeha-gaṇa with the Audumbaras.[15]

Jainism, however, seems to have been in a flourishing state at Mathurā during the second century BCE onwards, as indicated by the excavations at Kaṅkālī-ṭīlā which brought to light the remains of a brick *stūpa* and images of Tīrthaṅkaras, sculptural fragments depicting incidents from the lives of the Tīrthaṅkaras, *āyaga-paṭas, toraṇas* and railing pillars, etc.[16] A baked clay seal with a hole on one side for passing a string, found from Ahrwan, 12 km southwest of Palwal, has the Brāhmī legend *Śamaṇasa* in the characters of the later half of the second century BCE. The word *Śramaṇa* in Sanskrit means an ascetic or religious mendicant or devotee in general and has also been used for both, the Buddha and Mahāvīra. If the word *Śramaṇa* was not a proper name, the seal may be interpreted to have belonged to a Jaina monk. But the Jaina monks cannot be expected to run commercial activities to use such seals, though its use by a monk to send some confidential messages to other or higher monks or teachers cannot be ruled out altogether. Even if we accept that the word does not signify a Jaina monk but a personal name, still the adoption of such a personal name indicates the proclivity towards Jainism. Corroborative evidence, however, will remain a desideratum to be fulfilled by future discoveries.[17]

A Jaina patriarch Lohāchārya is said to have propagated Jainism amongst the mercantile tribe of Agroha (i.e., Agrodaka *Janapada*) during the first century CE.[18] *Therīgāthā*, which forms part of the *Khuddakanikāya*, contains stanzas five each of Nanduttarā and Mittakali of Kururaṭṭha. The traditional mention of names with the lives of the *Bhikshuṇīs* 'nuns' is preserved in the commentary of Dhammapāla known as the *Parmatthadīpinī*, ascribable to the fifth century CE. Both the *therīs* (nuns) belonged to the Brāhmaṇa families of Kammāsadamma *nigama* 'corporation' in the Kuru country. Nanduttarā had earlier been initiated to Jainism.[19] There is, however, complete paucity of archaeological evidence regarding the prevalence of Jainism in Haryana and Punjab during the Kushāṇa and even Gupta period as no Jaina inscription, icon or *āyāga-paṭa* has so far been discovered from the regions.

From Kapiśā Xuan Zang came to the capital of Siṃhapura, which has been identified by Cunningham with Katas (Kaṭāksha), a place of Hindu pilgrimage, situated about 25 km from Pind Dadan Khan in the Salt Range in district Jhelum (Pakistan).[20] The Chinese pilgrim records that he saw an Aśokan *stūpa* there near which was situated the place where the first prophet of the white-clothed heretics attained enlightenment and delivered his maiden sermon. This place was marked by a memorial and there also existed a Deva-temple. The 'Śramaṇeras' and the disciples having little hair on the head and naked or wearing only white clothes, which distinguished them from the Buddhists, practiced severe austerities and worshipped the image of their teacher which was just like that of Buddha but was distinguished only by clothing.[21] It is interesting to note that Sir Aurel Stein visited this place in 1889 and discovered the remains of the Siṃhapura Jaina temple buried near Murti, a village two miles from Katas. Images and architectural pieces in large numbers were brought to Lahore by him in twenty-six camel loads and were deposited in the Punjab Central Museum where some of them were exhibited in the sculpture gallery while most of the material was preserved in the godown.[22] At the time of the partition of India in 1947, some part of the Murti finds came to India's share and is now housed in the Government Museum and Art Gallery, Chandigarh. Two of the pieces belonging to the Gupta period have been listed and described by Bhattacharya in his catalogue of sculptures in the museum.[23] Jaina relics of Gupta art tradition found from Murti and the presence of the Jainas in the Gandhāra region, as recorded by Xuan Zang, however, reveal that Jainism must have spread to those areas after having traversed the present day Haryana and Punjab states of India.[24]

Uddyotana Sūri refers to a town named Pavvaiyā (Pārvatikā) on the bank of the river Chandrabhāgā (Chenab) in the introduction of his *Kuvalayamālākathā*, which was finished in Śaka 700, i.e., CE 778. The ruler of Pavvaiyā was Torarāya, a name which reminds us of the Hūṇa ruler Toramāṇa whose capital was Śākala (Sāṅgalā Hill), generally believed to be modern Sialkot in Pakistan now. It is probable that Pārvatikā was another name of Śākala which was situated close to the modern Pabbi hills and hence the city was called Pārvatikā.[25] Toramāṇa (*circa* CE 500) issued coins with rude copy of Sassanian bust on the obverse and wheel with bold Brāhmī legend Tora on the reverse.[26] The equation of Torarāya with Toramāṇa thus seems to be quite logical. Harigupta, a Jaina monk, was the guru of Torarāya, the reigning monarch of Pārvatikā, and stayed with him.[27] Pārvatikā may have therefore been an important centre of Jainism during the fifth century.[28] It must, however, be admitted, as noted above also, that no evidence of the existence of Jaina temples or sculptures of a period prior to the early medieval times has as yet been found from the present-day Punjab though their existence is quite probable.

An atheistic religion like Buddhism initially, Jainism later adopted paradoxically, like the latter, image-worship and the twenty-four Tīrthaṅkaras came to be worshiped as Supreme Deities along with their attendant *Yakshas* and *Yakshīs*. Severe discipline, self-control, renunciation and austerity, characteristic of the Jainas, did not allow much embellishments to be introduced in their sculptural representations. Still, some superb examples do exist amongst the numerous

Jina images found from different parts of the country. These images are generally found carved either in *kāyotsarga* (also called *khaḍgāsana*)[29] or *padmāsana* (also called *paryaṅkāsana*).[30] Śrutadevīs or Vidyādevīs are other important but secondary deities of Jainism represented in art. Since converts could not dissociate themselves from their former faith completely, we find many Hindu deities like Śrī-Lakshmī, Gaṇeśa, Vaiśravaṇa-Kubera, etc. included in the fold of Jainism. *Dikpālas, Navagrahas, Apasarases, Gandharvas, Vidyādharas, Kinnaras*, etc., too, came to be adopted as the sculptural embellishments on religious edifices.

*Chhattra-traya* or *Chhattrāvali* (triple umbrella); *lāñchhana* (cognizance); *Chaumukhī* or *Sarvatobhadrikā*,[31] a type of shrine-model with openings on all the four sides; *Chaubīsī* or *Chaturviṃśatikā*, a stele frieze or image with the twenty-four Tīrthaṅkara figures; *tri-* and *pañcha-tīrthikās*, images with three or five Jina figures, etc., absent in Kushāṇa and Gupta sculptures, make their appearance later. Decorated glorioles and *śrīvatsa*-mark on the chest of the Jina figures, however, continued throughout from the early period.[32]

Carved in purely human form having two arms (in contradistinction to Hindu deities who are often shown with multiple hands) and without ornaments in *kāyotsarga* or *dhyāna-mudrā*, the Jina images, shown as sky-clad in Digambara tradition and wearing only a (white) *dhotī* and no other garment in Śvetāmbara tradition, are depicted as young and beautiful in appearance, with a tranquil expression, arms reaching down to the knees, eyes centred on the tip of the nose in meditation, and *śrīvatsa* on the chest.[33] Iconographical texts[34] refer to the eight *Prātihāryas* which should be seen in a complete image of a Tīrthaṅkara: (1) divine (Aśoka) tree, (2) shower of celestial blossoms, (3) drum, (4) fly-whisks, (5) throne seat (a lion throne), (6) aureole, (7) tri-linear umbrella, and (8) heavenly music. Initially, the images of all the Tīrthaṅkaras were alike except Ṛishabhanātha (also called Ādinātha for being the first Tīrthaṅkara), Pārśvanātha who was generally shown with a canopy of three or seven or eleven snake-hoods (sometimes exceptionally with five snake-hoods also) and Supārśvanātha who was represented with one or five or nine snake-hoods overhead. Their images in *dhyāna-mudrā* were similar to the images of Buddha but were distinguished by the *śrīvatsa* mark on the chest. Emblems, *yakshas* and *yakshīs*, acolytes, *Kevala-vṛikshas* (trees under which they got enlightenment), etc. provide us clues to recognize and identify later Jina images. The *lāñchhanas* were introduced in the Gupta period with some images but got finally fixed by about the 10th century only.[35] The position of the *lāñchhana*, according to Āśādhara (CE 1228), was to be in the centre below the *pāda-pīṭha*, while the *yaksha* and *yakshī* were to be on the right and left side of the pedestal respectively.[36] *Dharmachakra* flkanked by a deer on either side, which was a Buddhist motif signifying Buddha's first sermon at Sarnath, was also adopted by the Jainas on the pedestal of the images of Tīrthaṅkaras sometime between eighth and tenth century CE. The *lāñchhana* of the Jina was then placed on top of the pedestal below the seat of the Jina or on the lower edge of the pedestal.

Like the neighbouring states of Rajasthan and Haryana, Jainism seems to have become popular in Punjab during the early medieval period and quite a few of Jaina images, both in stone and metal, have been found from the state.

## STONE SCULPTURES

Dholbaha, as we have seen above, had developed as a great trade centre between the plains of northern India and the hill region of Himachal Pradesh. It seems that Jainism came to Punjab with those traders, probably from Rajasthan, a notable number of whom settled at Dholbaha as is indicated by architectural and sculptural remains recovered from the site. A badly mutilated *Sarvatobhadrikā* 'quadruple' showing four Jina figures, seated back to back on all the four sides in *padmāsana* on a high-pedestalled and cushioned seat with crossed legs slanting slightly towards the front (Pl. 269), probably represents the earliest Jaina icon from Dholbaha. The image seems to have suffered the rage of iconoclastic vandals and centuries of climatic vagaries and no details worth noting can be discerned. Traces indicate that there may have been the depiction of an enface *dharma-chakra* flanked by deer on either side in the lower register and worn out figures of two lions with their back towards the centre in the upper register of the pedestal. The lions on the pedestal symbolize the *chakravartin* status of the Jinas. Their posture and depiction near the ends of the pedestal indicate the lingering on of the early tradition. It is difficult to guess its date but it looks like a piece of *circa* eighth century CE. Another *sarvatobhadra* measuring 17.5 X 11.25 cm made of black stone found from Bhalur in district Moga, however, is in a much better state of preservation though even in this case, deliberate vandalism has taken toll of the heads and arms of the Jinas (Pl. 270).[37] Even other parts seem to have been struck heavily but the nature of the stone has helped in the survival of the figures in meditation seated against a column whose upper part gets square with railing-like decoration, dormer windows and a double-inverted lotus design at the top. Lozenge-shaped *śrīvatsa* marks engraved on the chest of the Jina figures are quite clear. The seat is adorned with a sheet which hangs in the form of two pleated semi-circles on the pedestal which carries the depiction of a wheel in profile in the centre flanked by seated deer on and outward leaping lions. We are not sure whether only one Jina was depicted on all the four facets or four different Tīrthaṅkaras were carved facing the cardinal directions. One cannot be definite to assert that the image was imported from elsewhere or carved at the place but the stone is certainly not found in the region and the former proposition looks more probable. Stylistically, the four-fold image may be dated to *circa* tenth century CE.

A headless sandstone image of Neminātha from Khizrabad near Chandigarh seated in *padmāsana* (Pl. 271) indicates that by the ninth century CE, Jainism had spread and gained popularity in different parts of the state. The Jina has a stout bust with broad chest, attenuated waist with a deep navel mark, long arms folded at the elbows for the hands to be placed one upon the other in the lap over the crossed legs. The hands have suffered some damage. The throne on which the Jina sits has ribbed legs. The frontal edge of the throne is also rounded and ribbed at the ends. The sheet covering the seat falls in front in a wavy fashion. Between the legs of the throne is a wheel in profile in the centre with outward moving lions having their backs towards the wheel. A vertical conch with its spiral head placed on the *tri-ratha* pedestal at the lower end of the wheel helps us to recognize the image as that of Neminātha, the twenty-second pontiff. The extreme buttresses of the pedestal carry human figures, probably of the *yaksha* and *yakshī* of the Tīrthaṅkara, but it is difficult to be certain as all details are lost. A much mutilated small figure found from Mard Khera near Sunam shows the Tīrthaṅkara seated similarly on a square pedestal or seat with two lions having their back towards each other and front paws raised up with their heads turned to front flanking the central wheel in profile (Pl. 272). However, it defies proper identification because of its indifferent state of preservation and the absence of any cognizance. The head of the Jina has been broken deliberately but the body seems to be well modelled and muscular. The pedestal is *tri-ratha* and shows standing human figures on the extreme recesses. They are, however, beyond recognition. The image may have almost been contemporary or later by a few years to the preceding one. Broken above the belly is another *kankar* stone figure from Mard Khera showing the meditative Jina seated on a cushion cross-legged with hands in the lap (Pl. 273). The hands and the left knee, too, are broken. An embroidered sheet or carpet covers the seat and a part of the pedestal, which as usual carries the depiction of outward moving but enface lions supporting the fore part of their body on one leg while the front paw is raised up. The different type of ṣtone indicates the existence of more than one temple at this site which might have catered to the needs of a larger population in ancient times. An architectural piece from the same place, probably a part of the door-surround of a Jaina temple, shows a Jina in *khaḍgāsana* (Pl. 274). A notable feature of this figure are the extraordinarily long arms reaching the knees (*ājānu-lamba-bāhu*) indicating that the craftsmen paid heed to the textual prescriptions of the images. As usual, the head of the pontiff is broken. Stylistically, it may be placed in the ninth or early tenth century CE.

According to Mr. Rameshwar Dass of Sunam, a local enthusiastic archaeologist, a very beautiful buff-coloured sandstone *tri-tīrthika* of about half a metre height was recovered from the old mound between Baghraul and Kapial near Samuran, about 15 km southeast of Mard Khera and nearly 25 km southeast of Sangrur on Patran road near the border of Sangrur with Patiala, about three decades back and was taken away by the wife of a high official of the district. Later, some very badly mutilated Jina figures were also obtained from the site. No details of these images are, however, available now.

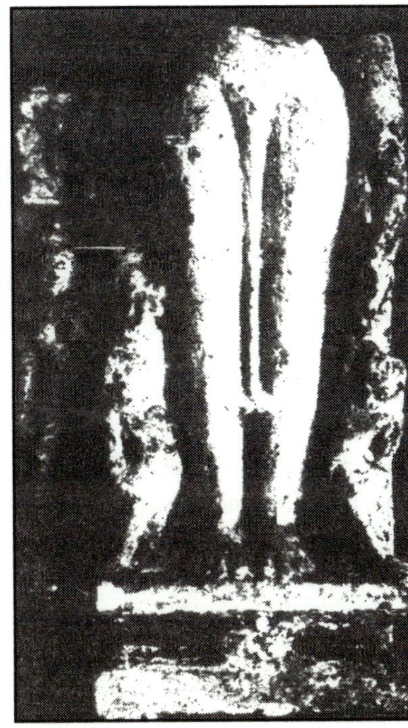

**Fig. 59.** *Kāyotsarga* Ādinātha, Kalyan (from *IAR*, 1978-79).

An independent image of Ādinātha in *kāyotsarga* posture is known from Kalyan near Patiala (Fig. 59).[38] This sandstone image is broken above the waist but can be identied with the help provided by the depiction of a small figure of bull seated to right on the pedestal as well as by the extant long left arm of the pontiff going well below the left knee. The free end of the *dhotī* falling down vertically between the two legs leaves little doubt to its being a Śvetāmbara image. Near the feet of Ādinātha are shown the fly-whiskers with their waist accentuated towards the main figure, keeping balance of the body by supporting the weight with one hand placed on the thigh and holding the fly-whisk in the other hand above the head. As per the Jaina iconographic tradition, they should be Bharata and Bāhubalī but there is absolutely no clue to identify them. The receding buttress on either side may have carried female figures as indicated by the one extant on the proper right hand side. The image is not in a good state of preservation. The extant legs of the figure of the Tīrthaṅkara betray elongation. It may be assigned to *circa* eleventh century CE on stylistic grounds. A complete sculpture of a Jaina Tīrthaṅkara of the same period is also reported from Kalyan but no details of its identification, posture, distinguishing marks, cognizance, vehicle, acolytes, *yaksha* and *yakshī* are available. The name of the village Kalyan (also called Panj Kalyan) seems to have derived from the Jaina term *Kalyāṇaka* or *Pañcha-Kalyāṇa* as there may have been the depiction of the scenes of life (*chyavana* 'before birth', *janma* 'birth', *dīkshā* 'consecration', *kaivalya* 'perfection', and *nirvāṇa* 'liberation') in the temple/s here.

Displayed in the Hoshiarpur museum, we have three Jaina reliefs from Dholbaha. One of these seems to have originally been the cult image worshipped in the Jaina temple there during the tenth century CE but has unfortunately survived only partially. The Jina, broken above the waist, is shown as seated in *padmāsana* on an embroidered cushion placed on an inverted lotus flower (Pl. 275). There is no cognizance, no *yaksha* and *yakshī* figure and no other clue for definite identification but since Dholbaha has not yielded any Buddhist images, it can be said with certainty that the extant relief belonged to a Jaina Tīrthaṅkara. There are some traces of the *dhotī* on the legs. The temple in which this image may have been installed originally must have thus belonged to the Śvetāmbara sect. The second piece is a broken fragment of a larger image or perhaps an architectural component having a square abacus at the top decorated with vase and foliage design with a Jina seated in meditation in a small pillared *rathikā* below (Pl. 276). On the viewer's right is an *aśva-vyāla* serving as the bracket while a female figure is shown in a pedimented niche below the Jina. The left side bears vertically a double lotus leaf design. The ribbed pillars, window dormer and the style of carving suggest tenth century date. The state of preservation is indifferent and worn out, indicating a long period of exposure. The third Jaina relief from Dholbaha on display in the said museum may also be an architectural piece or a part of *chaubīsī,* as it shows a miniature temple or *nāgara-kūṭa* bedecked with a lozenge-shaped diamond on the right with two registers on its right depicting three meditative figures in the upper row and two in the lower register (Pl. 277). Since the frieze is broken on the other side and below, it is difficult to determine the exact number of figures which were carved. The stone used is coarse grained on which very fine carving was not possible perhaps. As such the temple may have belonged to the laity built without any royal or substantive support, thus indicating that Dholbaha contained substantial Jaina population during the medieval period.

Some utterly worn-out and mutilated fragments of *nāgara-kūṭas* from Kharar furnish evidence of the existence of Jaina temples at this place in the tenth century CE. They show successively diminishing flatish tiers of the spire having *chaitya-gavāksha* design in front capped by a massive *āmalaka,* Jina seated in meditation in a pillared niche below flanked by female figures holding perhaps lotus flowers in the receding recesses on either side (Pl. 278). Stone used is greyish shale available in the nearby hills indicative of the utilization only of local resources. One piece (Pl. 279) recovered from now dereilict and extinguished Aja-Sarovara indicates that the sculptures were immerced in the tank fearing some imminent attack or after the temple was destroyed.

From Sanghol has been found a fragment measuring 29 X 24 cm with a *nāgara-kūṭa* (Pl. 280). It is actually the right hand top part of the *parikara* or a magnificent Jaina image as can be judged from the bead-stringed and lotus-petalled rim of the aureole and the semi-celestial beings on its outer edge coming out of the mouth of the mythical *makara-mukha* on its left and *vyāla* figure on the other end. The *nāgara-kūṭa* shows a Jina figure seated under triple umbrella in meditation within a ribbed pillared niche flanked on either side in the receding recesses by half-diamond designs. Like the *pīḍhā-deuls* of Orissa, the *nāgara-kūṭa* itself shows three successively receding slabs which are centrally covered by exquisitely carved *chaitya-gavāksha* over the niche containing the figure of the Jina. A huge *āmalaka* supports another *āmalaka* over a circular slab and on the top may be seen *kalaśa* or *stūpikā*. The overall balance and harmony bespeaks of the magnificence of the Jaina temple which must have once adorned Sanghol during the tenth-eleventh century CE.

Similar bead-stringed lotus-spacered rim of the halo with semi-celestial figures on it has been recovered from Rupalon also (Pl. 281). The *tilaka* in its centre has the seated Jina figure with attendant female and male figures in the receding recessed niches on the two sides and *vidyādhara* figures in flying postures supporting the Jina in the *tilaka* with upraised hands serving as *bhāraputras* and holding a stalked flower in their other hands below. The stone is coarse grained and the carving, too, is not very sharp indicating the utilization of local resources. Anyway, the fragment furnishes evidence of the proliferation of Jainism and existence of Jaina shrines in Punjab during the tenth-eleventh centuries.

A fragmentary sandstone image of a Jaina Tīrthaṅkara seated on an inverted lotus with pericarp in *dhyāna-mudrā* under the *chhattrāvali* flanked on either side by a sky-clad Jina in *kāyotsarga-mudrā* with meditative Jina figure atop from Majhur (Pl. 282) furnishes evidence of the existence of a Digambara shrine during the tenth century CE. The right knee and hands in the lap have suffered diminution. The lozenge-shaped auspicious mark on the chest is clearly marked. The main figure has a round face with drooping eyelids, sturdy nose, plump cheeks, thick lips, long ears, broad shoulders, strong arms and attenuated waist. The side figures of *khaḍgāsana* Jinas are canopied while the meditative Jina figures on the top corners look as if hooded.

Sunam seems to have remained a great stronghold of Jainism in the medieval period. It still has a large Jaina population and a Jaina temple which contains some very interesting and important material. Recovered from the old site of this town, however, are some stone images and architectural friezes which give us a glimpse of its heritage. One of these relics is a fragmentary relief measuring 23 X 19 cm, showing the folded legs of the pontiff seated on a full-blossomed lotus placed on two lions seated back to back with a small rhinoceros carved on the pedestal which helps us to identify it with the eleventh Jaina Tīrthaṅkara Śreyāṃsanātha, datable stylistically to about the ninth or early tenth century CE (Pl. 283).[39] Such an early image of this pontiff has not been found from anywhere as yet.

Also recovered from the site is a black stone inscribed *pañcha-ratha* pedestal of the twenty-second Tīrthaṅkara Neminātha (Pl. 284), identified as such because of a vertically placed conch with spiral head turned up engraved on it. The *bhadra-ratha* 'central projection' shows a wheel in profile in the centre flanked by seated deer looking at it. The *pratirathas* 'juxta-buttresses' carry the depiction of robust lions seated as usual on their haunches back to back with upper parts of the body raised above and poised on their yonder forepaws. The frontal paws are held near the chest and their faces are turned to front. Their tongues are lolling out and a double-stringed beaded cross-chain resembling *chhannavīra* may be seen on their bodies. They have erect ears and bear moustaches. Ribbed lathe-turned pillars stand on the extremities of the *pratirathas*. They are bedecked with four-petalled gemmed designs at their tops. The rounded frontal egde of the couch is also decorated with rings and rib-like designs. The sheet covering the seat of the pontiff falls in the form of a loop partially covering the backs of the lions and touching the upper edge of the wheel in the centre. Its pleats produce a pleasing effect. The portion of the suspended sheet bears five-stringed beaded ribbons clasped at their upper ends with vertically falling free ends. The extreme recesses show the *yaksha* and *yakshī* of the Jina. The uni-cephalous *yaksha* on the proper right hand side of the pedestal is seated in *lalitāsana* with left leg folded on a cushioned seat and the right one suspended gracefully. His hair is combed back and upwards and tied with a pearl string to keep them in position. The *yaksha* wears an *ekāvali* and probably the nether garment also, which provide a clue to its Śvetāmbara affiliation. He is holding a *bījapūraka* 'citrus' in his right hand and the left hand is placed on the corresponding knee. It is difficult to identify him with Gomedha, the *yaksha* prescribed for Neminātha in the Jaina canonical works. He is more probably Sarvānubhūti. The *yakshī* Ambikā on the other side, seated similarly supporting the child in its lap by left hand and holding an *āmra-lumbī* 'mango-bunch' in the right hand, supports such an identification as we find the representation of these two in numerous Tīrthaṅkara images in Rajasthan, Gujarat and elsewhere.[40] Minute care has been provided to all the figures. The two-lined inscription (Pl. 285), which has survived on the proper right hand side *pratiratha* facet of the pedestal, reads: (1) (Auspicious mark) *Jehavi-suta Dehi-* (2) *lena kāritā* //. The inscription meaning '(this image was) caused (to be made) by Dehila, son of Jehavi' seems to be complete and if any part of it existed on the other side of the central projection, it has completely rubbed off. The palaeography indicates a date close to the end of the ninth or early tenth century which later goes well with the carving style of the image. The use and availability of black stone was not local and it is difficult to say whether the image was carved at Sunam or imported ready-made.

In the latter case, the source may have been Rajasthan where we find the use of black stone for sculptures at various places in the medieval period. An inscribed white marble image dated Samvat 1495 and numerous others in same or black stone belonging to seventeenth through twentieth century in the same temple provide evidence of the continuing links with Rajasthan.

Evidence of the existence of a Jaina temple at Sunam during the tenth century is also furnished by an architectural piece which shows a female figure seated in *padmāsana* with folded legs holding a lotus in the left hand with right in *abhaya*, being adored by hybrid *nāga* couple having human bust and anguine tails (Pl. 286).[41] They stand slightly turned towards the main figure. The *rathikā* is pedimented and is flanked by smaller pedimented panels showing attendant male figures. The moulded base indicates it to have been a part of the socle or *vedībandha* of a temple. The absence of any cognizance renders it difficult to identify the niched female figure but it seems to have been the depiction of some *yakshī* associated with the Tīrthaṅkara to whom the shrine was dedicated. Jaina iconographic texts prescribe four or more hands for the Jaina *yakshīs* but according to the *Aparājitapṛichchhā* (chapter 221), Chakreśvarī, Naradattā or Bahurūpā, Ambikā, Padmāvatī and Siddhāyikā – the *yakshī* of Ādinātha (first Tīrthaṅkara), Munisuvrata (twentieth Tīrthaṅkara), Neminātha (twenty-second Tīrthaṅkara), Pārśvanātha (twenty-third Tīrthaṅkara) and Mahāvīra (twenty-fourth Tīrthaṅkara) respectively may have two hands. Chakreśvarī should hold citrus and *abhaya* and sit in *padmāsana* or on Garuḍa, Bahurūpā should hold sword and shield, Ambikā holding fruit and *varada* should have a child in lap and Siddhāyikā should sit in *bhadrāsana* holding book and *abhaya*. We thus see that our figure does not correspond to any of these and no textual prescription seems to have been adhered to. The hybrid adoring figures, however, suggest that she may be Padmāvatī, the *yakshī* of the penultimate Tīrthaṅkara Pārśvanātha. Shah has listed ten varieties of two-armed Padmāvatī distinguished on the basis of attributes, vehicles, traditions, etc. and this image corresponds to his variety 5, which as per tradition he has related to the Digambaras.[42] If this identification is accepted, there may have existed a temple of Pārśvanātha at Sunam belonging to the Digambaras during the tenth century to which this piece may be assigned stylistically.

Another fragment of the socle, measuring 37 X 25 cm, may be of the same temple as indicated by the use of the same coarse-grained sandstone and recovered from the same spot. It shows a kneeling female figure to right in profile with hands folded in front at the level of the head in a pedimented niche flanked by large-sized female figures each holding a lotus flower in one hand standing turned slightly towards the *rathikā*; the other hand is broken in both the figures (Pl. 287).[43] Besides the usual dress and ornaments, the extra-long pendant string of the beaded necklace falling from between their breasts and touching the knee of their leg is an interesting feature.

A much worn-out *sapta-ratha* pedestal (Pl. 288) in the Jaina temple at Ropar must have belonged to an image of Ādinātha as it shows *yaksha* Gomukha on the extreme proper right offset and Chakreśvarī on the corresponding recess on the left. Both are seated in *lalitāsana*. Gomukha bears a *karaṇḍa-mukuṭa* and his normal right hand is held in *varada-mudrā*. The attributes in the other three hands cannot be recognized because of the utterly indifferent state of its preservation. Similarly, Chakreśvarī on the other end may be recognized by the wheel held in her additional left hand. Her natural right hand is held in boon-giving posture. The attributes of the other hands cannot be made out. The central projection of the pedestal also carries a figure but it is also beyond proper recognition though the possibility of its being the Śrutadevī Sarasvatī cannot be ruled out keeping in view some other pedestals of this period. The lower facet of the pedestal shows an enface wheel probably flanked by deer seated on either side as normally seen in Jaina images. The successively receding recesses on either side of the *bhadra-ratha*, which probably carries the four-armed figure of Sarasvatī seated in *lalitāsana*, show elephant and lion figures. The image may have belonged to twelfth century CE. In spite of its deplorable condition, it provides evidence of the existence of a Jaina fane of Ṛishabhanātha at Ropar in the twelfth century CE. The present marble image of the main deity in this temple also belongs to Ṛishabhanātha and is dated Śaka 1796, i.e., CE 1874, a date which goes well with the old structure, beautiful murals and carved doorways of the temple.

While digging at the site of a derelict pond in the premises of the Gorakhnath Dera at Burail village, which now forms part of Sector 45 at Chandigarh, were found fourteen grey stone fragments of Jaina images in June 2004. These were acquired by the estate office and later transferred to the Government Museum and Art Gallery, Chandigarh where they are preserved now.[44] Unfortunately, these fragments do not represent any complete image but they furnish evidence of the existence here of a beautiful Jaina shrine in tenth-eleventh century CE. One piece depicts a Tīrthaṅkara standing in *khaḍgāsana* in a niche enclosed by a ribbed pillar on either side (Pl. 289). The figure is sky-clad and must have thus belonged to a Digambara shrine. The head has been defaced and the part above broken. Traces of locks of hair falling on the shoulders help us to identify the pontiff as Ādinātha. Below his feet is a *chaitya-gavāksha* with an enface lion stepping out. Just below the lions may be seen the top portions of the *bharaṇī* and abacus of the pillars, which must have formed another *rathikā* to enclose another image. Another notable fragment (Pl. 290) shows an exquisitely executed female head bearing a serene expression with drooping eyelids, bow-like eyebrows, long sturdy nose, thick lips and plump cheeks. Chin and the portion below are gone. Hair combed backwards and donned beautifully, gemmed earrings and a wheel behind the head add to the grace of the figure. Superposed over her head is a Jina in *dhyāna-mudrā* seated over an inverted lotus which also seems to serve as the canopy over the head of the female figure below. The Jina bears a topknot and a part of the umbrella above the head is also visible. Four full-blown flowers around his shoulders and bent knees have been utilized ingeneously to fill the gap. Standing gracefully in *tribhaṅga* on his proper left is a male attendant wearing *karaṇḍa-mukuṭa*, earrings, *ekāvali*, *aṅgadas*, *kaṅkaṇas*, sacred thread, nether garment with a sash on the thighs and secured by a waist band standing with waist accentuated towards the Jina and supporting his bust by resting his suspended left arm on the thigh of the slightly bent left leg. The right hand is not clearly visible but may have held a flywhisk. Next to it is the partially preserved figure of another sky-clad Jina standing in *kāyotsarga-mudrā*. The proper right hand side of the superposed figure of Jina may have similar depictions on his right also. The original image may have thus been a big and beautiful one representing perhaps Chakreśvarī, if the wheel behind her head provides the right clue. Stylistically, it may be assigned to *circa* tenth-eleventh century. There may have thus been a shrine dedicated to the first Tīrthaṅkara Ṛishabha. How beautiful the complete image must have been is only a matter of guess.

Two Jaina marble images of Naminātha and Neminātha, the twenty-first and twenty-second Tīrthaṅkaras, and a *parikara* consisting of the pedestal, two side pillars and the semi-circular top part, all detached from each other, were discovered accidentally while a brick-kiln owner was supervising farm operation in his agricultural fields near the milk plant on Dabwali road near Bathinda in October, 1979.[45] Naminātha is seated on a legged pedestal in meditative pose with both legs folded and palms of hand placed one over the other resting over the soles of the Jina in his lap (Pl. 291).[46] He has a youthful appearance bearing hair rendered in short spiral curls gathered round the head with a topknot. Diamond-shaped *śrīvatsa* has been carved on the chest. The round face on a constricted neck has elongated earlobes, eyes almost closed in meditation, long sturdy nose, lips suggesting subtle smile and bears a serene expression. A very interesting and unique feature of the image is the appearance of the free end of a garment coming from behind the back on his right shoulder. I am not aware of any similar instance in Jaina images discovered so far. Another pleated end of the *dhotī* is shown on the pedestal in the middle coming from under the folded legs. The *chīvara* or piece of cloth on the shoulder and the pleated end of the nether garment shown on the pedestal betray the Śvetāmbara affiliation of the image. A stalked lotus bud (*nīlotpala*) placed horizontally on the pedestal helps us to identify the pontiff with Naminātha whose independent sculptural depiction in Jaina religion is quite rare.

The second image from Bathinda belongs to Neminātha (Pl. 292).[47] The Jina is shown as seated on a cushioned seat in *padmāsana*. He has his hair donned in schematic curls gathered in rows one upon the other with a protuberance on the top of the head. The face bears drooping eyelids under *chāpākāra* 'bow shaped' eyebrows, long sharp nose, earlobes almost touching the shoulders and a very benign meditative expression. Diamond-shaped *śrīvatsa* on the chest has been carved quite prominently. The pontiff has a well-proportioned body with long and strong limbs. The pleated free end of the *dhotī* is shown spread over the seat coming from under his folded legs as in the preceding image. The frontal rounded facet of the cushioned *āsana* is exquisitely bedecked with floral and geometrical motifs. In the centre of it is carved the conch, the *lāñchhana* of Neminātha, in a unique fashion again. There is a linear lateral lozenge or quadrangle within a beaded enclosure. It is divided into five compartments, one in the centre and the other four in the corners of the quadrangle. The central division contains the conch placed horizontally with spiral head on the right or in the east. The position of the conch changes in the corner divisions to point towards the cardinal directions. The decoration and division of the *pīṭha,* and even the carving of the whole image, is so close to the marble image of Mahāvīra found from Amarsar (now preserved in the Ganga Golden Jubilee Museum, Bikaner), which according to the inscription engraved on it was consecrated by Ratnaprabha Sūri in Vikama Samvat 1232 (CE 1175),[48] that one wonders if the same artist has not carved this image of Neminātha and it is not an import from there. Fortunately for us, at the back of the seat is an inscription in three lines in Devanāgarī characters furnishing us the exact date of the consecration of the image as the sixth day of the bright fortnight of the additional month of Āshāḍha in the Vikrama Samvat 1236 corresponding to CE 1180.[49] The second half of the second line of the inscription seems to have been over-written and the third line has worn almost out of recognition. However, we give below our reading of the inscription (Pl. 293) –

Line 1. [Auspicious symbol] *Saṃvat 1236 dvir=Āshāḍha sudi 6 Śrī-Vīra-*
Line 2. *pāna-purīya Se Udyaṇ[ena]* [pratishṭhāpitaṃ]*[50] *Śrī-[Nemi-]*
Line 3. *jina biṃbaṃ //*

[(This) image of illustrious Tīrthaṅkara Nemi(nātha) was established by *Se* (*Śreshṭhin*) Udyaṇa of Śrī-Vīrapānapura on the sixth of the bright fortnight of the second Āshāḍha in the (Vikrama) Samvat 1236.]

The image comes from Bathinda and it may be pointed out that a town of the name of Chandbhan (< Chandpāna < Chandrabhānu) exists on Ferozepur-Bathinda section of the Northern Railway nearly 20 km north of Bathinda. Śrī-Vīrapānapura (< Śrī-Vīrabhānupura) may have been the name of another such town in the vicinity. The modern village Vireval near Kotkapura or Wirpal, now in the neighbouring Ferozepur district, may have derived its name from the old Vīrapāna. *Se* is used here as the abbreviation of *Seṭhi* or *Śreshṭhī* and such use has been very popular in inscriptions. However, it must be admitted that the name of the *Śreshṭhī* has not been deciphered satisfactorily and is conjectural. Be as it may, the epigraph gives us the definite date of the image and the style of carving prevalent at that time.

As noted above, five detached parts of the *parikara* were also found along with these two Jina figures. They were carved separately to be put together around the Jina image. The *pīṭha* showing the *siṃhāsana* or the lion throne is *sapta-ratha* and consists of the plain *bhiṭṭa* 'plinth', *jāḍyakumbha* 'inverted cyma recta', *karṇikā* 'knife-edged astragal', *antarpatra* 'recessed band' and *chhādyakī* 'cyma-cornice' mouldings. The *bhadra-ratha* 'central offset' shows an enface wheel flanked by deer on either side looking at the *dharma-chakra* as usual (Pl. 294). Above this is the figure of a female deity, Sarasvatī, seated in *lalitāsana* in a richly carved *rathikā* enclosed within turreted pillars with pediment above. The four-armed goddess has her natural right hand held in boon-giving posture and holds a manuscript in the *pralamba* 'suspended' normal left hand. In the additional right hand, there seems to be the long stalk of the lotus flower while the corresponding left supports what looks like the shaft of the *vīṇā*. She bears a *karaṇḍa-mukuṭa* on her head and usual ornaments and drapery, the details of which are difficult to make out properly because of the smallness of the figure. The successive recesses on the two sides show an attendant figure, elephant and lion each. The figures are quite lively and animated. At the extreme ends are carved the *yaksha* and *yakshī* of the Jina in pedimented niches, both are quadrumanous and sit in *lalitāsana*. Ambikā with a child in her lap on the left extreme of the pedestal can easily be recognized. The child is shown as touching her left breast. The attributes in her hands are not clearly visible and may only be presumed. The *yaksha* on the other side may be identified with Gomedha, probably three-faced. He is holding a spear in his additional right hand and an axe in the upper left. The attributes in the natural hands cannot be made out clearly. The depiction of the *yaksha* and *yakshī* figures are very important in Jaina iconography as they provide a clue to the identification of the Tīrthaṅkara even if other distinguishing marks are lost.

The *Ruchaka* or square pillars which supported the arched top of the *parikara* show very lavishly ornamented male *chaurī*-bearers standing on plain *mañchikās* 'pedestals' turned towards the Jina which must have been placed originally between these two pillars. Each fly-whisker wears a crown with leaf-shaped decorative ornament, big beaded earrings, guilded torque and triple-stringed necklaces with flower-like circular pendants and rectangular spacers, guilded armlets and wristlets, anklets and foot-bangles, nether garment secured by very elaborate waist band covering the thighs like sashes and having loose ends falling on the thighs, scarf and long garland (Pl. 295). Their waists are accentuated inwards with heads turned backwards to give free space to the hands holding the flywhisks above their heads. They stand bearing the weight of their body on the inner one leg with the toe of the other one touching the ground and heel raised up. The outer arms suspended almost vertically are placed on the respective thighs to maintain the balance. The top portion of pillars show vase and foliage designs and the brackets on the sides depict hybrid *siṃhāśva vyālas*.

The semicircular top of the *parikara* shows a crack in the middle, dividing the lotus-shaped halo in two parts (Pl. 296). The nimbus is capped by the triple parasol, characteristic of the Jaina images, with three unidentified human figures above crowning the image. The rectangular stele on either side of the aureole carry the figures of garland-bearing *vidyādharas* in flying postures followed by divine female musician minstrels. The *vidyādhara* figures are shown bearing *karaṇḍa-mukuṭa*, circular *earrings, ekāvali, hāra, aṅgada, kaṅkaṇa, nūpura*, etc. with head turned upwards. The *kinnarīs* behind are also shown with similar ornaments but bear buns on their heads. Huge elephants surmounting the stele are quite lively and equally richly ornamented. They have riders on their backs. Walking towards the *chhattrāvali,* the elephants anoint the Jina. The extreme recesses of this tympanum show *makara-mukhas* from which emanate flying *gandharvas* and *vidyādharas* adorning the rim all along.

D.R. Gehlot thought that this *parikara* belongs to the image of Naminātha even though he observed that:

> On the left and right extremities of the lion throne a *Yakṣa* and *Yakṣiṇī* of the Jina are depicted. According to the Jaina pantheon *śāsanadevatās* (governing deities) are always associated with the particular Tīrthaṅkaras. As per the tradition the *Yakṣa "Bhṛkuṭi"* and the *Yakṣī "Gandhari"* of Naminātha have not been shown here. In their place a four-armed seated *Kubera* or *Sarvānubhūti* and *Ambikā* with child on her lap, who is also called as *Kushmāndinī* and *Dharmadevī* in the Digambara School are depicted on the right and left corners of the *siṃhāsana*.[51]

While assigning this *parikara* to Naminātha he forgot that he himself noted the piece of cloth on the right shoulder of Naminātha. He also missed the flourish of the *dhotī* visible on the pedestal coming out from below the legs of the Tīrthaṅkara. As such the image does not belong to the Digambara but to the Śvetāmbara sect. The *yaksha* and *yakshī* shown on the *siṃhāsana*, therefore, are Sarvāubhūti or Gomedha and Ambikā as per the Śvetāmbara tradition. More than all these facts, Gehlot has illustrated this *parikara* around the image of Naminātha under discussion (Pl. 297) but could not realize that the image is too small for such a *parikara* and there is a huge gap between the head of the Jina and the lotus-petalled gloriole on the tympanum. We are illustrating here the *parikara* put around the image of Neminātha (Pl. 298) which fits so perfectly that one cannot have even an iota of doubt about it.[52]

Gehlot, however, rightly observed that

> The two sculptures of Naminātha and Neminātha from Bhatinda look alike in their art style and appear to be a product of the well-blended sculptural orders of Rajasthan and Gujarat. Jaina communities of Western India are mostly of Śvetāmbara persuation. The Jaina patrons used to import the finished images of marble from Rajasthan, which is the most reputed centre for marble carvings. The rear side of the Neminātha sculpture gives the date Samvat 1236 i.e. AD 1180. On stylistic grounds also both the sculptures can be dated to the same period and may be assigned to the Cahamana dynasty, as the elgant modelling of the figures with prominent facial features reflects the Cahamana art.[53]

The most probable source as pointed out above may, however, have been Amarsar in the Bikaner region. Jaina monks hailing from Rajasthan and Gujarat and consecrating metal images in Punjab, as we shall see subsequently, however, provide the desired evidence and corroborate the influence from Rajasthan.

Independent Jaina female images are very few and except the small figure of Vidyādevī Sarasvatī seated in *padmāsana* holding lotus in her right hand and a manuscript in the left (Pl. 135) found from Mard Khera and described above, we do not know of any other example in stone. A temple dedicated to Chakreśvarī is located near Sirhind close to the village Attewali on Fatehgarh Sahib-Chunian-Chandigarh road but it is a recent building and there is absolutely no old relic there to substantiate the heresay that it is the spot where the goddess whose image the Jaina Khandelwal pilgrims from Rajasthan, on a visit to the temple of Ādinātha at Kangra during the reign of Pṛithvīrāja Chauhan, were carrying refused to budge and was set up in an improvised shrine according to a divine wish.

## METAL IMAGES[54]

Interestingly, however, we have an independent metal image of Ajitā, also called Ajitabalā and Vijayā (Rohiṇī according to Digambara tradition), the *yakshī* of the second Tīrthaṅkara Ajitanātha now preserved in the Thakurdwara at Bhudan near Dhuri (Pl. 299). Seated in *padmāsana* on an iron seat (*lohāsana*), she holds a noose in her upper right hand and a goad in the corresponding left; the natural right hand is held in boon-giving pose and the natural left holds a citron. The details have rubbed off but the eyes closed in meditation, long earlobes, rotund breasts can be made out distinctly. She wears necklace, armlets and bangles besides an *uttarīya* and *dhotī* with its folded free end coming out from the *nīvi* and falling vertically on the legs. The face is heavier in comparison to other limbs of the body. Her hair is combed backwards and gathered in the form of a big bun on the head. The back slab consists of two sheets simulating a leaf with a *stūpikā* on the pinnacle. The sheets bear decorative engravings. The image is placed in a separately made pedestalled *chaukī* with a higher back showing perforations and front adorned with quaterfoil design, probably for daily worship and ablution. There is no inscription to help us date this image precisely. It must be noted that the iconongraphical details of the *yaksha-yakshī* images were discussed and finalized first in the *Nirvāṇakalikā* in the eleventh-twelfth centuries CE and followed by later writers.[55] Images of Ajitabalā are quite rare, a fact which endows greater significance to this image. Stylistically, it seems to belong to the sixteenth century. The image belongs to the Śvetāmbara sect as indicated by the dress and ornamentation of the figure.

Another very interesting metal image is preserved in the same temple. The intricately engraved pedestal with back frame is fully preserved with smaller side figures but the central figure is missing (Pl. 300). The five-hooded cobra rising from the middle of the back rest, however, indicates that this central figure was sheltered by the serpent. It may have been the image of the seventh Tīrthaṅkara Supārśva or the penultimate pontiff Pārśvanātha. On the evidence of *Vāstuvidyā*, 22.27, M.N.P. Tiwari has prescribed three or five snake-hoods for Supārśva and seven or nine for Pārśvanātha.[56] Though some confusion has remained even amongst the Jainas about the number of hoods of the serpent sheltering the pontiffs and there are some examples of Pārśvanātha also shown under five snake hoods,[57] yet the popularity of this pontiff being canopied by seven-hooded snake in the bronze and stone images of the neighbouring Haryana[58] and even in Punjab as we shall see subsequently indicates that the pontiff represented in the piece under discussion may have been Supārśvanātha.

More interesting, however, are the attendant figures of four-armed Gaṇeśa and another unidentified figure seated in *sukhāsana* on the right and left here. Both these figures are much worn out and it is difficult to identify properly all the attributes in their hands. Gaṇeśa has its trunk falling down almost vertically and its tip taking a twirl to its right. Over the head is shown a leaf-like hood with two perforations. Gaṇeśa was included in the Jaina pantheon in the eleventh-twelfth centuries and its popularity remained confined only to the Śvetāmbaras.[59] The temple at Bhudan, thus, must have belonged to this sect. The figure on the other side seems to hold a lotus and a conch in the right and left upper hands but the attributes in the normal hands are not clear but look like thunderbolts. Instead of the cylindrical crown, we see a mass of hair rolled like a *dhammilla* coiffure above which is the astral halo with two perforations, probably for further attachments. It is thus difficult to identify the figure as that of Vishṇu or Indra with certainty but both these deities have never been shown as acolyte figures of the Jinas and thus present an interesting feature. Stylistically, the piece may be dated to a period as late as the preceding one.

We have already noted above the existence of the very badly worn-out stone pedestal of an image of Ādinātha belonging to twelfth century at Rupnagar (Ropar). But Jainism seems to have spread to this place in tenth century if not earlier, as evidenced by some bronze images preserved in the local Śvetāmbara Jaina temple. Ashvini Agrawal[60] has referred to and illustrated some of these. An early bronze image shows Ādinātha seated in *dhyānamudrā* on a pedestal without any attendants and without *prabhāvali* at the back of his head (Fig. 60). The image is in

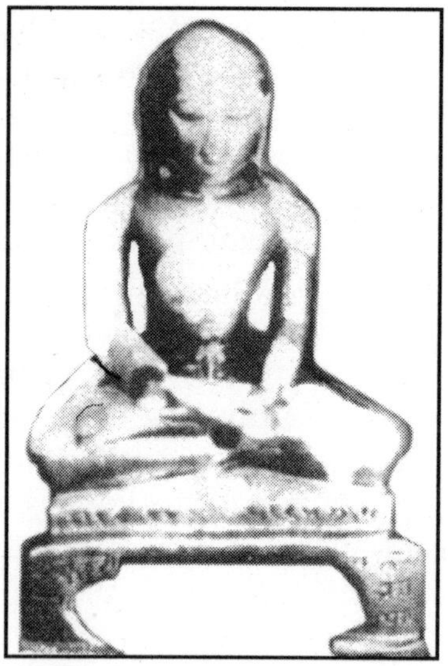

**Fig. 60.** Ādinātha from Ropar.

a very indifferent state of preservation but the quasi-closed meditative eyes, elongated earlobes, locks of hair falling on the shoulders, conch-like neck, broad chest, slim waist and a beautiful expression on the face may still be made out. There are traces of locks of hair on the shoulders. A part of the *dhotī* indicative of his Śvetāmbara affiliation may also be made out just below his navel. The image has remained in worship for centuries during which it has been anointed with sandal paste and water. As a result, it has worn out and some parts have even flaked off. The pedestal bears a short undeciphered inscription palaeographically datable to the tenth-eleventh century CE. Though the tradition of Jaina metal images is quite old, yet it is one of the earliest known figures from Punjab. Another small bronze figure of this pontiff at the same place is more indifferently preserved to show us the detailed features of the figure but it also bears the inscription at the back of the pedestal on the basis of which, it is also ascribable to the same period (Fig. 61). It is notable that bronzes from Amarsar in the Bikaner region belong to the period VS 1063-1160 (CE 1006-1103). A stylistic study of the above-mentioned Rupnagar bronzes with those of Amarsar will prove worth the labour.

A *pañcha-tīrthikā* of Pārśvanātha preserved in the Ropar Jaina temple shows the pontiff seated in meditation on a cushioned seat under the canopy of seven-hooded snake (Pl. 301). The legged *siṃhāsana* shows a part of the carpet covering it. The upright slabs of the back slab have *kāyotsarga* Jina figures while the small Jina figures in *dhyāna-mudrā* are depicted on their tops. The ornamental arch behind the head of the main figure going from above the serpent-hoods serves the purpose of the gloriole and is capped by a finial. It has flame-like decorations at the level of the back rest. There are traces of engravings on the back slab. Below the seat of the Tīrthaṅkara may be seen two lions back to back but with their fore parts raised up and facing. Outside the ribbed legs of the *siṃhāsana* are shown diminutive figures seated in *sukhāsana*. Normally, one may expect these figures to belong to the *yaksha* and *yakshī* of the Jina but both seem to be female figures. Their features are not very clear but the child in the lap of the *yakshī* on the right hand side indicates that Ambikā is represented here. *Yaksha* Sarvānubhūti could be expected on the other side as they were the most popular *yaksha* and *yakshī* figures who could be represented with all the Jinas as in Rajasthan and Gujarat. The depiction of Ambikā and another female figure, however, is enigmatic and perhaps unprecedented. What adds to our interest here is the depiction of a serpent-hooded female in the middle of the pedestal almost between the two lions standing and holding in her suspended left hand *kukkuṭa-sarpa* 'serpent-cock' which according to various Jaina texts[61] is the vehicle of Padmāvatī, the *yakshī* of Pārśva. This vehicle and the serpent-hood provide clues to identify this figure with Padmāvatī with certainty. As such this representation of Padmāvatī in the middle of the pedestal endows this image with uniqueness. On the lower *paṭṭikā*, of the pedestal may be seen eight fully globoid and the last half globular figures representing the planetary

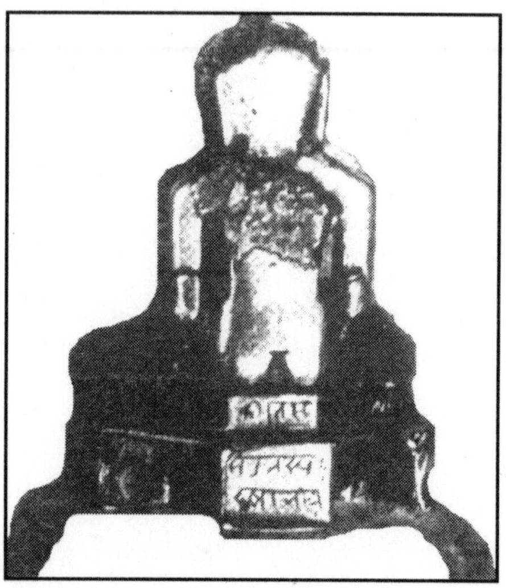

**Fig. 61.** Same, back side with inscription.

divinities. The inscription at the back has worn out completely except on the basal *paṭṭikā* and the legible portion reads 'Saṃvat 1152 (= CE 1095) siriyuta' (Pl. 302). The inscription being dated is very important for providing us the definite evidence of the date of the image.

There is an inscribed bronze *pañcha-tīrthikā* of Ādinātha in the Jaina temple at Ropar installed during the reign of Bahlul Lodi. Ādinātha seated on *siṃhāsana* in *dhyāna-mudrā* is cast elaborately. There is an astral *prabhāvali* behind the head of the Tīrthaṅkara and projecting semicircular *chhatrāvali* above with two anointing elephants on its sides. Two *khaḍgāsana* Jina figures flank him and above them may be seen two more in *padmāsana*. The attendant fanners are also there on the *parikara,* which as per the Jaina iconographical texts may be identified with his sons Bharata and Bāhubalī. The *yaksha* and *yakshī* figures exist on the right and left buttresses of the pedestal and may be identified with Sarvānubhūti and Ambikā rather than Gomukha and Chakreśvarī. The central portion of the pedestal shows as usual two outward moving lions. The lower moulding of the pedestal shows nine round globules representing the planetary divinities with Rāhu and Ketu. Worn-out and diminutive human figures at the ends of the lower moulding of the pedestal seem to carry the figure of the donors. The inscription on its back (Pl. 303) states that this image of the illustrious (Tīrthaṅkara) Ādinātha was caused to be made by Līlāde(vī), wife of *Sā*. (*Sāha* < *Śāha*, Seth) Hariā, son of Sūhaḍāde(vī), wife of *Sā*. Sādūla of Prāgvāṭa, together with the family, for their personal welfare and installed in Tapāgachchha on Sunday, the 5th day of the dark fortnight of the month of Mārgaśīrsha in Sam(vat) 1524 (CE 1467) by the illustrious Lakshmīsāgara Sūri. The full text runs thus:

> *Saṃ. 1524 varshe Mārga. Va.*[62] *5 Ravau Prāgvāṭa. Sā. Sādūla-bhāryā Sūhaḍāde putra Sā. Hariākena-bhāryā Līlāde pramukha kuṭumba-yutena nija-śreyorthaṃ Śrī-Ādinātha biṃbaṃ kā. pra. Tapāgachchhe Śrī-Lakshmī-sāgara-Sūribhiḥ Śrī//*

Prāgvāṭa was another name of Medapāṭa or Mewar in Rajasthan, with Chittore as its chief town. Members of the Poravāla business community, who are mostly Jainas, were known as Prāgvāṭas after the name of this region. Lakshmī-sāgara Sūri is known to us from the Soma-Saubhāgya-Paṭṭāvalī as a disciple of Ratna-śekhara Sūri and Soma-sundara Sūri (*Soma-suṃdara Sūri saṃtāne*). He was born in VS 1464 and was consecrated at the age of thirteen; he obtained the status of Sūri in VS 1508 and became the leader of the *gachchha* in VS 1517 (CE 1440). He was a popular monk whose qualities were lyricized even by the nymphs.[63] Puran Chand Nahar has listed thirty images consecrated by him at various places and now preserved in Delhi, Kolkata, Bihar, Rajasthan, etc. during VS 1517 and 1539, which also give an idea of his popularity and perambulations.[64] Though quite likely, yet we do not know for certain whether he came in contact with Jaya-sāgara Upādhyāya (CE 1450-1515) who was active with his missionary activities in the Punjab and Himachal Pradesh and authored amongst various works the historical *Vijñapti-Triveṇī,* which describes the Jaina *tīrthas* like Nagara-koṭṭa Kangra.[65] In VS 1510 (CE 1453), the Chief Minister of Dungarpur got big metal images installed by Lakshmī-sāgara Sūri.[66] It is likely that many of his followers may have shifted to Punjab as a result of the severe famine that occurred in Rajasthan in VS 1521. Lakshmī-sāgara Sūri also installed a *pañcha-tīrthikā* of Anantanātha at Sunam in Samvat 1537, as we shall see subsequently. Four years prior to the consecration of this latter image, he was at Pokaran in Rajasthan where he installed in the Tapāgachchha there a *pañcha-tīrthikā* of Ādinātha which is now preserved in the Ādinātha temple at Pokaran in Rajasthan.[67] It is thus clear that at least some of the metal images, if not all, installed at Ropar were consecrated by the Jaina monks who hailed from Rajasthan. The Pokaran *pañcha-tīrthikā* of Ādinātha is similar in format and concept to the *pañcha-tīrthikā* of Ropar under discussion and of course many others installed at Sunam, and point to the fact that they were in all probability obtained from Rajasthan. A good number of Khandelwal Jains now settled at Nakodar, Jalandhar, Garh Shankar, Garhdiwala, Tanda Urmur, Mukerian and Sunam as well as the Oswals (Ūkeśa-vāla) and Modis at Ludhiana and Patiala, and Dugars at Amritsar also point to their having migrated from Marwar and Bikaner regions and perhaps also from Gujarat as indicated by a *Kalpa-sūtra* copied at Patan in Gujarat in VS 1473 (= CE 1416), now in the Jaina collection at Zira[68] near Ferozepur. The Śvetambara Pārśvanātha temple at Zira was consecrated in 1896 and is said to contain old stone and metal images (one of which belongs to the fourteenth century of Vikrama Samvat) but nothing authentic is known about them.

One bronze image in the Ropar Jaina temple represents Pārśvanātha seated in meditation on a cushion placed on a legged pedestal with a seven-hooded serpent canopying his head (Pl. 304). A big chunk from the left of his bust and smaller chunks from the head, knees, shoulders and arms have flaked off exposing the rough core. The left shoulder of the Jina has suffered some diminution. The pedestal is plain and bereft of the depiction of the usual *dharmachakra* flanked by deer and outward moving lions. Even the *yaksha* and *yakshī* or any other acolyte figure is not there. Long earlobes, contemplating eyes, etc. may, however, be discerned. An interesting feature of the image is that the seven-hooded serpent has been carved in full, rising above from the bottom of the back in an anguine fashion to canopy the Jina (Pl. 305). There is an inscription on the back of the pedestal running on the three sides of the pedestal as well as on its back support (Fig. 62). But for the date portion, it is difficult to make out much of it. The date Samvat 1657 (=CE 1600), however, is fortunately clear to give us a definite evidence of the style prevalent here during the reign of Akbar to which it belongs.[69]

The Jaina temple at Ropar contains a very much worn out and corroded metal image of a Tīrthaṅkara in meditation which may be identified either with Padmaprabha (sixth Tīrthaṅkara) or with Naminātha (twenty-first Tīrthaṅkara) because of the depiction of a lotus, as the former has the red lotus as his cognizance while the latter has a blue lotus. It is dated 'Saṃ(vat) 1965' (=CE 1908) and indicates the continuing tradition of the worship of the different Tīrthaṅkaras by the people through the centuries (Pl. 306).

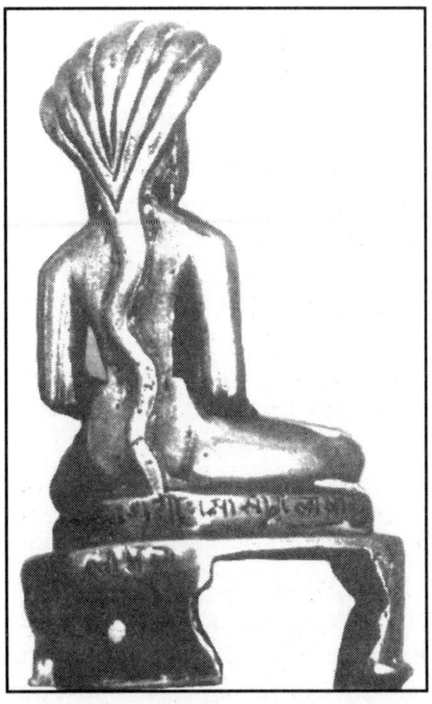

Fig. 62. Inscription at the back of the image of Pārśvanātha, Ropar.

Sunam was another stronghold of Jainism in the Punjab in the medieval period. We have already noted the Jaina stone sculptures and architectural pieces found from this place. The local Jaina temple was a great store-house of Jaina manuscripts, paintings, wooden objects, bronzes, etc. before the partition but many of these objects have been donated in the recent decades. However, it still possesses some important bronze images and other things which are of great interest, particularly when very little is known from Punjab.

A very badly mutilated and worn-out metal image represents Pārśvanātha standing probably on a lotus in *khaḍgāsana* sheltered by a seven-hooded serpent (Pl. 307). Another snake with its wavy or coily body (or perhaps the stem of a lotus) seems to rise vertically along his right side. Two attendant figures, probably a female on the right and a male on his left, are shown poised over what look like lotus flowers near his feet. All details are lost due to wearing, corrosion and mutilation. The image shows unique features and may tentatively be dated to *circa* tenth-eleventh century.

The earliest bronze figure (12.5 X 7.0 cm) belongs to Ṛishabhanātha (Pl. 308) seated in meditation on a round cushioned seat placed on the pedestal. The figure is worn out to the extent of wiping out all details except the contours of the body. However, locks of hair falling on the shoulders, hands placed in the lap and crossed legs slanting towards the front may be clearly discerned. The cognizance of bull seated to right may be seen on the pedestal. The diminutive figures seated in profile with folded hands on either side of the seat are probably the figures of the donor couple. The male figure on right is slightly damaged. Standing behind them flanking the Jina may be Bharata and Bāhubalī but there is very little to substantiate this identification. At the level of the head of Ādinātha are the garland-bearing *vidyādhara* figures, one each on either side, flying outwards on the arched back slab. At the top below the three-tiered finial seems to be a crowned corpulent figure just above the head of the Jina. The inscription on the back (Pl. 309) has completely worn out except on the basal *paṭṭikā* and reads '- - -ginādika-putrena' in the characters of about eleventh-twelfth centuries CE.

A *pañcha-tīrthikā* of Pārśvanātha (14.0 X 7.5 cm) shows the pontiff under the canopy of seven-hooded serpent seated on the *siṃhāsana* with legs crossed at right angles to the spinal column and hands placed on the soles of the feet with palms upward (Pl. 310). At the back is an apsidal *parikara* frame bedecked with spiral and flamboyant decorations on the rim and an architrave with finial atop. *Kāyotsarga* Jina figures flank Pārśvanātha while small *padmāsana* Jina figures are shown at the level of his head. A flourish of the *dhotī* coming out from under the crossed legs indicates the Śvetāmbara affiliation of the image. In the centre of the pedestal is a vertical column, may be the wheel in profile, with perhaps the looped part of the seat carpet above it. Two lions seated back to back looking retrorse with forepaws erect are placed on the pedestal as usual. The extreme buttress on either side shows standing male and female figures respectively on the proper right and left. The figures are too small to be detailed but the female with a child in her lap supported with her left hand certainly seems to be Ambikā. The male figure represents the *yaksha* who, in all likelihood, is Sarvānubhūti. The depiction of the *yaksha* and *yakshī* in standing postures is an interesting feature. In the centre of a lower *paṭṭikā* of the *pīṭha* are nine globules representing the nine planetary divinities. The inscription on the back of the apsidal *parikara* frame (Pl. 311) reads: *Saṃvat 1235 [Jyeshṭha] sudi 2 Gurau Śrī-Devasena-saṃghe Śrī-Ma[ṃgala]-chaṃdra-putrī Sahajā Pārśvanāthaṃ praṇamati//* [i.e., Sahajā, the daughter of the illustrious Ma(ṃgala)-chandra pays obeisance to Pārśvanātha in the illustrious Deva-saṃgha[70] on Thursday, the second day of the bright fortnight of the month of (Jyeshṭha) in the Vikrama year 1235].

The record gives us the name of Devasaṃgha and Sahajā, daughter of Maṃgala-chandra. There is no other record available to us to inform the presence of the Deva-saṃgha at Sunam and of course in Punjab. The date corresponds to CE 1165 when the Chāhamānas of Ajmer were ruling over this part of the country.

After the defeat of Pṛithvīrāja Chauhan at the hands of Muhammad Ghori started the era of iconoclasm, desecration and devastation of the Hindu religious places. Even the Jaina icons and fanes were not spared for quite some time till this merchantile community took to other forms of art like calligraphy, painting and making of smaller portable images in metal in particular. We find some Jainas realizing the necessity of peaceful conditions to carry on their avocations and getting closer to the rulers. Jinaprabha Sūri, a contemporary of the Delhi Sultan Muhammad Tughlaq, was a great scholar who impressed the Sultan by his erudition and charms and became his religious mentor. The area of his activities spread from Bihar to Gujarat and Punjab to Karnataka though mainly based at Delhi. He recovered from Muhammad Tughlaq's possession some Jaina sculptural pieces and re-enshrined them in a temple.[71] Ṭhakkara Pheru of Dhāṃdhiyā *gotra* 'sept' was a great polymath and staunch follower of Jainism. He served as a minister of

Jalaluddin Khilji (CE 1290-96) and a mint-master of Alauddin Khilji (CE 1296-1316).[72] The Tughlaqs, again, were religious bigots but the conditions seem to have started improving somewhat during the reign of the Sayyids and Lodis when people could follow, may be slightly calendestinely, their religious arts and undertakings. This is reflected by the metal images available in the Jaina temple at Sunam, as we have the next bronze dated to Samvat 1484 (= CE 1427) when Mubarak II of the Sayyid dynasty was the Sultan of Delhi. This is an image of the seventeenth Jaina Tīrthaṅkara Kunthunātha (15 X 8.5 cm). He was so named because his mother Śrīdevī, the queen of Vasu (or Sūryasena) of Hastināpura, saw a treasure of gems called 'Kunthu' in her dream before his birth. As per Jaina iconographical texts, his cognizance is goat. The name of his *yaksha* is Gandharva and *yakshī* Balā, also called Achyutā and Gādhāriṇī (Jayā or Jayadevī according to the Digambara tradition). The earliest image of Kunthunātha is datable to the eleventh century CE and the depiction of the *yaksha* and *yakshī* with him seems to have started a century later. As in the case of many other Tīrthaṅkara images, the depiction of Sarvānubhūti and Ambikā with him was more popular than the prescribed *yaksha* and *yakshī*. His images, both in stone and metal, are also quite rare.

Our image shows the pontiff in the stiff posture of meditation seated on the *siṃhāsana* under triple-umbrella, which has its lower portion projecting in semicircular shape and is bedecked with a triangular screen (Pl. 312). The eyes of the Jina are guilded and the face seems to be heavier than the bust. The figure does not reflect the mellifluous contours of the earlier forms and displays the tendency of increasing angularization. The serenity of expression is also lacking. The cushion below him is embroidered. The apsidal back slab is capped by a pitcher and has tiered and tapering finial within leaflike appendages. The outer rim shows twisted wire or rope pattern. The side slabs depict the fanners standing up to the level of the shoulders of the Jina, garland-bearing *vidyādhara* figures hovering in the sky above them and anointing elephants in profile atop. Small figures on the juxta-buttresses of the lion throne are corrode and not very clear but they seem to be of Sarvānubhūti and Ambikā seated in *sukhāsana*. The lower moulding shows five small roundels on the right and four on the left, representing the *navagrahas*. Small human figures sitting enface with folded hands at the end of the lower moulding may be identified as those of the donor couple or lay worshippers. The inscription at the back (Pl. 313) reads thus: *Saṃvat 1484 varshe Mārga*[73] *sudi 5 Ravau Dūgaḍa-gotre Sā. Jhāḍhā su. Sūrā bhāryā Rūpabāī [kār?]yīthākena pitṛi-mātṛi-puṇyārthaṃ Śrī-Kunthūnātha-biṃbaṃ kā. pratishṭitaṃ Śrī-Rudrapallīya-gachhe Śrī-Harsha-suṃdara Sūri-paṭṭe Śrī-Deva-suṃdara Sūribhiḥ//.*

[This image of the illustrious (Tīrthaṅkara) Kunthunātha was caused to be made by Rūpabāī, (resident) of (Kār?)thīyaka, wife of Sūrā (who is the) son of Seth Jhāḍhā, (born) in Dūgaḍa *gotra* 'sept', for the welfare of her father and mother and installed (consecrated) by the illustrious Deva-sundara Sūri, pupil of the illustrious Harsha-sundara, in Rudrapallī-gachha on Sunday, the fifth of the bright half of (the month of) Māgha (or Mārgaśīrsha) in Saṃvat 1484.]

Deva-sundara Sūri was the (third) disciple of Soma-tilaka Sūri. He was born in VS 1430, tonsured in 1437, became Sūri in 1457 and left this world in 1499. He added to the dignity and excellence of his teacher and had surprising power. He had miraculous powers like removing the poison; tearing the fear of water, fire, griffins and wild animals; knowing the past and the future and was respected by even the royal officials.[74]

Next we have a *chaturviṃśati-paṭṭa* of Ṛishabhanātha (15.0 X 9.5 cm) dated Samvat 1487 (Pl. 314). Ādinātha is seated in *dhyāna-mudrā* on the lion throne showing probably a wheel in profile (which looks like a column) supporting the falling looped part of the carpet which gives the impression of a bull depicted on it. The lions with their back towards the wheel are depicted as facing. The buttress on the proper right carries the small figure of the *yaksha* seated in *sukhāsana* and *yakshī* seated similarly occupies the corresponding buttress on the left. Interestingly, the *yaksha* is shown as having bovine face and can therefore be identified with Gomukha without any hitch. In the absence of visible *chakras* in her hands, the *yakshī* can only be presumed to have been Chakreśvarī. Because of the smallness of the figures, it is difficult to ascertain the number of hands of the *yaksha* and *yakshī*. Ṛishabhanātha occupies the central place in the *chaturviṃśati* and has a halo around his head. There are only some traces of the locks falling on his shoulders. Branches of the banyan tree winding down from the back of his gloriole indicate the moment of his perfection. Triple umbrella is shown above his head. Very interesting is the fact that the two *khaḍgāsana* Jinas which flank him on his right and left are shown as standing under the canopy of five- and seven-hooded snakes which helps us to identify them as Supārśvanātha and Pārśvanātha respectively. Such distinction is not visible in the case of the remaining Tīrthaṅkaras who have all been represented in the form of very small meditative figures on the back frame. Another notable point is the presence of full-blown lotus flowers flanking the Jina seated just above the *chhatrāvali* of the main figure. The central projection of the *triratha pīṭha* shows five spherical dots while the juxta-buttresses show two each. They are obviously the nine planetary divinities. Suspended from the central globular dot is a diminutive human figure difficult to recognize. This may be the representation of Śāntidevī. The *chaubīsī* is not in a good state of preservation. Most of the figures are worn out and have lost sharpness.

The inscription on the back of this *chaturviṃśati-paṭṭa* (Pl. 315) is worn out at places. It reads: *Saṃvat 1487 Māgha sudi 5 Kāshṭhā-saṃghe bha. dramekā [- - ī]devāna si[- -] Jina-chaṃdradeva [- - -]śikshārthaṃ [ - ]bāī Sahajāī chaturviṃśati kāritaṃ//*

The undeciphered gaps in the inscription do not allow us to translate the text satisfactorily but the inscription tells us that this *chaturviṃśati-paṭṭa* was caused to be made by some lady for the education of Jina-chandradeva, probably her son, by making a donation of some *drammas*[75] and it was installed in the Kāshṭhā-saṃgha on the fifth day of the bright half of the month of Māgha in the Samvat year 1487 (= CE 1430).

The next image is somewhat unconventional and shows the pontiff sheltered by a nine-hooded serpent seated in *dhyāna-mudrā* on a solid tapering stool (Pl. 316). It measures 6.5 X 3.5 cm. The face of the Jina is heavier in comparison to his elongated body. The facial features are not sharply engraved. The earlobes touch the shoulders. Of the Jaina Tīrthaṅkaras, Supārśva and Pārśva are invariably shown with a serpent canopying their head with his hoods. According to B.C. Bhattacharyya,[76] Supārśva is sheltered by a serpent having one, five or nine hoods (*Ekaḥ pañcha nava cha phaṇāḥ Supārśve saptame jine*) but *Vāstuvidyā* (XXII.27) prescribes three or five hoods for Supārśva and seven and nine for Pārśva (*Tri-pañcha-phaṇaḥ Supārśvaḥ Pārśvaḥ sapta-navastathā*). This confusion exists even in actual examples of the images of the two Tīrthaṅkaras.[77] The cognizance of Supārśva is *Svastika* and his *yaksha* and *yakshī* are Mātaṅga and Śāntā (Kālī or Kālikā according to Digambara tradition), whereas the cognizance of Pārśva is serpent and he is served by Pārśva or Vāmana (Dig. Dharaṇa) as his *yaksha* and Padmāvatī as his *yakshī*. The confusion to distinguish the images of the two serpent-hooded Jinas gets more confounded when the cognizances and *yaksha-yakshī* figures are not shown with them. And this is what exactly the case here is also. This little metal image does not show any of the adjuncts. Even the inscription running around the stool (Pl. 317) does not help us to decide the issue. The inscription reads: *Saṃvat 1505 varshe Vaiśāsh(kh)a sudi 5 Somavāre [Śrī-]mūla-saṃghe Chaṃdradeva//.*

Chandradeva mentioned in this inscription may be the same as mentioned in the previous epigraph, according to which his mother got the *chaturvṃśati-paṭṭa* installed for his education. There is a difference of eighteen years between the two records during which Chandradeva may have completed his education and grown to adulthood.

We have seen above that the images of Pārśvanātha as found at Sunam are sheltered by seven-hooded snakes. That the nine-hooded snakes also canopied him will be clear a bit later. We, therefore, feel inclined to regard even this nine-hooded image as that of Pārśvanātha whose worship seems to have been quite popular at this place.

Our next image (16.5 X 10.5cm) is a *pañcha-tīrthikā* of Ajitanātha installed only four years later in Samvat 1509 (= CE 1452) during the reign of Bahlol Lodi (CE 1451-89). Ajitanātha is depicted as seated on a decorated cushion placed on the lion throne (Pl. 318). He has a square face, pointed top-knot, long earlobes, conch-like neck, broad chest and seems to wear a *dhotī*. Flanking him are the small figures of *khaḍgāsana* Jinas and fanners on successively receding buttresses. *Makara-mukhas* are shown above the heads of the fly-whiskers while meditating Jinas are placed above the standing pontiffs. Superposed over the meditating figures are elephants in profile anointing or perhaps carrying the crowns in their trunks. A circular projecting and triangularly screened shade shown between the elephants and above the head of the Tīrthaṅkara, represents the umbrella with a finial. The figures of *yaksha* Mahākāya and *yakshī* Ajitabalā occupy their fixed places but are beyond recognition because of corrosion and diminutive size. Between the lions is engraved a tusker furnishing evidence for the identification of the Tīrthaṅkara which is corroborated by the inscription at the back. The moulding below the lion throne has five globular pellets on viewer's left and four on right as an indication of the *navgrahas*. At the extreme ends of this and the lower moulding are two kneeling human figures with hands folded in front. Geometrical formalism, idealization, severely linear arrangement with emphasis on strict symmetry, angularization and employment of stereotype figures seem to characterize the bronzes of this period.

The inscription at the back (Pl. 319) may be deciphered as follows: *//Saṃ.// 1509 varshe Māgha sudi 10 Śanau Ūkeśa-vaṃśe Sāhū-gotre Sā. Sāliga-bhā. Bhojalade-putra Sā. Saṃgrāmeṇa bhā. Sahajalade Sā. putra Soḍhādi-sahitena sva-puṇyārthaṃ/ Śrī-Ājitanātha-biṃbaṃ kā. pra. Śrī-Kharataragachhe Śrī-Jinasāgara-Sūribhiḥ// Śrī: //.*

[This image of the illustrious Ajitanātha was caused to be made for their own merit by Seth Saṃgrāma, son of Bhojalade wife of Seth Sāliga, born in Ūkeśa[78] family in Sāhū gotra 'sept', together with his wife Sahajalade (and) sons Seth Soḍhā etc., and consecrated by the illustrious Jinasāgara Sūri in Kharatara-gachha[79] on Saturday, the tenth day of the bright fornight of Māgha in the Saṃvat year 1509.]

Jina-sāgara Sūri belonged to the Pippalaka-śākhā and was a good scholar. He is the author of *Karpūra-prakara-Ṭīkā, Siddha-hema-śabdānuśāana-laghu-vṛitti* and *Shashṭi-śataka-Bālāvabodha*, the last one completed in Samvat 1491.[80]

A *pañcha-tīrthikā* of the sixteenth Tīrthaṅkara Śāntinātha in the Jaina temple at Sunam is a close copy of the preceding *pañcha-tīrthikā* with the only difference that the *makara-mukhas* have given way to the back rest at the level of the shoulders of the Tīrthaṅkara (Pl. 320). The vertical slab between the backs of the lions is worn out to the extant that it has lost even the traces of the cognizance (*Mṛiga* 'deer') of the pontiff if there was any. The figures of the *yaksha* and *yakshī* too have lost details of distinction. It is, however, the inscription at the back (Pl. 321) which furnishes details of its installation. A part of it is too blurred to be deciphered but the rest of it reads: *Saṃ. 1512 varshe Phāguṇa sudi 11 dine/ U [O]savāla-jñātīya/ Loḍhā-gotre/ Sā. [Gh]ullā[putra?] Sā. Vallātena nija-bhrātṛi-Vaṇavīra-nimitte Śrī-Śāṃtinātha-viṃvaṃ kārāpitaṃ pra. Rudrapallīya-gachchhe/Śrī-Deva-suṃdara-Sūri-paṭṭe Śrī-Soma-[suṃdara-Sūribhiḥ//*].*

[This image of of the illustrious (Tīrthaṅkara) Śāṃtinātha was caused to be made by *Śāha* Vallāta, son of *Śāha* Ghullā, of Osavāla caste (and born) in the Loḍhā *gotra* 'sept', for his brother Vaṇavīra and was consecrated on the eleventh day of the bright half of Phāguṇa in the Saṃvat year 1512 in Rudrapallī-gachchha by the illustrious Soma-suṃdara-Sūri, disciple of the illustrious Deva-suṃdara-Sūri.]

We have seen above that the *pañcha-tīrthikā* of the seventeenth Tīrthaṅkara Kunthunātha (Pls. 312-13) was also established in the Rudrapallī-gachchha by Deva-suṃdara Sūri in Saṃvat 1484, i.e., twenty-eight years earlier. The present record gives us the name of his disciple Soma-suṃdara Sūri. The two inscriptions thus furnish the names of three teachers Harsha-suṃdara-Sūri, his disciple Deva-suṃdara-Sūri and the latter's disciple Soma-suṃdara-Sūri connected with the Rudrapallī-gachchha. Soma-sundara Sūri was a Rajasthani Jaina writer and poet and has written *Neminātha Navarasa Phāga* (S. 1481), *Upadeśamālā, Yogaśāstra, Sītā-Rāma-Charita, Dhanapāla Kathā, Tatva-vichāra Prakaraṇa, Kālikāchārya Kathā, Shashṭi-Śataka-Bālāvabodha* (S. 1496) and *Tapāgachchha-gurvāvalī* (S. 1497).[81] As such he may have impressed the people by his poetic and speaking talents and had a very large following. Soma-sundara Sūri had an immaculate character and qualities and is known as the jewel of the great Tapā-gachchha.[82] Soma-sundara Sūri belonged to Ranakpur in district Pali in Rajasthan where he consecrated in VS 1496 Chaturmukha Ādinātha Jaina temple.[83] He consecrated an image of Ādinātha in VS 1516 which is now preserved in Mahāvīra-svāmī temple, Maniktala, Kolkata; a metal image of Kunthunātha in VS 1525 now housed in Śītalanātha temple at Balotara and an icon of Ṛishabhanātha in VS 1501 now lying in the Jaina temple at Alwar.[84] He died at Palanpur (Gujarat).

The similarity in the form and concept of the *pañcha-tīrthikā* is also notable and it seems to be possible that a scion of the person who made Kunthunātha's image created the present *pañcha-tīrthikā*. The preceding *pañcha-tīrthikā,* too, may have been the creation of the same artist as it also bears very close affinity with the two referred to above. The constraint to work within the limitations of style and iconography is obvious.

Another similar *pañcha-tīrthikā*, measuring 12.0 X 8.5 cm, of the fourteenth Tīrthaṅkara Anantanātha (Pl. 322) forms part of the collection of the Jaina temple, Sunam. The only differences are the revertion to *makara-mukhas* at the level of the back rest extremities and double fish motif instead of the finial at the top. The square tablet between the backs of the lions of the *siṃhāsana,* however, shows the engraved falcon which is the cognizance of Anantanātha. All other figures including the central Jina, *khaḍgāsana* and meditative miniature pontiffs, fly-whiskers, anointing elephants, donors or worshippers, *yaksha* and *yakshī, navagraha* globules and even the decorations remain constant. The inscription at the back (Pl. 323) reads: *Saṃ. 1537 varshe Jeṭha va. 7 Sukre Prāgvāṭa-jñā. Sā. Ṭīlhākena bhā. Tejalade putra Gajā bhā. Gaṃgāde pra. Kuṭuṃba-yutena Śrī-Anaṃtanātha-biṃba(ṃ) kā. pra. Śrī Lakshmī sāgara-Sūribhiḥ.*

[This image of Śri Anantanātha was caused to be made by Śaha Ṭilha of the Prāgvāṭa caste, with (his) wife Tejalade, son Gajā, (his) wife Gaṅgāde together with the family and consecrated by the illustrious Lakshmī-sāgara-Sūri on Friday, the seventh day of the dark fortnight of (the month of) Jeṭha in the Saṃvat year 1537.]

The date Samvat 1537 corresponds to CE 1480, which falls during the reign of Bahlol Lodi (CE 1451-89). We have noted above that Lakshmī-sāgara Sūri had installed a *pañcha-tīrtikā* of Ṛishabhanātha in the Tapāgachchha at Ropar in Samvat 1524. It is possible that Lakshmī-sāgara Sūri, who consecrated this image thirteen years later, was the same person. He was the disciple of Jina-sāgara Sūri who had consecrated Ajitanātha's *pañcha-tīrthikā* in Samvat 1509 described above. The two *pañcha-tīrthikās* are quite similar to each other.

Quite interesting is the image of Pārśvanātha (20.0 X 11.0 cm) sitting in *dhyāna-mudrā* with folded legs slanting forward (Pl. 324). The Jina bears schematic curls with a topknot on the head. The facial expression is placid with eyes concentrating at the tip of the nose. Long earlobes touch the shoulders. There is a big lozenge-shaped *śrīvatsa* on the chest. The palm of the left hand is placed on the lap and that of the right hand over that. What, however, are the most interesting features are that the pontiff is sheltered by a nine-hooded snake and two entwined snakes are shown on the pedestal and the standing *yaksha* and *yakshī*, Pārśva or Vāmana and Padmāvatī, as prescribed in the Jaina canonical works, are also depicted with snake-hoods. The moulding of the *pīṭha* just below the entwined snakes shows nine heads, obviously representing the planetary divinities. At the bottom in the centre of the pedestal is a diminutive human figure, probably of Śāntidevī. The nine-hooded snake sheltering Pārśvanātha rises straight at his back parallel to his spinal cord (Pl. 325). The inscription at the back (Pl. 326) tells us that this image was set up in the *Mūla-saṃgha* on Monday, the tenth day of the bright half of Vaiśākha in Samvat 1545: *[Saṃvat 1545] varshe Vaiśāsh(kh)a sudi 10 Some Śrī-Mūla-saṃghe [pratishṭhitaṃ].* The complete inscription cannot be deciphered as most part of it, particularly on the lower moulding, has worn out badly.

We refer back to the nine-hooded image dated Samvat 1505 (Pls. 315-16) described above and the discussion about the number of snake-hoods under which Pārśvanātha and Supārśvanātha are depicted in Jaina art and iconography. The present image does not leave any doubt to its being that of the twenty-third Tīrthaṅkara Pārśvanātha. As such we feel that even in the fifteenth century, lay followers of Jainism and even the artists were not sure about the exact number of the serpent-hoods to be shown in the images of the two pontiffs. Another point to be noted is the different art styles of the earlier and the present image. It is quite likely that this image was acquired from a different place or from a different artist.

There is an undated metal image of Pārśvanātha (14.0 X 8.0 cm) also preserved in the Sunam Jaina temple. It shows the Tīrthaṅkara seated in meditation on an emberoidered cushion placed on the lion throne (Pl. 327). The Jina bears a prominent diamond-shaped *śrīvatsa* on the chest besides other usual features. The intuitive expression with almost closed eyes and the elongation of the figure are evidently signs of change that had appeared in course of time. The pedestal also shows interesting features. In its centre is the hubbed wheel in profile as if yoked. Above this wheel is a snake, the cognizance of Pārśvanātha. The lions are looking facing. *Yaksha* and *yakshī* are missing altogether. At the back may be seen the body of the winding serpent rising from the uppermost moulding of the pedestal towards the head but has a gap between the level of the shoulders to the back of the head and its forepart with hoods is missing (Pl. 328). It was perhaps meant to be attached separately. We thus miss the evidence of the number of hoods which sheltered the Jina but the depiction of the cognizance on the pedestal makes sure that the image belongs to Pārśvanātha and not Supārśva. The image may be assigned to the sixteenth century on stylistic grounds.

The continuing poularity of Pārśvanātha at Sunam is vouched by another small white metal image (7.0 X 3.0 cm) in the same temple showing the Jina seated in meditation on a multiple-moulded high pedestal sheltered by a seven-hooded serpent (Pl. 329). Interestingly, the Jina is shown as wearing an upper garment which covers both his shoulders as seen in some early images of Buddha. As we have been noting even in the foregoing account, this feature lends further support to the supposition that Sunam was a great stronghold of the Śvetāmbaras. Unlike the winding fashion in which the serpent rises at the back of the Jina, as seen in some of the images described above, the serpent here is depicted with coils (Pl. 330) at the back and bears serration marks on its body. At the back of the hoods is shown a full-blown lotus flower. Overall, the image gives an impression of the degradation which was taking place. The use of white metal is another deviation. I feel inclined to assign it to the seventeenth century CE.

Before passing on to the next site, it will not be improper to refer to some other symbolic representations in the Jaina temple at Sunam. The most attractive one is the model of a

*Samavasaraṇa* in metal (Pl. 331). Literally meaning assemblage, the *samavasaraṇa* is a Sermon-hall fascinatingly planned by Indra or other gods where every Tīrthaṅkara is believed to have delivered his first or some important sermon after attaining enlightenment 'where heavenly beings, human beings and the animal world assemble, take their apportioned seats, and attend to the sermon'.[85] This special structure is generally round or square with three fortifications, each having four ornamental and well-guarded gateways. Inside, there are forest groves, parks, ponds, swimming pools for heavenly damsels, artificial hillocks, platforms, houses, palaces, picture-galleries, wish-fufilling trees, and what not, every part divinely bedecked and provided with every desired thing. In the centre of the uppermost fortification is a pavilion with four archways in four different directions with a big platform for the Jina to deliver the sermon. The concept of the *samavasaraṇa*, thus, seems to have been inspired by the *sarvatobhadrikā* or *chaumukhī* images meant for the whole gathering around to see the Jina while delivering the sermon. Tiwari remarks that independent examples of the *samavasaraṇas* have been found only from Śvetāmbara sites.[86]

Interestingly, the *samavasaraṇa* in the Sunam temple is hexagonal containg the depiction on its three fortifications of almost all the elements referred to above. It is a beautiful model and deserves a detailed study.

The *ashṭa-maṅgala*, the depiction of eight auspicious symbols, has remained popular with both the Digambaras and the Śvetābaras from ancient times. According to the Śvetāmbara canonical texts, they are *svastika*, *śrīvatsa*, *nandyāvarta*, *vardhamānaka* (powder-flask), *pūrṇa-ghaṭa* 'full vase', *darpaṇa* 'mirror' and *matsya* or *matsya-yugama* 'pair of fish'. While they were used as decorative measures, small metal platters of these *ashṭa-maṅgalas* are also dedicated in Jaina temples and worshipped along with other Jaina metal images.[87] An example of a pedestalled brass-tablet of *ashṭa-maṅgala* exists in the Jaina temple at Sunam (14.5 X 8.5 cm), indicating the popularity of the Śvetāmbara sect at this place through the centuries (Pl. 332).

In Jaina theology, Arhat, Siddha, Āchārya, Upādhyāya and Sādhu constitute the 'Five Supreme Ones', Pañcha-Parameshṭhins. They command high respect and are regarded as equal to the Jinas in importance. They are invoked daily by the Jainas in the famous *mantra* 'incantation' – *Namo Arahantāṇaṃ, Namo Siddhāṇaṃ, Namo Āyariāṇaṃ, Namo Uvajjhāyāṇaṃ, Namo Loe Savvasāhūṇam*.[88] The *mantra* is obtained in the beginning of the *Bhagavatī-sūtra* and the *Kalpa-sūtra* and special sanctity is attached to it from old times because the *Pañcha-Parameshṭhīs* are regarded as the 'Devādhidevas, the highest of objects of veneration for a pious Jaina'.[89] In about the ninth century, 'Four Essentials of Salvation' were added to the list of 'Five Supreme Ones' to form the 'Nine Dignities' (Nava-pada) These four essentials are, however, different in the two Jaina sects – for the Śvetāmbaras they are *Samyak-jñāna* (Right Knowledge), *Samyak-darśana* (Right Faith), *Samyak-charita* (Right Conduct) and *Samyak-tapa* (Tight Penance), while the Digambaras believe them to be the *Chaitya* (Jina-image), *Chaityālaya* (Jina temple), *Dharma-chakra* (Sacred Wheel of Law) and *Śruta* (Jaina Scriptures). The Nine Dignities (Nava-Pada) came to be worshipped popularly in the form of tantric *yantras* 'diagrams' called Siddha-Chakra and Nava-Devatā by the Śvetāmbaras and Digambaras respectively. Absence of early specimens indicates that the form of Siddha-Chakra known to us now developed quite late. Shah has published a bronze tablet of the Siddha-Chakra worshipped by the Śvetāmbaras, now preserved in the Vadodara Museum.[90] The *yantra* has the form of an eight-petalled lotus showing the Arhat in the centre and the Siddha, Āchārya, Upādhyāya and Sādhu represented in the petals pointing to the four cardinal directions and the following four *Namaskāra-mantras* 'obeisance formulae', in the intervening petals, beginning clockwise from the North-East corner, i.e., between the Siddha and the Āchārya: (1)- *Oṃ Hrīṃ namo daṃsanassa*, (2) *Oṃ Hrīṃ namo ṇānassa*, (3) *Oṃ*

*Hrīṃ namo Chāritassa*, and (4) *Oṃ Hrīṃ namo tavassa*. While describing the figures of the *Pañcha-Parameshṭhins*, Shah observed that

> The Arhat and the Siddha sit in the padmāsana showing the dhyāna-mudrā, while the remaining three Parameṣṭhins are in the same posture; they seem to carry some object in one hand with the other resting on the lap. As figures are indistinct in this bronze, it is not possible to identify the symbol held by them. But paintings of the Siddha-Cakra are common and in these, each of these figures lets his left hand rest on the lap while the right one, held in the *vyākhyāna-mudrā*, carries a mukha-paṭṭī (mukha-paṭṭikā) or mouth-piece.[91]

In paintings, different colours are prescribed for the *Parameshṭhins* – white for the Arhat, red for the Siddha, yellow for the the Āchārya, blue for the Upādhyāya and black for the Sādhu. Interestingly, we have an old painted Siddha-Chakra in the Jaina temple, Sunam corresponding to this description (Pl. 333). It has a diameter of 12.5 cm. The paper has become brittle and colours have also faded slightly. The tantric word *Hrīṃ*, however, is not there in the obeisance formulae which even otherwise also seem to have been changed slightly as we read *Oṃ name Saṃghassa* in the North-eastern petal. All figures except the one at the top are shown as wearing an *uttarīya* 'upper garment'. The figure at the top does not show *vyākhyāna-mudrā;* both the hands are placed on the lap in meditation. Another painted Siddha-Chakra from a manuscript from Faridkot district is much more elaborate, has illegible text added to the Siddha-Chakra at various places and, interestingly enough, has a wide range of Hindu deities painted all around it (Pl. 334).

The Śvetāmbara Jaina temple at Ropar possesses a bronze Siddha-Chakra[92] similar in concept and form to the one published by Shah but for the fact that the gargoyle attached to it has detached (Pl. 335). The Arhat is seated in *padmāsana* on a cushion in a dotted circle in the centre. The *dhotī* worn by him is indicated by incised parallel lines in the form of a necklace on the chest but with upper ends going outwards on the shoulders. The Arhat has long earlobes, almost touching the shoulders. Five petals pointing upwards adorn his head. The back-frame, square up to the shoulders with a circular aureole behind the head, is indicated by dotted outline with ornamental flourishes at the upper corners at the level of the shoulders. The petal on top shows the Siddha seated similarly but without the back-frame. He too has five-petalled head-decoration, long earlobes and wears a *dhotī*. The Āchārya, Upādhyāya and the Sādhu have also been provided with cushioned seats and sit in *padmāsana* with right hand in *vyākhyāna-mudrā* and left in the lap. In a marked contrast to the figures in the Siddha-Chakra published by Shah, they have been provided with haloes behind their heads indicating their elevation to the status of divinity. The petals between the Parameshṭhins carry the obeisance formulae mentioned above. The third and fourth incantations are somewhat corrupt in form. The third shows a strange symbol for *ri* followed by a letter which looks like *ma*. In the fourth, the word *tavassa* seems to begin with *sa*. The pattern of putting the legend, too, differs from the Vadodara example. Here, all the formulae are written in three lines, *namo* . . . . (followed by the respective *Pada*) in the middle, with the genitive suffix *ssa* in the third. The second and third formulae show redundant double vertical strokes at the end of the middle line. There is, however, no doubt that the intended *mantras* were the same as those noted by Shah.

The eight petals around the cental circle are shaped like the three-arched *chaityas* and are indicated by dotted lines with double loops at the ends. The space between the upper parts of the petals is bedecked with floral designs consisting of three circlets simulating the shape of club with leaves and branches on the sides. All around is a beaded border. The depiction of the figures and the palaeography indicate that it may have been made in about the seventeenth century CE.

In the *dhyāna-mantra* of the Jainas, the Siddhas come next to the Arhats. Shah has observed that "Tīrthaṅkaras or Arhats and the Siddhas are separately invoked only because the former as Arhat are worshipped as embodied souls, the Siddhas are worshipped in their disembodied stage when even the last bondage of the material body does not remain . . . Being disembodied, his body is not shown and the metal plaque is made like a stencil, the whole standing figure of the Siddha being cut away . . . Such images are found in Digambara shrines."[93] He has remarked further that since "A Siddha is said to be free from the bondage of his body (*a-śarīrī*), so he is represented without the body. No early stencil-cut Siddha images are known. The practice of representing Siddhas in this way seems to be very late."[94]

The Jaina temple at Ferozepur has preserved such a stencil-cut Siddha figure (Pl. 336) which bears an inscription on its pedestal dated Samvat 1632 (CE 1575), which falls during the reign of Akbar. It is well known that Akbar was a tolerant and inquisitive emperor who had established at Agra in CE 1573 an 'I'bādat khānā' or house of worship where representatives of various religions assembled and held discussions on religious topics. Jaina monk Hīra-vijaya Sūri was also invited to participate in the discussions and Akbar was highly impressed by his exposition. Once during Akbar's visit to Lahore, Jina-chandra Sūri (S. 1598-1670) also exhorted him and was endowed with the title of 'Yuga-pradhāna' by the emperor.[95] Some Jaina temples were founded at Lahore with Akbar's permission and several grand functions were held under royal patronage. A large number of Jaina families fom Mewar came to settle in the cities and towns of Punjab and many *Upāśrayas* or *ḍerās* (religious establishments) were set up there.[96]

There is a Digambara *tri-tīrthikā* also in the Jaina temple at Ferozepur (Pl. 337) showing the sky-clad Jinas standing in *kāyotsarga* pose under the triple umbrella. The image is in an indifferent state of preservation but the artistic execution certainly shows a degenerating trend. The image may belong to the seventeenth century CE. The temple, however, possesses a beautiful *chaturviṃśati-paṭṭa* (Pl. 338) with Ṛishabhanātha having locks of hair falling on the shoulders seated in *padmāsana* in the centre under the triple umbrella flanked by a *khaḍgāsana* Jina on either side with small meditating figures above them. The *yaksha* and *yakshī*, which seem to be Sarvānubhūti and Ambikā, occupy their prescribed positions on the right and left of the *siṃhāsana*. Above the ornamental arch is a meditating Jina figure flanked by diminutive *khaḍgāsana* Jinas with two meditating figures on their sides and two more slightly lower below. The juxta-buttresses on either side also show five meditatig Jinas one above the other with temple-spire atop. At the base of the extreme recesses are again two very small figures of *khaḍgāsana* Jinas above which are the *vyāla* figures. The lower moulding of the pedestal carries planetary divinities in human form, seven seated on the central projection and two on the extremities. A good balance seems to have been maintained within the constraints of format and iconography. The image may be dated to the sixteenth century on stylistic grounds. We thus see that the temple seems to have flourished during the reign of Akbar.[97]

## NOTES AND REFERENCES

1. Some scholars prefer 467 BCE as the date of Mahāvīra's *nirvāṇa* [A. Ghosh (Ed.), *Jaina Art and Architecture*, 3 vols., New Delhi, 1974-75 (*JAA*), I, p. 16; Rhys Davids in *Encyclopaedia Britannica*, 9th ed., Vol. XII, p. 543].
2. Somewhat Jainistic views regarding the spread of Jainism in Punjab and northwestern India and Central Asia have been given by Hira Lal Duggar (*Madhya Eśiyā aura Pañjāba meṃ Jaina Dharma*, Delhi, 1979) and Banarsi Das Jain ('Jainism in the Punjab', in Jagan Nath Agrawal and Bhim Dev Shastri (Eds.), *Sarūpa – Bhāratī or the Heritage of Indology Being the Dr. Lakshman Sarup Memorial Volume*, Hoshiarpur, 1964, pp. 238-47). Hemachandra, a great Jaina scholar and poet, has recorded in his *Trishashṭiśalākāpurushacharitra*

(Parva I, Canto 3, vv. 335, 380 and Canto 5) a Jaina tradition that when Bharata, the elder brother proclaimed himself as a *chakravartin*, all except Bāhubalī submitted to his authority. A battle ensued between Bharata and Bāhubalī for suzerainty and the matter was referred to Ṛishabha who advised Bāhubalī to yield. Dismayed at the decision, Bāhubalī renounced the world to undertake severe penance.

3. *JAA*, I, p. 51.
4. Sir John Marshall, 'Excavations at Taxila', *ARASI*, 1914-15, pp. 1-35; *Guide to Taxila*, Cambridge, 1960, pp. 69, 72-74; Jain, *op. cit.*
5. Ghosh, *op. cit.*, p. 8, fn. 2.
6. *Sacred Books of the East*, Vol. XVII, pp. 38-39; V. Fausboll, *The Jātaka*, London, 1963, Vol. VI, p. 62.
7. O.P. Bharadwaj, *Studies in the Historical Geography of Ancient India*, Delhi, 1986, p. 154.
8. J.W.C. McCrindle, *Ancient India as Described by Megasthenes and Arrian*, Revised 2nd ed., Calcutta, 1960, pp. 98ff.
9. S.B. Deo in A. Ghosh, *op. cit.*, pp. 22-25.
10. Topra village lies about 11 km southwest of Jagadhari in district Yamunanagar of Haryana. For details see *CASR*, XIV, pp. 78-79; E. Hultzsch, "Delhi-Topra Pillar Edicts", *Corpus Inscriptionum Indicarum*, Vol. I, London, 1925, pp. 119-37; D.C. Sircar, *Inscriptions of Aśoka*, Publication Division, Delhi, March 1957, pp. 73-77,
11. A.K. Roy, *A History of the Jainas*, New Delhi, 1984, p. 75.
12. *JAA*, I, p. 26.
13. Roy, *op. cit.*, pp. 75-76.
14. Roy, *loc. cit.*; Cf. Jagdish Chandra Jain, *Bhārata ke Prāchīina Jaina Tīrtha* (Hindi), Banaras, 1952, pp. 17-18 and 27.
15. Devendra Handa, *Jaina Bronzes from Hansi*, Shimla-New Delhi, 2002, pp. 7-8; *Tribal Coins of Ancient India*, pp. 25-38.
16. *JAA*, I, pp. 28, 51-55.
17. Devendra Handa, "A Terracotta Seal from Ahrwan (District Palwal, Haryana)", *Indian Coin Society Newsletter*, No. 45 (Oct.-Dec. 2007), pp. 107-109.
18. Jyoti Prasad Jain, *The Jaina Sources of the History of Ancient India*, Delhi, 1964, p. 106.
19. *Therīgāthā*, which forms part of the *Khuddaka-nikāya*, contains stanzas of Nanduttarā and Mittakālī (five each), of Kururaṭṭha. The traditional mention of the names with the lives of the *Bhikshuṇīs* 'nuns' is preserved in the commentary of Dhammapāla known as the *Paramatthadīpanī*, ascribable to the fifth century CE. Both the *therīs* 'female recluses' belonged to the Kammāsadamma *nigama* 'corporation' in the Kuru country. Kammāsadamma is identified with village Kamaspur in Haryana by Bharadwaj (*op. cit.*, pp. 157-58). Nanduttarā had earlier been initiated to Jainism – *Imasmiṃ buddhuppāde Kururaṭṭhe Kammāsadamma-nigame brāhmaṇa-kule nibbattitvā ekachchānaṃ vijjāṭṭhānāni sippāyatanāni cha ugga-hetvā nigaṇṭhapabbajjaṃ upagaṃtvā vādasutā jambusākhaṃ gahetvā bhaddā. . .*(*Therīgāthā*, ed. N.K. Bhagwat, Bombay, 1956, p. 63).
20. *CAGI*, pp. 104-08.
21. Watters, *op. cit.*, pp. 248-51; Samuel Beal (Eng. Tr.), *Buddhist Records of the Western World*, London, 1884, Vol. I, pp. 143-45. Hira Lal Dugar (*op. cit.*, pp. 108-109) quotes *Vividha Tīrthakalpa* of Jinaprabha Sūri (fourteenth century CE) which refers to the temples of Nemīnātha and Vimalanātha at Siṃhapura: *Śrī Siṃhapure liṅgābhidhaḥ Śrī-Nemināthaḥ. . . . Śrī Siṃhapure cha Vimalanāthaḥ//.*
22. *Gazetteer of Jhelum District*, Lahore, 1904, pp. 43-46. Aurel Stein and Fred H. Andrews discovered Murti in 1889. Stein and Fabri revisited it in 1931. For details see M.A. Stein, *Archaeological Reconnaissances in North-Western India and South-Eastern Iran*, London, 1937, pp. 52-57, Pls. 20-21; Charles Fabri, "Archaeology in the Punjab", *Marg*, X (2), March 1957, p. 13; etc.
23. D.C. Bhattacharyya, *Medieval Indian Sculpture* (*In the Government Museum and Art Gallery, Chandigarh*), Chandigarh, 1981, pp. 10-11. 93-94, Fig. 47. The second image, a Jaina tutelary couple, described by Bhattacharyya as coming probably from Murti (*Ibid.*, pp. 96-98, Fig. 48) actually belongs to Rohtak. There are, however, numerous other pieces of the Gupta period recovered from Murti and obtained by the Chandigarh Museum from the Lahore Museum, which have not been included by Bhattacharyya in his catalogue, may be probably because they belong to the Gupta period.

24. It is interesting to note that a wall painting in Chinese Turkestan depicting a headless naked male standing tiptoe with the right leg brought in front of the left was identified by A. Von Le Coq (as quoted by Banarsi Das Jain, *op. cit.*, p. 242) as a Digambara Tīrthaṅkara and N.C. Mehta also endorsed the view saying that the old wall-paintings in Chinese Turkestan depict many scenes from Jaina history taking a cue from C.J. Shah (*Jainism in Northern India*, London, 1932, p. 194); but the fact that the genital of this figure is pierced by a heavy metallic ring goes against such an identification.
25. Banarsi Das Jain, *op. cit.*, pp. 242-43. The city itself may have given the name to the hills as Pabbi may be derived from Pārvatikā.
26. Vincent A. Smith, *Coins of Ancient India: Catalogue of the Coins in the Indian Museum Calcutta*, Vol. I, Oxford, 1906 (reprint, Delhi-Varanasi, 1972), pp. 233-34, Pl. XXV.4.
27. Harigupta himself seems to have belonged to a royal family because his copper coin datable palaeographically to fifth century is known to have been found from Ahichchhatrā (Alexander Cunningham, *Coins of Medieval India*, London, 1894, p. 19, Pl. II.6). For different views regarding the identification of Harigupta, see D.C. Sircar, *Studies in Indian Coins*, Delhi, 1968, pp. 221-26.
28. C.J. Shah, *op. cit.*, pp. 209-15.
29. It is described as 'the standing posture with feet at a distance of about two inches from each other, the hands resting naturally by the sides, but not so as to touch the body' (B.C. Bhattacharya, *Jaina Iconography*, 2nd revised edition, Delhi-Varanasi-Patna, 1974, pp. 139-40). It is enjoined that Ajitanātha, Sambhavanātha and Abhinandana should be especially sculptured in this posture.
30. It has been prescribed for Mahāvīra, Ṛishabha, and Neminātha: *Vīraḥ Ṛishabhaḥ Nemiḥ eteshāṃ Jinānāṃ paryaṅkāsanam/ Śesha Jinānām-utsargāsanam //*
31. *Sarvatobhadra* (four-fold) Tīrthaṅkara images were also carved from the late Kushāṇa period.
32. *JAA*, I, pp. 111-16.
33. *Bṛihatsaṃhitā* LVII.45:

    *i. Ājānulambabāhuḥ śrīvatsāṅkaḥ praśāntamūrtiścha/*

    *ii. Digvāsastaruṇo rūpavāṃścha kāryyo'rhataṃ devaḥ//*

34. *Aśoka-vṛikshaḥsurapushpavṛishṭirdivyadhvaniśchāmaramāsanañcha/*

    *Bhāmaṇḍalaṃdundubhirātapatramashṭa pratihāryāni Jineśvarānām//*

    As quoted by D.R. Bhandarkar, "Jaina Iconography", *Indian Antiquary*, 1911. Cf. *Jaina Iconography*, p. 20, fn. 1 -

    *Divyatarusurapushpavṛishṭidundubhirāsanayojanaghoshau/*

    *Ātapavāraṇachāmarayugame yasya vibhāti chāmaṇḍalatejaḥ//*

    See also *Rūpa-Maṇḍana* VI.33-34.
35. U.P. Shah, *Jaina-Rūpamaṇḍana*, Vol. I, Delhi, 1987, pp. 83-86 and 152-53, Figs. 26-27, 34-35.
36. *Pratishṭhā-sāroddhāra*, I.77:

    *Sthiretrārchayoḥ pāda-pīṭhasyādho yathāyatham/*

    *lāñchhanaṃ dakshiṇe pārśve yaksham yakshīm cha vāmake//*

    Cf. *Pratishṭhāsārasaṃgraha*, V.12: *Yakshaṃ cha dakshiṇe pārśve vāme śāsanadevatā* (as quoted by M.N.P. Tiwari, *Jaina Pratimā-vijñāna* (Hindi), Varanasi, 1981, p. 155).
37. Devendra Handa, "A Sarvatobhadrika Pratima from Punjab", *Arhat Vacana*, Indore, Year 1, Nos. 3-4 (June-Sept. 1989), pp. 55-56 & plate.
38. *IAR*, 1978-79, p. 99, Pl. LIII A.
39. Handa (1987), *op. cit.*, p. 116, Pl. XXIV.
40. Tiwari, *op. cit.*, pp. 117-24.
41. Handa (1987), *op. cit.*, Pl. XXV.
42. Shah (1997), *op. cit.*, p. 280.
43. Handa (1987), *op. cit.*, Pl. XXVI.
44. *Times of Chandigarh*, Thursday, July 24, 2008, p. 3.
45. *The Tribune*, dated 13.10.1979; *IAR*, 1979-80, p. 105.
46. D.R. Gehlot, "A Rare Marble Sculpture of Naminātha from Bhatinda, District Bhatinda, Punjab", in R.T. Vyas (Chief Editor), *Śilpasaṃvit; Consciousness Manifest – Studies in Jaina Art and Iconography and Allied Subjects in Honour of Dr. U.P. Shah*, Oriental Institute, Vadodara – Abhinav Publications, New Delhi, 1995, pp. 73-75, Pls. I-II.

47. *Ibid.*, Pl. III.
48. Cf. Chandramani Singh (Ed.), *Museums of Rajasthan*, Jawahar Kala Kendra, and Department of Archaeology and Museums, Rajasthan, Jaipur in association with Mapin Publishing, 2009, p. 85. See also V.S. Srivastava, *Catalogue & Guide to Ganga Golden Jubilee Museum, Bikaner*, Jaipur, 1960-61, p. 14 (& 17-19 for bronzes from Amarsar).
49. Gehlot (*op. cit.*, p. 74, Pl. IV) did not take note of the expression 'dvir-Āshāḍha' and read the name of the donor as Shri Virupan Puriya.
50. The engraver seems to have committed some error and tried to rectify his mistake by engraving over the earlier part and this has resulted in jumbling of this part of the epigraph.
51. Gehlot, *loc. cit.*
52. U.P. Shah, however, published the photograph of this image with the *parikara* on the last cover page of the *Journal of Oriental Institute*, Baroda, Vol. 31, No. 3 as that of Ṛishabhanātha.
53. Gehlot, *op. cit.*, p. 75.
54. The metal images described here have not been examined metallographically. They may be of brass, bronze or octo-alloy or some other alloy. I have, therefore, used the commonly employed term 'bronze' for these images in general.
55. Tiwari, *op. cit.*, p. 157.
56. *Ibid.*, p. 101, fn. 3: *Tri-pañcha-phaṇaḥ Supārśvaḥ Pārśvaḥ sapta-navastathā.*
57. Shah (1995-96), pp. 285-90.
58. Handa (2002), *op. cit.*, pp. 18-24, Pls. 10-28; (2006), *op. cit.*, pp. 261-63, Pls. 358-70.
59. Tiwari, *op. cit.*, p. 44.
60. Ashvini Agrawal, "Jaina Bronzes at Ropar", *Newsletter, INTACH (Chandigarh Pinjore Kalka Regional Chapter*, March 1993, pp. 24-28.
61. *Rūpa-maṇḍana* VI.21; *Devatāmūrtiprakaraṇa* VII.63; *Trishashṭi-ślākā-purusha-charita* IX.3, 364-65; etc.
62. The abbreviations commonly used in these bronze images are: *kā*. for *kāritam* 'caused to be made'; *pra*. for *pratishṭhitam; bhā*. for *bhāryā* 'wife'; *va*. for *vadi* 'dark fortnight'; *sā* for *Sāha* or *Śāha*, i.e., *Śreshṭhin* or *Seth; su*. for *suta* 'son' and also for *sudi* 'bright fortnight'; etc.
63. According to the *Paṭṭāvalī-Samuchchaya* (pp. 39, 67-68, 133, 146, 157, 162 and 172) Lakshmī-sāgara Sūri was a favourite disciple of Soma-sundara Sūri who left the world in VS 1517. He had a large following and shed light of the faith like a lamp (*Ibid.*, p. 133)–

    *Lakshmīsāgarasūriśītamahasā Lakshmīravāpe tato*
    *Dīpeneva guṇodayaṃ kalayatā jyotibṛihadbhānutaḥ/*
    *Gāyantīḥ sarasundarīguṇagaṇānyasyāshṭadiksaṅgiṇī-*
    *R-vijñāyāshṭa vinirmame kimu vidhiḥ śrotuṃ śrutīrātmanaḥ//*
64. Puran Chand Nahar, *Jaina Inscriptions*, Part I, Calcutta, 1918, various numbers on different pages.
65. Agarchand Nahta *et al* (Eds.), *Rājasthāna kā Jaina Sāhitya* (Hindi), Jaipur, 1977, p. 67. See also Mul Raj Jain, "A Jain Pilgrimage to Nagarkot in Saṃ. 1484", *Proceedings and Transactions of All India Oriental Conference*, Thirteenth Session, Nagpur, 1946, pp. 398-403.
66. K.C. Jain, *Ancient Cities and Towns of Rajasthan*, Delhi-Varanasi-Patna, 1972, p. 360. Lakshmī-sāgara Sūri visited Jirāvalā and Abu also (*Ibid.*, p. 428).
67. Devendra Handa, "Pokaraṇa ke kuchha Aprakāśita Abhilekha", *Maru-Bhāratī*, Pilani, Year 29, No. 4 (January 1982), p. 34, fig. 2. The complete text of the epigraph runs thus: *Saṃ. 1533 Śrā. sudi 1 Ūkeśa Sā. Bhādrā bhāryā Saramāde-putra Sā. Phāmaṇeta bhā. Śrī-Dū pramukha kuṭuṃba-yutena sva-śreyāsa (=Śreyase) Śrī-Ādi-biṃbaṃ kā. pra. Tapā Śrī-Lakshmī-sāgara-Sūribhiḥ//.* It is also notable that slightly more than a year earlier, Hīra-vijaya Sūri consecrated an image of Śītalanātha in the Tapā-gachchha at Pokaran (*Ibid.*, p. 35). He was born in VS 1583 (= CE 1526) in Ukeśa (Oswal) family, obtained *dīkshā* 'consecration' in VS 1607, attained the status of Sūri in VS 1610 at Sirohi in Rajasthan, founded Chintāmaṇi-Pārśvanātha temple at Agra in VS 1640 and died at Unnatapura in Gujarat in VS 1652. He exhorted Akbar and was honoured by the emperor. He was at Lahore in Punjab also for some time. His disciple Vijaya-sena Sūri too visited Lahore (*Paṭṭāvalī-Samuchchaya*, pp. 73-79, 160 and 176). It is thus very clear that Jaina monks from Rajasthan visited Punjab quite often and were very active in spreading and strengthening Jainism in the Punjab.

68. As quoted by Umakant P. Shah (Ed.), *Treasures of Jaina Bhaṇḍāras*, Ahmedabad, 1978, p. 19.
69. Ashvini Agrawal, *loc. cit.*
70. The original or *Mūla-saṃgha* of the Jainas was divided into four *saṃghas* – Nandi, Sena, Deva and Siṃha – each subdivided into *gaṇas* and further into *gachchhas* (*JAA*, III, p, 185).
71. Muni Jina-vijaya (Ed.), *Vividha-tīrtha-kalpa*, Santiniketana, 1934, p. 45.
72. B.L. Nahata (Ed.), *Dravya-parīkshā aura Dhātūtpatti* (of Ṭhakkara Pheru) (Hindi), Vaiśālī, 1976.
73. Mārga has probably been used here as the abbreviated form of Mārgaśīrsha. It is equally possible that 'rga' is engraved mistakenly for 'gha'.
74. *Śrī-Deva-suṃdara-gururgarimābhirāmaḥ śrī-vāchakasya kali-śatru-bhayānakasya/ (Paṭṭāvalī-Samuchchaya, p. 39). . . Yaṃ {Aṇahilla-]pattane guṃgaḍīrasraḥkṛitasthitiḥ pradhānatarayogiśatatrayaparivṛito maṃtra-taṃtrādi-samṛiddhi-maṃdiraṃ sthāvara-jaṃgama-visha-pāpa-hārī jalānala-vyāla-hari-bhaya-bhettā atītānāgatādi-vastu-vettā rāja-maṃtri-pramukha-bahujana-bahumāna-pūjitaḥudayīpā yogī prajā-samakshaṃ stutiṃ kurvāṇaḥ prakaṭita-parama-bhakti-ḍaṃbaraḥ sāḍaṃbaraṃ vaṃditavāna//* (*Ibid*, p. 64). A metal image of Pārśvanātha consecrated by him in VS 1454 is preserved in a Jaina temple in Delhi (Nahar, *op. cit.*, no. 461, p. 110).
75. The word *dramma* is derived from the Greek coin term drachm, which was a silver coin weighing 4.27 grammes. Later, however, *dramma* seems to have been used for copper coins also. It finds mention in medieval Jaina literature and inscriptions. See for details R.C. Agrawala, "Dramma in Ancient Indian Epigraphs and Literature", *JNSI*, XVII (2), 1955, pp. 64-82.
76. B.C. Bhattacharyya, *op. cit.*, p. 60.
77. Umakant P. Shah, "Some Interesting Images of Pārśvanātha", *Indologica Taurinensia*, Vol. XXI-XXII (1995-96), Torino (Italy), pp. 285-90, Figs. 1-18.
78. For the history and people connected with Ūkeśa, see Darshan Vijay Muni (Ed.), *Upakeśagachchhapaṭṭāvali*, Viramgam, 1933; Devendra Handa, *Osian: History, Archaeology, Art & Architecture*, Delhi, 1984.
79. See for details Jina Vijaya Muni (Ed.), *Kharataragachchhabṛihadgurvvāvali*, Bombay, 1956. The Kharataragachchha has remained more popular and effective in Rajasthan as compared to other *gachchhas* and the presence of the people belonging to this *gachchha* at Sunam indicates their migration from Rajasthan or at least having been influenced by the monks popularizing it.
80. Nahta *et al.*, *op. cit.*, pp. 73 and 228.
81. *Ibid.*, pp. 142, 170 and 228.
82. *Śrī-Yuga-pradhān=āvatāra-śrī-bṛihat=Tapāgachchha-śṛiṅgāra-hāra-bhaṭṭāraka-Puraṃdara-pūjya-śrī-Soma-suṃdara-Sūri* (*Paṭṭāvalī-Samuchchaya*, p. 38).
83. Govind Lal Shrimali, *Rājasthāna ke Abhilekha*, Part II, Jodhpur, 2000, pp. 282-84; *Paṭṭāvalī-Samuchchaya*, p. 172: *Somasuṃdarasūriḥ prāgvaṃśī Rāṇapura-pratishṭhā-kṛit Pālaṇapure bhaginyāḥ saha saṃyamaṃ jagrāha.*
84. Nahar, *op. cit.*, nos. 122, 734 and 990.
85. *JAA*, III, pp. 529-33, Tiwari, *op. cit.*, pp. 152-53; Shah (1987), *op. cit.*, pp. 23-26. For a good example of the ornamented metal *samvasaraṇa* installed during the reign of Chālukyan ruler Bhīmadeva II in Samvat 1252 (CE 1195) at Cambay, see B. Bandyopadhyay, *Survey of Indian Metal Sculpture*, Delhi, 1987, p. 39, Pl. 35.
86. Tiwari, *loc. cit.*
87. U.P. Shah, *Studies in Jaina Art*, Banaras, 1955, pp. 109-12, fig. 60; (1987), *op. cit.*, Fig. 153.
88. Umakant P. Shah, "Beginnings of Jaina Iconography", *Bulletin of Museums & Archaeology in U.P.*, Lucknow, No. 9, pp. 8-9; (June 1987), pp. 41-46, Fig. 38.
89. Shah (1987), *op. cit.*, p. 41.
90. Shah (1955), *op. cit.*, p. 98, fig. 85; (1987), *op. cit.*, Pl. XXII, fig. 39.
91. *Ibid.*
92. Devendra Handa, "A Bronze Siddha-Cakra from Punjab", in P.K. Mishra and S.K. Sullerey (Eds.), *Heritage of India: Past and Present (Essays in Honour of Prof. R.K. Sharma)*, 2 vols, Delhi, 1994, I, pp. 239-41, Pl. 41.1.
93. Shah (1987), *op. cit.*, p. 42.
94. *Ibid.*, Fig. 185.
95. Nahta *et al* (eds.), *op. cit.*, p. 67.

96. *Paṭṭāvalī-Samuchchaya*, pp. 73-74, 78-79 and 160; Banarsi Das Jain, *op. cit.*, pp. 246-47. A mutilated green stone image of about 20 cm height belonging to the eighth Tīrthaṅkara Chandraprabhu installed in VS 1643 (= CE 1586), as per the inscription on its pedestal, was recovered from a well and is now preserved in the Śvetāmbara Jaina temple at Samana (Hira Lal Dugar, *op. cit.*, p. 228). It also confirms the congenial religious atmosphere created by Akbar during his reign.
97. The Jaina temple at Ferozepur contains some inscribed marble images also, the earliest of which is that of Ajitanātha dated Samvat 1546 (= CE 1489). Important amongst others installed later are those of Padma-prabha or Naminātha and Śāntinātha. All these seem to have been imported later from Rajasthan.

# 11

# Epilogue

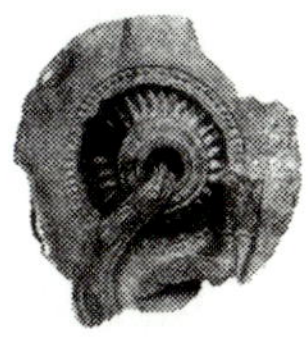

The foregoing account makes it clear that art activity started in Punjab, as also in many other parts of the country, during the Mauryan period and continued to flourish till about the advent of iconoclastic hordes in the medieval period. The ring-stone found from Ropar bearing the typical Mauryan polish and some hand modelled terracotta figurines, however, remain the few specimens of the earliest period. Ring-stones have been found from various early historic cities of north India and the specimen from Ropar betrays the continuation of the tradition and relationship with other early centres of art and trade. Though the vast empire established by Chandragupta Maurya and extended further by his grandson Aśoka disintegrated during the Śuṅga period yet the craze for artistic objects seems to have increased and become popular even with the common men as is evidenced by the terracotta figurines found from Ropar, Sunet, etc. Hand made figurines continued to be made some times, but the significant technical change which is noticeable in the Śuṅga period is the use of moulds on a large scale which distinguishes them from the Mauryan repertoire and augurs the inception of a truly native and indigenous physiognomy and idiom. The new style is characterized by the cherubic nude boys and *Yakshī* figures wearing elaborate jewellery, which are proportionate and betray modelling in bold relief and are generally treated with a red slip. They show complete control of contours, linear rhythm, sensitive treatment, elegance, sophisticated expressions, elaborate coiffures, diaphanous drapery, profuse ornamentation, multiplicity of poses and attitudes. The terracotta figurines found from Ropar and Sunet betray stylistic and socio-cultural affinity with those discovered from other centres of northern India like Mathurā, Ahichchhatrā, Kauśāmbī, etc.

The Indo-Greek, Scytho-Parthian and Kushāṇa impact is discernible in the terracotta and stone images found from Sunet, Sunam, Hathur, Sanghol and elsewhere. Alien physiognomic features, dress and ornamentation, furniture and crockery and Gandhāra style as elucidated above furnish fresh data regarding ethnology, history, culture, religion, and art of the state leaving little doubt to its trade with northwestern parts of the subcontinent. Assimilative and accommodating spirit of the people is also reflected by the recovered specimens. The richness and affluence of the Kushāṇa period is indicated by the abundant use of imported mottled Sikri sandstone used for the railing pillars at Sanghol. Comparative scarcity of Gupta specimens betrays the decline which may have occurred with the withdrawal of the Kushāṇa power. The devastation wrought by the Hūṇas is indicated by the destruction of the *stūpa* at Sanghol and the subsequent rarity of objects of art. The reign of Harshavardhana provided some respite to which the account of Xuan Zang also points out but the real fillip seems to have come during the Pratihāra period to which belong most of the images and architectural remains described above. Numerous temples must have been built during this period. The use of buff sandstone and stylistic similarities indicate employment of artists from almost all surrounding regions, as far as Madhya Pradesh even. Impact from Kashmir, particularly on the sculptures found from Dholbaha located just at the foot of the Shiwalik hills adjoining Himachal Pradesh, may have trickled as a result of Avantivarman's invasion and the geographical location of the site on a trade route which connected the Himachal region of Kangra and Kullu with the plains of Punjab. Employment of artisans from the hills too is quite probable. Pratihāra rule also provided an opportunity for the Jainas of Rajasthan to establish themselves and expand towards the Punjab plains and Himachal hills. The missionary activities of the Jaina monks got further encouragement during the Chauhan rule and this is well evidenced by the use of marble and metal images of the subsequent periods.

The Chauhan power was an important pillar of strength to fall before the depredations of the iconoclasts and we find that art activity almost ceases in Punjab with the establishment of Islamic rule towards the end of the twelfth century CE. During the Sultanate rule the Jainas seem to have continued their missionary activities and set up small metal images in their homes or establishments but the construction of temples and images for general public remained a rare occurrence. The reign of the Mughal emperor Akbar (CE 1556-1605) was a great respite and some religious forbearance was witnessed. But reversion to the same old policy of discrimination, imposition of *jaziya* (religious cess) and iconoclasm by the subsequent rulers remained a great deterrent to the erection and establishment of religious edifices and carving of images. Centuries of Islamic rule resulted in complete decline in the art of construction and iconography.

Figures of Śiva holding a sword and Lakshmī supporting a lotus in right hand with left hand akimbo on some early clay sealings found from Sanghol furnish evidence of the evolving iconographic features. The badly mutilated terracotta figurine of Kārttikeya from Sanghol may have originally been hex-cephalic shown with six Kṛittakās touching their breasts as if eager to suckle the divine babe. This unique figurine reminds us of the six-headed Kārttikeya and Shashṭhī depicted on Yaudheya coins. Such an iconographic prescription may have thus evolved during the Yaudheya rule in this region. Beautiful Gupta terracottas from Ropar, Sanghol, Janer, Zahura and other places vie with any of their class betraying stylistic affiliation with the Gangetic valley in general.

Dholbaha presents an ideal picture of the evolution of styles and influences from different quarters during nearly half a millennium years of its existence as a great art centre of the region from about CE 700 to 1200. The unfinished images found from this site furnish undoubted evidence of the existence of art ateliers here mostly utilizing locally available stone. Numerous Vishṇu heads, Harihara, Hara-Gaurī, Śiva with a long *jaṭā-jūṭa*, Śiva with a goose, and the Rāmāyaṇa panel are some remarkable specimens from this site. Images from Bathinda, Velore, Janer, Ghanauli, Khanpur, Lalru, Majhur, Mard Khera, Zahura, etc. provide rare glimpses of the artistic, aesthetic and iconographic achievements of the artists. The bronze mask from Ropar and other metal images from Bhudan, Sunam, Kharar and Ferozepur are significant not only from the viewpoint of art and iconography but also of the movement of styles and missionary activities of the Jaina monks from Rajasthan and elsewhere. Jaina images from Bathinda, Bhudan, Sunam, Ferozepur and Ropar show very interesting iconographic innovations.

More than three hundred specimens illustrated in this work may convince anyone that Punjab is no more a terra incognita in sculptural art. It is hoped that persistent work and systematic explorations in future will bring to light many more figures to present a complete picture of the art activities of the state in ancient and medieval times.

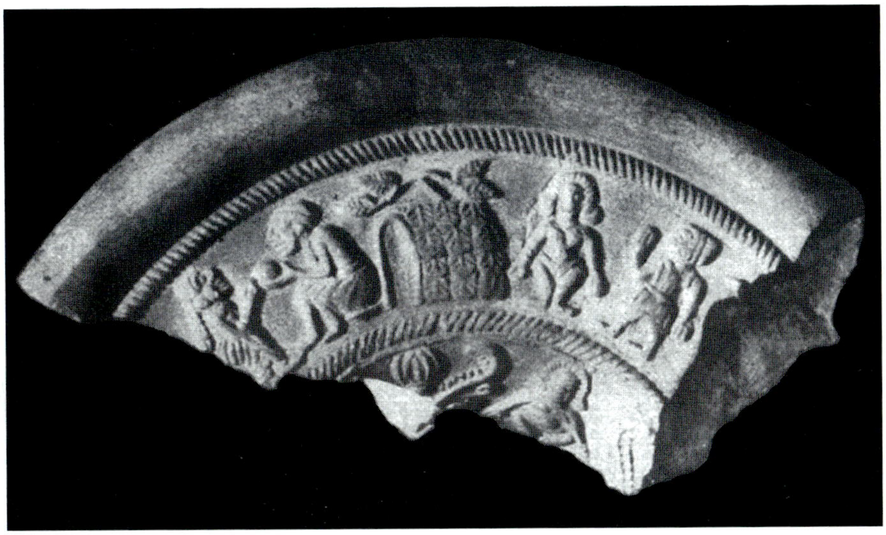

**Pl. 1.** Mauryan ring stone, Ropar.

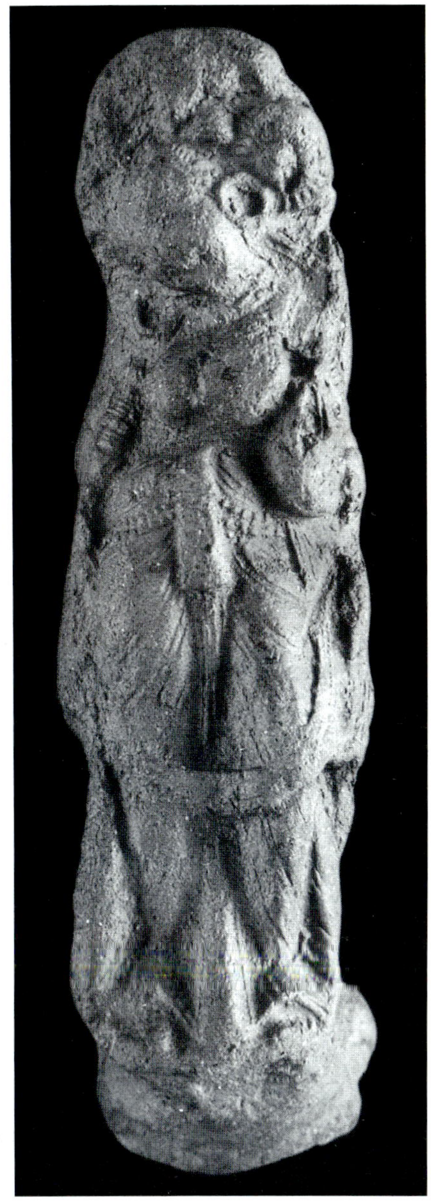

**Pl. 3.** Śuṅga *yakshī*, terracotta, Sunet.

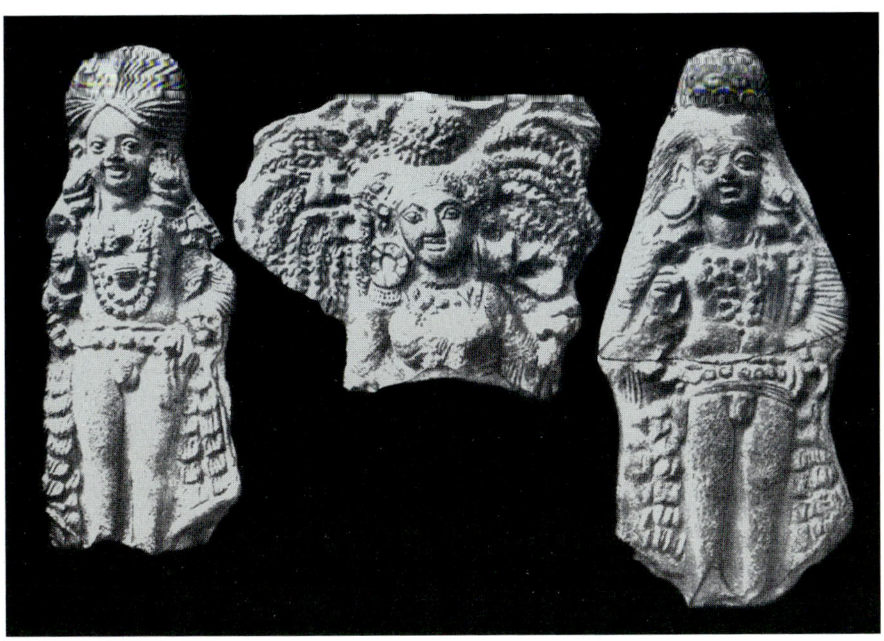

**Pl. 2.** Śuṅga terracottas, Ropar.

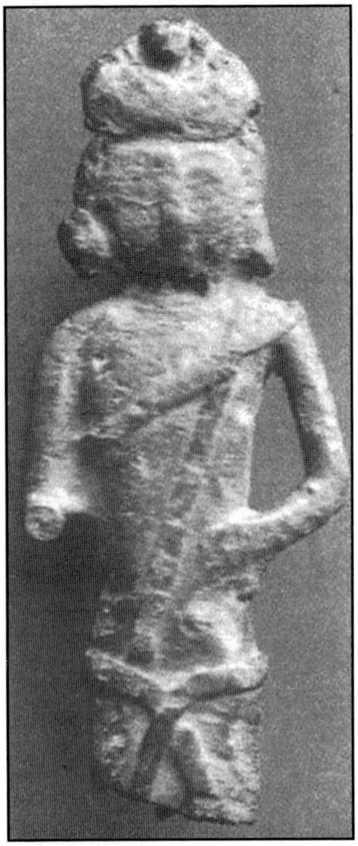

**Pl. 4.** *Yājñika* Brāhmaṇa, bronze, Ropar.

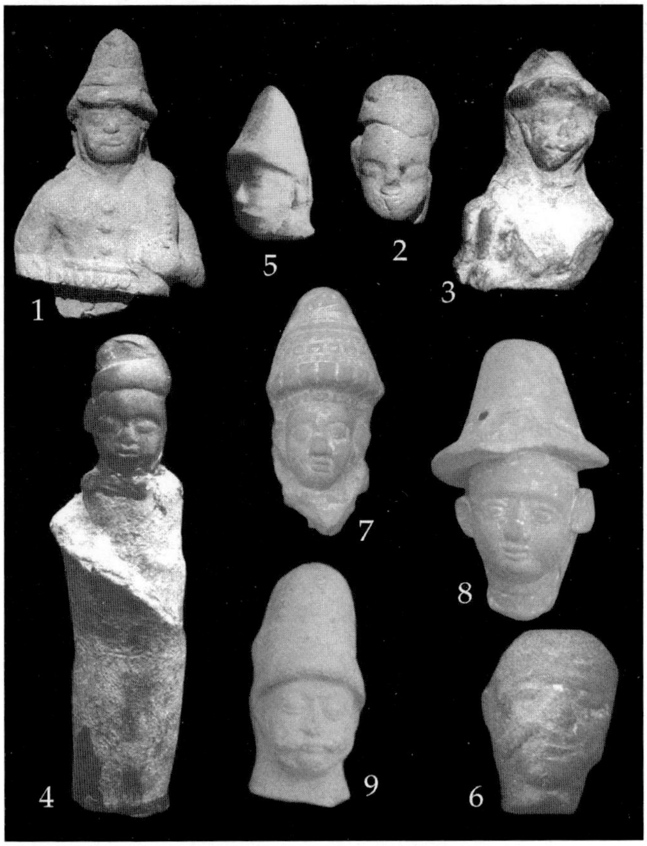


**Pl. 5.** Terracottas figurines from Sunam, Sunet, Hathur, etc.

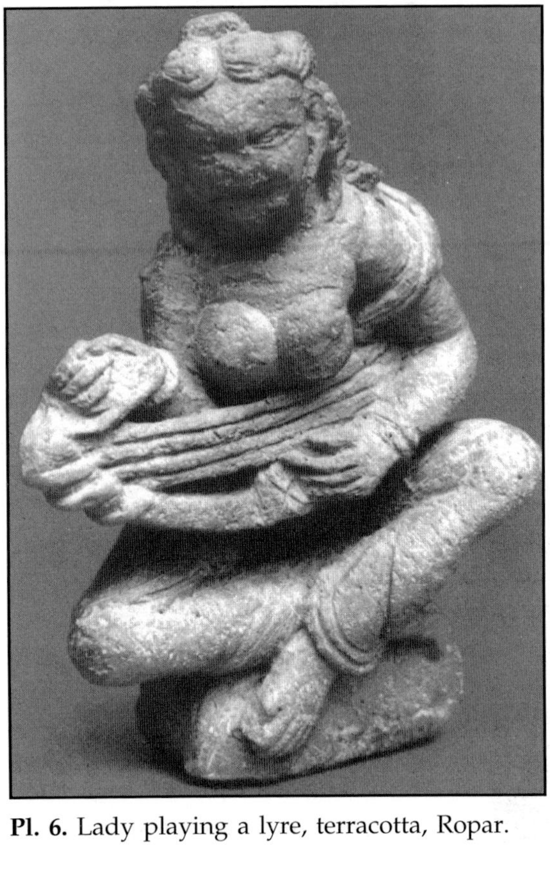

**Pl. 6.** Lady playing a lyre, terracotta, Ropar.

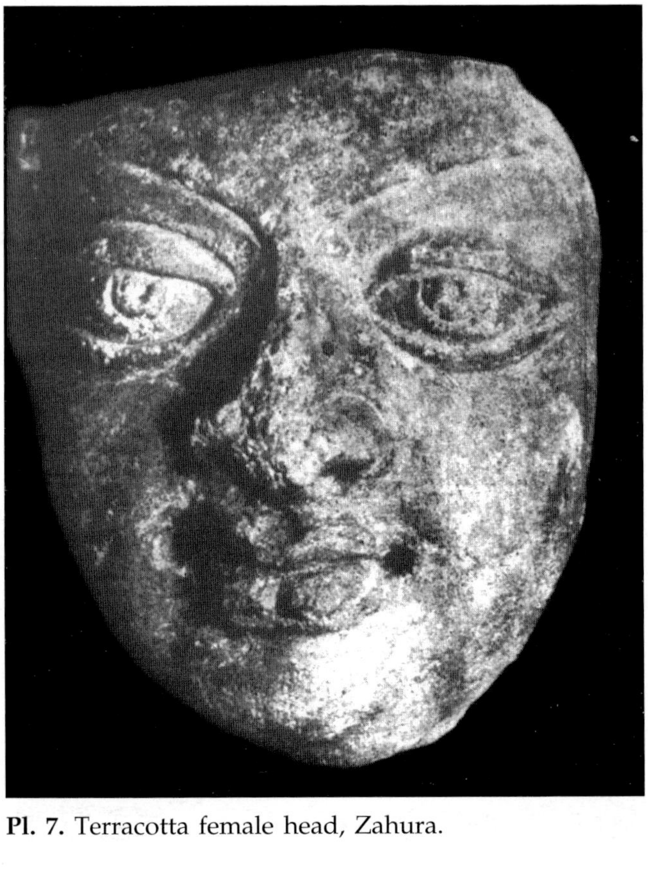

**Pl. 7.** Terracotta female head, Zahura.

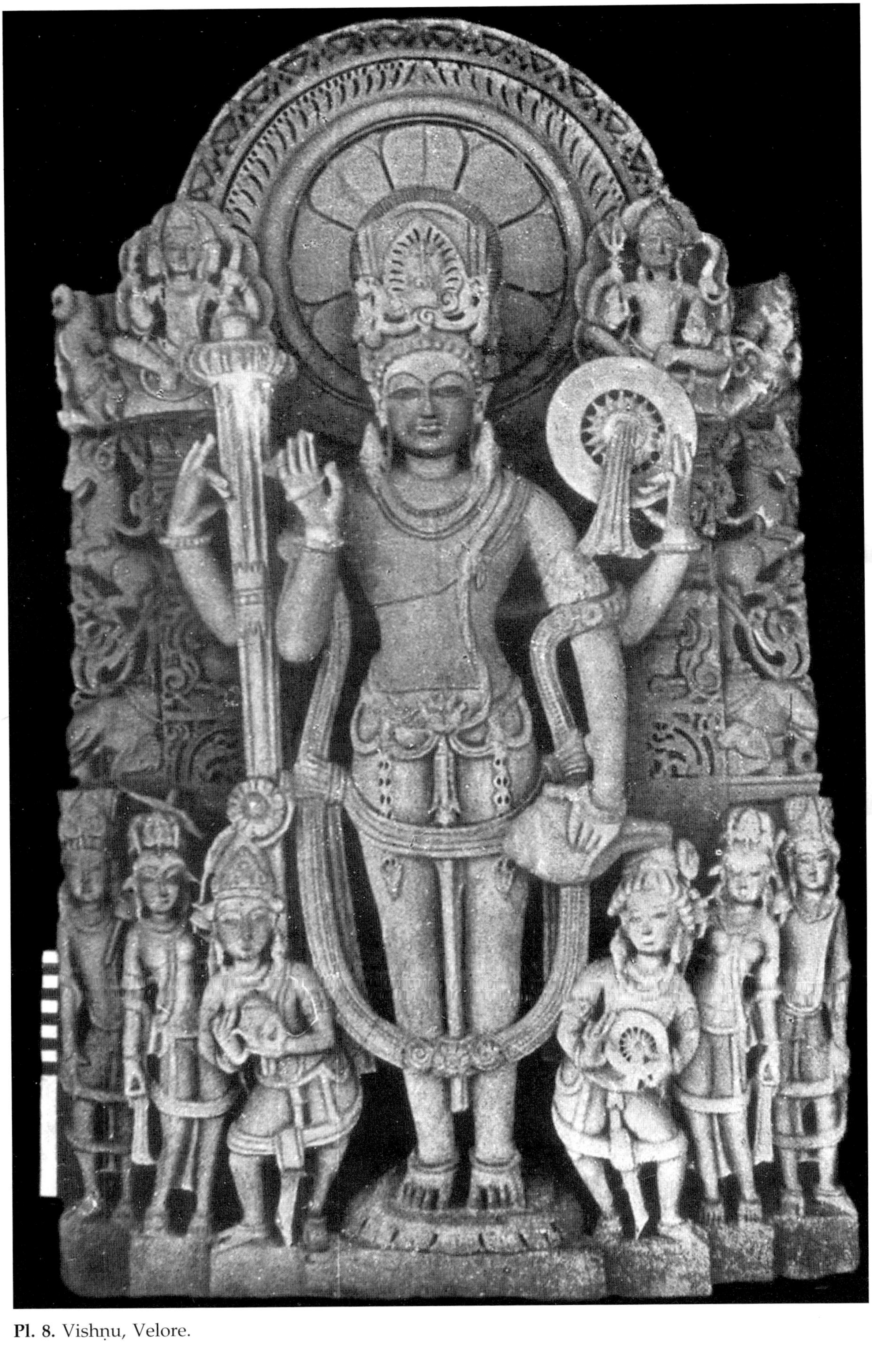

**Pl. 8.** Vishṇu, Velore.

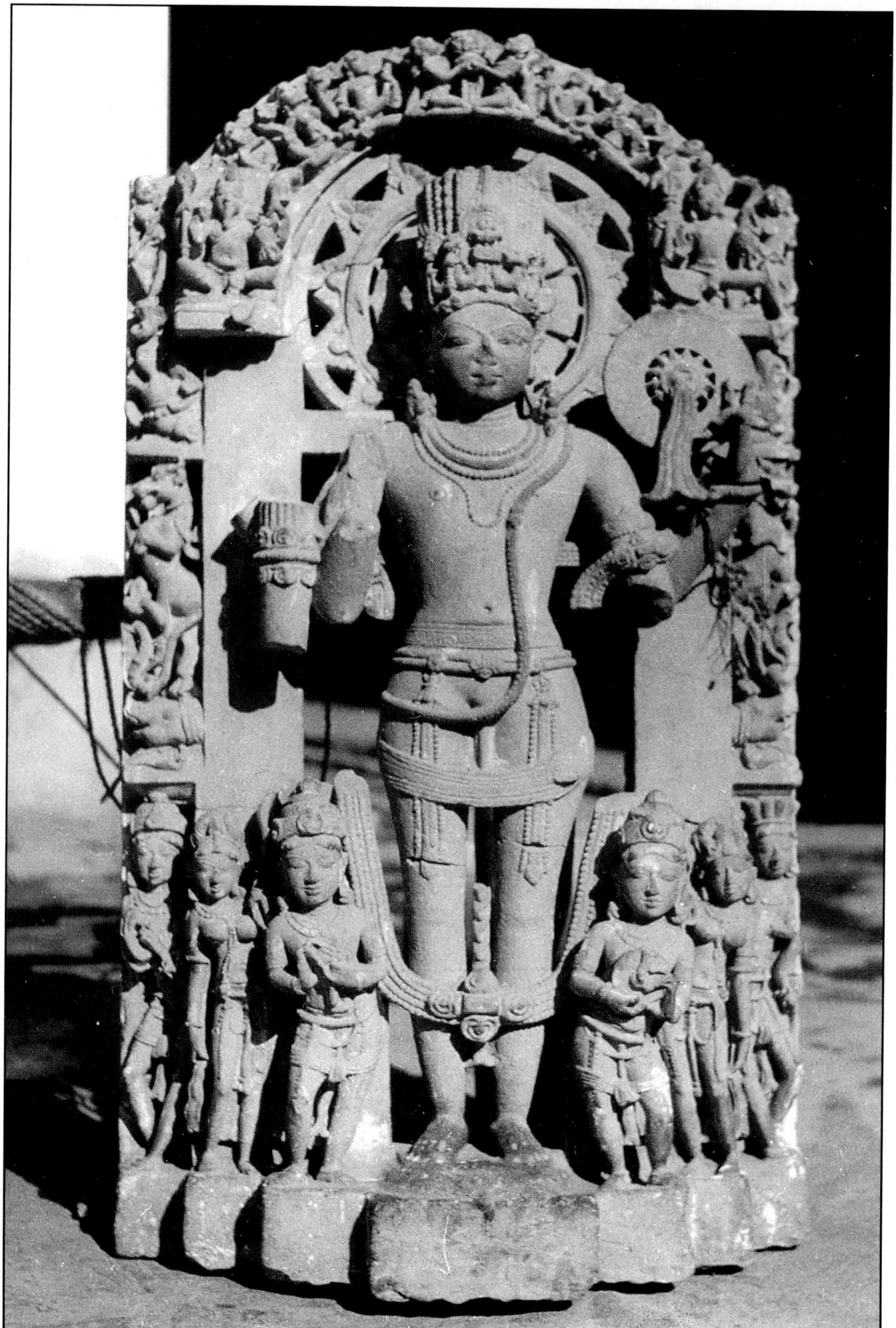

**Pl. 9.** Vishṇu, Khanpur.

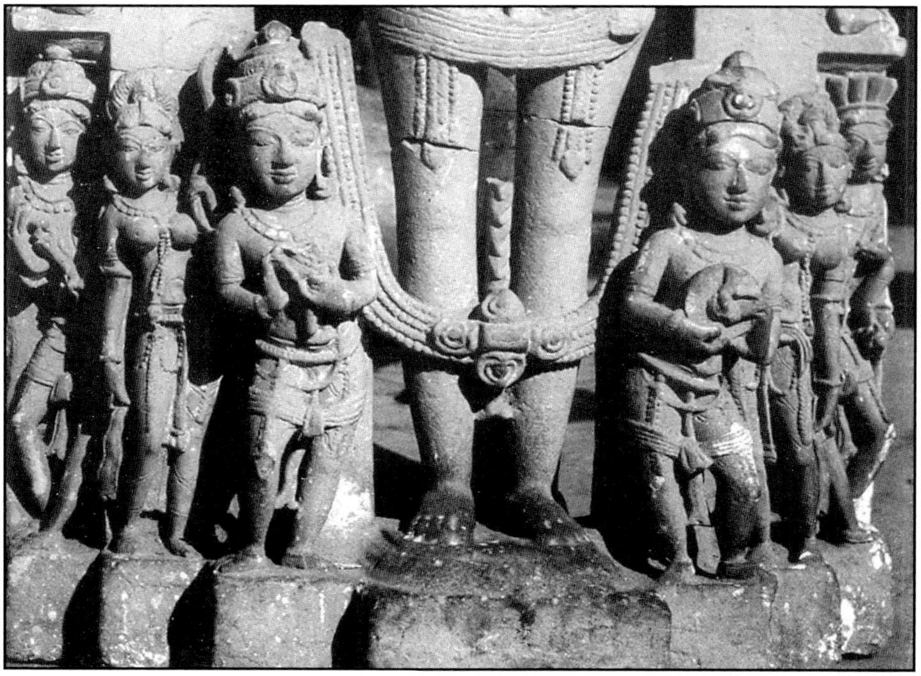

**Pl. 10.** Same, details of the pedestal.

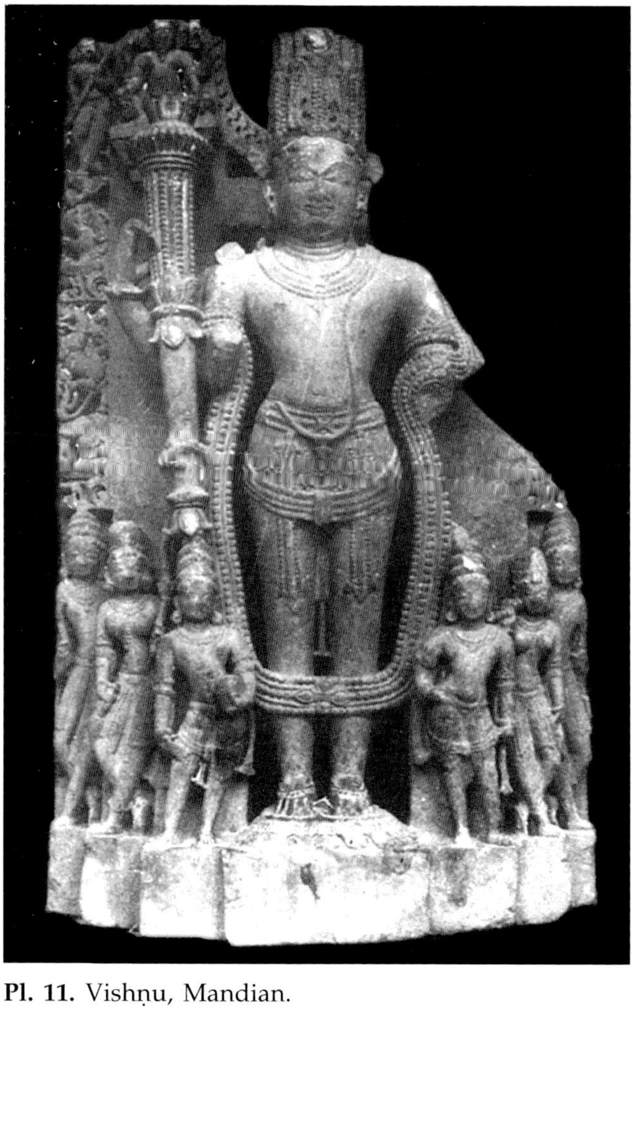

**Pl. 11.** Vishṇu, Mandian.

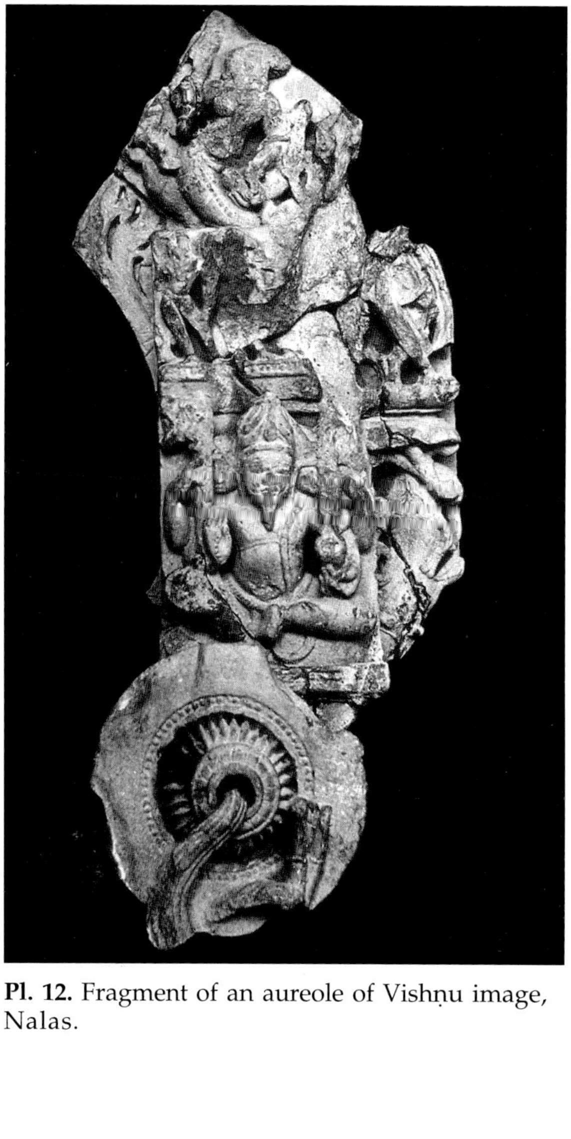

**Pl. 12.** Fragment of an aureole of Vishṇu image, Nalas.

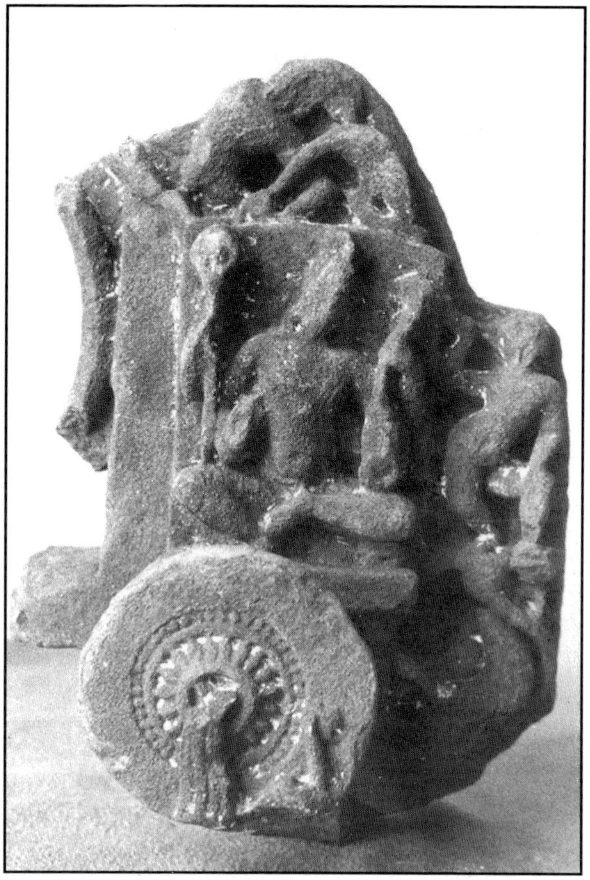

**Pl. 13.** Stele with *Chakra*, Kharar.

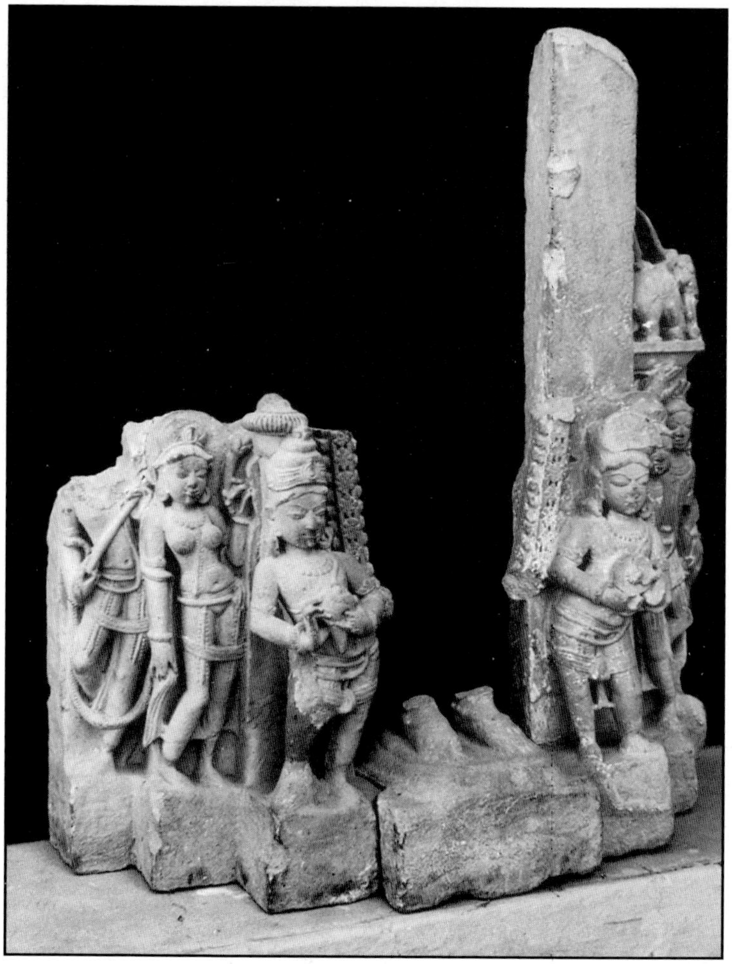

**Pl. 14.** Pedestal of an image of Vishṇu, Khanpur.

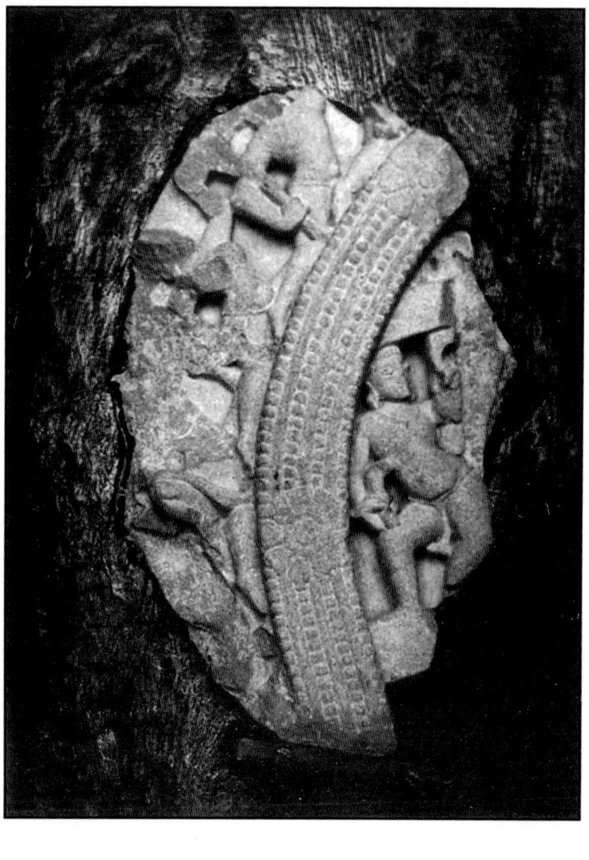

**Pl. 15.** Fragment of the halo of a Vishṇu image, Kharar.

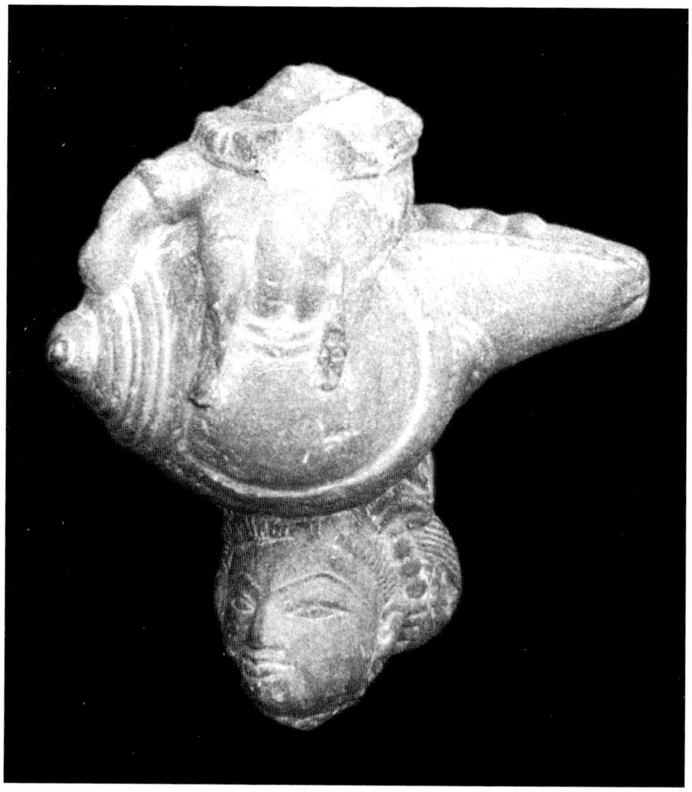

**Pl. 16.** Vishṇu's hand holding conch, Khanpur.

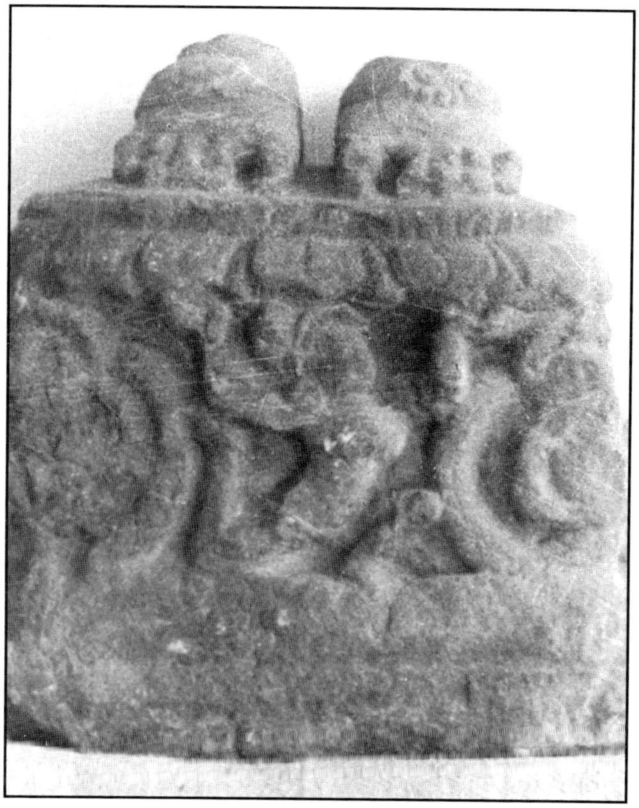

**Pl. 18.** Fragmentary pedestal showing Vishṇu's feet, Kharar.

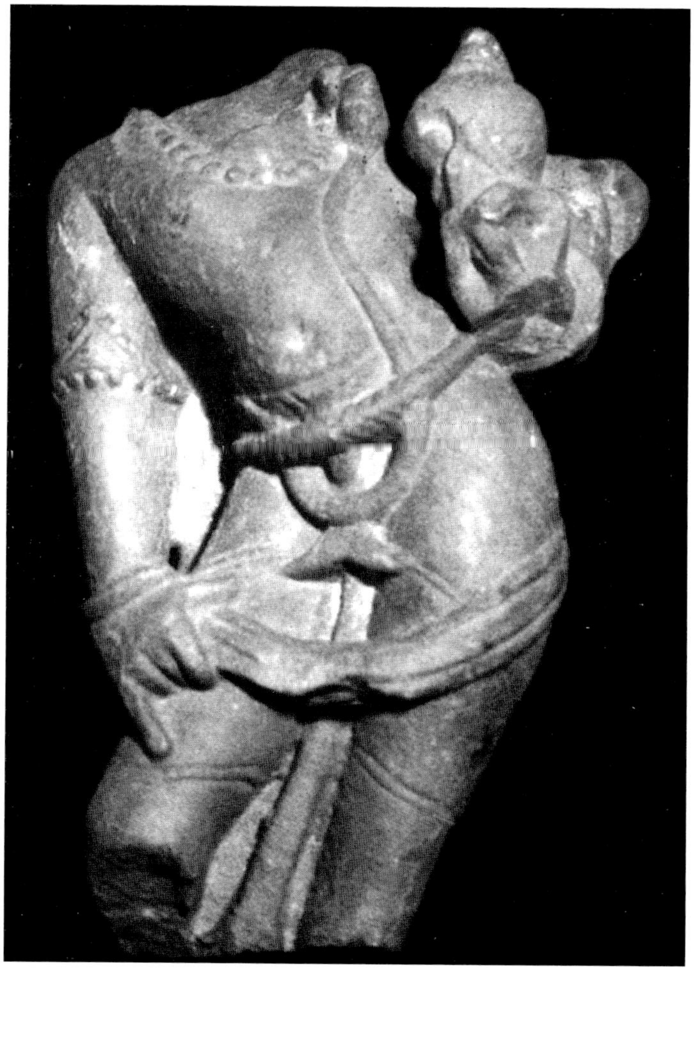

**Pl. 17.** Śaṅkha-purusha, Majhur.

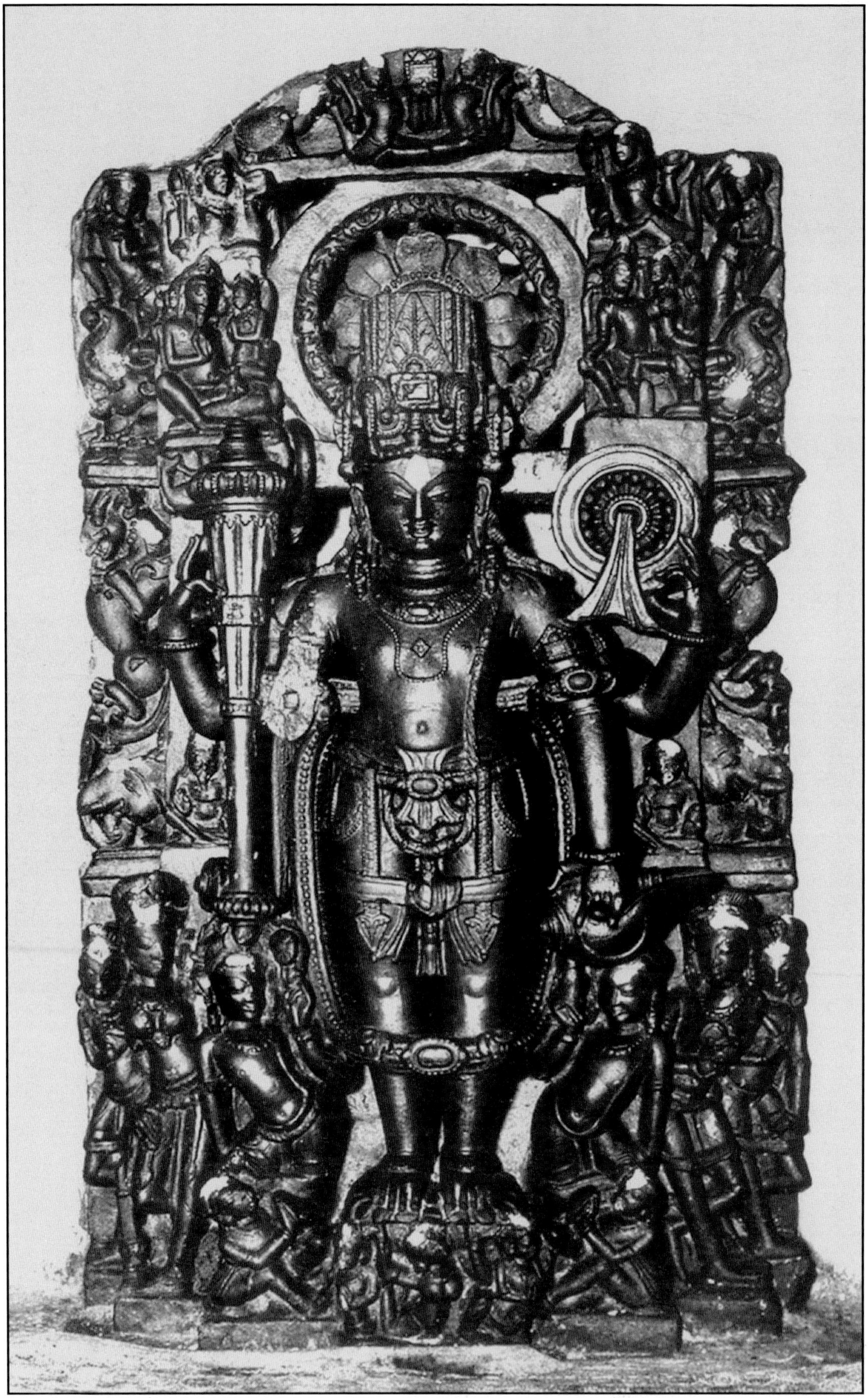

**Pl. 19.** Vishṇu, Janer.

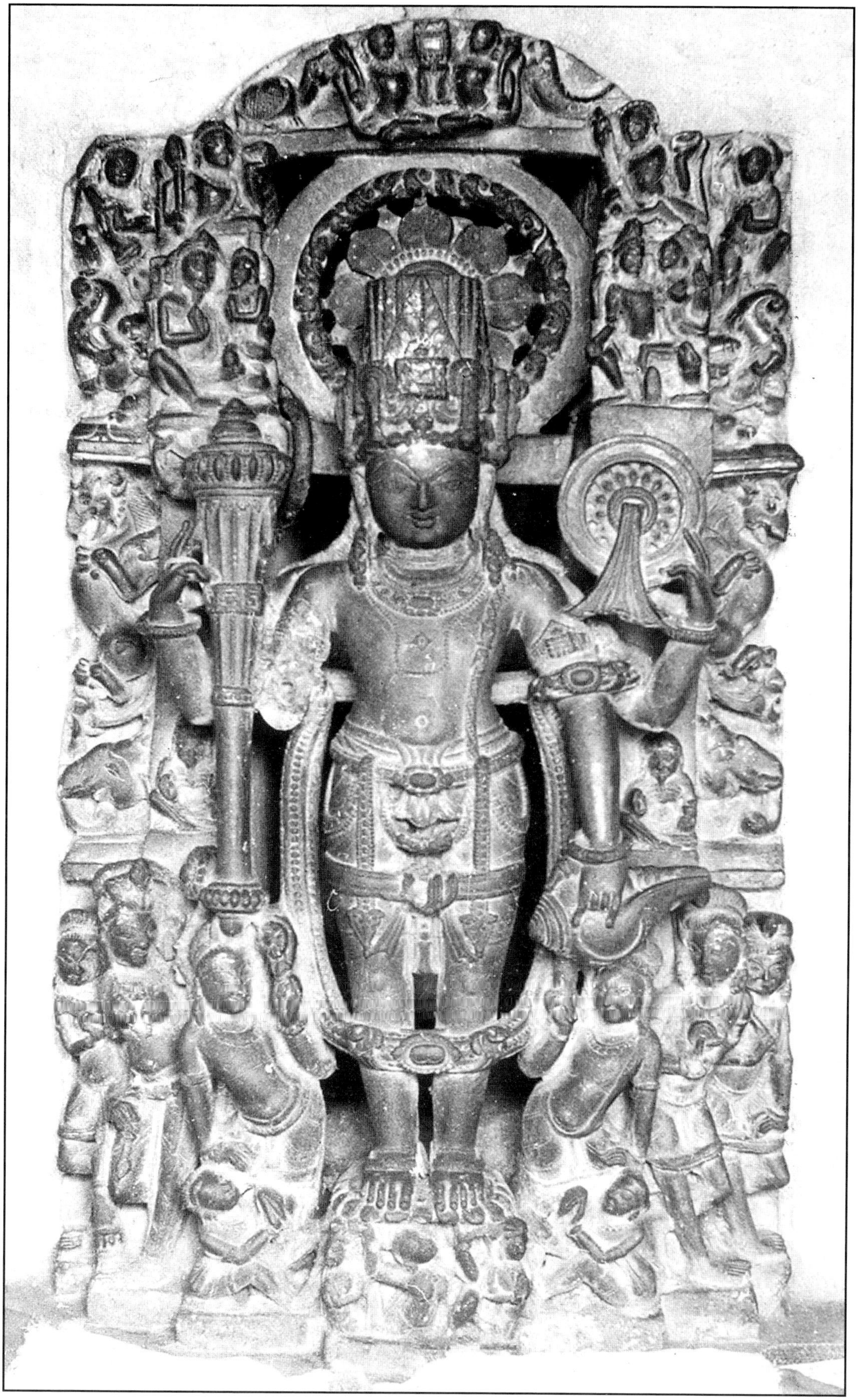

**Pl. 20.** Same, before treatment.

**Pl. 22.** Bust of Vishṇu, Dholbaha.

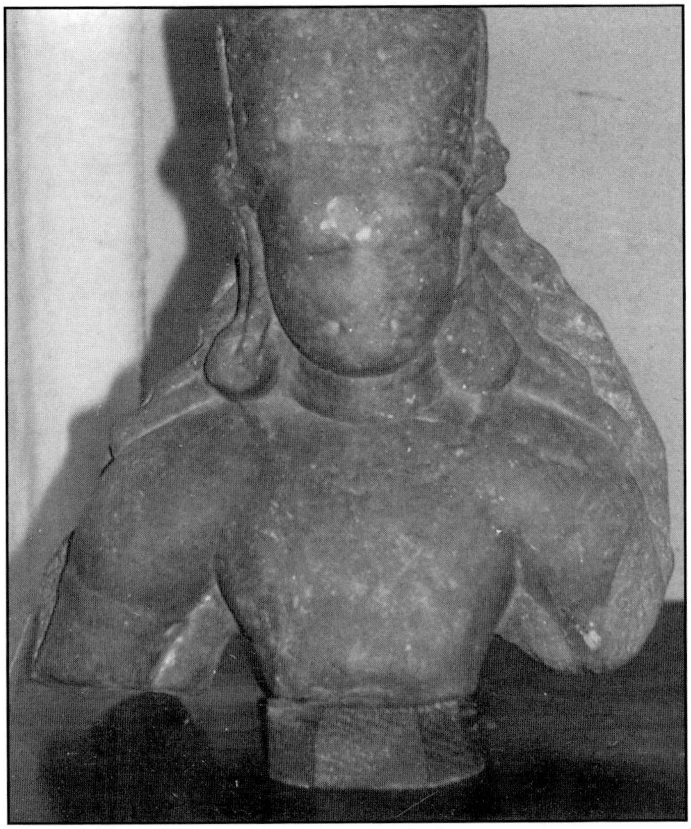

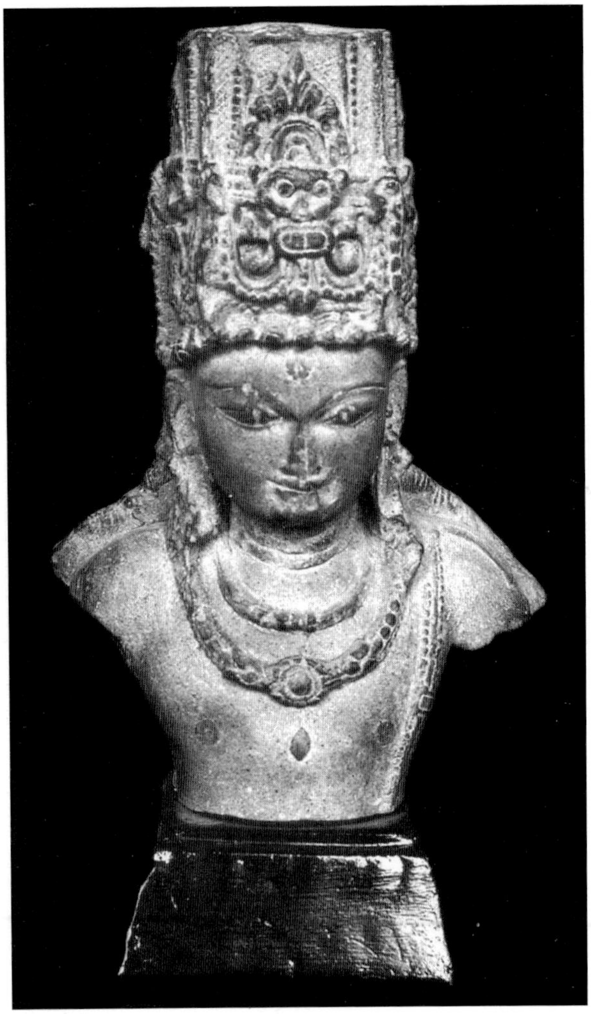

**Pl. 21.** Bust of Vishṇu, Majhur.

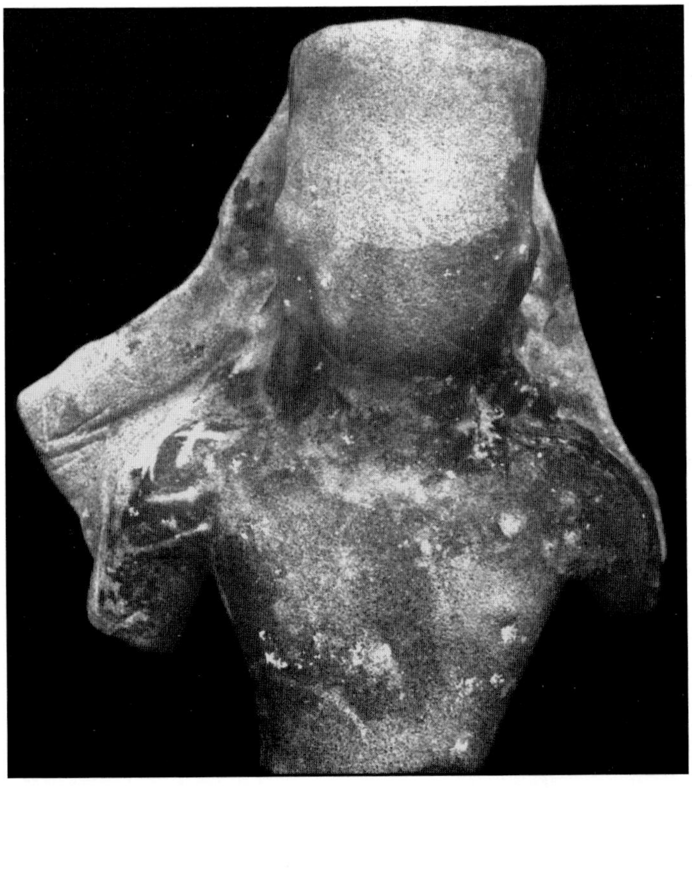

**Pl. 23.** Bust of Vishṇu, Dholbaha.

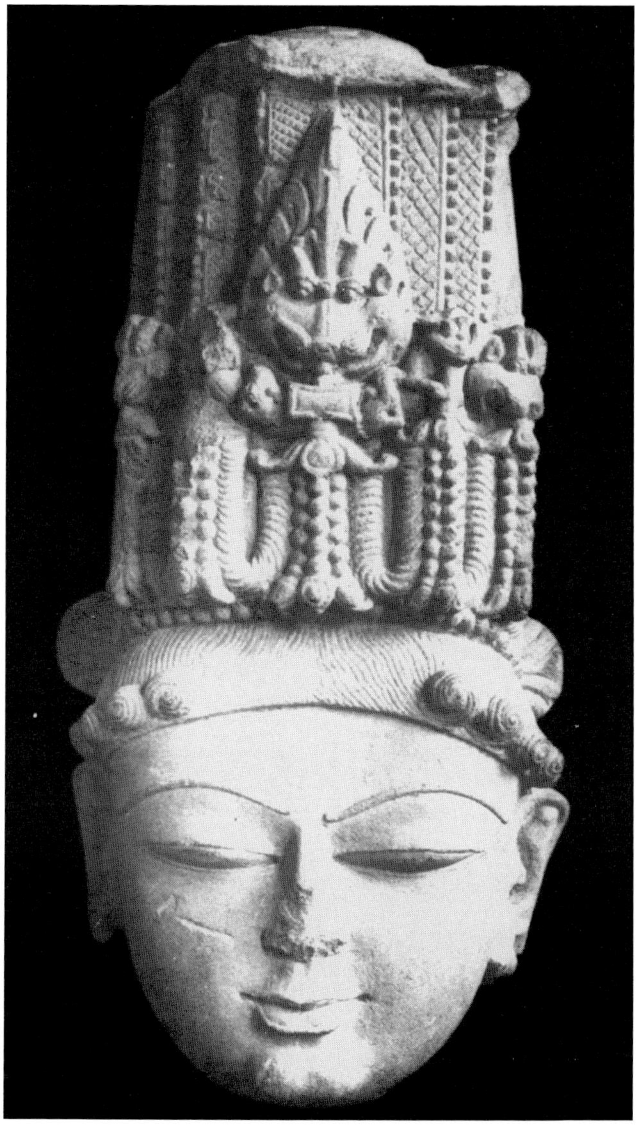

**Pl. 24.** Head of Vishṇu, Dholbaha.

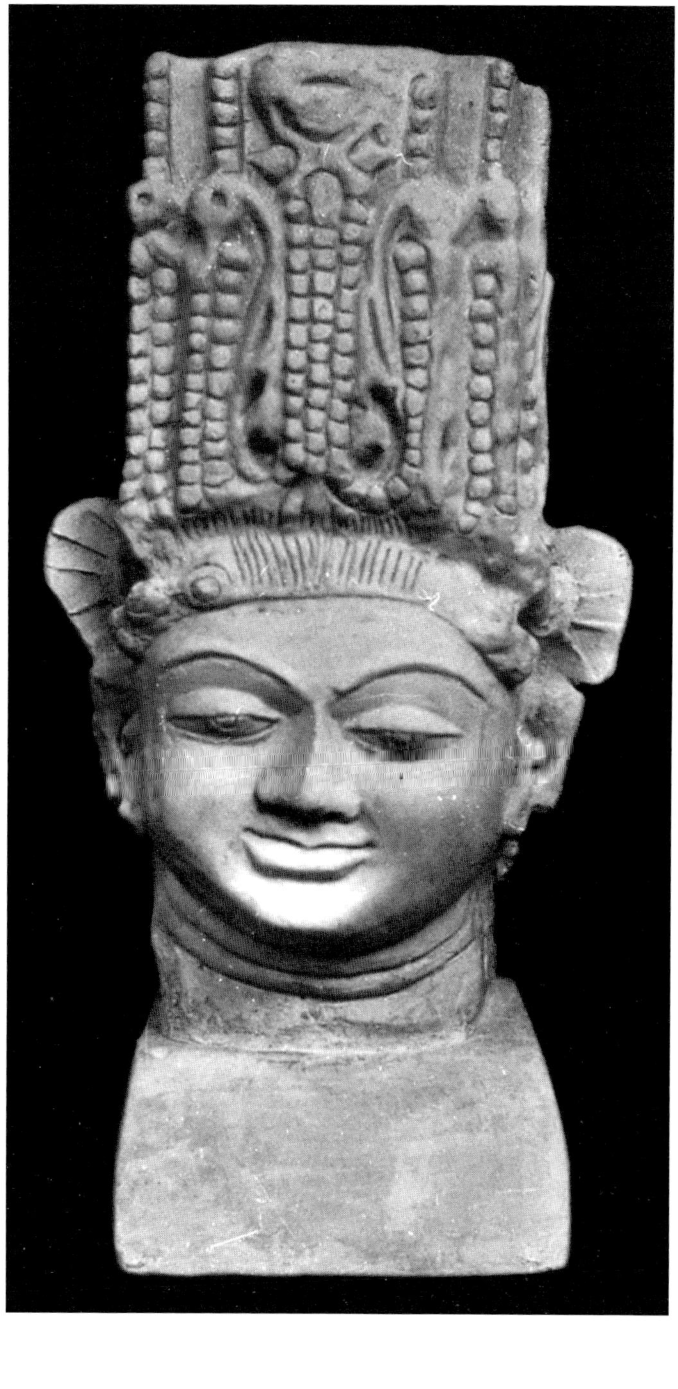

**Pl. 25.** Head of Vishṇu, Dholbaha.

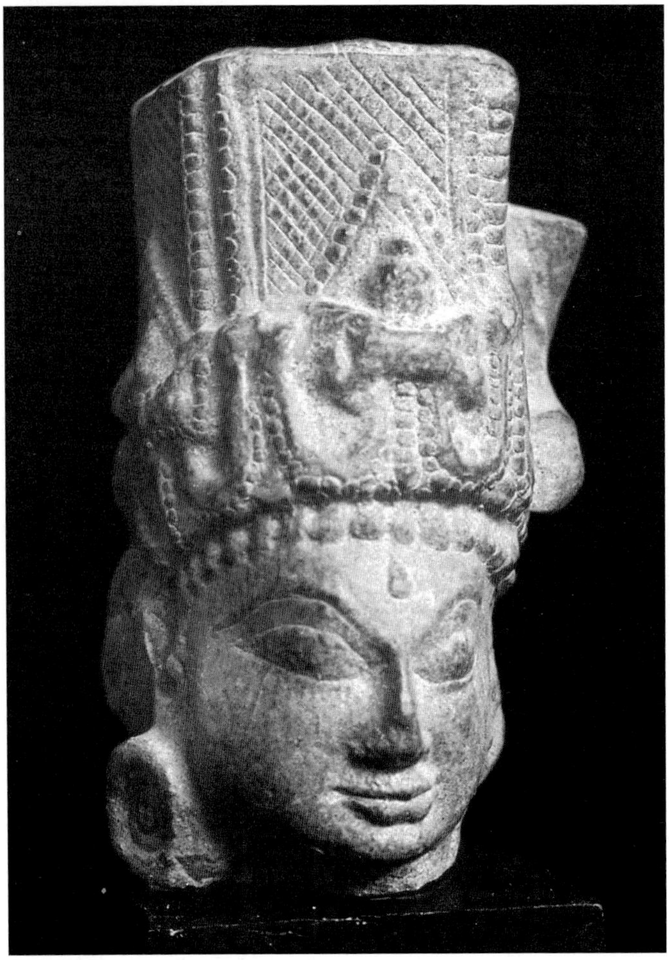

**Pl. 26.** Head of Vishṇu, Dholbaha.

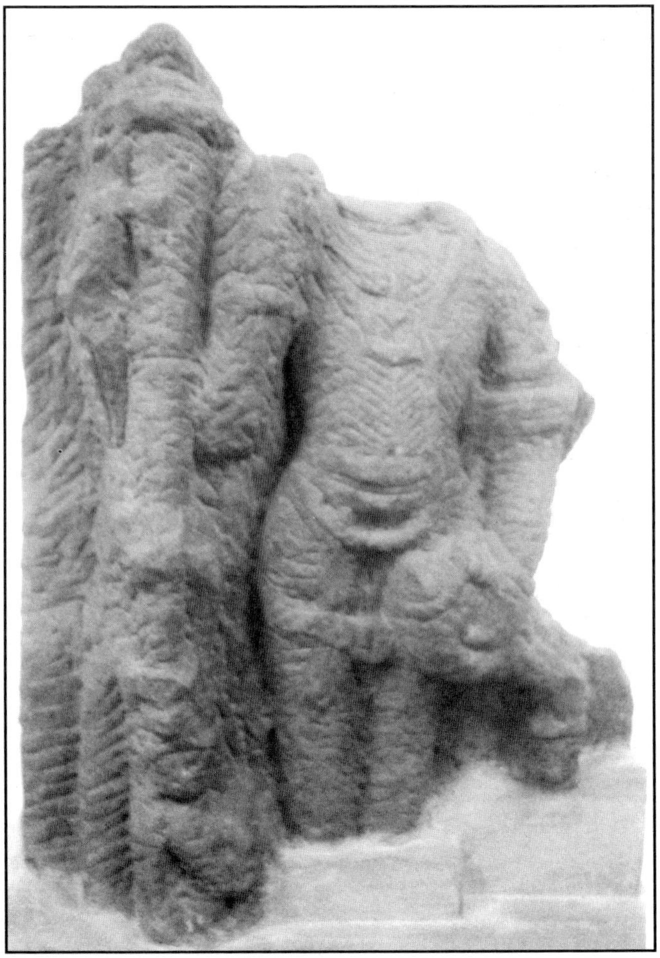

**Pl. 27.** Unfinished image of Vishṇu, Dholbaha.

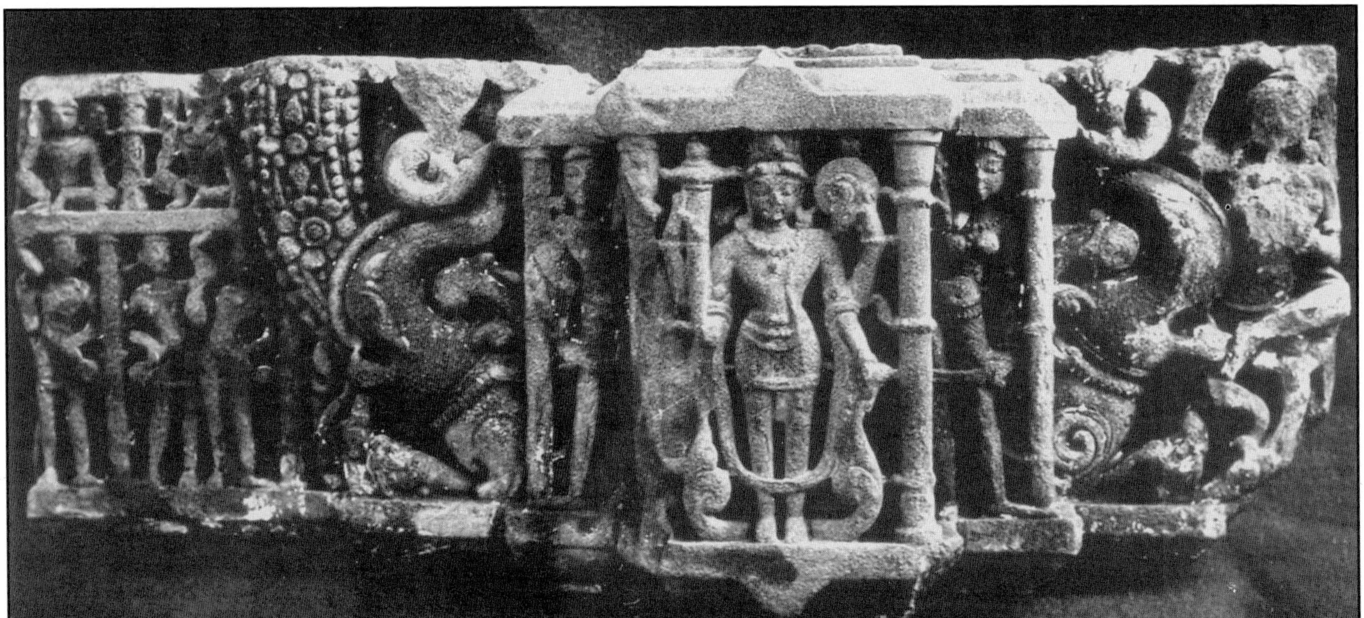

**Pl. 28.** Frieze showing standing Vishṇu, Dholbaha.

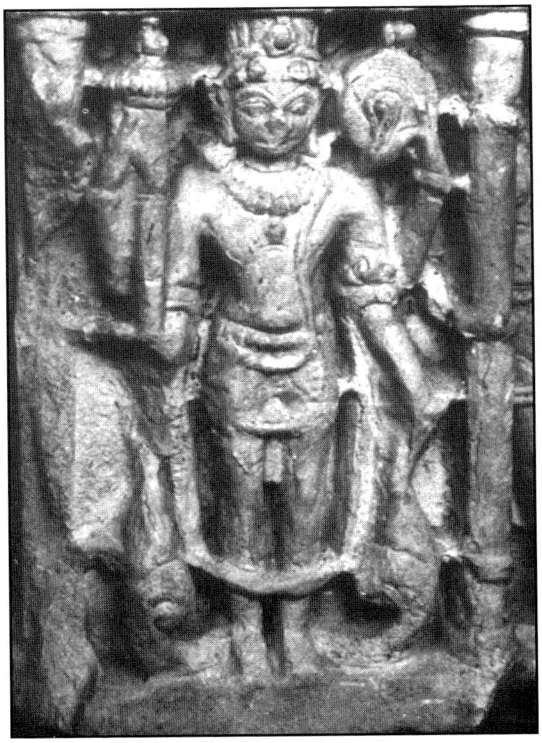

**Pl. 29.** Same, details of the Vishṇu image.

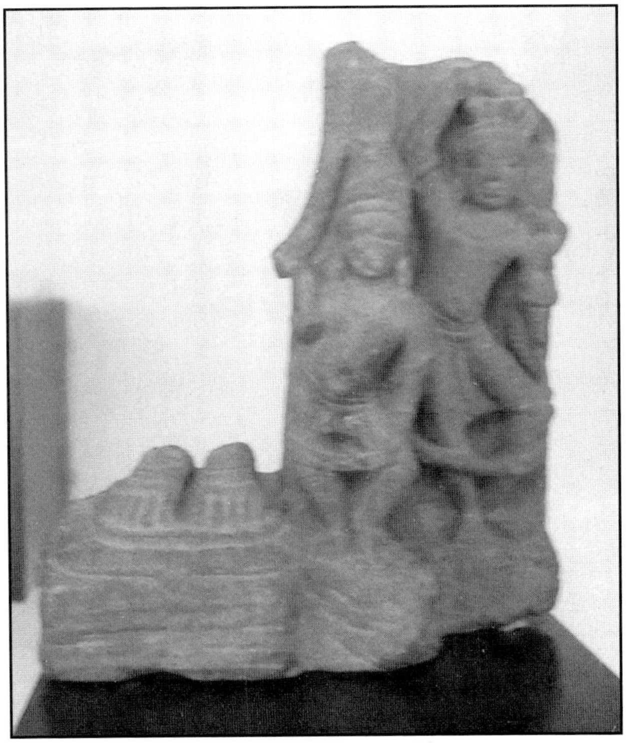

**Pl. 30.** Pedestal of an image of Vishṇu showing attendant figures, Dholbaha.

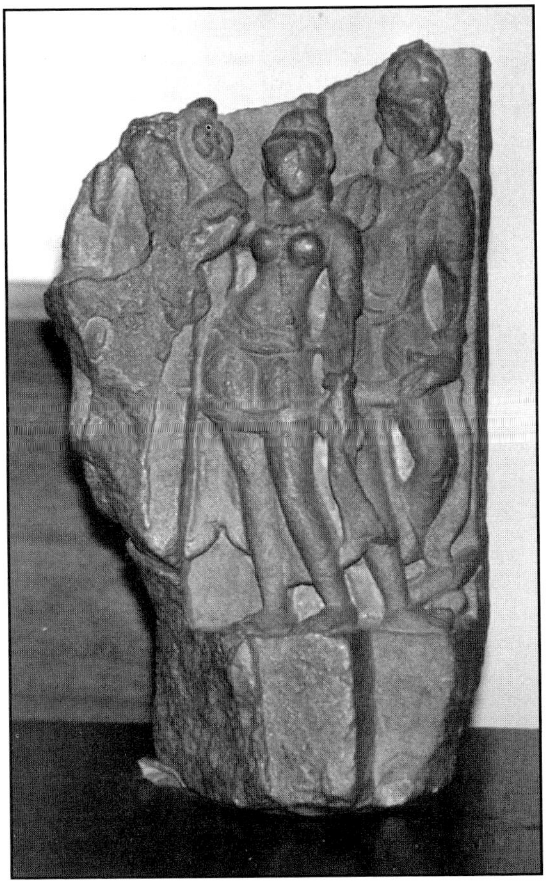

**Pl. 31.** Fragmentary pedestal showing Vaishṇava acolytes, Dholbaha.

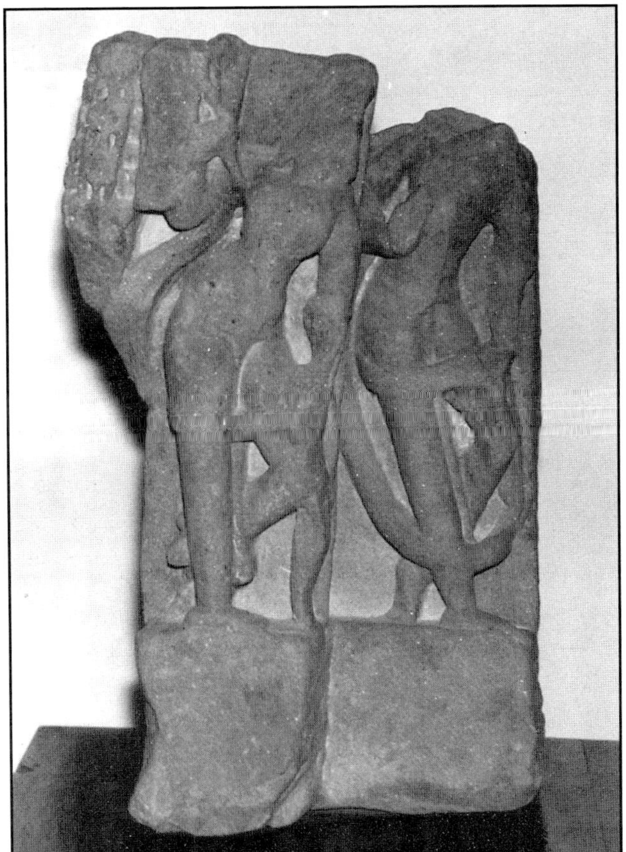

**Pl. 32.** Another fragment, Dholbaha.

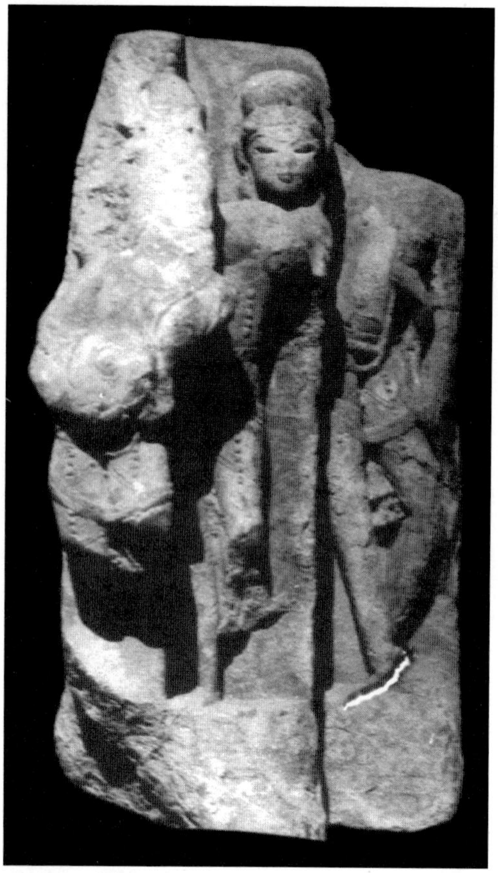

**Pl. 33.** Chakra-purusha and other acolytes, Dholbaha.

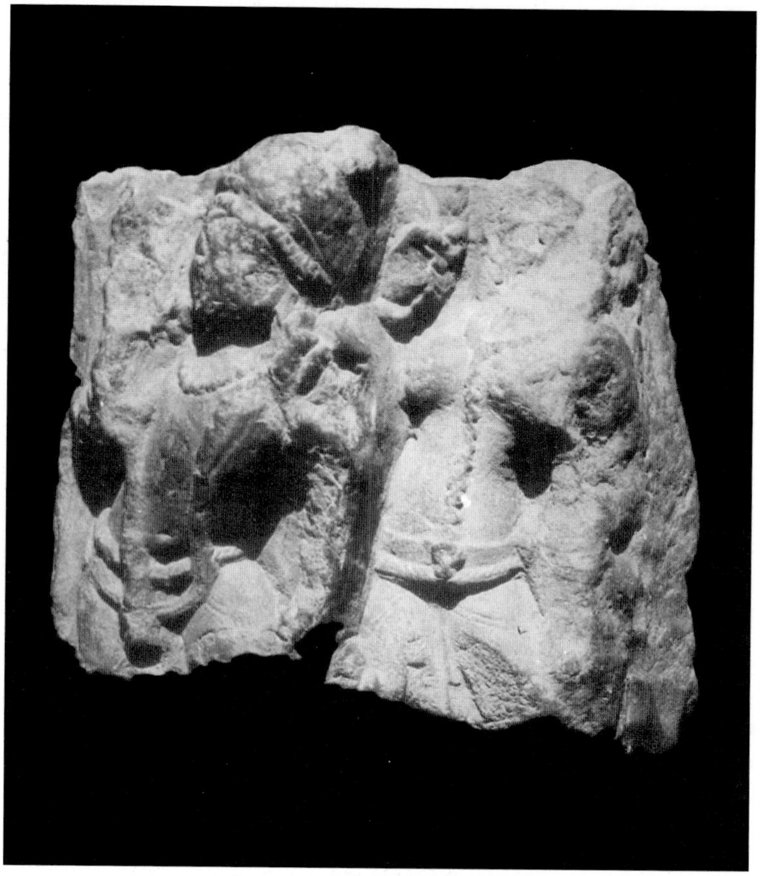

**Pl. 34.** Fragment of a pedestal, Dholbaha.

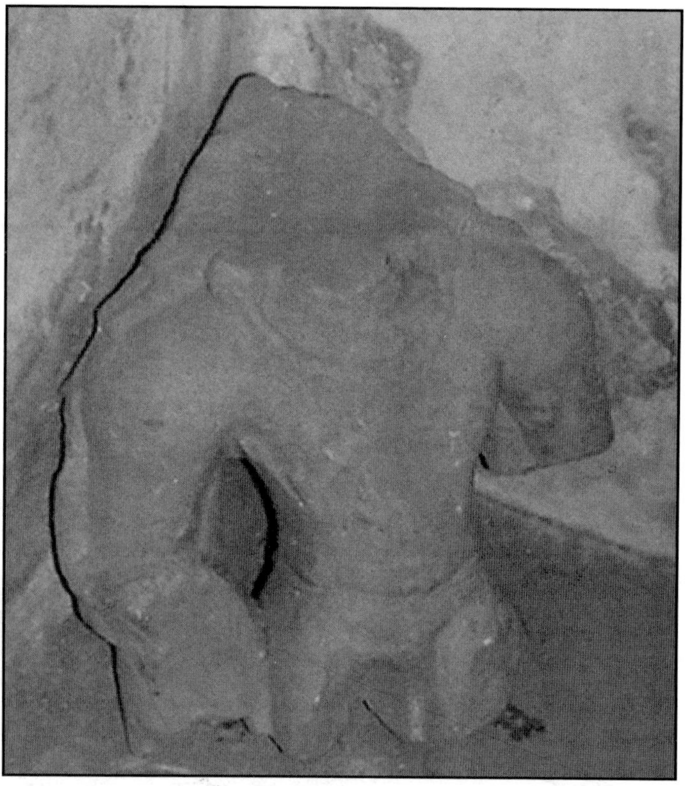

**Pl. 35.** Fragmentary bust, Dholbaha.

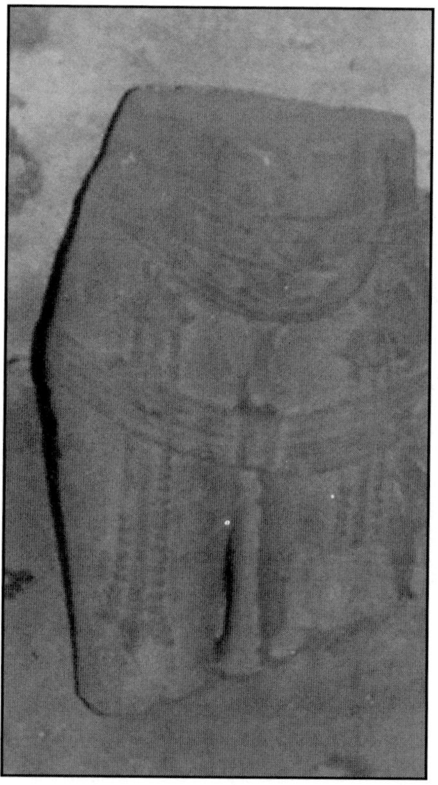

**Pl. 36.** Fragmentary image, Dholbaha.

**Pl. 38.** Attendant figures, Mandian.

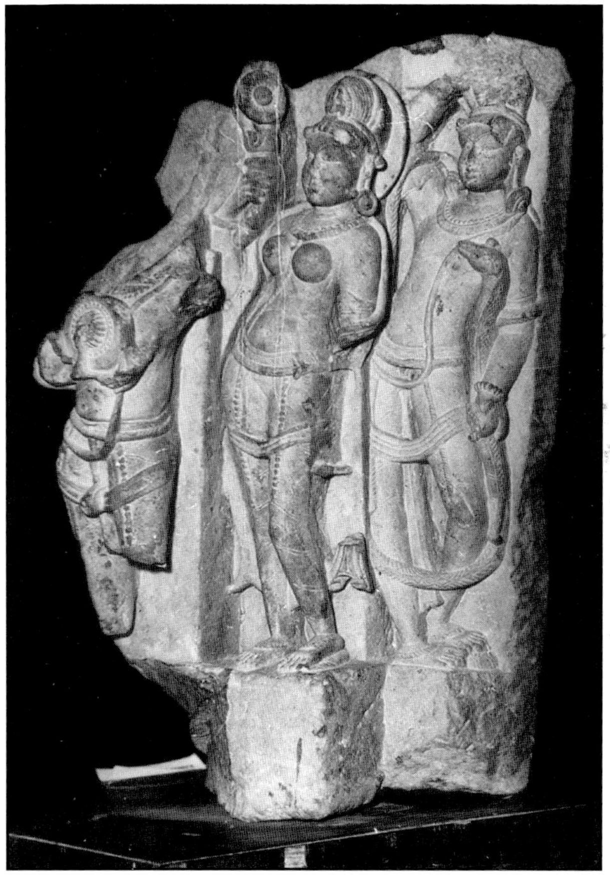

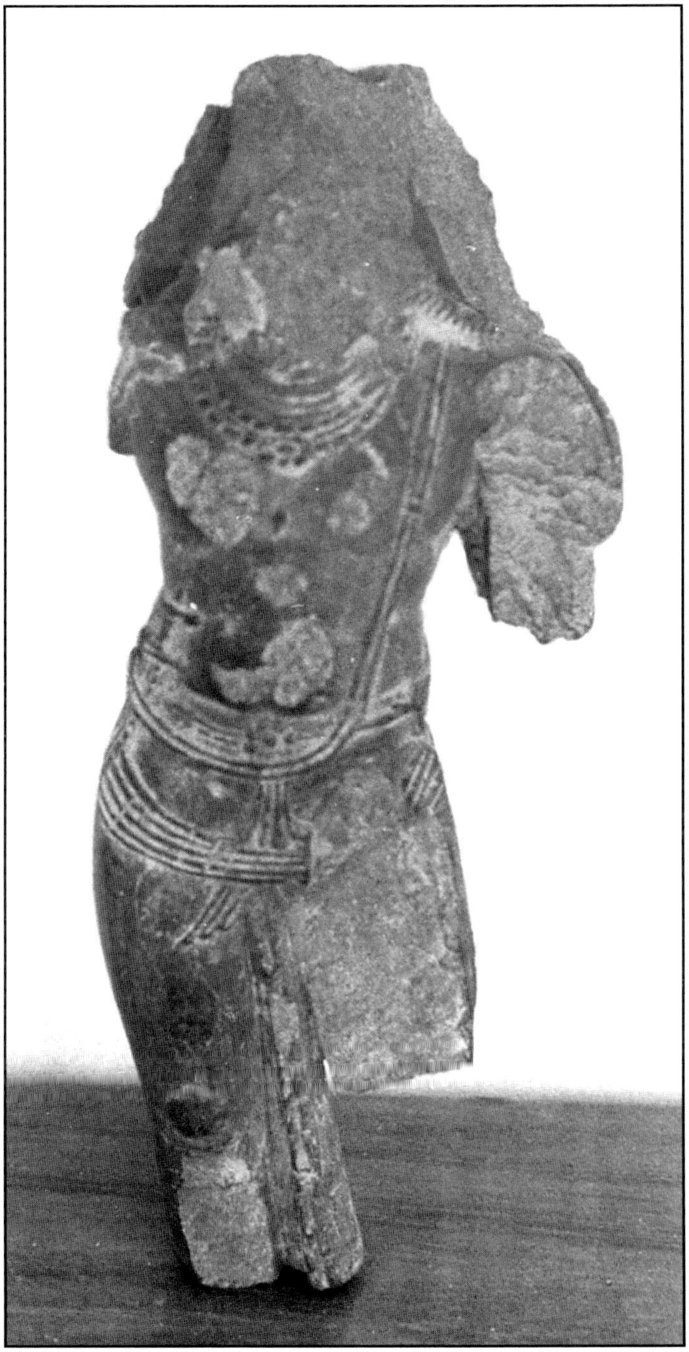

**Pl. 37.** Image of Vishṇu, Singh-Bhagwantpur.

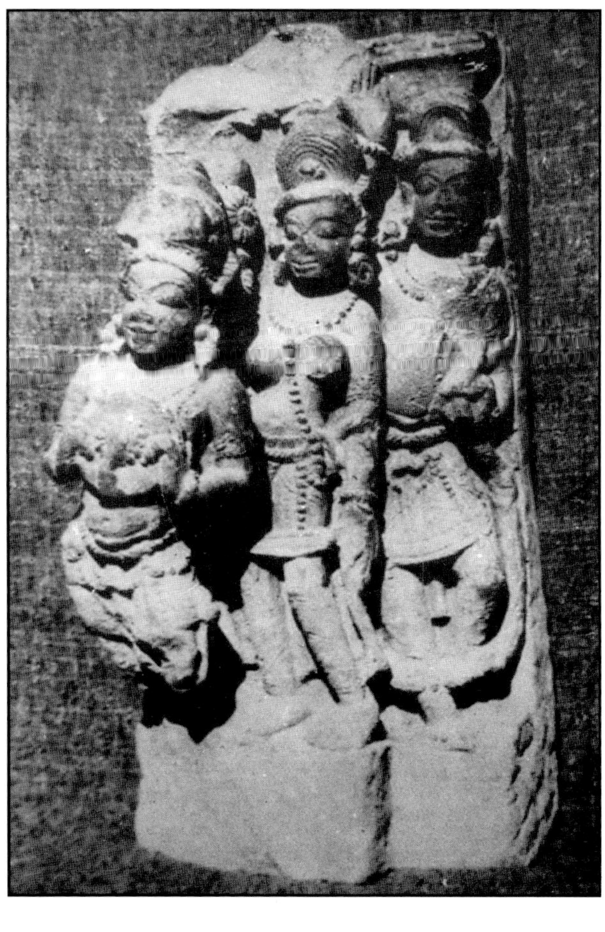

**Pl. 39.** Attendant figures, Sunam.

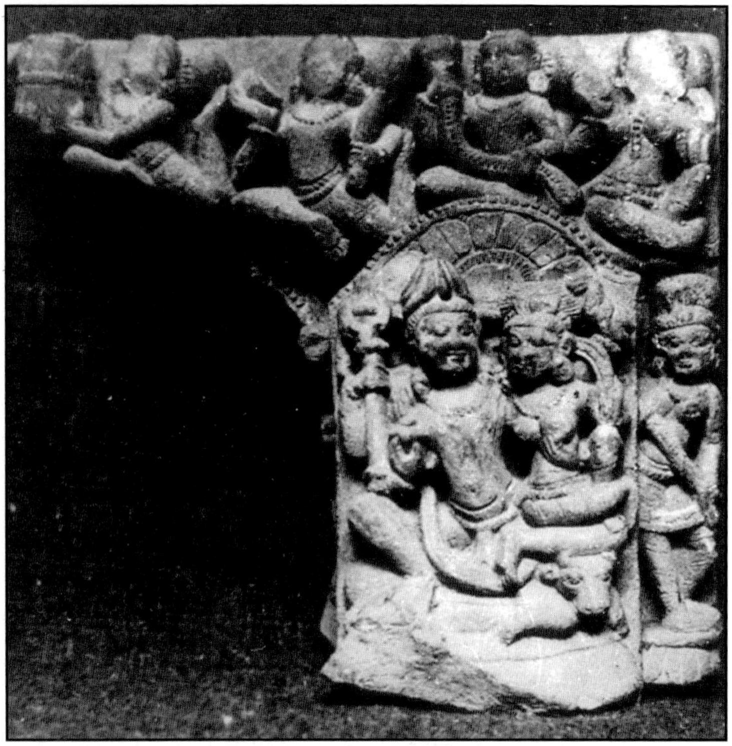

**Pl. 40.** Stele showing Umā-Maheśvara, Sunam.

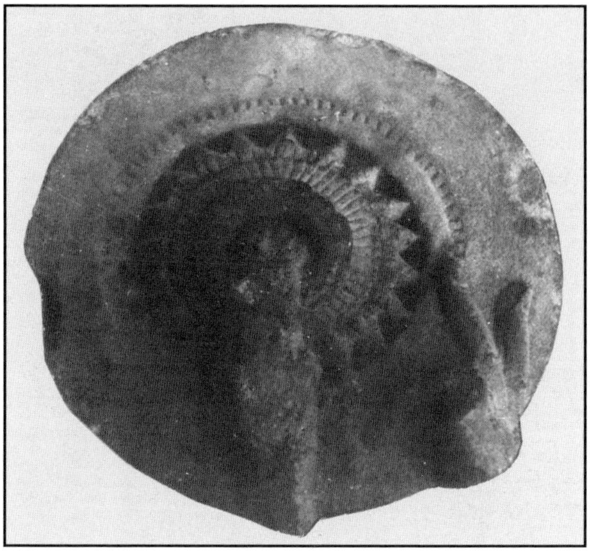

**Pl. 42.** *Chakra*, Sunam.

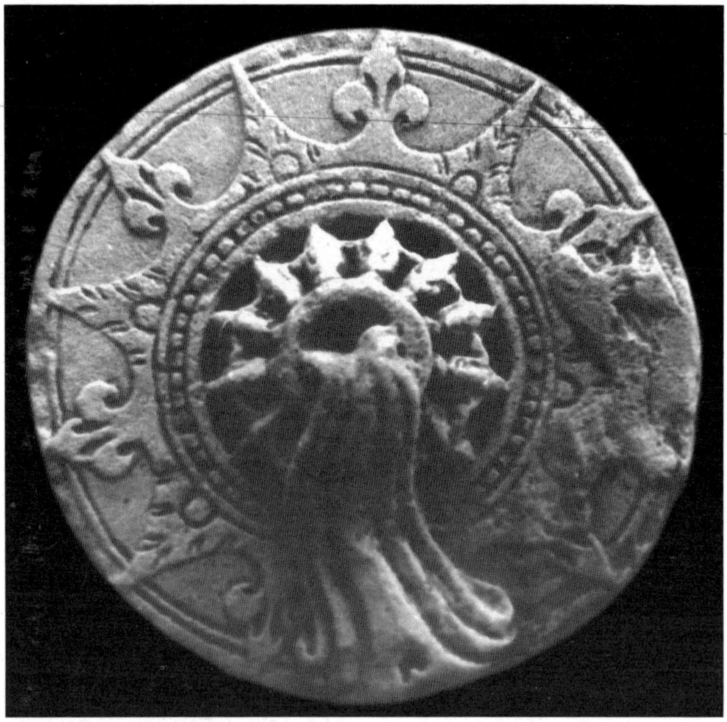

**Pl. 41.** *Chakra* detached from an image of Vishṇu, Sunam.

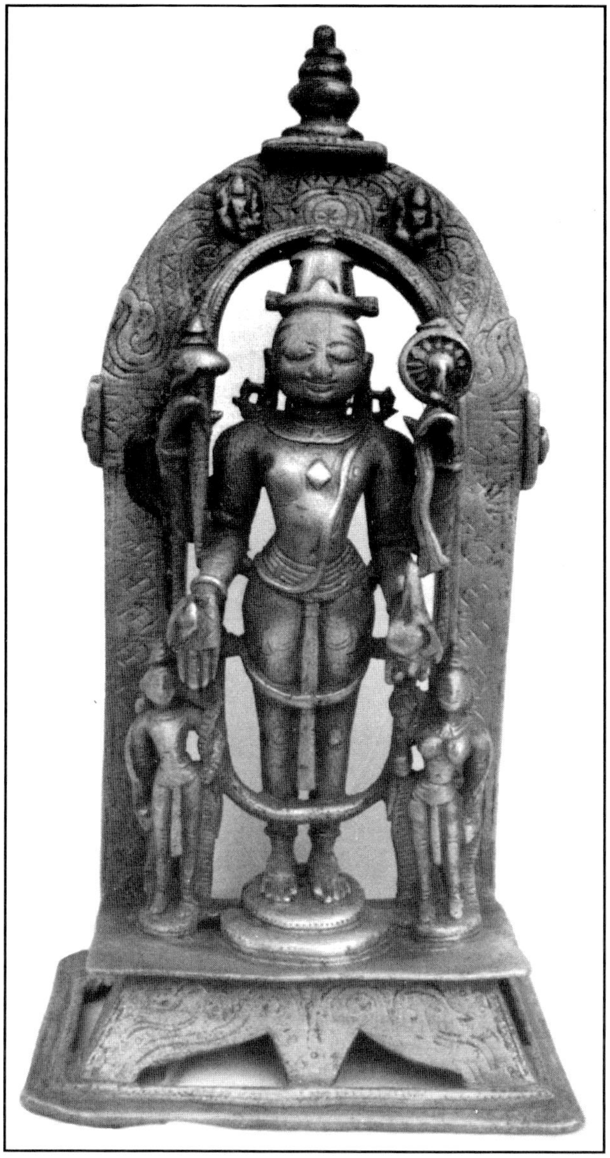

**Pl. 43.** Bronze image of Vishṇu, Sunam.

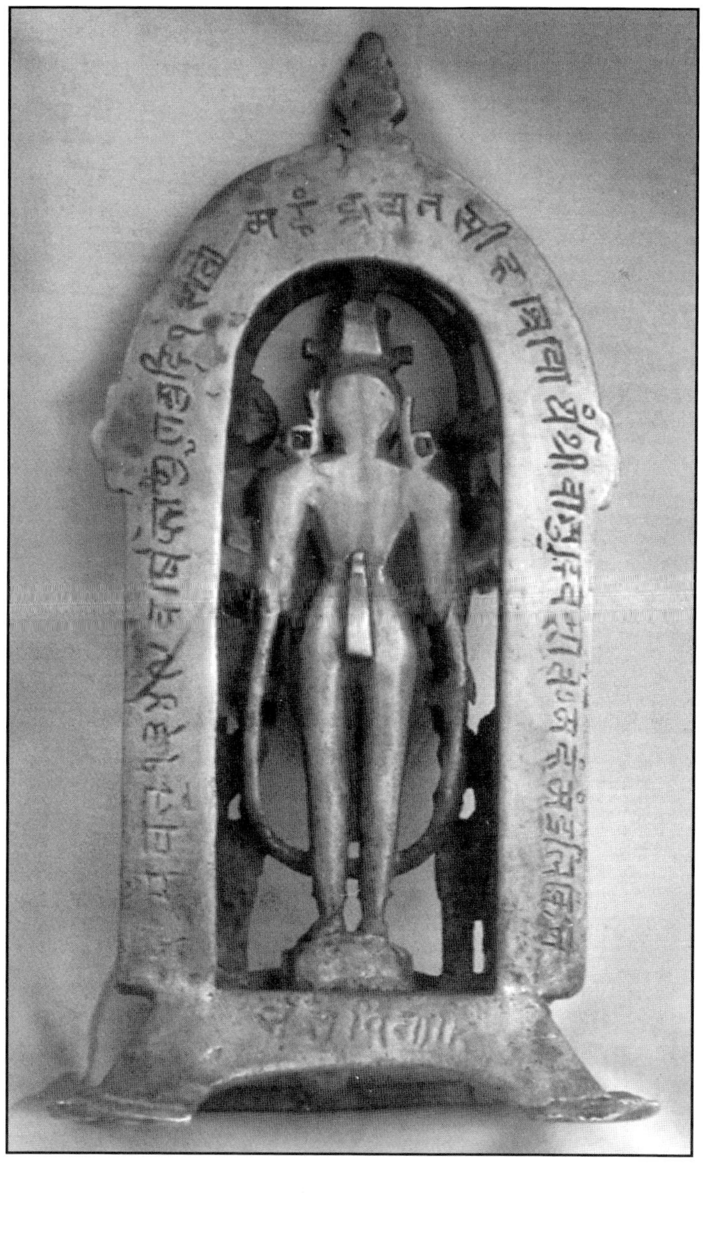

**Pl. 44.** Same, inscribed back portion.

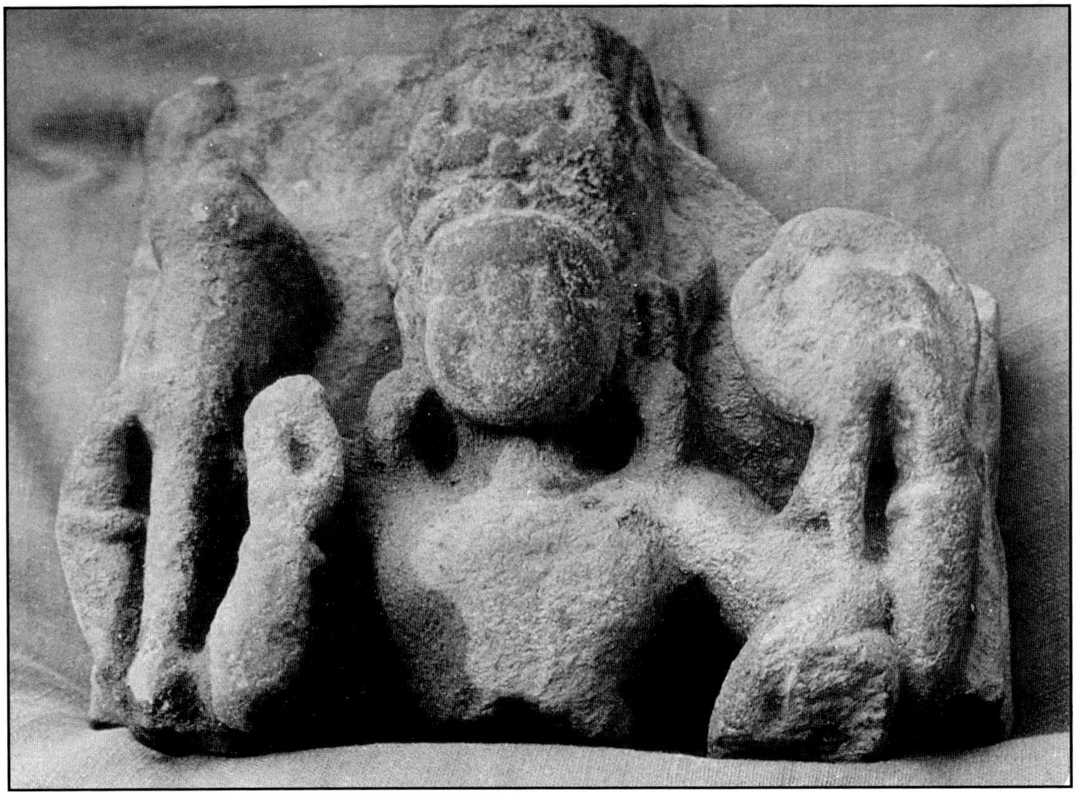

**Pl. 45.** Bust of Vishṇu, Janer.

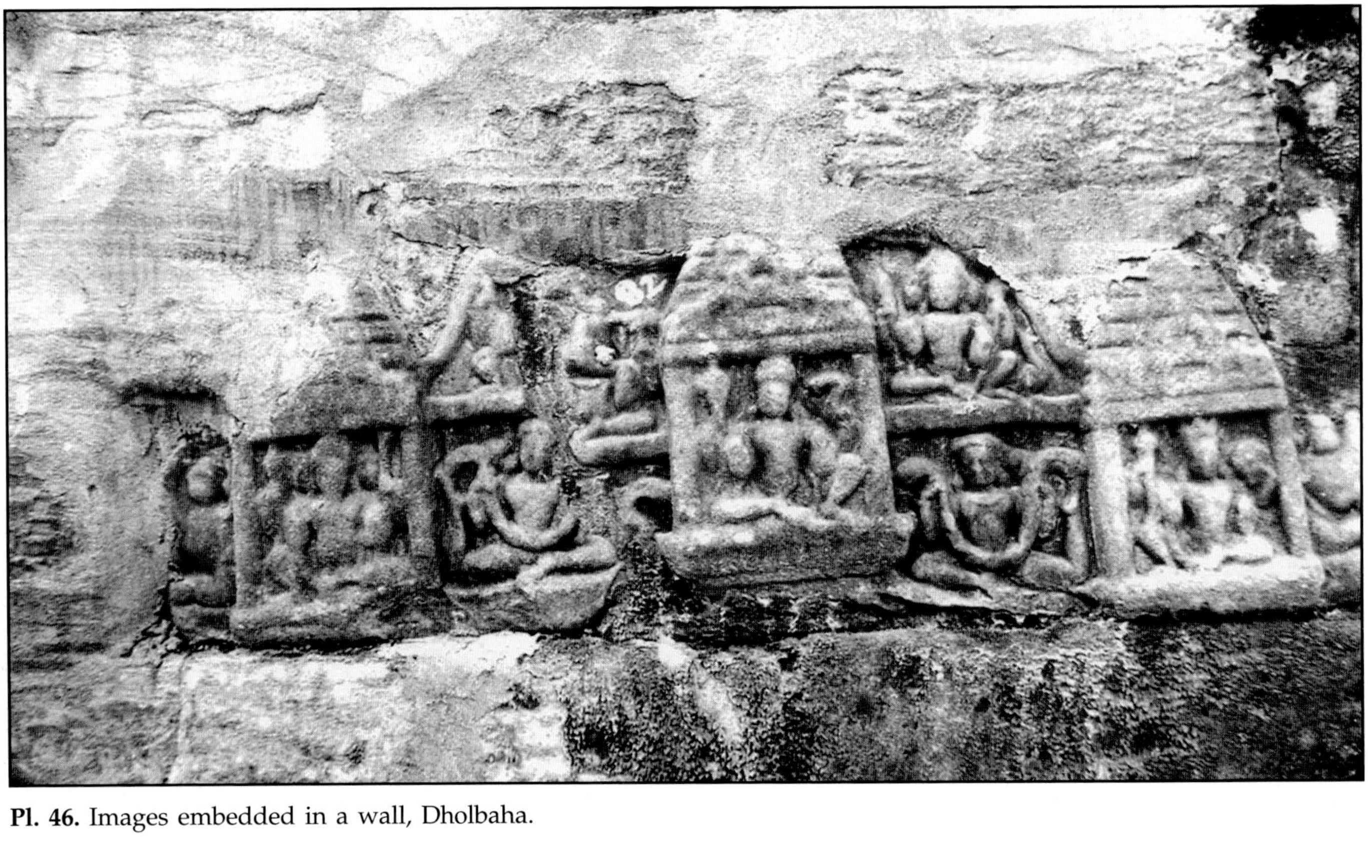

**Pl. 46.** Images embedded in a wall, Dholbaha.

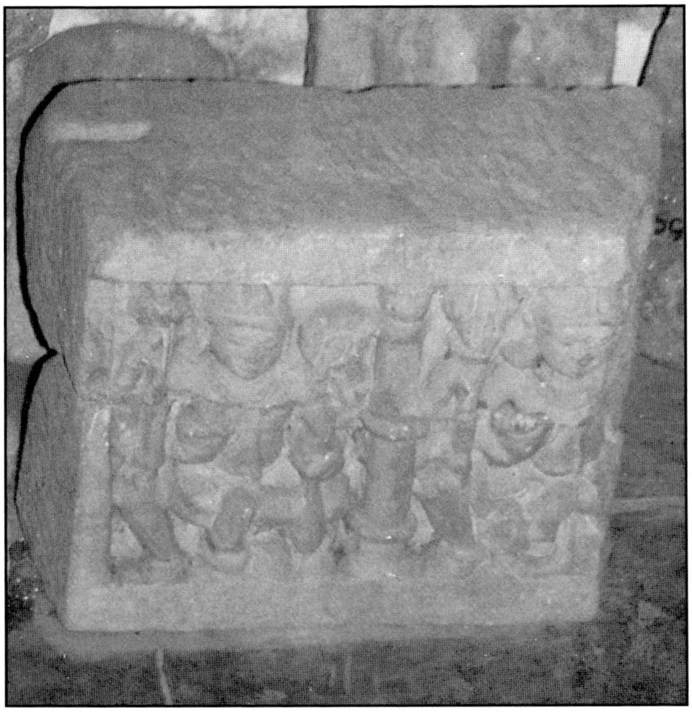

**Pl. 47.** Panel showing seated Vishṇu and Śiva, Dholbaha.

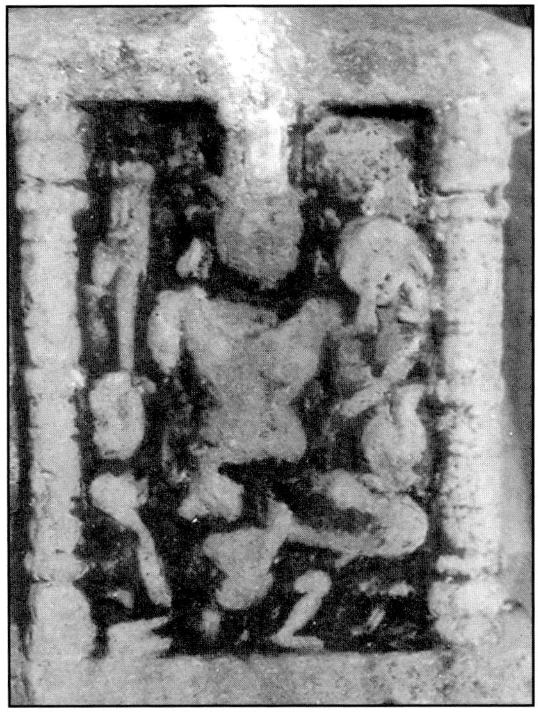

**Pl. 48.** *Garuḍavāhī* Vishṇu, Sunam.

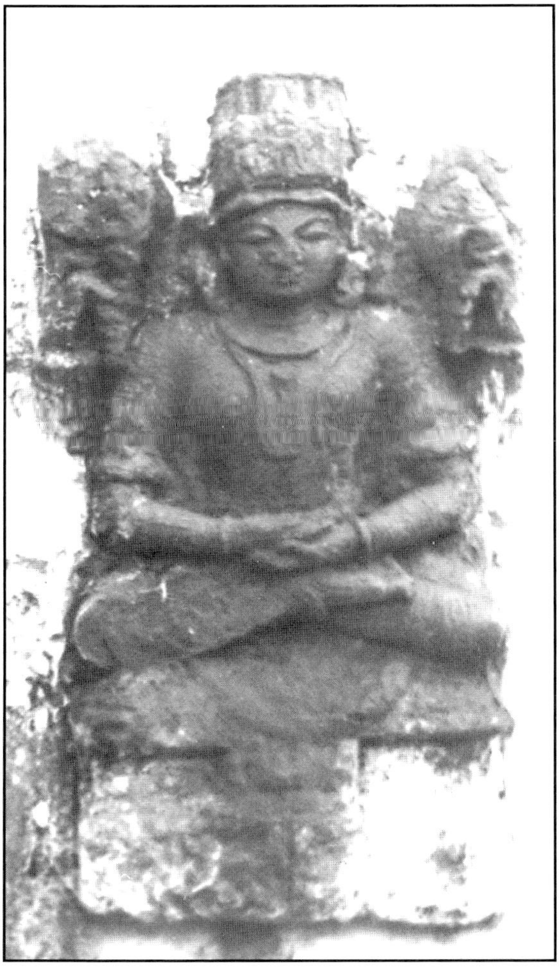

**Pl. 49.** Yoga-Nārāyaṇa, Lalru.

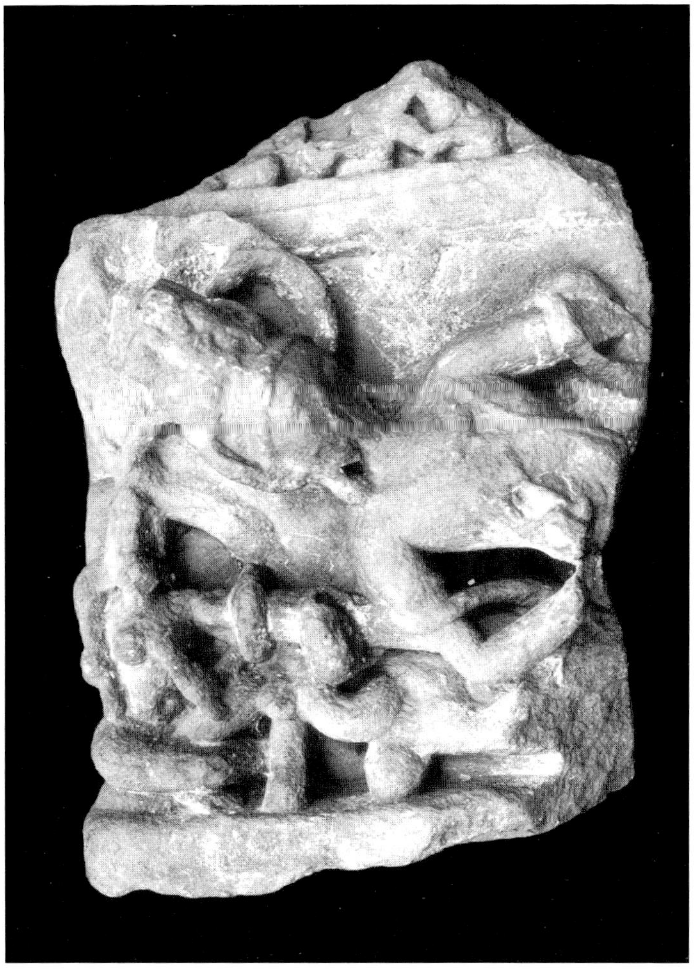

**Pl. 50.** Śeshaśāyī, Kharar.

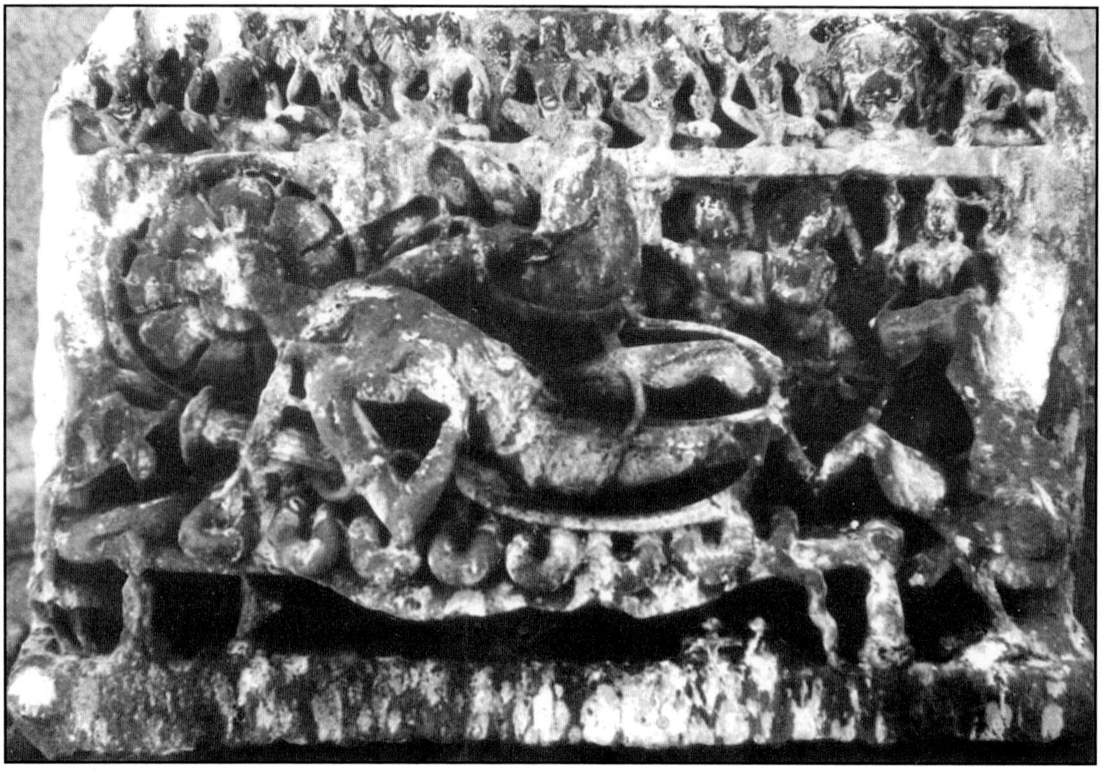

**Pl. 51.** Śeshaśāyī, Siswan.

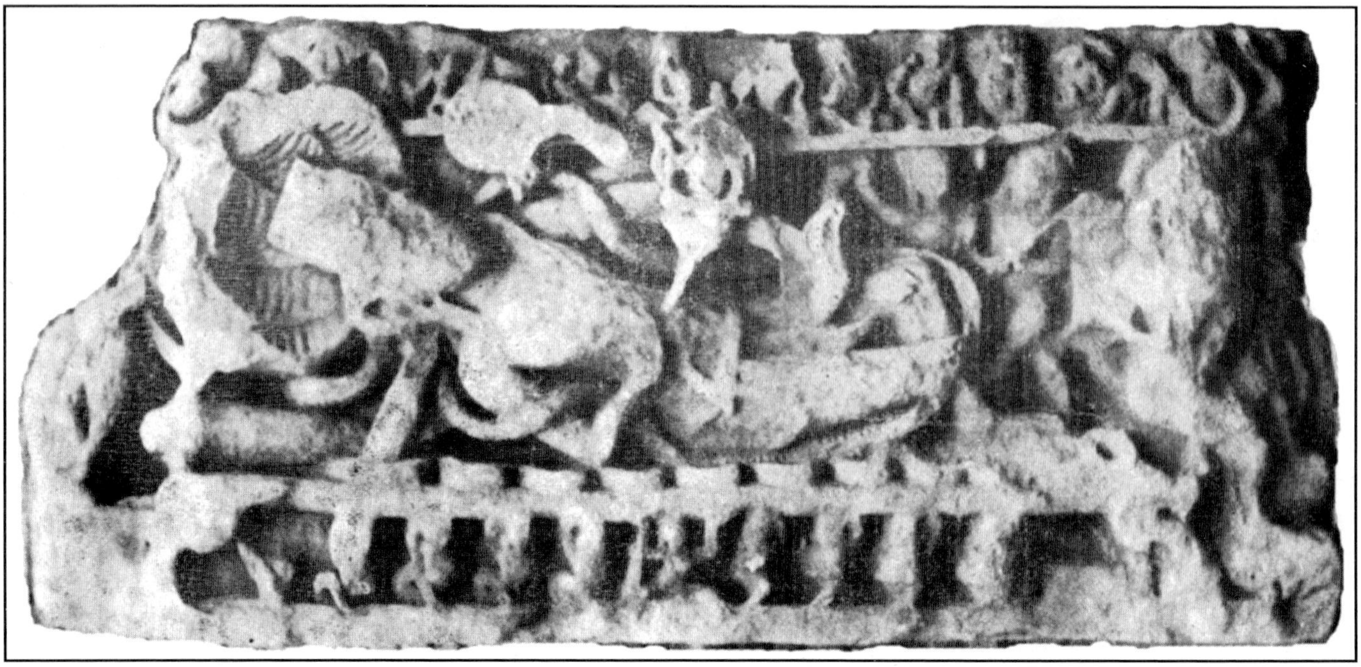

**Pl. 52.** Śeshaśāyī, Ghuram.

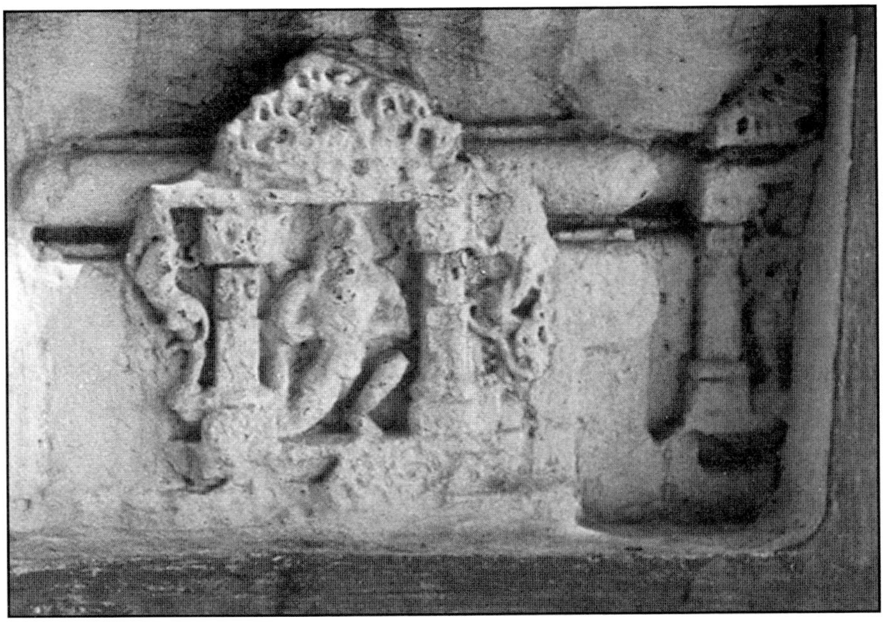

**Pl. 53.** Garuḍa, Sunam.

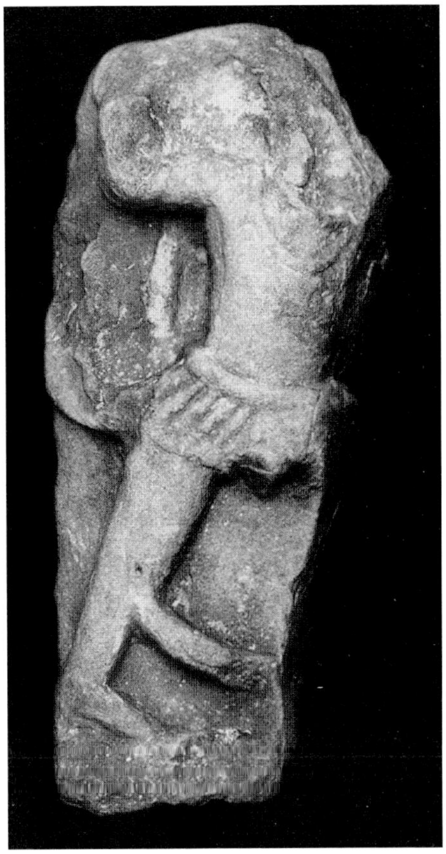

**Pl. 55.** Fragmentary Varāha image, Kharar.

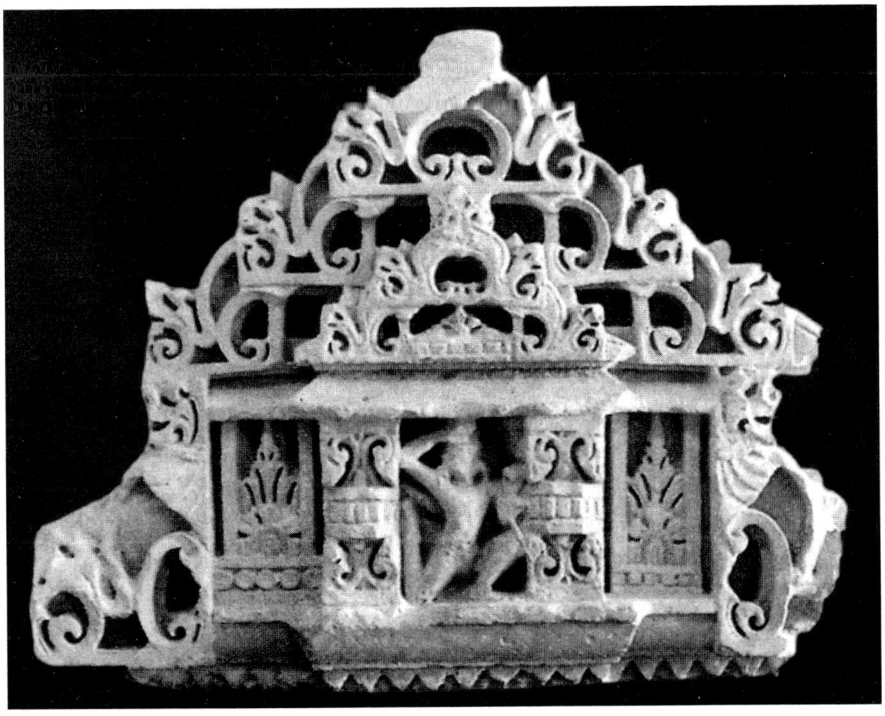

**Pl. 54.** Garuḍa, Samana.

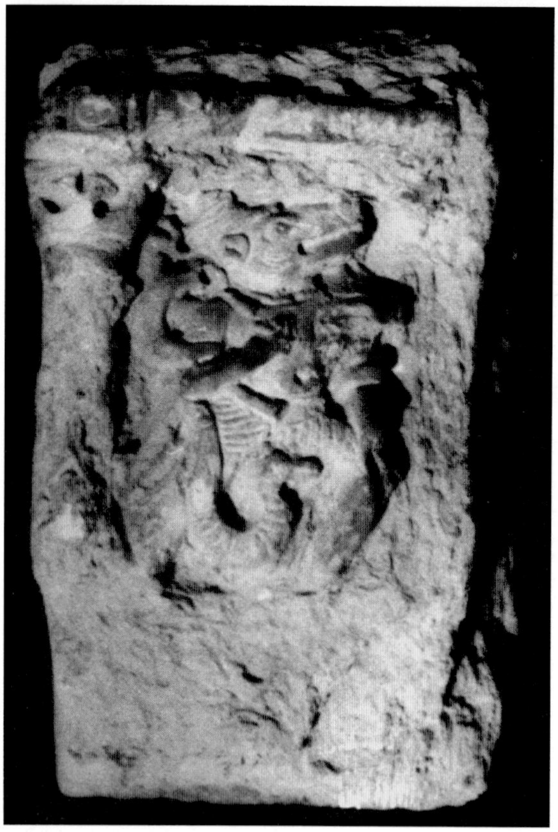

**Pl. 56.** Sun baked clay figure of Varāha, Janer.

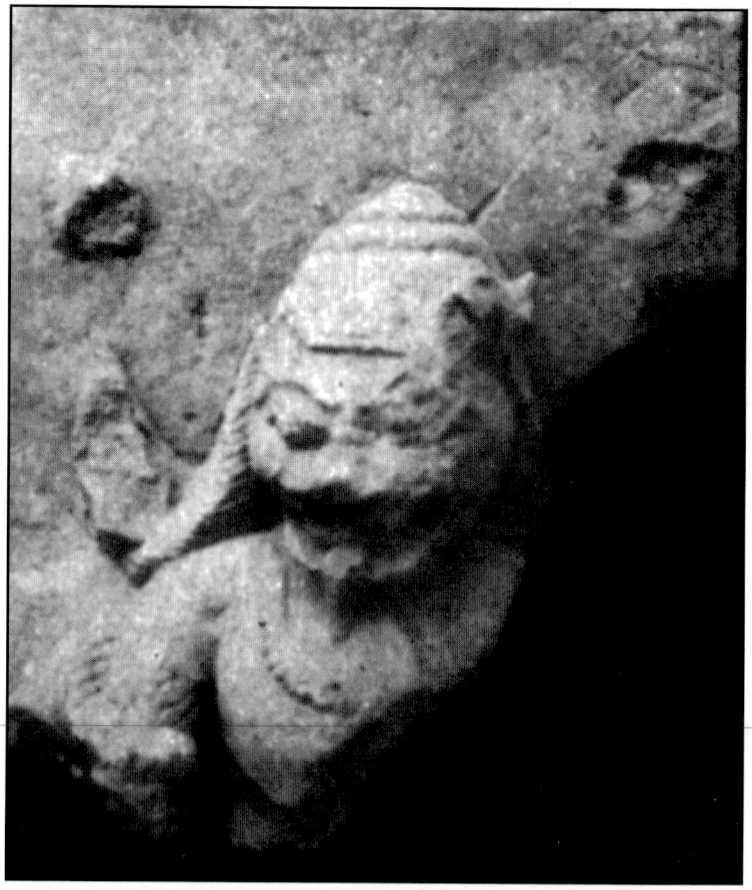

**Pl. 57.** Bust of Narasiṃha, exact provenance unknown.

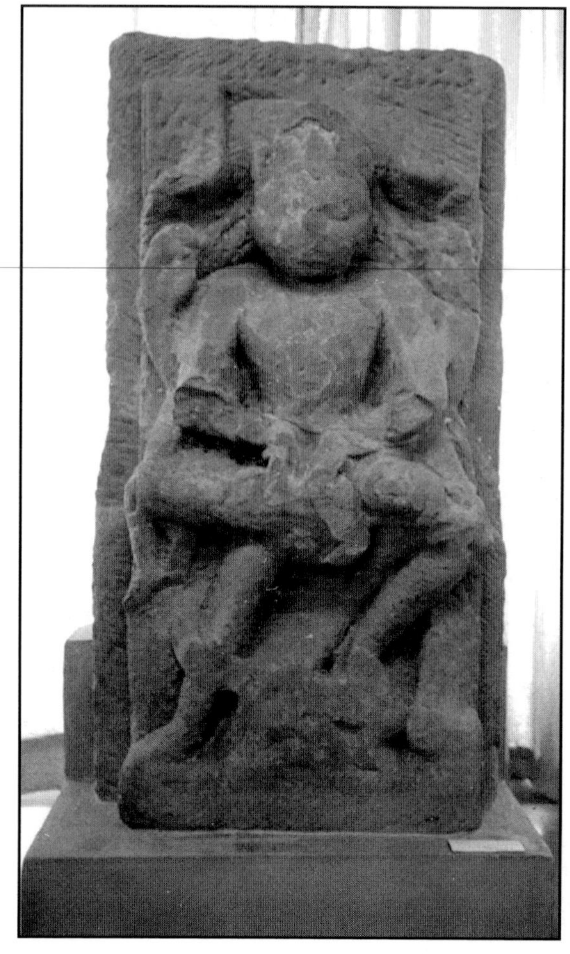

**Pl. 58.** Narasiṃha, Dholbaha.

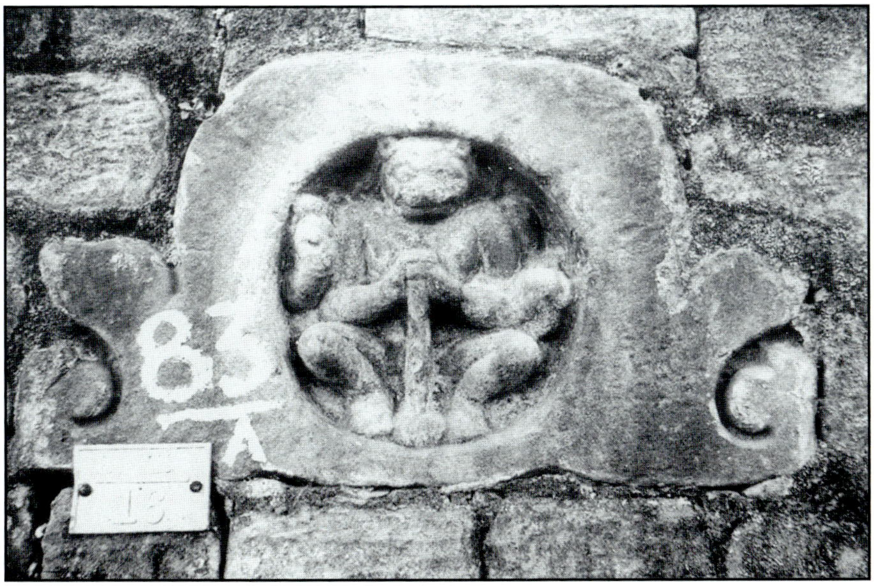

**Pl. 59.** Narasiṃha in a dormer window, Dholbaha.

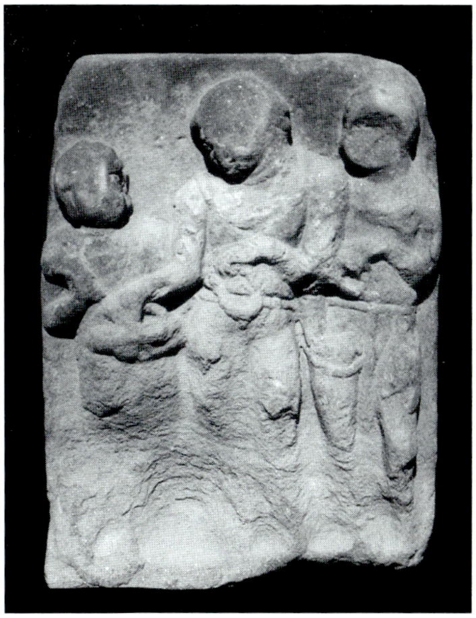

**Pl. 60.** Rāmāyaṇa panel, Dholbaha.

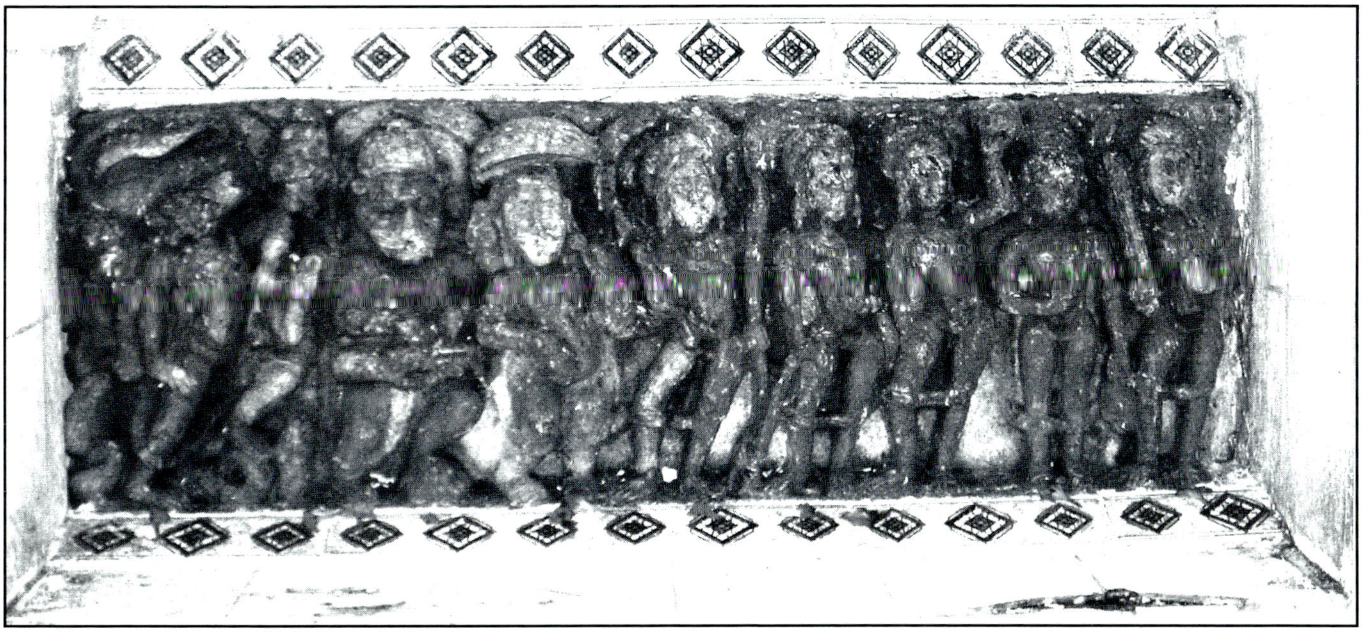

**Pl. 61.** Daśāvatāra panel, Humayunpur-Tasimbli.

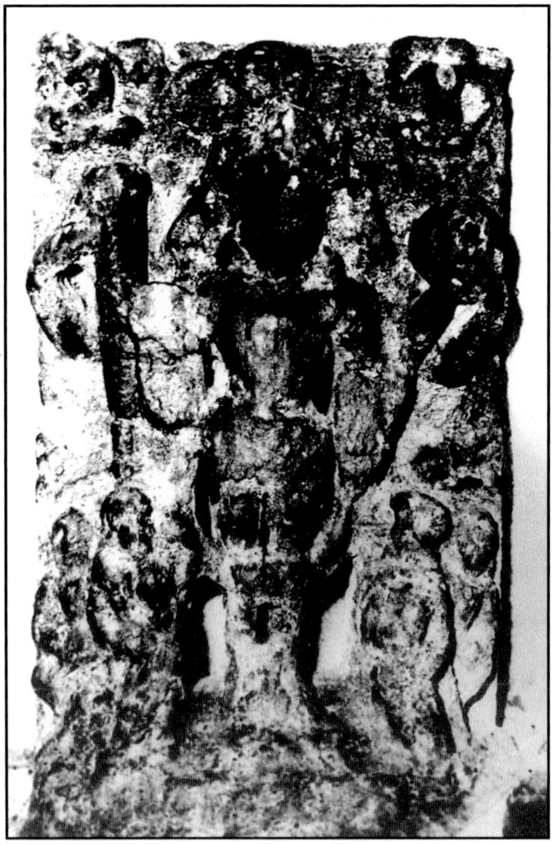

**Pl. 62.** Vaikuṇṭha, Chandpur-Rahon.

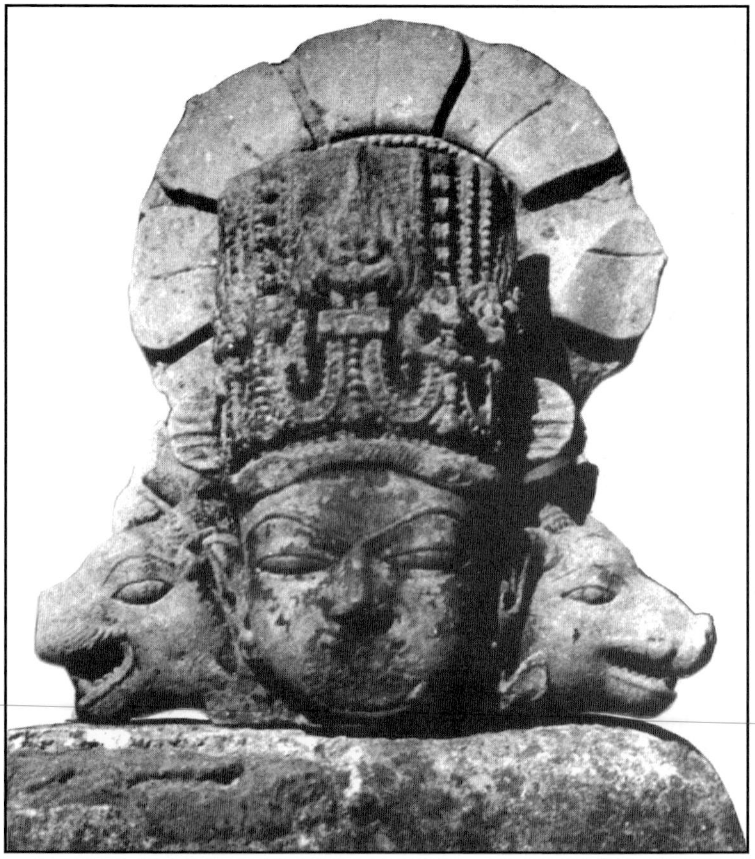

**Pl. 63.** Vaikuṇṭha head, Kharar.

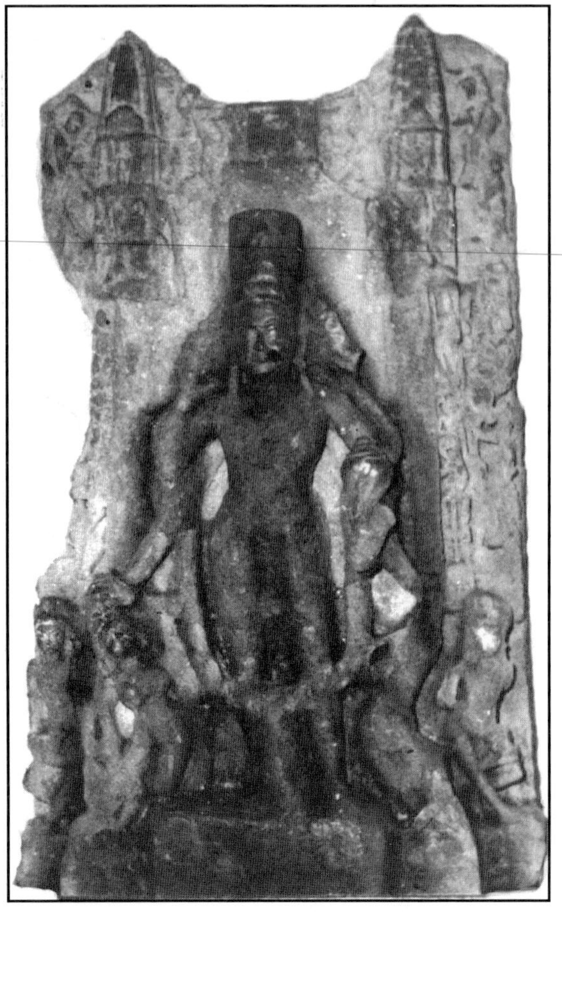

**Pl. 64.** Vaikuṇṭha under worship, Kharar.

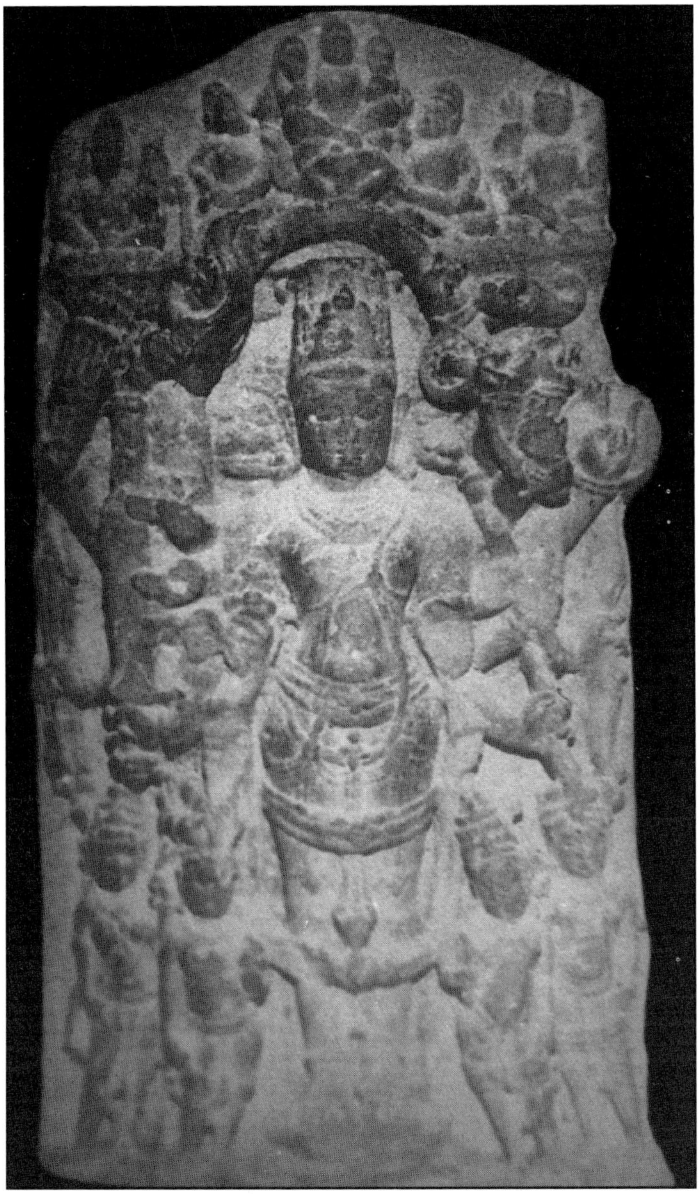

**Pl. 65.** Vaikuṇṭha, Amritsar.

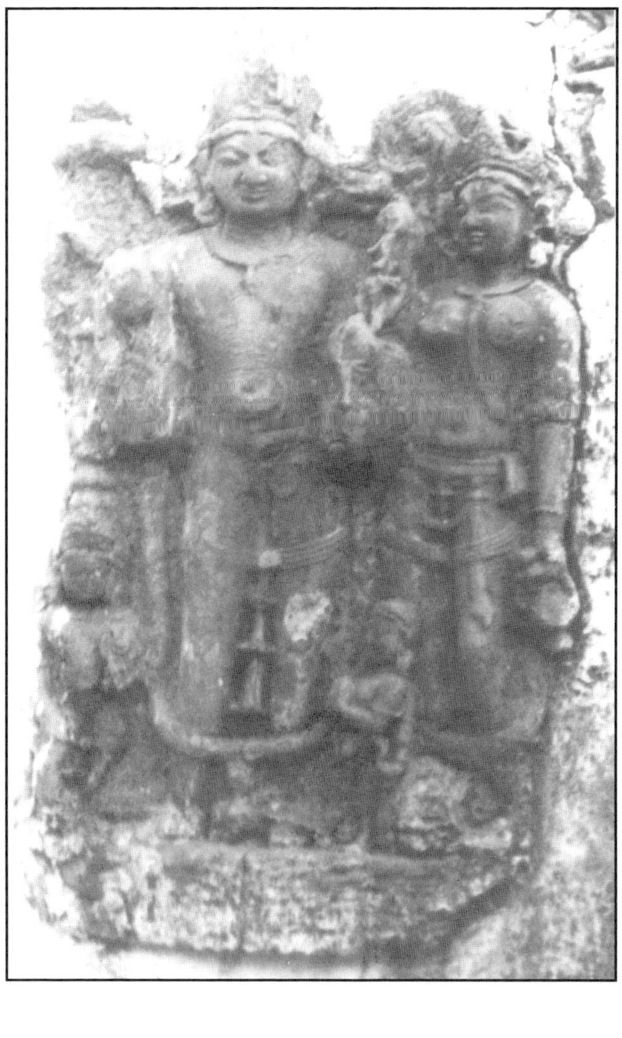

**Pl. 66.** Vaikuṇṭha-Lakshmī, Lalru.

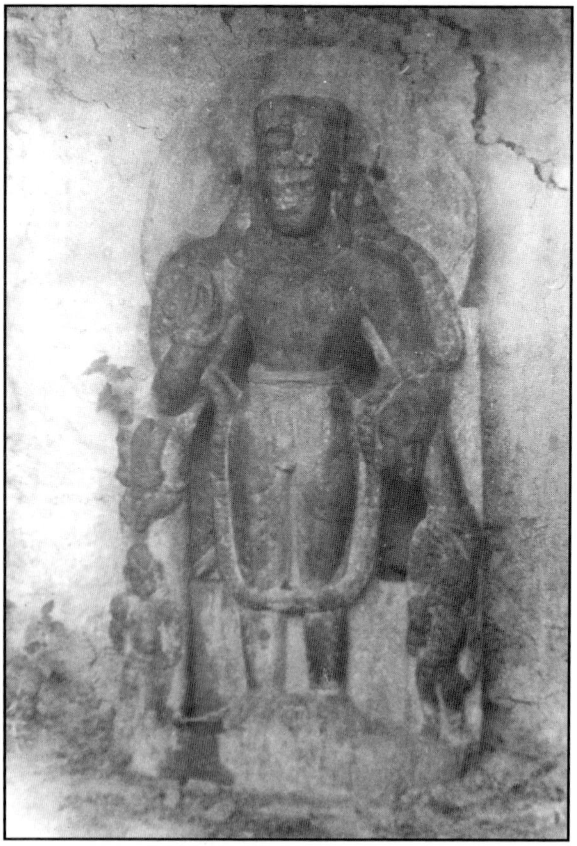

**Pl. 67.** Harihara, Dholbaha.

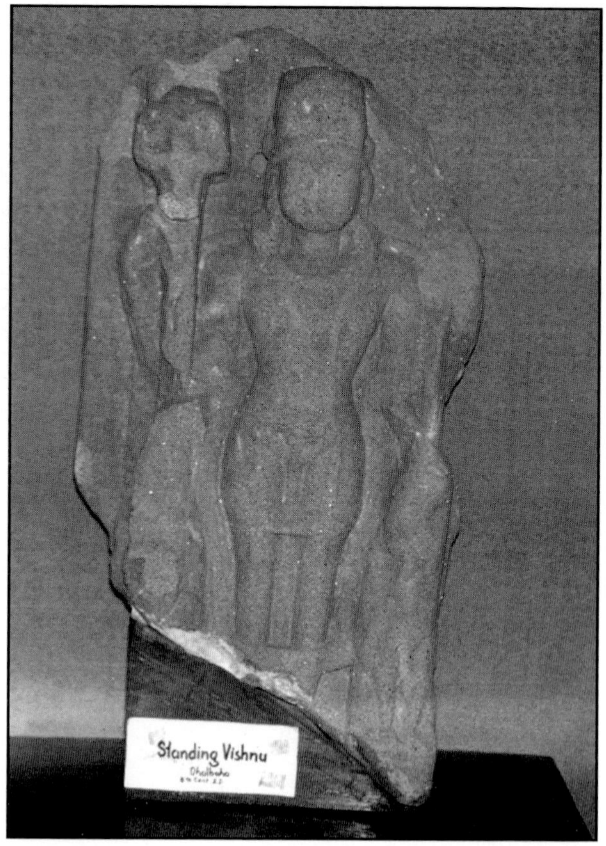



**Pl. 69.** Harihara, Dholbaha.

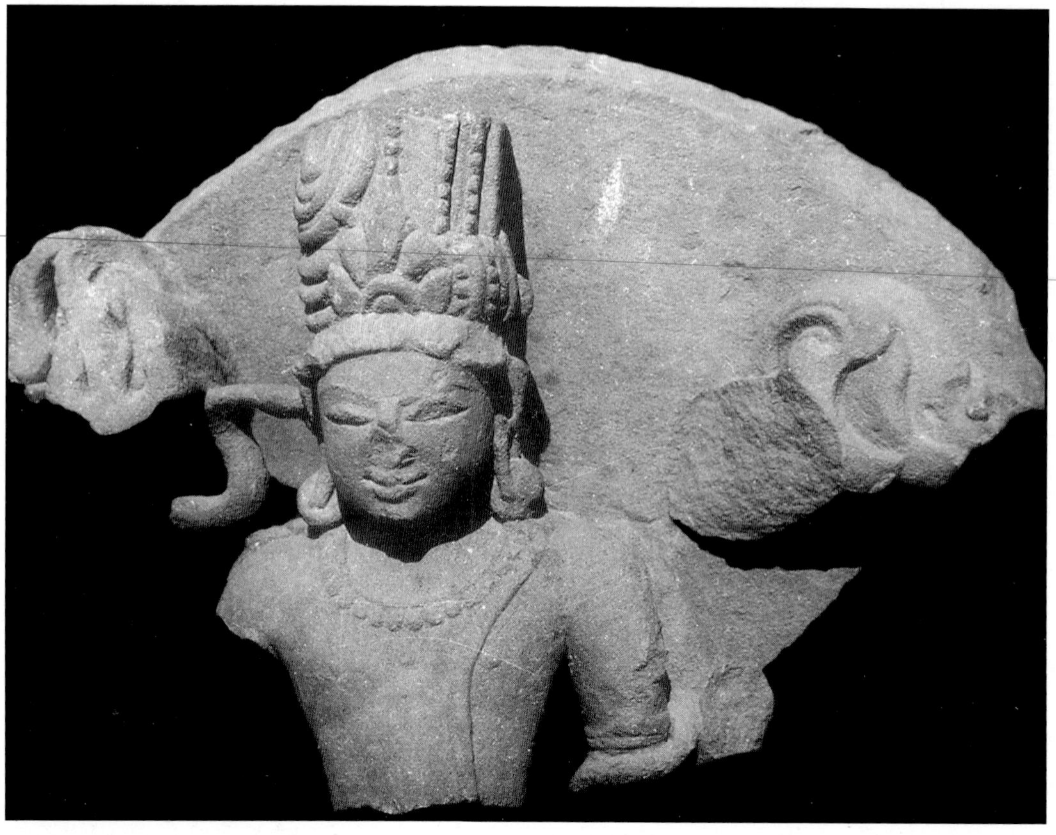

**Pl. 68.** Harihara, Kharar.

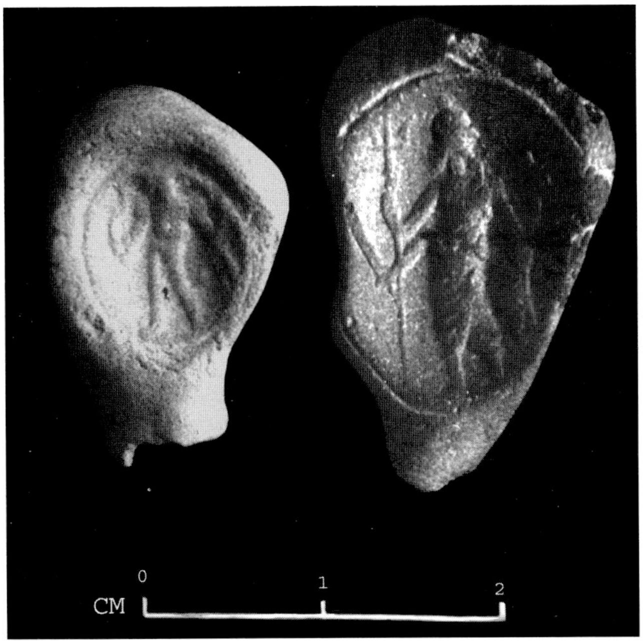


**Pl. 70.** Sealings showing Śiva, Sanghol.

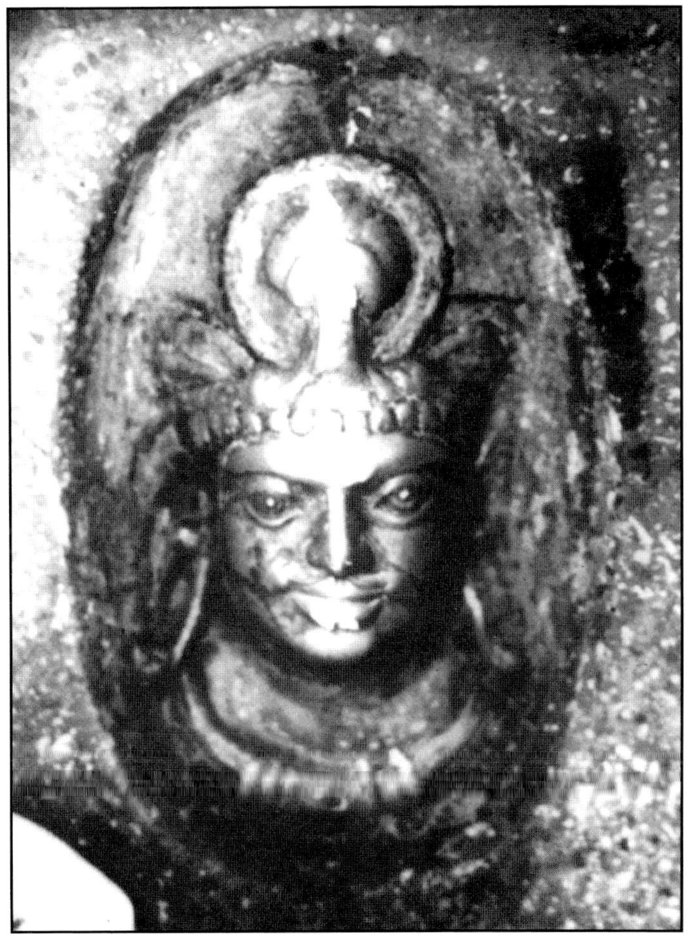

**Pl. 71.** Bronze mask of Śiva, Ropar.

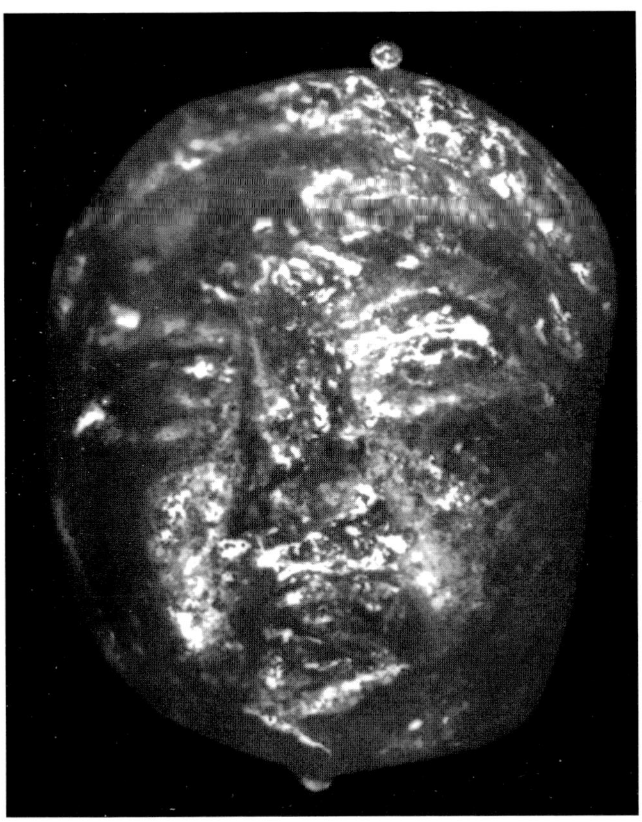

**Pl. 72.** Head with horizontal eye, Sanghol.

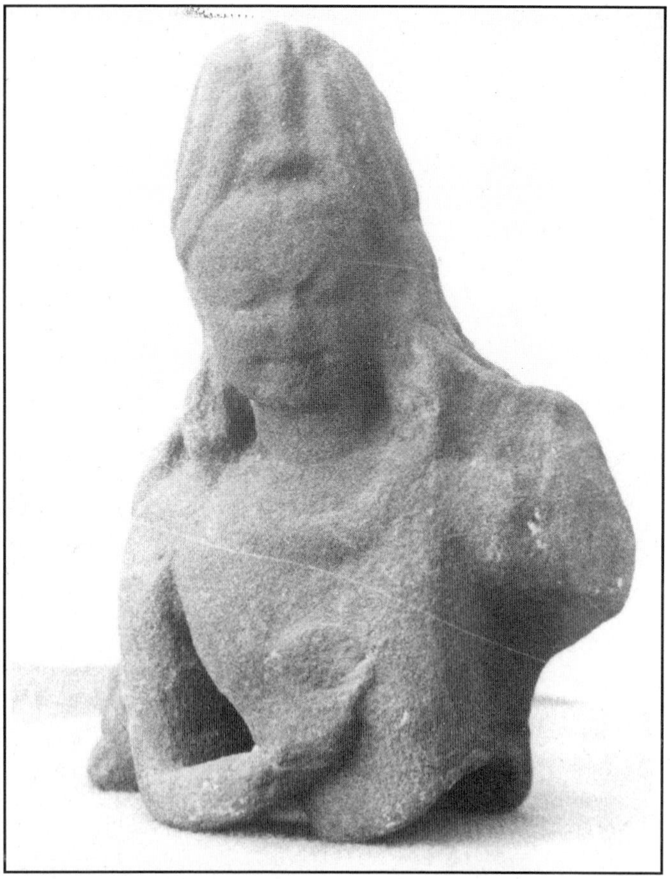

**Pl. 73.** Bust of Śiva, Dholbaha.

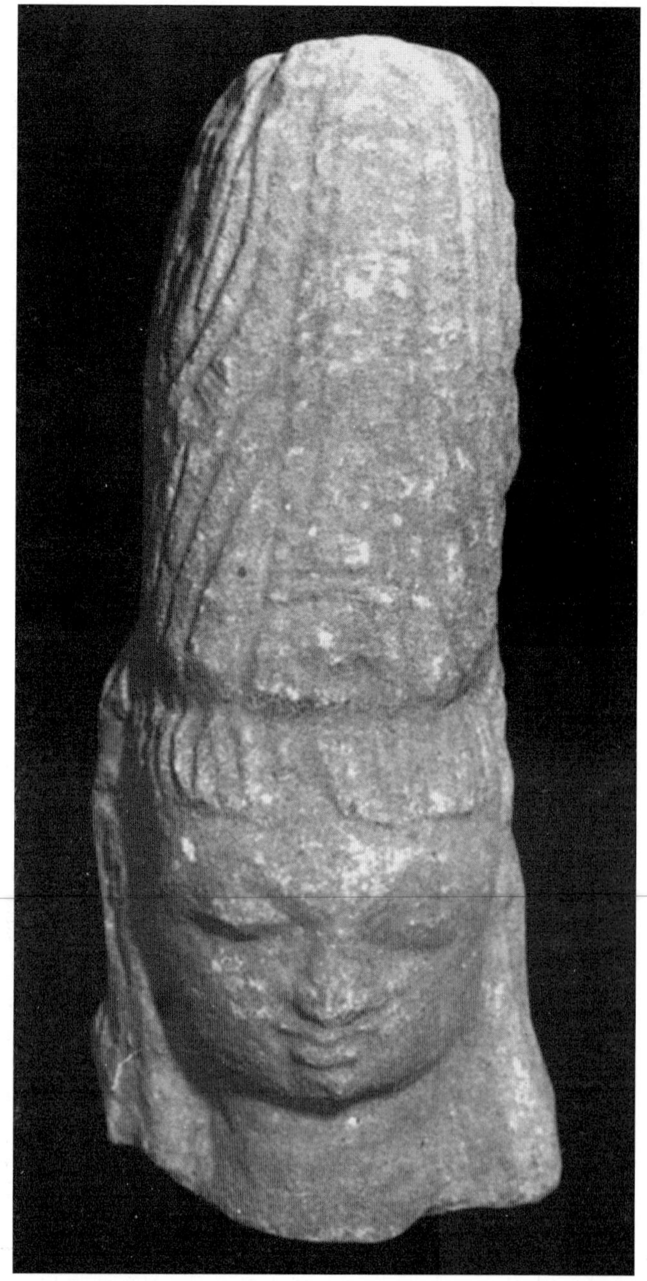

**Pl. 75.** Head with long *jaṭā-jūṭa*, Dholbaha.

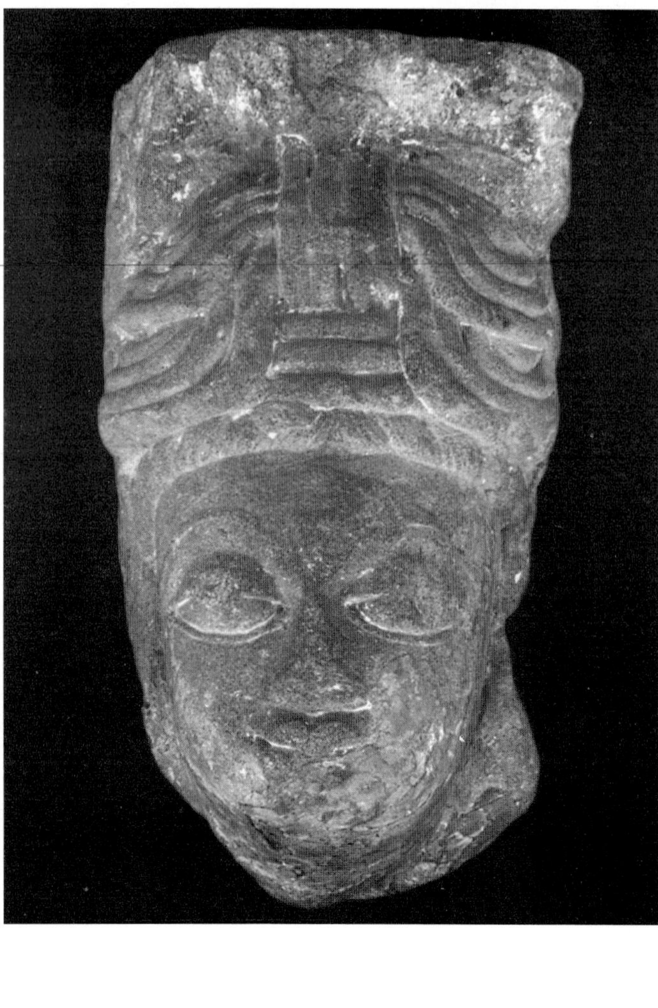

**Pl. 74.** Head of Śiva, Dholbaha.

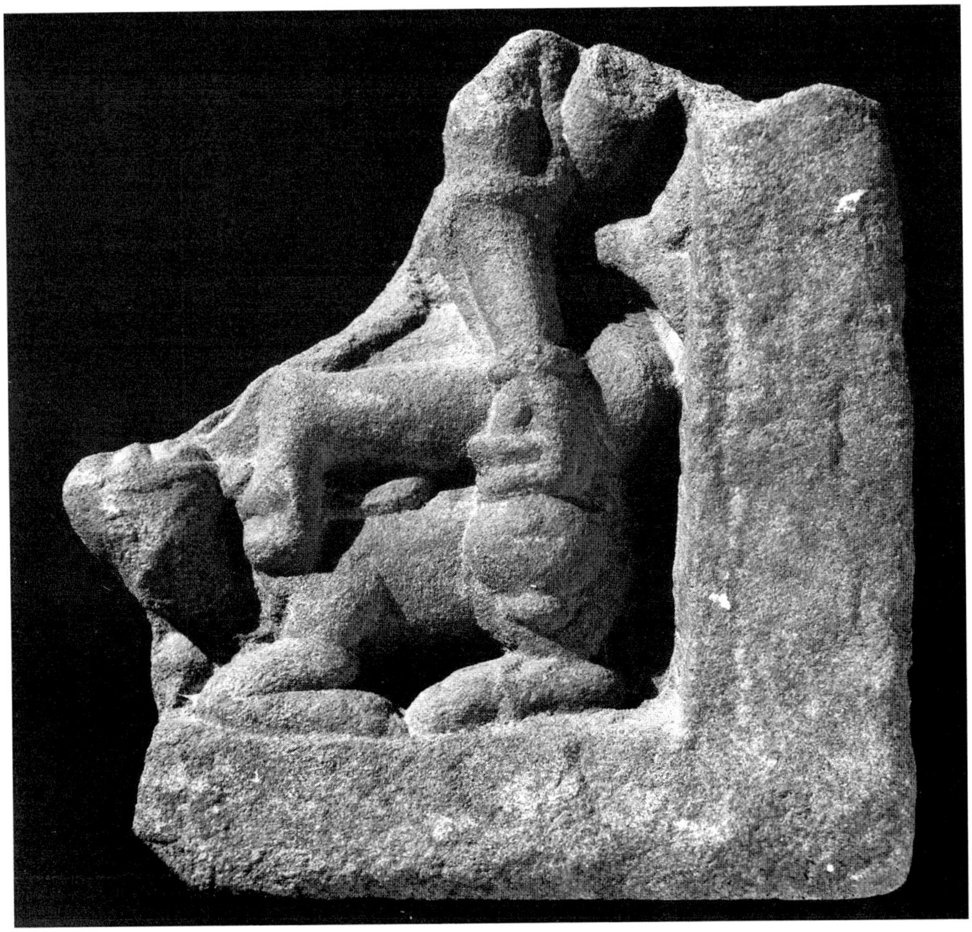

**Pl. 76.** Śiva seated on Nandī, Dholbaha.

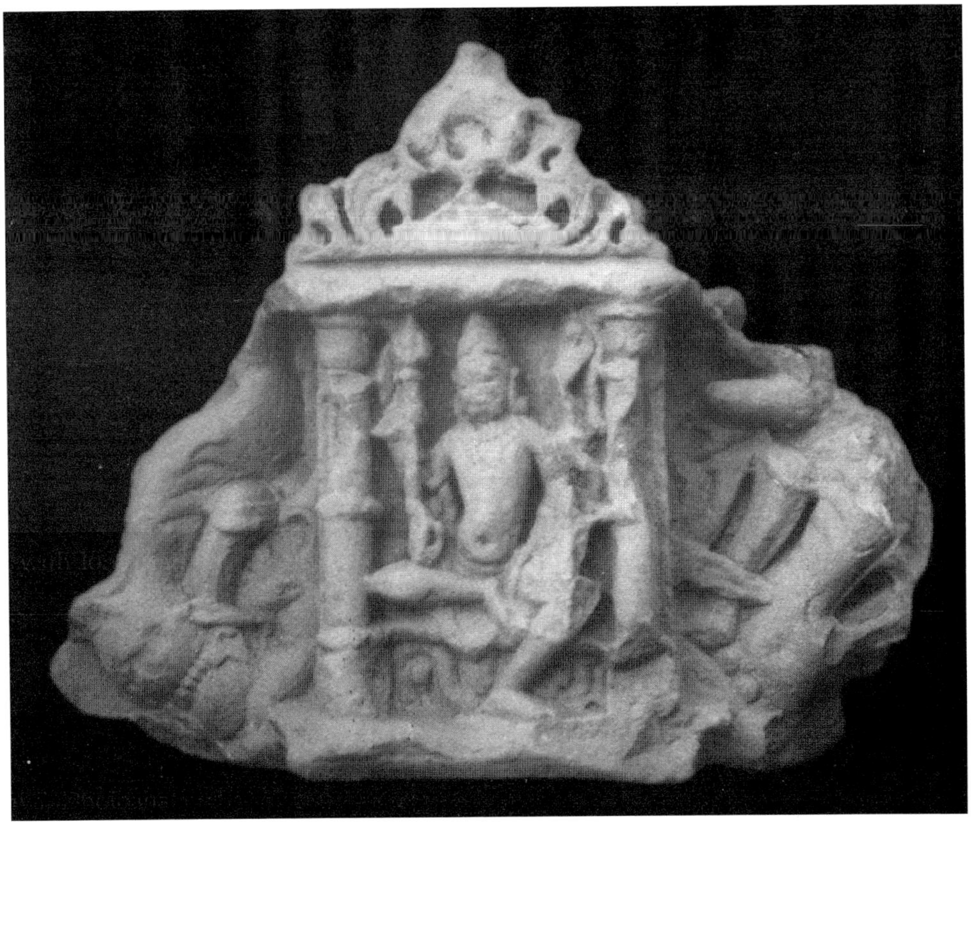

**Pl. 77.** Śiva in a *rathikā*, Dholbaha.

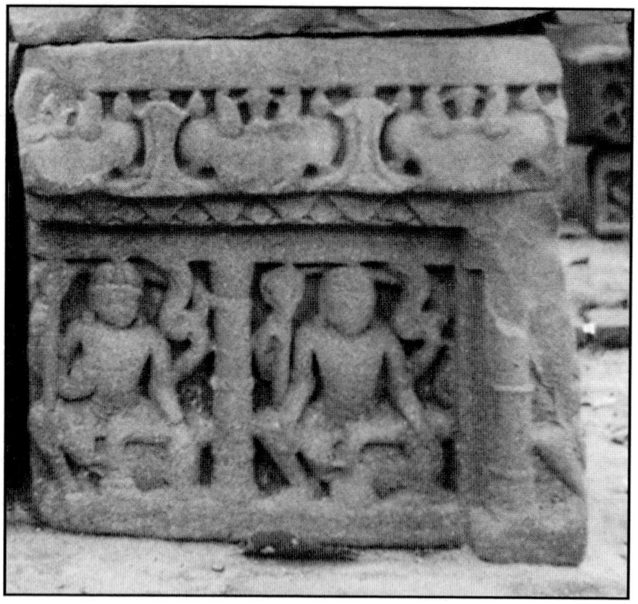

**Pl. 78.** Seated images of Śiva, Dholbaha.

**Pl. 79.** Standing images of Śiva, Dholbaha.

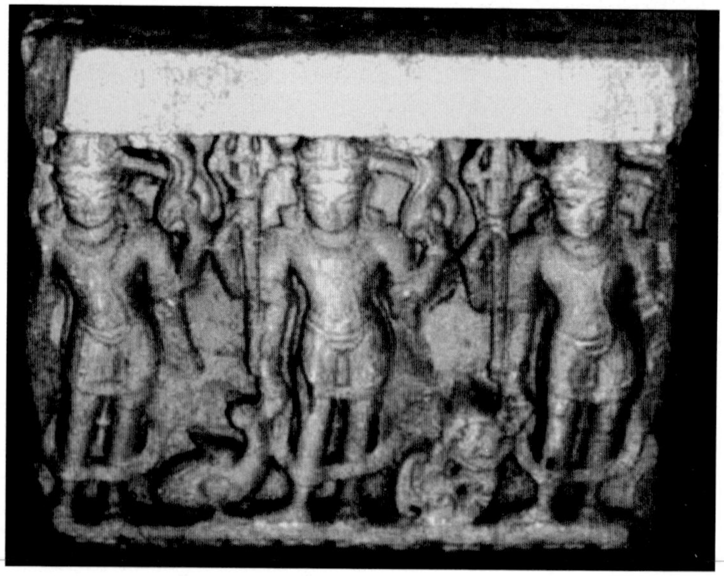

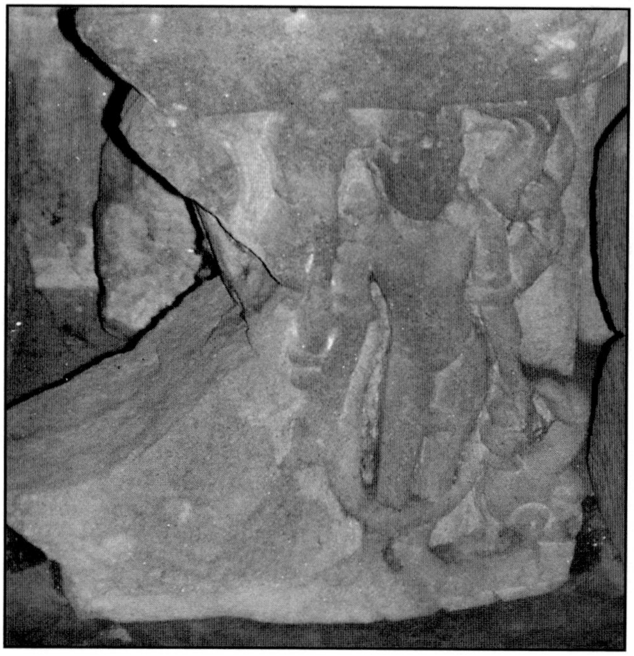

**Pl. 80.** Standing figure of Śiva with goose, Dholbaha.

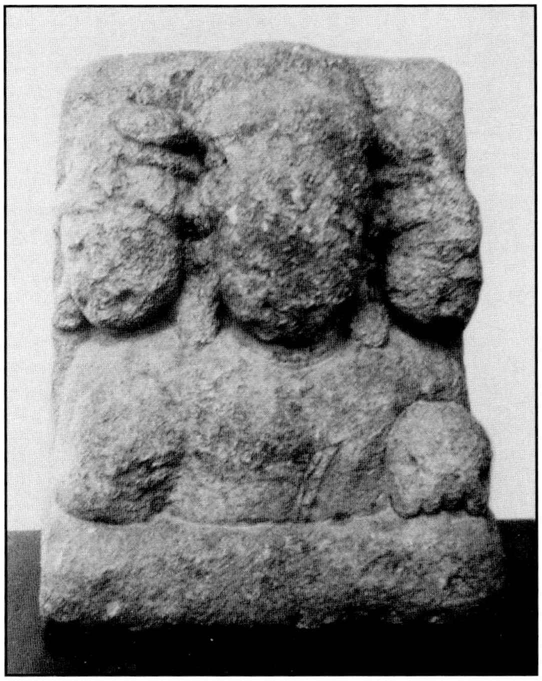

**Pl. 81.** Bust of Maheśa, Dholbaha.

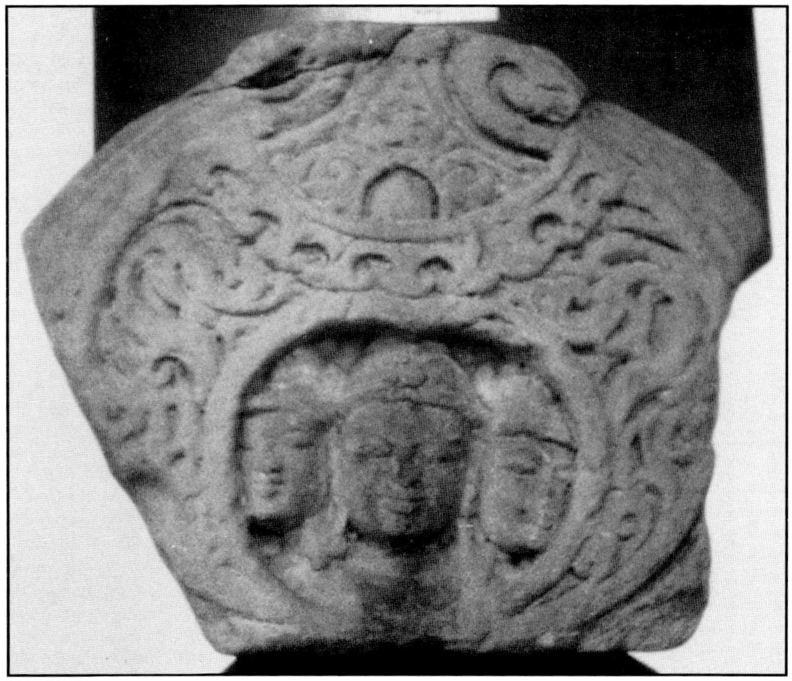

**Pl. 82.** *Bhadramukha* with Śaiva heads, Dholbaha.

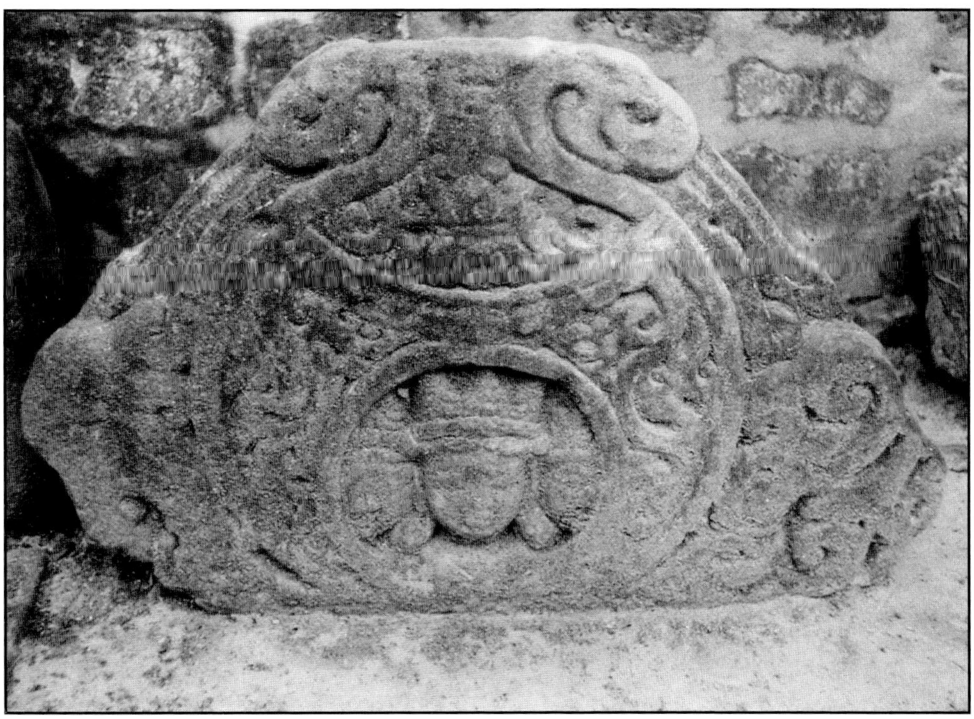

**Pl. 83.** Bhadramukha showing Śaiva heads, Dholbaha.

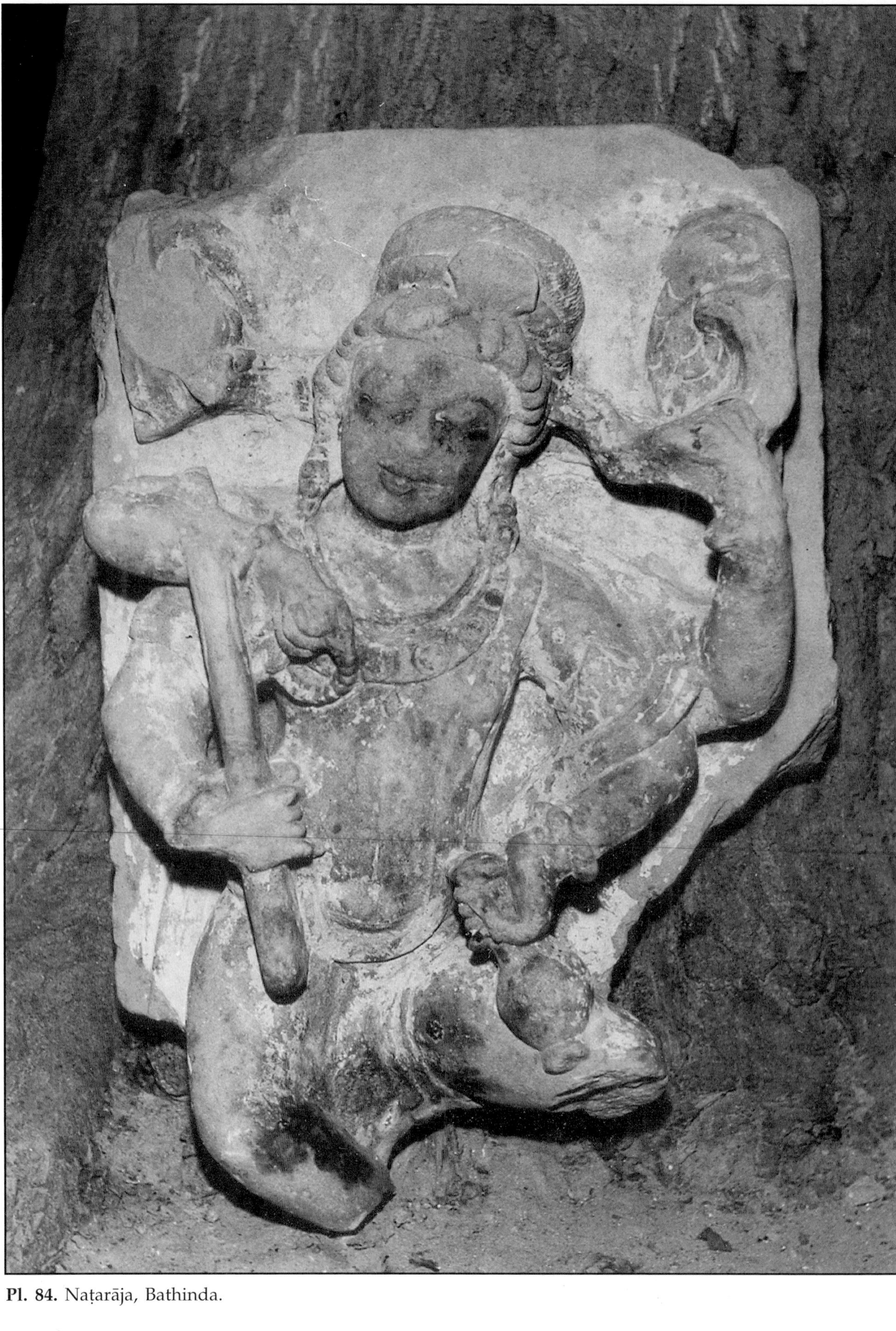

**Pl. 84.** Naṭarāja, Bathinda.

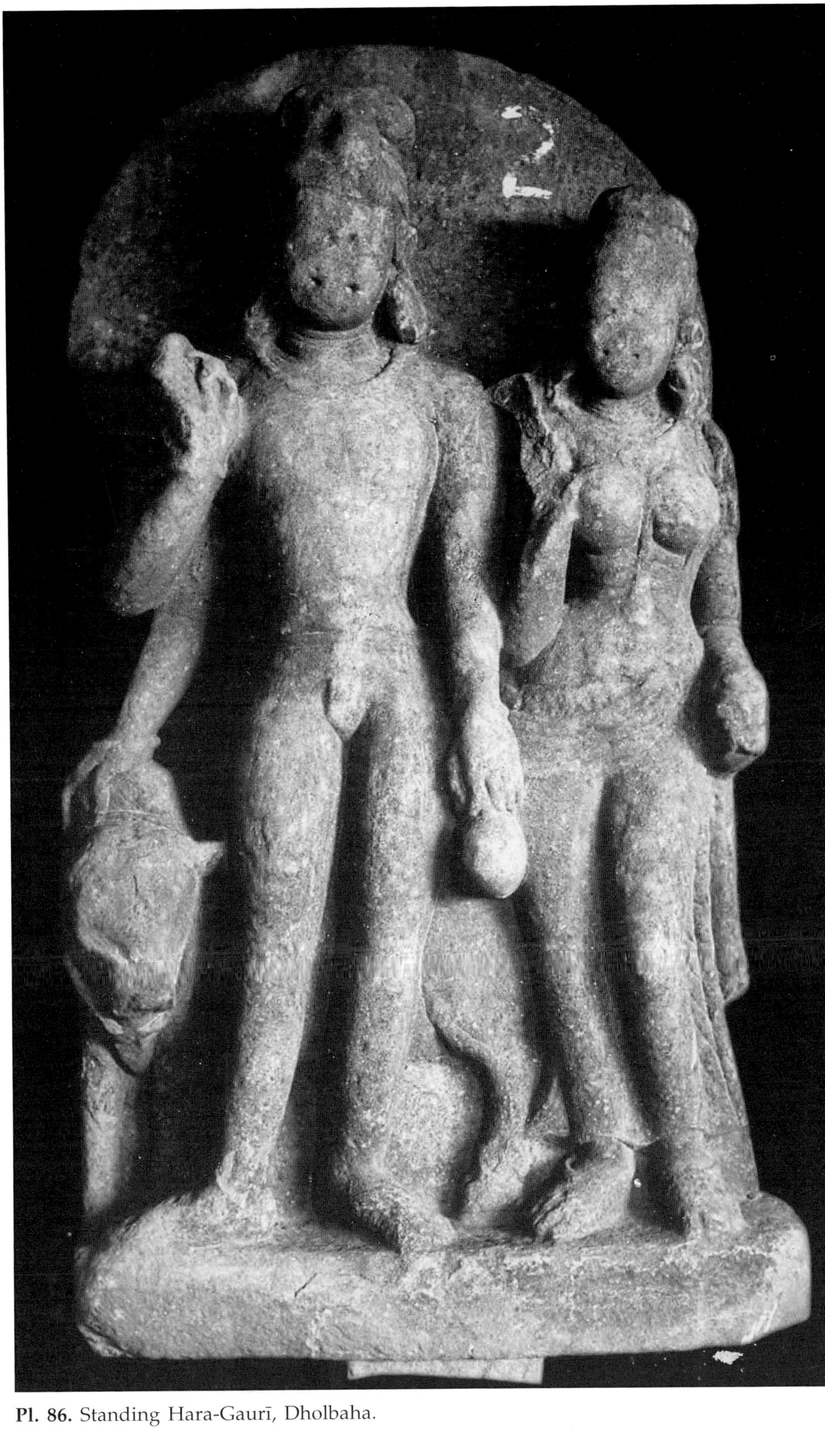

**Pl. 86.** Standing Hara-Gaurī, Dholbaha.

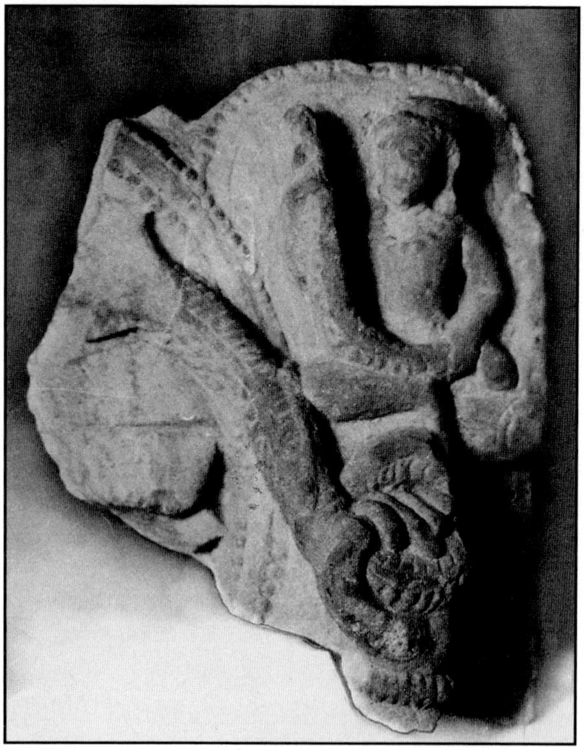

**Pl. 85.** Fragmentary hand of Śiva holding snake, Sunam.

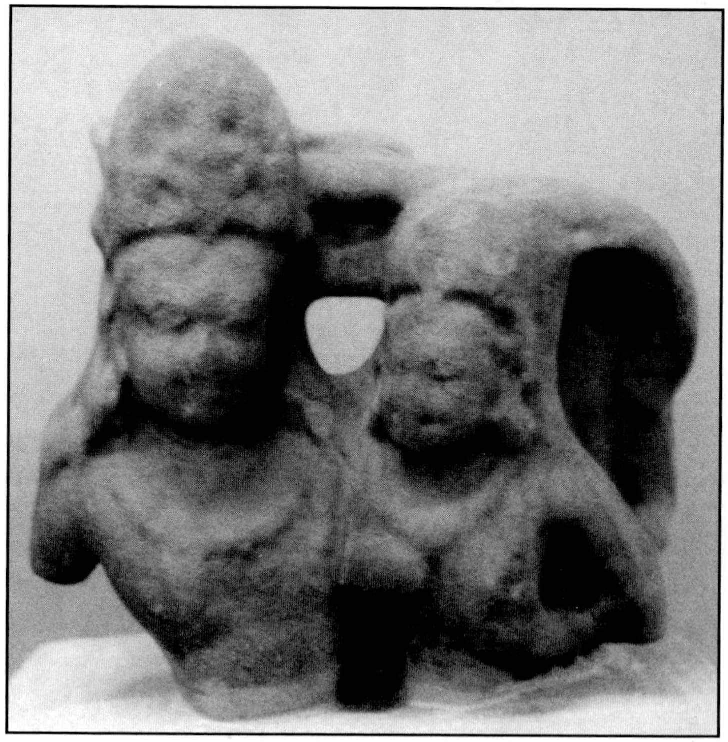

**Pl. 87.** Fragmentary Umā-Maheśvara, Dholbaha.

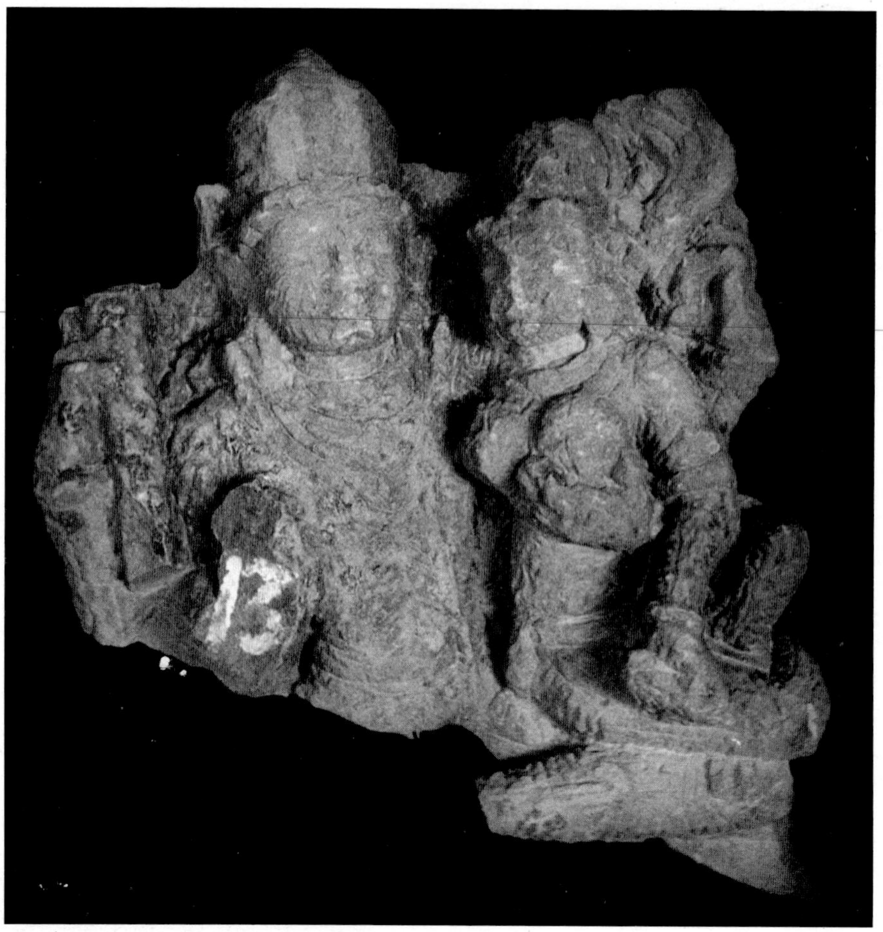



**Pl. 88.** Unfinished Umā-Maheśvara, Dholbaha.

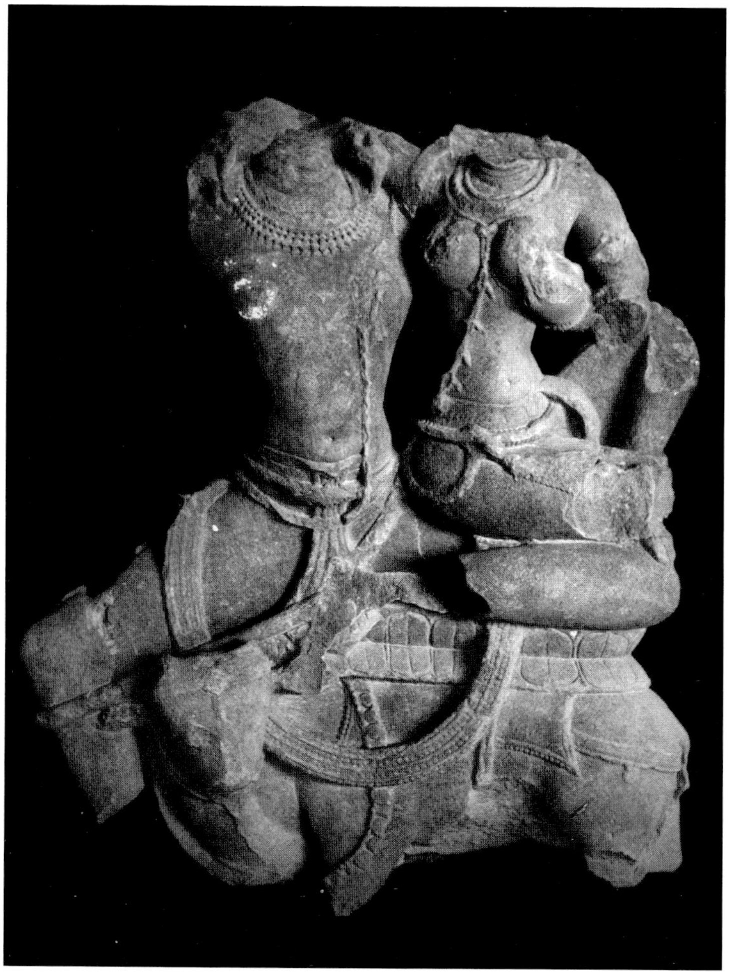

**Pl. 89.** Headless Umā-Maheśvara, Dholbaha.

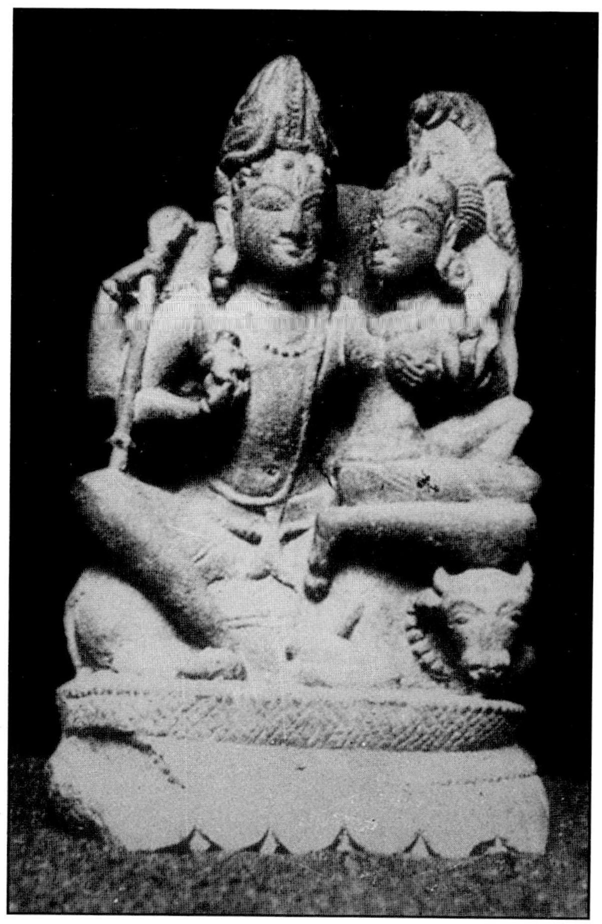

**Pl. 91.** Umā-Maheśvara, Sunam.

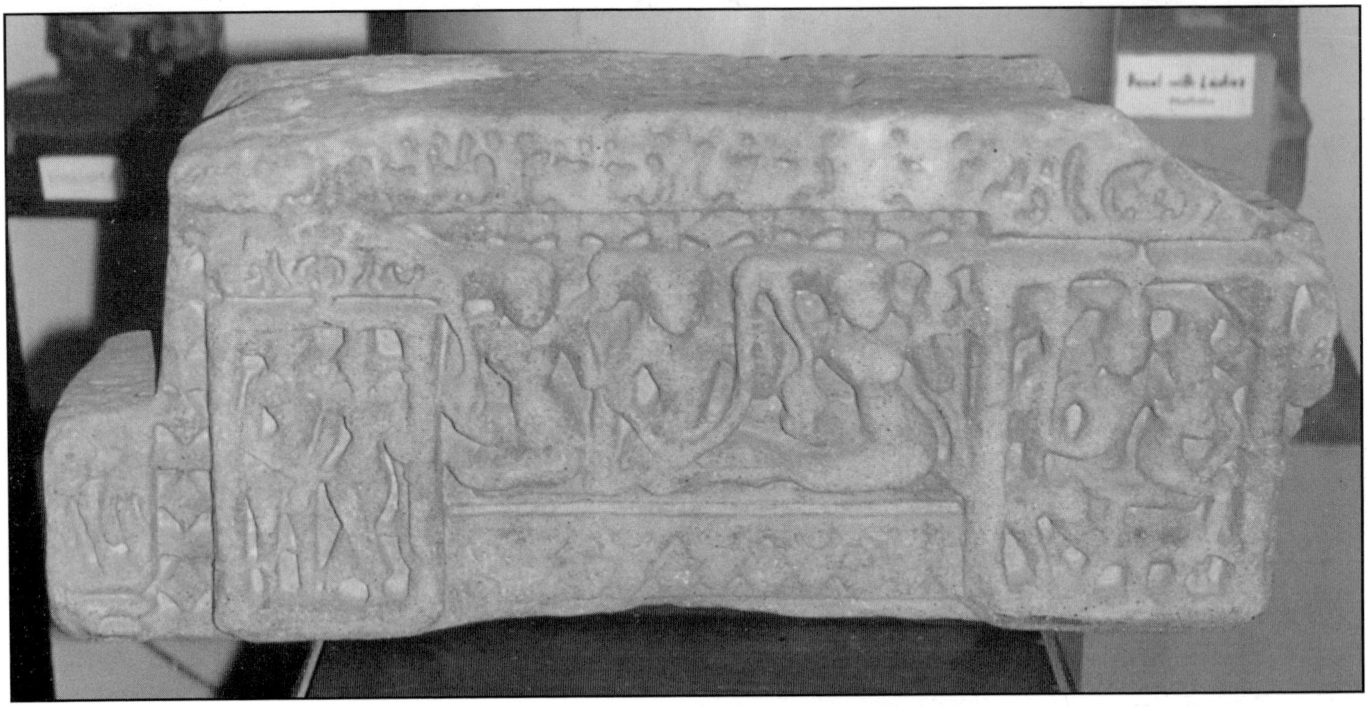

**Pl. 90.** Umā-Maheśvara on *lalāṭa-bimba*, Dholbaha.

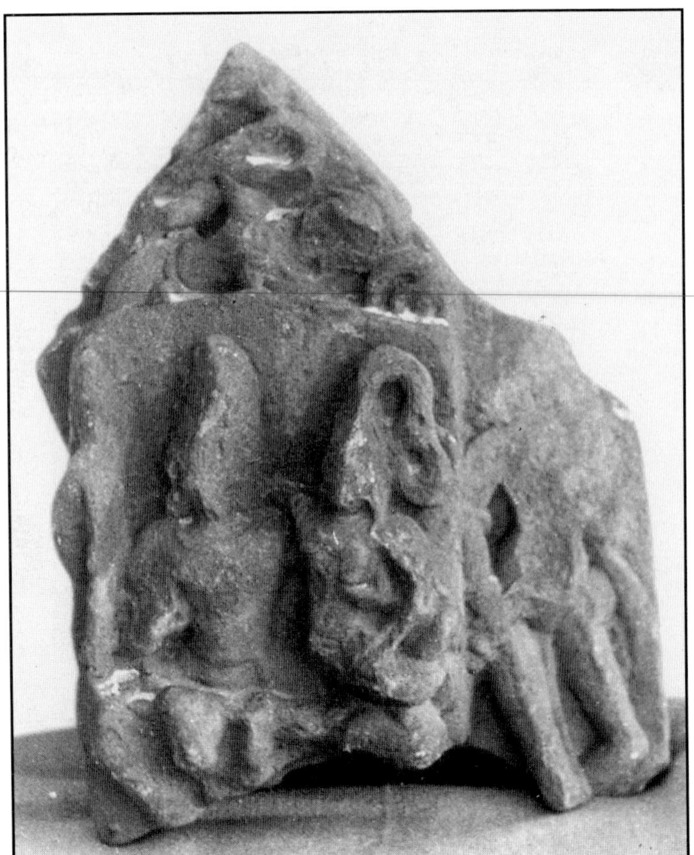

**Pl. 92.** Umā-Maheśvara on a stele, Kharar.

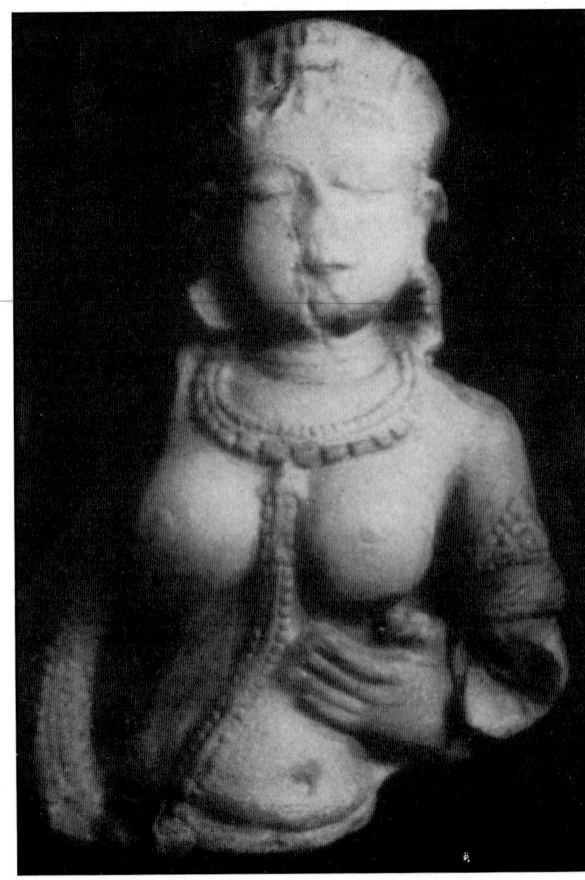

**Pl. 93.** Probably a fragment of Umā-Maheśvara image, Majhur.

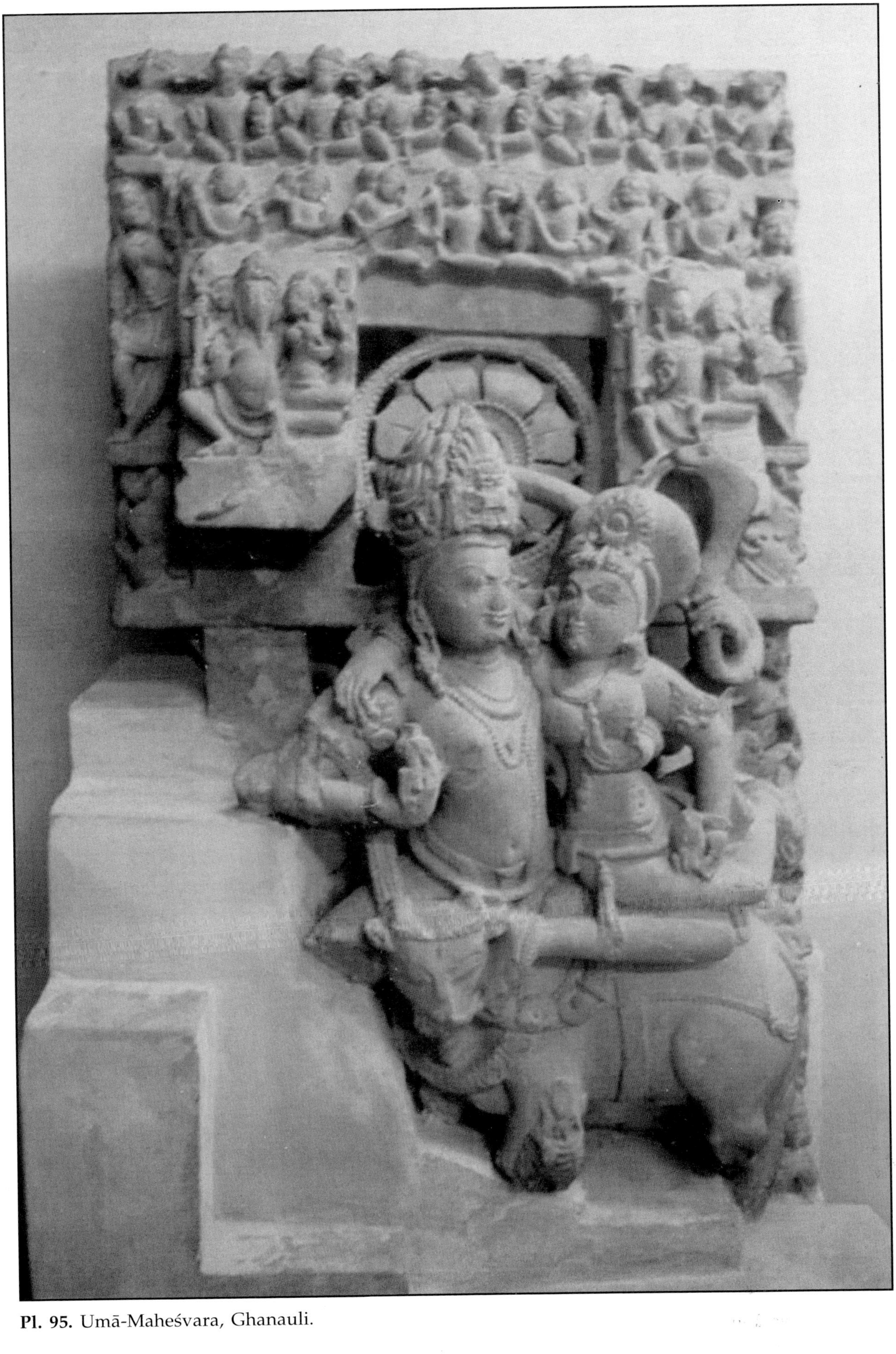

**Pl. 95.** Umā-Maheśvara, Ghanauli.

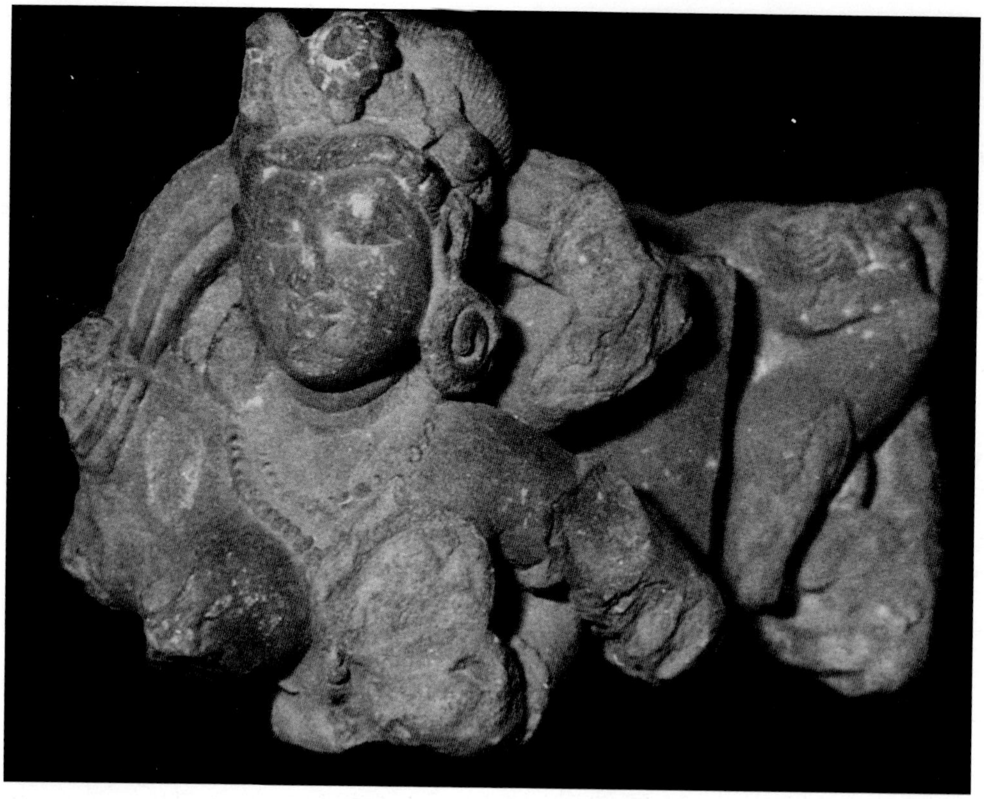

**Pl. 94.** Fragment of an Umā-Maheśvara image, Dholbaha.

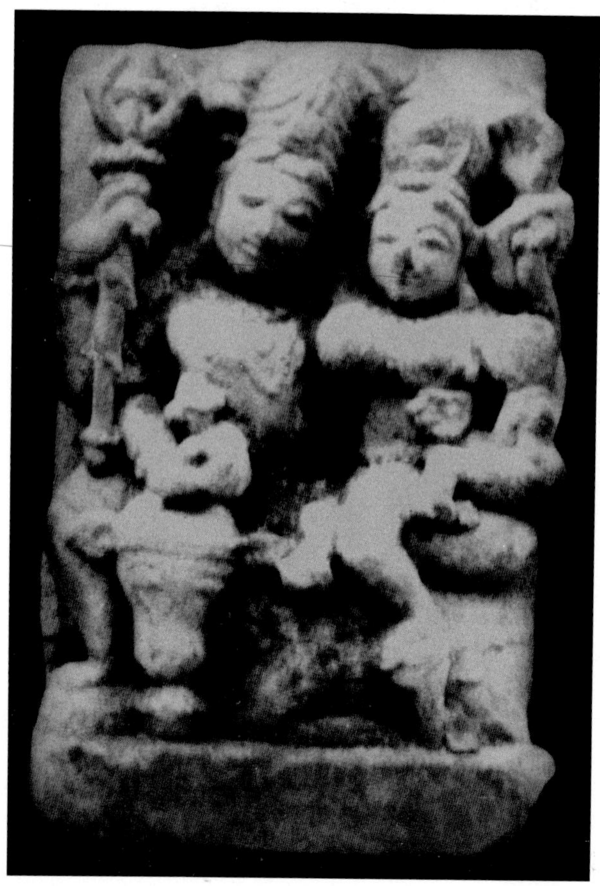

**Pl. 96.** Umā-Maheśvara in a private collection.

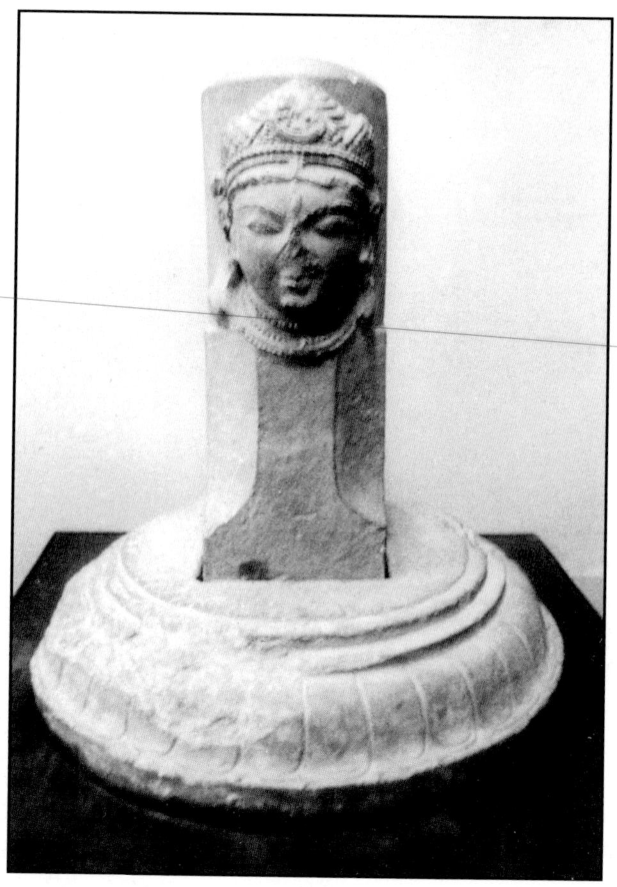

**Pl. 98.** *Mukha-liṅga*, Sultanpur Lodi.

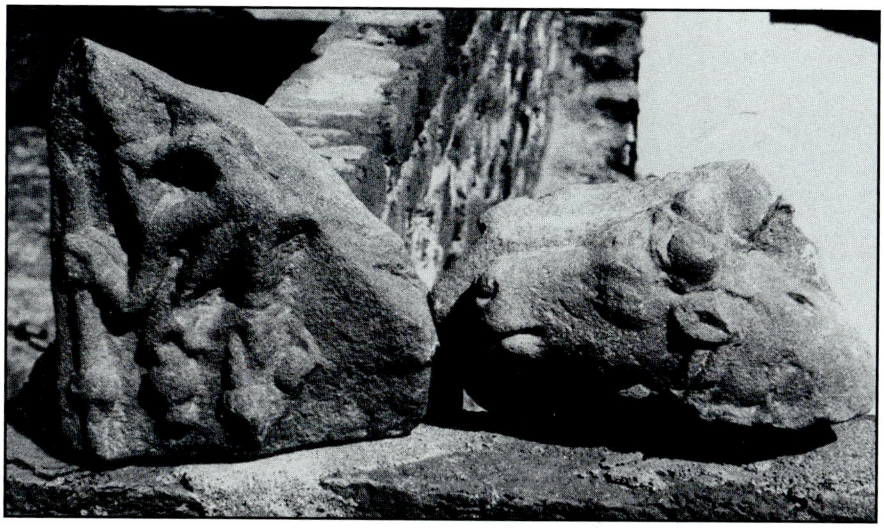

**Pl. 97.** Bull's head, Siswan.

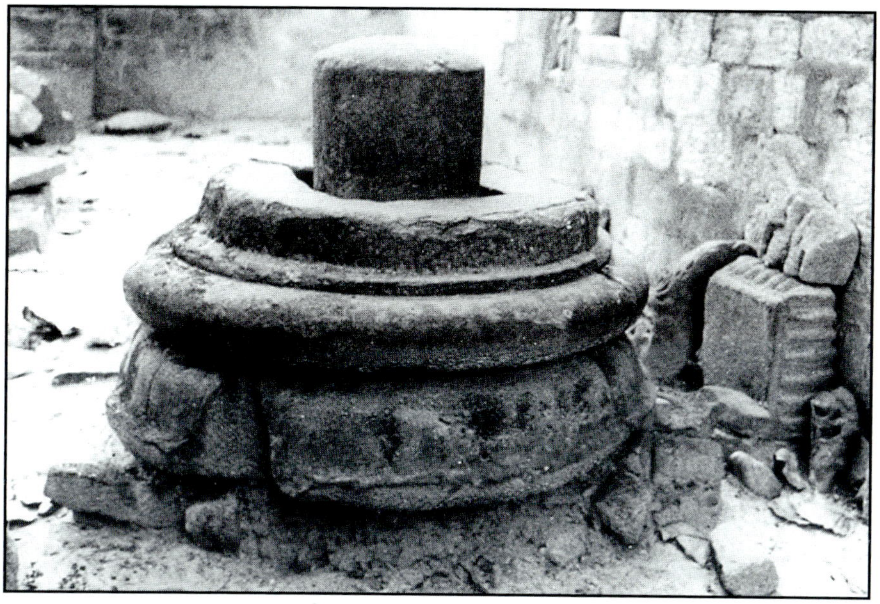

**Pl. 99.** Śiva-liṅga, Dholbaha.

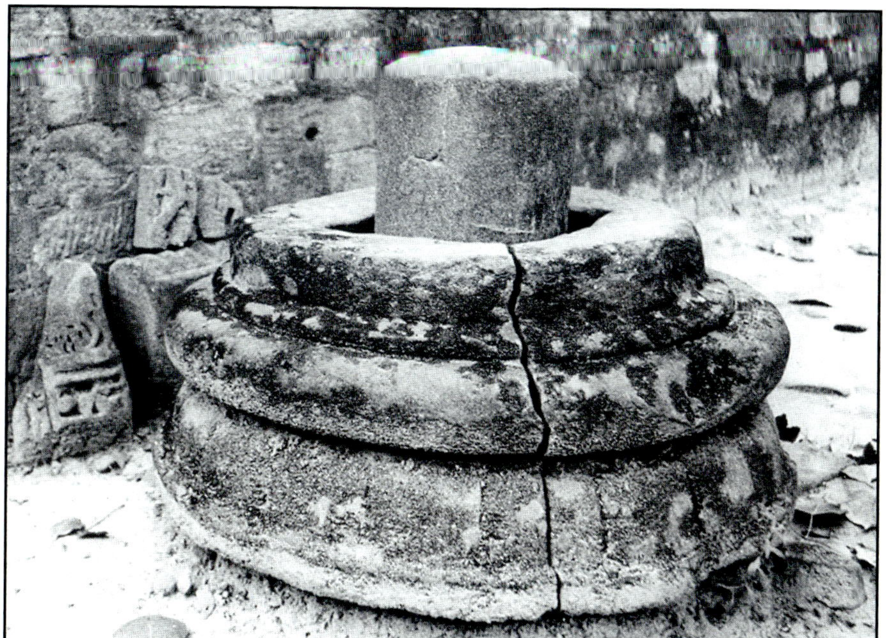

**Pl. 100.** Śiva-liṅga in a decorated *yonipīṭha*, Dholbaha.

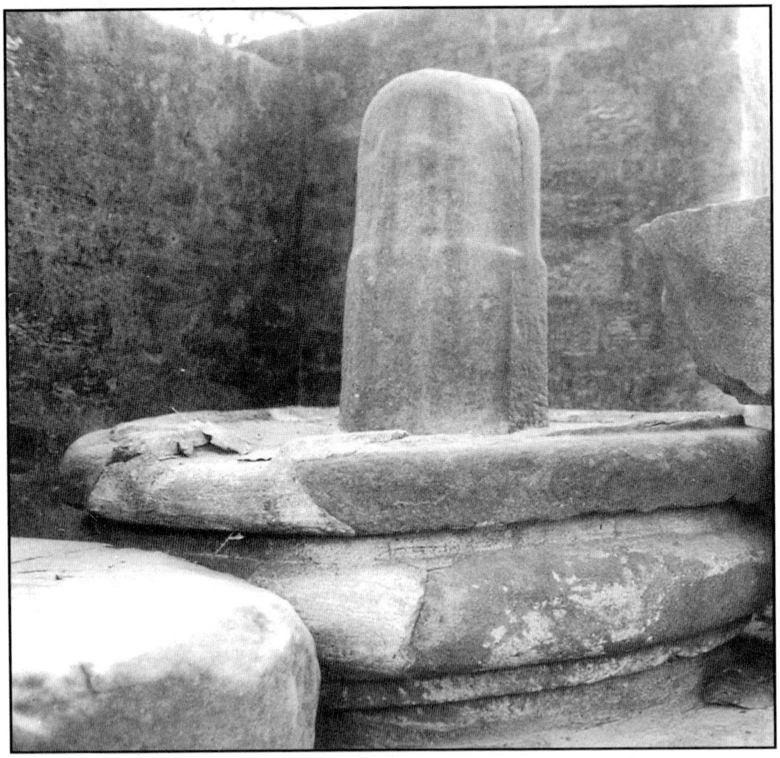

**Pl. 101.** Fluted Śiva-liṅga, Dholbaha.

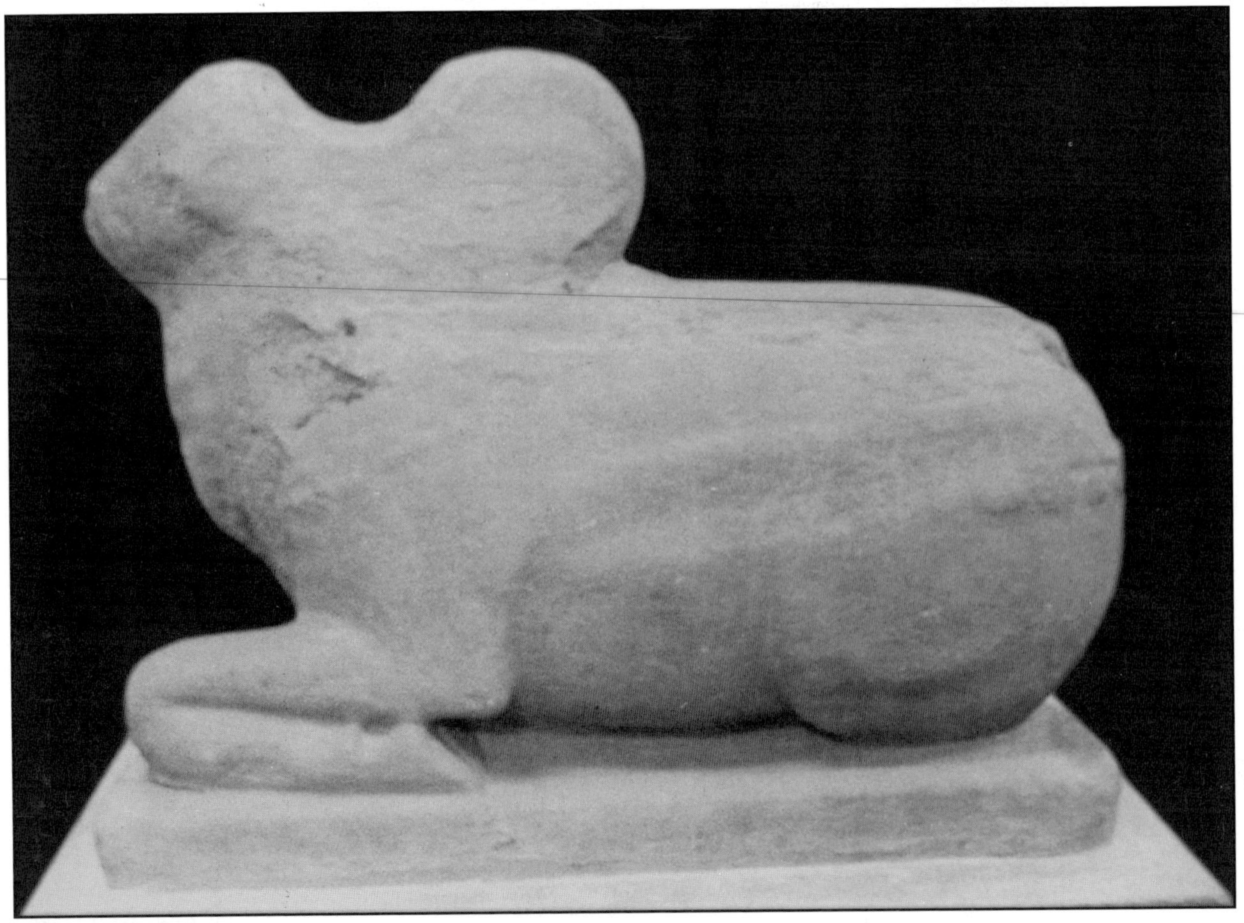

**Pl. 102.** Nandī, Dholbaha.

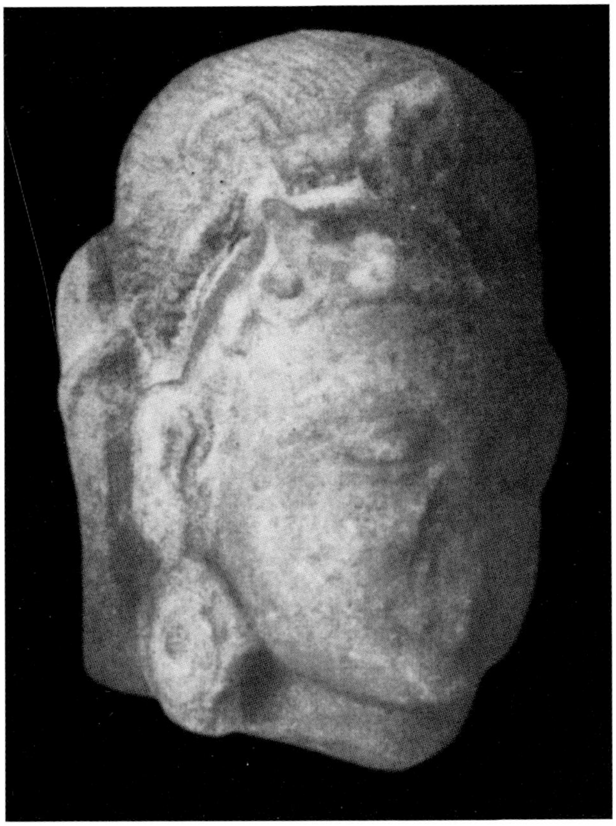

**Pl. 103.** Pārvatī head, Sarai Naga.

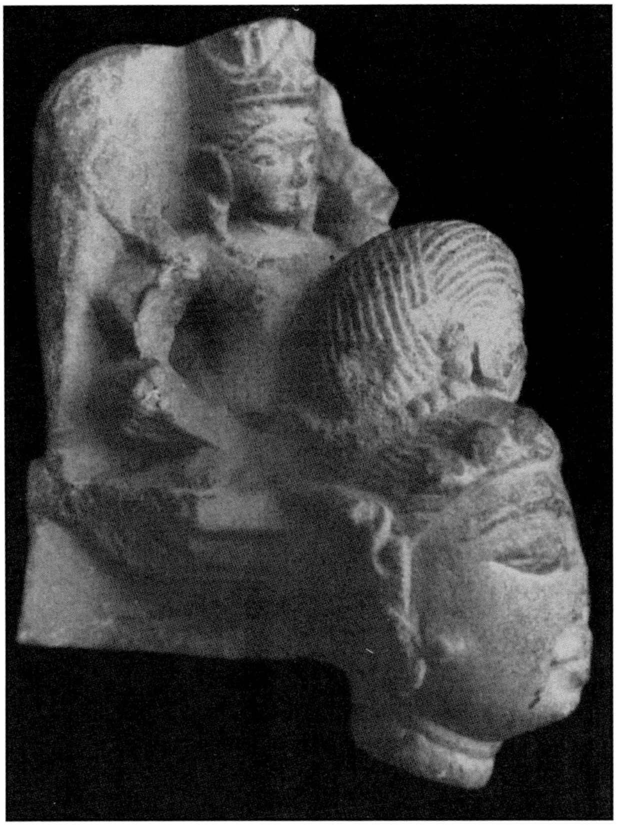

**Pl. 104.** Pārvatī head with another figure, Sarai Naga.

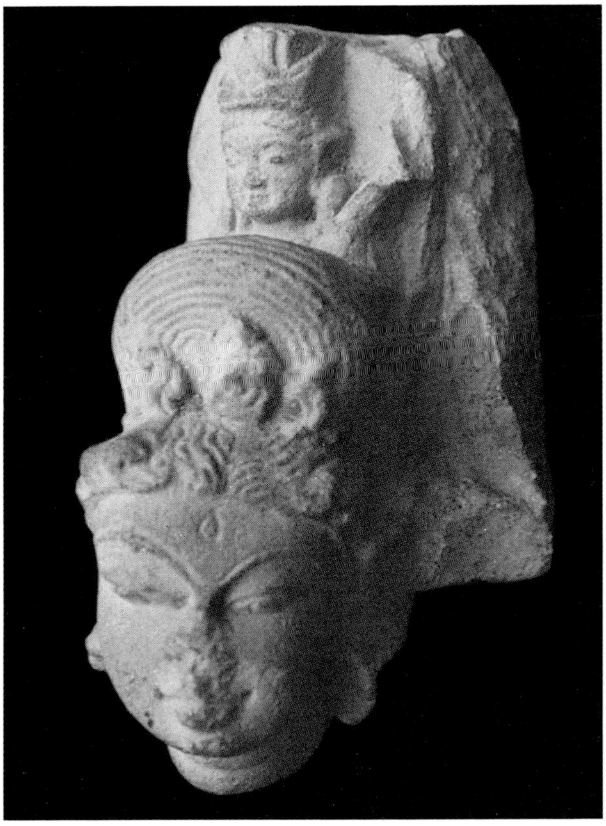

**Pl. 105.** Same, another view.

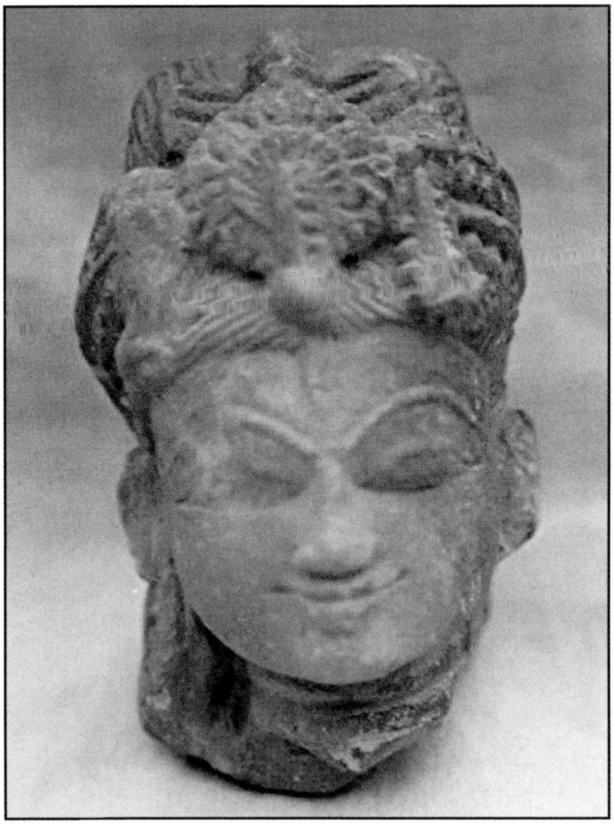

**Pl. 106.** Pārvatī head, Mard Khera.

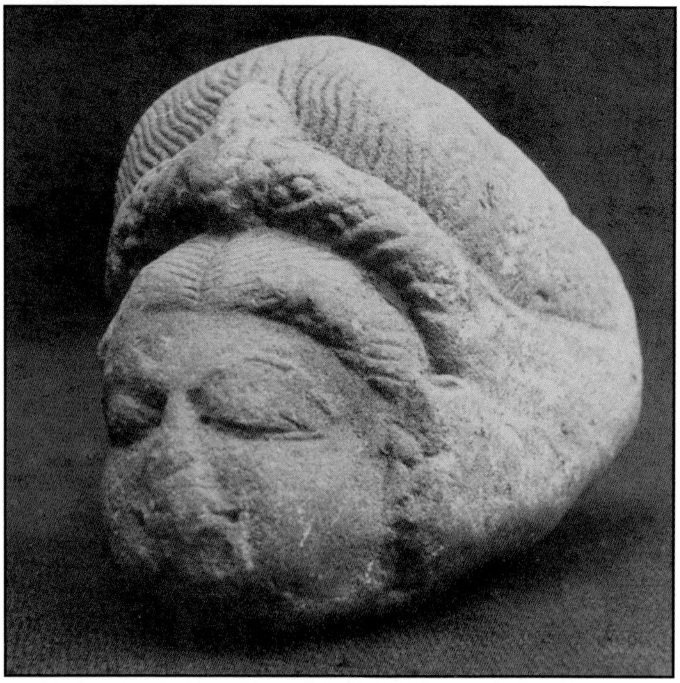

**Pl. 107.** Pārvatī head, Sunam.

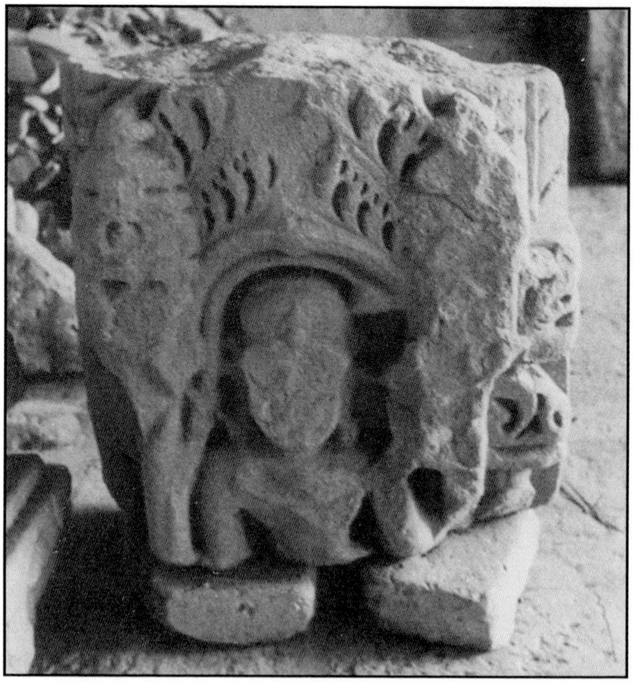

**Pl. 108.** Badly mutilated image of Pārvatī, Dholbaha.

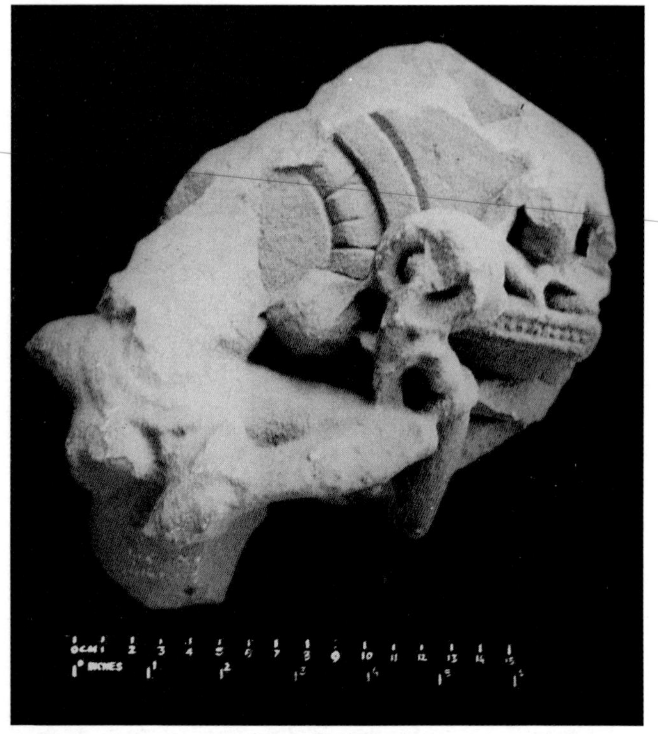

**Pl. 109.** Bust of Pārvatī(?), Sirhind.

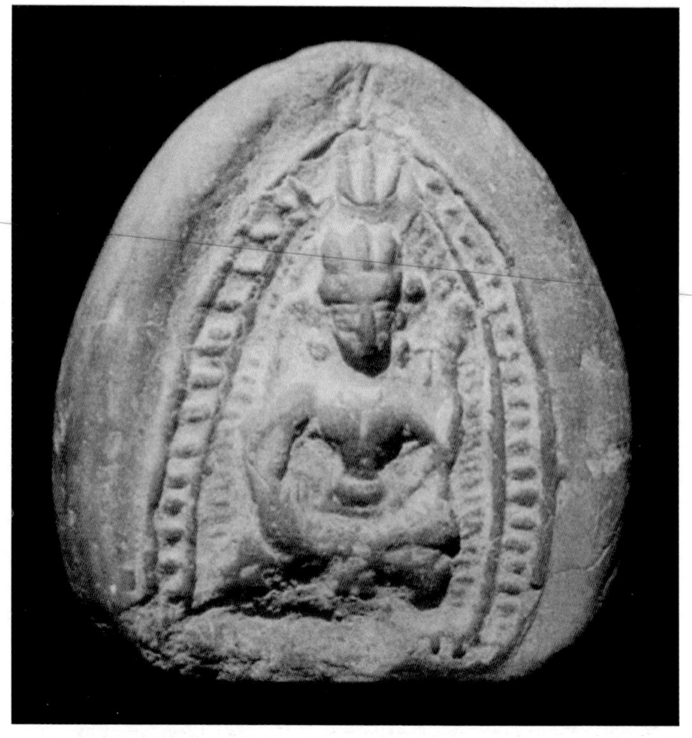

**Pl. 110.** Moulded plaque of Durgā, Hawara.

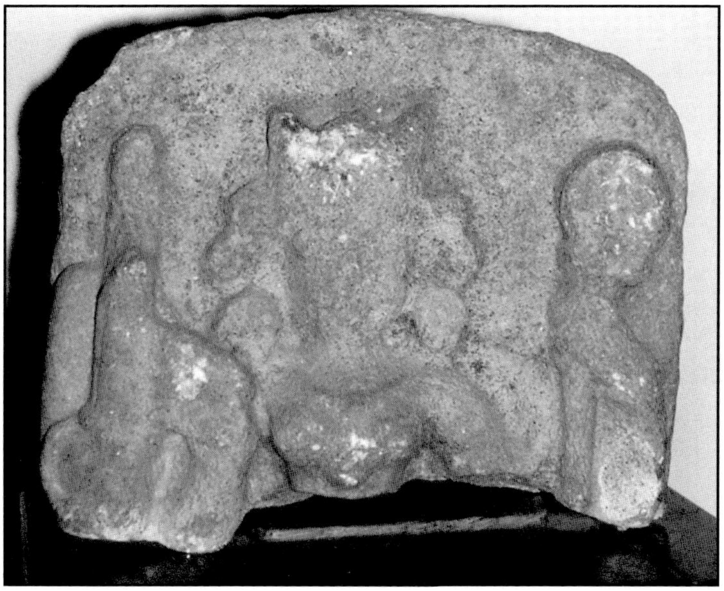

**Pl. 111.** Durgā, Dholbaha.

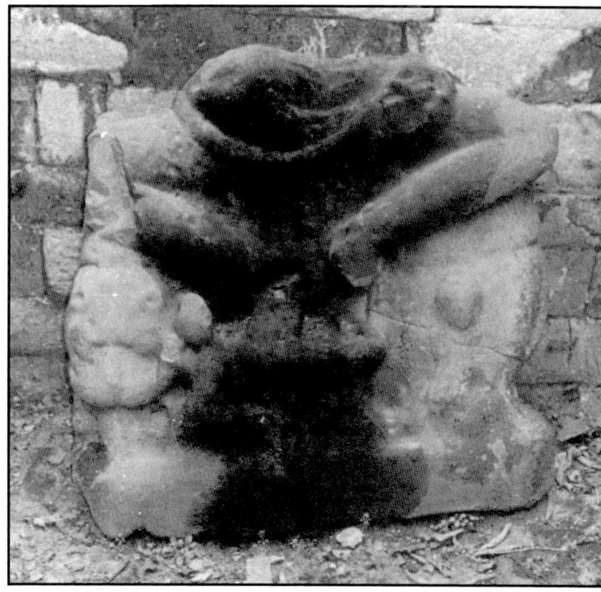

**Pl. 112.** Fragmentary Durgā, Dholbaha.

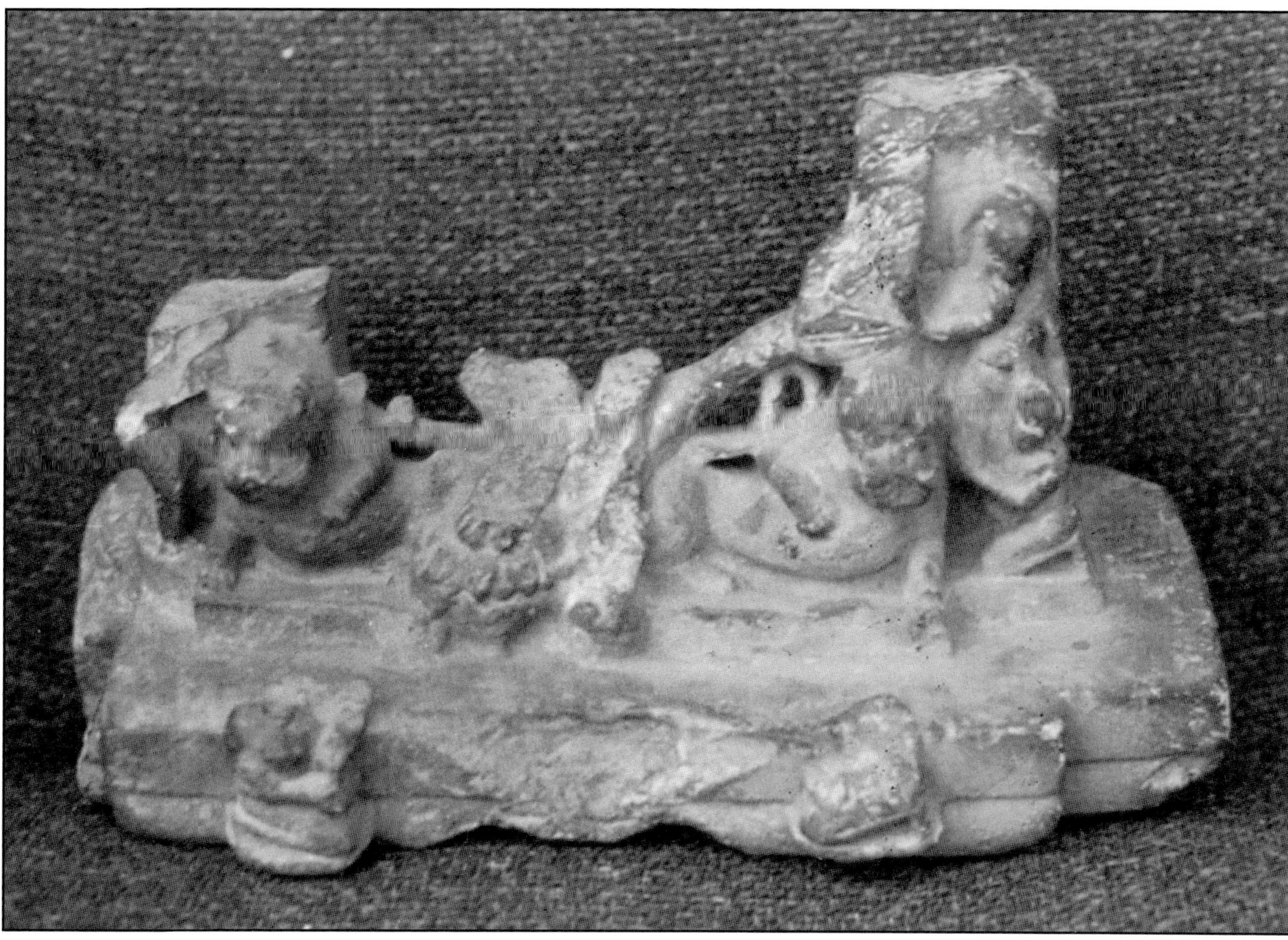

**Pl. 113.** Kshemaṅkarī, Sunam.

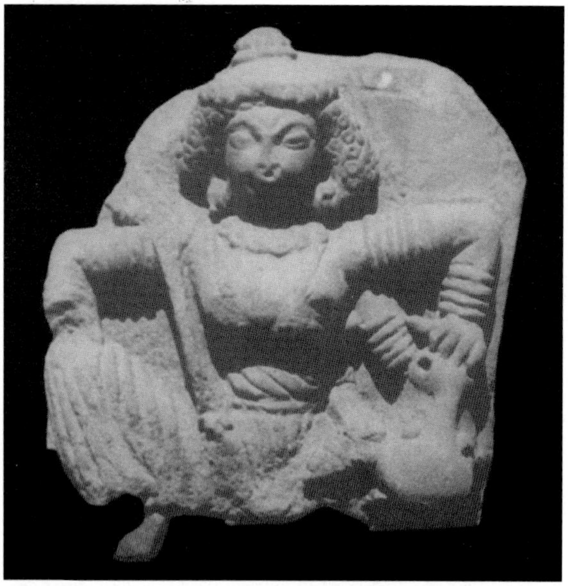

**Pl. 114.** Mahishāsuramardinī, terracotta, Sanghol.

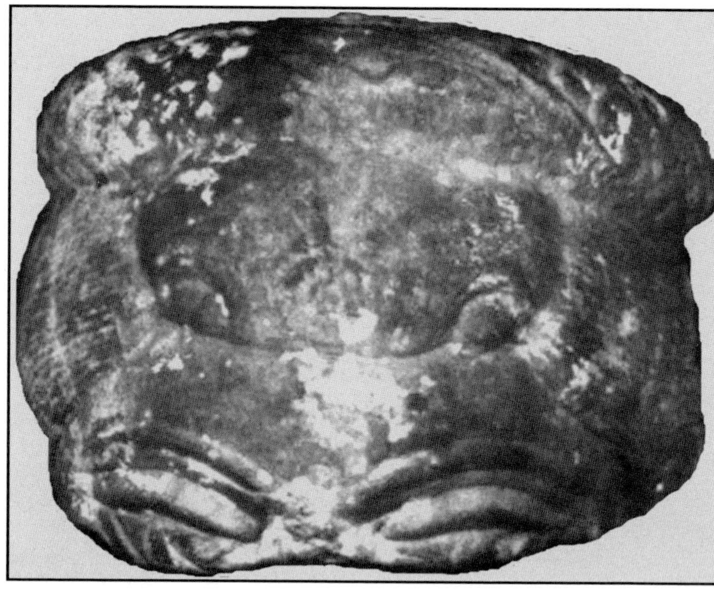

**Pl. 115.** Head of Mahishāsuramardinī (?), Sanghol.

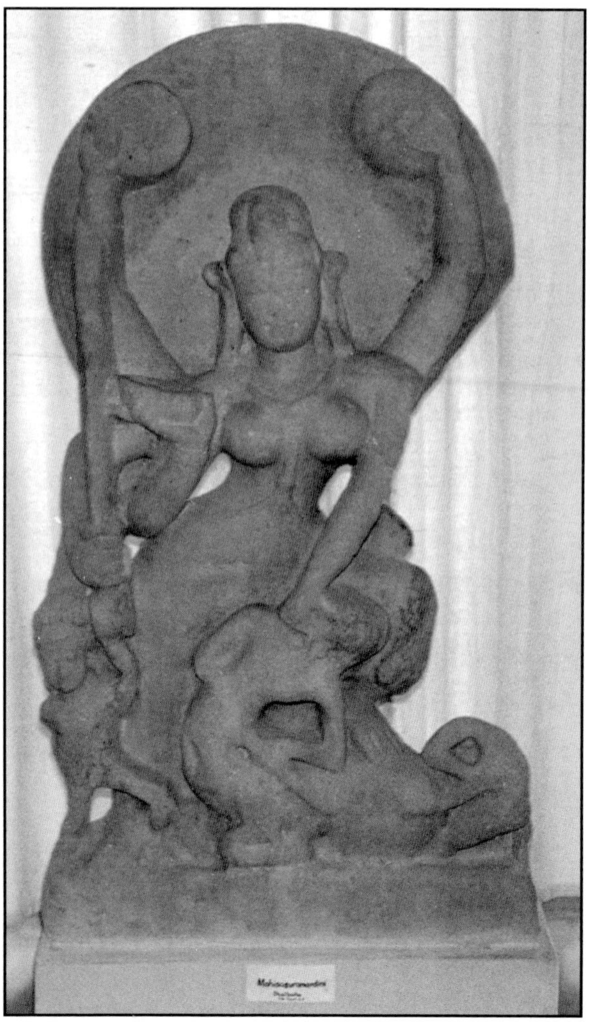

**Pl. 116.** Mahishāsuramardinī, Dholbaha.

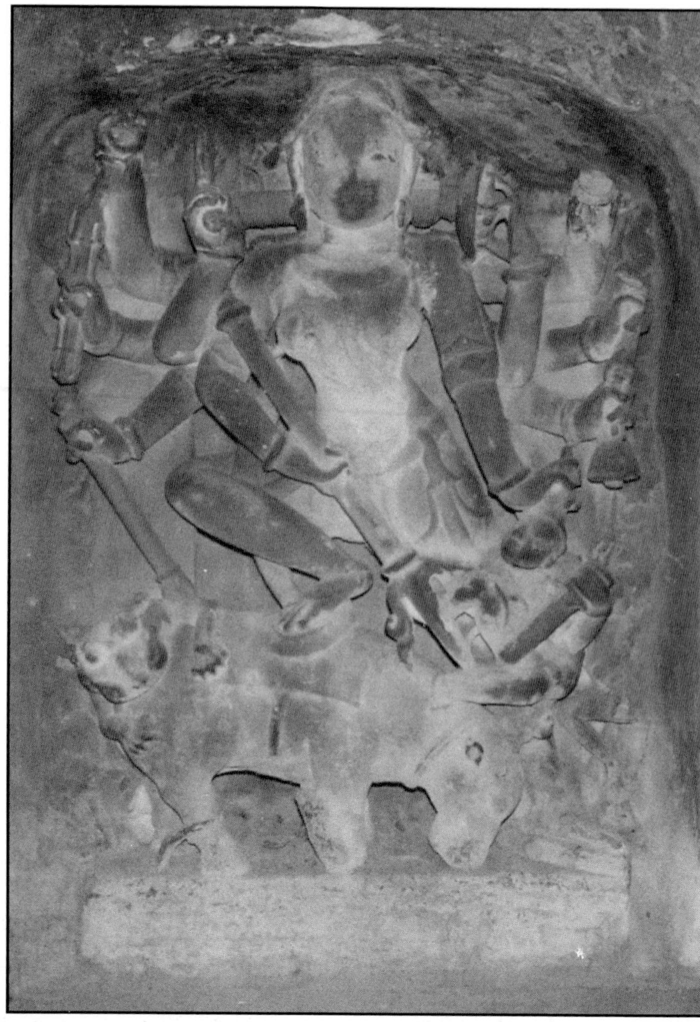

**Pl. 117.** Kātyāyanī under worship, Dholbaha.

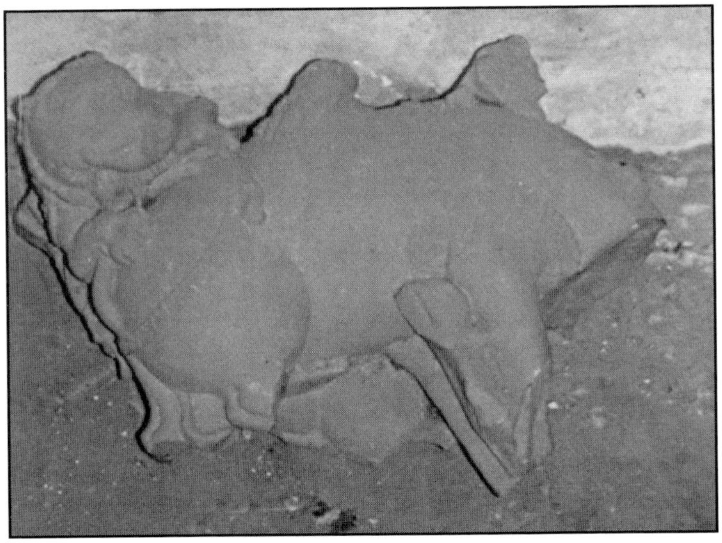

**Pl. 118.** Fragment of a Mahishāsuramardinī image, Dholbaha.

**Pl. 119.** Fragmentary Mahishāsuramardinī, Samuran.

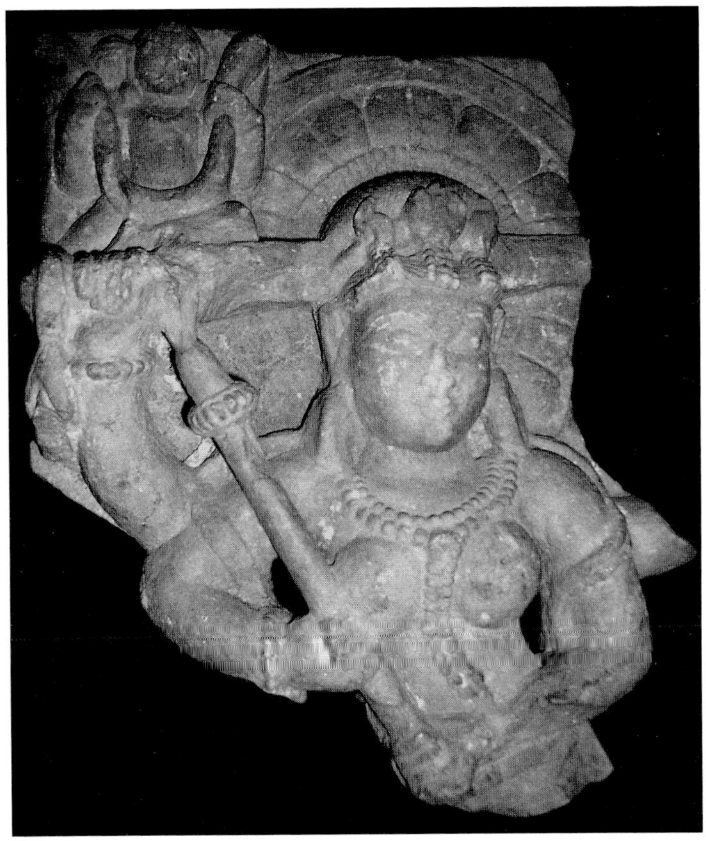

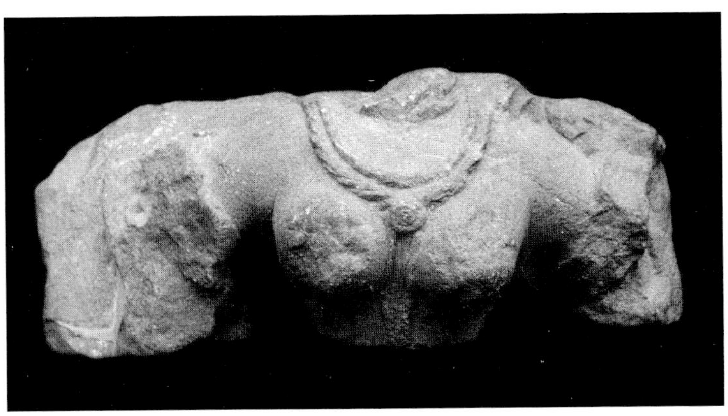

**Pl. 120.** Fragmentary bust of Mahishāsuramardinī, Kharar.

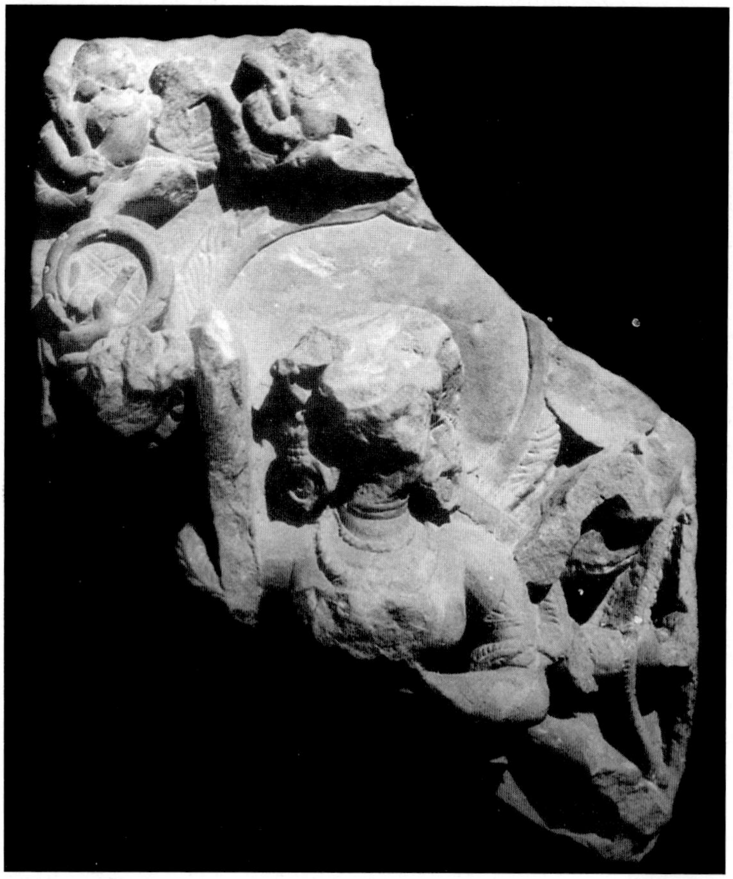

**Pl. 121.** Fragment of a Mahishāsuramardinī image, Sirhind.

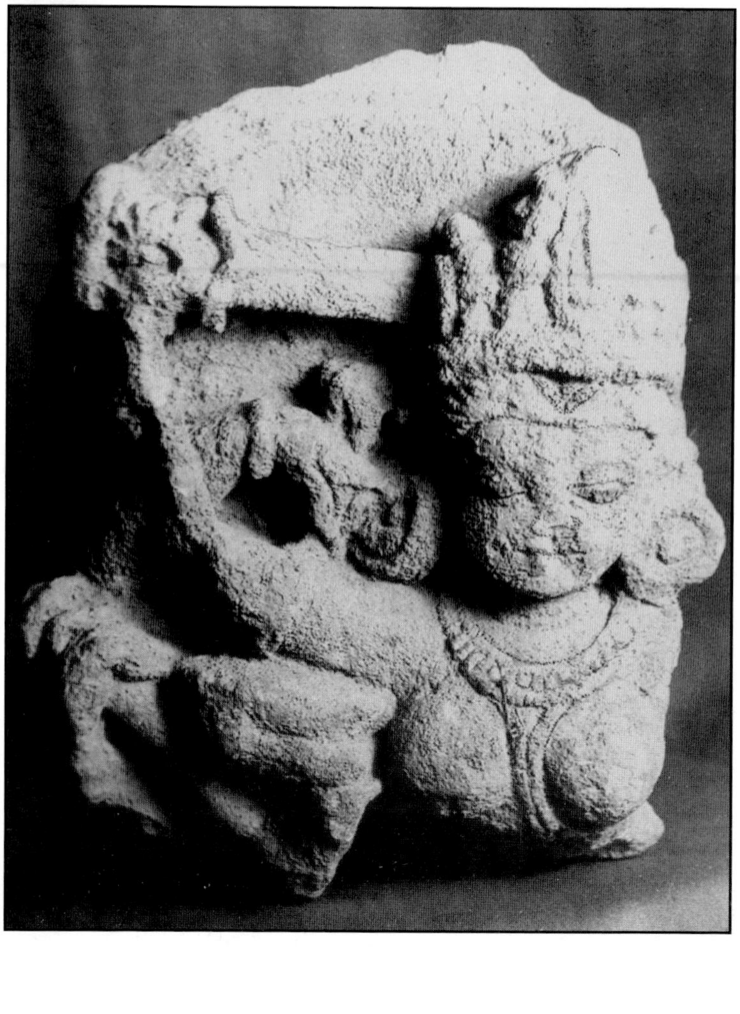

**Pl. 122.** Mahishāsuramardinī, Sunam.

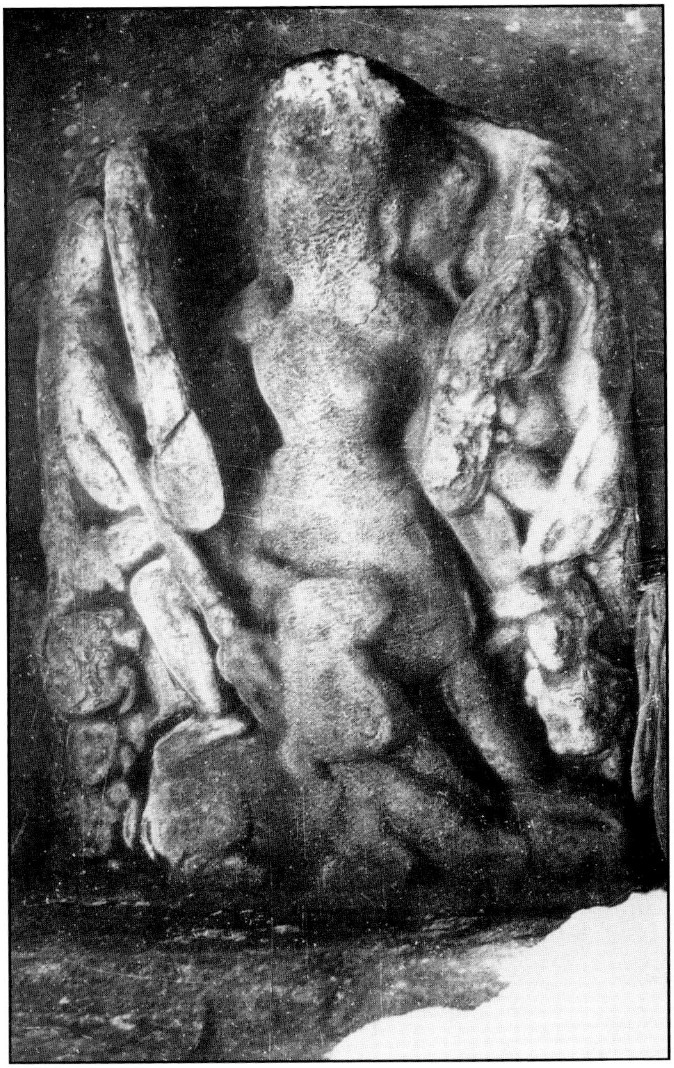

**Pl. 123.** Mahishāsuramardinī with additional elephantine head, Zahura.

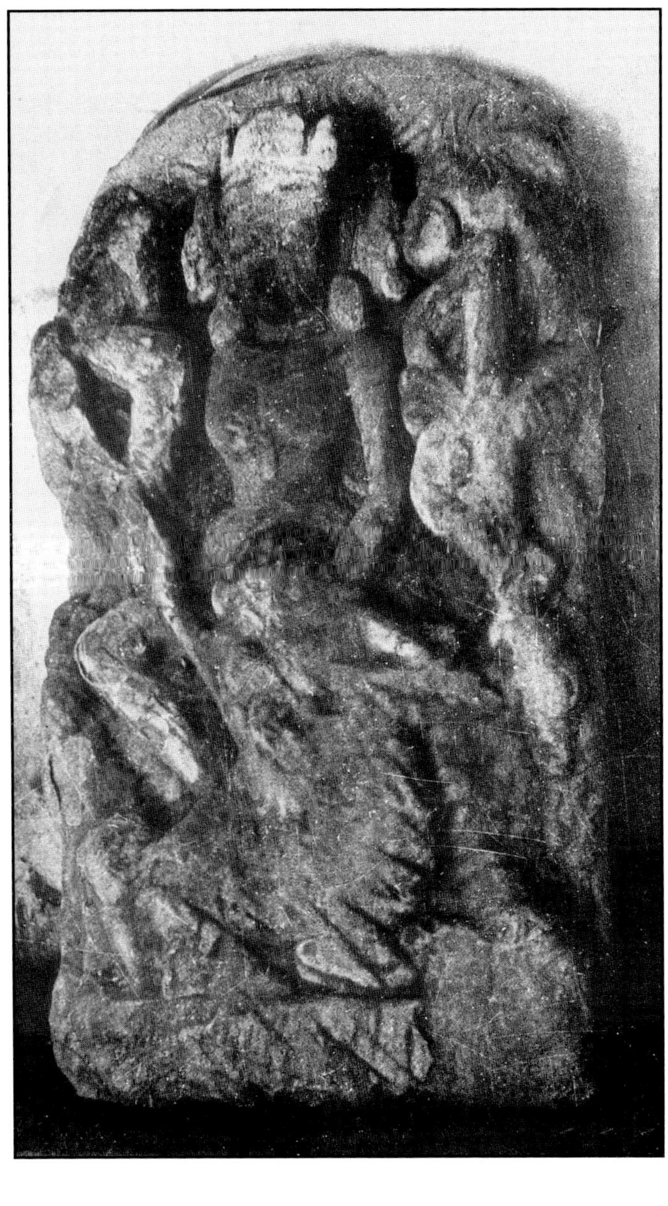

**Pl. 124.** Tri-cephalous Mahishāsuramardinī, Zahura.

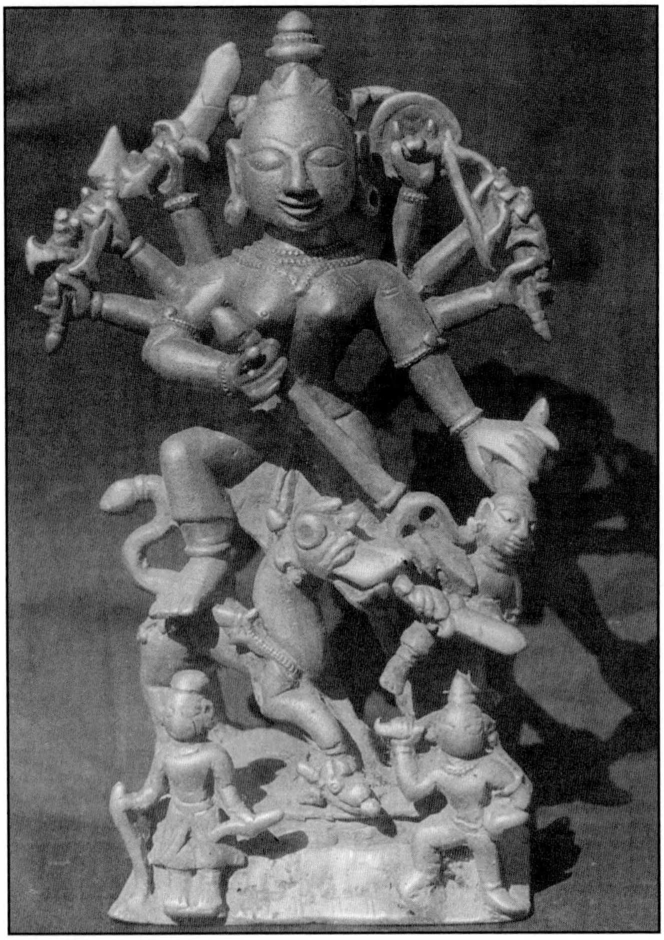

**Pl. 125.** Eight armed Mahishāsuramardinī, bronze, Kharar.

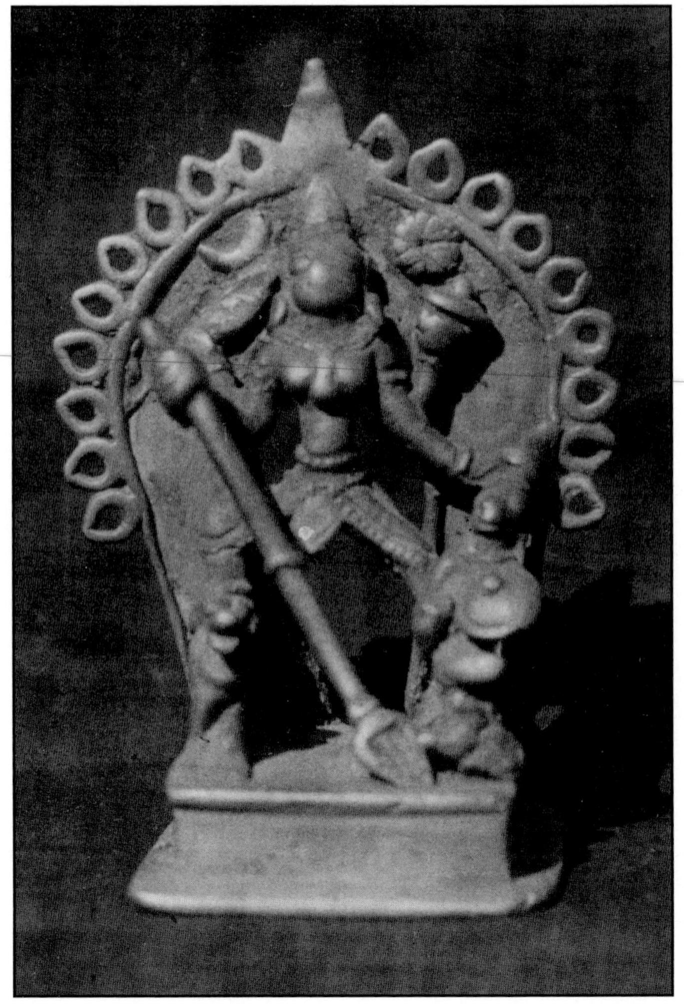

**Pl. 126.** Four armed Mahishāsuramardinī, bronze, Kharar.

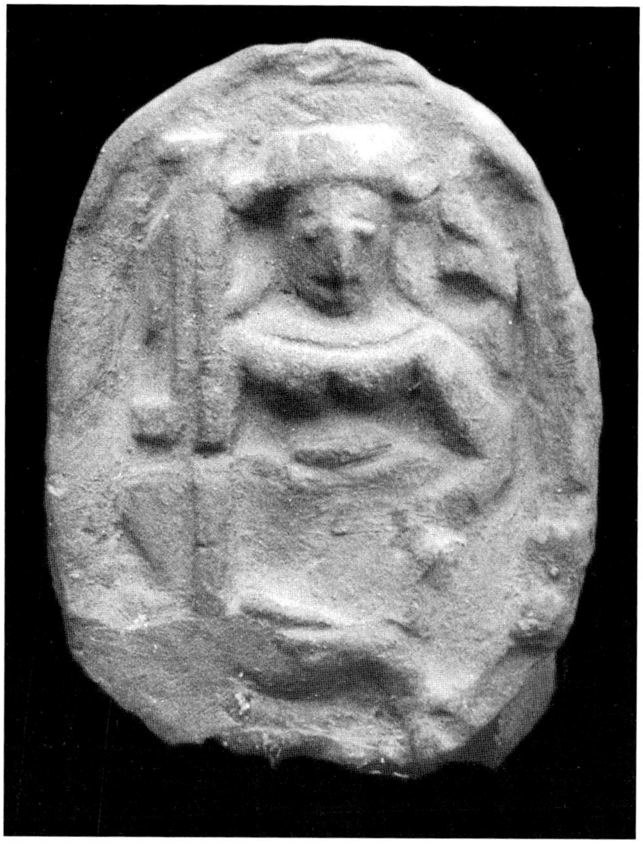

**Pl. 127.** Moulded plaque of Mahishāsuramardinī, Hawara.

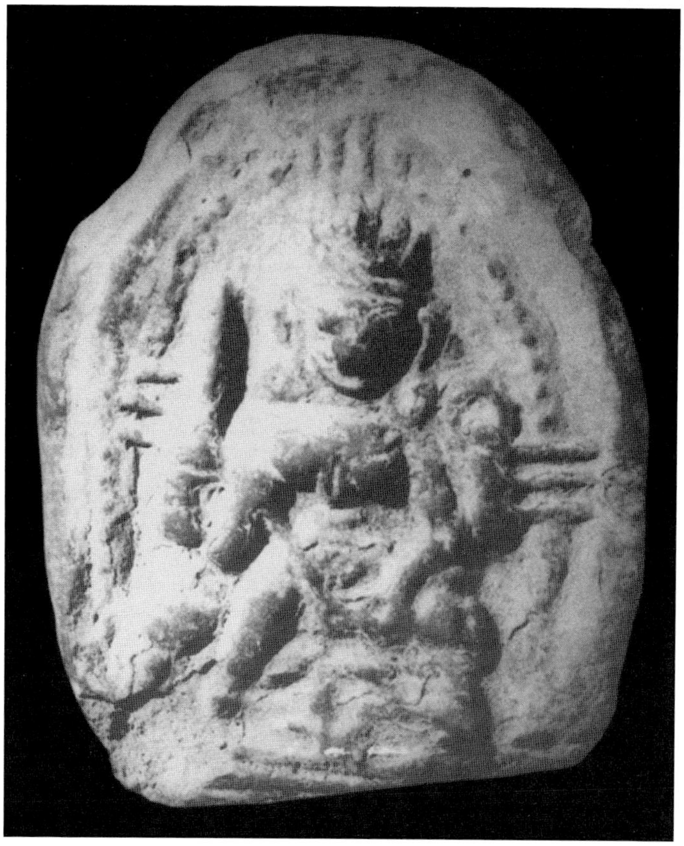

**Pl. 128.** Clay mould of Mahishāsuramardinī, Sahana.

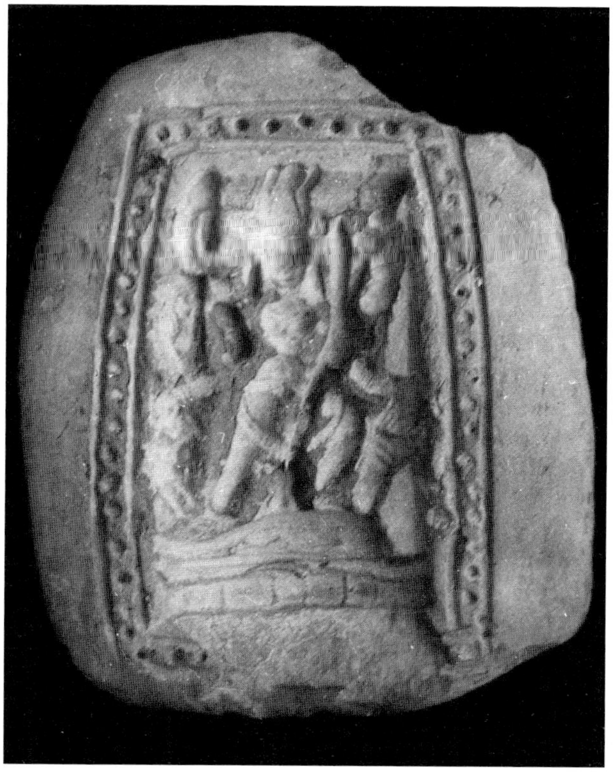

**Pl. 129.** Terracotta mould of Kālī, Hawara.

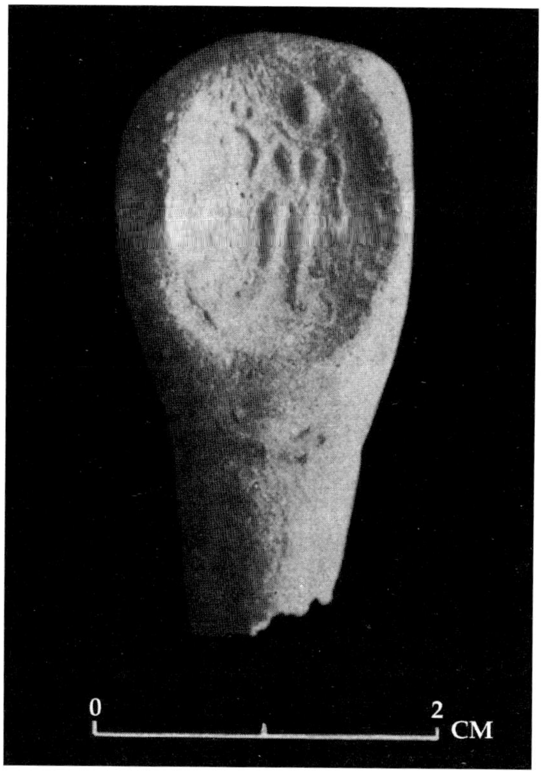


**Pl. 130.** Clay sealing showing Lakshmī, Sanghol.

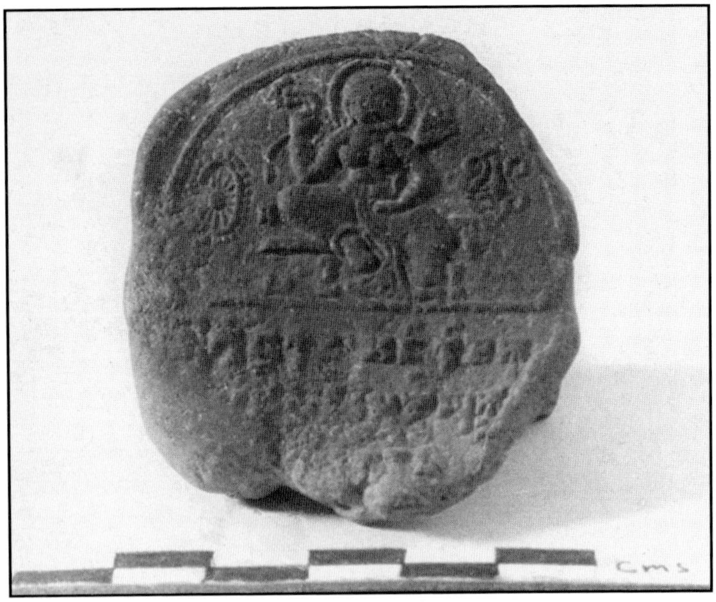

**Pl. 131.** Inscribed terracotta sealing showing Lakshmī, Ropar.

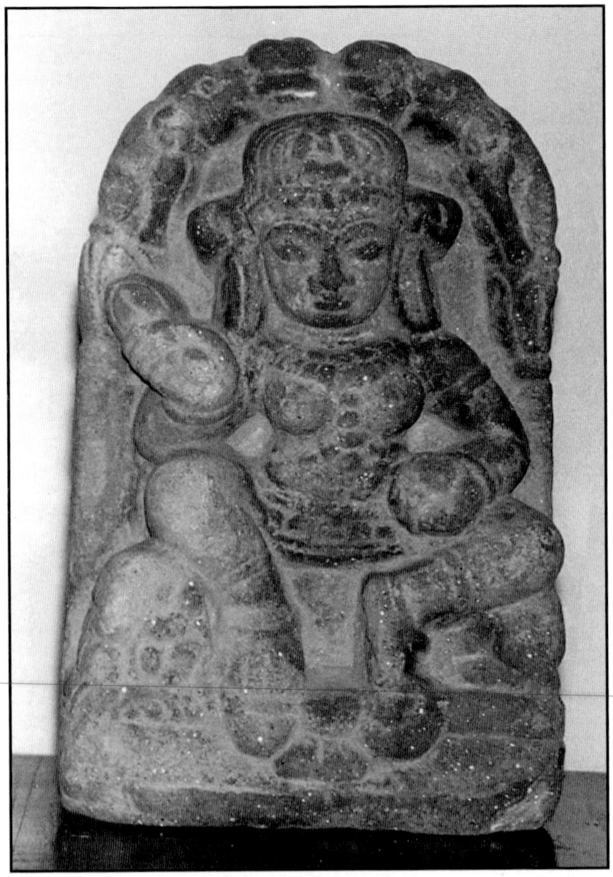

**Pl. 133.** Gaja-Lakshmī, Dholbaha.

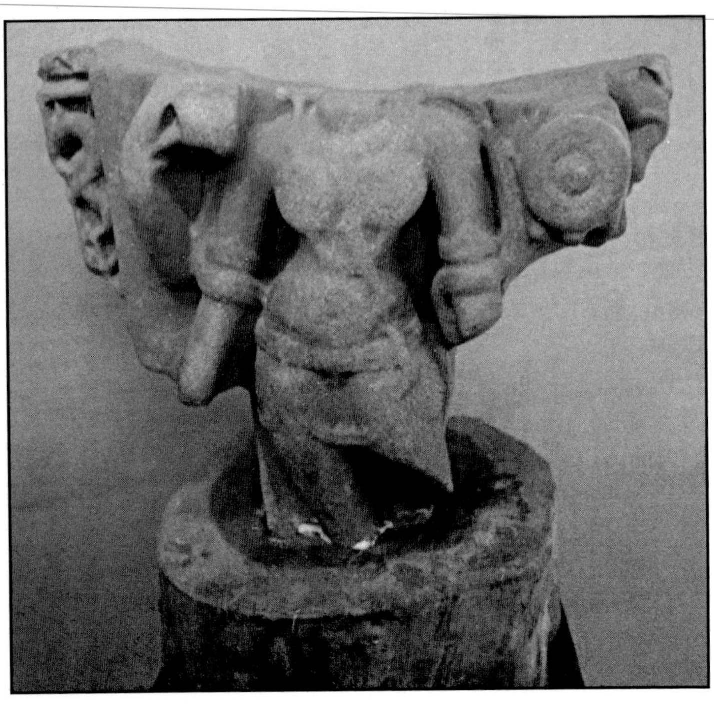

**Pl. 132.** Fragmentary Lakshmī, Dholbaha.

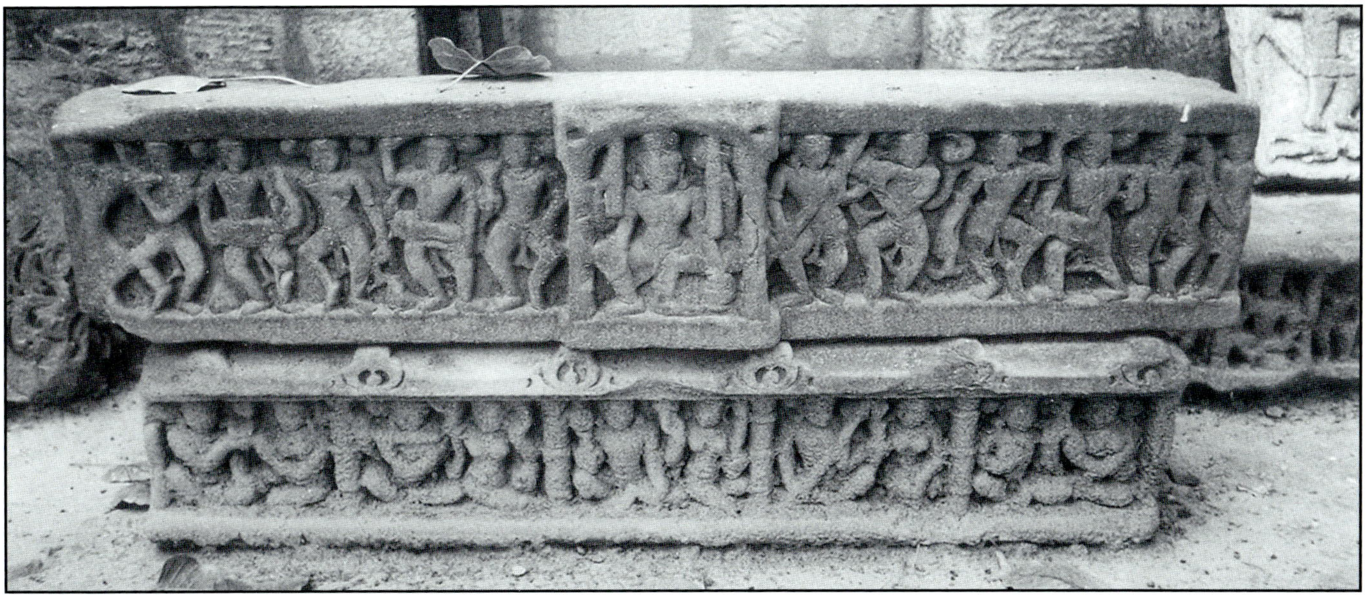

**Pl. 134.** Aechitectural frieze showing Sarasvatī, Dholbaha.

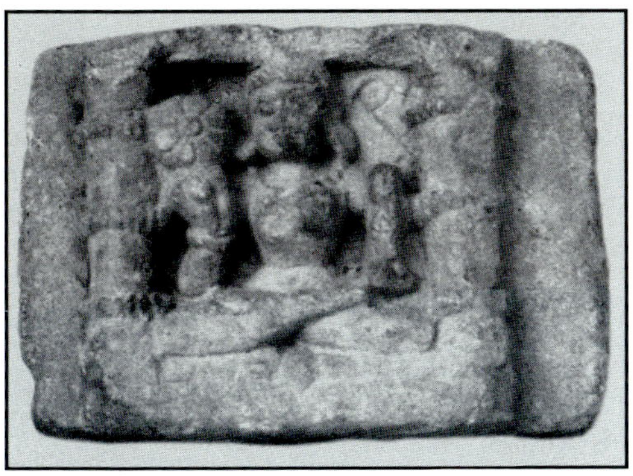

**Pl. 135.** Sarasvatī, Mard Khera.

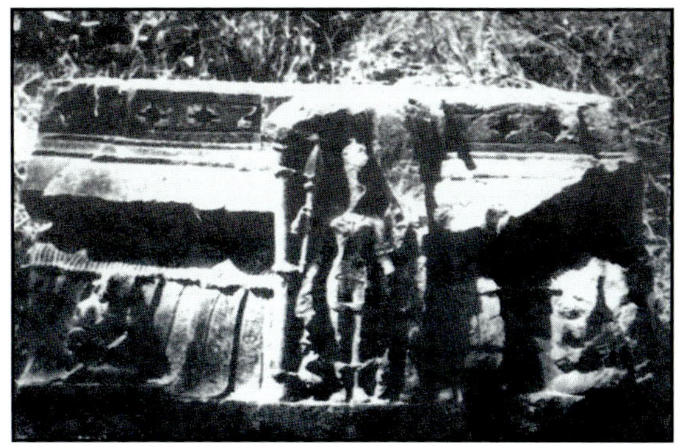

**Pl. 138.** Kaumārī, Majhur.

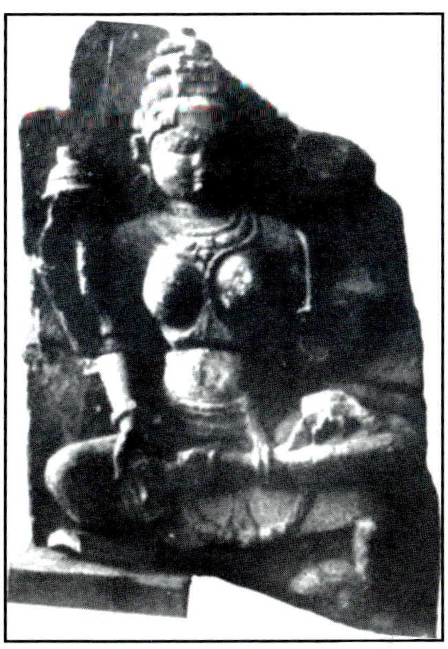

**Pl. 136.** Brahmāṇī, exact provenance unknown.

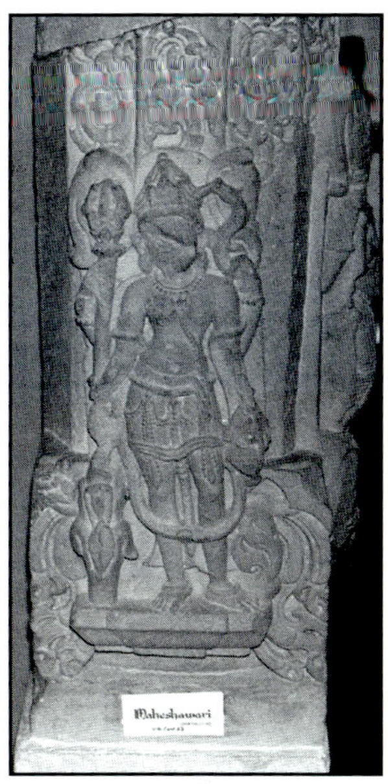

**Pl. 137.** Māheśvarī, Majhur.

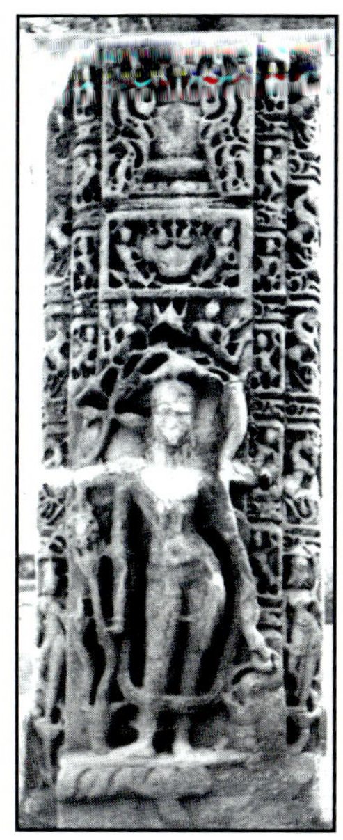

**Pl. 139.** Gaṅgā, Dholbaha.

Pl. 141. River Goddesses, Kharar.

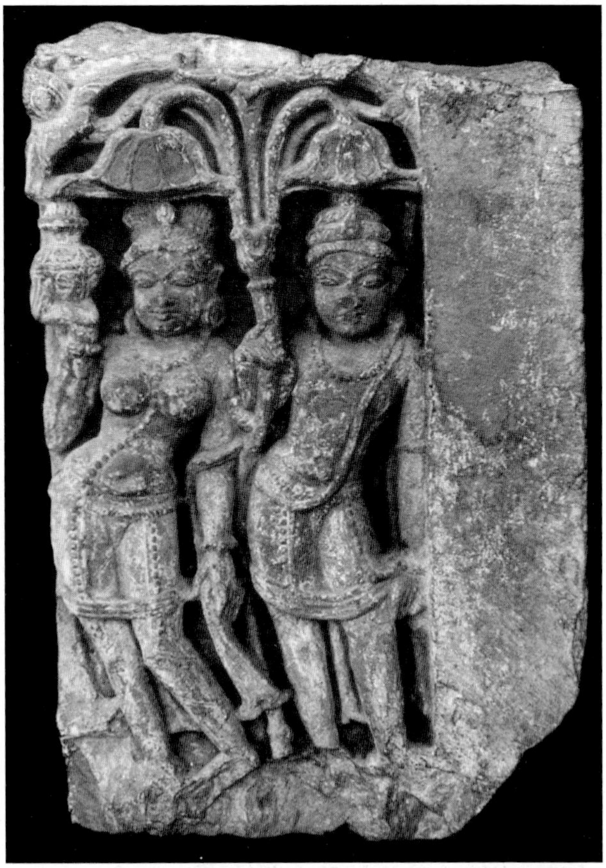

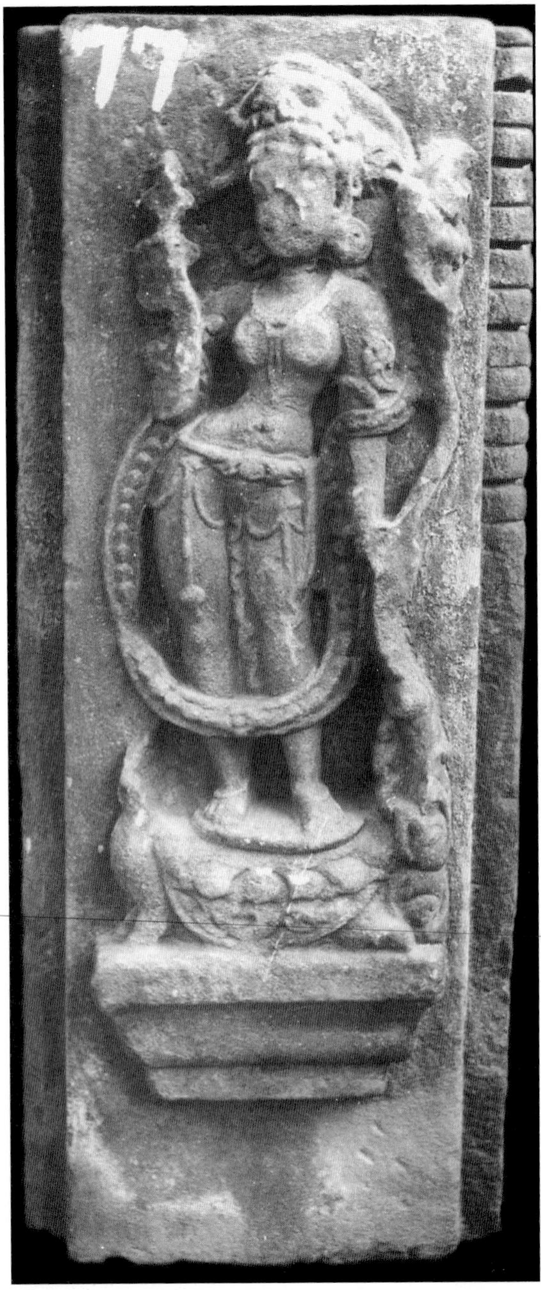

**Pl. 140.** Yamunā, Dholbaha.

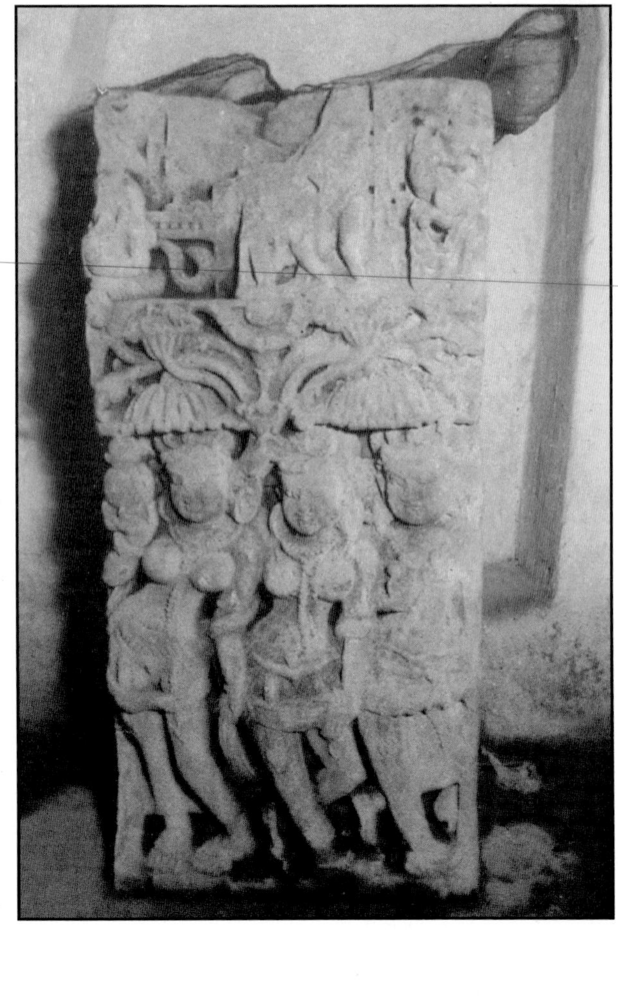

**Pl. 142.** Doorjamb with river goddesses, Sunam.

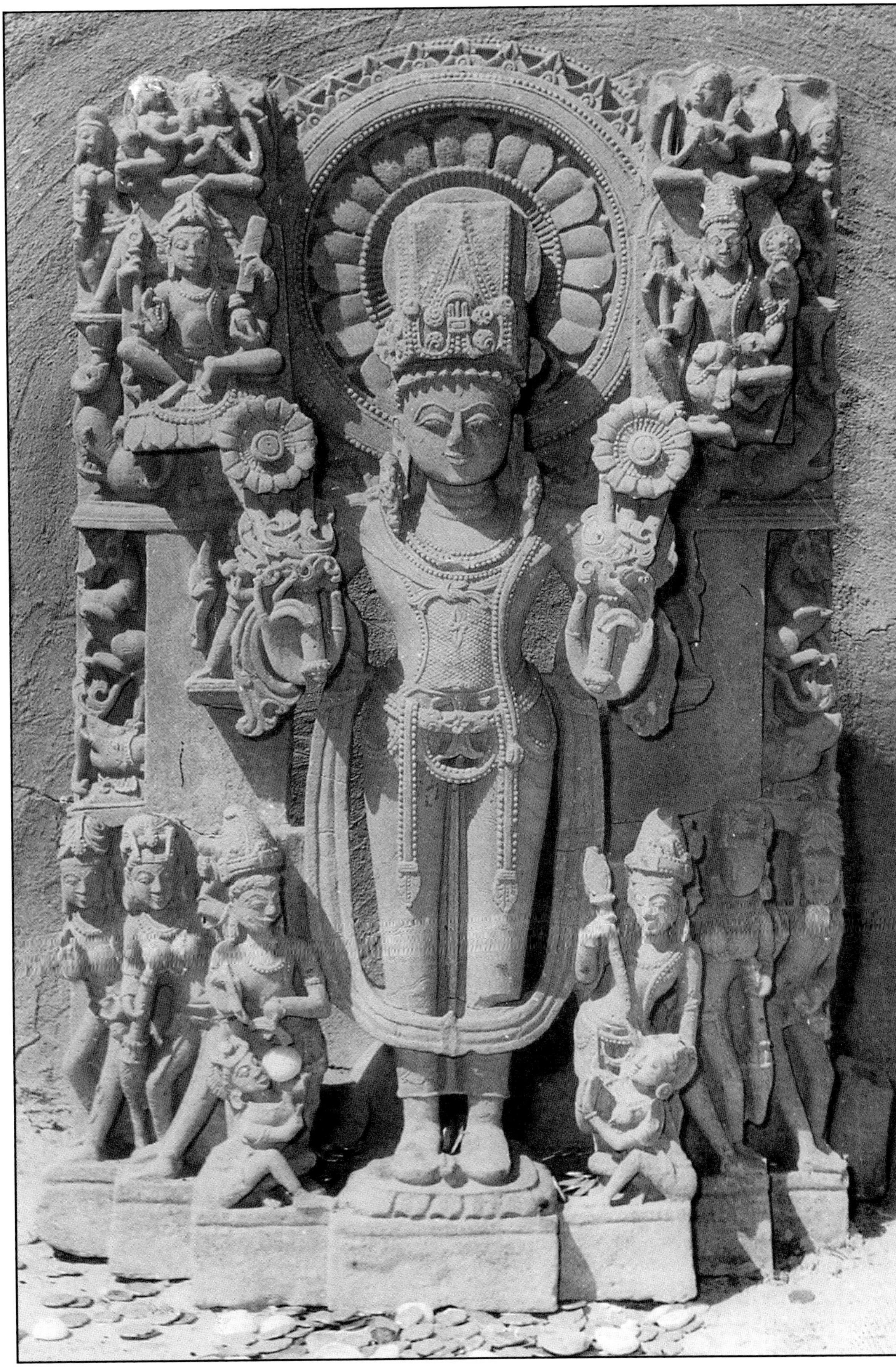

**Pl. 143.** Sūrya, Mard Khera.

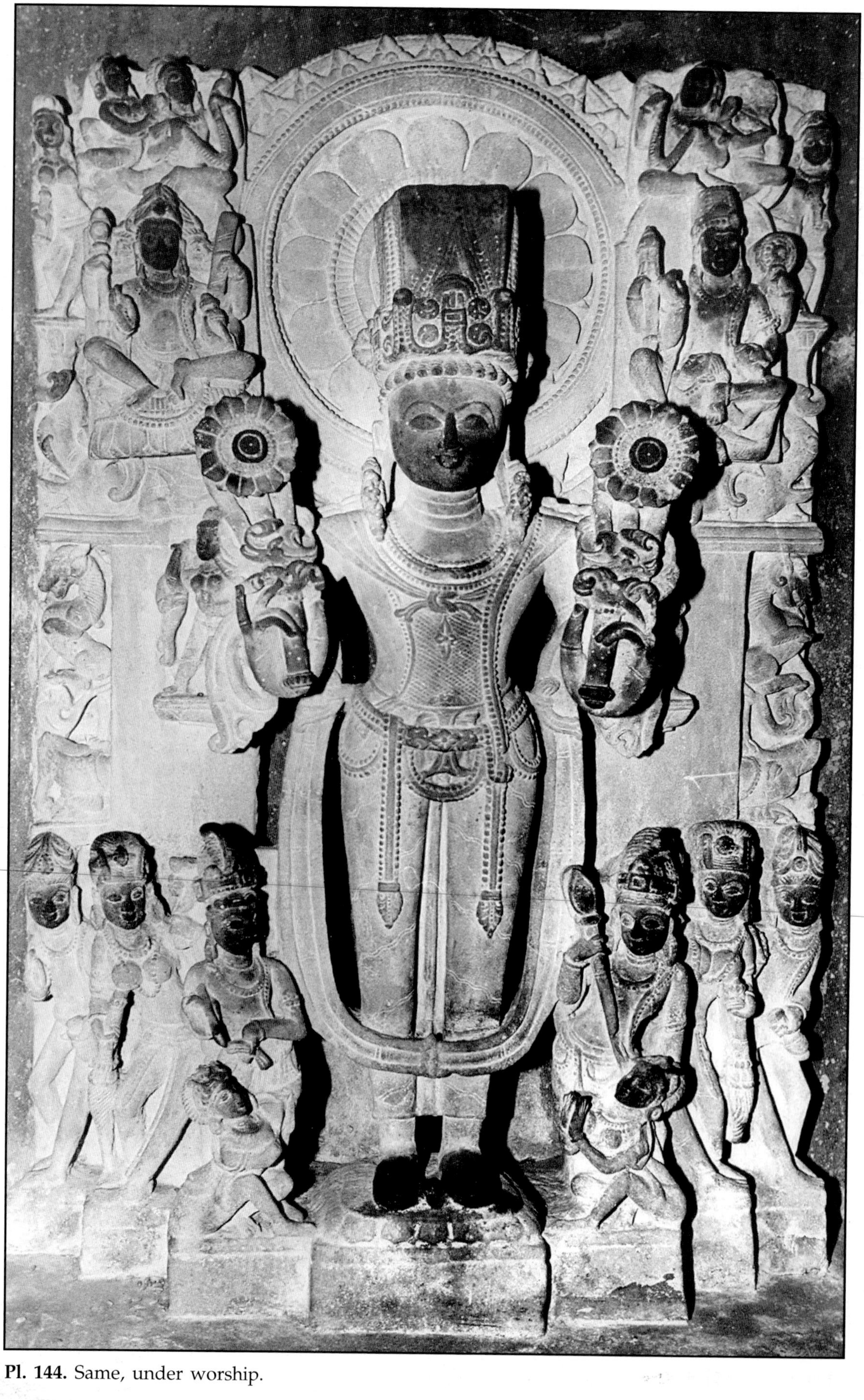

**Pl. 144.** Same, under worship.

**Pl. 146.** Standing Sūrya, Sunam.

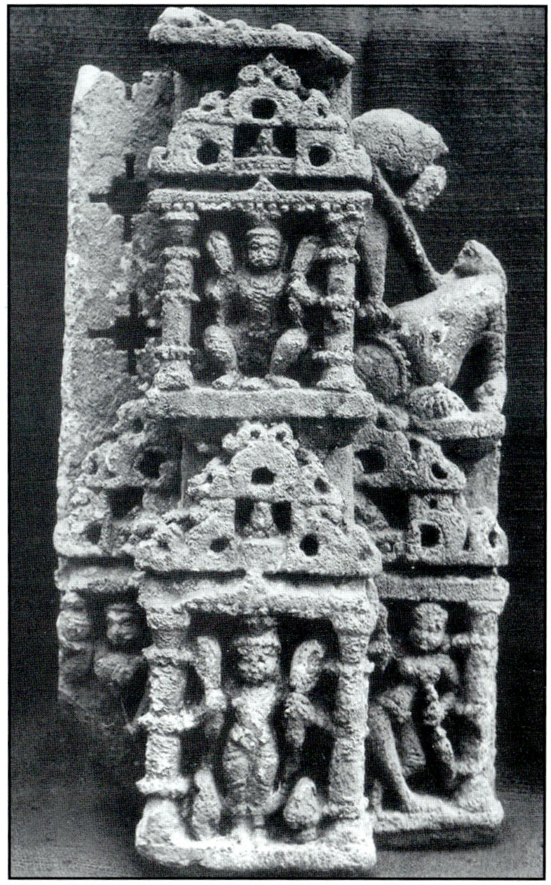

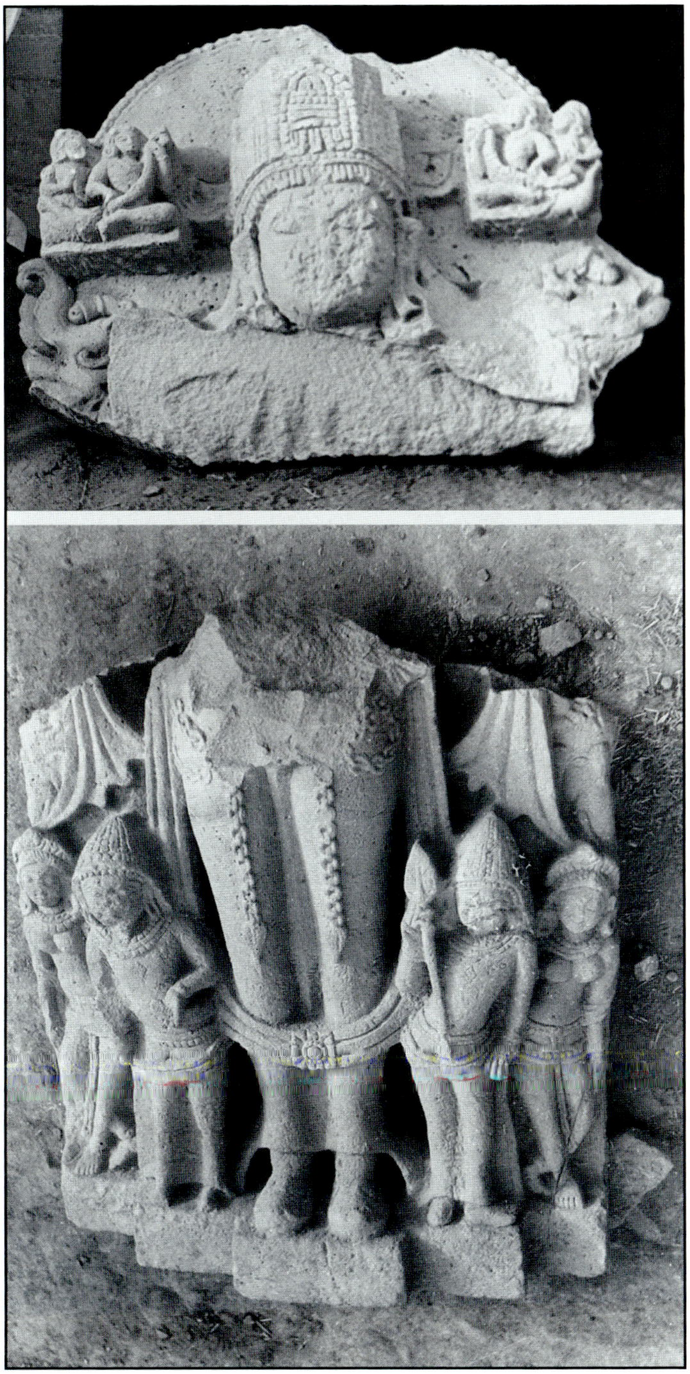

**Pl. 145.** Fragments of Sūrya image, Sunam.

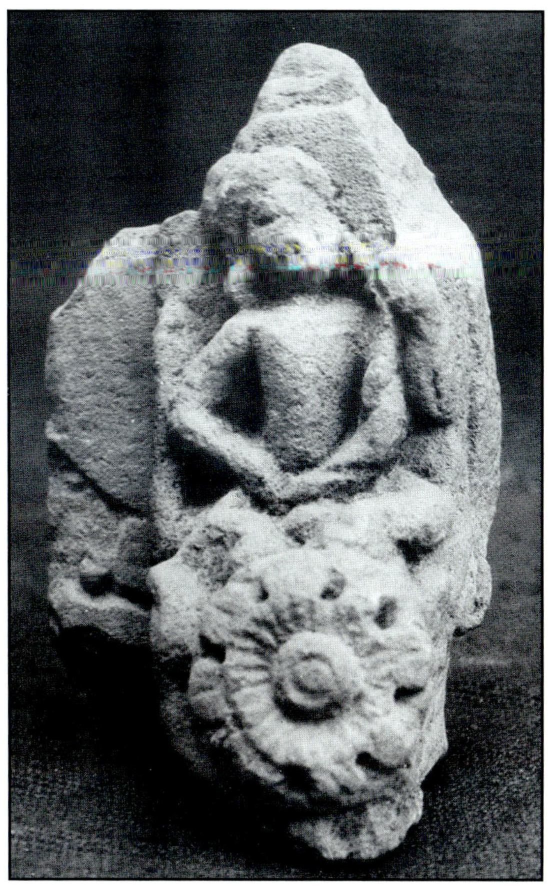

**Pl. 147.** Stele of a Sūrya image, Sunam.

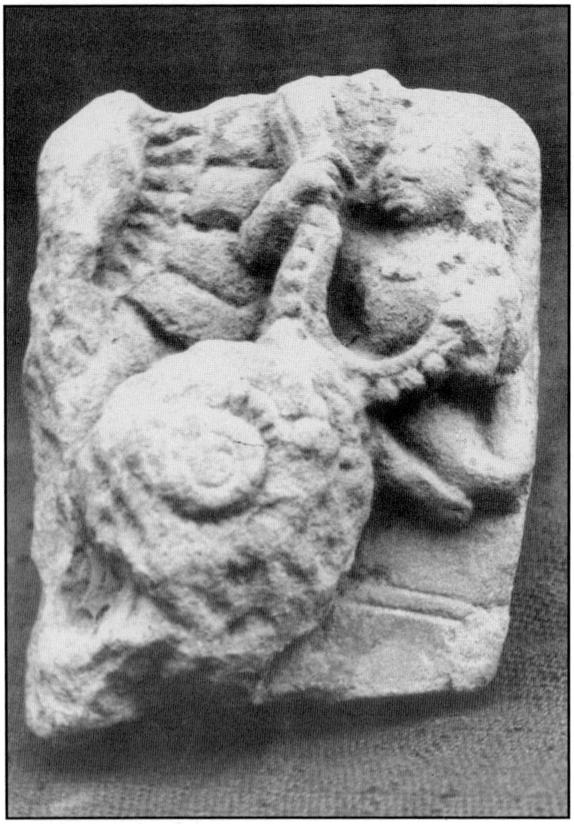

**Pl. 148.** Stele of a Sun image, Sunam.

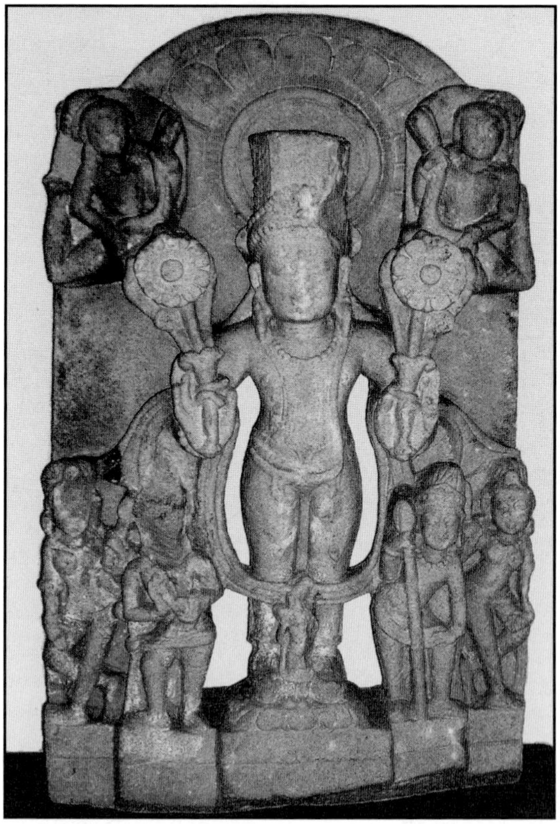

**Pl. 149.** Sūrya, Samuran.

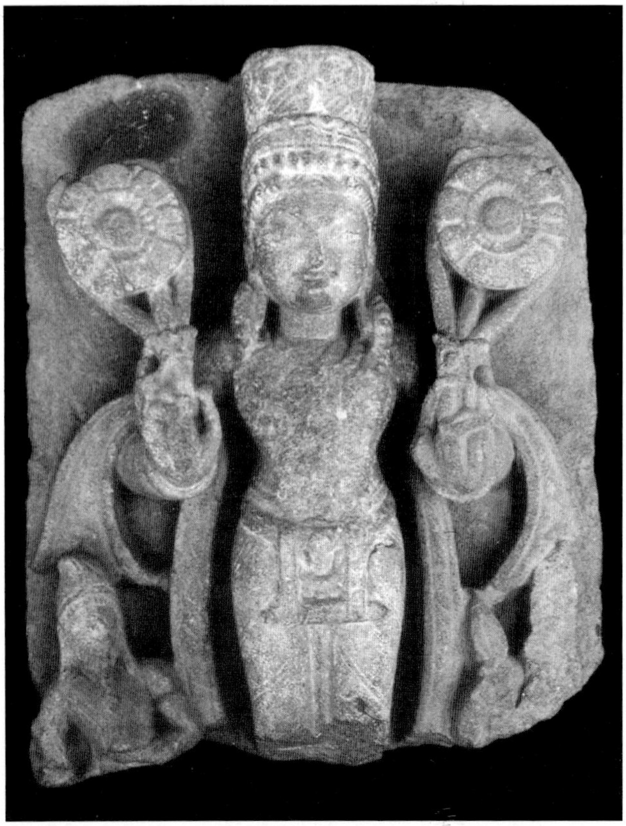

**Pl. 150.** Sūrya, Singh-Bhagwantpur.

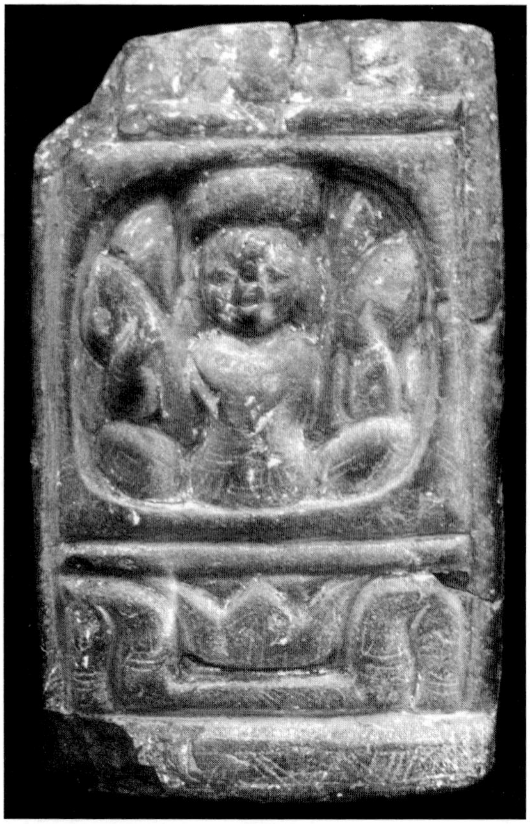

**Pl. 151.** Stone plaque showing seated Sūrya, Gujar Kheri.

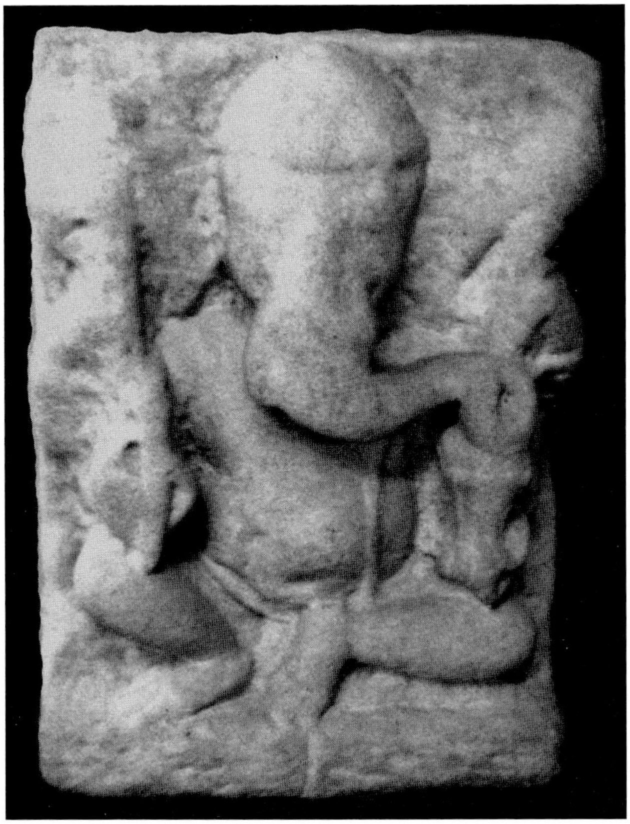

**Pl. 152.** Gaṇeśa, Dholbaha.

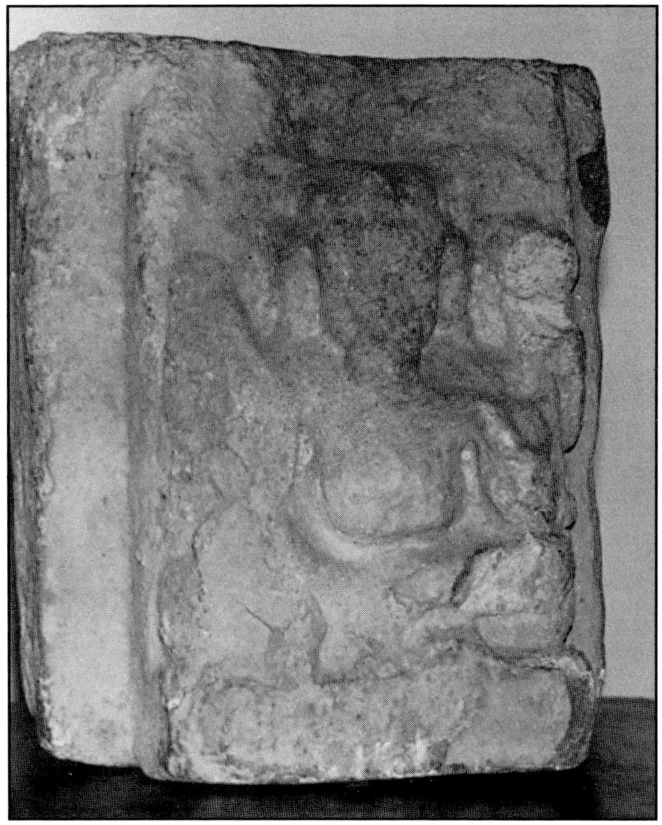

**Pl. 154.** Gaṇeśa (Hoshiarpur Museum), Dholbaha.

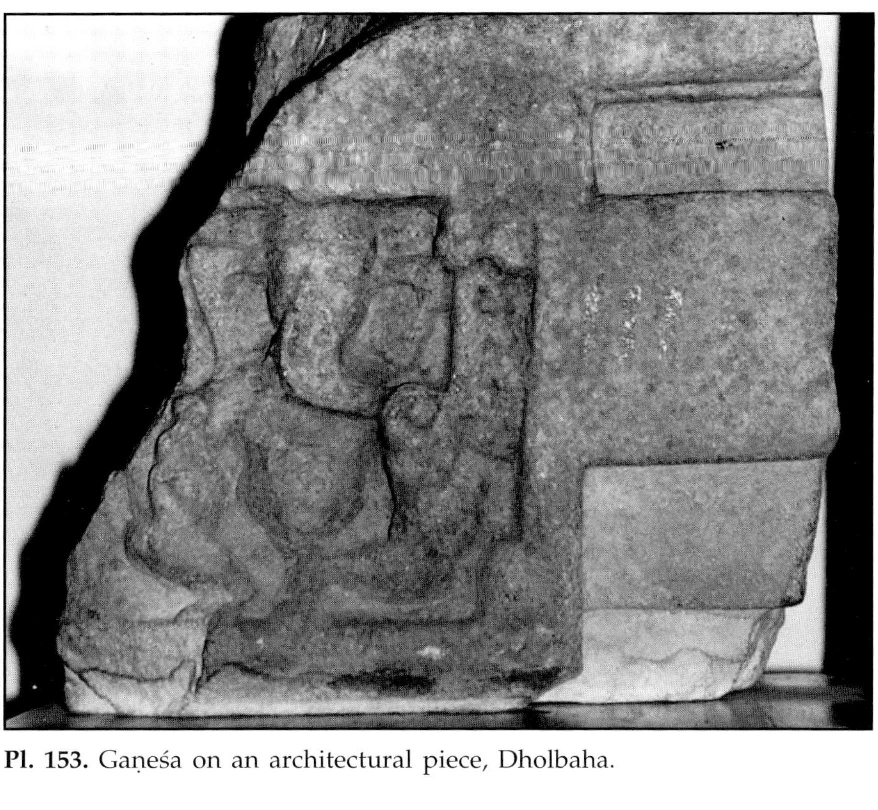

**Pl. 153.** Gaṇeśa on an architectural piece, Dholbaha.

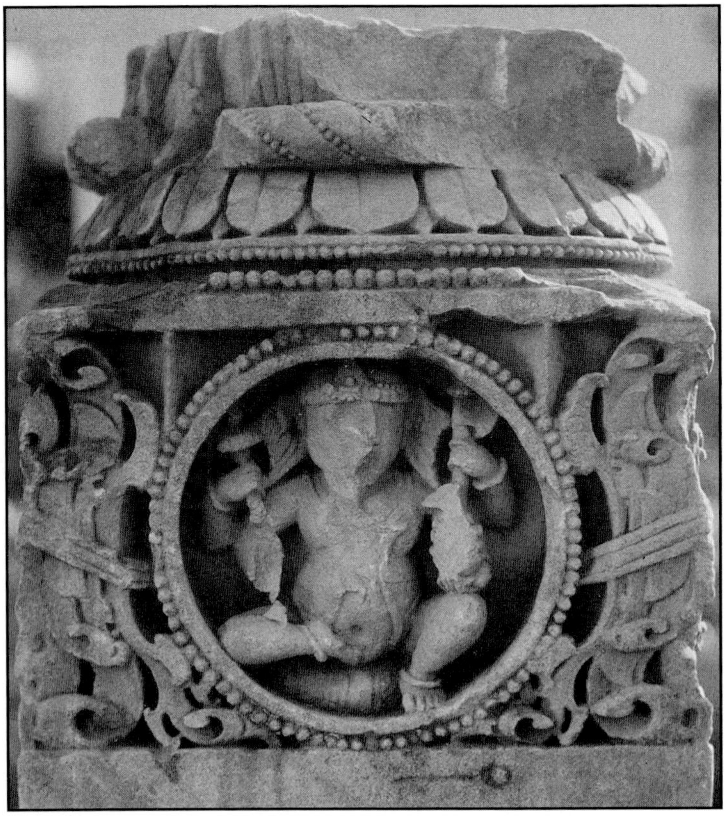

**Pl. 155.** Gaṇeśa in a medallion on a pillar, Sirhind.

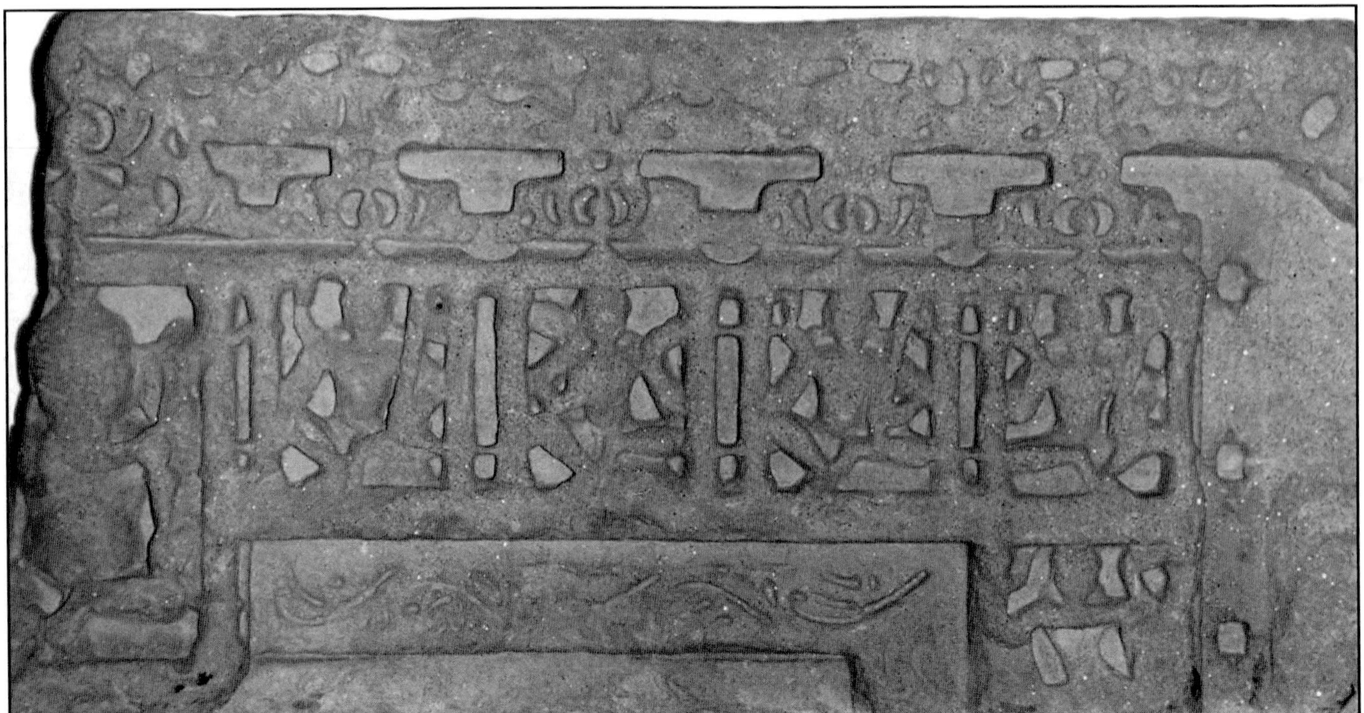

**Pl. 156.** Gaṇeśa on the lintel of a door-surround, Dholbaha.

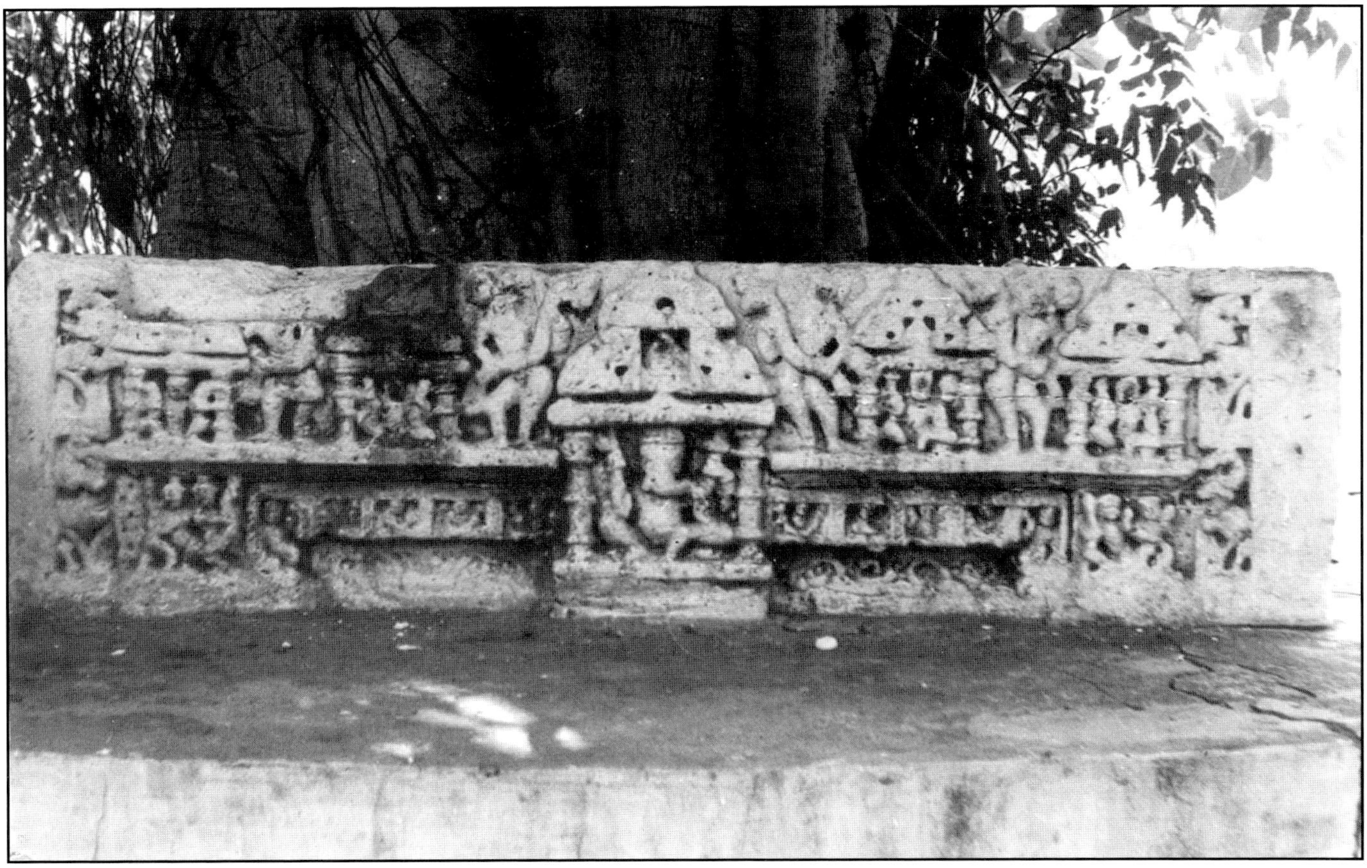

**Pl. 157.** Gaṇeśa on the lintel of a door-surround, Sunam.

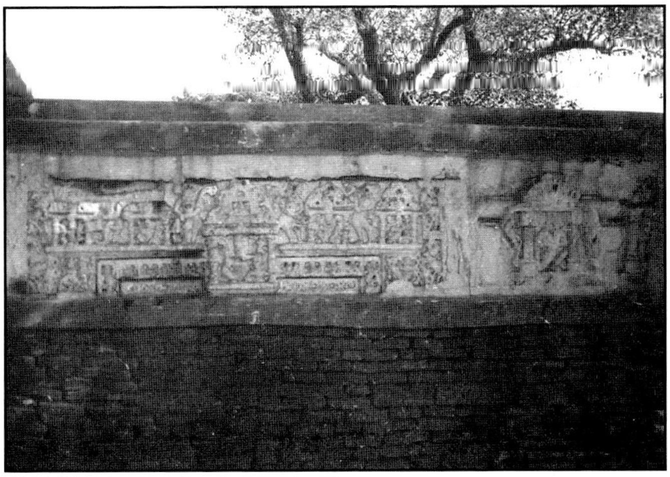

**Pl. 158.** Gaṇeśa on the lintel of another door-surround, Sunam.

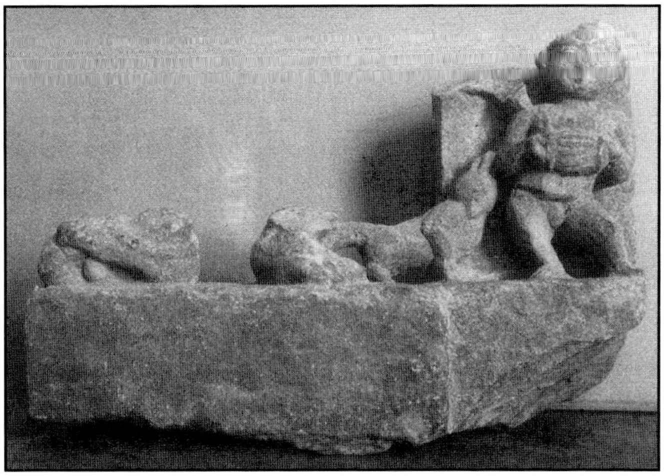

**Pl. 159.** Fragment of a dancing Gaṇeśa, Rajinidevi.

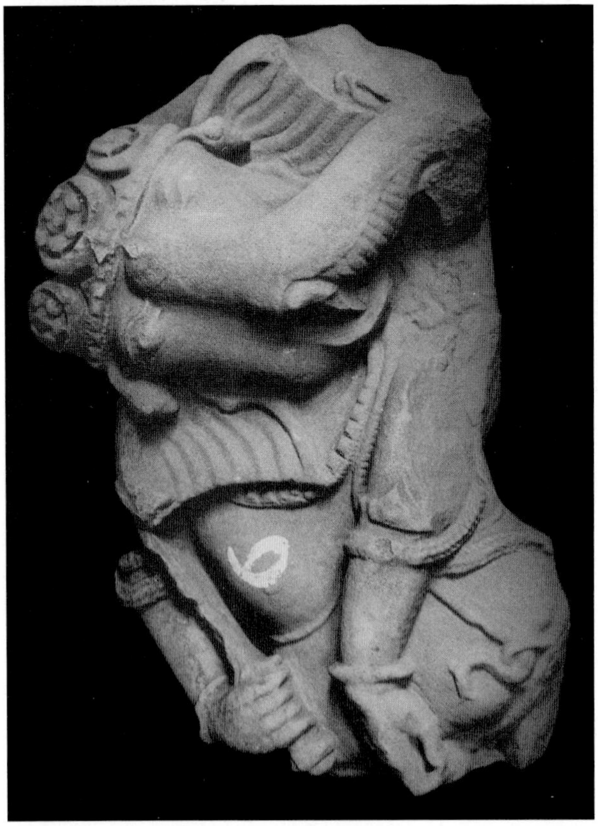

**Pl. 160.** Dancing Gaṇeśa, Dholbaha.

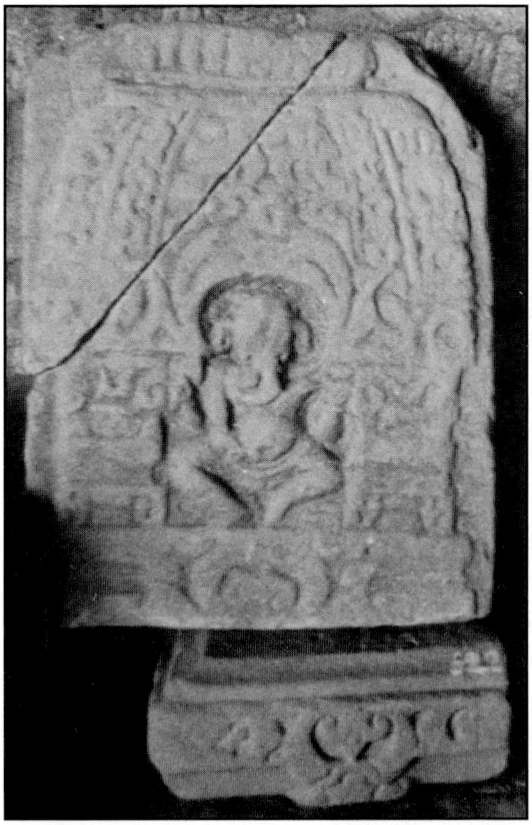

**Pl. 161.** Gaṇeśa on a *nāgara-kūṭa*, Dholbaha.

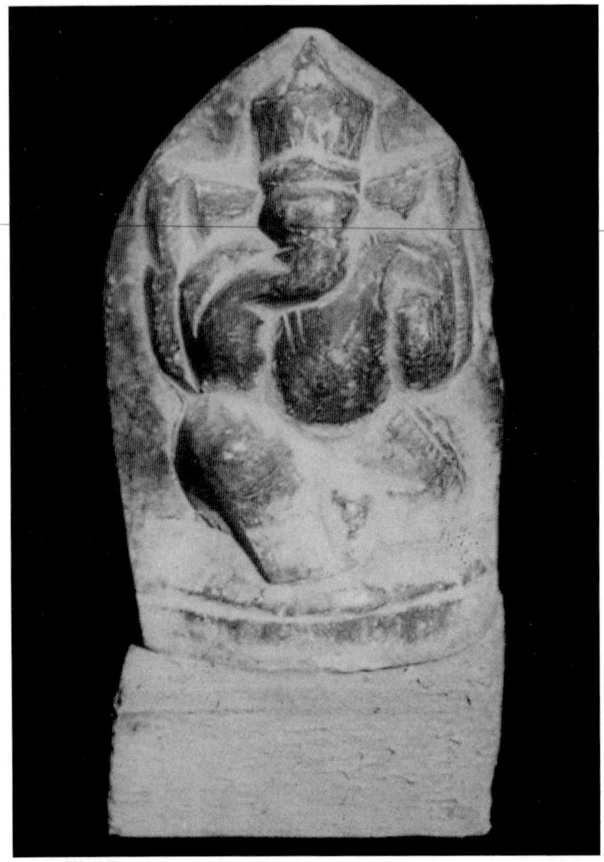

**Pl. 162.** Wooden Gaṇeśa, Rau ke Kalan.

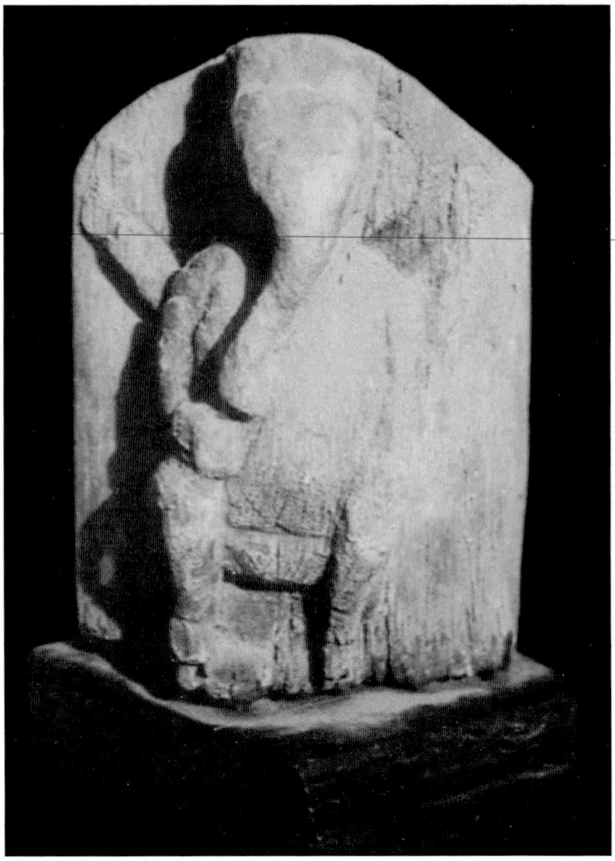

**Pl. 163.** Wooden Gaṇeśa, Panj Kalyan.

Pl. 165. Brahmā on a stele, Dholbaha.

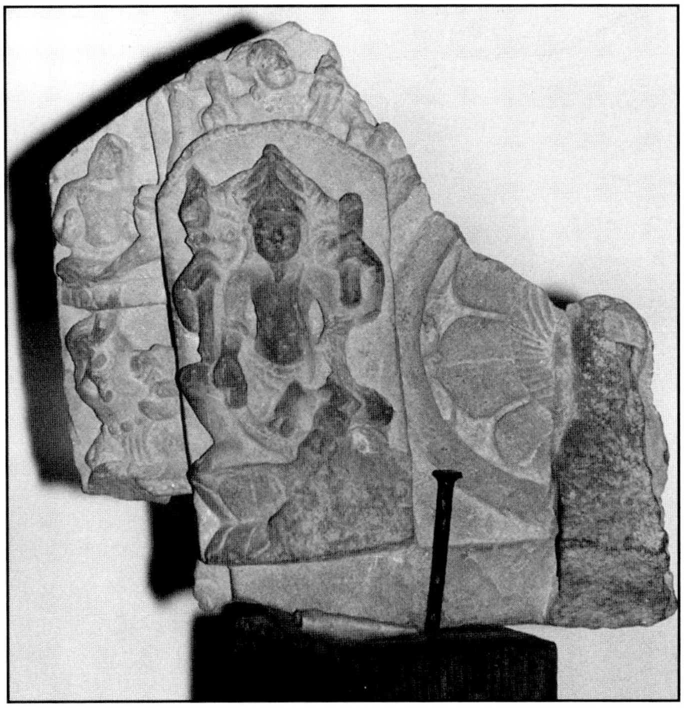

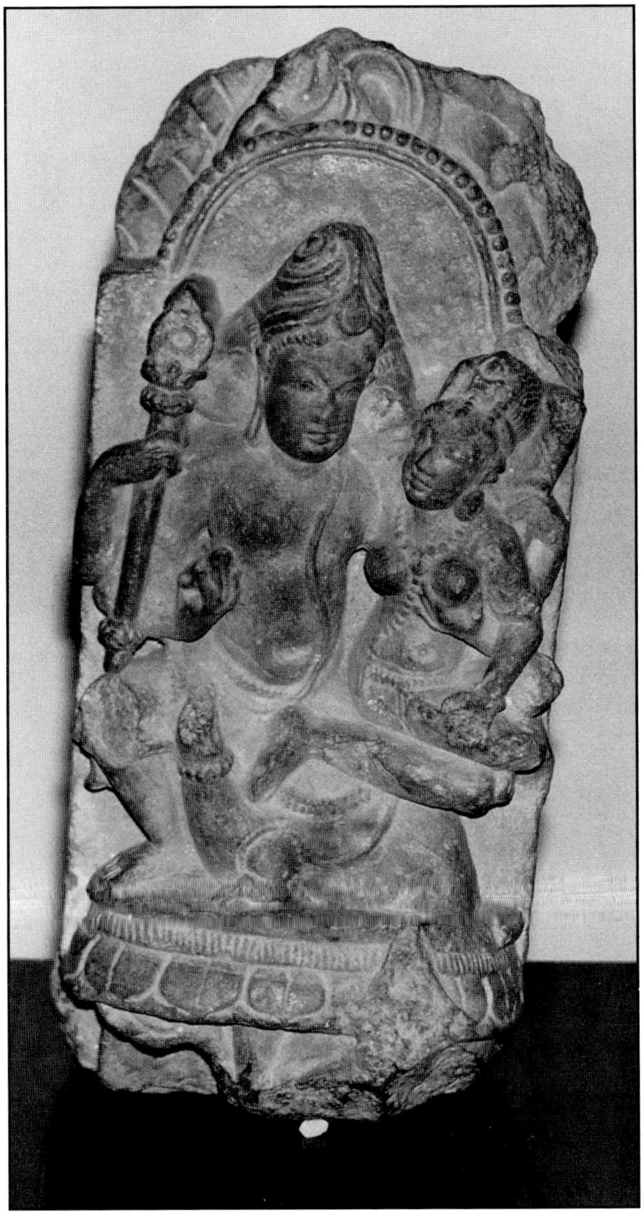

Pl. 164. Brahmā-Sarasvatī, Majhur.

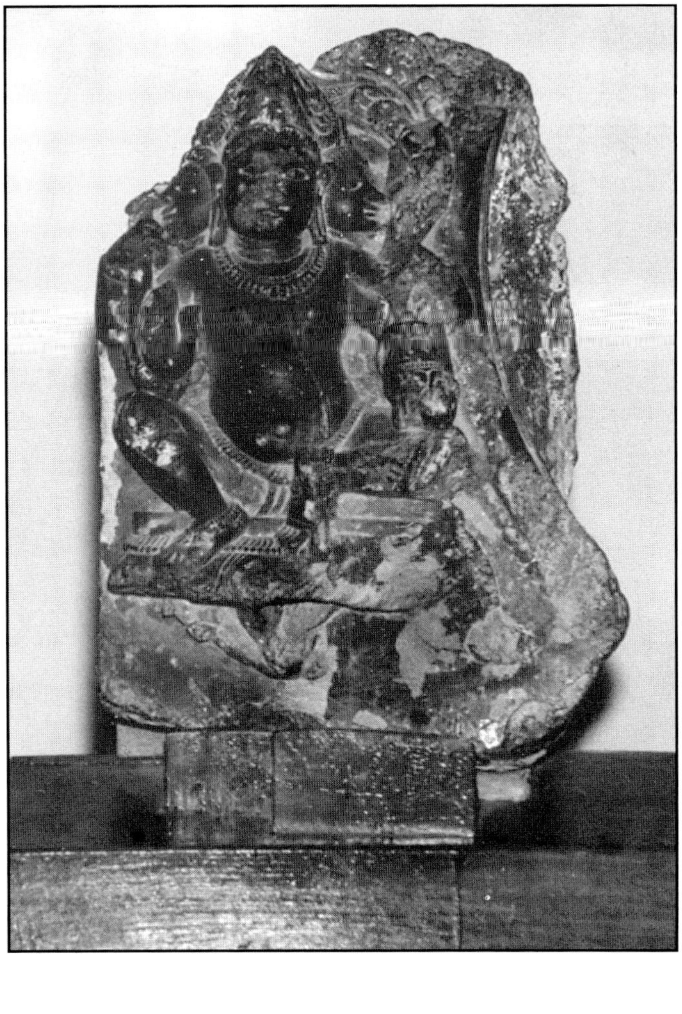

Pl. 166. Brahmā on a stele of black stone, Dholbaha.

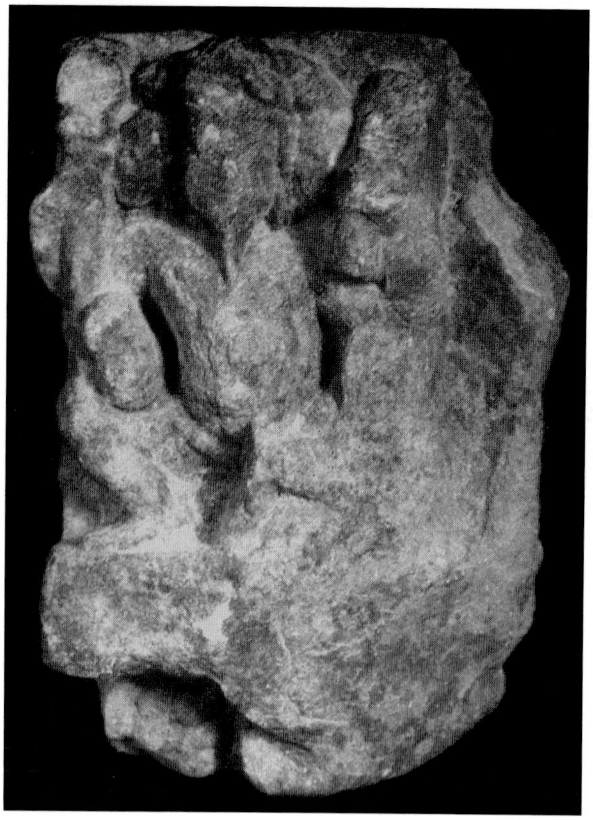

**Pl. 167.** Brahmā, Kharar.

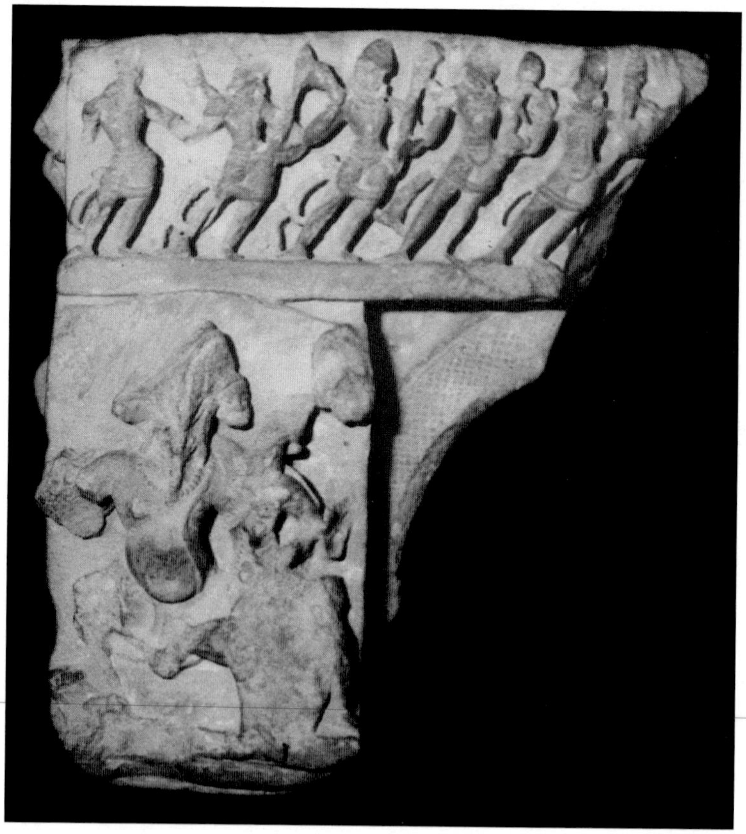

**Pl. 168.** Brahmā on a stele, Kharar.

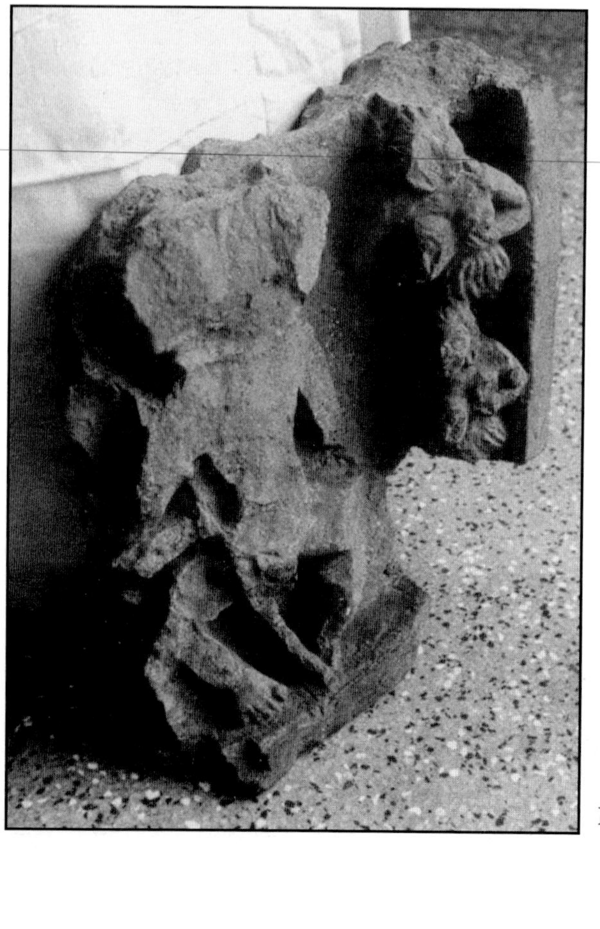

**Pl. 169.** Kārttikeya with Kṛittikās, terracotta, Sanghol.

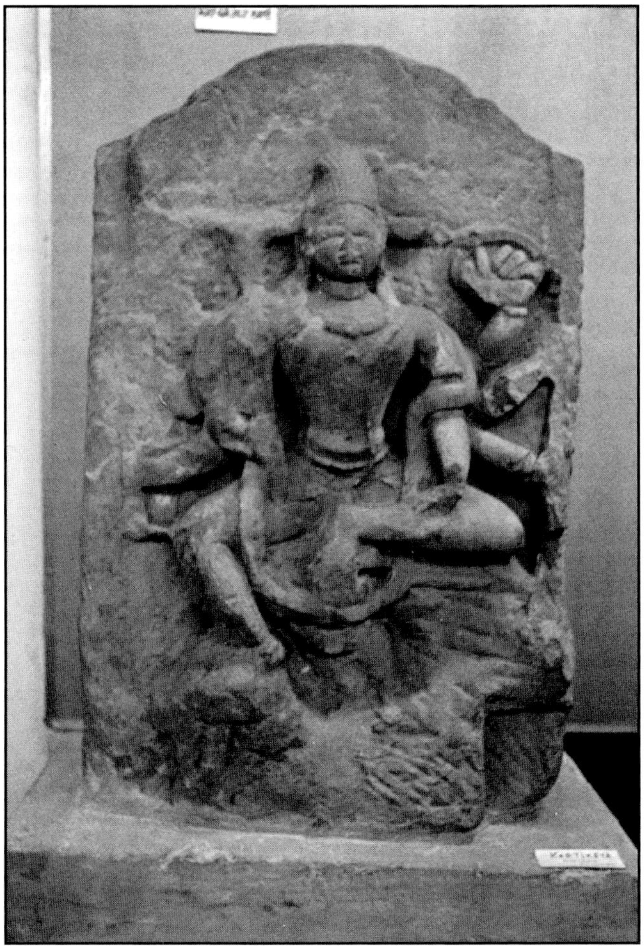

**Pl. 170.** Seated mono-cephalous Kārttikeya, Dholbaha.

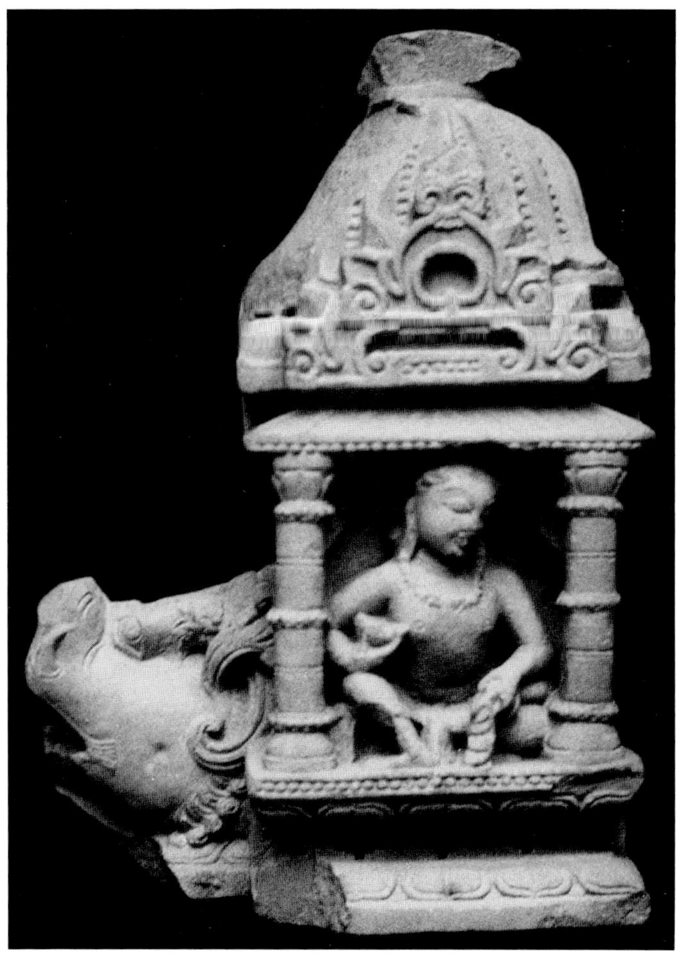

**Pl. 174.** Kubera, Sanaur.

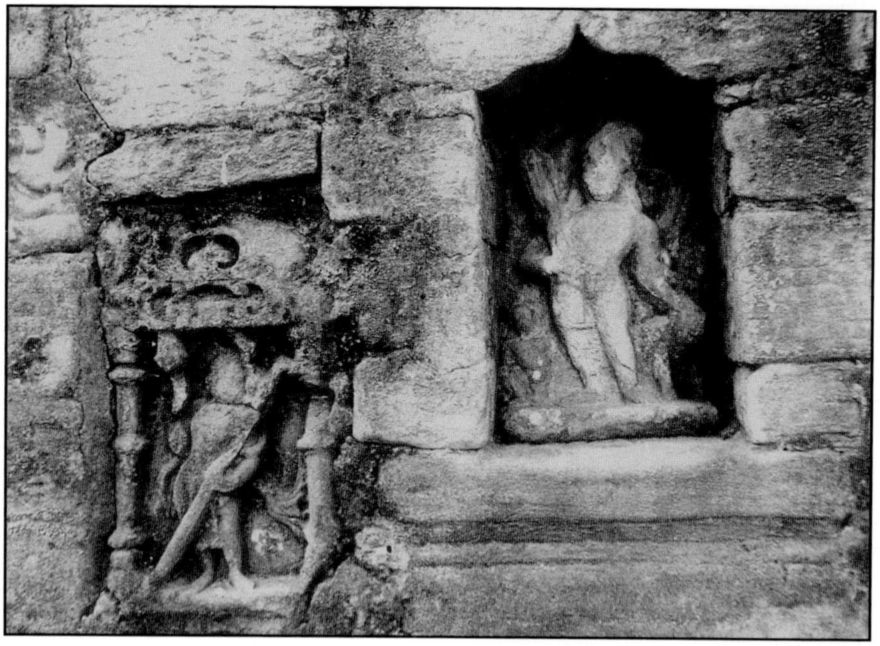

**Pl. 171.** Standing figures of Kārttikeya, Dholbaha.

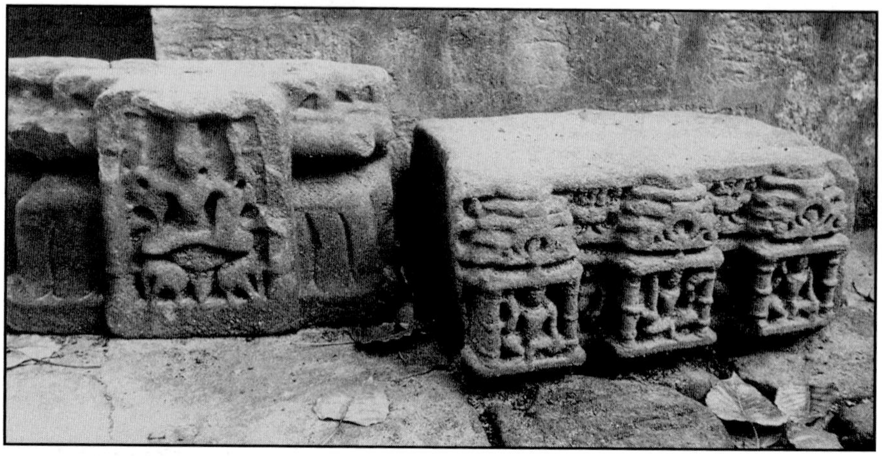

**Pl. 172.** Indra, Dholbaha.

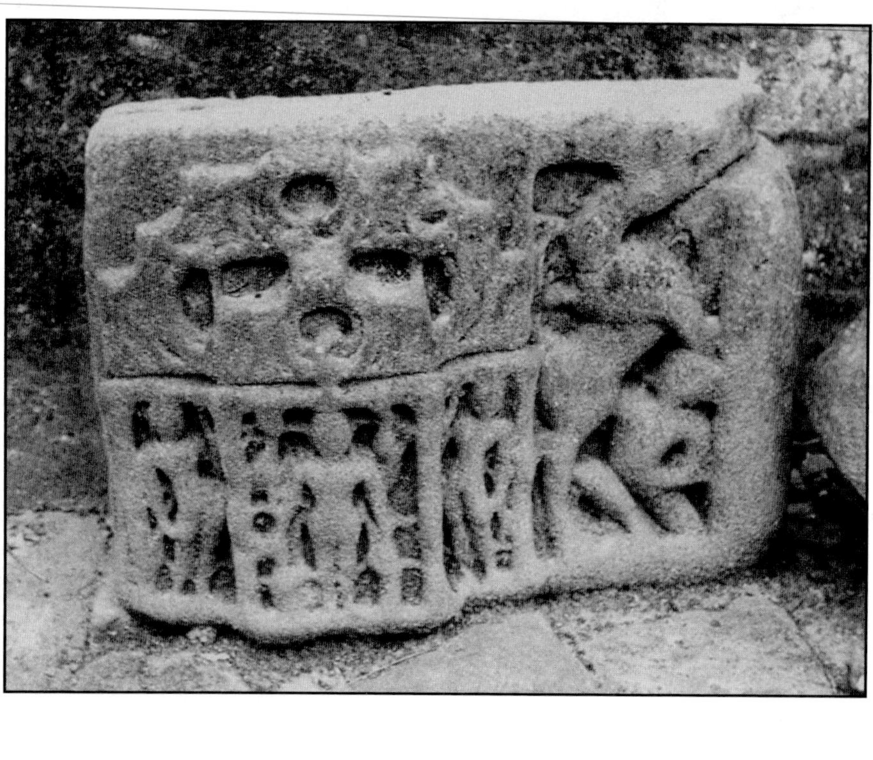

**Pl. 173.** Īśāna, Dholbaha.

**Pl. 175.** Minstrels and angels, Dholbaha.

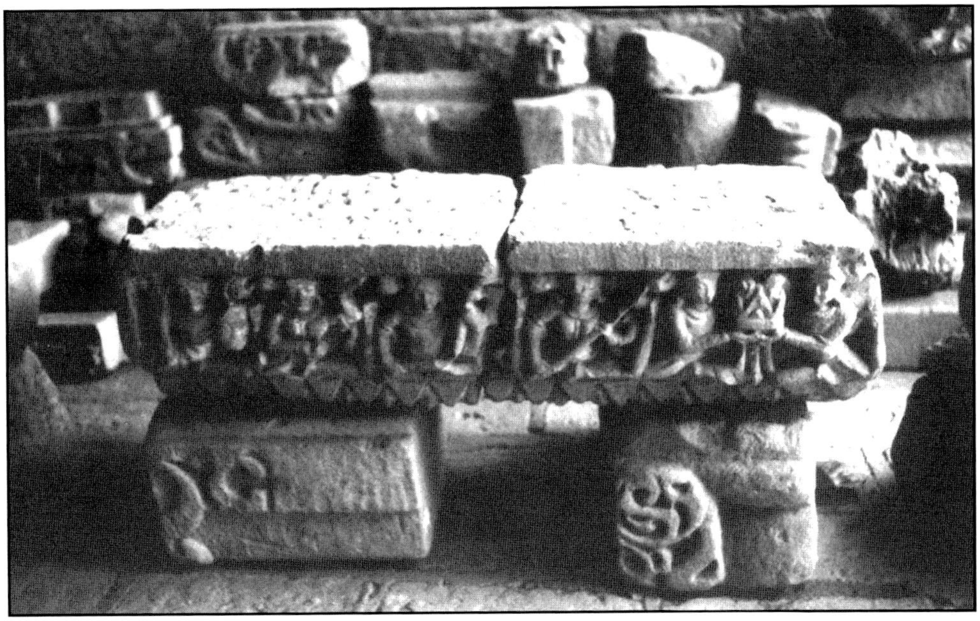

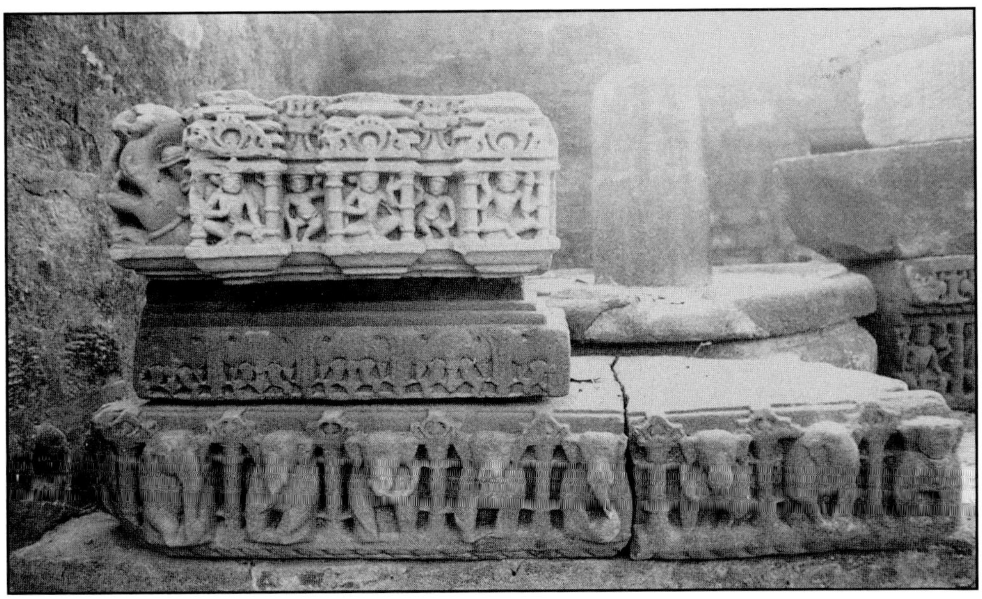

**Pl. 176.** Dancers, Dholbaha.

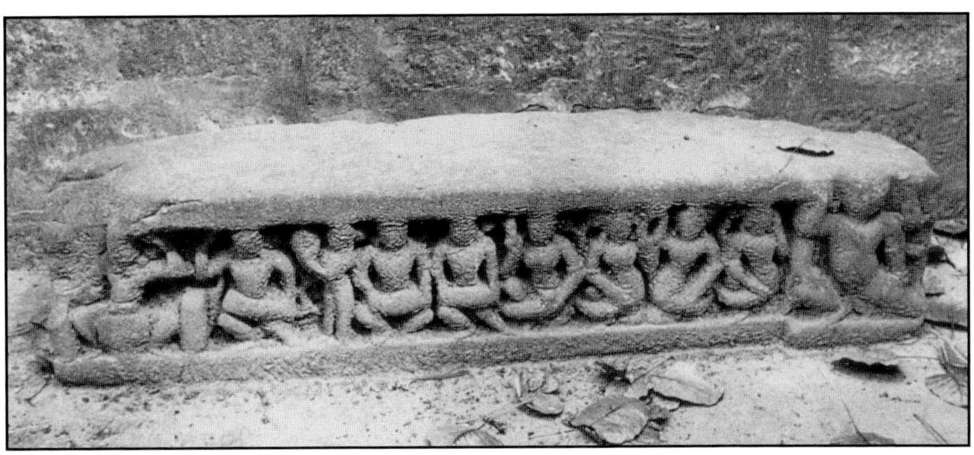

**Pl. 177.** Musicians, Dholbaha.

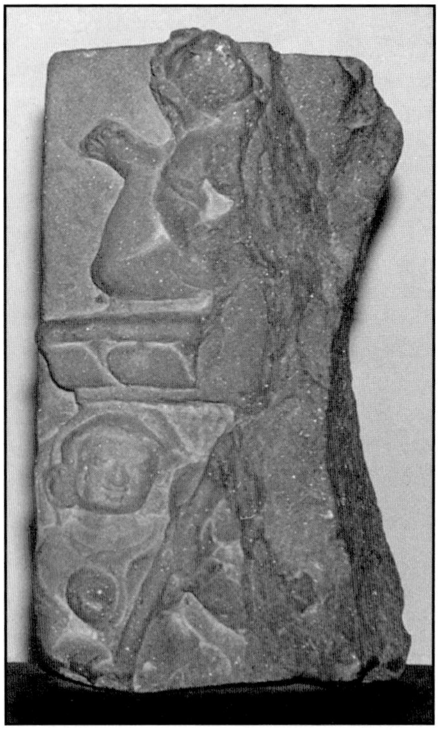

**Pl. 178.** *Vidyādhara* and *Gandharvī*, Dholbaha.

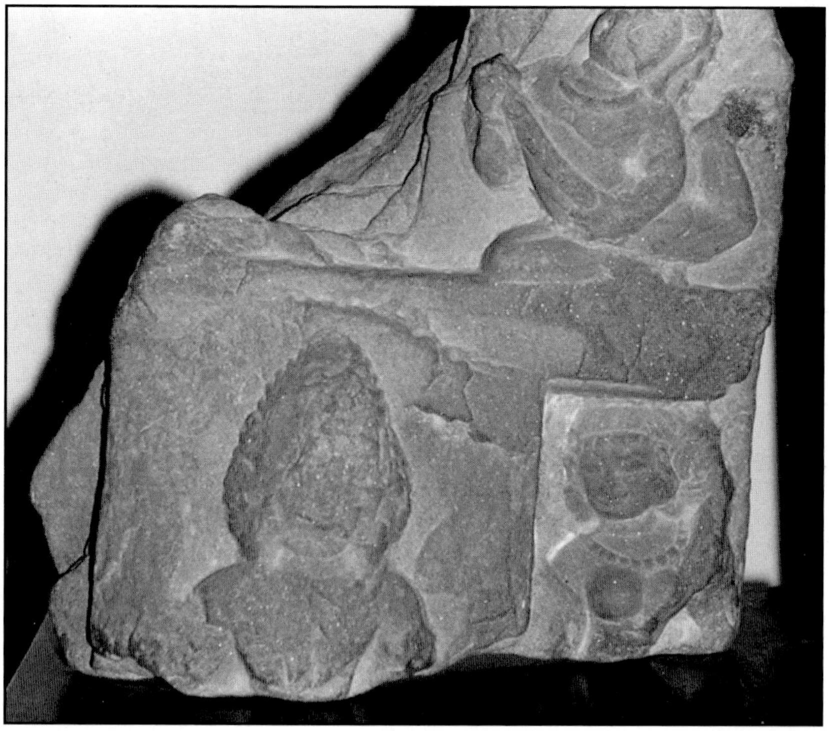

**Pl. 179.** *Vidyādhara* and *Gandharvī*, Dholbaha.

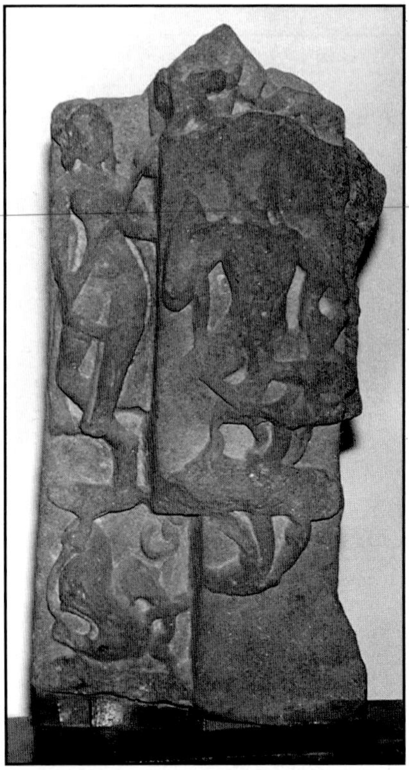

**Pl. 180.** Female musician, Dholbaha.

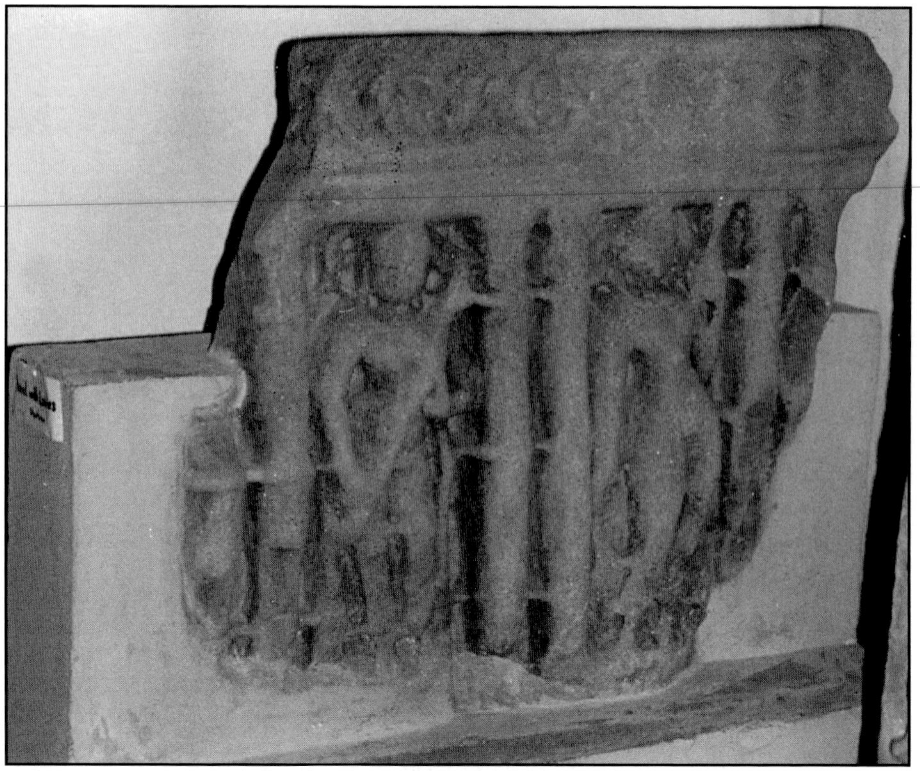

**Pl. 181.** Lady with a lyre, Dholbaha.

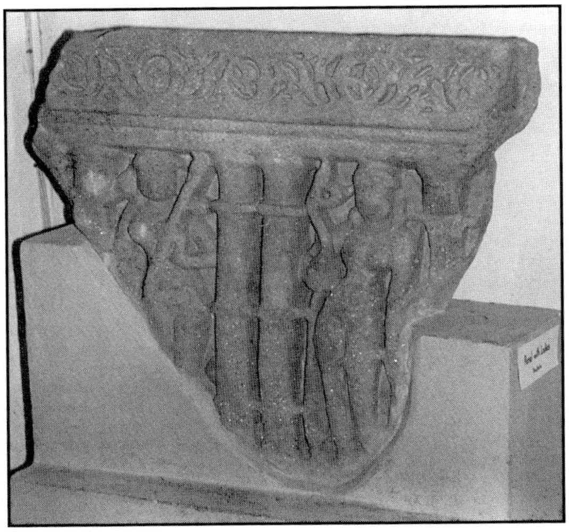

**Pl. 182.** Female musician, Dholbaha.

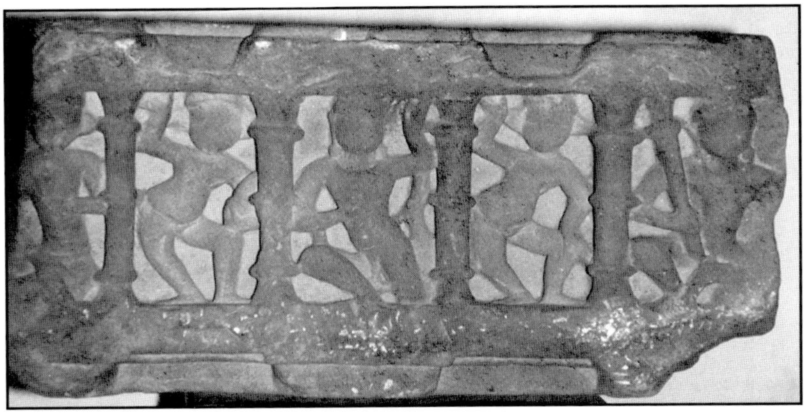

**Pl. 183.** Dancers and musicians, Dholbaha.

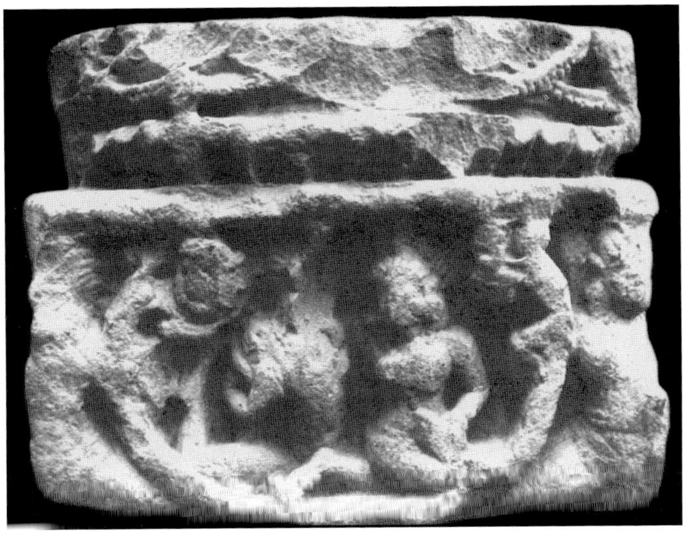

**Pl. 184.** *Gandharva* couple, Sunam.

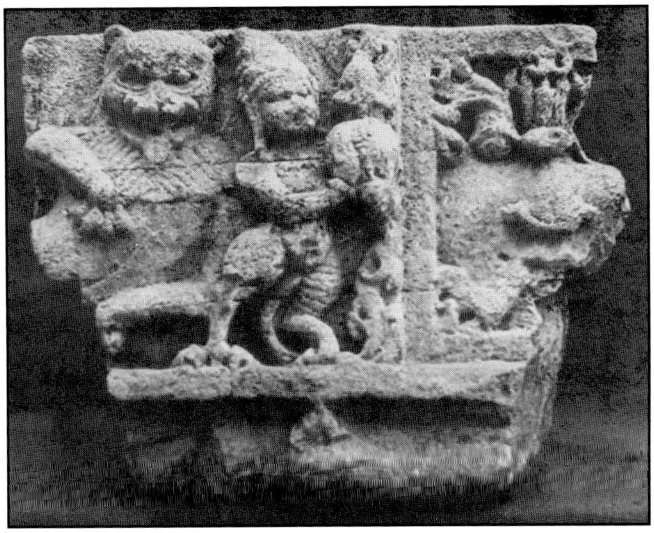

**Pl. 185.** Lion, Udadhikumāra and *Kīrttimukha*, Sunam.

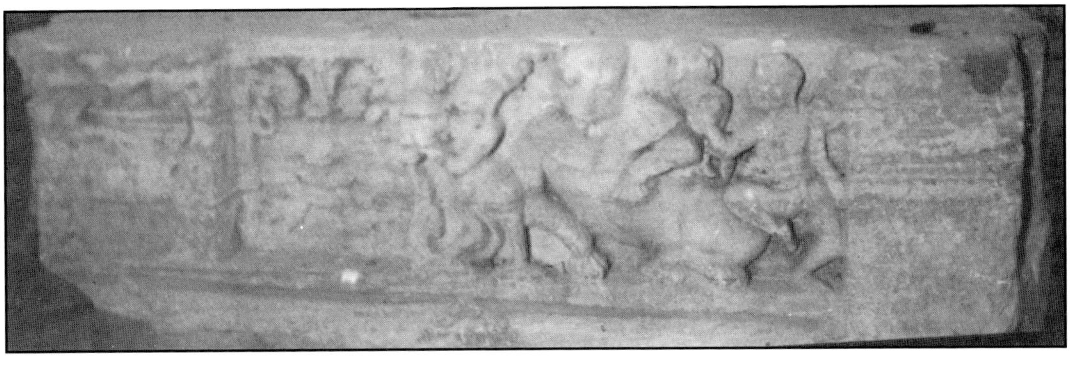

**Pl. 186.** Door sill, Sunam.

**Pl. 188.** *Chāmarikā*, Dholbaha.

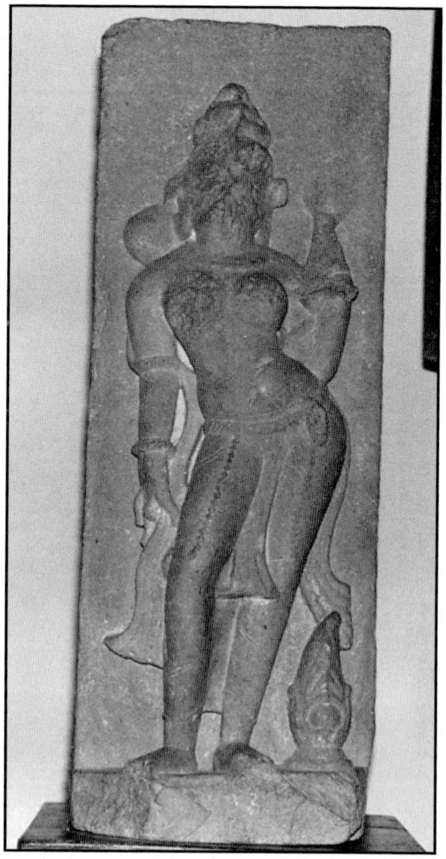

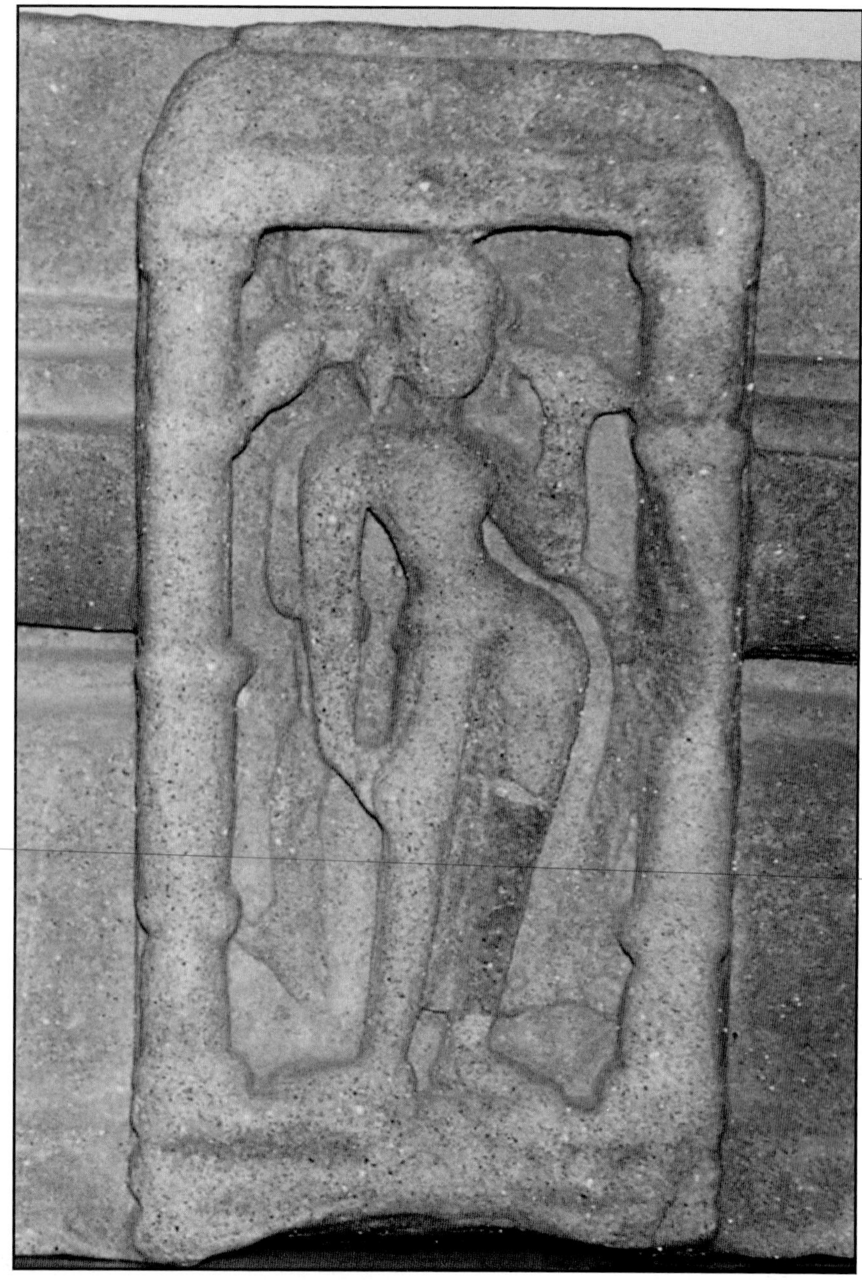

**Pl. 187.** Fly-whisker, Dholbaha.

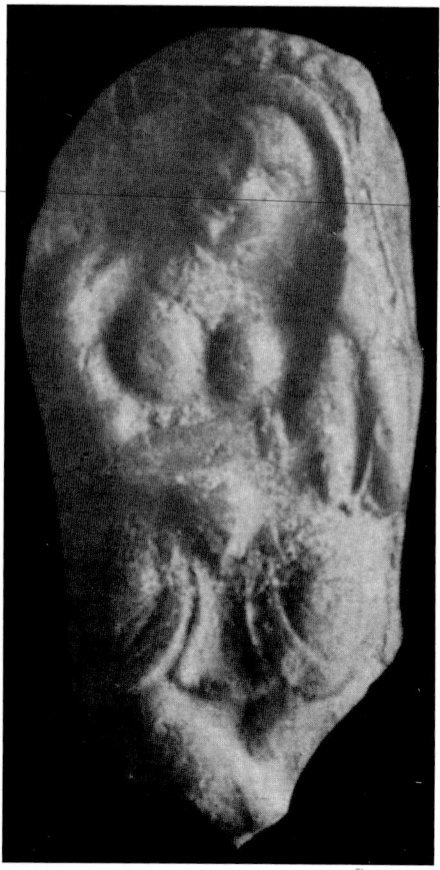

**Pl. 192.** *Keśagumphinī*, terracotta, Sunet.

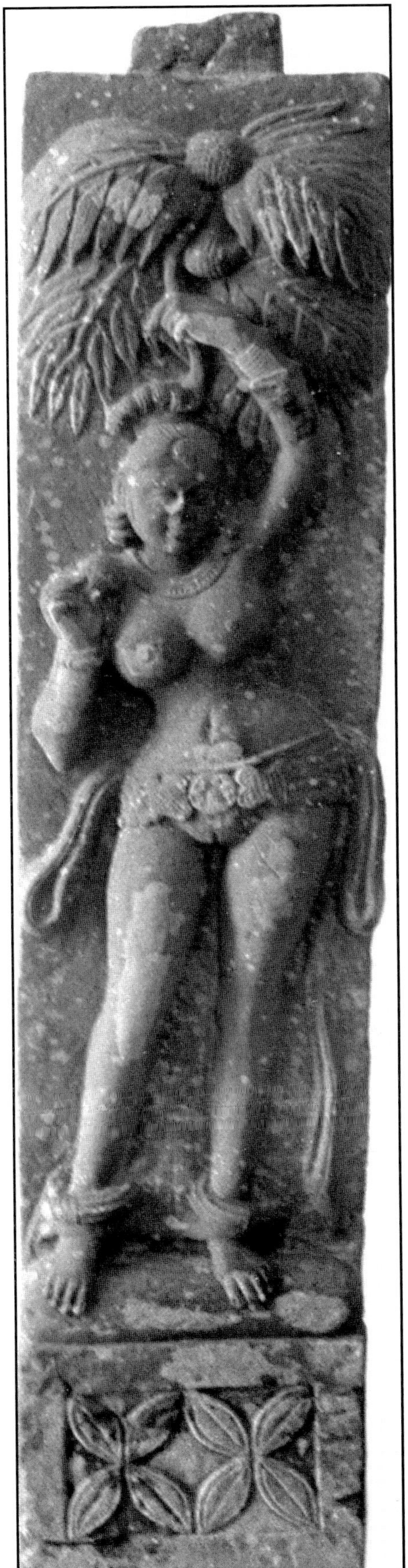

**Pl. 189.** *Sālabhañjikā* on a railing pillar, Sanghol.

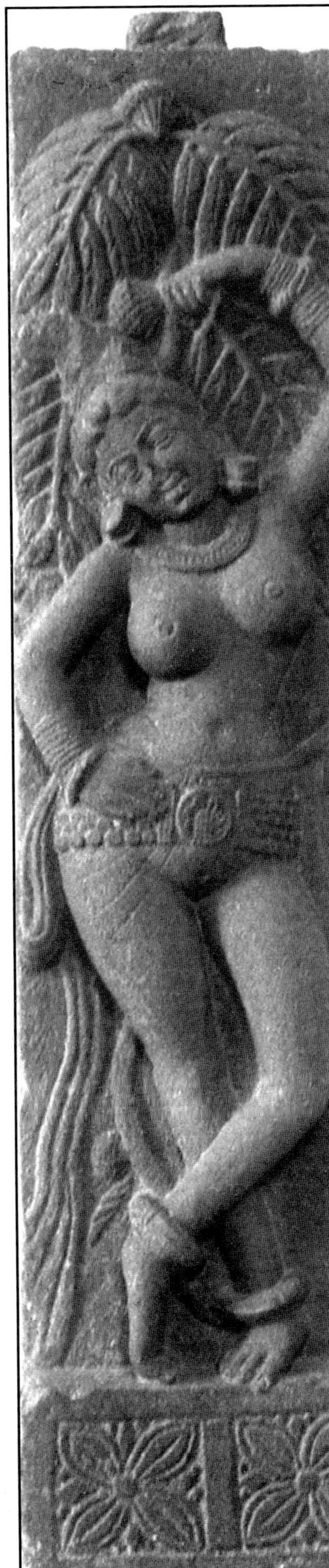

**Pl. 190.** *Sālabhañjikā* on a railing pillar, Sanghol.

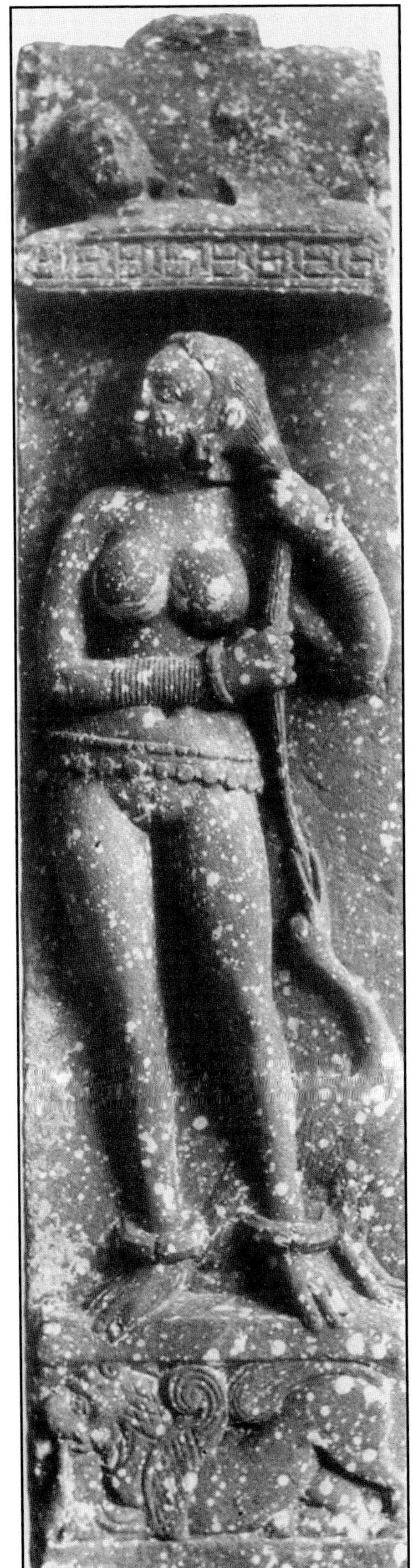

**Pl. 191.** *Karpūramañjarī* squeezing her wet tresses, Sanghol.

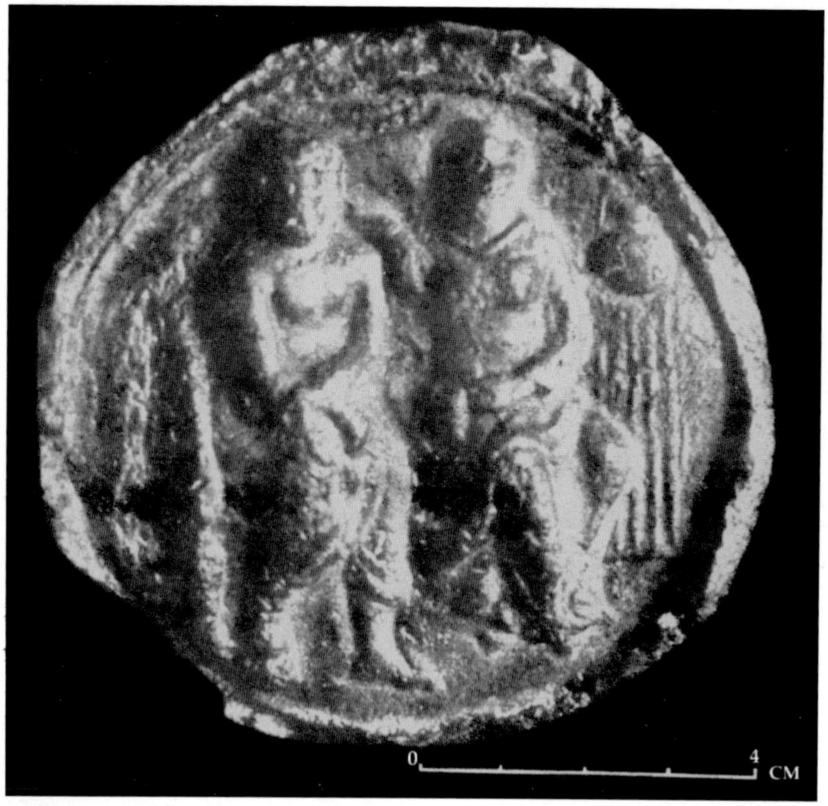


**Pl. 193.** Terracotta plaque depicting a couple in Hellenistic dress, Sanghol.

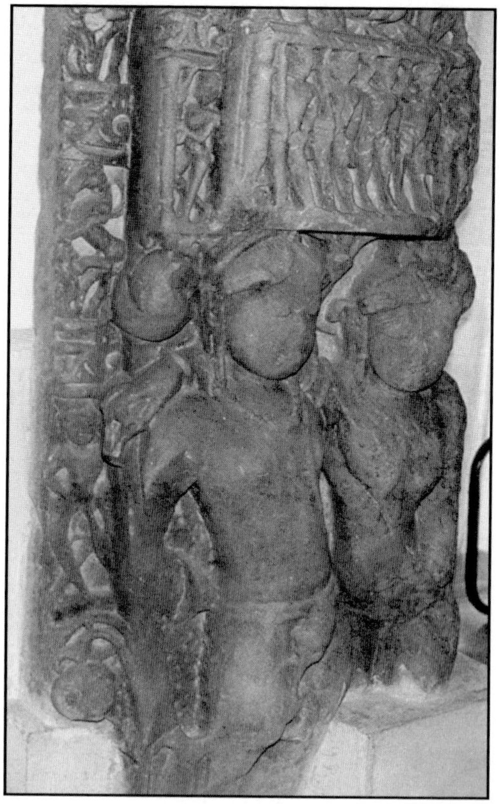

**Pl. 194.** Doorjambs, Dholbaha.

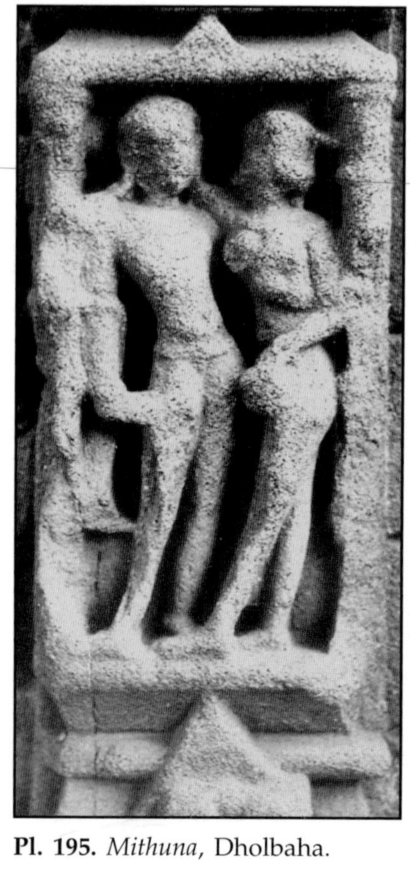

**Pl. 195.** *Mithuna*, Dholbaha.

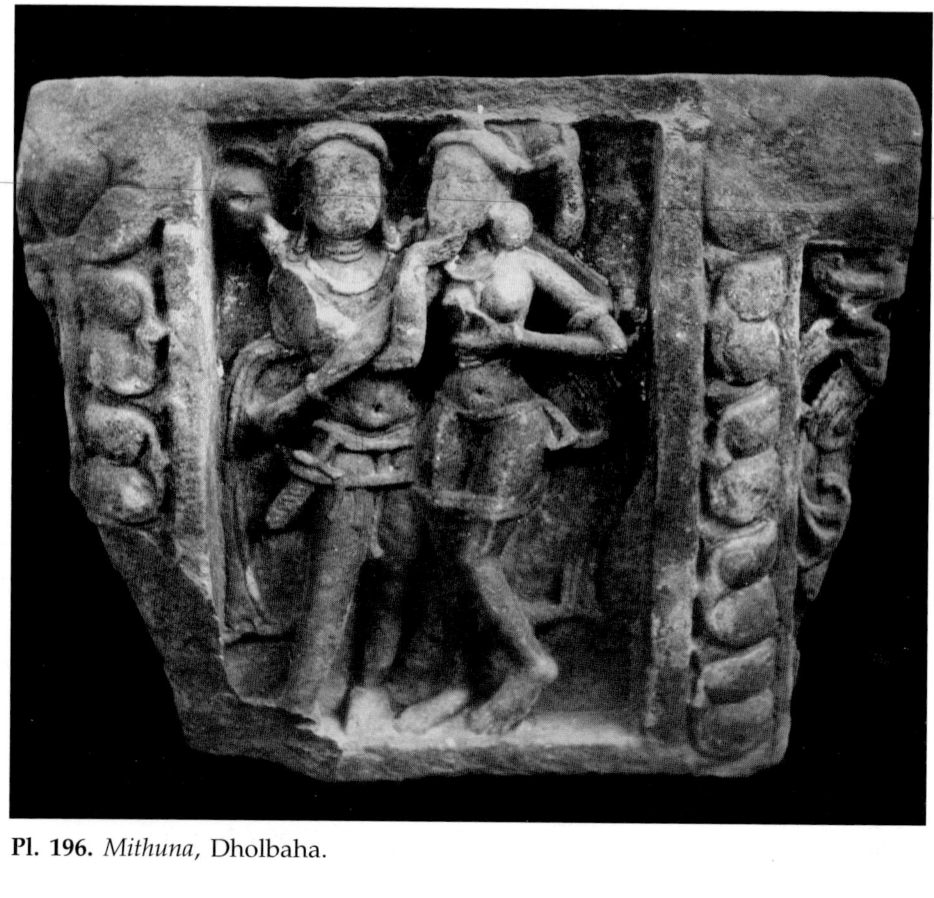

**Pl. 196.** *Mithuna*, Dholbaha.

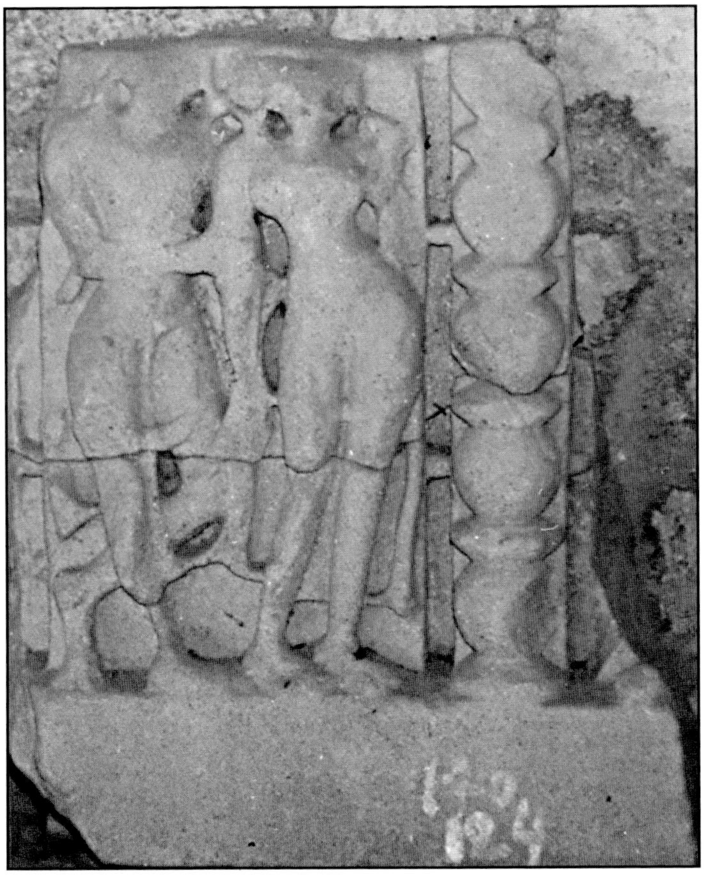

**Pl. 197.** *Mithuna*, Dholbaha.

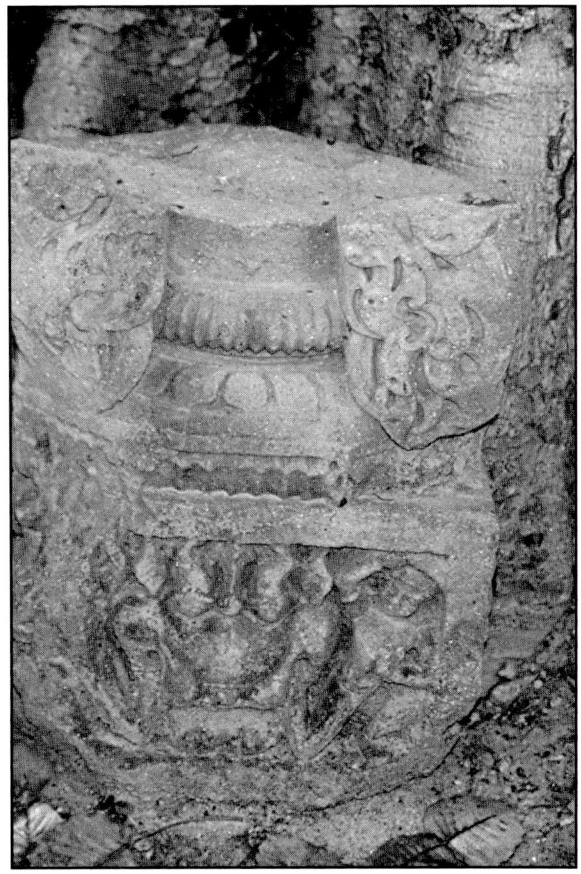

**Pl. 199.** *Ghaṭa-pallava* and *Kīrttimukha*, Dholbaha.

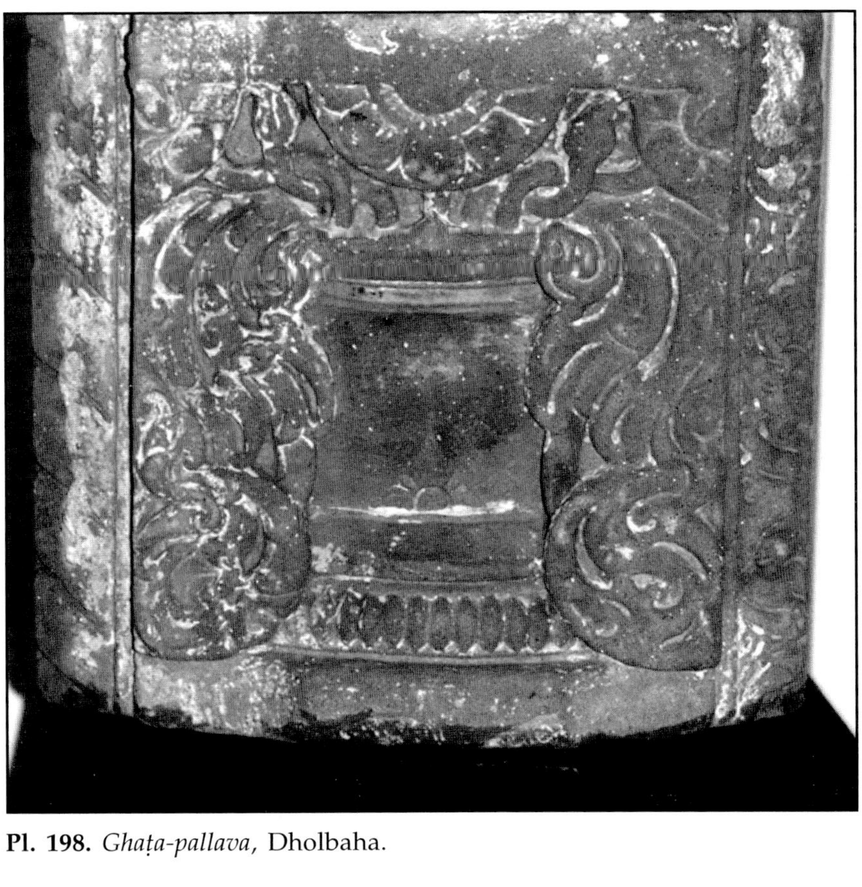

**Pl. 198.** *Ghaṭa-pallava*, Dholbaha.

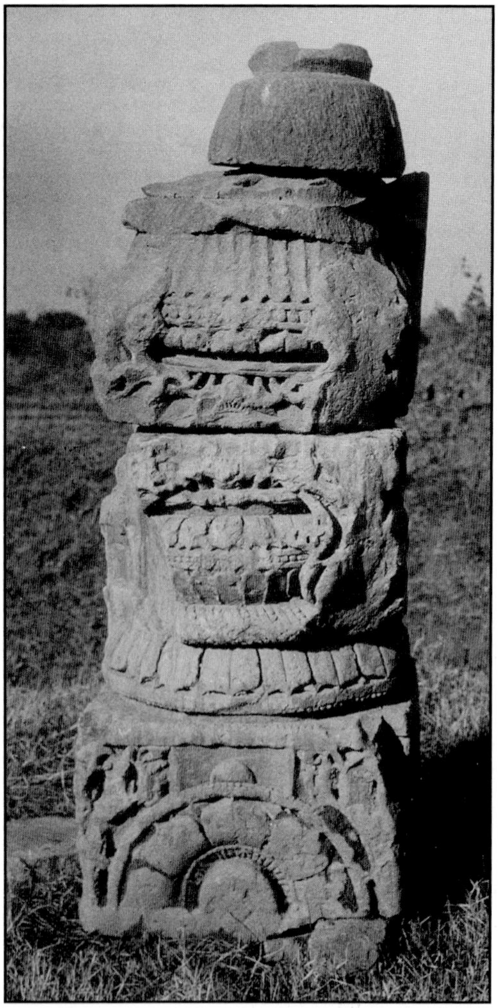

**Pl. 200.** Pillar with *Ghaṭa-pallava* and *Ardha-padma* motif, Sirhind.

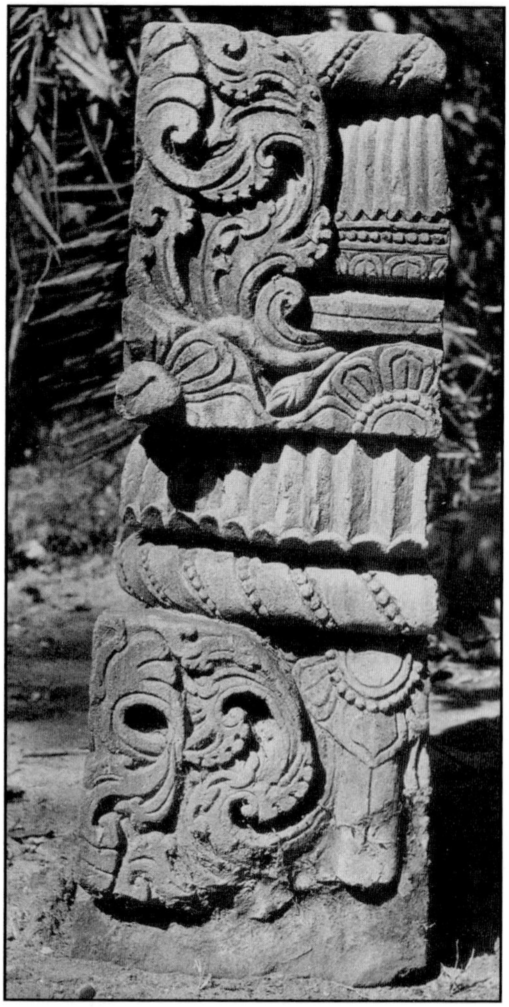

**Pl. 201.** Fragment of a pillar, Sirhind.

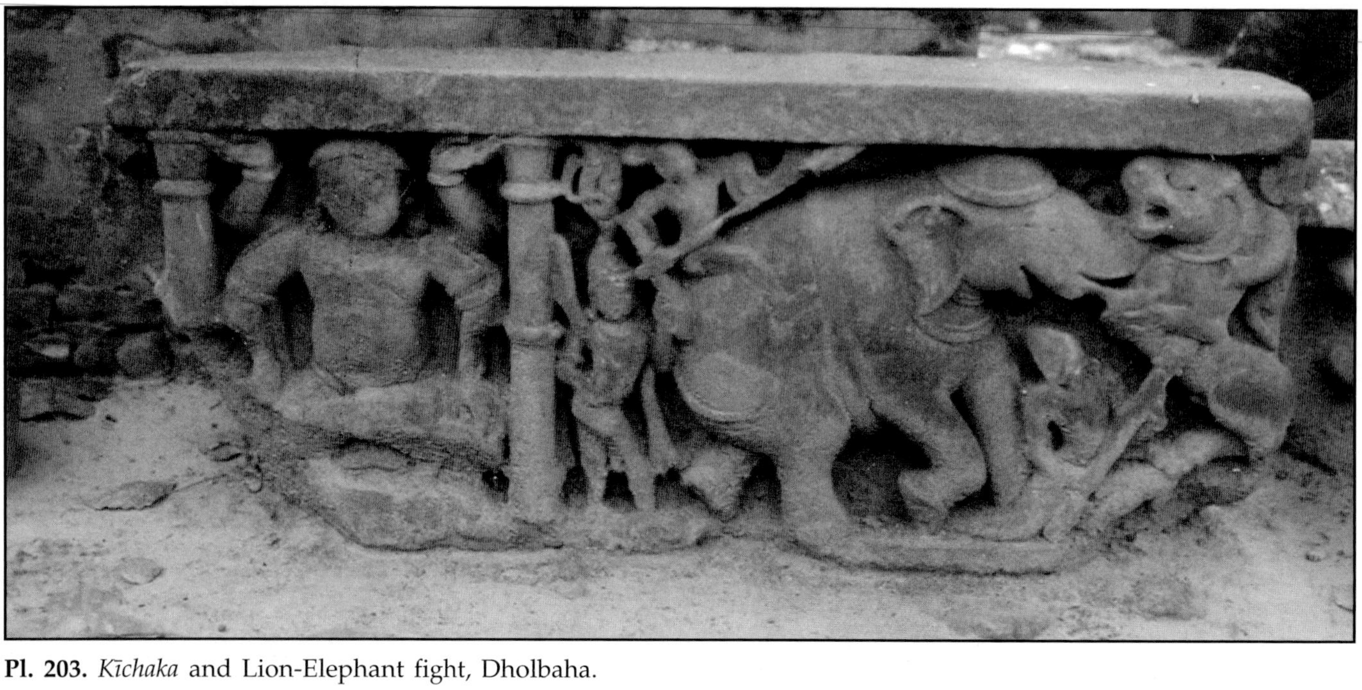

**Pl. 203.** *Kīchaka* and Lion-Elephant fight, Dholbaha.

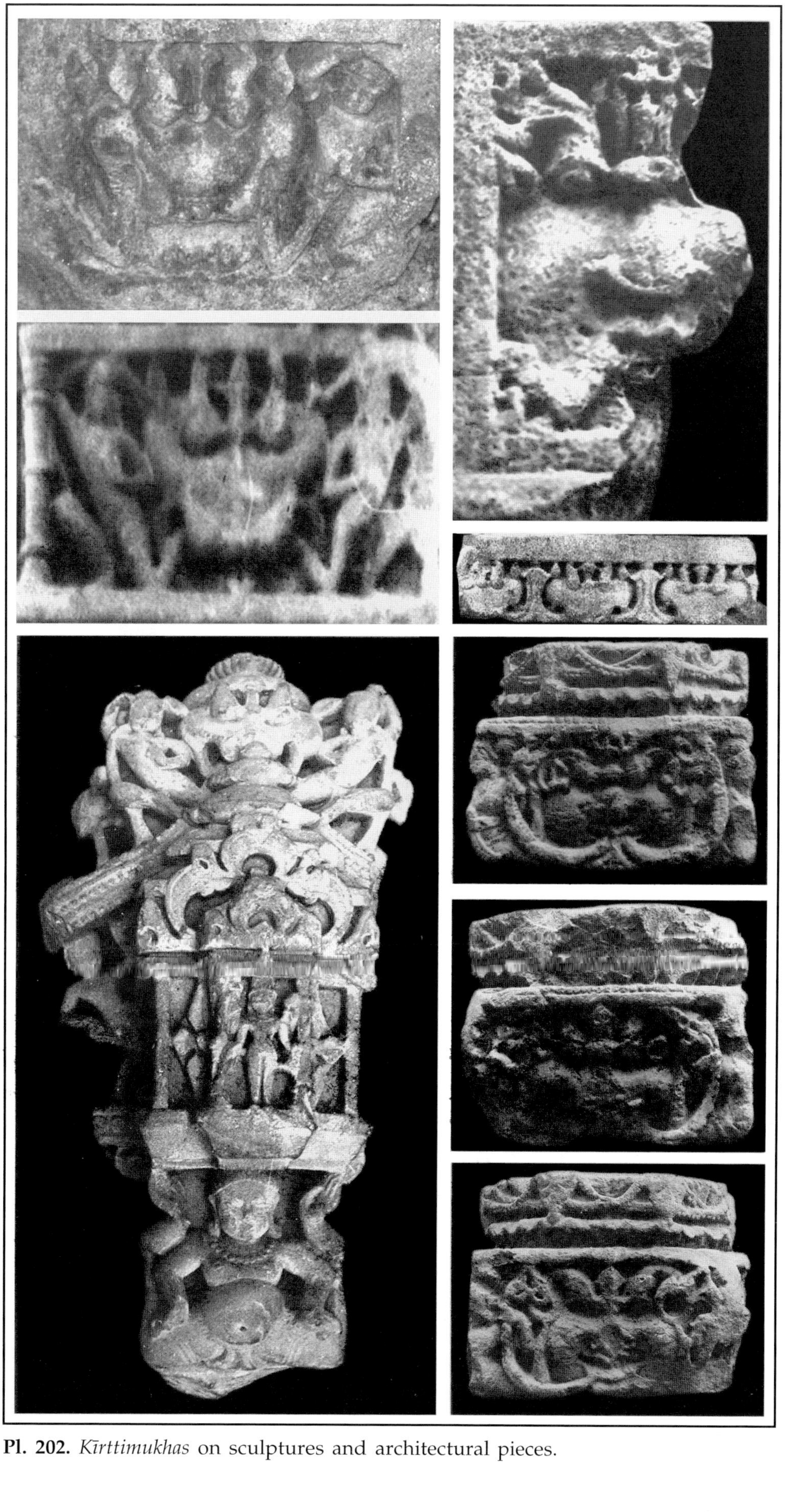

**Pl. 202.** *Kīrttimukhas* on sculptures and architectural pieces.

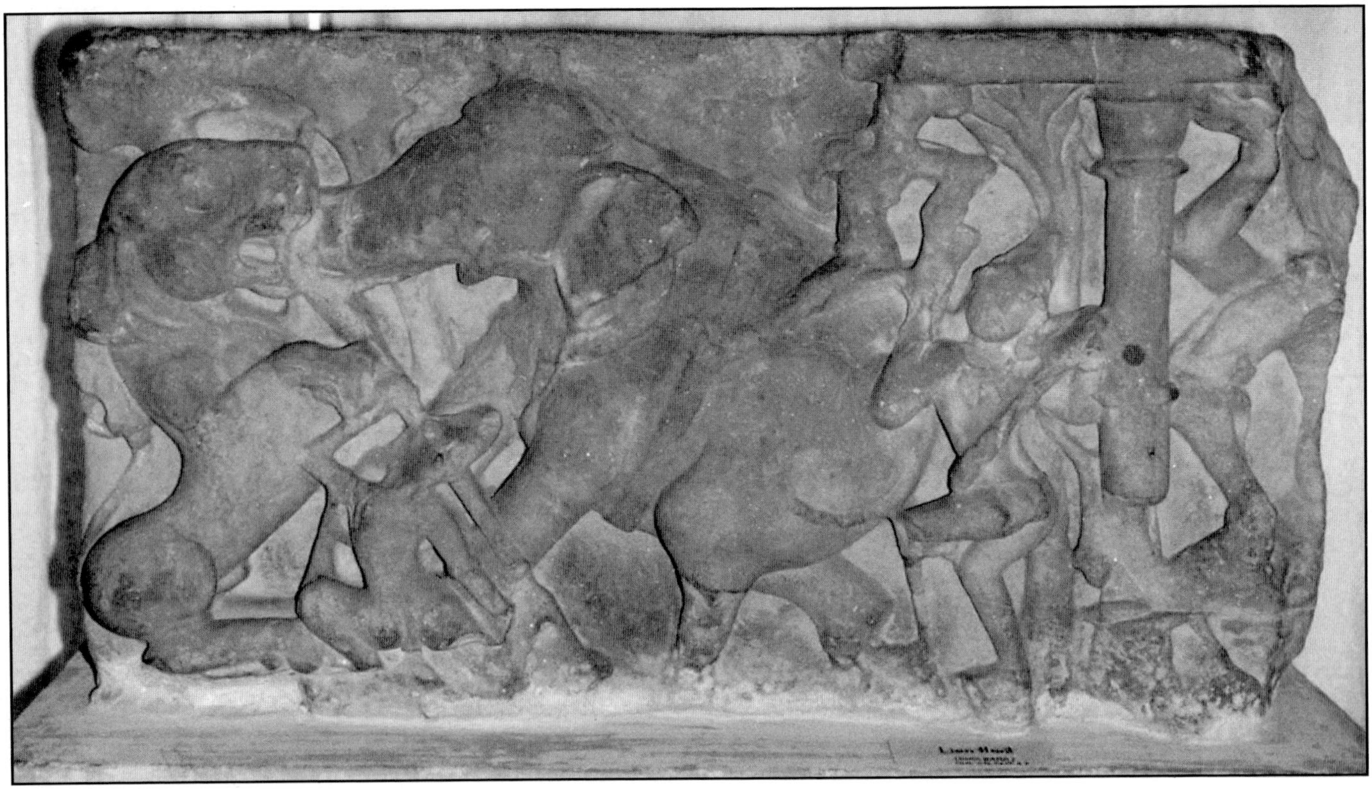

**Pl. 204.** Lion-hunting scene, Dholbaha.

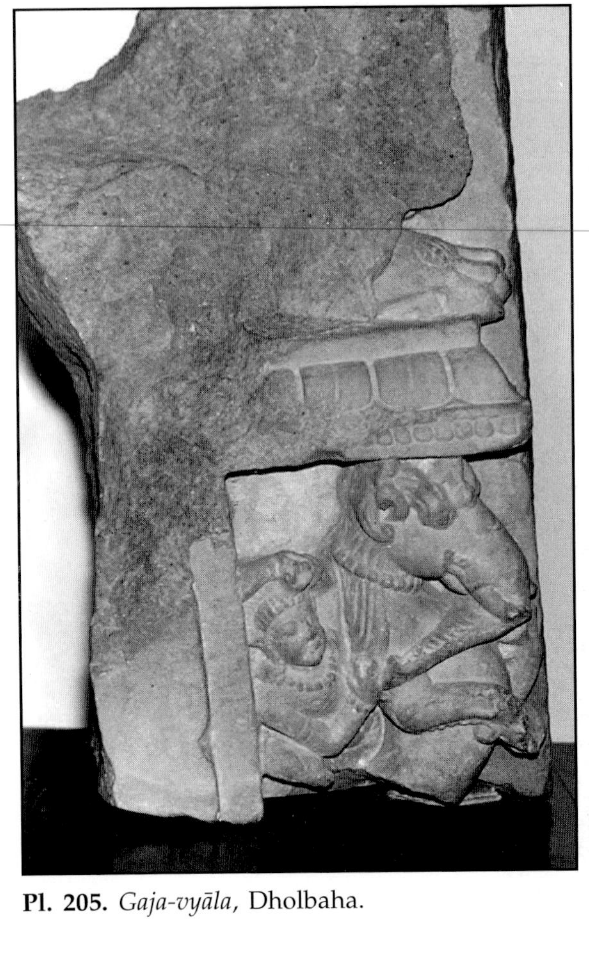

**Pl. 205.** *Gaja-vyāla*, Dholbaha.

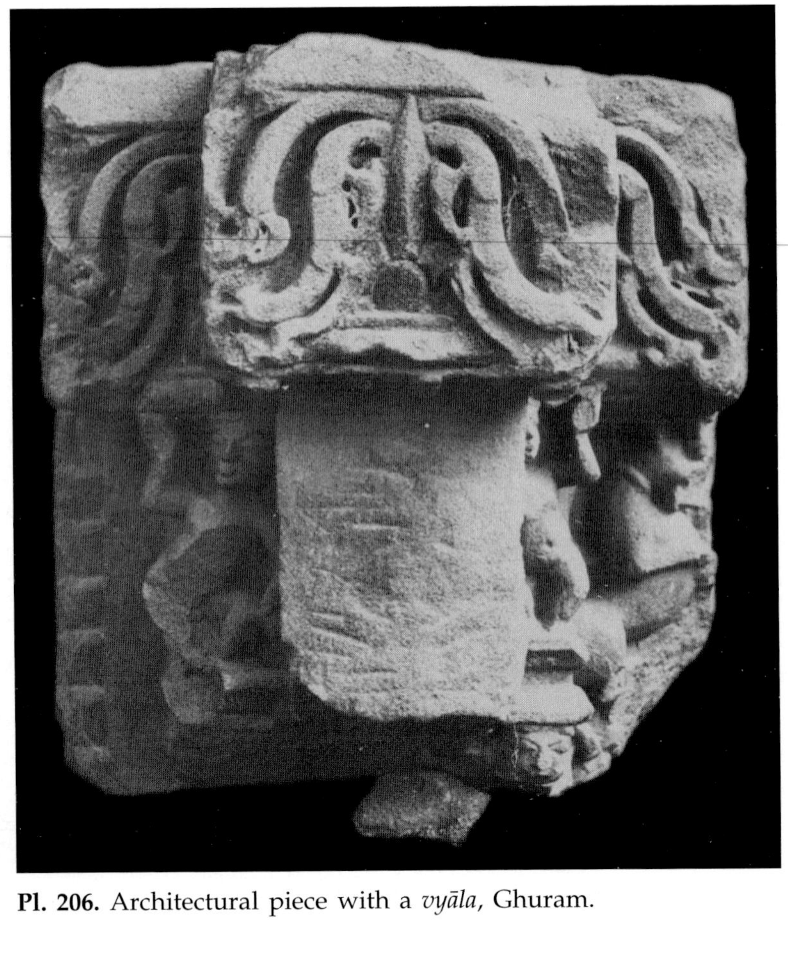

**Pl. 206.** Architectural piece with a *vyāla*, Ghuram.

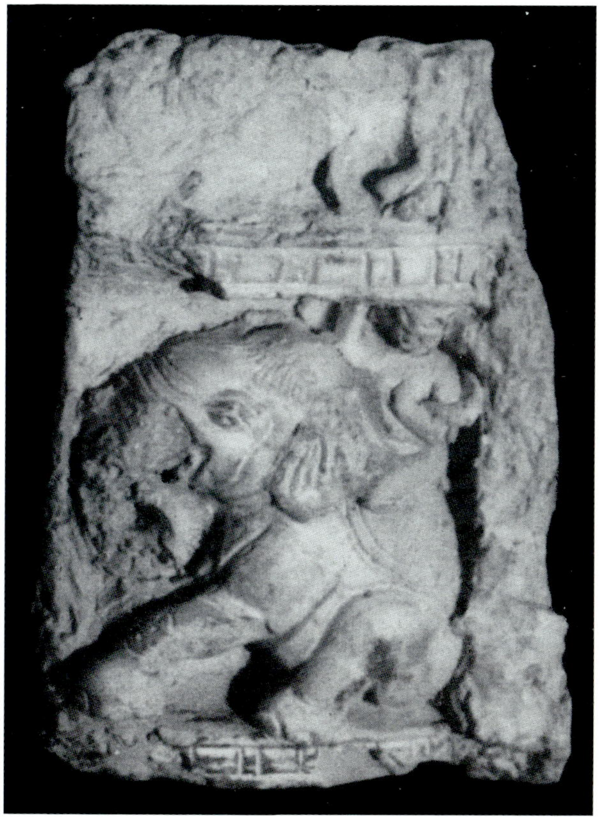

**Pl. 207.** Elephant with rider, unbaked clay, Janer.

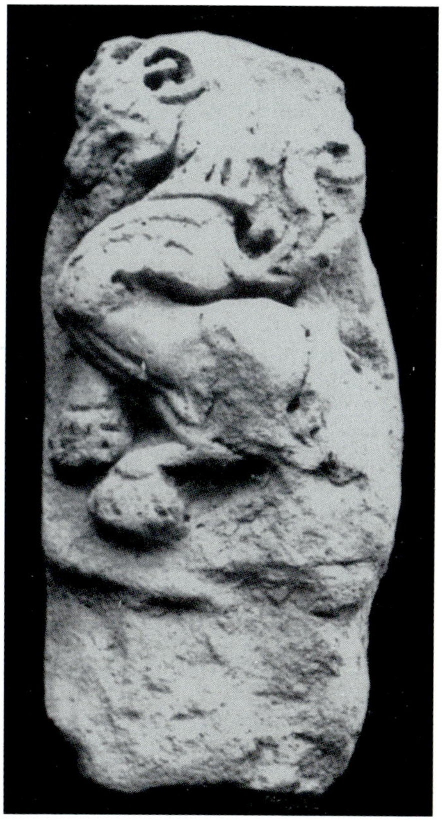

**Pl. 208.** Winged lion, unbaked clay, Janer.

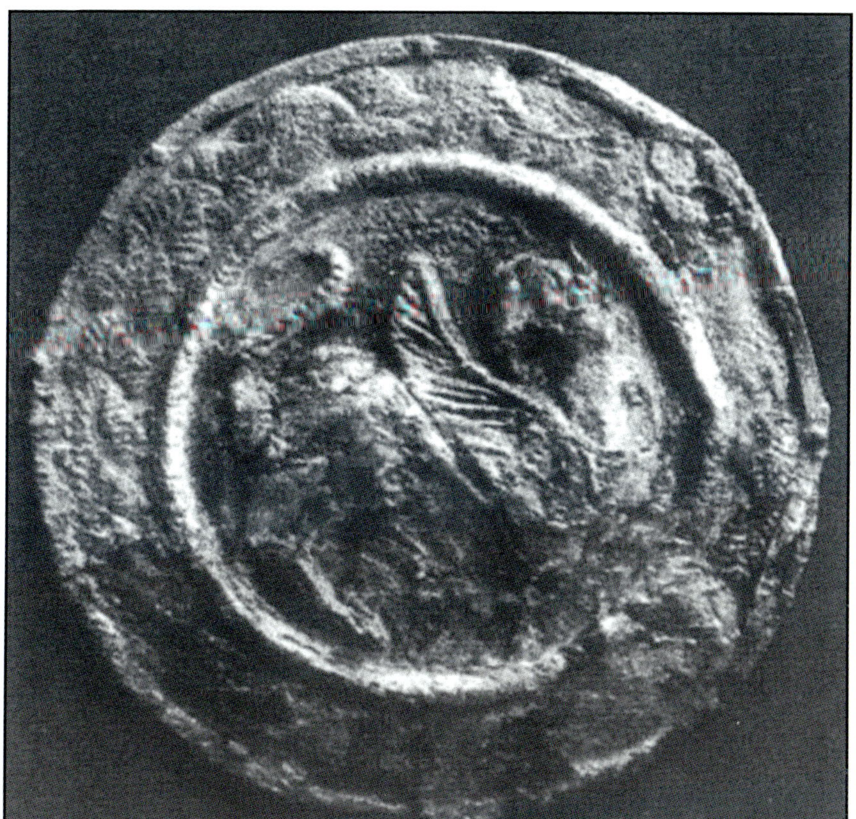

**Pl. 209.** Winged griffin in a medallion, bronze, Ropar.

Pl. 211. Doorjamb, Siswan.

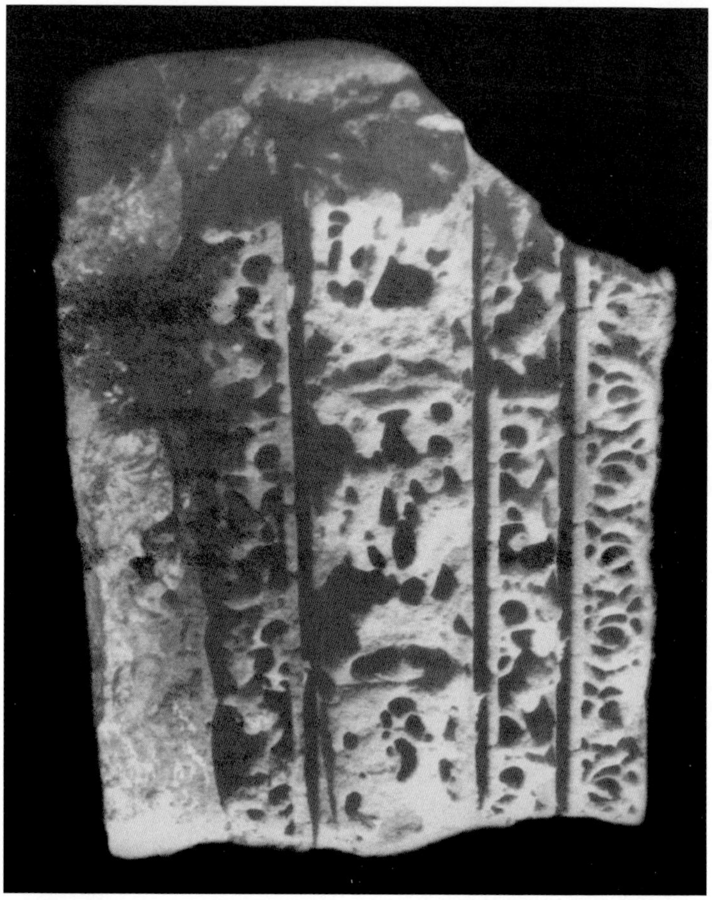

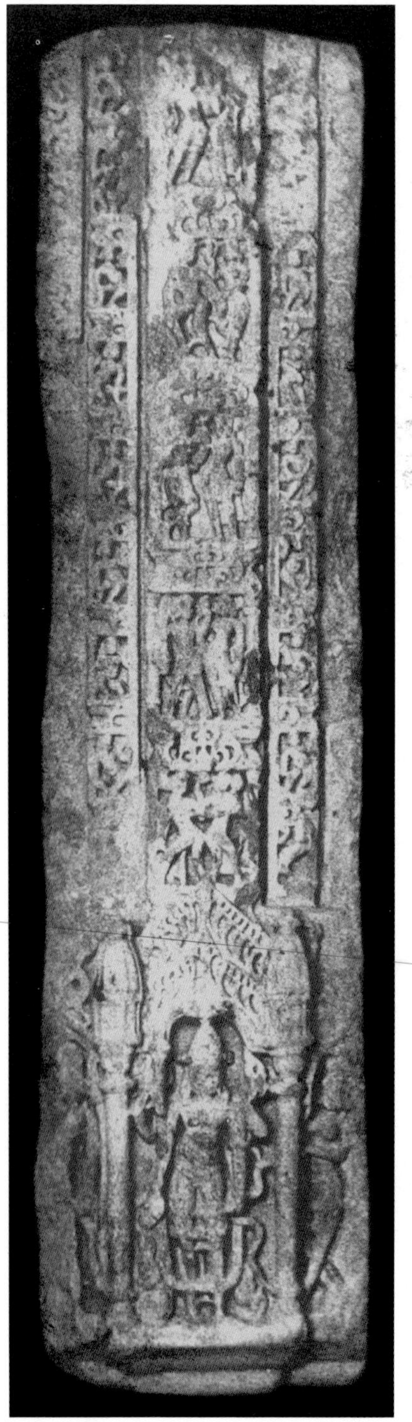

Pl. 210. Doorjamb, Majhur.

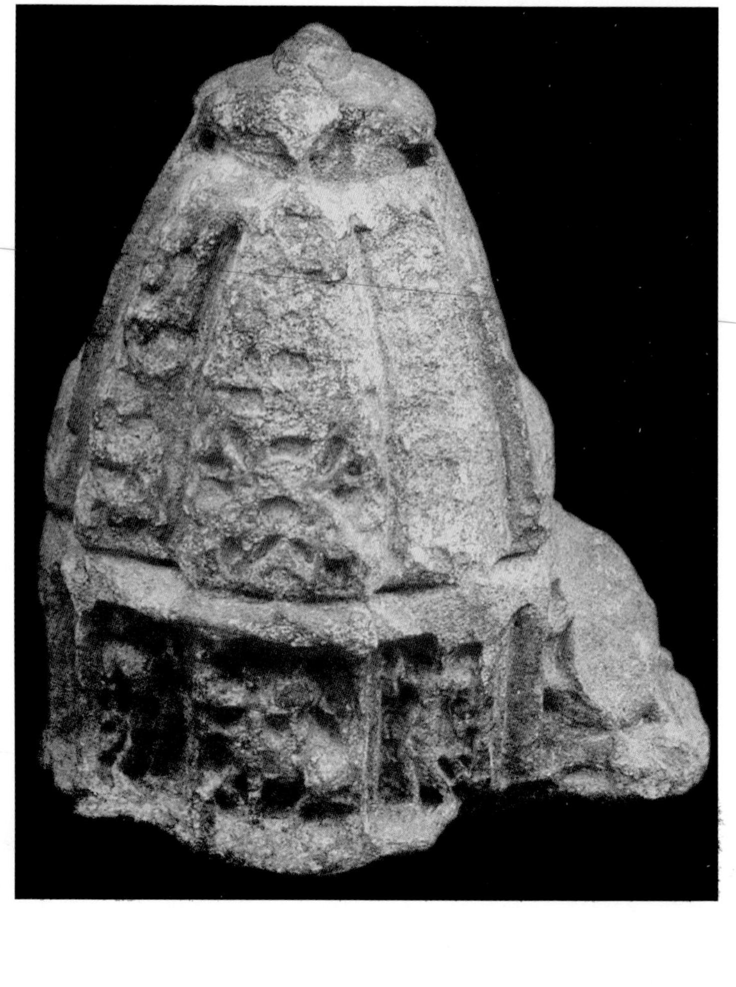

Pl. 212. *Nāgarakūṭa*, Kharar.

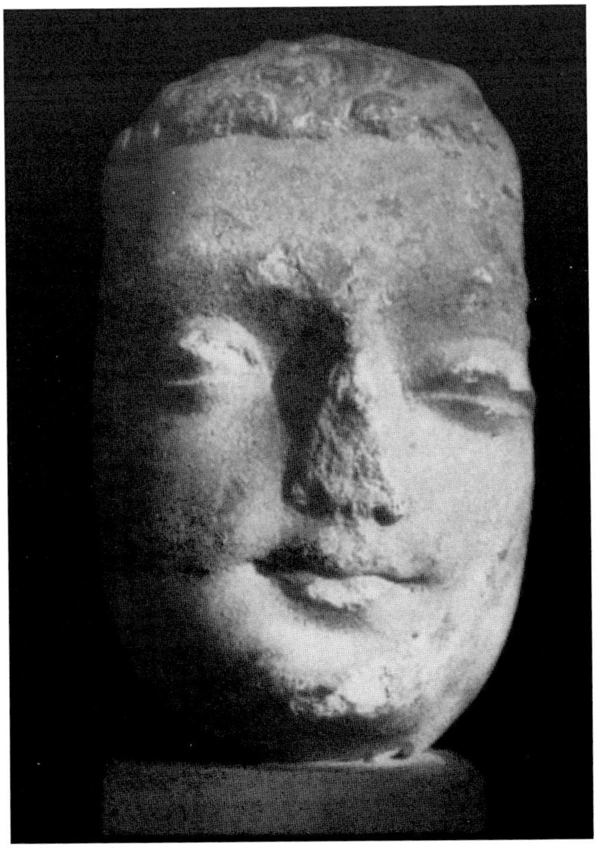

**Pl. 213.** Buddha head, stucco, Sanghol.

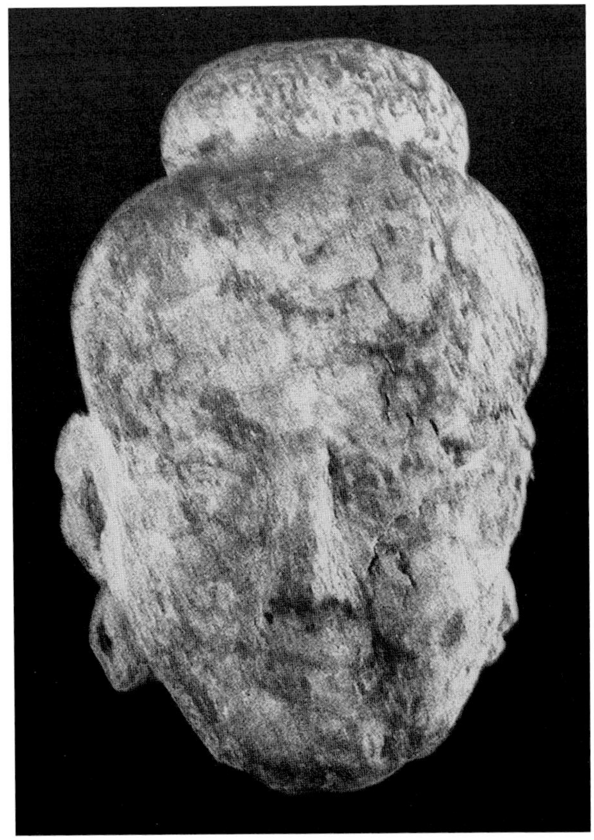

**Pl. 214.** Buddha head, clay, Sanghol.

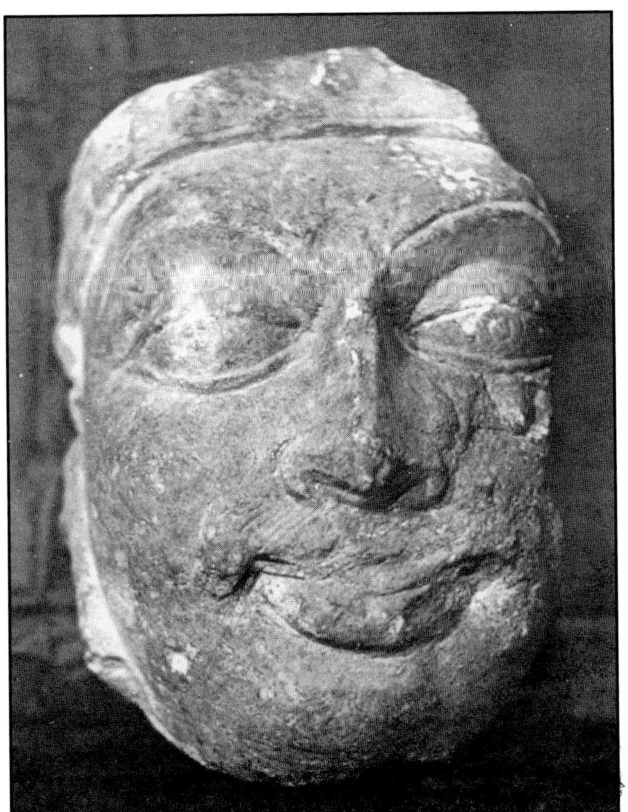

**Pl. 215.** Moustached head, Sanghol.

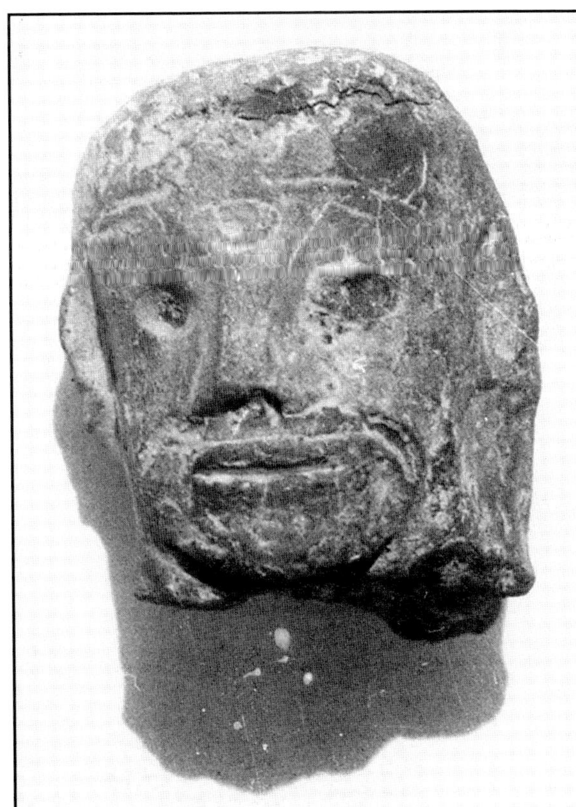

**Pl. 216.** Head with drooping moustache, Sanghol.

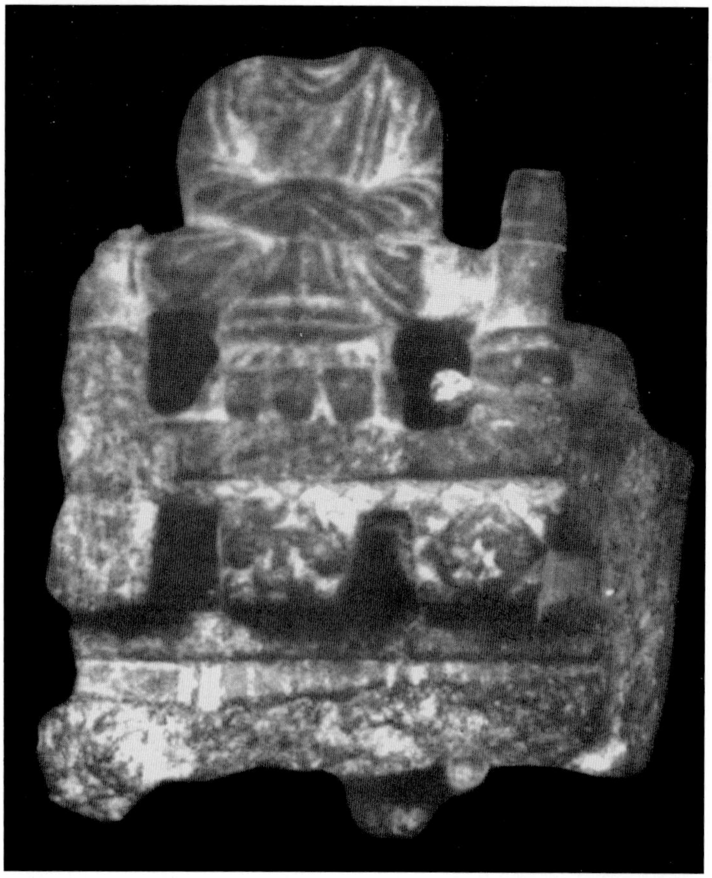

**Pl. 217.** Architectural piece with headless Buddha, Sanghol.

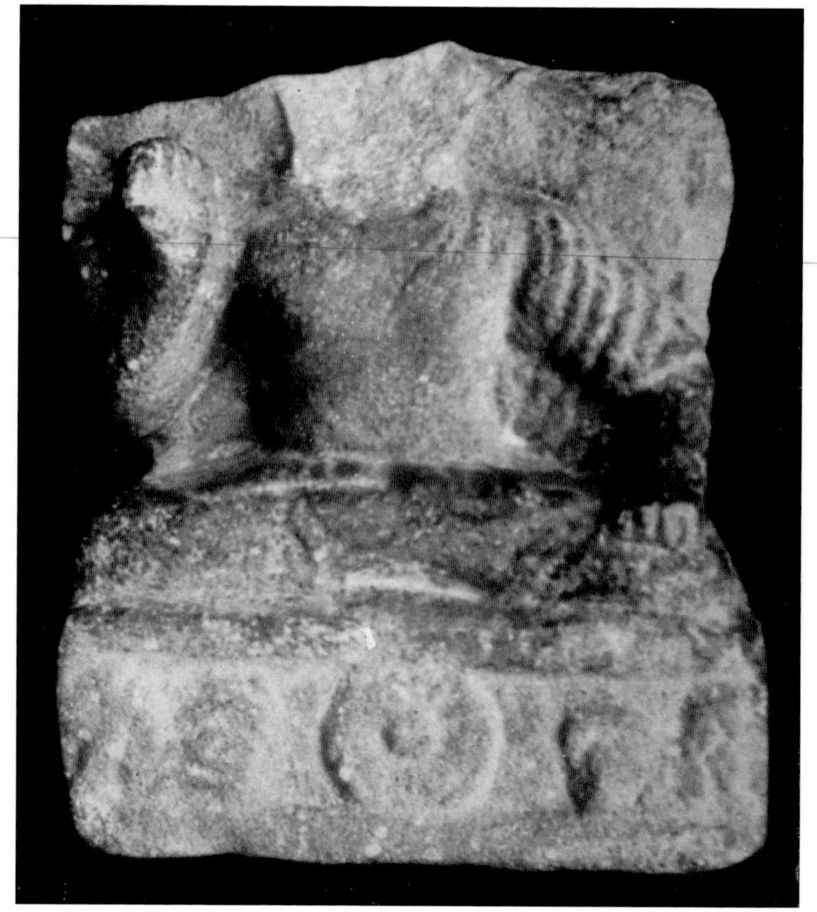

**Pl. 218.** Bodhisattva, Sanghol.

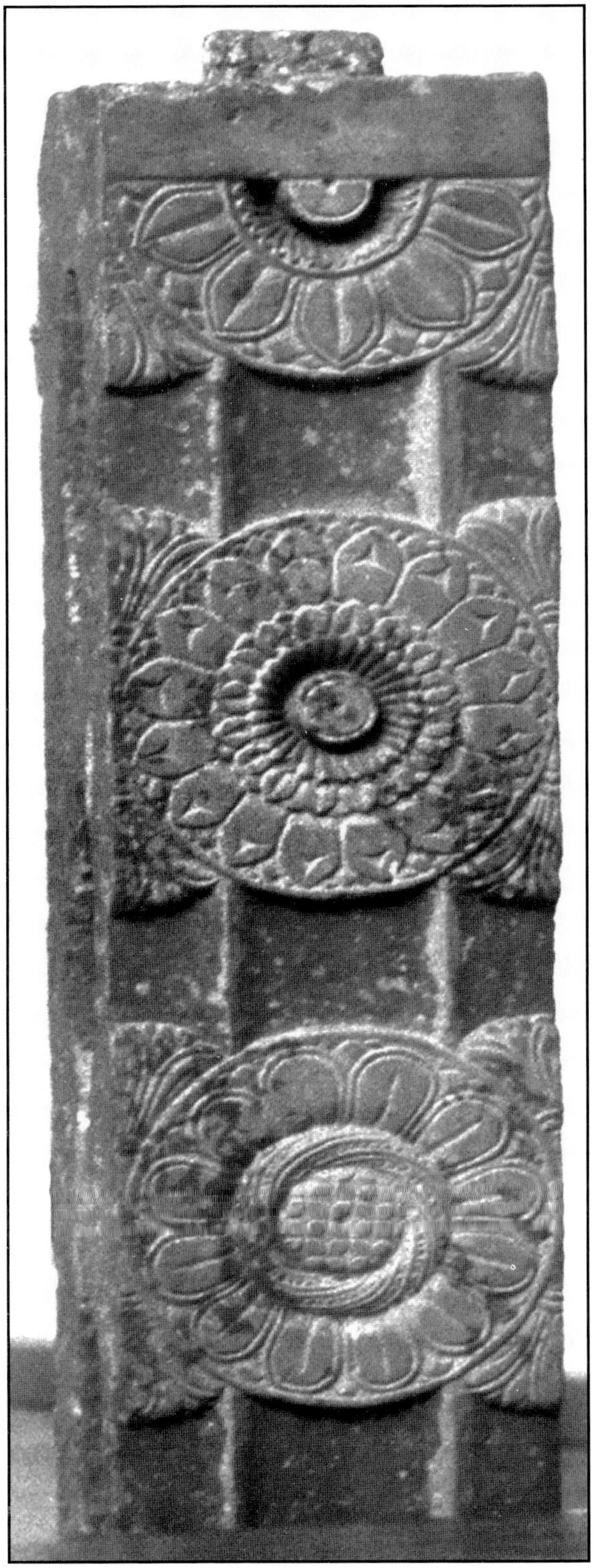

**Pl. 219.** Lotus flowers on the back of a railing pillar, Sanghol.

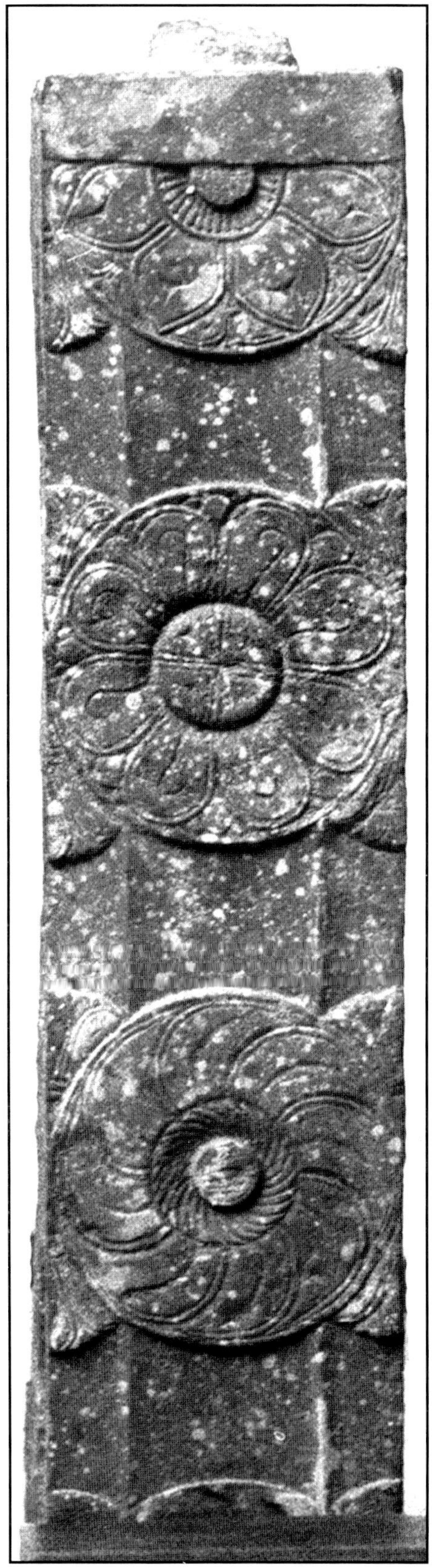

**Pl. 220.** Lotus flowers on the back of another railing pillar, Sanghol.

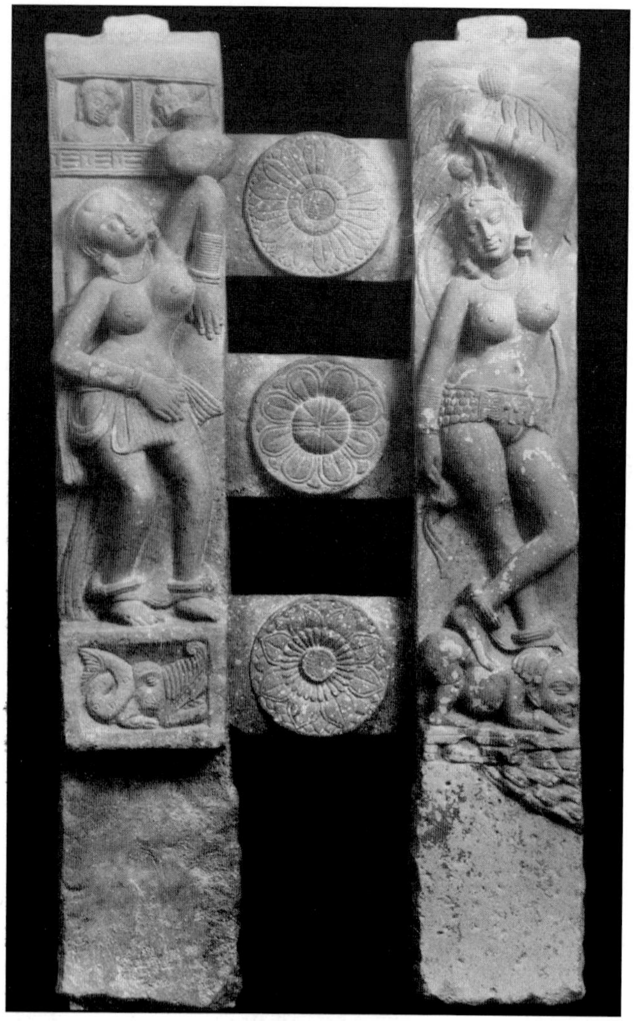

**Pl. 221.** Lotus flowers on a cross-bar, Sanghol.

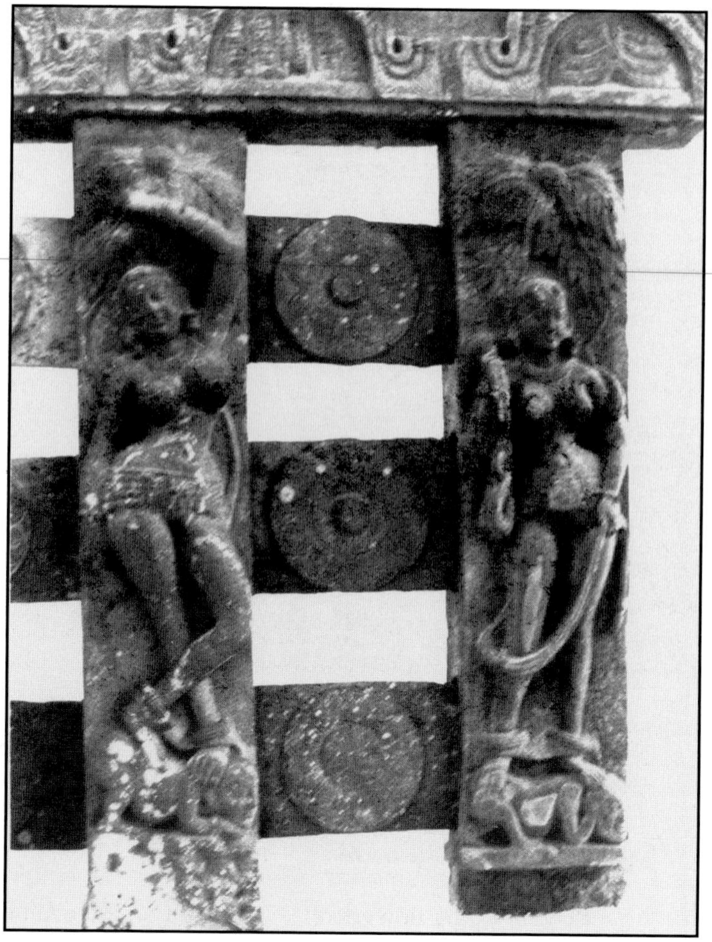

**Pl. 222.** Similar, Sanghol.

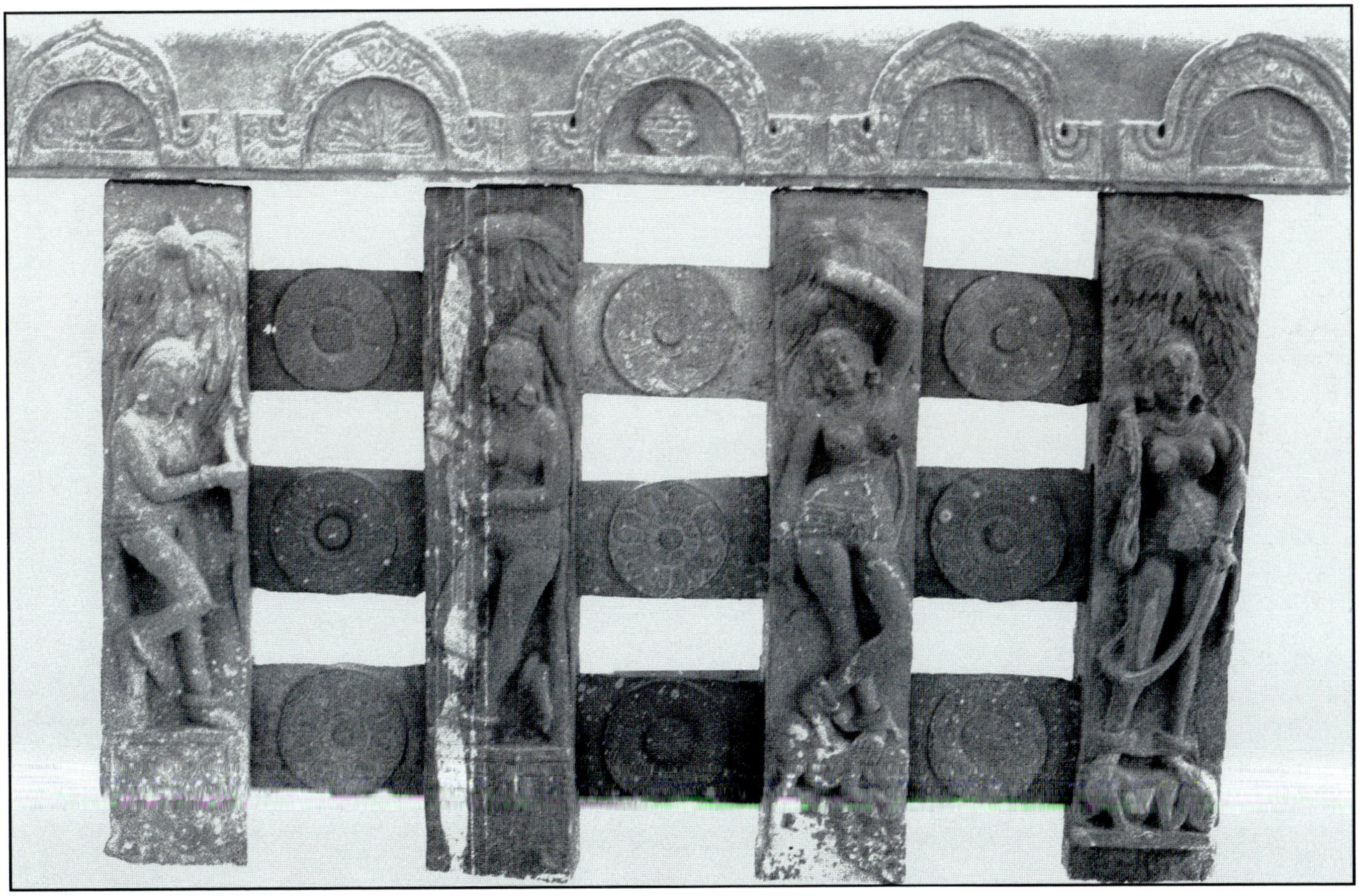

**Pl. 223.** Reconstructed railing with cross-bars and coping stones showing lotuses and other motifs, Sanghol.

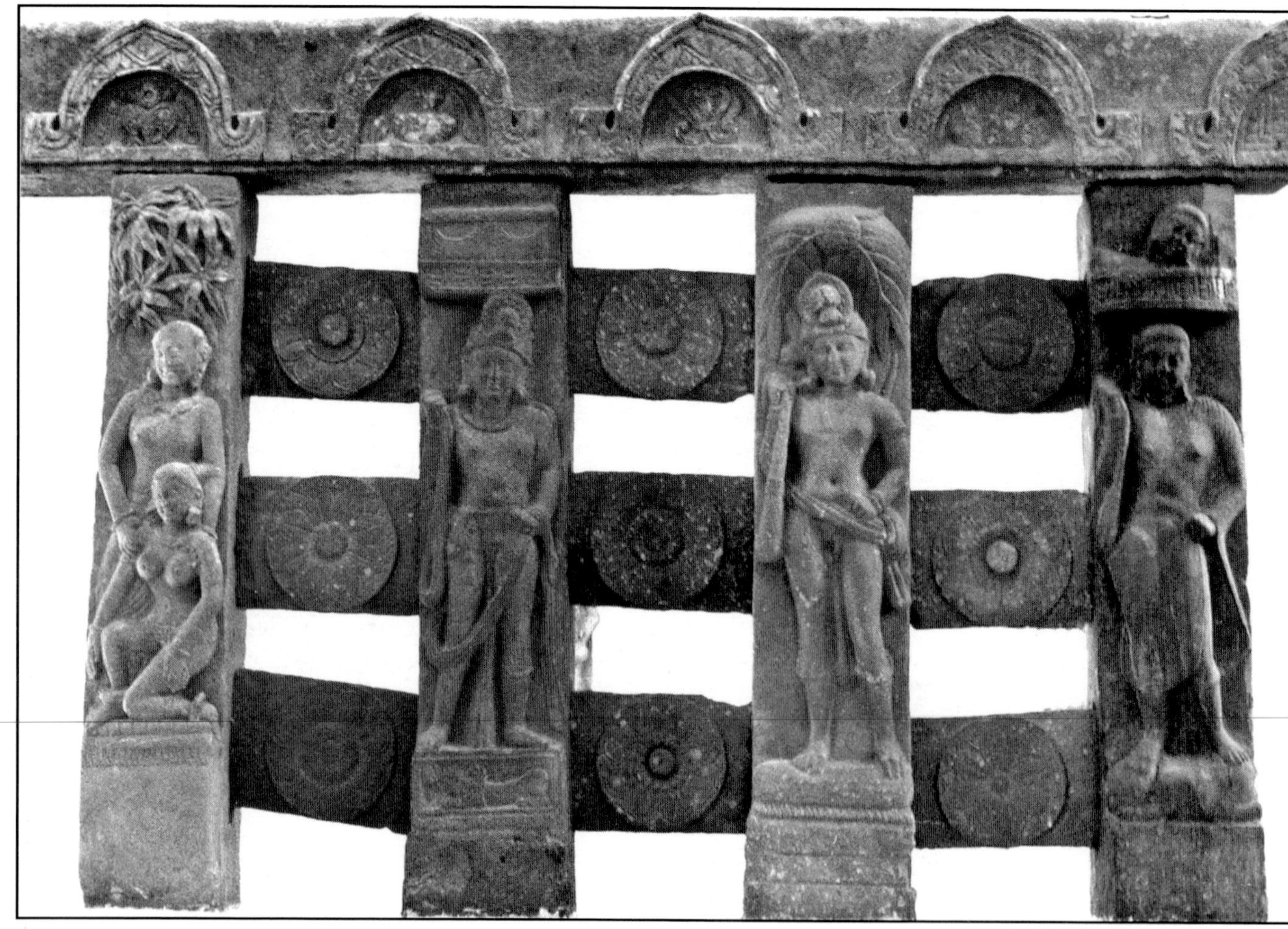

**Pl. 224.** Similar, Sanghol.

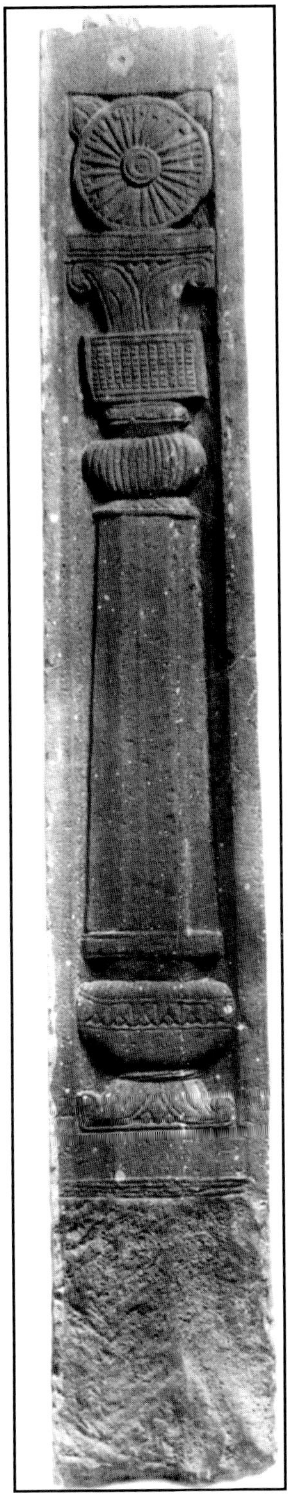

**Pl. 225.** Corner pillar showing *dharmachakra*, Sanghol.

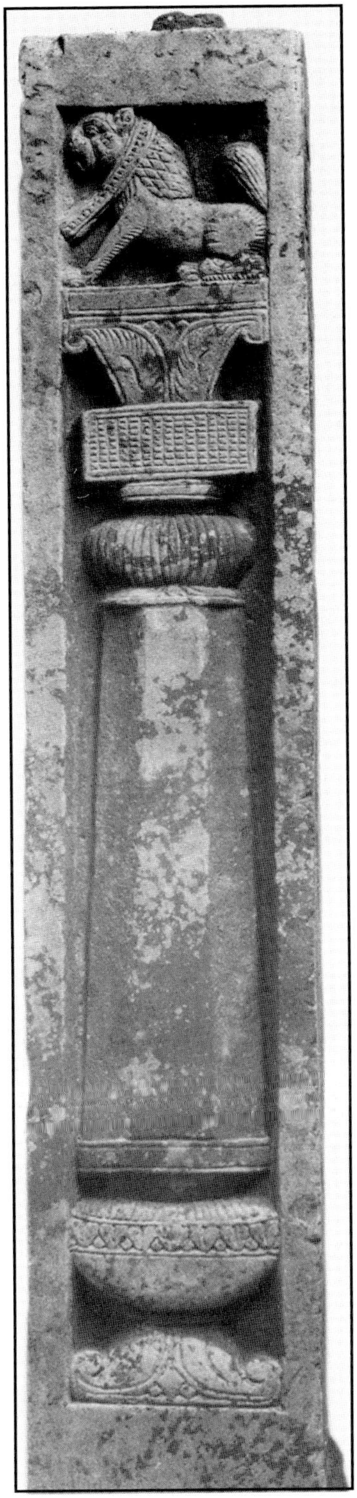

**Pl. 226.** Same, with sejant lion atop on another facet, Sanghol.

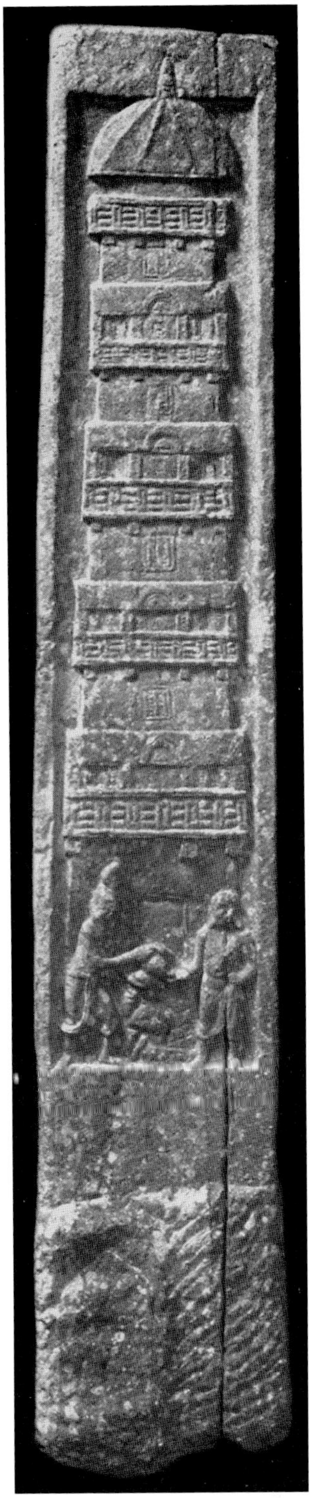

**Pl. 227.** Corner pillar with a towering shrine, Chandigarh Museum.

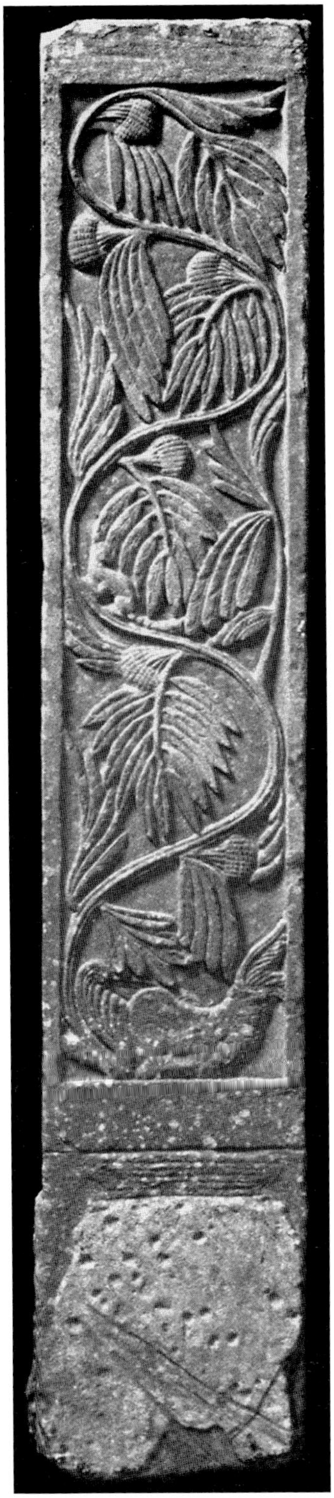

**Pl. 228.** Same, back side with creeper motif.

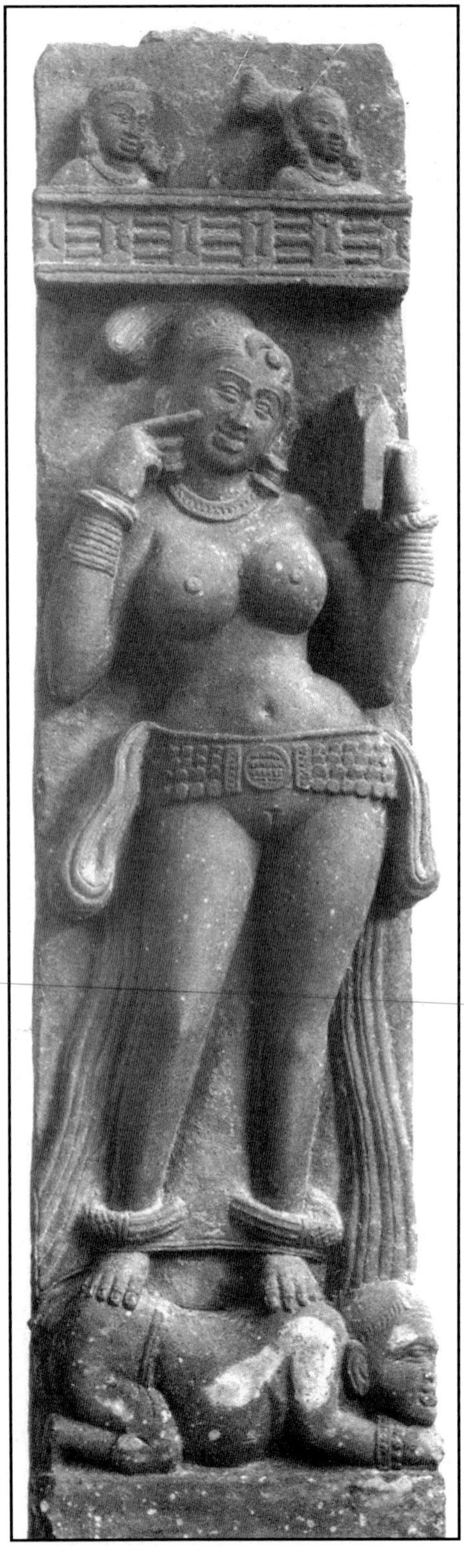

**Pl. 229.** Paribhogadarśinī, Sanghol.

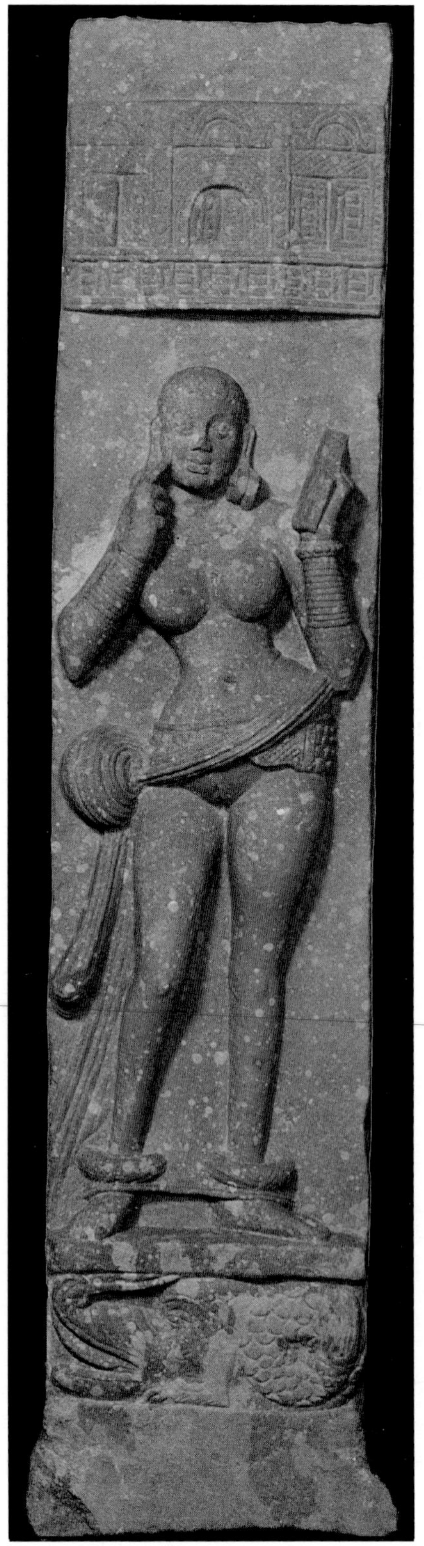

**Pl. 230.** Paribhogadarśinī, Chandigarh Museum.

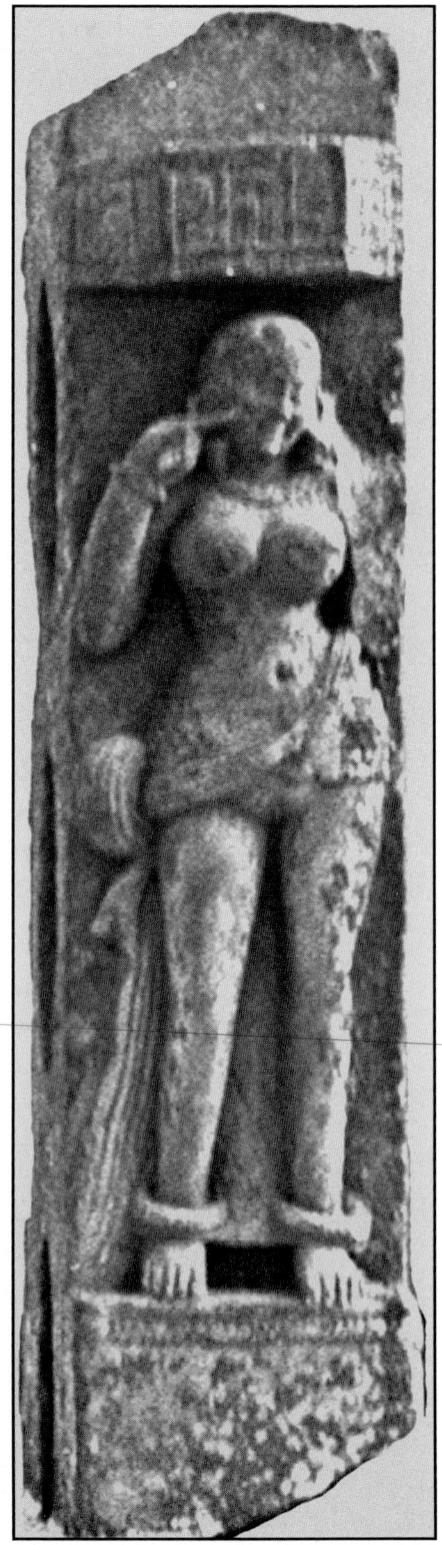

**Pl. 231.** Another pillar with Paribhogadarśinī, Sanghol.

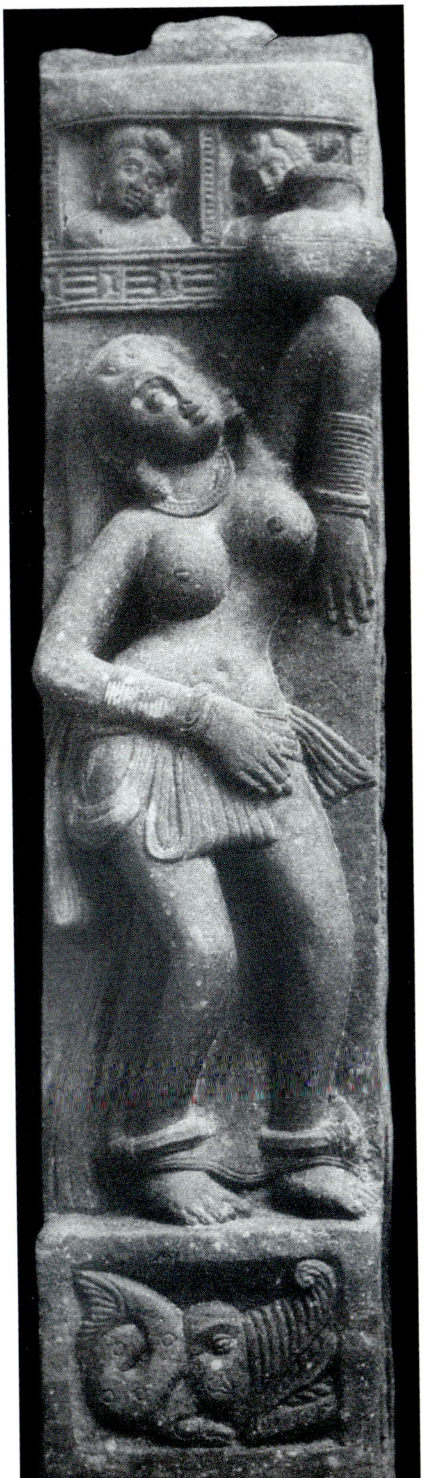

**Pl. 232.** Naṭī, Sanghol.

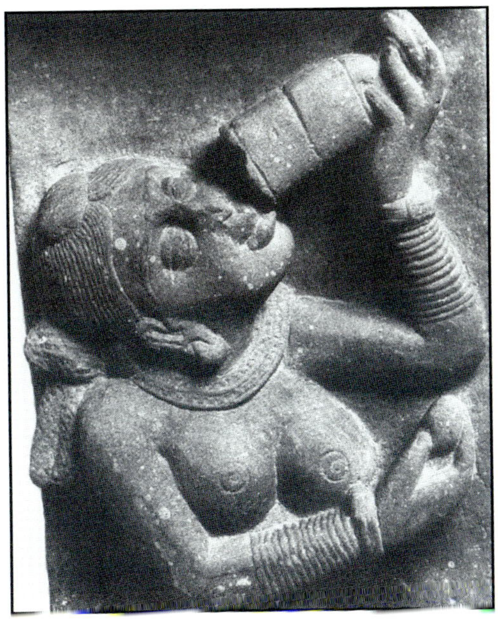

Pl. 234. Same, closer view.

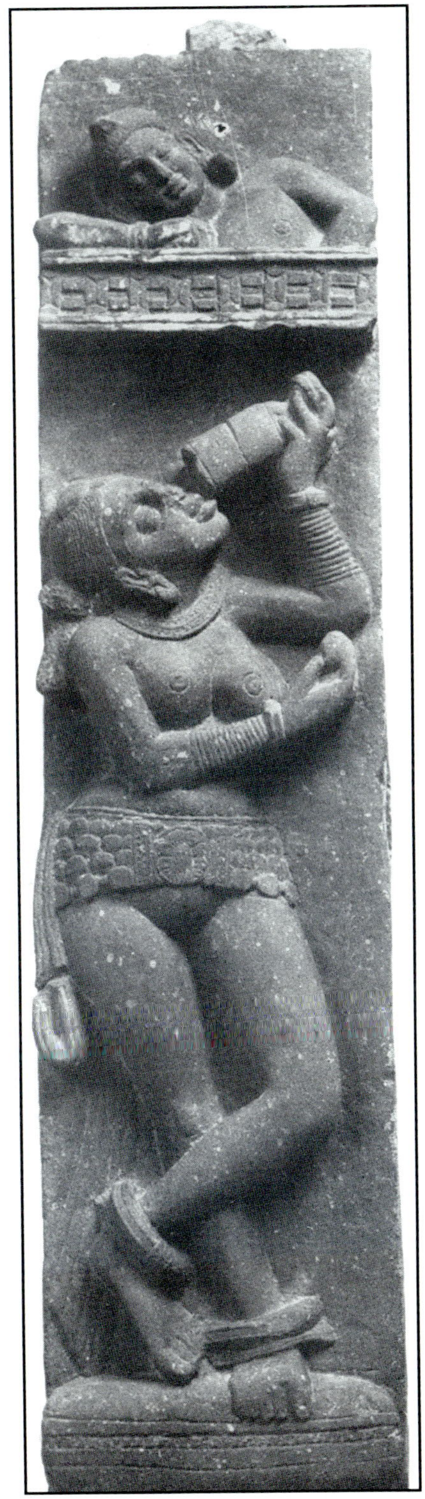

**Pl. 233.** Madhupāna, Sanghol.

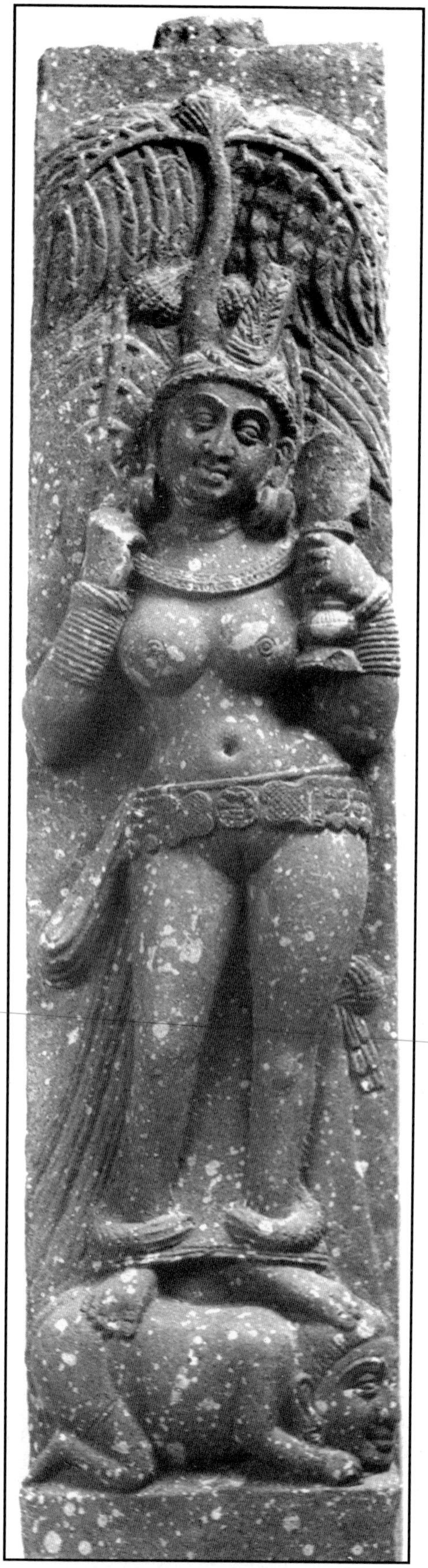

**Pl. 235.** *Yakshī* with a mirror.

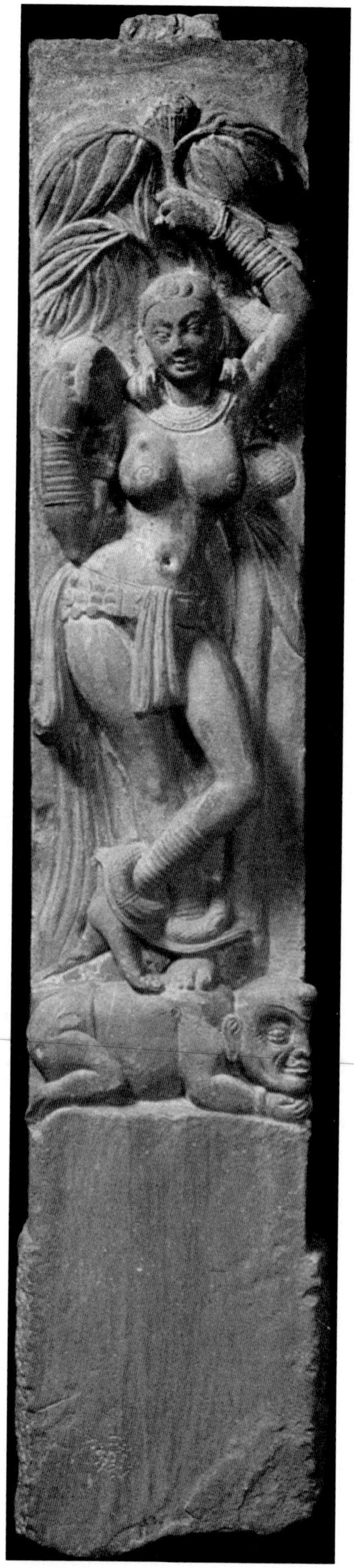

**Pl. 236.** Darpanadhāriṇī, Chandigarh Museum.

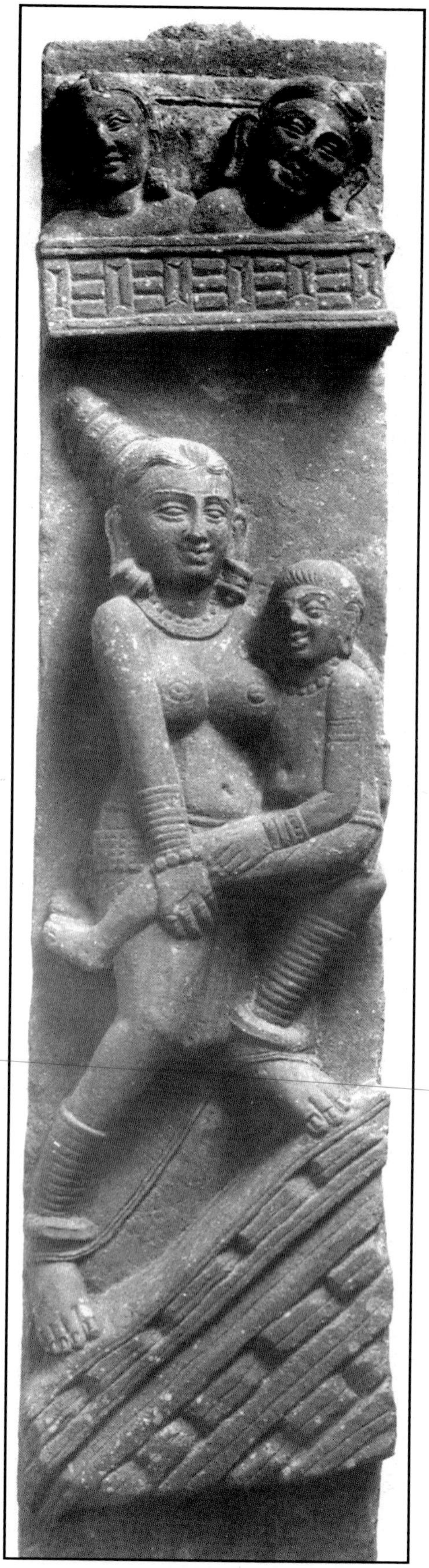

**Pl. 237.** Mother and child, Sanghol.

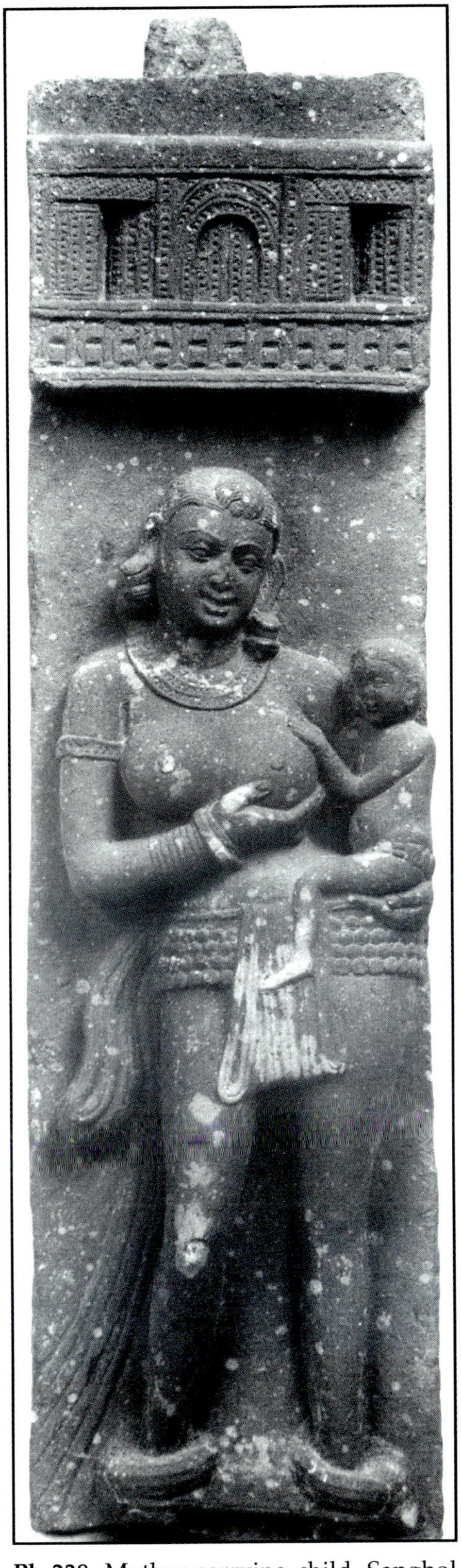

**Pl. 238.** Mother carrying child, Sanghol.

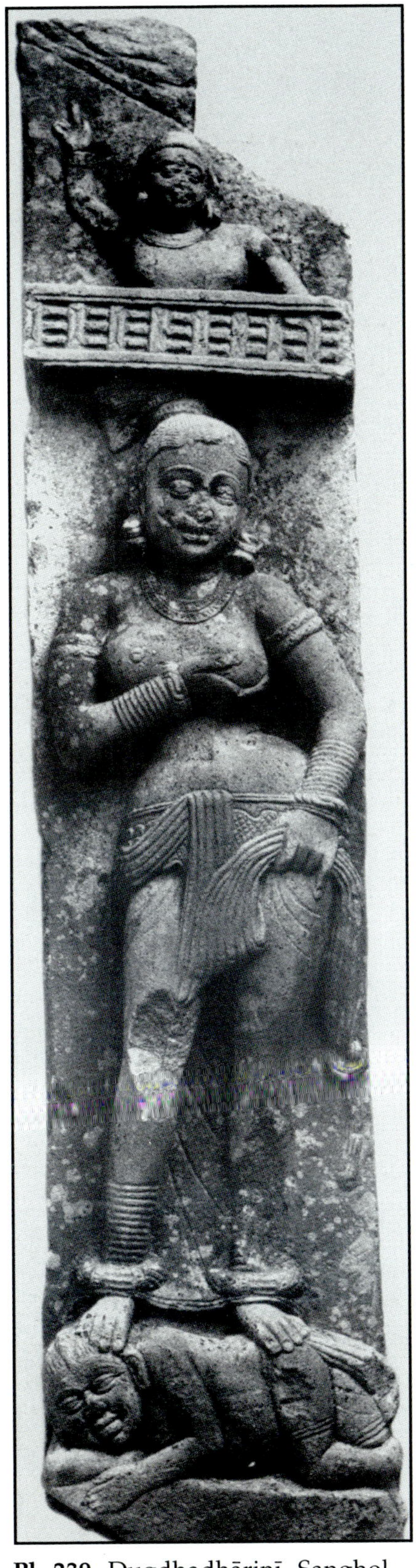

**Pl. 239.** Dugdhadhāriṇī, Sanghol.

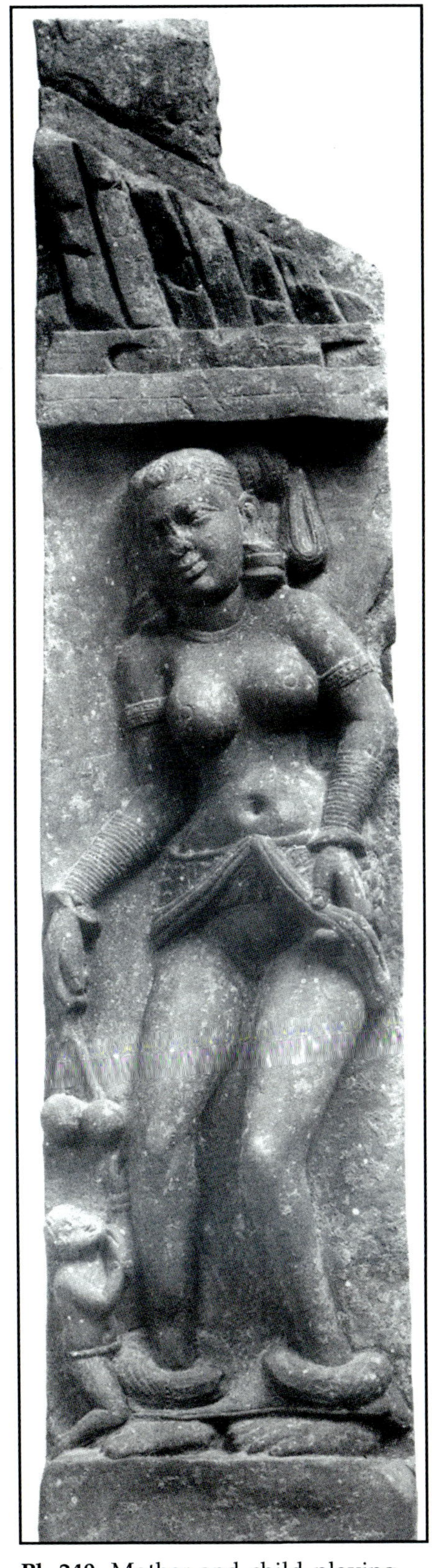

**Pl. 240.** Mother and child playing with rattle, Sanghol.

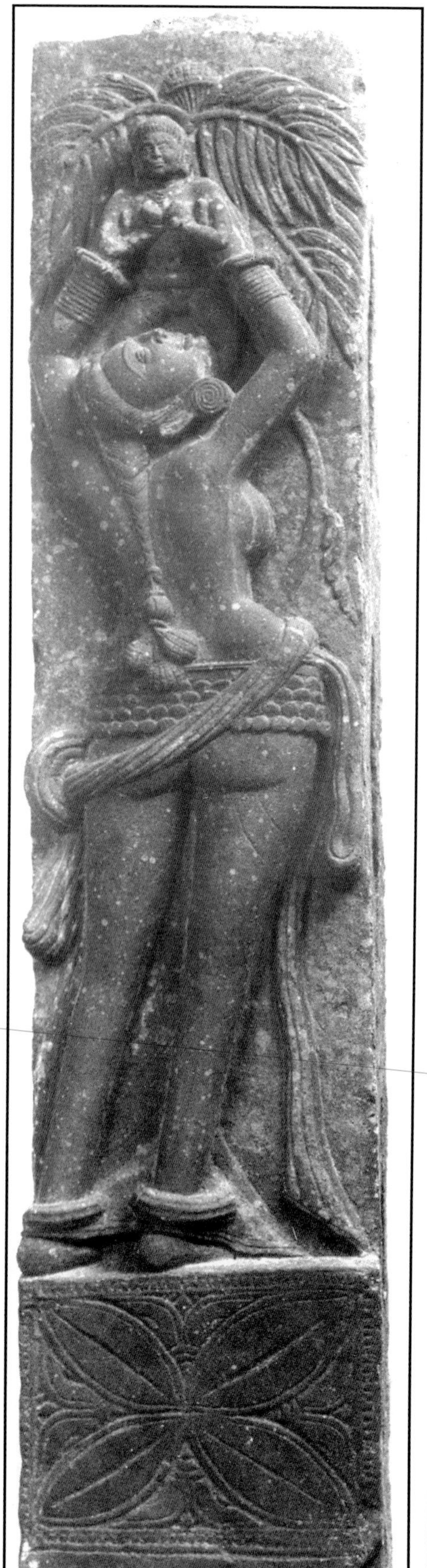

**Pl. 241.** Mother playing with child, Sanghol.

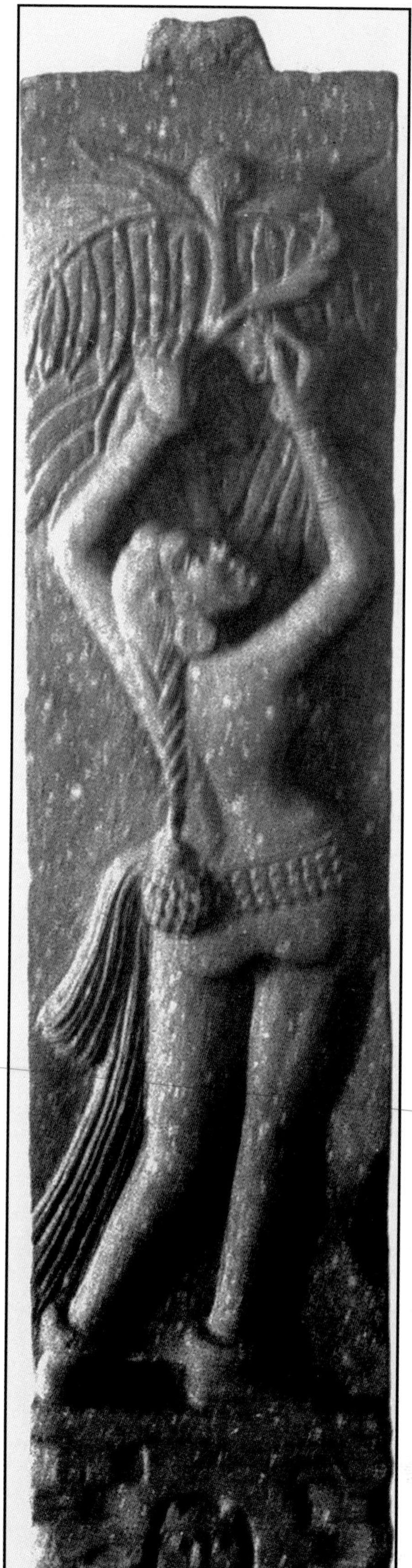

**Pl. 242.** *Yakshī* plucking flowers, Sanghol.

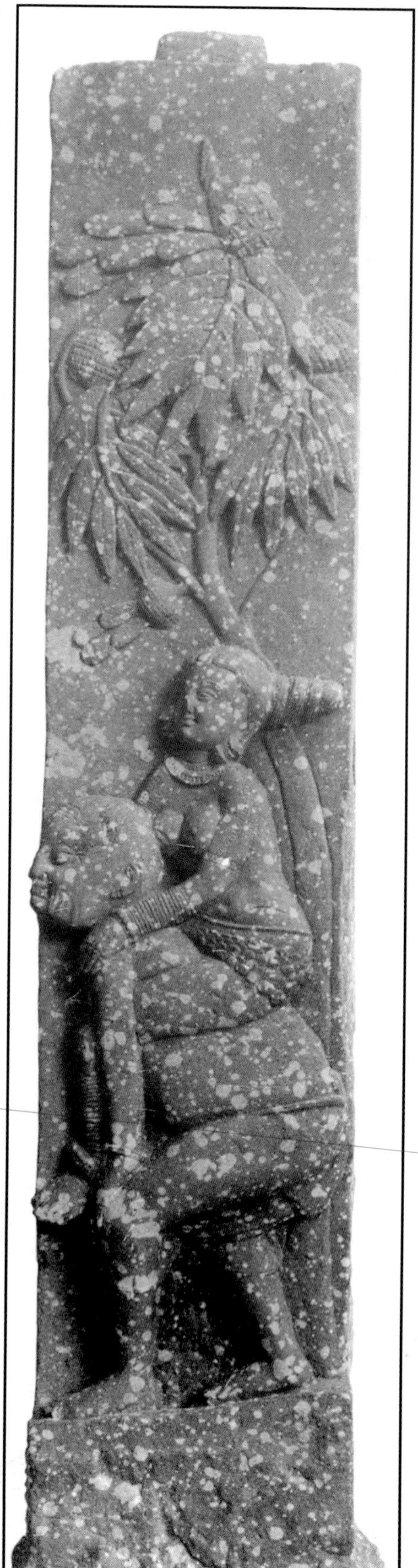

**Pl. 243.** Yakshārohī, Sanghol.

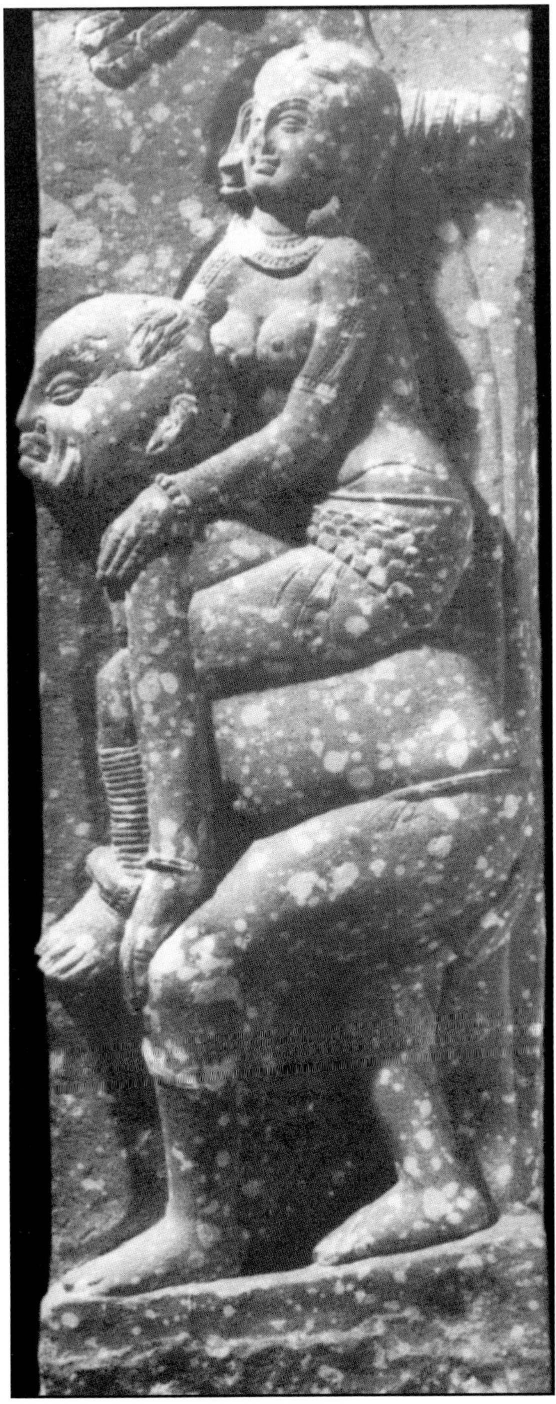

**Pl. 244.** Same, closer view.

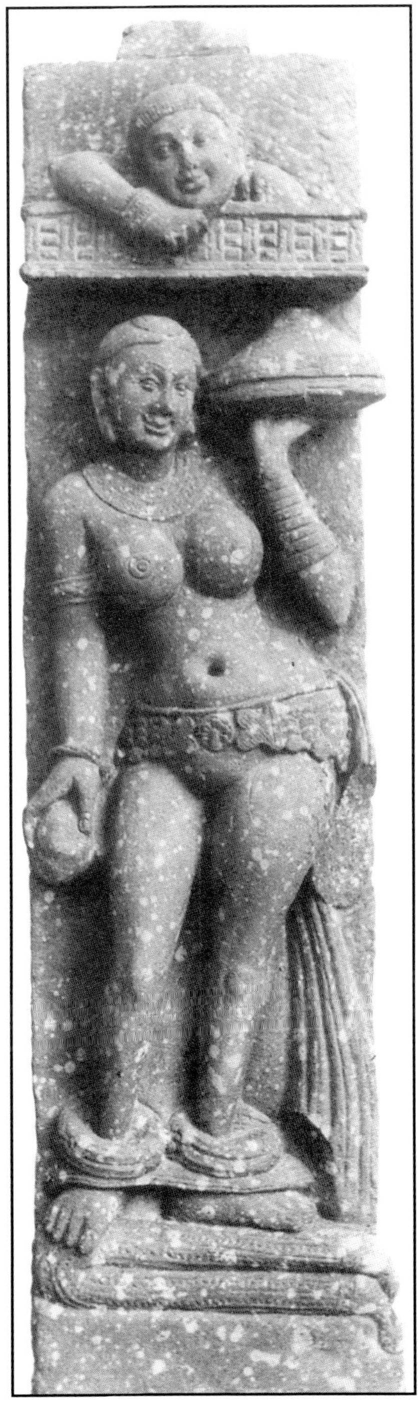

**Pl. 245.** Prasādhikā, Sanghol.

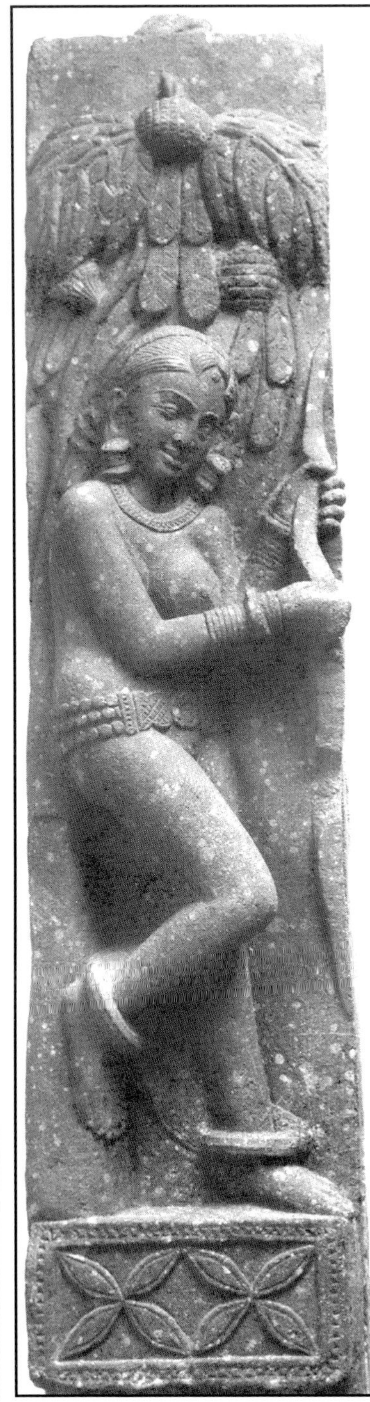

**Pl. 246.** Aśoka-dohada, Sanghol.

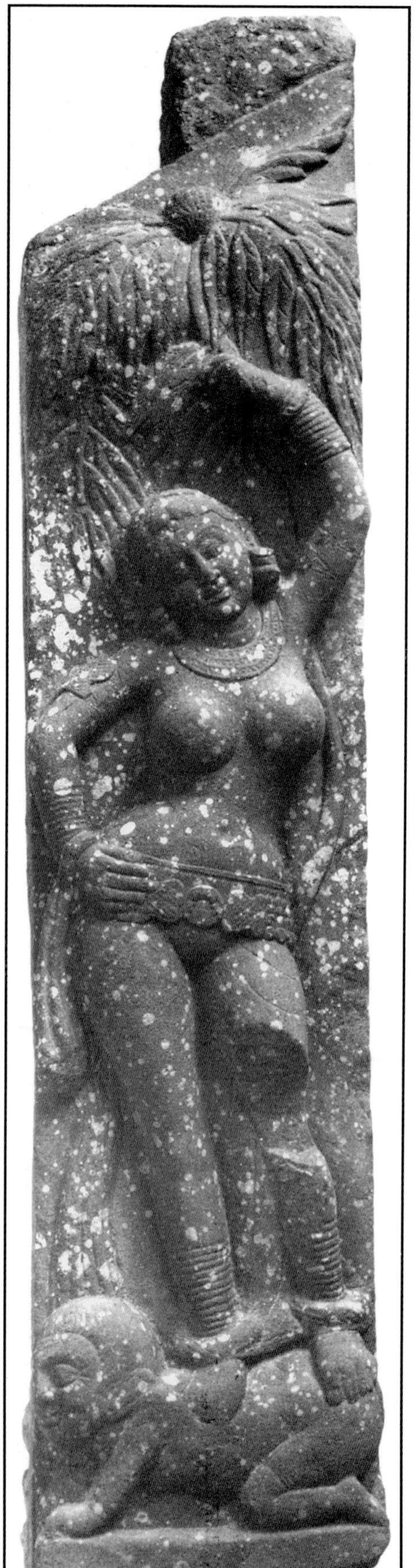

**Pl. 247.** *Śālabhañjikā*, Sanghol.

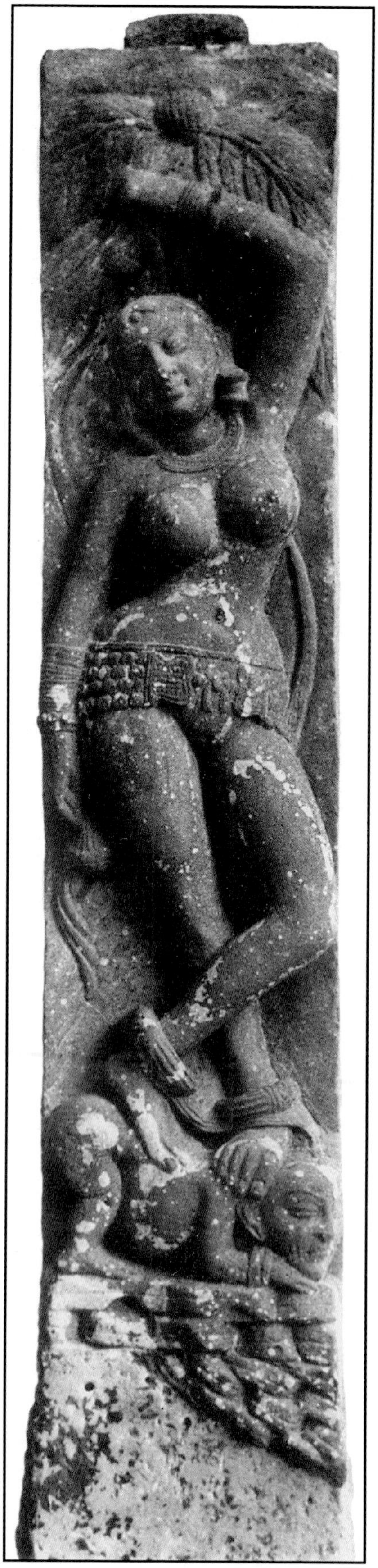

**Pl. 248.** *Śālabhañjikā*, Sanghol.

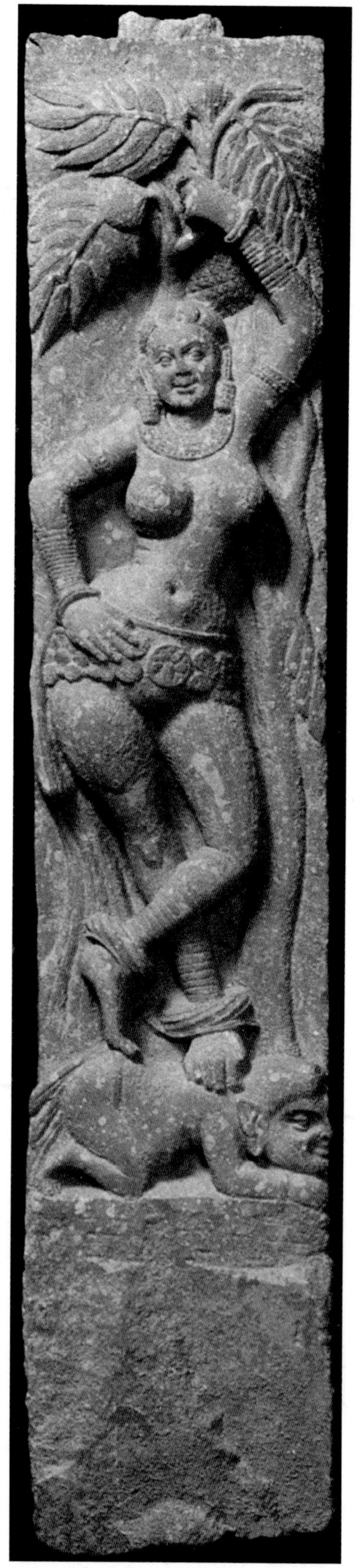

**Pl. 249.** *Śālabhañjikā*, Chandigarh Museum.

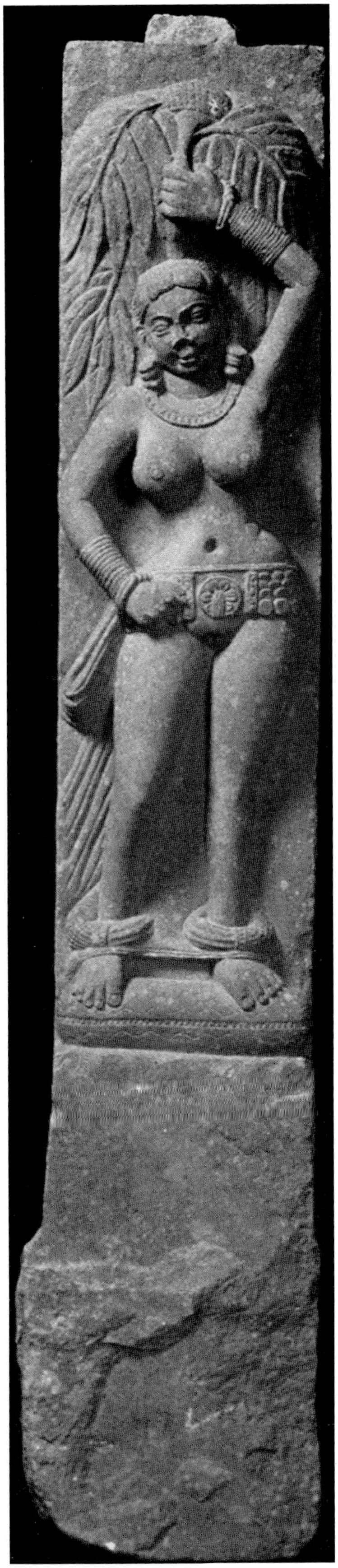

**Pl. 250.** *Śālabhañjikā*, Chandigarh Museum.

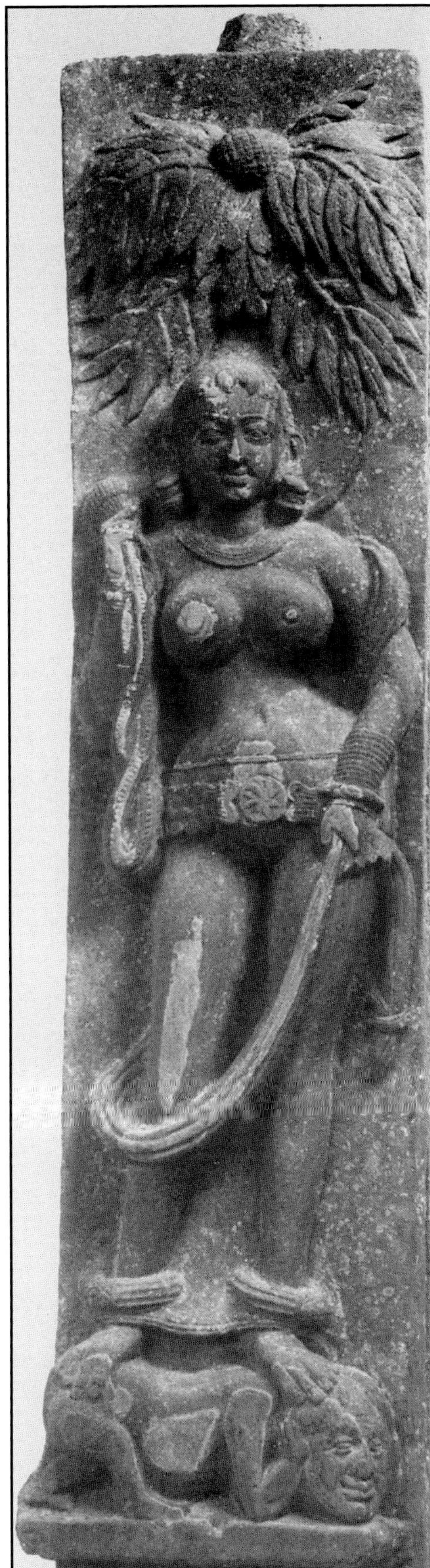

**Pl. 251.** Upāsikā, Sanghol.

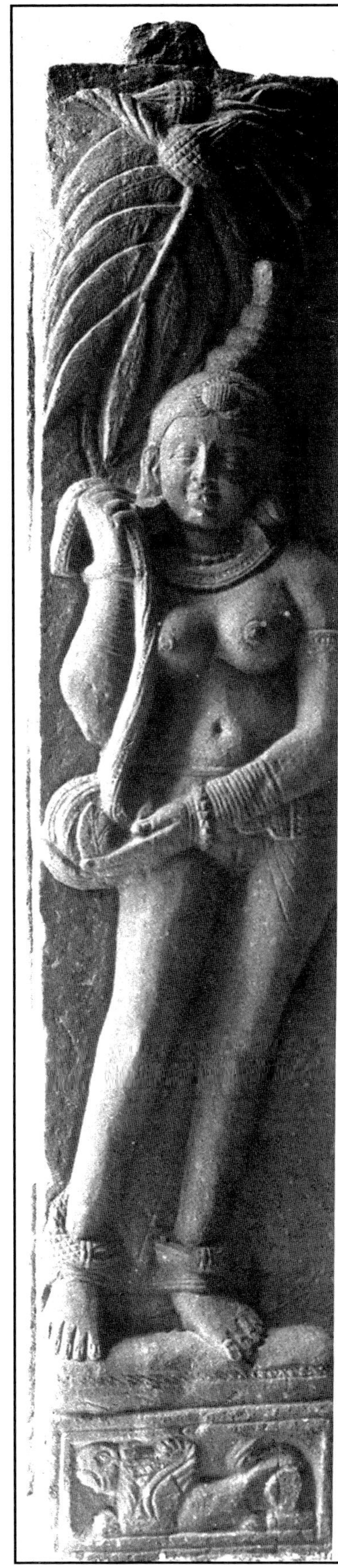

**Pl. 252.** Another female devotee, Sanghol.

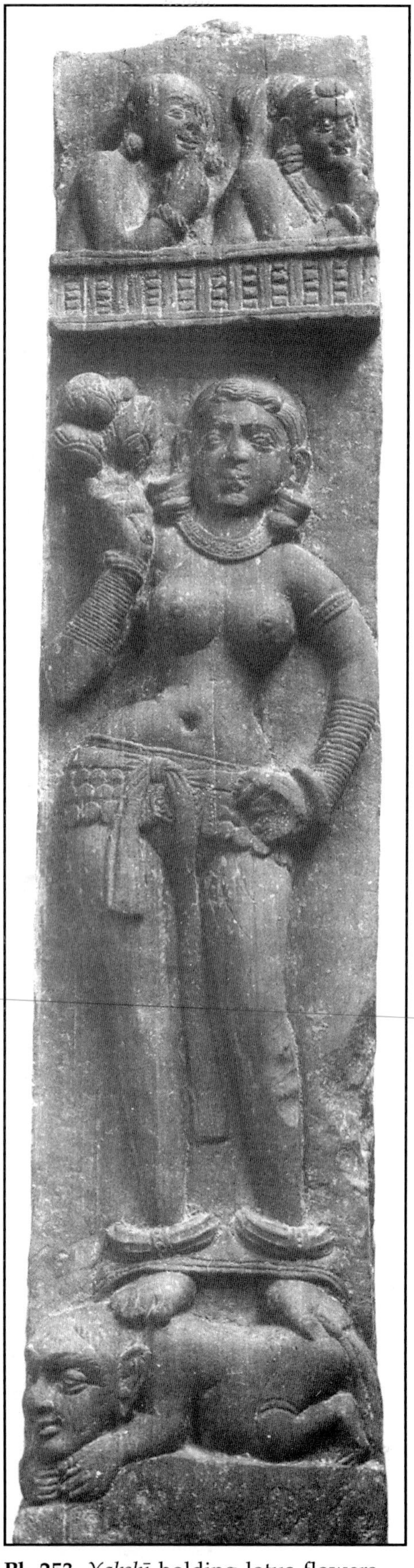

**Pl. 253.** *Yakshī* holding lotus flowers, Sanghol.

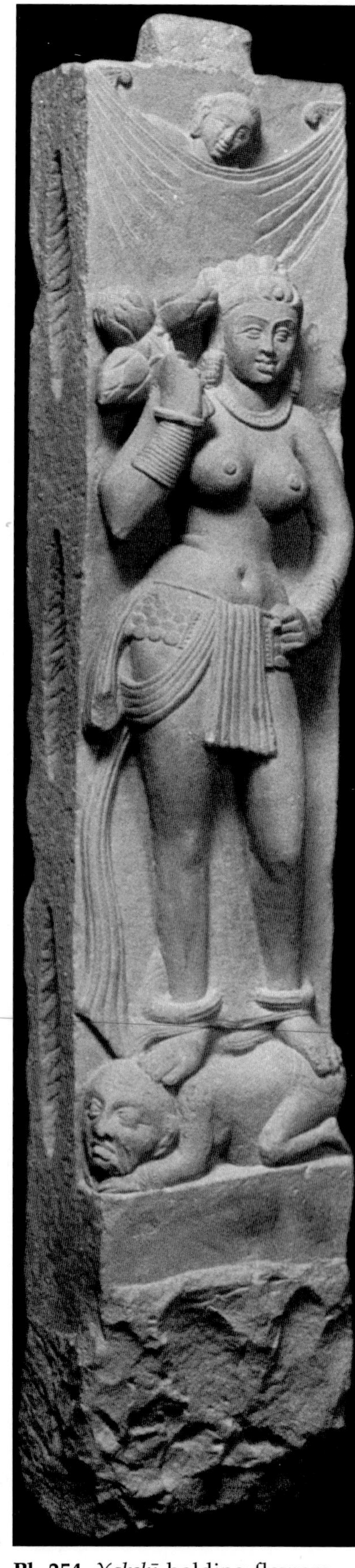

**Pl. 254.** *Yakshī* holding flowers, Chandigarh Museum.

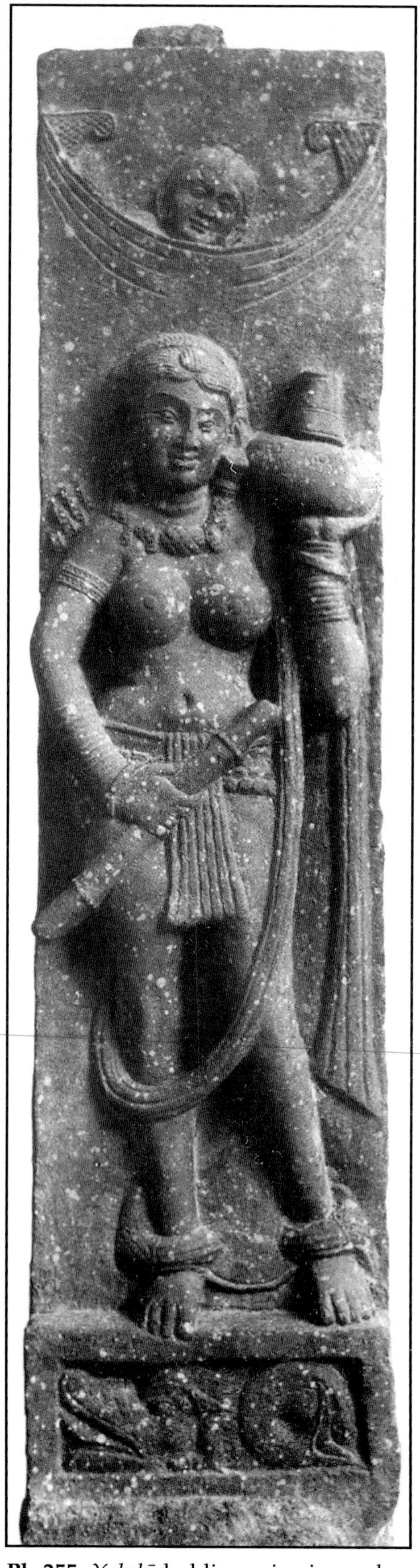

**Pl. 255.** *Yakshī* holding wine-jar and flute, Sanghol.

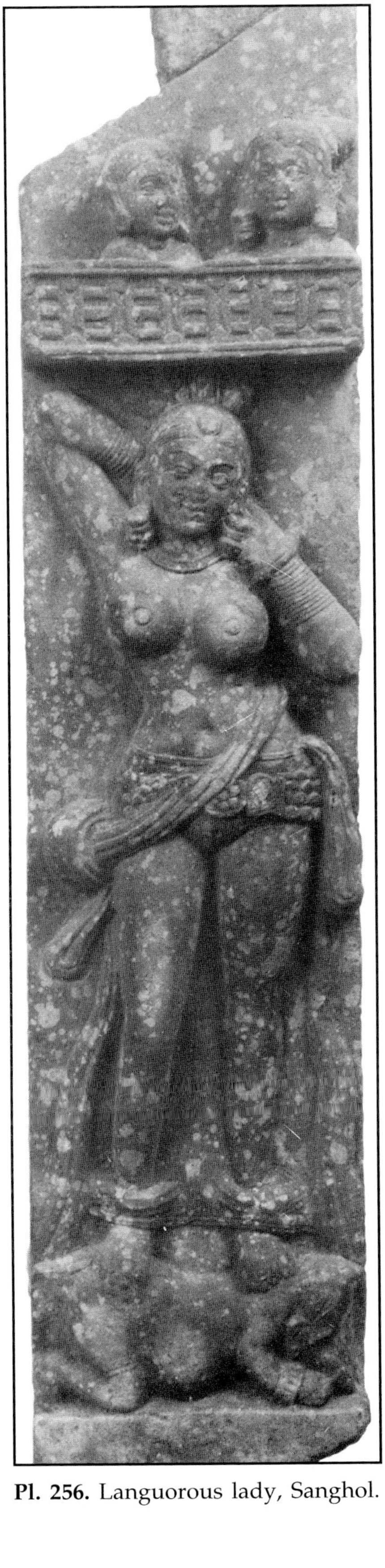

**Pl. 256.** Languorous lady, Sanghol.

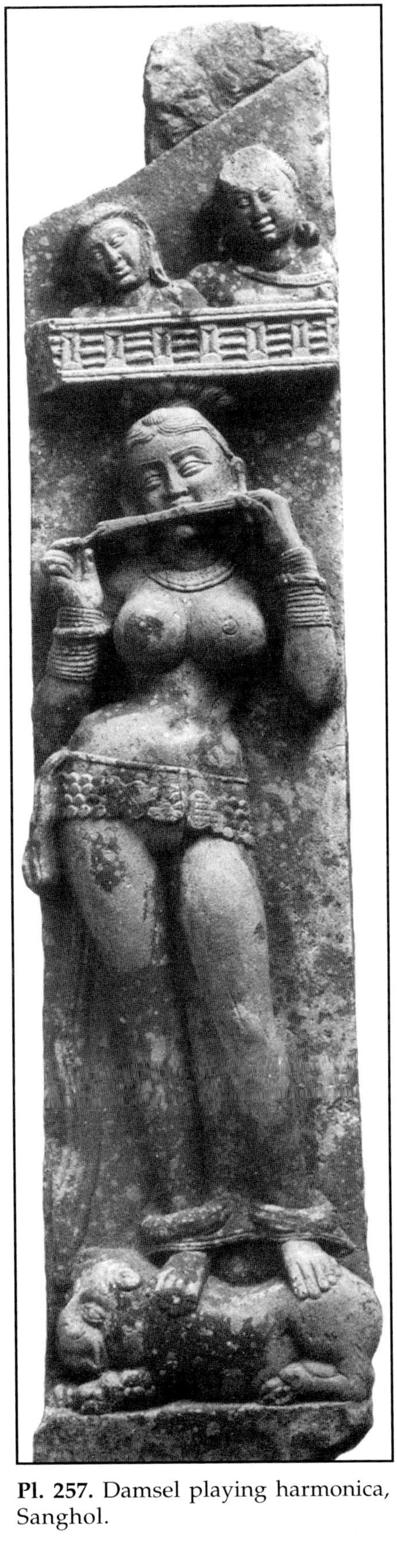

**Pl. 257.** Damsel playing harmonica, Sanghol.

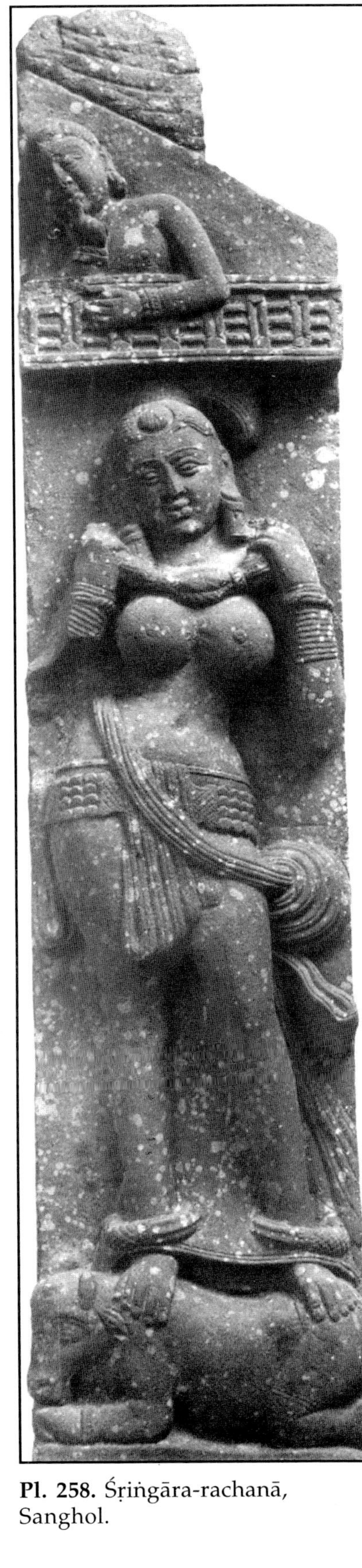

**Pl. 258.** Śṛiṅgāra-rachanā, Sanghol.

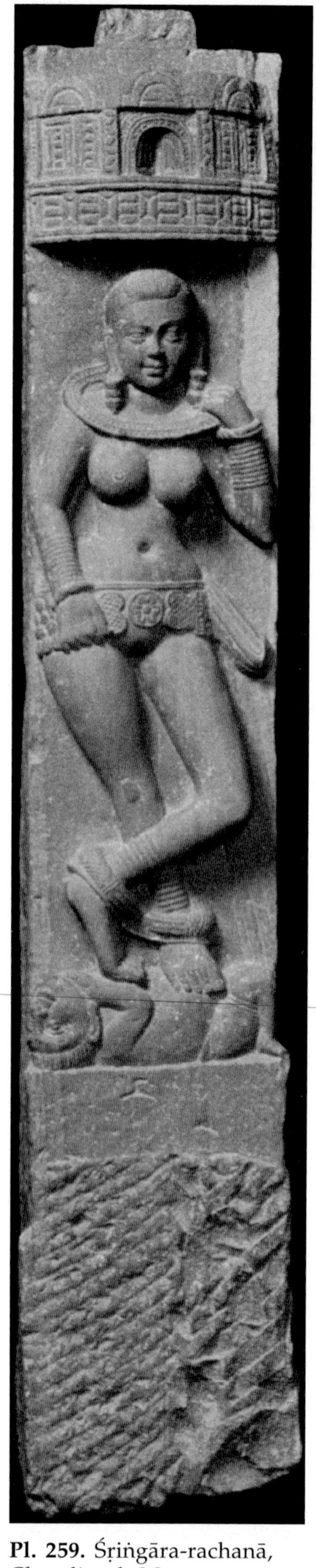

**Pl. 259.** Śṛiṅgāra-rachanā, Chandigarh Museum.

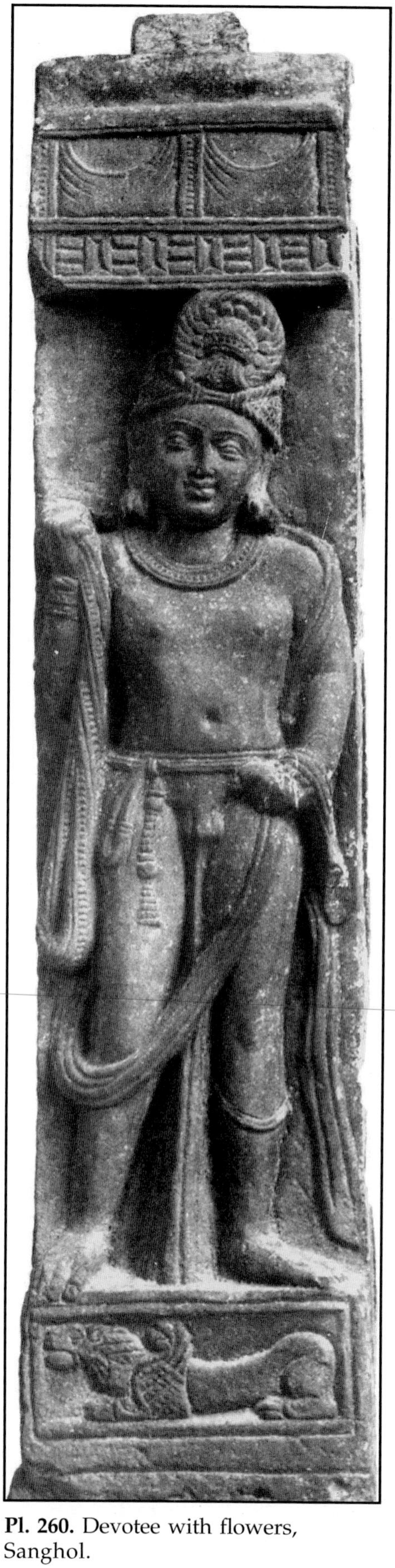

**Pl. 260.** Devotee with flowers, Sanghol.

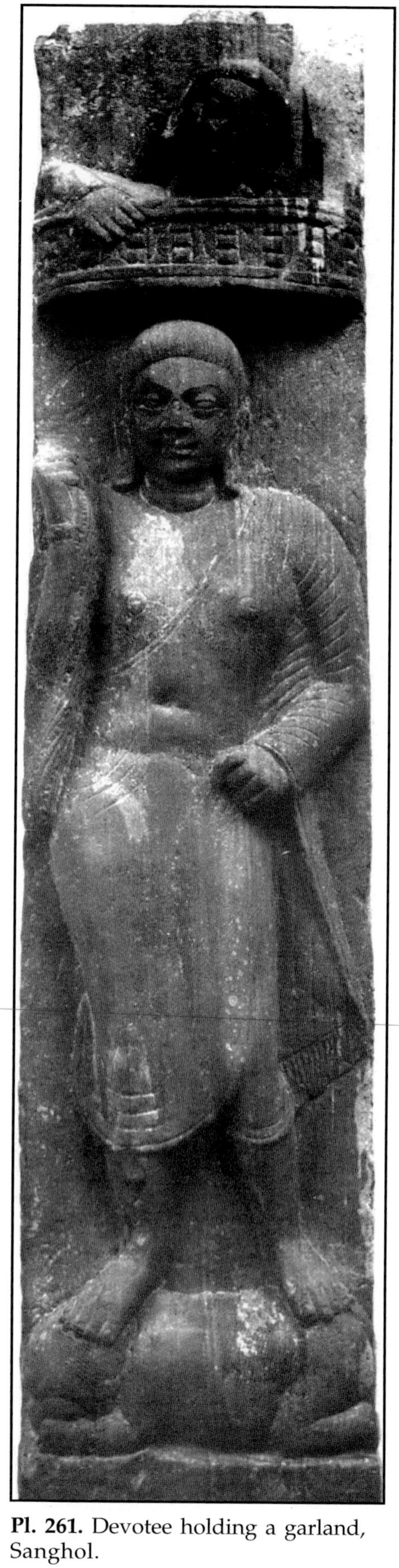

**Pl. 261.** Devotee holding a garland, Sanghol.

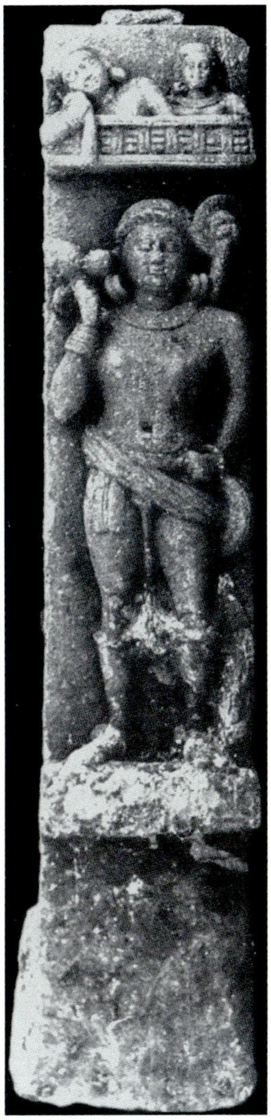

**Pl. 262.** Devotee holding a bunch of flowers, Sanghol.

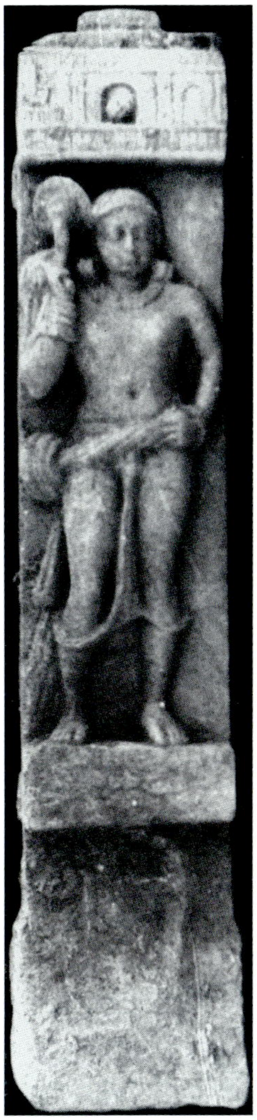

**Pl. 263.** Fly-whisker, Sanghol.

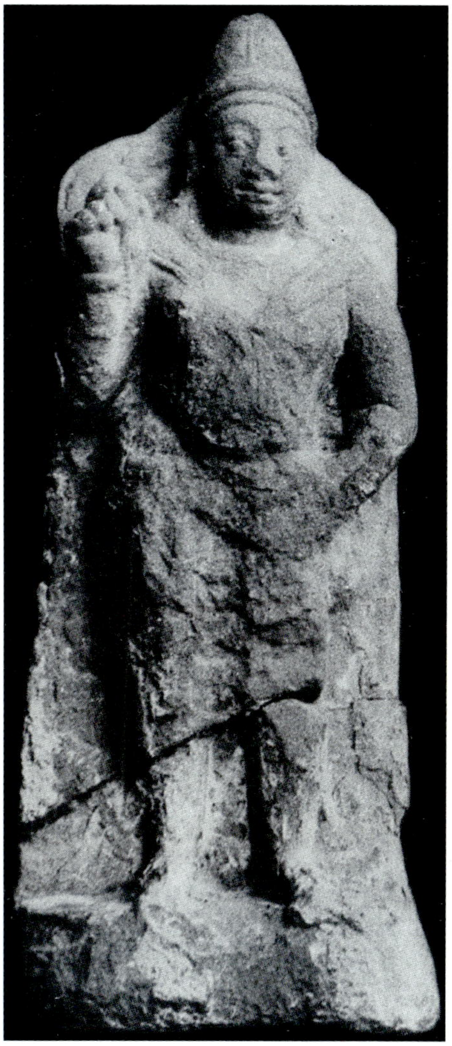

**Pl. 264.** Śaka devotee, Karhali.

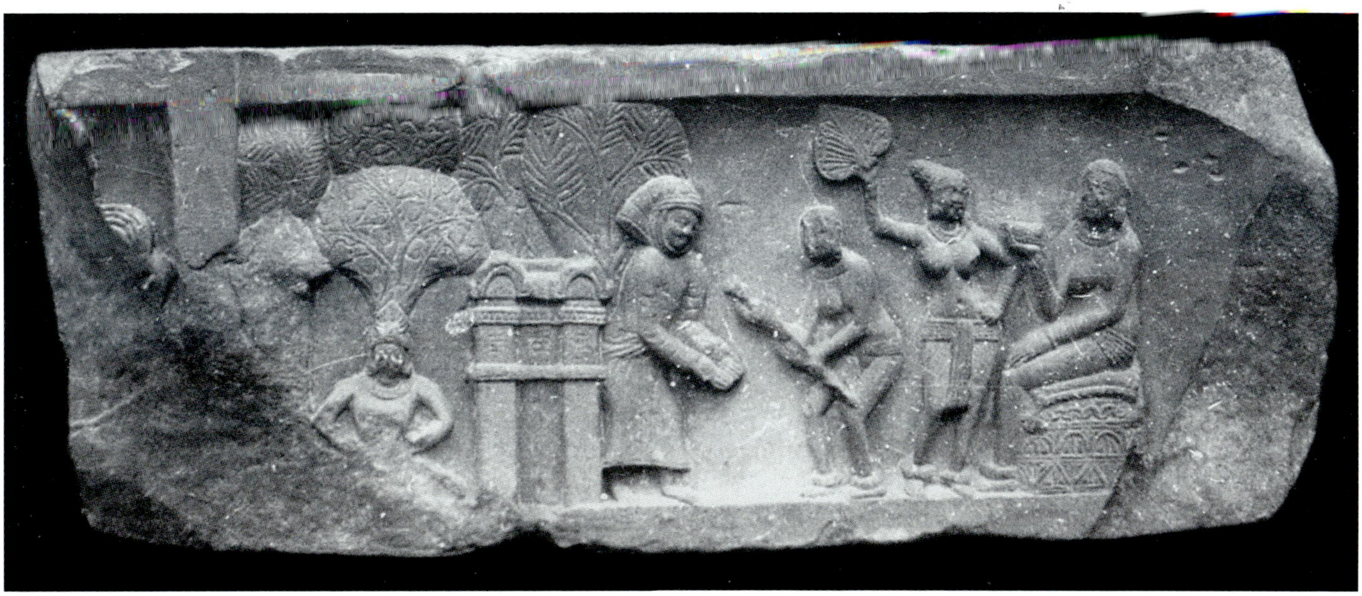

**Pl. 265.** Architrave showing meditating male, female passing on a babe to another and a royal female being fanned by a maid, Sanghol.

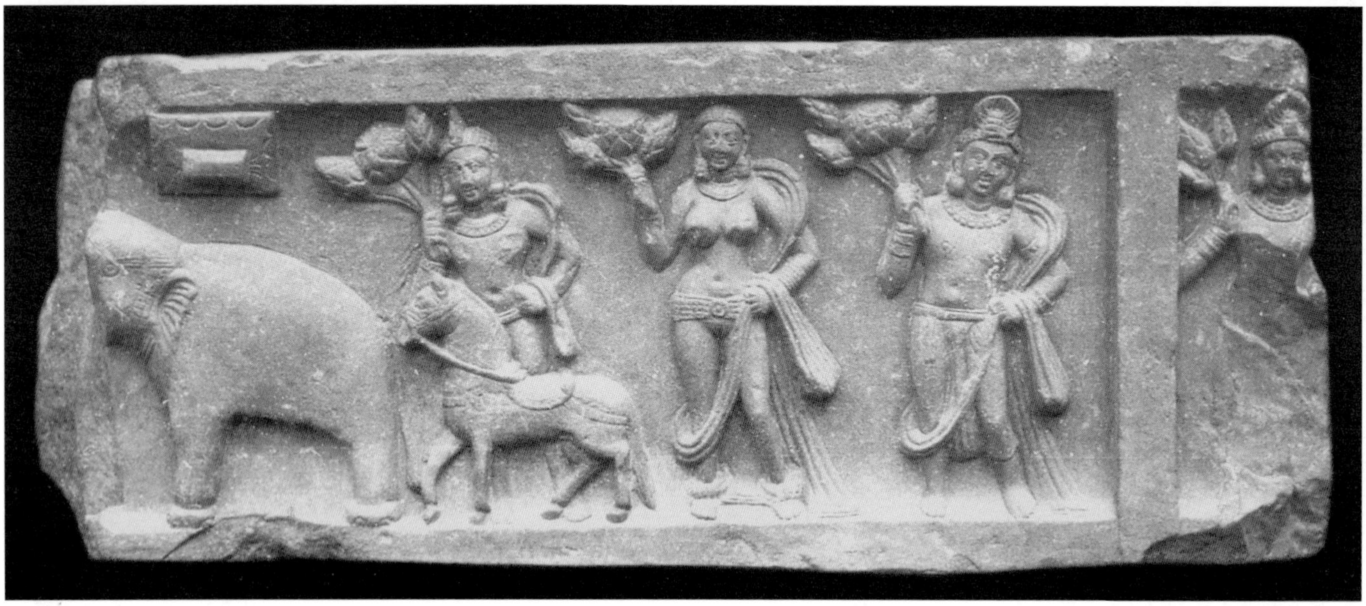

**Pl. 266.** Other side of the architrave showing elephant, horse and three human figures holding flower bunches, Sanghol.

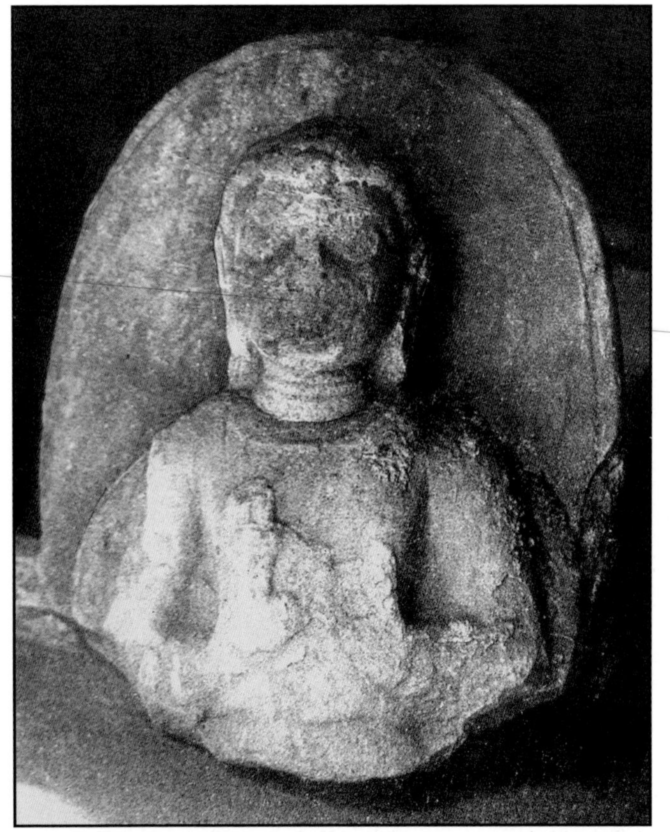

**Pl. 267.** Buddha in *dharmachakra-pravartana-mudrā*, Zahura.

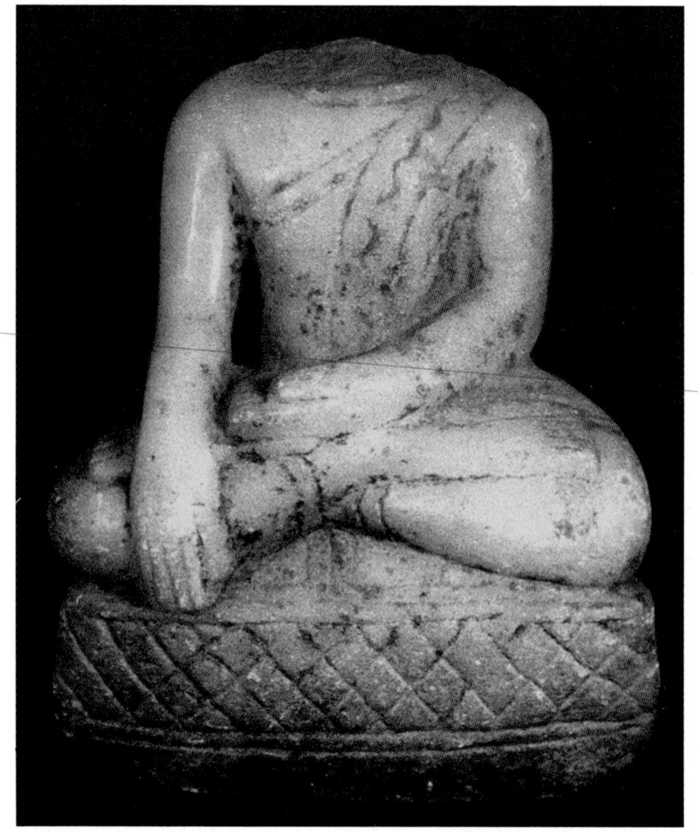

**Pl. 268.** Headless marble Buddha in *bhūmisparśa-mudrā*, Kharar.

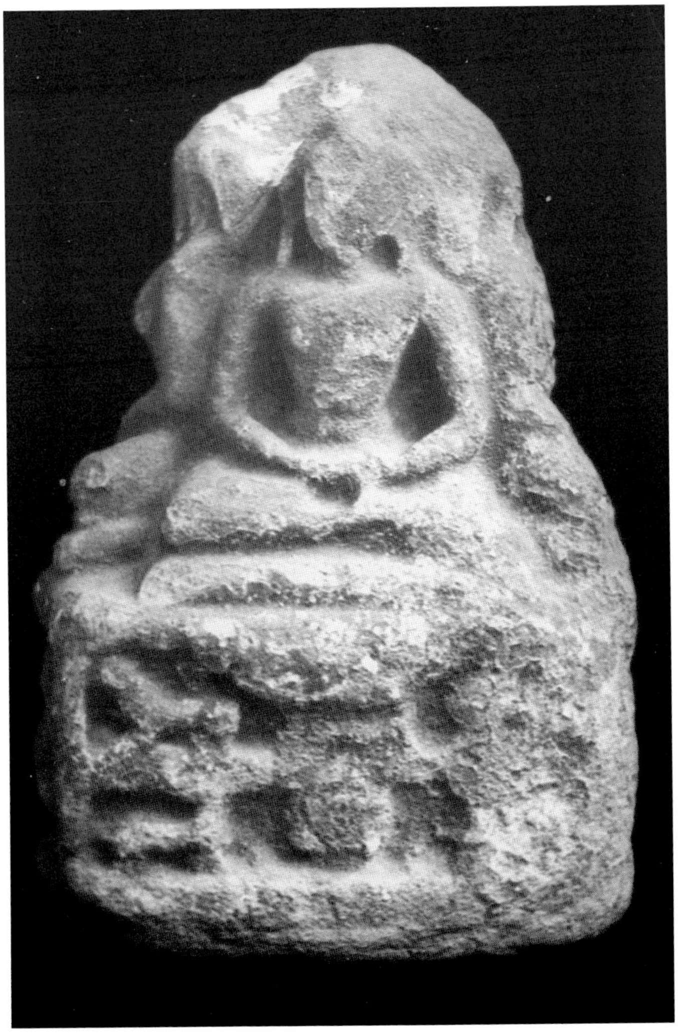

**Pl. 269.** Sarvatobhadra, Dholbaha.

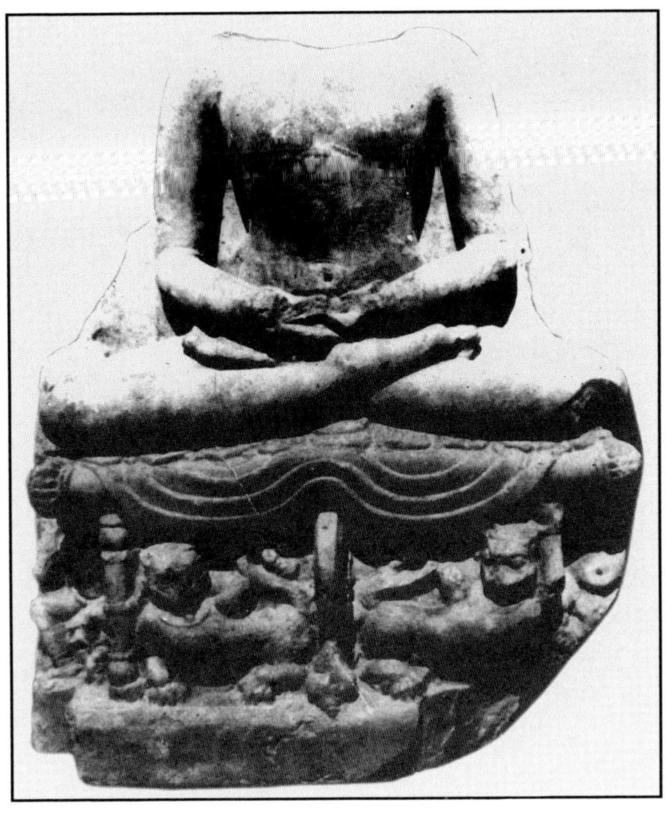

**Pl. 271.** Neminātha from Khizrabad.

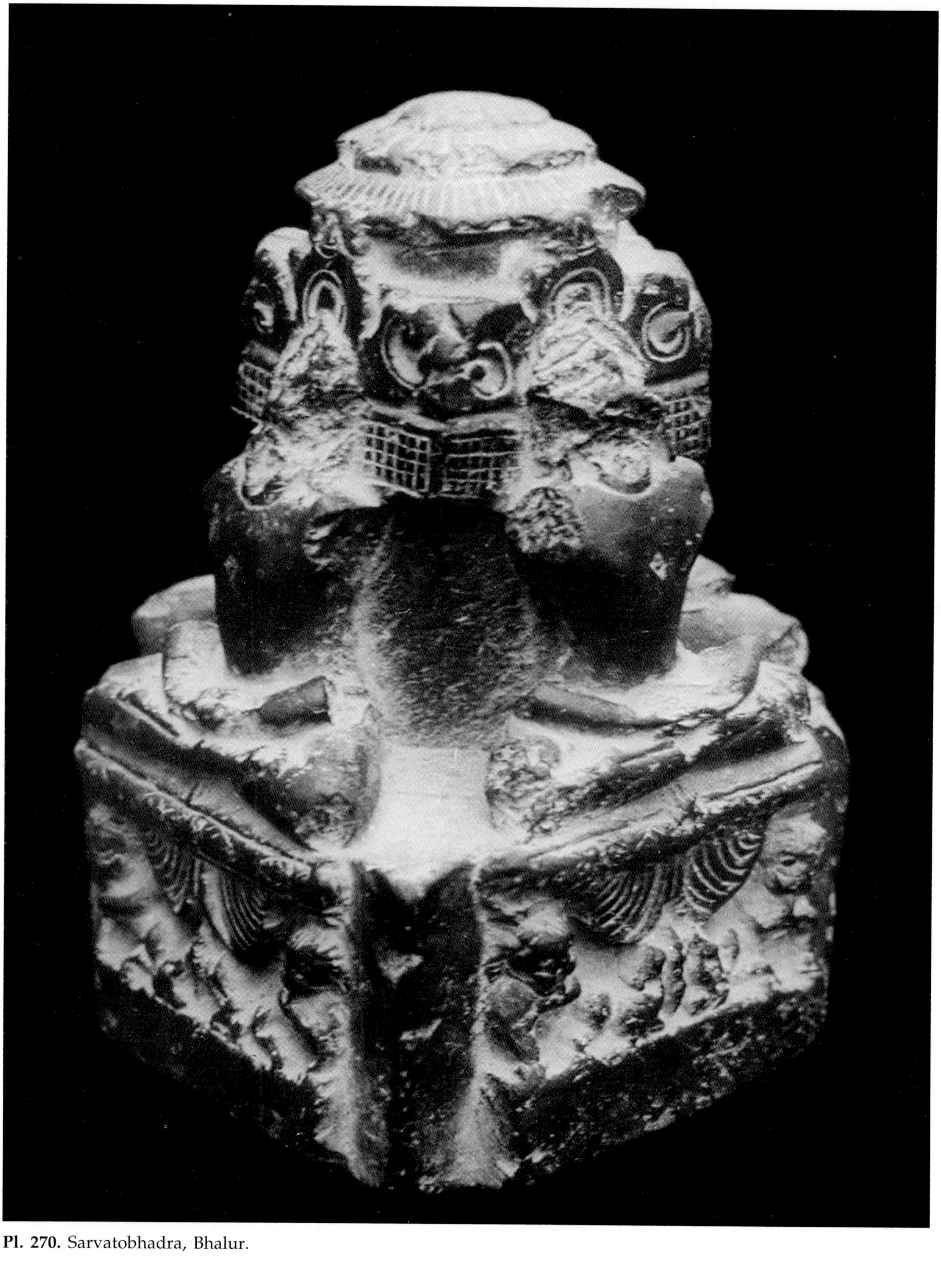

**Pl. 270.** Sarvatobhadra, Bhalur.

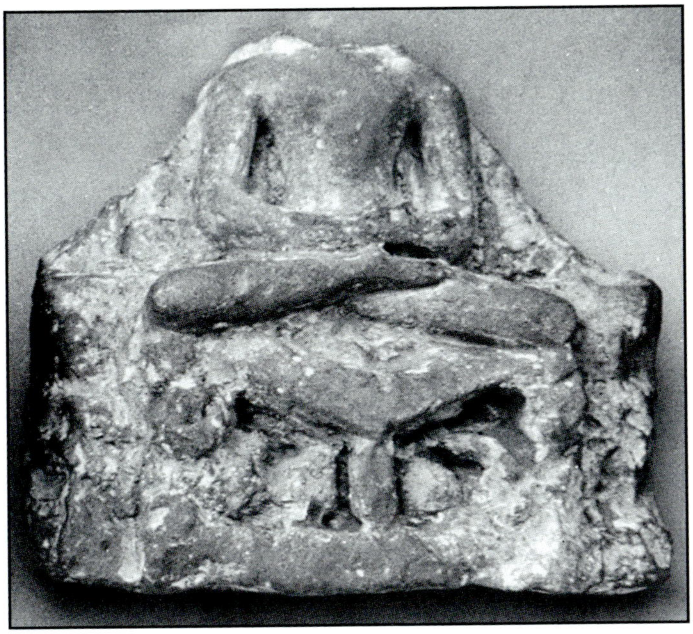

**Pl. 272.** Seated Jina, Mard Khera.

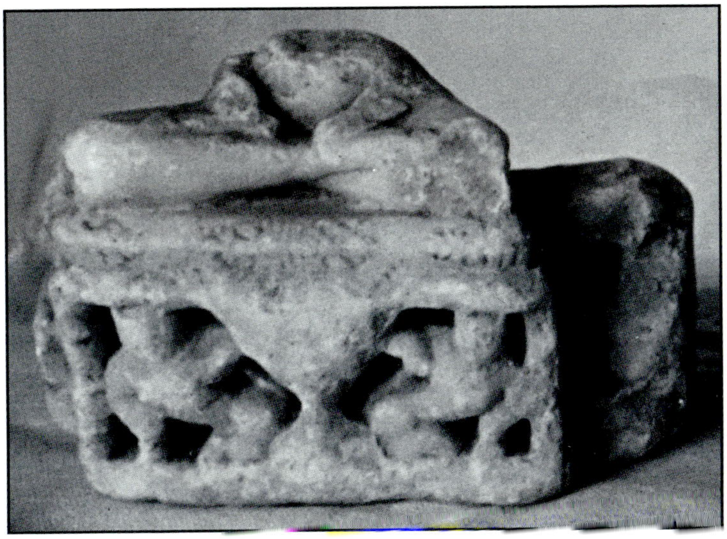

**Pl. 273.** Meditative Jina, Mard Khera.

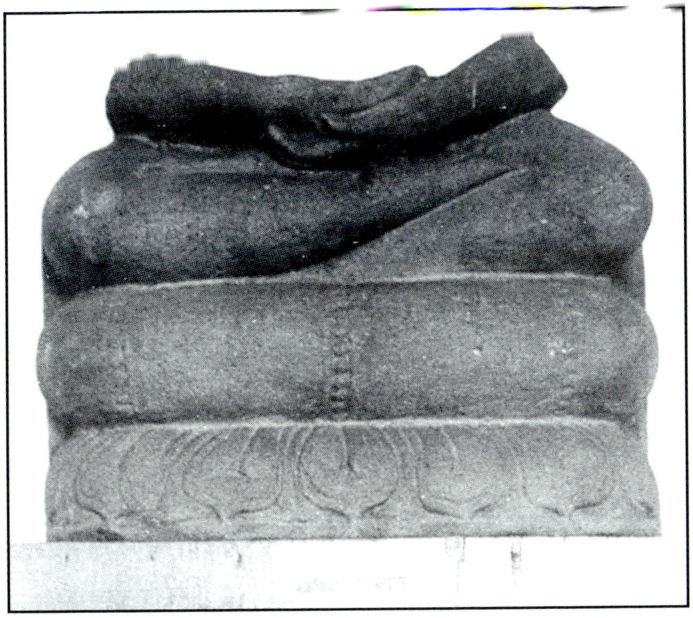

**Pl. 275.** Broken Jina figure in *padmāsana*, Dholbaha.

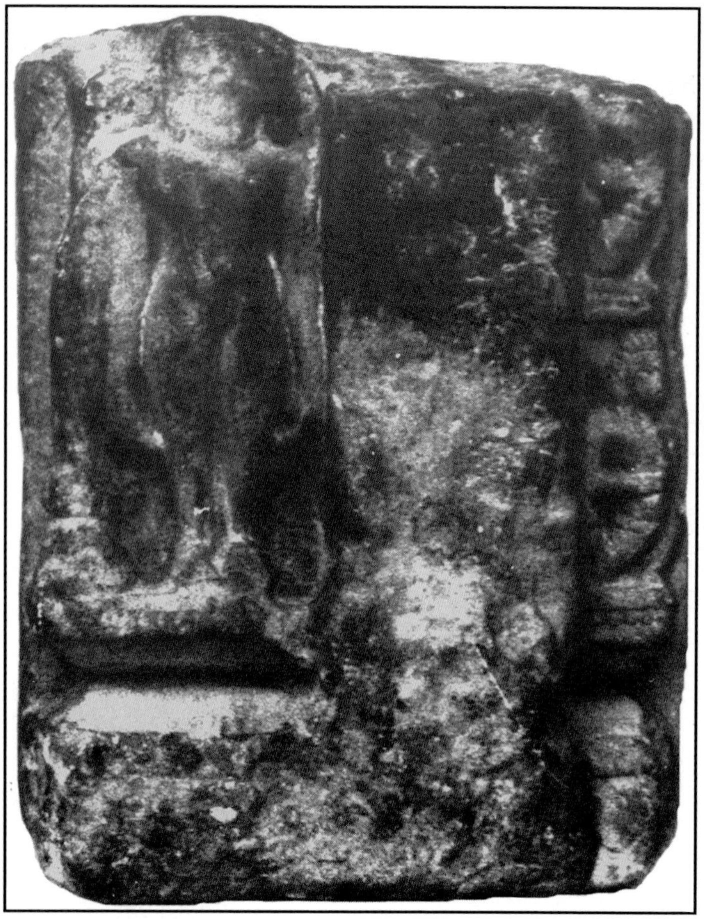

**Pl. 274.** Jina in *khaḍgāsana*, architectural piece, Mard Khera.

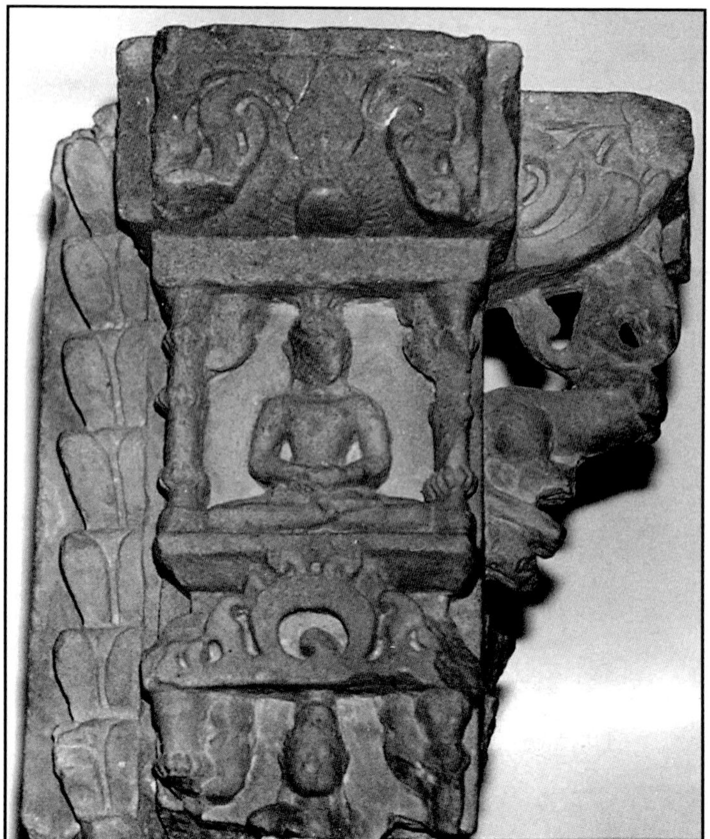

**Pl. 276.** Architectural piece showing a Jina, Dholbaha.

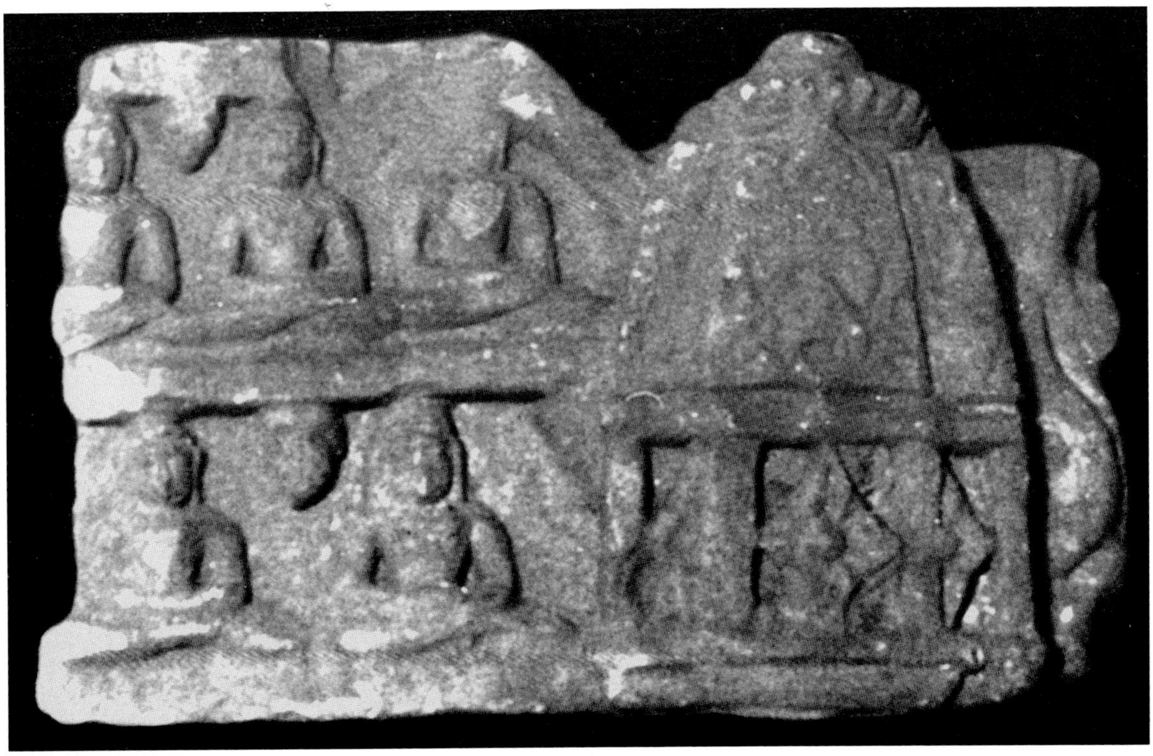

**Pl. 277.** Fragmentary piece, Dholbaha.

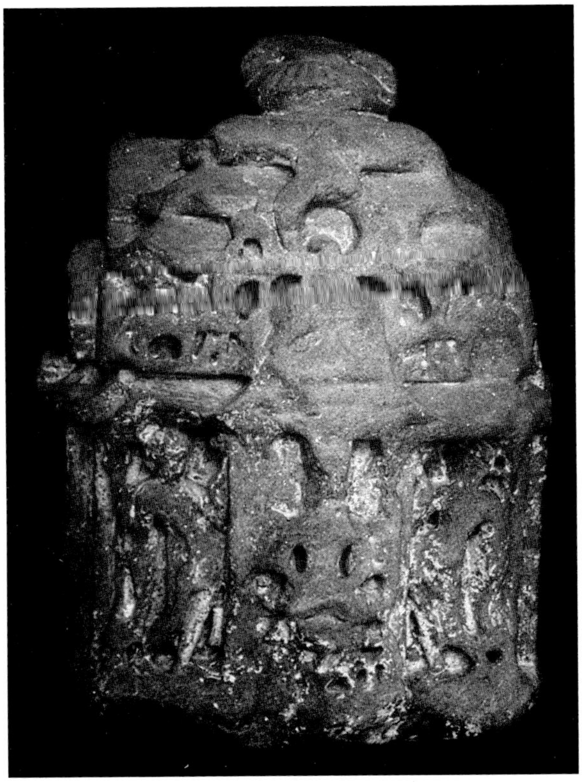

**Pl. 278.** Fragmentary *nāgara-kūṭa*, Kharar.

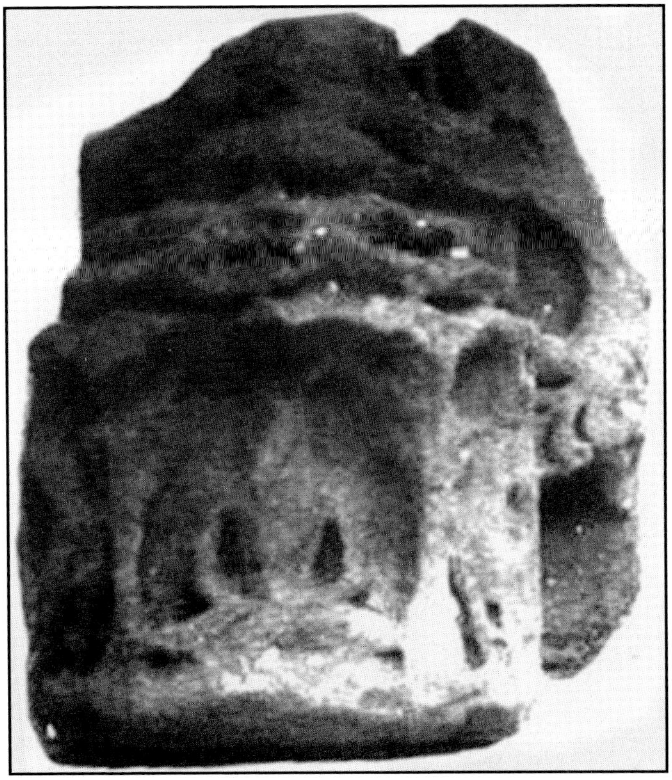

**Pl. 279.** Fragmentary *nāgara-kūṭa*, Kharar.

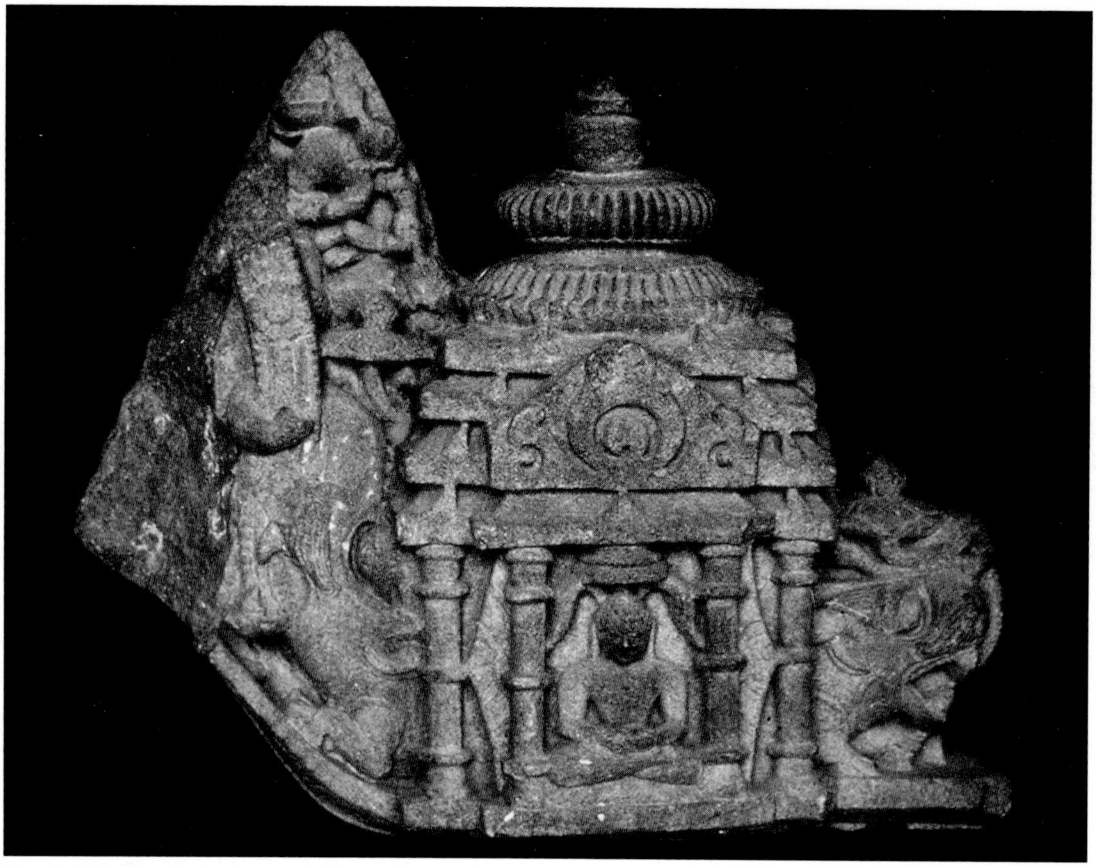

**Pl. 280.** Fragmentary *nāgara-kūṭa*, Sanghol.

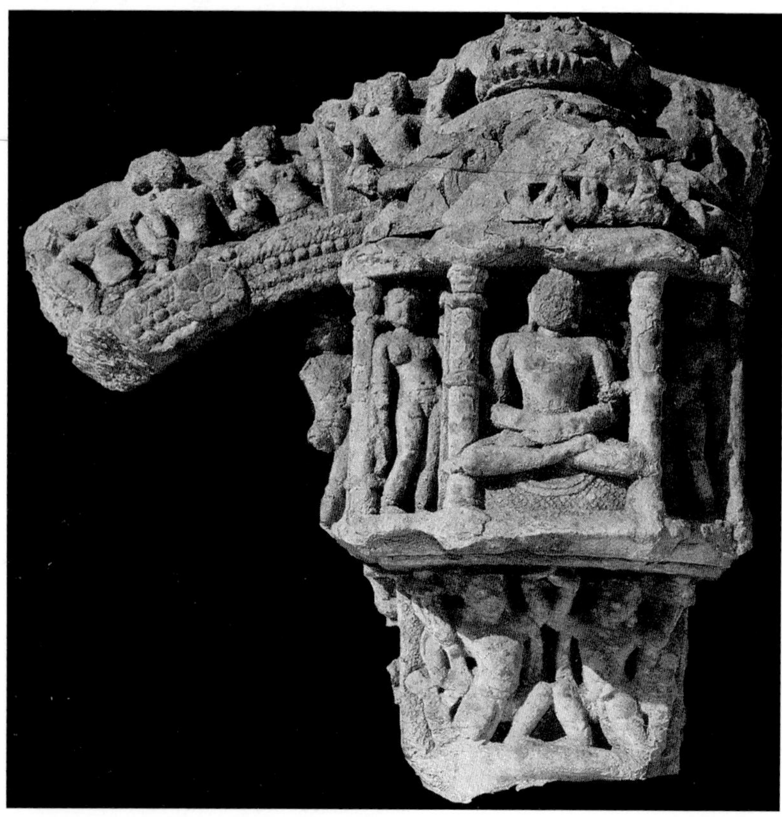

**Pl. 281.** Fragment of a Jina figure, Rupalon.

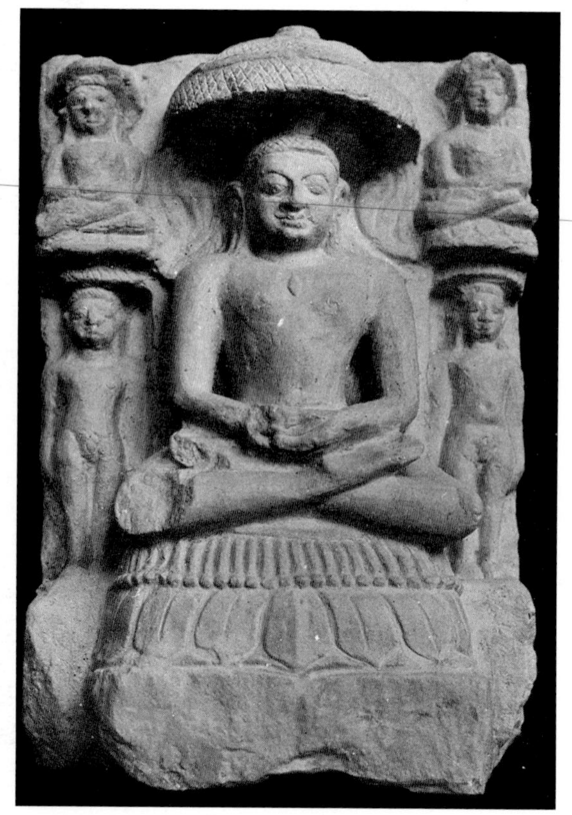

**Pl. 282.** Meditative Jina figure, Majhur.

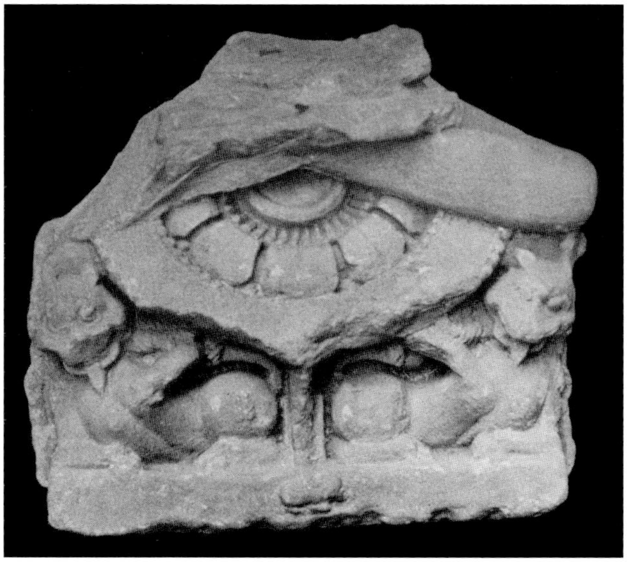

**Pl. 283.** Jaina Tīrthaṅkara Śreyāṃsanātha, Sunam.

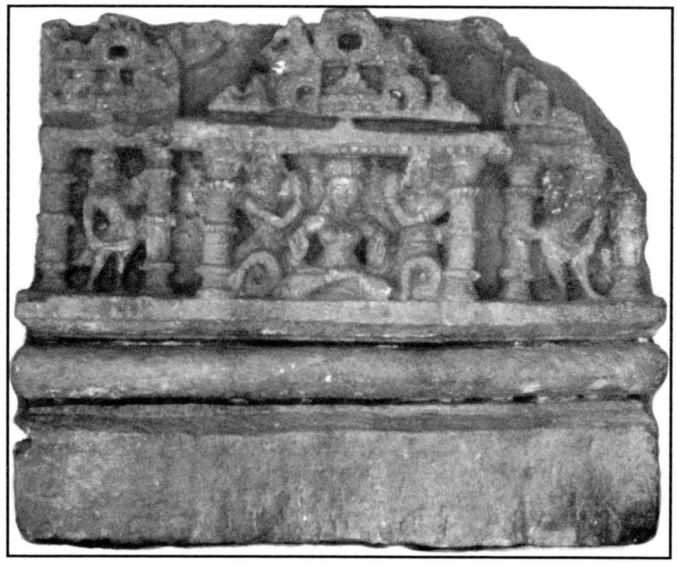

**Pl. 286.** Architectural piece of the wall of a Jaina temple, Sunam.

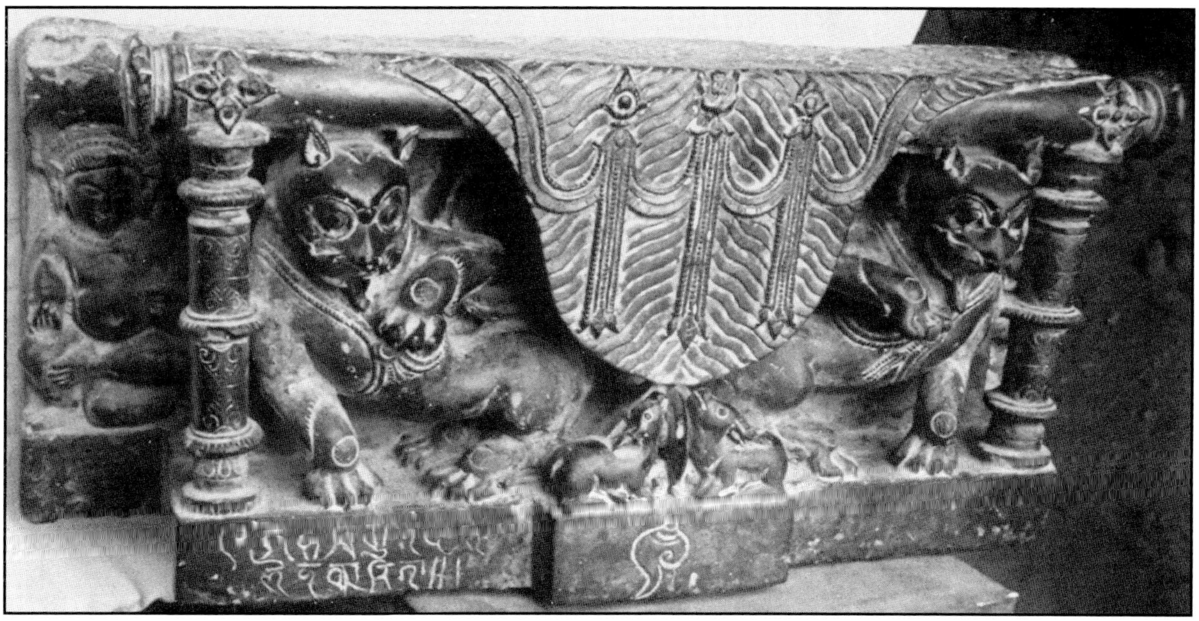

**Pl. 284.** Pedestal of an image of Neminātha, Sunam.

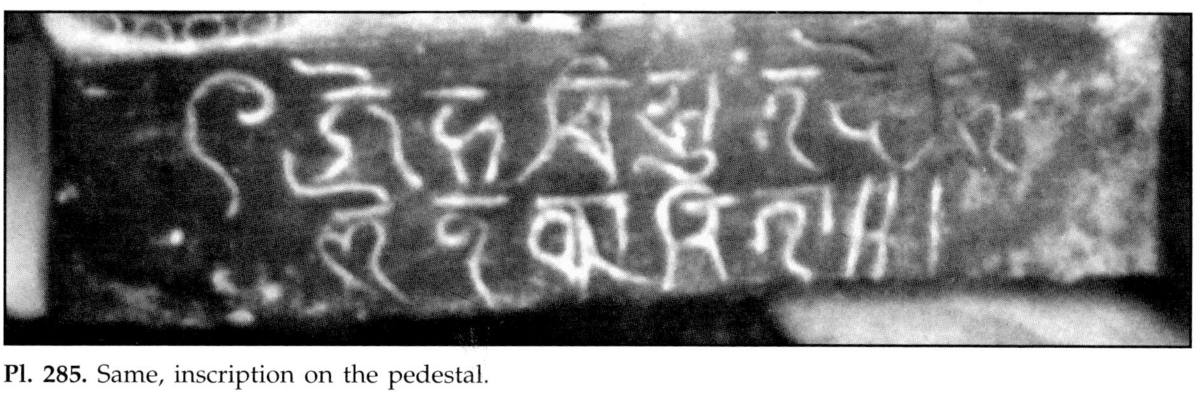

**Pl. 285.** Same, inscription on the pedestal.

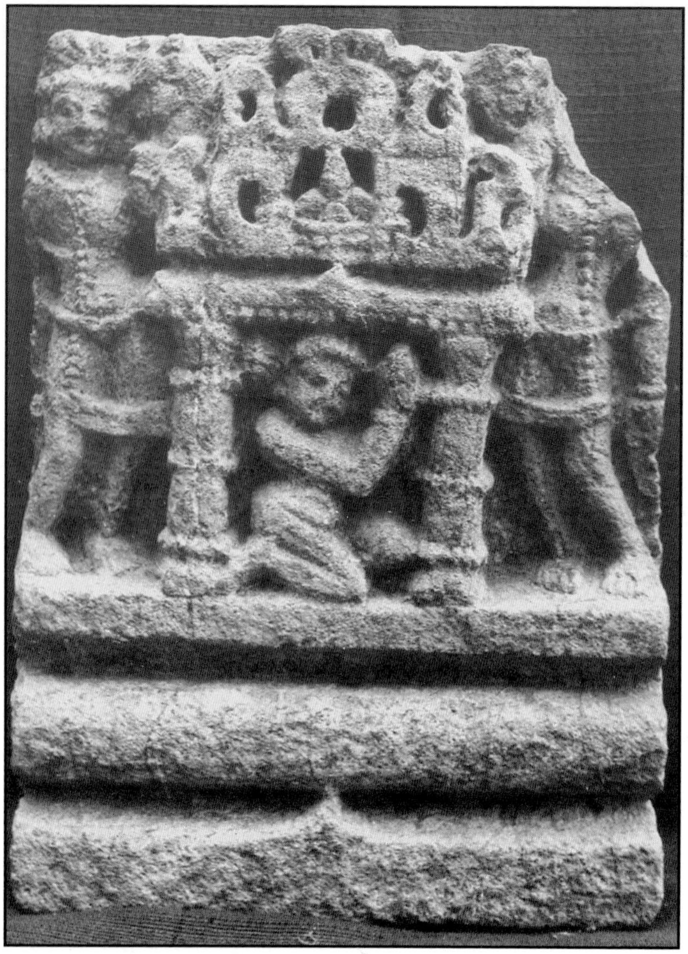

**Pl. 287.** Fragment of the socle of a Jaina temple, Sunam.

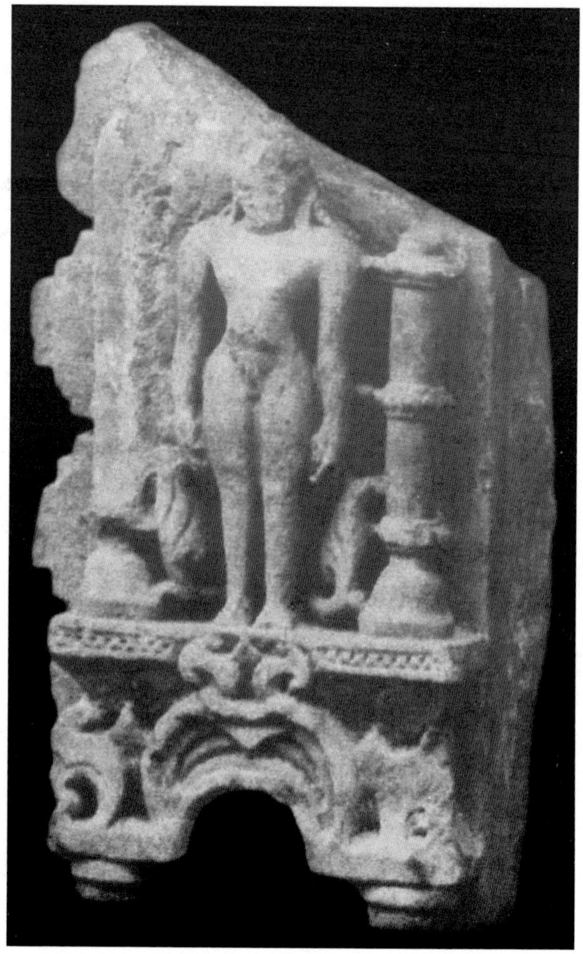

**Pl. 289.** Tīrthaṅkara standing in *khaḍgāsana*, Burail (Chandigarh).

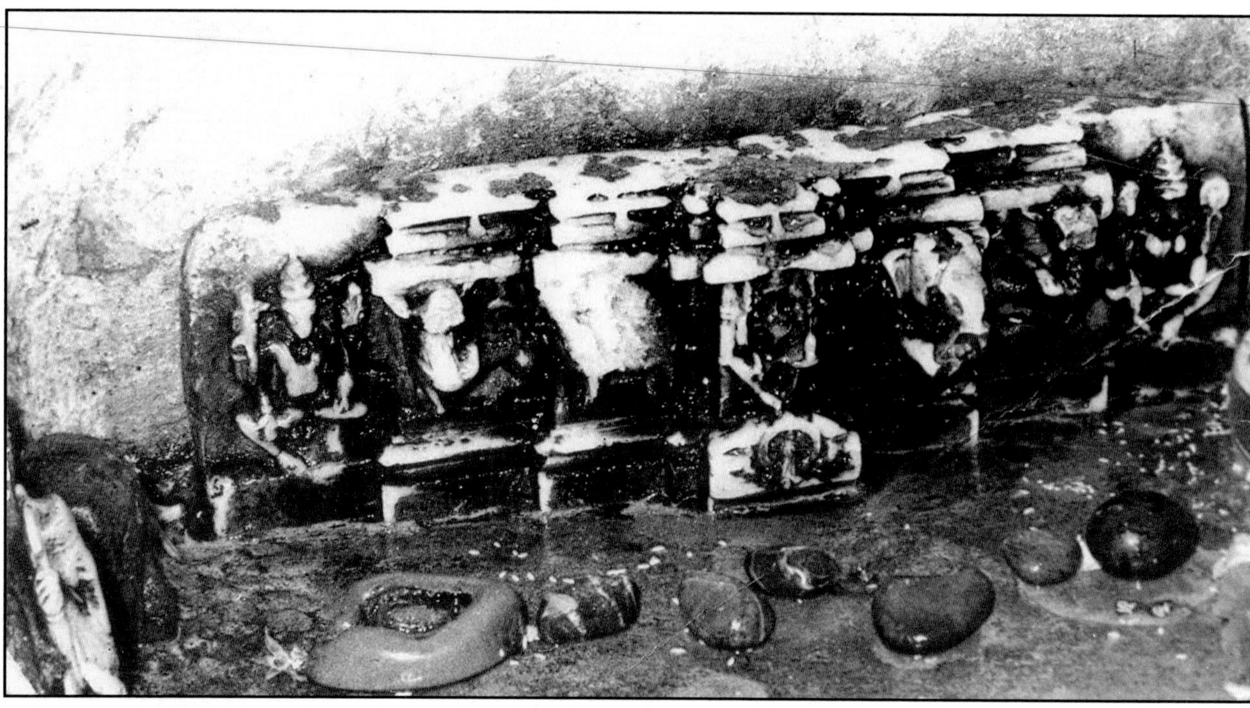

**Pl. 288.** Pedestal of an image of Ādinātha, Ropar.

**Pl. 291.** Meditative Naminātha, Bathinda.

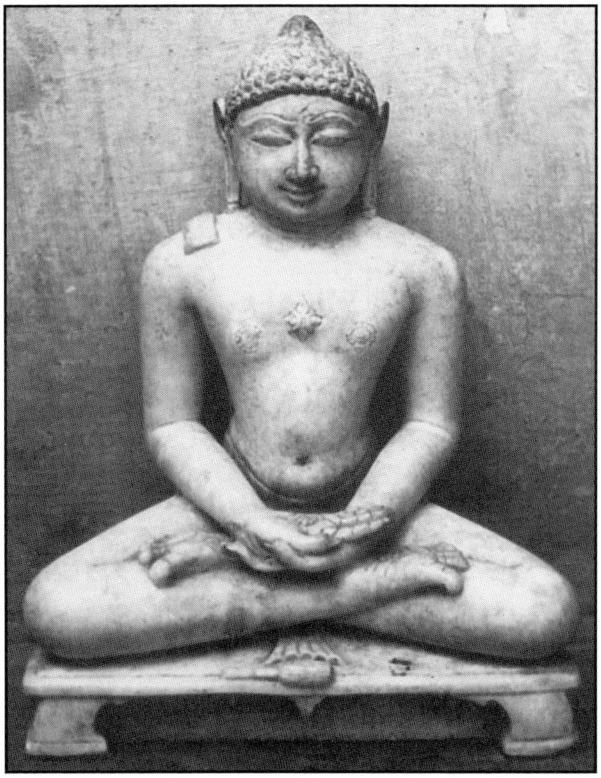

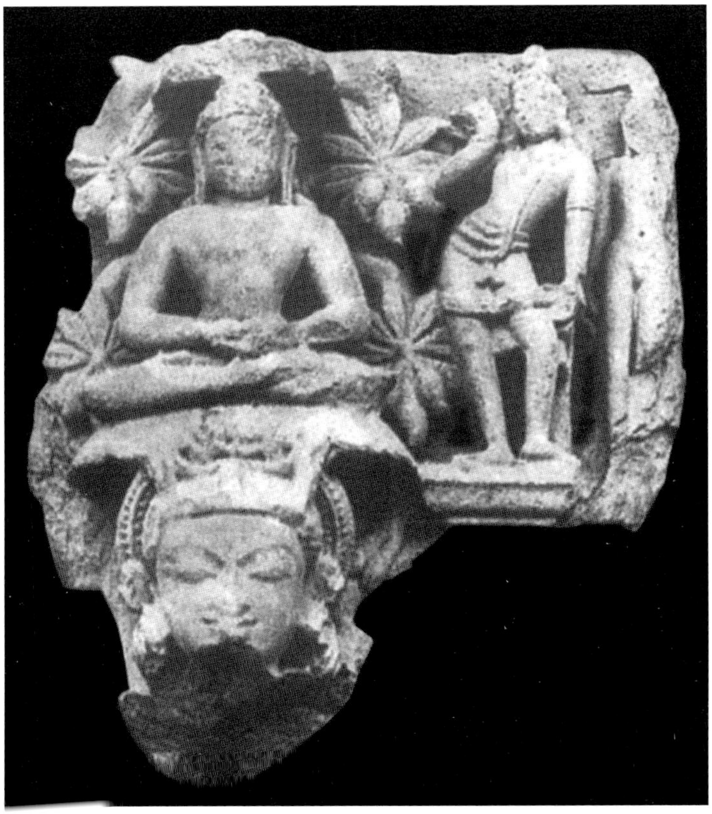

**Pl. 290.** Fragment of a Jina image, Burail (Chandigarh).

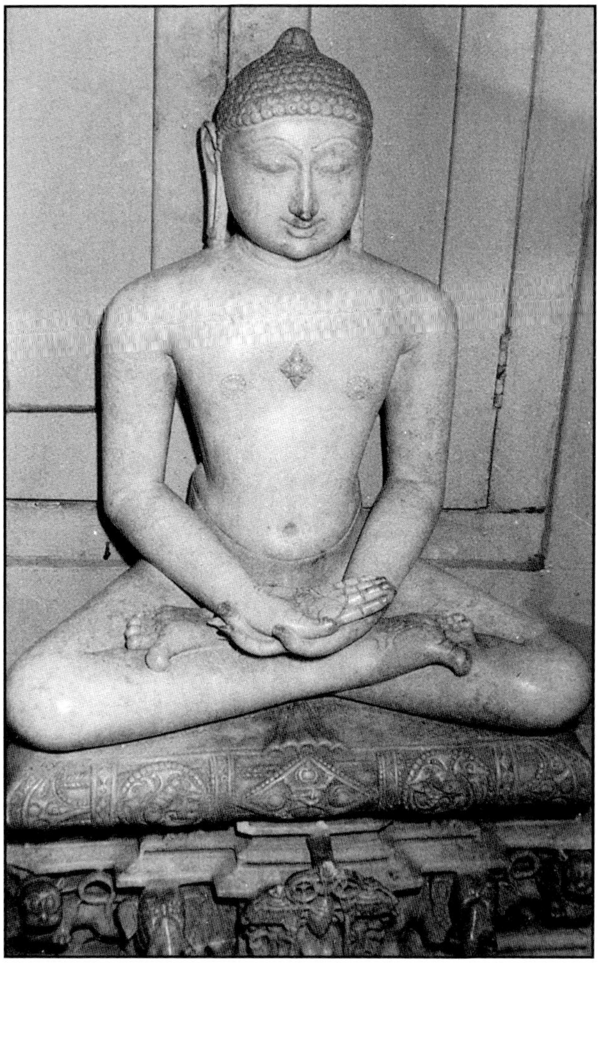

**Pl. 292.** *Padmāsana* Neminātha, Bathinda.

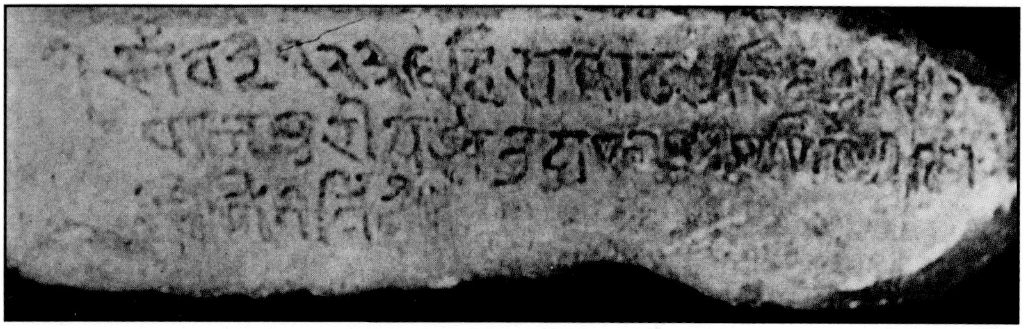

**Pl. 293.** Same, inscription on the back.

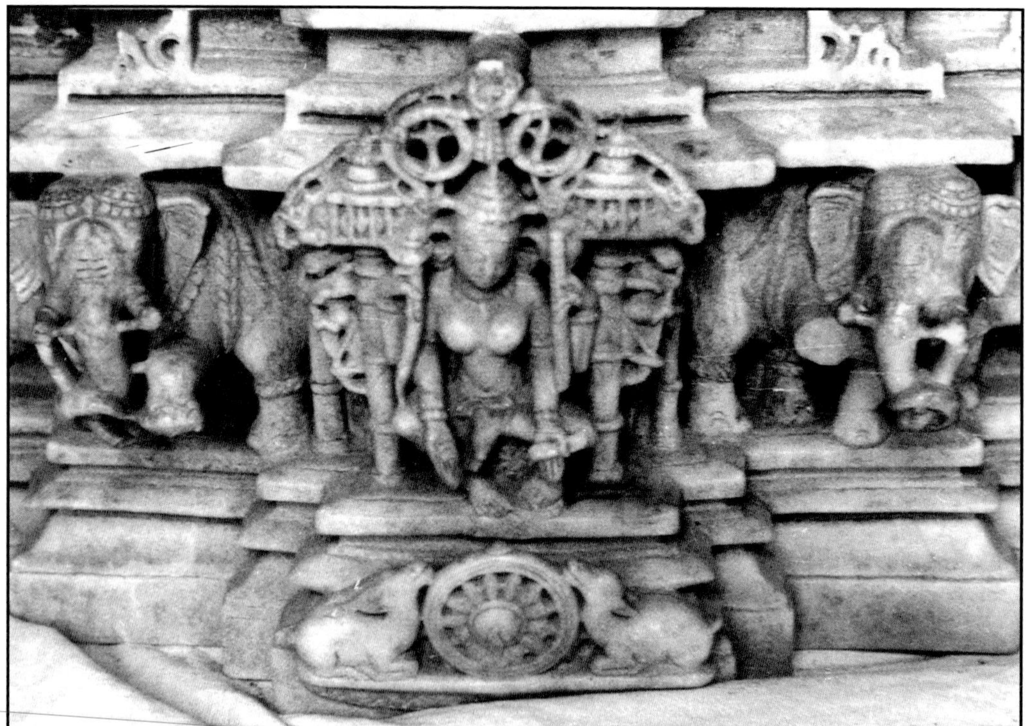

**Pl. 294.** Pedestal of the Jaina image, Bathinda.

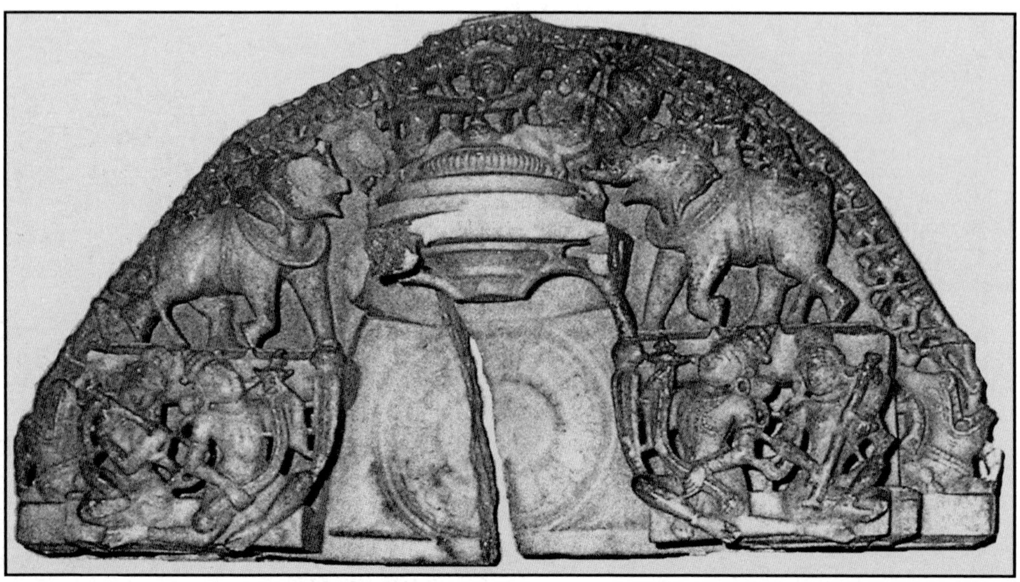

**Pl. 296.** Top part of the *parikara*, Bathinda.

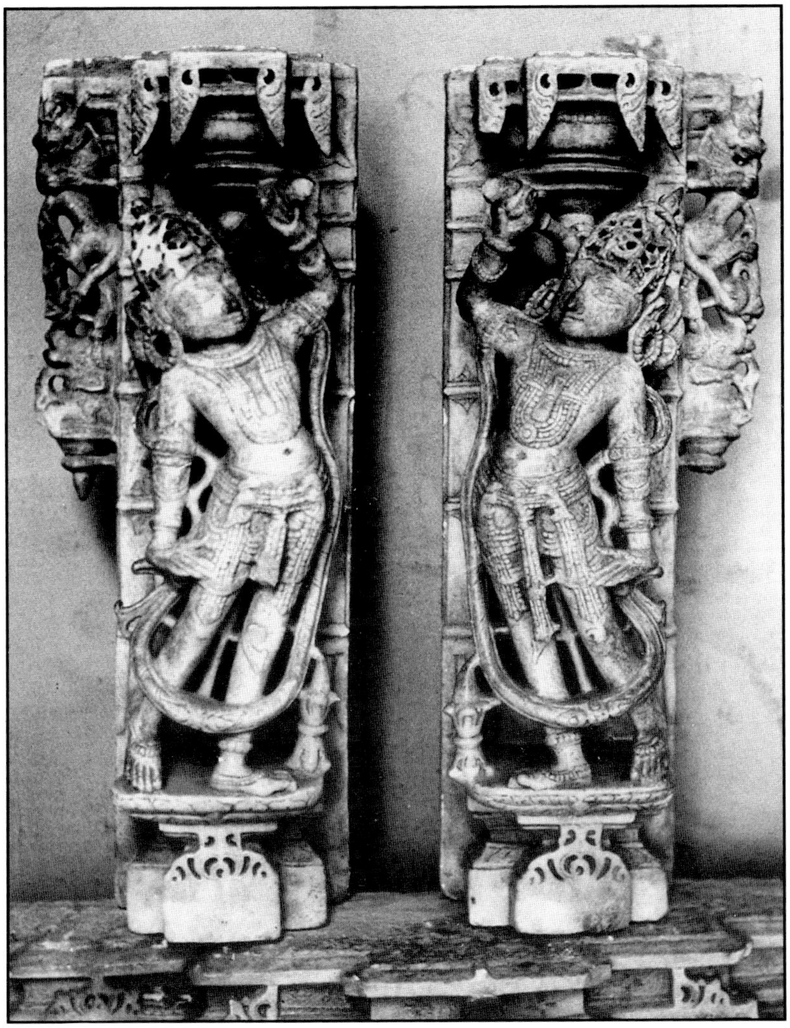

**Pl. 295.** Pillars of the *parikara*, Bathinda.

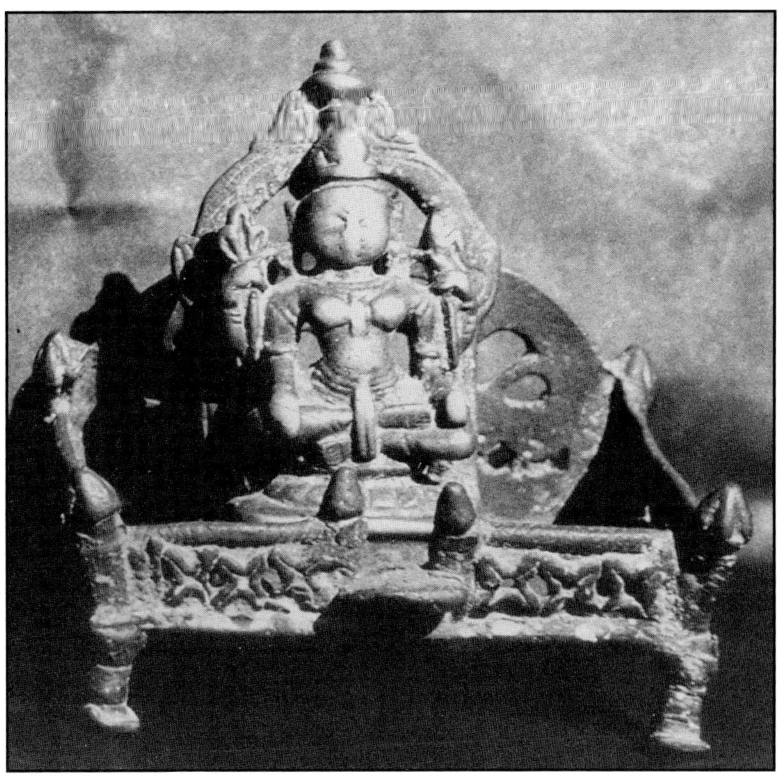

**Pl. 299.** *Yakshī* Ajitabalā, Bhudan.

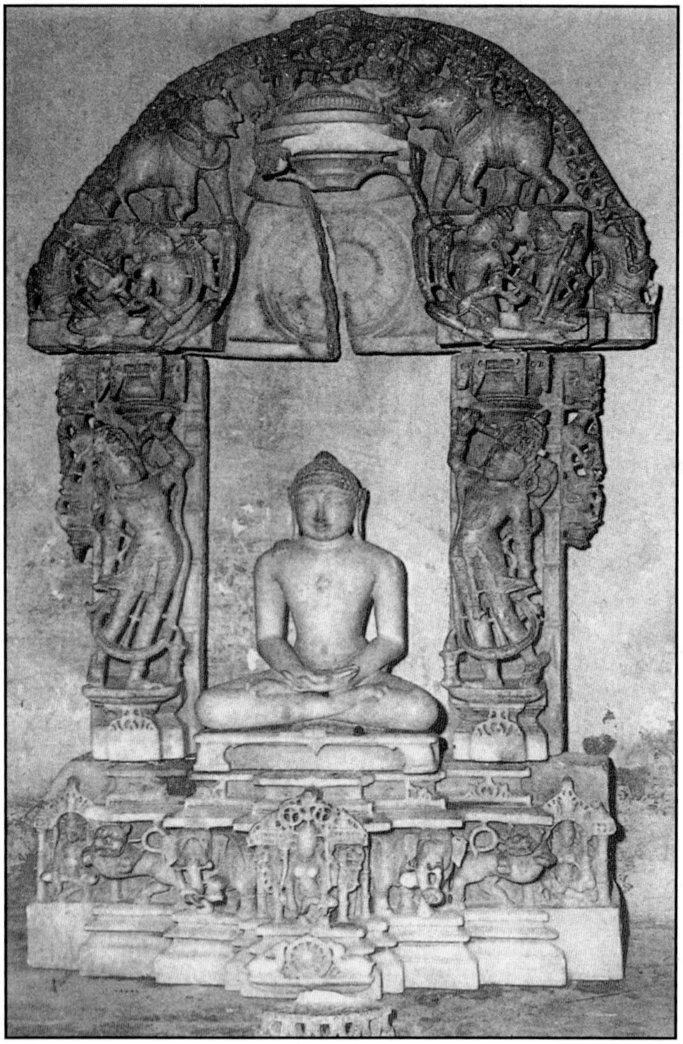

**Pl. 297.** *Parikara* around the image of Naminātha, Bathinda (after D.R. Gehlot).

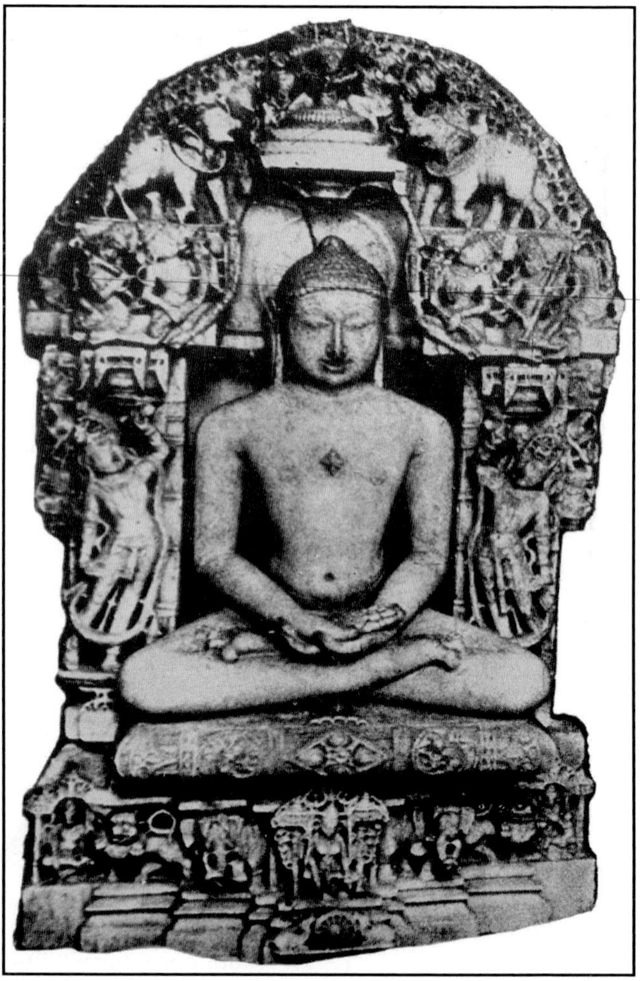

**Pl. 298.** *Parikara* around the image of Neminātha, Bathinda.

**Pl. 301.** *Pañcha-tīrthikā* of Pārśvanātha, Ropar.

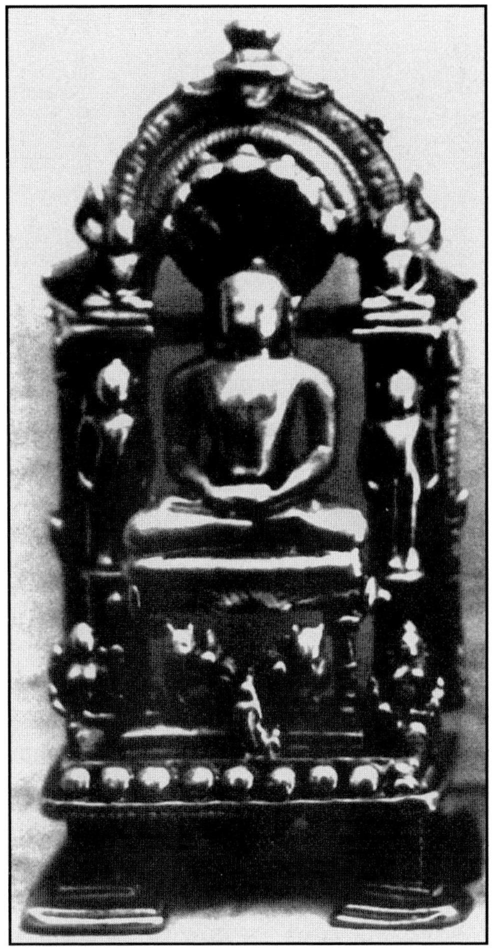

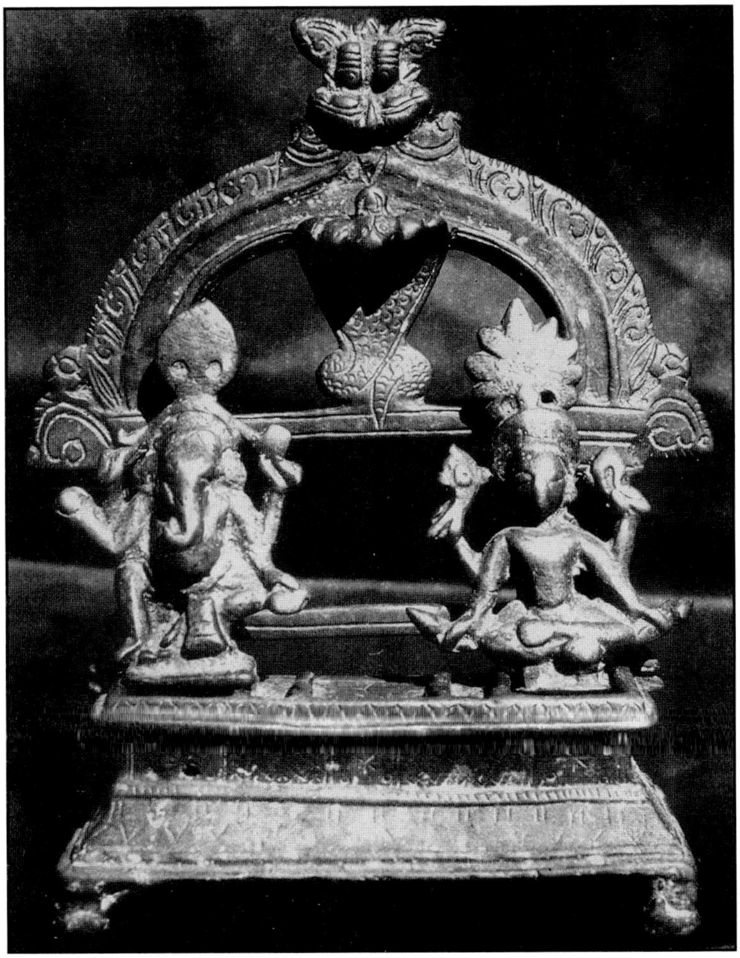

**Pl. 300.** Acolyte figures, Bhudan.

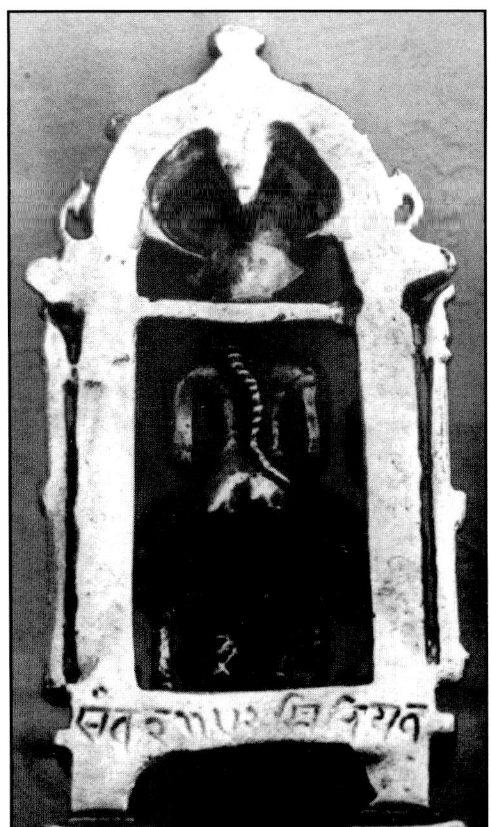

**Pl. 302.** Same, inscription at the back.

**Pl. 304.** *Padmāsana* Pārśvanātha, Ropar.

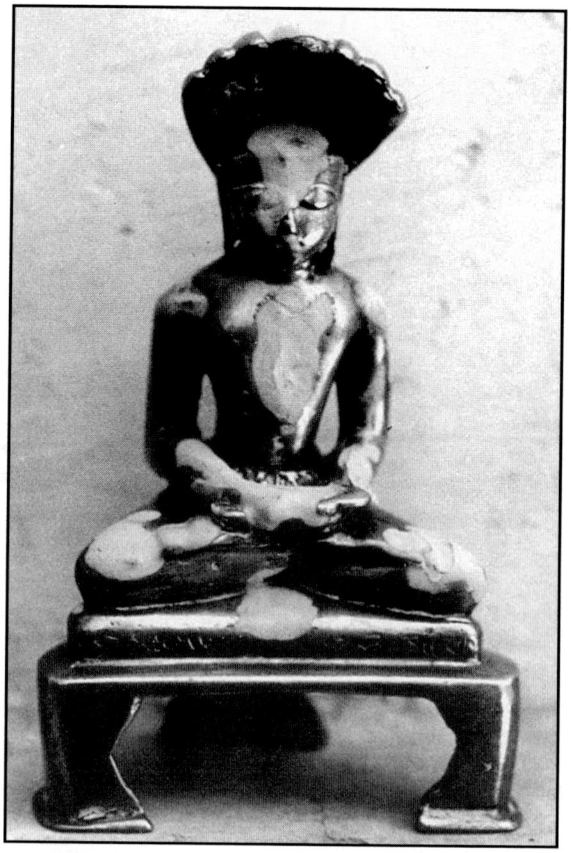

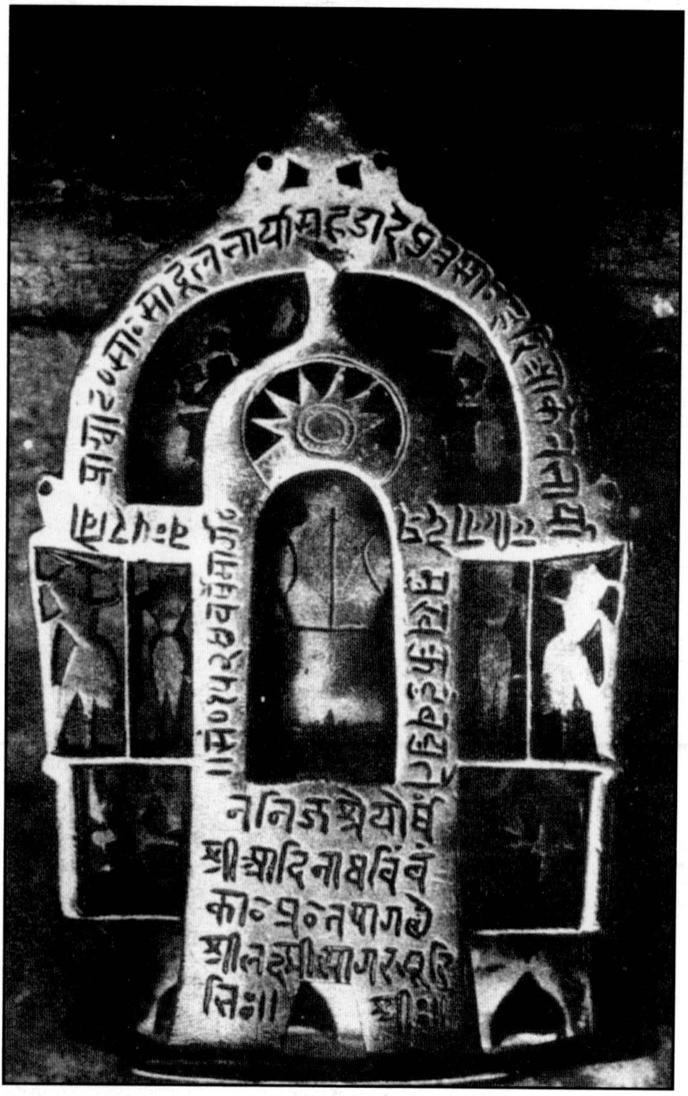

**Pl. 303.** Inscription on the back of a *Pañcha-tīrthikā* of Ādinātha, Ropar.

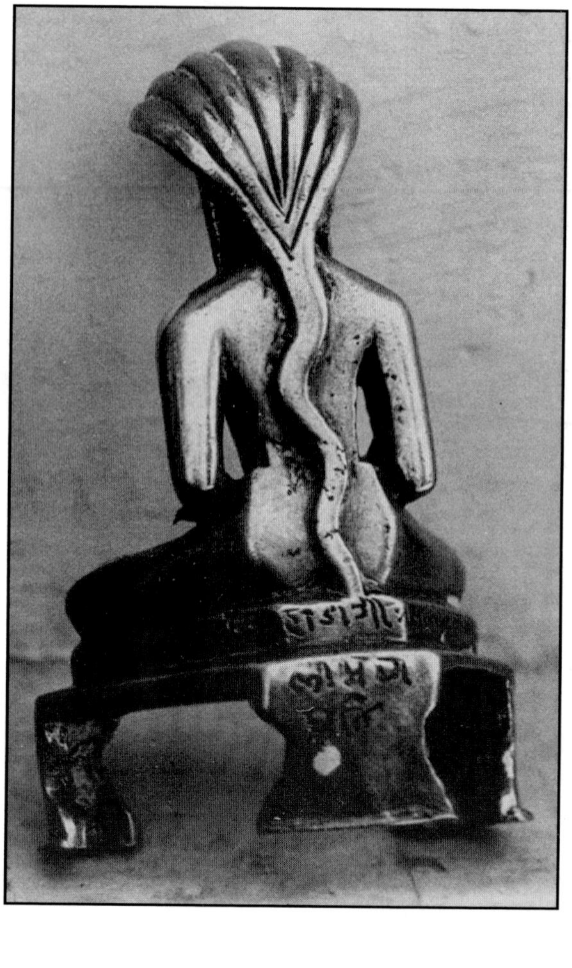

**Pl. 305.** Same, back view.

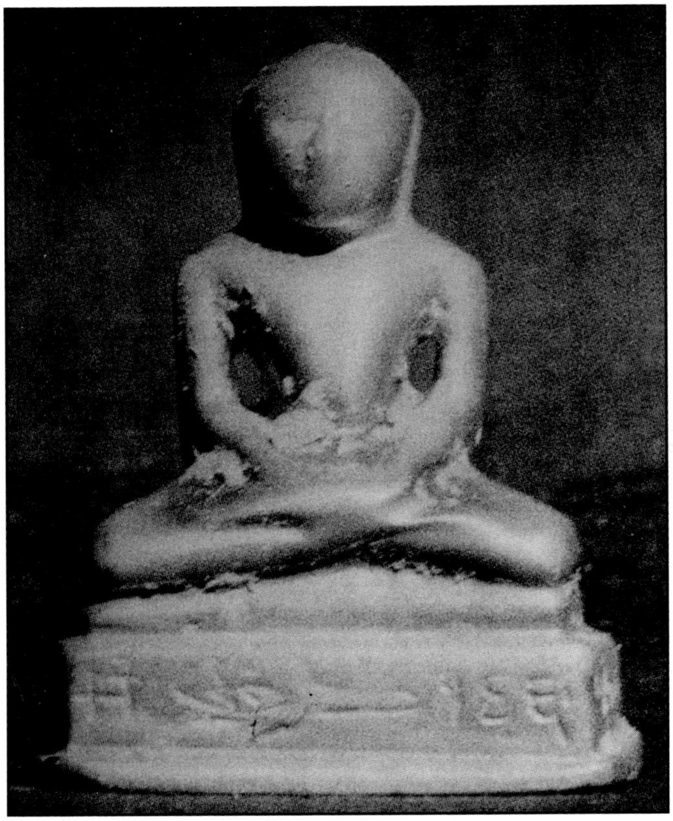

**Pl. 306.** Padmaprabha or Naminātha, Ropar.

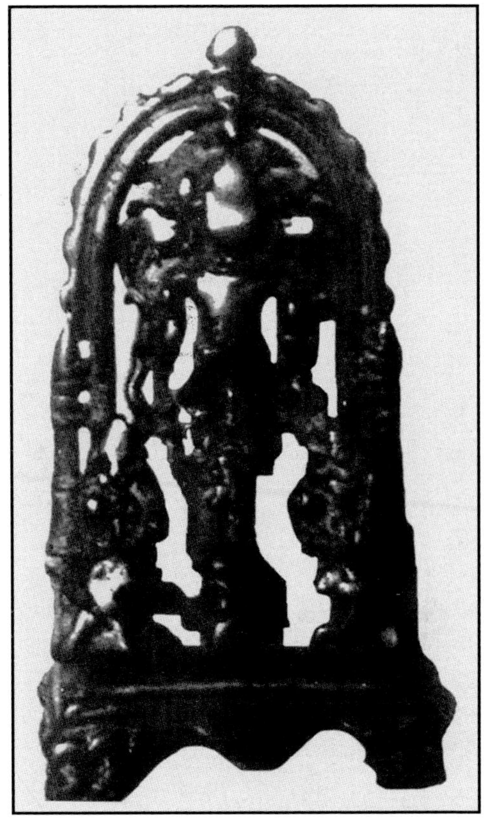

**Pl. 307.** Pārśvanātha in *khaḍgāsana*, Sunam.

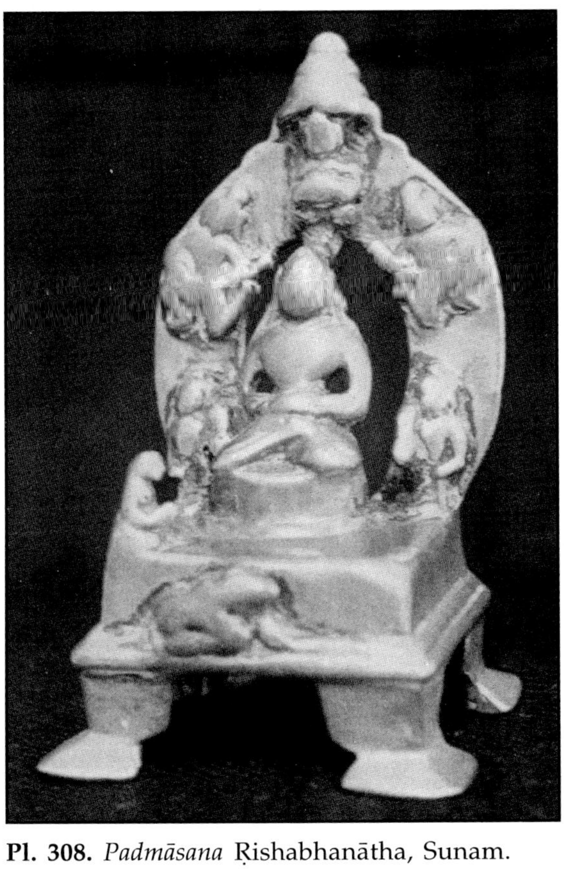

**Pl. 308.** *Padmāsana* Ṛishabhanātha, Sunam.

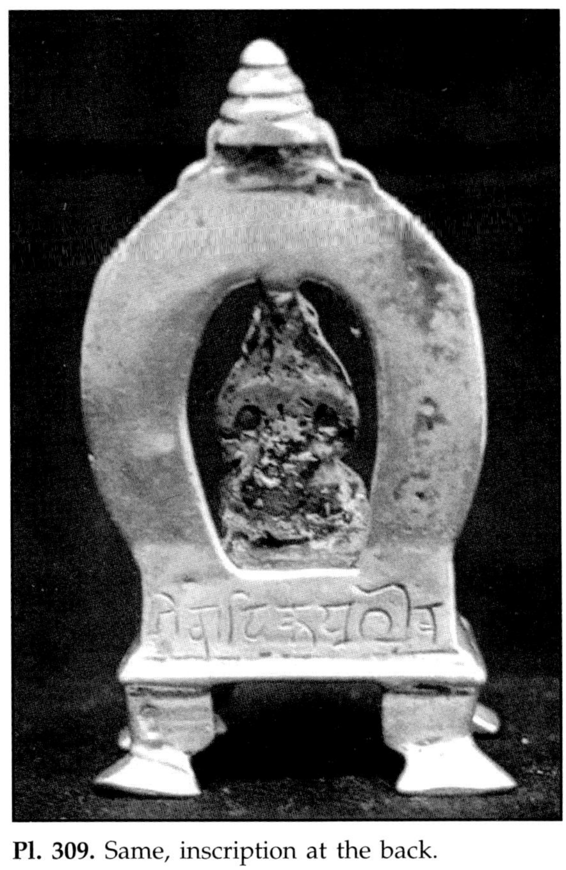

**Pl. 309.** Same, inscription at the back.

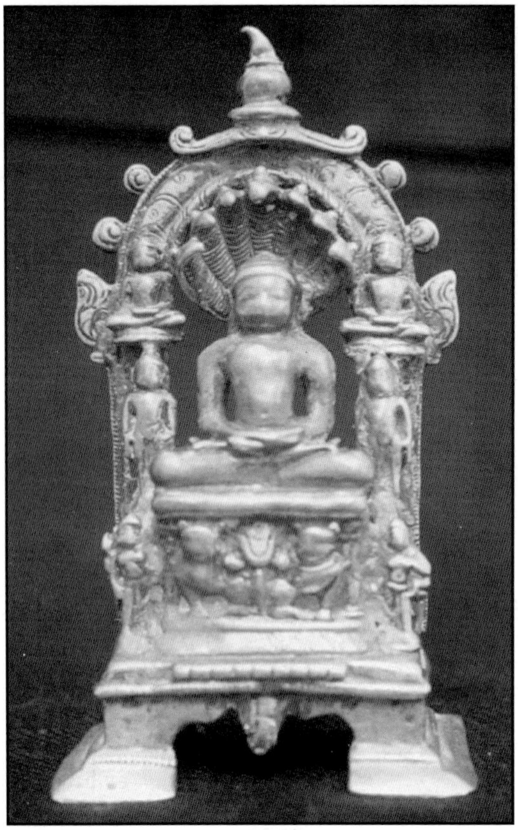

**Pl. 310.** *Pañcha-tīrthikā* of Pārśvanātha, Sunam.

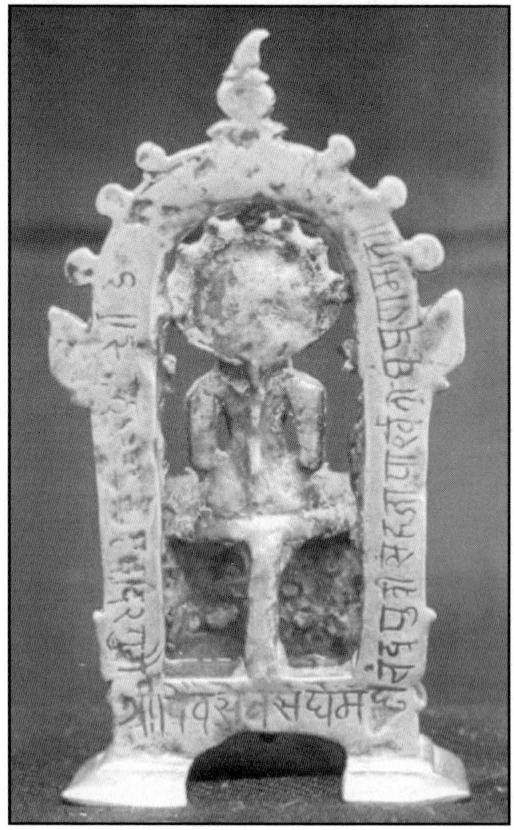

**Pl. 311.** Same, inscription on the back.

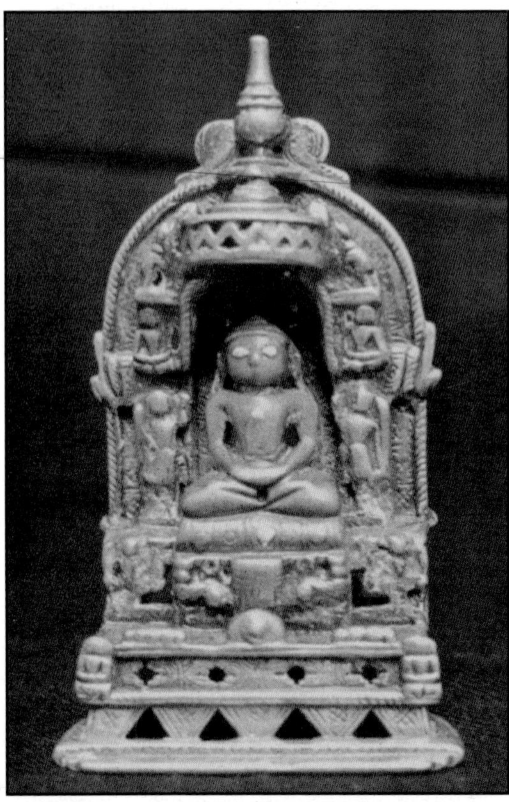

**Pl. 312.** Jaina Tīrthaṅkara Kunthunātha, Sunam.

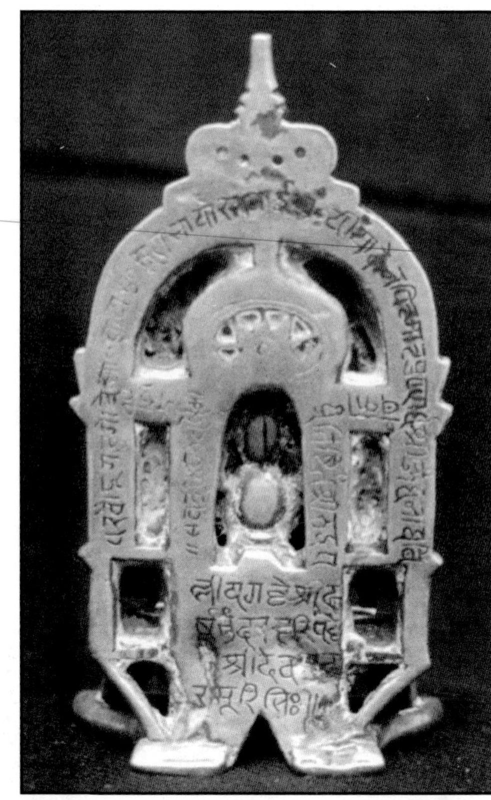

**Pl. 313.** Same, inscription at the back.

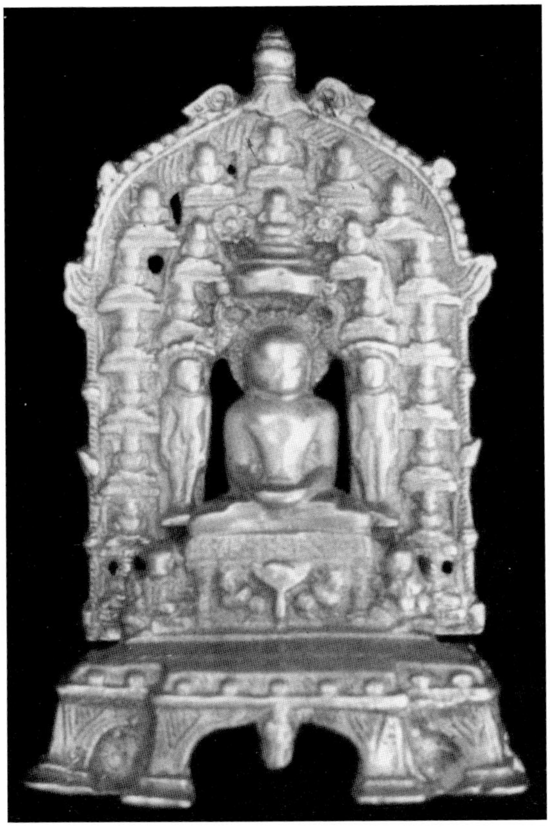

**Pl. 314.** *Chaturviṃśati-paṭṭa* of Ṛishabhanātha, Sunam.

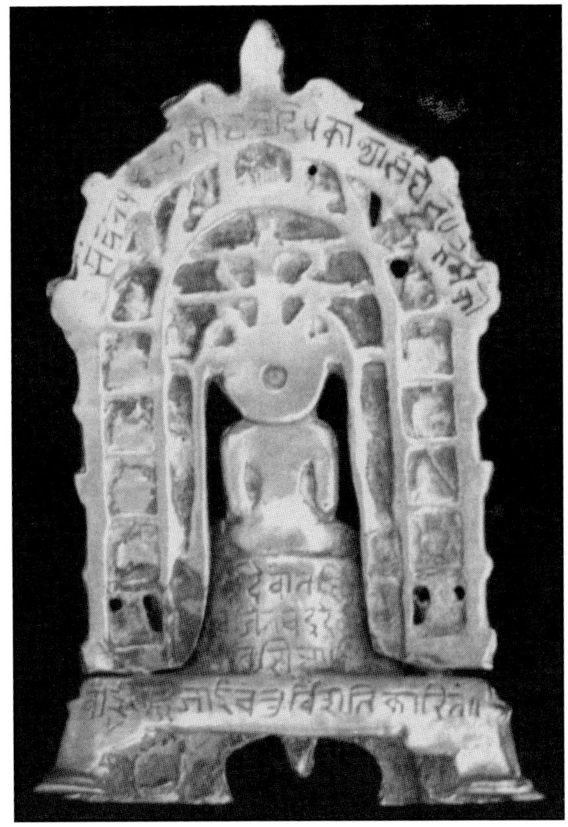

**Pl. 315.** Same, back view with inscription.

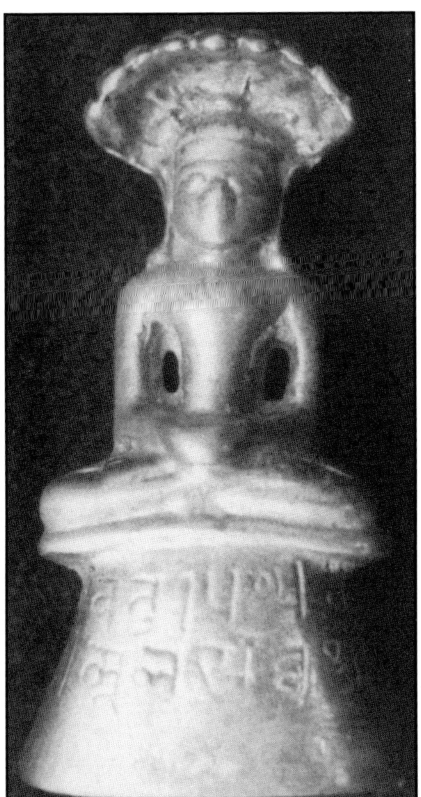

**Pl. 316.** Jina sheltered by nine-hooded snake, Sunam.

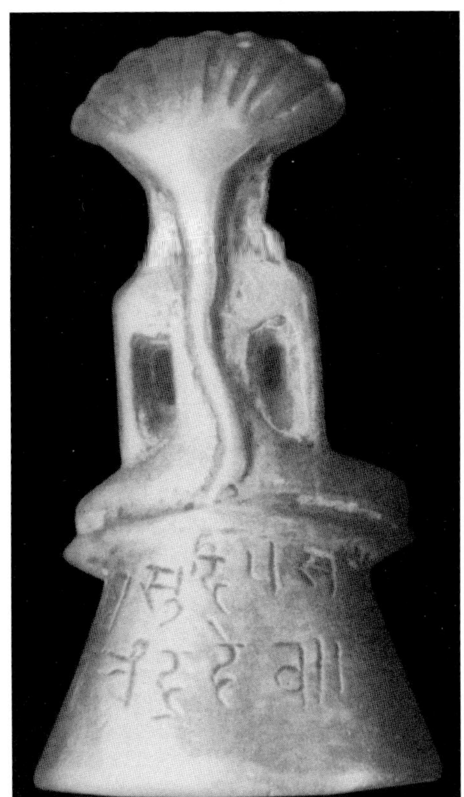

**Pl. 317.** Same, back view.

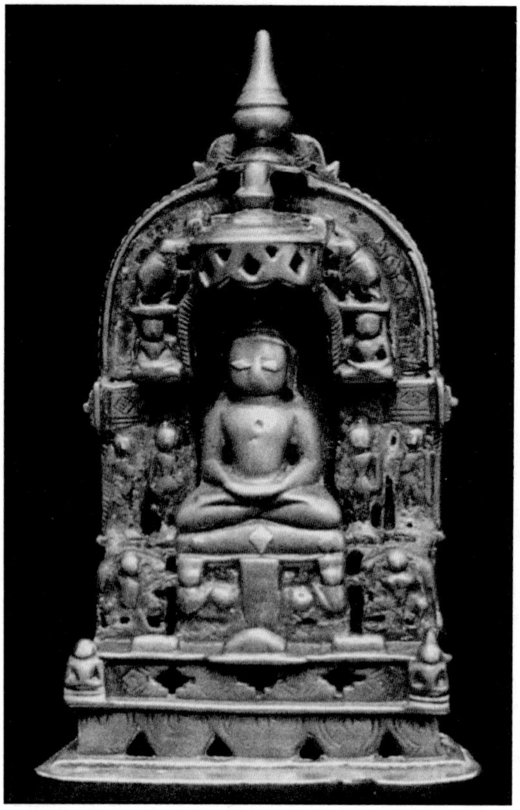

**Pl. 318.** *Pañcha-tīrthikā* of Ajitanātha, Sunam.

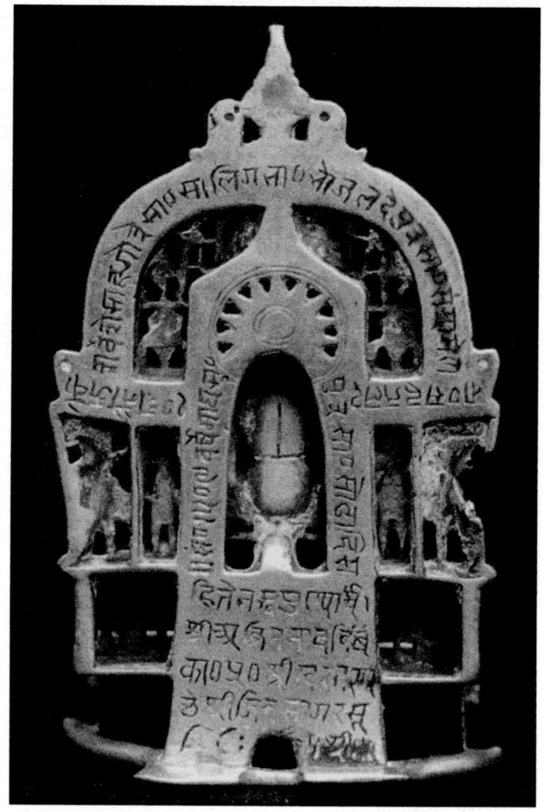

**Pl. 319.** Same, inscription at the back.

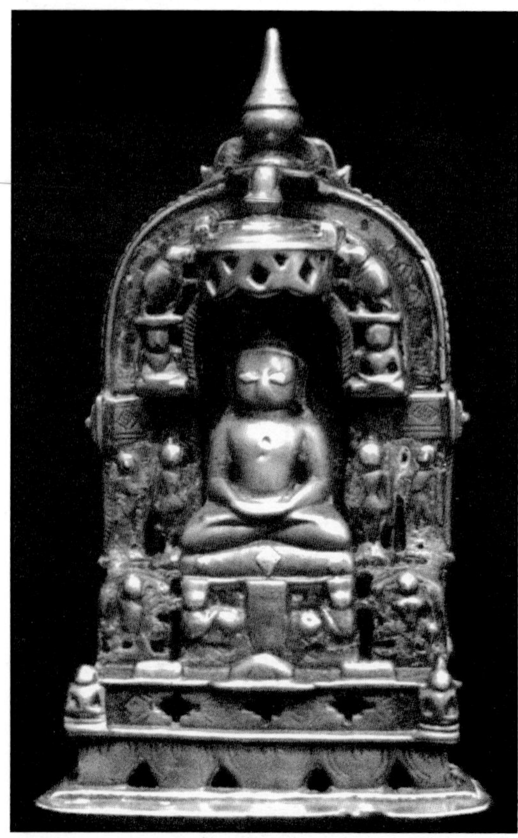

**Pl. 320.** *Pañcha-tīrthikā* of Śāntinātha, Sunam.

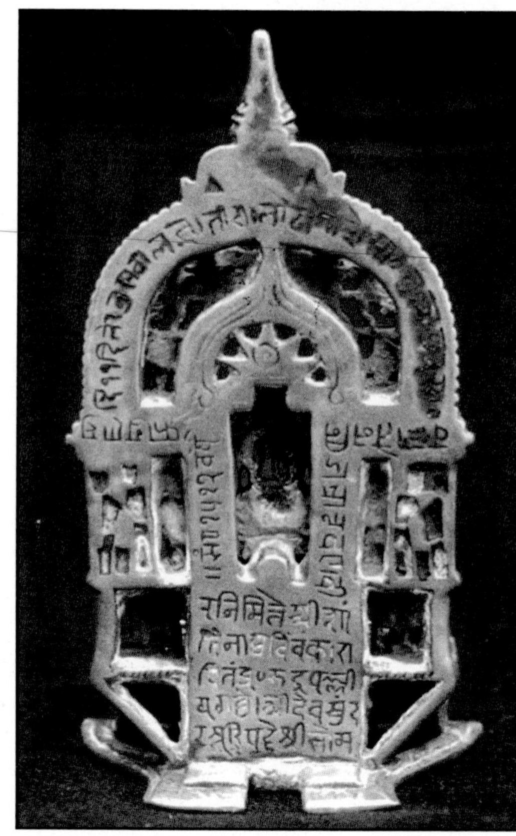

**Pl. 321.** Same, inscription at the back.

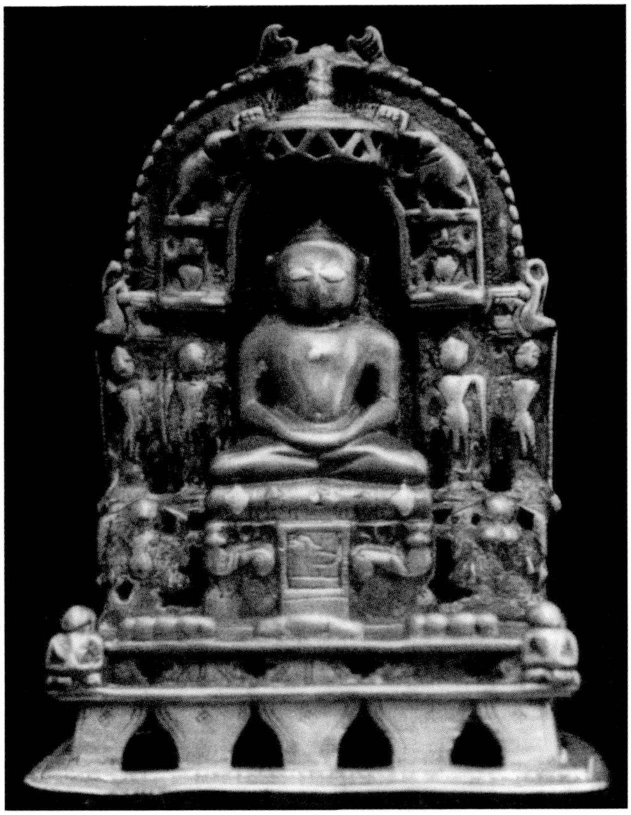

**Pl. 322.** *Pañcha-tīrthikā* of Anantanātha, Sunam.

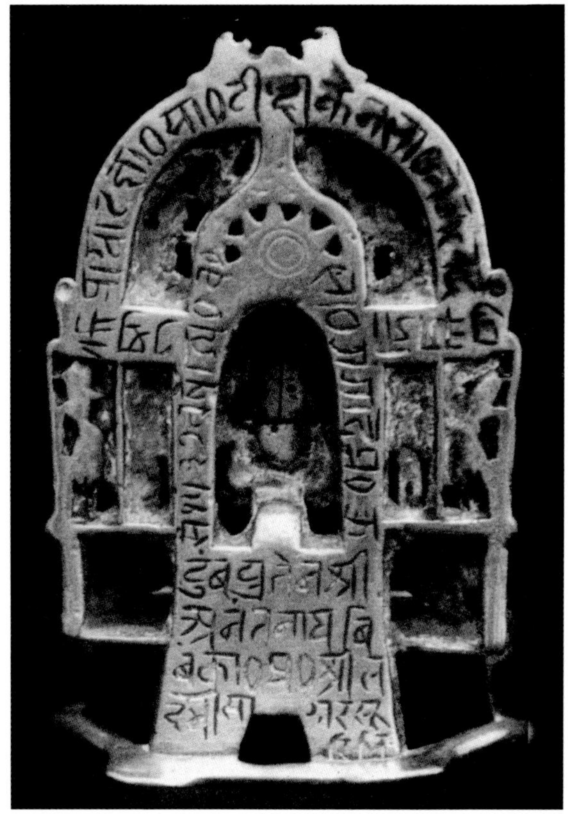

**Pl. 323.** Same, inscription at the back.

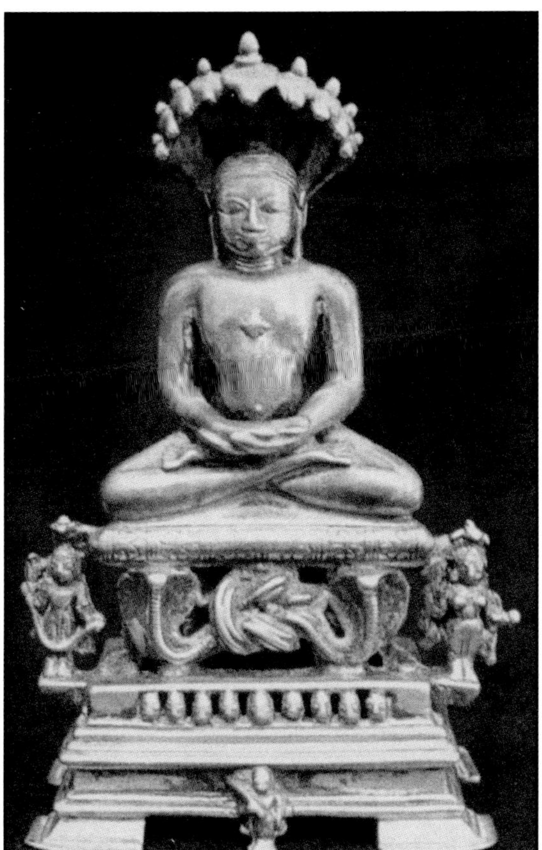

**Pl. 324.** Meditative Pārśvanātha, Sunam.

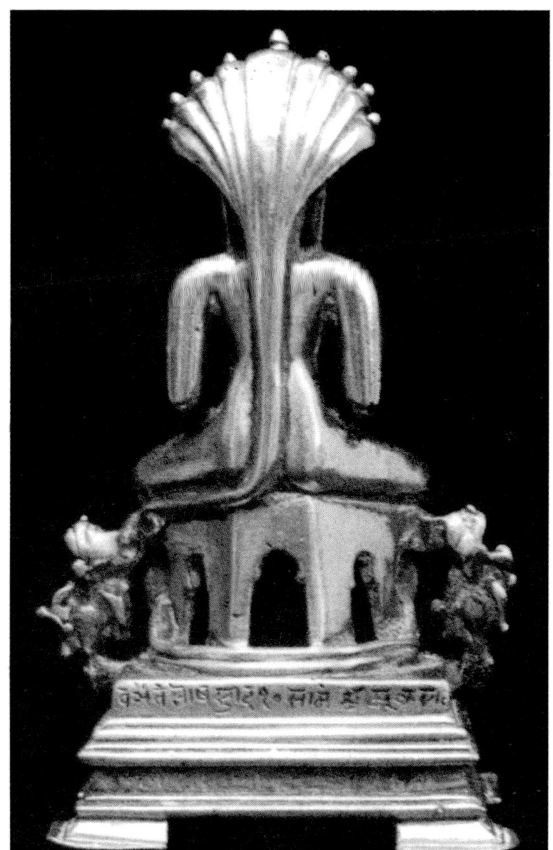

**Pl. 325.** Same, back view.

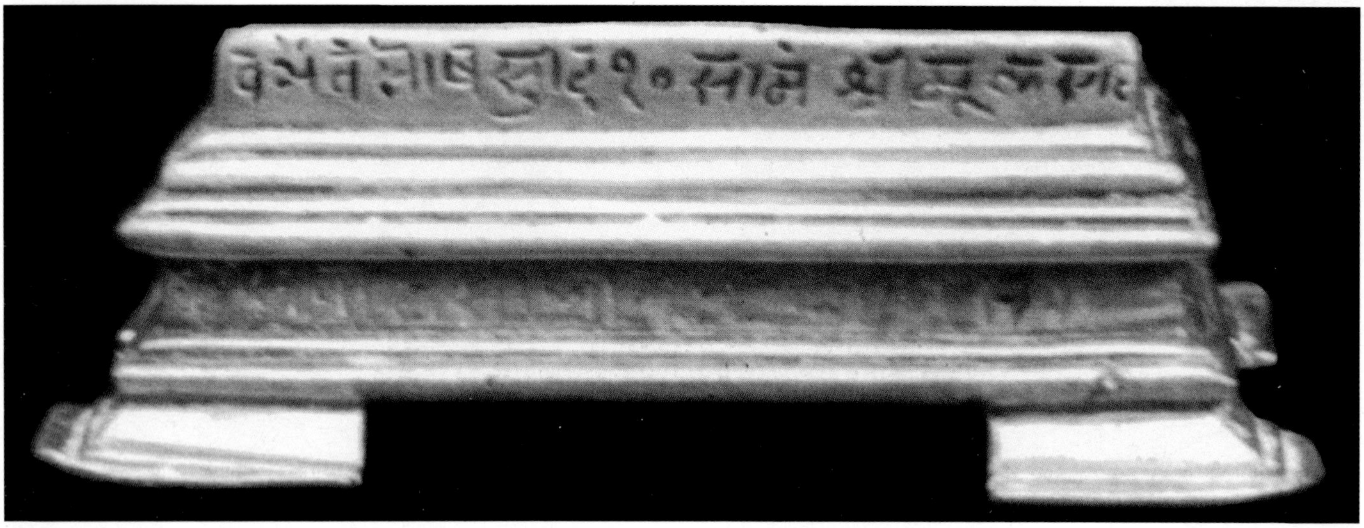

**Pl. 326.** Same, inscription on the back.

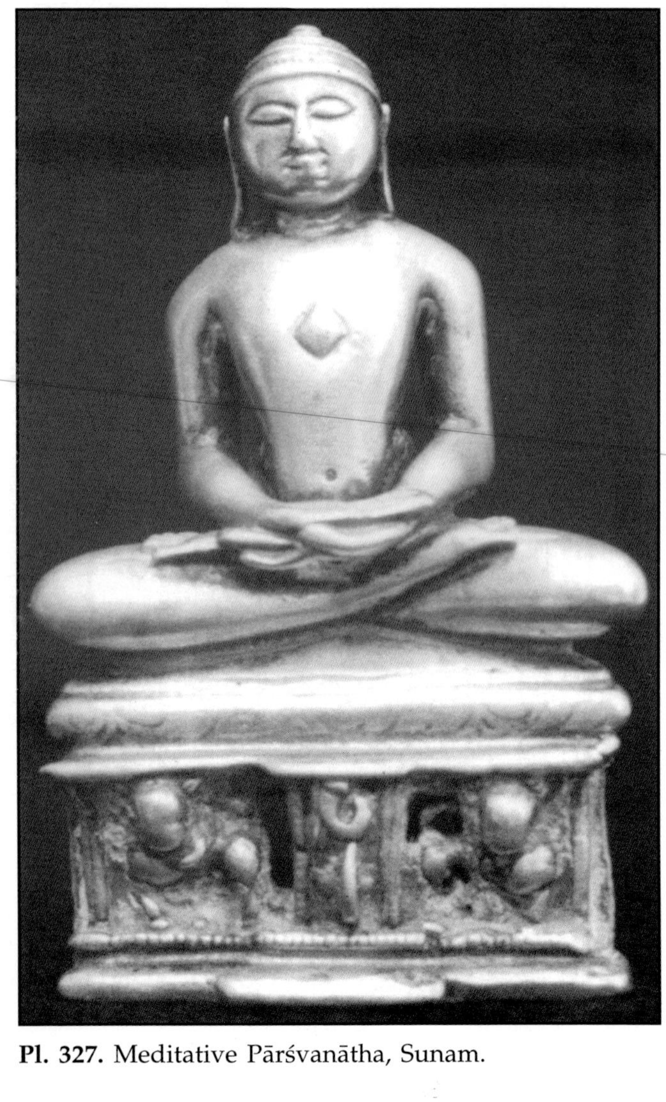

**Pl. 327.** Meditative Pārśvanātha, Sunam.

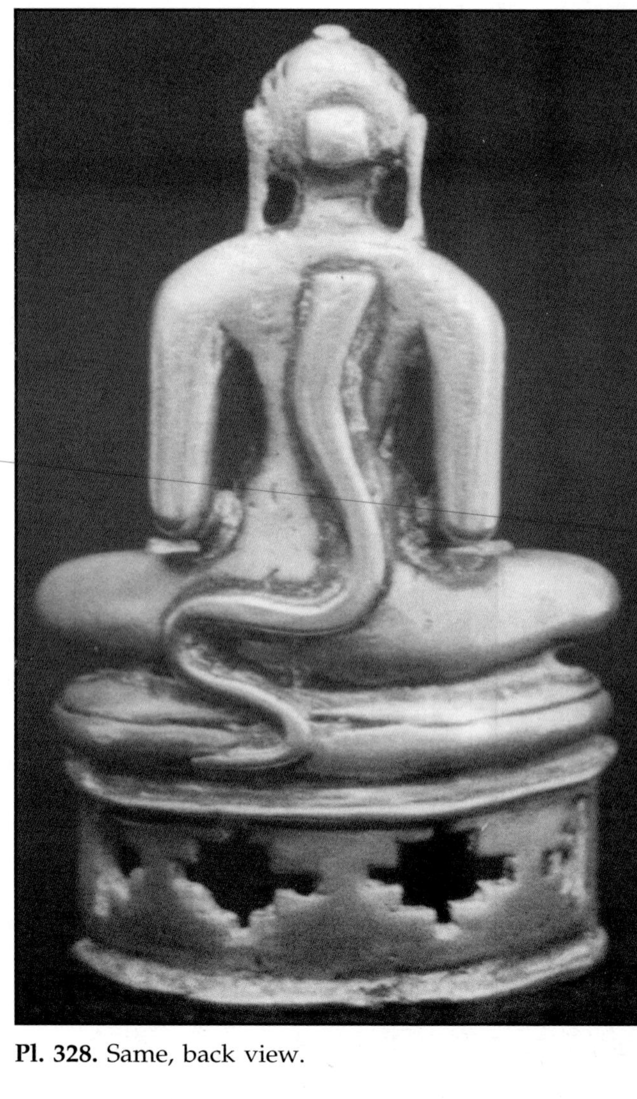

**Pl. 328.** Same, back view.

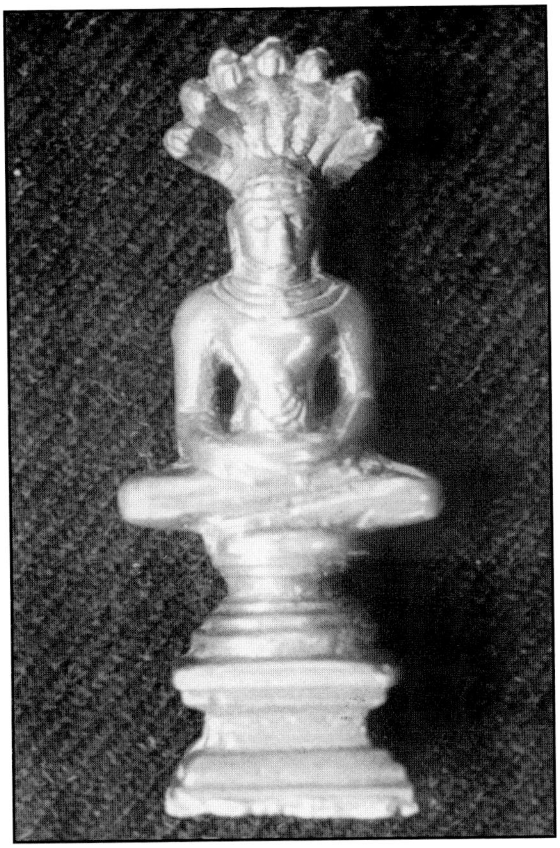

**Pl. 329.** Pārśvanātha, white metal, Sunam.

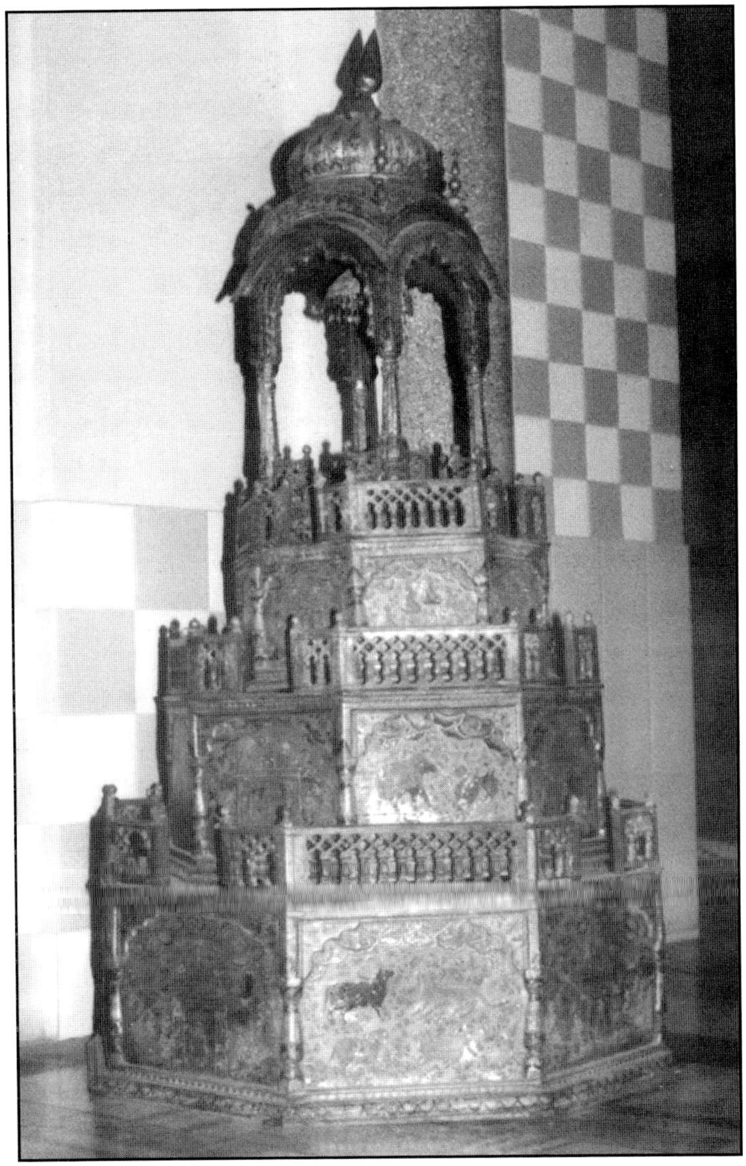

**Pl. 331.** *Samavasaraṇa* in the Jaina Temple, Sunam.

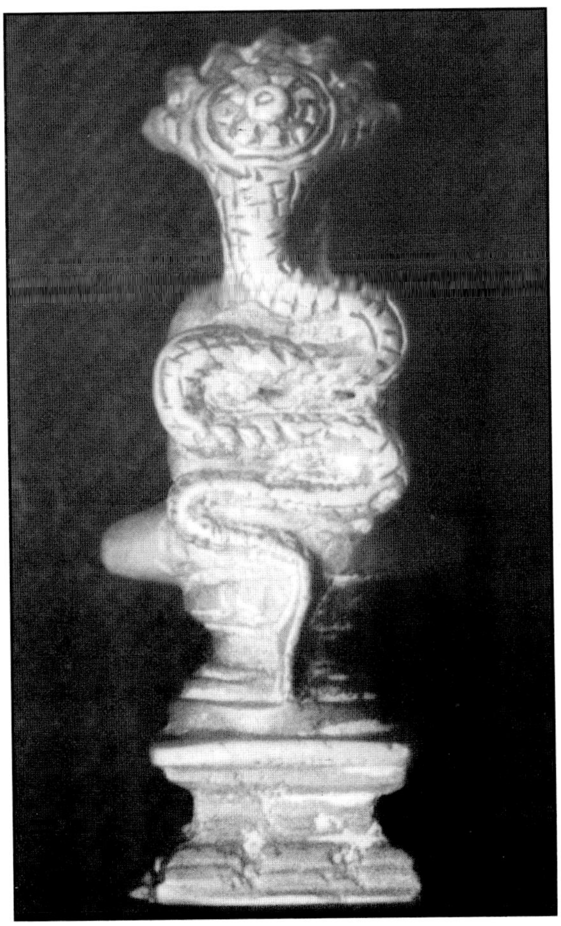

**Pl. 330.** Same, back view.

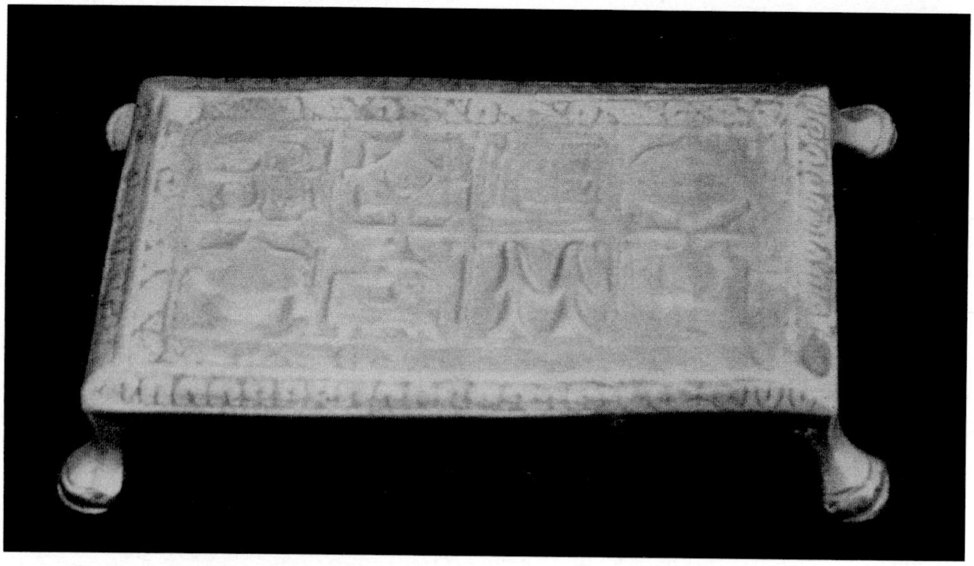

**Pl. 332.** Brass-tablet of *ashṭa-maṅgala*, Jaina temple, Sunam.

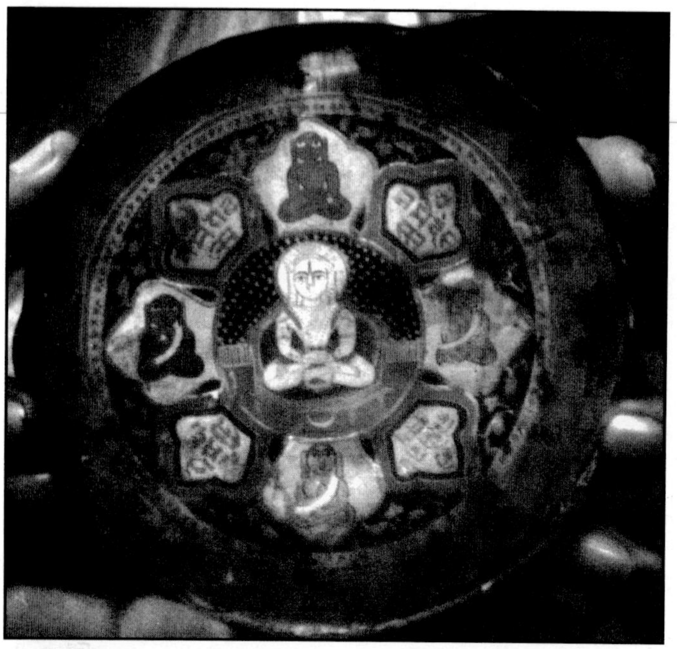

**Pl. 333.** Painted Siddha-Chakra in the Jaina temple, Sunam.

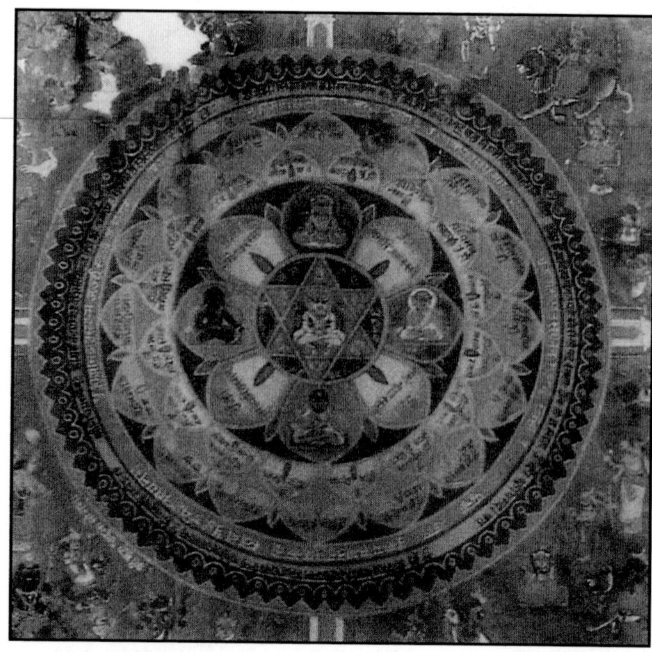

**Pl. 334.** Painted Siddha-Chakra from a manuscript from Faridkot.

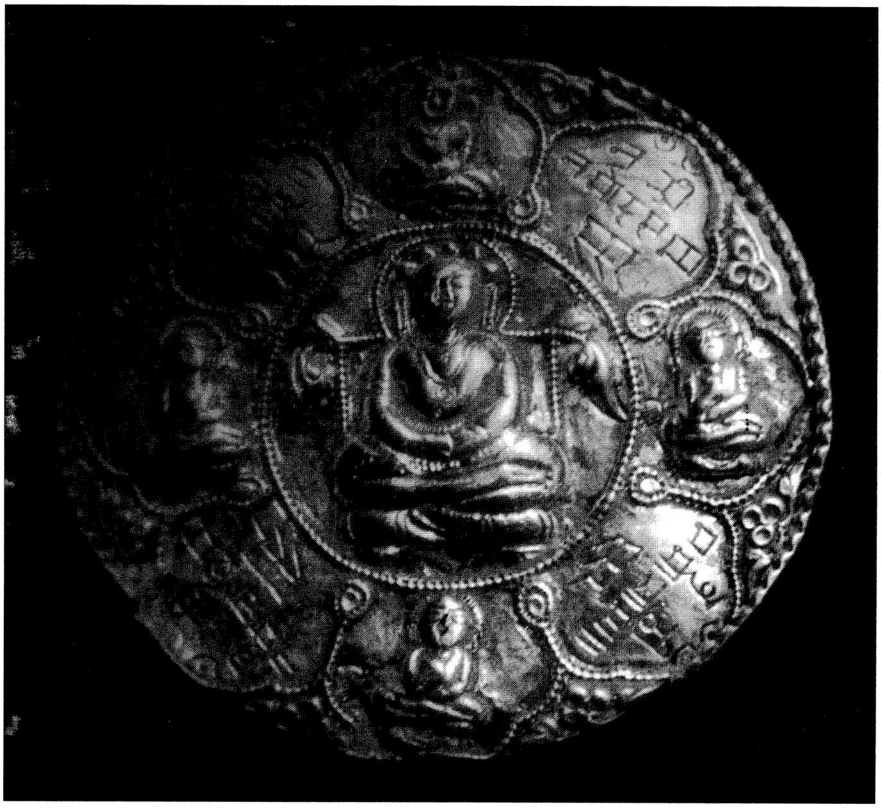

**Pl. 335.** Bronze Siddha-Chakra, Ropar.

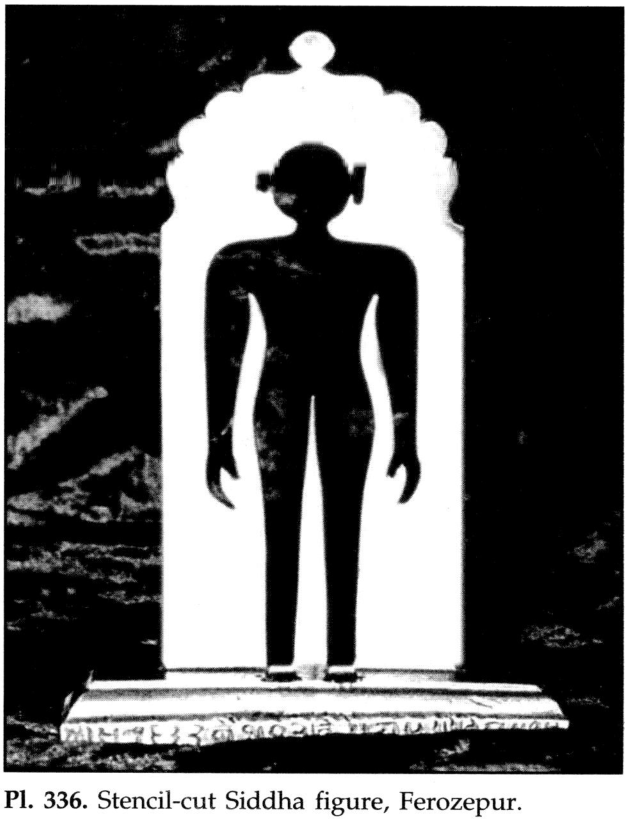

**Pl. 336.** Stencil-cut Siddha figure, Ferozepur.

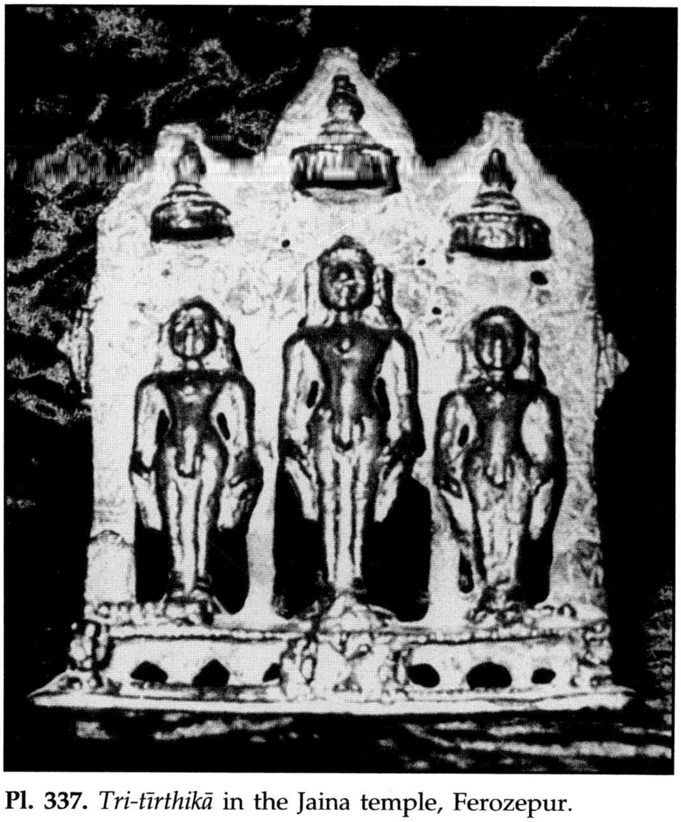

**Pl. 337.** *Tri-tīrthikā* in the Jaina temple, Ferozepur.

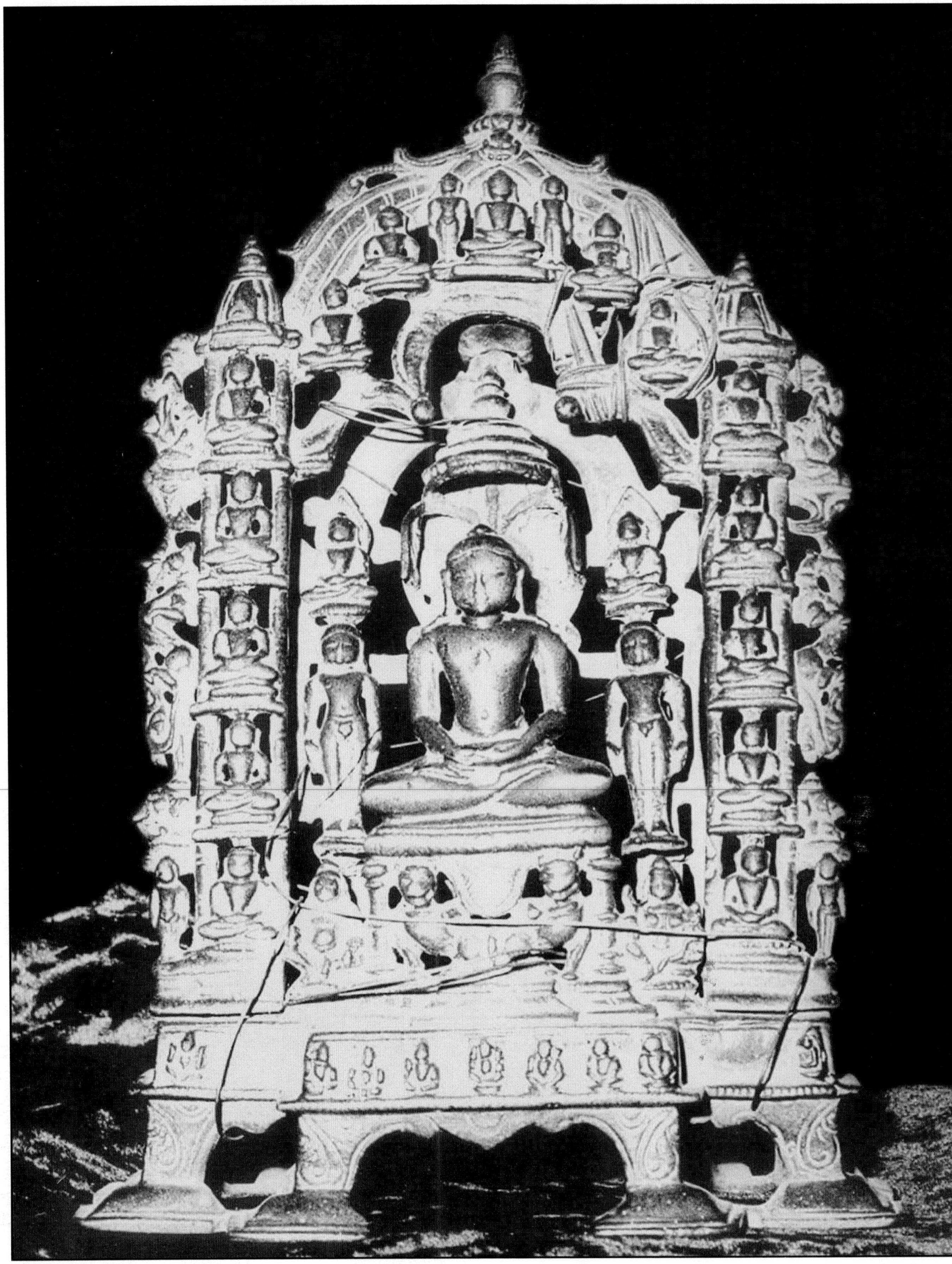

**Pl. 338.** *Chaturviṃśati-paṭṭa* of Ṛishabhanātha, Ferozepur.

# Glossary

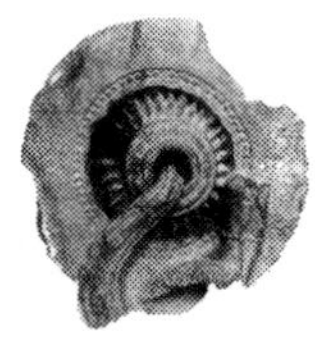

| | |
|---|---|
| *ābhaṅga* | body posture with one bend |
| *abhaya* | fear-allaying posture |
| *abhaya-mudrā* | fear-allaying or protection-affording posture of hand |
| *ābhūshaṇa* | ornament |
| *āchārya* | preceptor, holy teacher |
| *adhishṭhāna* | moulded base (of a temple) |
| *adhovastra* | nether garment |
| *akshamālā* | rosary |
| *ālīḍha* (*āsana*) | the posture of a warrior; body position with left leg drawn back and right knee bent |
| *āliṅgana* | embrace |
| *āmalaka* | myrobalan, flat-fluted melon-shaped member or cogged wheel like stone crowning the spire of temples |
| *āmra-lumbī* | mango-bunch |
| *amṛita-kalaśa* | pot of nectar |
| *aṅgada* | armlet |
| *aṅgulikā* | finger ring |
| *aṅgushṭha* | thumb |
| *añjali-mudrā* | gesture of respect and worship consisting of palms of hands joined to each other near the chest |
| *antaḥ-patra* or *antarapatra* | a moulding of the basement or pedestal, recessed band |
| *antaḥ-śākhā* | inner band, inner jamb of a door surround |
| *antarpaṭṭa* | recessed face between projecting mouldings |
| *antaśśākhā* | inner jamb of the door surround |
| *anuratha* | auxiliary offset flanking the central offset |
| *apasmāra-purusha* | dwarf demon personifying ignorance |

| | |
|---|---|
| *apsarā* | celestial maiden, heavenly damsel |
| *ardha* | half |
| *ardha-padma* | half-lotus motif |
| *ardha-paryaṅkāsana* | a sitting posture in which one leg is drawn up on the seat and the other with knee bent rests on the ground, same as *lalitāsana* |
| *ardha-ratna* | (decorative motif of) half-diamond |
| *arhat* | Buddhist or Jaina monk of the highest rank |
| *āsana* | seat, sitting posture |
| *āsana-mudrā* | sitting posture |
| *āsana-mūrti* | seated image |
| *ashṭa-maṅgala* | the depiction of eight auspicious symbols |
| *asura* | demon |
| *aśva-vyāla* | horse-like mythical animal |
| *atibhaṅga* | body posture with complex flexions, exaggerated flexion |
| *āvaraṇa-devatās* | surrounding deities |
| *avatāra* | incarnation |
| *avyaṅga* | chest-cover in Sun images, coat of mail |
| *āyāga-paṭa* | slab carved with sacred Jaina figures and symbols |
| *āyudha* | attribute, weapon |
| *āyudha-purusha* | personified form of a deity's attribute |
| | |
| *bāhya-śākhā* | outer band |
| *bhadra* | cardinal, main or central projection of the wall |
| *bhadra-pīṭha* | variety of a pedestal |
| *bhadra-ratha* | central offset |
| *bhakti* | religious devotion |
| *bharaṇī* | pillar-capital, fluted echinus with arris, circular myrobalan-like part of a pillar supporting the abacus |
| *bhāra-putraka* | Atlantes, dwarfish or *yaksha*-like figure supporting superstructure |
| *bhāra-vāhaka* | (same) |
| *bhāryā* | wife |
| *bhikkhu, bhikshu* | Buddhist mendicant |
| *bhikshuṇī* | nun |
| *bhiṭṭa* | plinth below the wall, sub-base of a temple |
| *Bhūmi* | Earth Goddess |
| *bhūmisparśa-mudrā* | earth-touching gesture |
| *bījapūraka* | a kind of fruit |
| *biṃba* | image |
| *Bodhisattva* | Buddha in a previous birth |
| | |
| *chaitya* | a (Buddhist) shrine, assembly hall, place of worship |
| *chaitya-gavāksha* | dormer-window, horseshoe-shaped motif, a decorative motif |
| *chaitya-gṛiha* | sanctuary, Buddhist temple |
| *chakra* | wheel or discus; weapon of Vishṇu |
| *chāmara* | fly-whisk |
| *Chakra-purusha* | personified form of Vishṇu's discus |
| *Chandraśāla* | *chaitya*-dormer motif |

| | |
|---|---|
| *chāpākāra* | bow-shaped |
| *chaturmukha* | four-faced |
| *chaturmukha-liṅga* | *liṅga* with four heads attached at cardinal points |
| *chaturmūrti* | image with four faces or combining four deities |
| *chaturviṃśatikā* | frieze or image with twenty-four Tīrthaṅkara figures |
| *chaubīsī* | same |
| *chaurī* | fly-whisk |
| *chhādyakī* | hood, cyma-cornice |
| *chhatra* | parasol |
| *chhatrākāra* | parasol-like |
| *chhattrāvalī* | multiple parasols atop a *stūpa* |
| *chhattra-traya* | triple parasols atop a *stūpa* |
| *chīvara* | Rag garment, particularly of Buddha or a Buddhist mendicant |
| *chūḍāmaṇi* | crest-jewel |
| *ḍamaru* | dumb-bell |
| *daṇḍa* | scepter, staff |
| *darpaṇa* | mirror |
| *darpaṇa-dhāriṇī* | female holding a mirror |
| *daśāvatāra* | the ten incarnations of Vishṇu |
| *ḍerā* | religious establishment |
| *devāṅganā* | divine damsel |
| *dhammilla* | braided and ornamental hair coiffure with hair swept into a circular chignon on the top of the head and adorned with flowers, pearls, etc. |
| *dharmachakra* | Buddha's wheel, (Buddhist) wheel of the Law |
| *dhotī* | Indian nether garment |
| *dhvaja* | banner, cognizance |
| *dhvaja-stambha* | banner-pillar, post in front of a temple carrying the cognizance of a deity |
| *dhyāna* | meditation |
| *dhyāna-mantra* | meditative incantation or invocation |
| *dhyāna mudrā* | meditative posture |
| *digambara* | sky-clad, naked |
| Digambara | sky-clad, one of the main Jaina sects |
| *dīkshā* | consecration |
| *dikpāla* | regent, guardian of a direction |
| *dīnāra* | Denarius, gold coin |
| *dohada* | motif showing a beautiful young woman standing by Aśoka tree pressing its stem by her left foot |
| *dvārapāla* | doorkeeper |
| *dvāra-śākhā* | door jambs, door surround |
| *dvibhaṅga* | double flexion, body position with two bends |
| *dhyāna-mudrā* | gesture of meditation in which the legs are folded and crossed with soles turned up and hands placed one upon the other with palms turned upwards |
| *ekamukhaliṅga* | *liṅga* with single head attached to it |

| | |
|---|---|
| *ekāvalī* | pearl necklace of single strand |
| | |
| *gadā* | mace |
| *Gadā-devī* | Vishṇu's personified mace |
| *gaja-śārdūla* | mythical animal combining features of elephant and lion |
| *gaja-vyāla* | Griffin with elephant head |
| *gaṇa* | soldier in Śiva's army, dwarfish playful creature |
| *gaṇa-śākhā* | doorjamb ornamented with dwarf figures |
| *gandharva* | celestial musician |
| *Garuḍa* | the divine eagle, Vishṇu's vehicle |
| *Garuḍāsana* | riding on Garuḍa |
| *Garuḍārūḍha* | riding on Garuḍa |
| *Garuḍa-vāhī* | having Garuḍa as the vehicle |
| *gavāksha* | decorative window motif |
| *ghaṇṭā* | bell |
| *ghaṭa* | vase, pot |
| *ghaṭa-pallava* | vase with foliage, an ornamental motif consisting of a pot with overflowing foliage, often used as the base or capital of pillars and pilasters |
| *godhā* | alligator |
| *gopālāsana* | standing cross-legged posture |
| *gotra* | sect |
| *graha* | planet, planetary divinity |
| *graiveyaka* | neck ornament |
| *grāsa-mukha* | Gorgon face or head, *kīrti-mukha* |
| *grīvā* | neck |
| *guṇa* | quality, property, attribute |
| | |
| *haṃsa* | goose |
| *hāra* | necklace |
| *harmikā* | square railing atop a *stūpa* containing a *chhatrāvalī* |
| *hasta* | hand |
| | |
| *Jāḍyakumbha* | inverted cyma recta |
| *Janapada* | tribe, state |
| *jātaka* | stories of the previous lives of Buddha |
| *jaṭā* | matted lock |
| *jaṭā-jūṭa* | high hair lock |
| *jaṭā-mukuṭa* | matted hair coiffure, head-gear or crown of matted locks |
| Jina | a term used for the Arhats/Tīrthaṅkaras of the Jainas |
| | |
| *kalaśa* | vase, pot, pitcher-finial |
| *kamalāsana* | lotus seat |
| *kamaṇḍalu* | spouted water vessel; a typical vase carried by ascetics, sages and some gods |
| *kambu-grīva* | having a conch-like neck |
| *kanishṭhikā* | little finger |

| | |
|---|---|
| *kaṅkaṇa* | bangle, bracelet |
| *kapāla* | skull, skull-cup |
| *karaṇḍa-mukuṭa* | crown or coiffure with basket-like pile |
| *kārita* | caused to be made |
| *karṇa* | corner, ear |
| *karṇābhūshaṇa* | ear ornament |
| *karṇaka, karṇikā* | knife-edged astragal |
| *karṇa-kuṇḍala* | earring |
| *kaṭi-sūtra* | waist band |
| *kaṭyavalambita* | with hand resting on the waist |
| *kāyotsarga* | standing body posture of abandonment |
| *kevala-vṛiksha* | tree of enlightenment or emancipation |
| *keyūra* | armlet, bracelet |
| *khaḍga* | sword |
| *khaḍgāsana* | same as *kāyotsarga* or the posture adopted by standing Tīrthaṅkaras |
| *kīchaka* | atlantes, *bhāra-vāhaka* |
| *kinnara* | a semi-divine being half-human half-bird |
| *kirīṭa-mukuṭa* | cylindrical crown worn by Vishṇu, Sūrya, etc. |
| *kīrttimukha* | face of glory, an auspicious symbol looking like a lion face |
| *kumbha* | pot |
| *kumbhaka* | pillar base |
| *kuṇḍa* | tank |
| *kuṇḍala* | earring |
| *kuṇḍikā* | nectar flask |
| *kūrcha* | a handful of *kuśa* grass, beard |
| *kuśa* | a type of grass |
| *kuṭhāra* | hatchet |
| | |
| *lahara-vallarī* | decorative wavy vegetal motif |
| *lalāṭa bimba* | central figure on door lintel or architrave |
| *lalāṭikā* | ornament of the forehead |
| *lalitāsana* | sitting posture of ease with one leg placed on the ground and the other folded on the seat |
| *lāñchhana* | distinctive sign, attribute |
| *līlā* | sport, divine play |
| *liṅga* | aniconic phallus-like emblem of Śiva |
| | |
| *madhupāna* | drinking wine |
| *madhyamā* | middle finger |
| *mahārājalīlāsana* | sitting posture of royal relaxation |
| *makara* | crocodile, alligator, mythic aquatic creature, ornamental motif |
| *makara-mukha* | face or fore part of crocodile |
| *makara-toraṇa* | *makara* emitting overreaching arch, gateway arch emanating from the mouth or tail of *makara* |
| *mālā* | garland, decorative band |
| *mālya-dhara* | garland-bearing |
| *mañchikā* | pedestal |

| | |
|---|---|
| *maṇi-bandha* | wrist, string or ornament of pearls or set with jewels |
| *mantra* | aphorism, incantation, invocation |
| *mātṛikā* | the divine mother |
| *matsya-yugam* | pair of fish |
| *mekhalā* | waist-band, girdle |
| *mithuna* | couple, male/female pair, an auspicious motif in Indian art |
| *mithuna-śākhā* | doorjamb bearing couples (sometimes erotic) |
| *modaka-pātra* | bowl of sweet balls |
| *mṛidaṅga* | drum |
| *mṛiga* | deer |
| *mudrā* | symbolic hand or arm position |
| *mukha-liṅga* | Śiva-*liṅga* with one or more faces around it |
| *mukha-paṭṭī(ikā)* | mouth-piece, a piece of white cloth used by Jainas to cover the mouth |
| *muktāhāra* | pearl necklace |
| *mukuṭa* | crown, tiara, headdress of god |
| *mūla-kanda* | turnip of dark foliage root |
| *mūrti* | icon, image of a deity |
| *nakha-kshata* | nail mark |
| *nāga* | snake, serpent, cobra |
| *nāga-pushpa* | honeysuckle |
| *nāgara-kūṭa* | shrine-model with North Indian type spire |
| *nāga-śākhā* | doorjamb with intertwined *nāgas* |
| *Nandī* | Śiva's bull |
| *Nandyāvarta* | an auspicious symbol |
| *naṭī* | female acrobat, acrobatic danseuse |
| *Navagraha* | nine planetary divinities |
| *nigama* | corporation |
| *nīlotpala* | blue lotus |
| *nirvāṇa* | final liberation or emancipation |
| *nīvi* | knot of the lower garment |
| *nūpura* | anklet/s |
| *pada/ pāda* | foot, a quarter part, step, place, position, name |
| *padma* | lotus |
| *Padma-purusha* | Vishṇu's personified lotus-attribute |
| *padmāsana* | meditation posture, lotus throne |
| *pañcha* | five |
| *Pañcha-Parameshṭhins* | Five Supreme Ones in Jainism |
| *pañchāgni-tapas* | penance of five fires |
| *pañcha-ratha* | having five recesses or offsets |
| *pañcha-tapas* | performing of five austerities |
| *pañcha-tīrthikā* | image with five Jina figures |
| *pañchāyatana* | quincunx, five-shrined |
| *parameshṭhin* | spiritual teacher |
| *paraśu* | battle-axe |
| *parikara* | ornamental arch or image-frame |

| | |
|---|---|
| *pāśa* | noose |
| *patra-śākhā* | jamb adorned with foliage |
| *paṭṭikā* | slab-like moulding |
| *pedyā* | lower sections of doorjambs showing river goddesses and/or guardians |
| *piṅgalorddha* | a type of hair coiffure |
| *pīṭha* | socle, moulded base or pedestal of an image or temple |
| *pīṭhikā* | image-pedestal |
| *prabhā-maṇḍala* | halo, nimbus |
| *prabhāvali* | aureole, halo, nimbus |
| *pradakshiṇā* | circumambulation |
| *pradakshiṇā-patha* | processional passage or circumambulatory path |
| *pralamba* | hanging |
| *pralamba-hasta* | with hand hanging down |
| *pratiratha* | companion of *ratha*, wall offset flanking the central projection, juxta-buttress |
| *pratishṭhita(ṃ)* | installed, consecrated |
| *pratyālīḍha* | body posture with right leg drawn back and left knee bent |
| *Pṛithvī* | Earth Goddess |
| *Purāṇa* | religious text on Hindu myths, legends, pilgrimage, worship, etc. |
| *pūrṇaghaṭa* | vase of plenty, vase and foliage, an auspicious motif |
| *pūrṇa-kumbha* | (same) |
| *purusha* | man |
| *pustaka* | book, manuscript |
| *ratha* | lit. a car, recess, Pagoda |
| *rathikā* | deep niche, framed niche to shelter an image |
| *ṛishi* | sage, seer |
| *ruchaka* | square-sectioned pillar |
| *rūpaśākhā* | jamb with figures |
| *sādhu* | pious, virtuous |
| *sadyaḥ snātā* | fresh from bath |
| *sā/sāha* | *Śāha*, rich person |
| *śākhā* | branch, jamb of a door frame |
| *śakti* | female energy, wife of god |
| *śālabhañjikā* | tree dryad, an art motif showing a *yakshī* holding the branch of a tree |
| *sallekhanā* | prolonged religious fast unto death in Jainism |
| *sama* | straight, even |
| *samabhaṅga* | frontal body posture without flexion |
| *samapādasthānaka* | frontal standing body posture, standing posture in which the figure is equipoise with weight equally distributed on the two feet |
| *samavasaraṇa* | divinely devised assembly-hall for the first sermon of every Tīrthaṅkara |
| *saṃgha* | Church, congregation |
| *śaṅkha* | conch shell |
| *śaṅkha-patra* | conch-shaped leaf |
| *Śaṅkha-purusha* | personified form of Vishṇu's conch |
| *santāna-mañjarī* | a cluster of flower buds of a plant in Indra's paradise |

| | |
|---|---|
| *sapta-mātṛikā* | seven mothers, group of female divinities |
| *sapta-ratha* | with seven offsets |
| *śārdūla* | composite animal used as decoration |
| *sarpa* | snake, serpent |
| *sarpa-yajñopavīta* | sacred thread of a snake |
| *sarvato-bhadra* | *chaturmukha*, quadruple, temple or image looking similar on all the four sides, a shrine-model with image on the four faces |
| *śāsanadevatā* | governing deities |
| *śayana-mūrti* | reclining image |
| *siddha* | perfected being |
| *śikhara* | spire, head or upper part of a temple |
| *śilpa* | art, skill, sculpture, ingenuous manual work |
| *siṃha* | lion |
| *siṃhāsana* | lion-throne; seat with legs in the form of lion's feet |
| *siṃhāśva* | hybrid lion-horse |
| *siṃha-vyāla* | mythical leonine creature |
| *śiraśchakra* | halo, nimbus, aureole |
| *śramaṇa* | ascetic, religious mendicant, term used for both Buddha and Mahāvīra and their follower monks |
| *śrāvaka* | Jaina lay disciple |
| *śreshṭhī* | *Śāha*, the head or president of a mercantile or other guild |
| *śrīvatsa* | an auspicious mark generally shown on the chest of Vishṇu and Jaina tīrthaṅkaras |
| *sruk/sruch/sruva* | wooden ladle used for pouring ghee (clarified butter) in the sacrificial fire |
| *stambha* | pillar, column |
| *sthānaka* | standing |
| *sthānaka-mūrti* | standing image |
| *stūpa* | Buddhist relic or votive mound |
| *stūpī, stūpikā* | finial of a temple |
| *sūchī* | cross-bar |
| *śuka-nāsa, śukanāsikā* | antefix above the roof of the porch, pediment-shaped roof over the vestibule resembling a parrot's nose or beak |
| *sukhāsana* | sitting posture with both legs resting comfortably on ground |
| *sura-sundarī* | heavenly damsel |
| Śvetāmbara | white-clothed, a Jaina sect |
| | |
| *tāla-patra* | palm leaf |
| *tapasvinī* | female ascetic performing penance/s |
| *tarjanī* | pointing finger |
| *thera* | monk |
| *therī* | *bhikshuṇī*, female monk |
| *tilaka* | auspicious mark on the forehead, a variety of turret-design |
| *tīrtha* | a holy place, pilgrimage centre |
| *Tīrthaṅkara* | Jaina religious reformer, pontiff |
| *toraṇa* | cusped arch at the entrance, ornamental arch or gateway |
| *tribhaṅga* | body position with triple flexion |

| | |
|---|---|
| *tripuṇḍa* | a three-line mark on the forehead |
| *tri-ratha* | having three projections |
| *triratna* | a three-pronged auspicious symbol |
| *triśūla* | trident |
| *tri-tīrthikā* | frieze or image with three Jina figures |
| | |
| *Udadhikumāra* | a divinity with human body and avian legs generally shown as carrying a pot on the doorsills |
| *udgama* | pediment |
| *udīchya-veśa* | Northerners' dress |
| *udumbara* | threshold, door-sill supporting the door-jambs |
| *Upāśraya* | Jaina religious establishment for the stay of monks |
| *ūrdhvaliṅga* | with phallus erect |
| *ushṇīsha* | coping stone, turban |
| *utakuṭikāsana* | posture of sitting on haunches |
| *uttaraṅga* | door-architrave or lintel |
| *uttarīya* | upper garment, scarf |
| *vāhana* | vehicle or mount |
| *vaijayantīmālā* | long garland worn by Vishṇu |
| *vaikakshyaka* | a cross-chain ornament |
| *vāma* | dwarfish, low |
| *vanamālā* | long garland worn by gods |
| *varada* | boon-giving |
| *varada-mudrā* | boon-giving hand posture, wish-granting gesture |
| *vedī-bandha* | podium, basal wall mouldings |
| *vedikā* | railing, balustrade |
| *vedikā-stambha* | railing pillar |
| *vibhavavāda* | theory of different forms or incarnations of the god |
| *vidyādhara* | 'bearer of knowledge', semi-celestials generally shown as hovering or flying in the sky and carrying a garland above the principal deity |
| *vīṇā* | lyre, lute, a kind of stringed musical instrument |
| *vīṇā dhara* | one who holds the *vīṇā* |
| *vyāghra charma* | tiger skin |
| *vyāla* | mythical composite animal, leogryph, griffin |
| *vyāla-śākhā* | jamb decorated with *vyāla* figure/s |
| *vyākhyāna-mudrā* | the posture of explaining the essential doctrines of Dhamma |
| *vyūha* | emanation |
| | |
| *yajñopavīta* | sacred thread |
| *yaksha* | nature divinity, male fertility godling; object of cult worship, semi-divine being, acolyte of a Jaina *tīrthaṅkara* |
| *yakshī/yakshiṇī* | female fertility godling; beautiful figures depicted on railing pillars |
| yoga | deep meditation, concentration of mind, contemplation of the Supreme Spirit |
| *yogāsana* | seated in meditation, yogic posture |
| *yoni-pīṭha* | pedestal of the shape of a female organ of generation |
| *yūpa* | sacrificial pillar |

# Bibliography

## ORIGINAL SOURCES


*Agnipurāṇa*
*Aitareya Brāhmaṇa*
*Aitareya Upanishad*
*Aparājita-pṛichchhā*
*Ashṭādhyāyī*
*Bhagavadgītā*
*Bhāgavata Purāṇa*
*Bhavishya Purāṇa*
*Brahma Purāṇa*
*Brahmāṇḍa Purāṇa*
*Brahma-Vaivarta Purāṇa*
*Bṛihatsaṃhitā*
*Devatāmūrtiprakaraṇa* (Calcutta, 1936)
*Dīghanikāya*
*Divyāvadāna*
*Garuḍa Purāṇa*
*Gauḍavaho* (edited by S.P. Pandit, Bombay, 1887)
*Harivaṃśa* (Gita Press ed.)
*Jayākhya Saṃhitā* (GOS, Baroda, 1931)
*Kāṭhaka Saṃhitā*
*Kharatara-Gachchha-Bṛihad-Gurvāvali*
*Kshīrārṇava* of Viśvakarmā
*Kumārasambhava* of Kālidāsa
*Kuvalayamālākathā* of Uddyotana Sūri
*Liṅga Purāṇa*
*Mahābhārata*
*Mahābhāshya*
*Mahāmāyūrī* (ed. Sylvan Levi, *Journal Asiatique*, 1915)
*Mahāvaṃsa*

*Maitrāyaṇī Saṃhitā*
*Manusmṛiti*
*Matsya Purāṇa,* (Ānandāśrama Sanskrit Series, Poona, 1907)
*Nārada Purāṇa*
*Nṛisiṃhatāpan Upanishad*
*Padma Purāṇa*
*Paṭṭāvalī-Samuchchaya* (edited by Muni Darshanvijay, Viramgam, 1933)
*Paushkarasaṃhitā*
*Pratishṭhā-sāroddhāra*
*Rājataragiṇī* of Kalhaṇa, Eng. tr. by R.S. Pandit, Sahitya Academi, New Delhi, 1977 (reprint)
*Rāmāyaṇa*
*Ṛigveda*
*Rūpa-maṇḍana*
*Śāradātilaka*
*Śatapatha Brāhmaṇa*
*Saura Purāṇa*
*Skanda Purāṇa*
*Śiva Purāṇa*
*Taittirīya Āraṇyaka*
*Taittirīya Brāhmaṇa*
*Taittirīya Saṃhitā*
*Tṛishashṭiśalākāpurushacharitra* of Hemachandra
*Vaikhānasāgama*
*Vājasaneyī Saṃhitā*
*Vāmana Purāṇa*
*Varāha Purāṇa*
*Vāyu Purāṇa*
*Vāyu Saṃhitā*
*Vishṇudharmottara Purāṇa* (GOS, Baroda, 1958)
*Vishṇu Purāṇa*
*Yajurveda*

## MODERN BOOKS

Agrawal, Jagannath (1991), *Inscriptions of Haryana, Punjab, Himachal & Kashmir*, ICHR, New Delhi.
Agrawal, Jagannath and Shastri, Bhim Dev (Eds.) (1964), *Sarūpa – Bhāratī or the Heritage of Indology Being The Dr. Lakshman Sarup Memorial Volume*, Hoshiarpur.
Agrawala, P.K. (1967), *Skanda-Kārttikeya*, Varanasi.
——. (1983), *Mithuna, the Male-Female Symbol in Indian Art and Thought*, Delhi.
——. (1993), *Ancient Indian Mother-Goddess Votive Discs*, Varanasi.
——. (1994), *Gupta-kālīna Kalā evaṃ Vāstu*, Varanasi.
Agrawala, V.S. (1933), *Handbook of the Sculptures in the Curzon Museum of Archaeology in Muthra*, Allahabad.
——. (1964), *Indian Art*, Varanasi.
——. (1966), *Śiva-Mahādeva*, Varanasi.
——. (1977), *Gupta Art (A History of Indian Art in the Gupta Period 300-600 AD)*, compiled and edited by P.K. Agrawala, Varanasi.
Ahir, D.C. (2009), *Buddhism in the Punjab, Haryana and Himachal Pradesh*, New Delhi.
Ahluwalia, J.S. (Ed.) (1987), *Historico-Archaeological Linkages of Punjabiat*, Department of Cultural Affairs, Archaeology, Archives and Museums, Punjab, Chandigarh.
Allan, John (1936), *Catalogue of the Coins of Ancient India in the British Museum*, London.
Altekar, A.S. (1957), *Coinage of the Gupta Empire*, Varanasi.
Apte, V.S. (1959), *Sanskrit-English Dictionary*, Delhi-Varanasi-Patna.

Bandyopadhyay, B. (1987), *Survey of Indian Metal Sculpture*, Delhi.
Banerjea, J.N. (1956), *The Development of Hindu Iconography*, 2nd ed., Calcutta.
Banerji, R.D. (1928), *Bas Reliefs of Badami*, Memoirs of the Archaeological Survey of India, No. 25.
Bapat, P.V. (Ed.) (1964), *2500 Years of Buddhism*, Delhi.
Beal, Samuel (Eng. Tr.) (1884), *Buddhist Records of the Western World*, 2 Vols., London.
Begley, W.E. (1973), *Viṣṇu's Flaming Wheel: The Iconography of the Sudarśana Cakra*, New York.
Berkson, Carmel (2000), *The Life of Form in Indian Sculpture*, New Delhi.
Bhagwat, N.K. (Ed.) (1956), *Therīgāthā*, Bombay.
Bhandarkar, D.R. (1921), *Carmichael Lectures on Ancient Indian Numismatics*, Calcutta.
Bhandarkar, R.G. (1928), *Vaiṣṇavism, Śaivism and Minor Religious Systems*, Poona.
Bhan, Suraj (1975), *Excavations at Mitathal (1968) and Other Explorations in the Sutlej-Yamuna Divide*, Kurukshetra University, Kurukshetra.
Bharadwaj, O.P. (1986), *Studies in the Historical Geography of Ancient India*, Delhi.
Bhattacharya, B.C. (1924), *Jaina Iconography*, 2nd revised edition, Delhi-Varanasi-Patna.
Bhattacharyya, D.C. (1981), *Medieval Indian Sculpture* (*In the Government Museum and Art Gallery, Chandigarh*), Chandigarh.
——. (Ed.) (2002), *Gandhāra Sculpture in the Government Museum and Art Gallery, Chandigarh* (*in the light of the International Colloquium held in 1998 at Chandigarh*), Chandigarh.
Bhattacharya, U.C. (1960-61), *Catalogue & Guide to Rajputana Museum, Ajmer, Rajasthan*, Part I, Sculptures, Jaipur.
——. (1960-61), *Catalogue & Guide to State Museum, Bharatpur (Rajasthan)*, Jaipur.
Briggs, John ((Eng. Tr.) (1966), *Tarikh-i-Farishta: The Rise of the Mohammadan Power in India*, Calcutta.
Chakrabarti, Dilip K. and Saini, Sukhdev (2009), *The Problem of the Sarasvati River and Notes on the Archaeological Geography of Haryana and Indian Panjab*, New Delhi.
Chakravarti, Mahadev (1986), *The Concept of Rudra-Śiva Through the Ages*, Delhi.
Champakalakshmi, R. (1981), *Vaiṣṇava Iconography in the Tamil Country*, New Delhi.
Chandra, Lokesh and Jain, Jyotindra (Eds.) (1986), *Dimensions of Indian Art (Pupul Jayakar Seventy)*, Delhi.
Chandra, Pramod (1970), *Stone Sculpture in the Allahabad Museum*, American Institute of Indian Studies, Publication No. 2, Poona.
Chandra, Rai Govinda (1964), *Prāchīna Bhārata meṃ Lakshmī Pratimā – Eka Adhyayana*, Varanasi.
Chatterjee, Asim Kumar (1970), *The Cult of Skanda-Kārttikeya in Ancient India*, Calcutta.
Coomaraswamy, A.K. (1927), *History of Indian and Indonesian Art*, New York.
——. (1948), *The Dance of Siva*, Bombay.
——. (1956), *La Sculpture de Bharhut*, Paris.
——. (1969), *Introduction to Indian Art*, Delhi
Cunningham, Alexander (1891), *Coins of Ancient India*, London.
——. (1894), *Coins of Medieval India*, London.
——. (1963), *The Ancient Geography of India*, Reprint, Varanasi.
Czuma, S. (1985), *Kushana Sculpture – Images from Early India*, Cleveland.
Daivakaraṇi, Virajānanda (2010), *Bhārata ke Prāchīna Mudrāṃka* (Hindi), Jhajjar.
Desai, Devangana (1996), *The Religious Imagery of Khajuraho*, Mumbai.
Desai, Kalpana S. (1973), *Iconography of Viṣṇu*, New Delhi.
Desai, Nileshvari Y. (1968), *Ancient Indian Society, Religion and Mythology as Depicted in the Markandeya Purana: A Critical Study*, Baroda.
Dey, Nundo Lal (1971), *The Geographical Dictionary of Ancient and Mediæval India*, 3rd edition, Delhi.
Dhaky, M.A. (1965), *The Vyāla Figures on the Medieval Temples of India*, Varanasi.
Dugar, Hira Lal (1979), *Madhya Eśiyā aura Pañjāba meṃ Jaina Dharma*, Delhi.
Encyclopaedia Britannica, 9th ed.
Fleet, John Faithful (1888), Corpus Inscriptionum Indicarum, Vol. III: *The Inscriptions of the Early Gupta Kings and their Successors*, Calcutta.
Fowler, H.N. (Eng. Tr.) (1936), Plutarch's *Moralia*, Oxford.
Frauwallner, E. (1956), *The Earliest Vinaya and the Beginnings of Buddhist Literature*, Rome.

Ganguli, K.K. and Biswas, S.S. (Eds.) (1986), *Rupanjali in Memory of O.C. Gangoly*, Calcutta.
Gardner, Percy (1966), *The Coins of the Greek and Scythic Kings of Bactria and India in the British Museum*, Chicago.
Gaston, A-M (1982), *Śiva in Dance, Myth and Iconography*, Delhi.
Gautam, Chamanlal (1967), *Devavāda kā Vaijñānika Svarūpa* (Hindi) I, Vishṇu-Rahasya, Bareilly.
*Gazetteer of Jhelum District*, Lahore, 1904.
Geiger, W. (1912), *The Mahāvaṃsa or The Great Chronicle of Ceylon*, London.
Getty, Alice (1936), *Gaṇeśa*, Oxford.
Gonda, J. (1954), *Aspects of Early Viṣṇuism*, Utrecht.
Goswamy, B.N. (1985-86), *Essence of Indian Art*, Festival of India 1985-86, Mapin Publishing Private Ltd. Ahmedabad and Asian Art Museum of San Fransisco.
Goyal, Shankar (Ed.), *Śrīrāmābhinanam Reconstructing Indian History for S.R. Goyal*, Vol. II, Jaipur, 2003.
Growse, F.S. (1883), *Mathura, a district memoir*, (3rd ed.), Allahabad.
Gupta, P.L. and Hardaker, T.R. (1985), *Ancient Indian Silver Punchmarked Coins of the Magadha-Maurya Karshapana Series*, Anjaneri.
Gupta, S.P. (Ed.) (1985), *Kushāṇa Sculptures From Sanghol (1st-2nd Century AD): A Recent Discovery*, National Museum, New Delhi.
Haertel, H. (1960), *Indische Sculpturen*, 1, Berlin.
——. (Ed.) (1976), *German Scholars on India*, Vol. II, Bombay.
Haig, Wolseley (1958), *Cambridge History of India*, Reprint, Delhi.
Handa, Devendra (1984), *Osian: History, Archaeology, Art & Architecture*, Delhi.
——. (1985), *Studies in Indian Coins and Seals*, Delhi.
——. (Ed.) (1987), *Indological Studies (Essays in Memory of Shri S.P. Singhal)*, Delhi.
——. (Ed.) (1989), *Ajaya-Śrī: Recent Studies in Indology (Prof. Ajay Mitra Shastri Felicitation Volume)*, 2 Vols., Delhi.
——. (2002), *Jaina Bronzes From Hansi*, Shimla-New Delhi.
——. (2004), *An Epic Pilgrimage – History and Antiquity of Pehowa: Ancient Pṛithūdaka – A Mahābhārata Site on the Sarasvatī*, New Delhi.
——. (2006), *Early Indian Coins from Sugh*, Delhi.
——. (2006), *Sculptures from Haryana: Iconography & Style*, Shimla-New Delhi.
——. (2007), *Tribal Coins of Ancient India*, New Delhi.
Handa, Devendra and Agrawal, Ashvini (eds.) (1989), *Ratna-Chandrikā: Panorama of Oriental Studies (Shri R.C. Agrawala Festschrift)*, New Delhi.
Harle, J.C. (1986), *The Art and Architecture of the Indian Subcontinent*, London.
Hopkins, E.W. (1895), *The Religion of India*, Boston.
——. (1915), *Epic* Mythology, Strassburg (Indian reprint, 1968).
Hussain, Agha Mahdi (Ed.) (1938), Islami's *Fatuh-us-Salatin*, Agra.
Jain, Jagdish Chandra (1952), *Bhārata ke Prāchīna Jaina Tīrtha* (Hindi), Banaras.
Jain, Jyoti Prasad (1964), *The Jaina Sources of the History of Ancient India*, Delhi.
Jain, K.C. (1972), *Ancient Cities and Towns of Rajasthan*, Delhi-Varanasi-Patna.
Jash, Pranabanand (1974), *History of Śaivism*, Calcutta.
Joshi, Jagat Pati (Chief Editor) (1997), *Facets of Indian Civilization: Recent Perspectives – Essays in Honour of Prof. B.B. Lal*, 3 Vols., New Delhi.
Joshi, N.P. (1965), *Mathurā kī Mūrtikalā* (Hindi), Mathura.
——. (1972), *Catalogue of the Brahmanical Sculptures in the State Museum, Lucknow*, Part I, Lucknow.
——. (1979), *Iconography of Balarāma*, New Delhi.
Kala, S.C. (1980), *Terracottas in the Allahabad Museum*, New Delhi.
*Kalyāṇa* (Tīrthāṅka) (Jan. 1957), Gita Press, Gorakhpur.
Kanta, Surya (1961), *Vaidika Devaśāstra* (Hindi), Delhi.
Keith, A.B. (1964), *Indian Mythology*, New York.
Kielhorn, F. (Ed.) (1880-85), *Mahābhāshya* of Patañjali, 2 volumes, Bombay.
Konow, S. (1929), Corpus Inscriptionum Indicarum, Vol. II, Part I, *Kharoshṭhī Inscriptions with the Exception of those of Aśoka*, Calcutta.

Kumar, Jitendra (1989), *Masterpieces of Mathura Museum, Mathura.*

Law, B.C. (1954), *Indological Studies*, Part III, Allahabad.

Macdonell, A.A. (1963), *Vedic Mythology*, Varanasi.

Maheshwari, K.K. (2010), *Imitations in Continuity: Tracking the Silver Coinage of Early Medieval India*, IIRNS, Mumbai.

Majumdar, R.C. (Ed.) (1955), *The Struggle for Empire*, Bombay.

——. (Ed.) (1968), *The Age of Imperial Unity*, 4th ed., Bombay.

Malla, Bansi Lal (1990), *Sculptures of Kashmir (600 – 1200 AD)*, Delhi.

Marshall, Sir John (1931), *Mohenjodaro and the Indus Civilization*, Vol. I, London.

——. (1960), *Guide to Taxila*, Cambridge.

Maxwell, T.S. (1988), *Viśvarūpa*, Delhi (OUP).

McCrindle, J.W.C. (1960), *Ancient India as Described by Megasthenes and Arrian*, Revised 2nd ed., Calcutta.

Mehta, N.C. (1932), *Jainism in Northern India*, London.

Mevissen, Gerd J.R. and Banerji, Arundhati (Eds.) (2009). *Prajñādhara: Essays on Asian Art History Epigraphy and Culture in Honour of Gouriswar Bhattacharya*, 2 vols., New Delhi.

Mishra, P.K. and Sullerey, S.K. (Eds.) (1994), *Heritage of India Past and Present (Essays in Honour of Prof. R.K. Sharma)*, 2 vols., Delhi.

Mittal, Kewal Krishan and Agrawal, Ashvini (Eds.) (1993), *Buddhist Art and Thought*, New Delhi.

Mookerji, R.K. (1960), *Ancient Indian Education*, Delhi.

Muni, Darshan Vijay (Ed.) (1933), *Upakeśagachchhapaṭṭāvali*, Viramgam.

Muni, Jina Vijaya (Ed.) (1934), *Vividha-tīrtha-kalpa*, Santiniketana.

——. (Ed.) (1956), *Kharatara-Gachchha-Bṛihad-Gurvāvali* of Jinapāla Upādhyāya and others, Bombay

Nagar, Shanti Lal (1989), *Composite Deities in Indian Art and Literature*, New Delhi.

——. (1995), *Sūrya and Sun Cult*, New Delhi.

Nagaswami, R. (1982), *Tantric Cult of South India*, Delhi.

——. (2002), *Foundations of Indian Art*, Chennai.

——. (2006), *The Art and Religion of the Bhairavas*, Chennai.

Nahata, B.L. (Ed.) (1976), *Dravya-parīkshā aura Dhātūtpatti* (of Ṭhakkara Pheru) (Hindi), Vaiśāli.

Nahta, Agarchand *et al.* (Eds.) (1957), *Rājasthāna kā Jaina Sāhitya* (Hindi), Jaipur.

Narain, A.K. (1957), *The Indo-Greeks*, Oxford.

Nath, R. (1980), *The Art of Khajuraho*, New Delhi.

Navaratnam, R. (1973), *Kārttikeya – The Divine Child*, Bombay.

Ohri, V.C. (Ed.) (1975), *Arts of Himachal*, State Museum, Simla.

——. (1991), *Sculpture of the Western Himalayas (History and Stylistic Development)*, Delhi.

Pal, Pratapaditya (1985), *Vaisnava Iconology in Nepal – A Study in Art and Religion*, Calcutta

——. (1996), *The Peaceful Liberators: Jaina Art from India*, Los Angeles & London, 1996.

Panchamukhi, R.S. (1951), *Gandharvas & Kinnaras in Indian Iconography*, Dharwar.

Pandey, Lalta Prasad (1971), *Sun-Worship in Ancient India*, Delhi-Patna-Varanasi.

Pandit, R.S. (Eng. Tr.) (1977), *Rājataraṅgiṇī of Kalhaṇa*, (reprint, Sahitya Academi) New Delhi.

Parihar, Subhash (2006), *History and Architectural Remains of Sirhind – The Great Mughal City on Delhi-Lahore Highway*, New Delhi.

Phadke, H.A. (1990), *Haryana: Ancient and Medieval*, New Delhi.

Pillai, J.M. Somasudaram (1925), *Śiva Naṭarāja – The Cosmic Dancer in Cidambaram*, Chidambaram.

Prinsep, James (1858), *Essays in Indian Antiquities*, edited by Edward Thomas, London.

*Panjab District Gazetteers*, Vol. VII, Part A: Ambala District 1923-24, Lahore, 1925.

*Punjab Government Museum, Hoshiarpur*, Chandigarh (no date).

Puri, B.N. (1967), *History of the Gurjara Pratiharas*, Bombay.

Pusalkar, A.D. (1955), *Studies in the Epics and Puranas*, Bombay.

Rani, Archana (2007), *Saṃghola evaṃ Mathurā kī Kalā* (Hindi), Delhi.

Rao, M.S. Nagaraja (Ed.) (1987), *Kusumāñjali: New Interpretation of Indian Art & Culture – Sh. C. Sivaramamurti Commemoration Volume*, 2 Volumes, Delhi.

Rao, T.A. Gopinatha (1971), *Elements of Hindu Iconography* (Reprint, Indological Book House), Delhi.

Ray, Himanshu Prabha (Ed.) (2010), *Sanghol and the Archaeology of Punjab*, New Delhi.

Reynolds, James (Eng. Tr.) (1858), Al-Utbi's *Kitab-i-Yamini, Memoirs of Mahmud of Ghazni*, London.

Rhys Davids, T.W. (1882), *The Questions of King Milinda*, Sacred Books of the East Series, Vols. 35-36 (reprint, MLBD, Delhi, 1965).

Rodgers, Charles Jas. (1890), *Report of the Panjab Circle of the Archaeological Survey for 1888-89*, Lahore.

——. (1891), *A Revised List of Objects of Archaeological Interest in the Punjab*, Lahore.

Rosenfield, T.J.M. (1967), *The Dynastic Arts of the Kushans*, Berkeley.

Roy, A.K. (1984), *A History of the Jainas*, New Delhi.

Sachau, Edward (Ed.) (1989), *Al-Beruni's India* (reprint), Delhi.

Sampurnananda, Dr. (vs 2001), *Gaṇeśa* (Hindi), Varanasi.

Sant, Urmila (1997), *Terracotta Art of Rajasthan*, New Delhi.

Sarasvati, Swami Omanand (vs 2031), *Ancient Seals of Haryana*, Jhajjar.

Sarma, I.K. (1982), *The Development of Early Saiva Art and Architecture (with special reference to Andhra Pradesh)*, Delhi.

Sashtry, H.K. (1986), *South Indian Images of Gods and Goddesses* (reprint), New Delhi.

Schrader, Otto E. (1916), *Introduction to the Pañcarātra and the Ahirbudhnya Saṃhitā*, Madras.

Sethi, S.M. (2002), *A Catalogue of Stone Sculptures in the Museums of Himachal Pradesh*, Shimla.

Shah, C.J. (1932), *Jainism in Northern India*, Bombay.

Shah, U.P. (1955), *Studies in Jaina Art*, Banaras.

Shah, Umakant P. (1987), *Jaina-Rūpa-Maṇḍana*, Vol. I, New Delhi.

Sharma, Dasharatha (Gen. Ed.) (1966), *Rajasthan Through the Ages*, Vol. I, Bikaner.

——. (1975), *Early Chauhān Dynasties*, 2nd revised edition, Delhi.

Sharma, G.B. and Kumar, Manmohan (1986), *Coins, Seals and Sealings from Sanghol*, Chandigarh.

Shrimali, Govind Lal (2000), *Rājasthāna ke Abhilekha* (Hindi), 2 Parts, Jodhpur.

Shukla, D.N. (1958), *Bhāratīya Vāstuśāstra* (*Pratimā Vijñāna*), Vol. IV, Gorakhpur.

Siddhantashastree, R.K. (1975), *Śaivism Through the Ages*, Delhi.

Singh, Chandramani (Ed.) (2009), Museums of Rajasthan, Jawahar Kala Kendra, and Department of Archaeology and Museums, Rajasthan, Jaipur in association with Mapin Publishing.

Singh, Jai Prakash and Ahmad, Nisar (Eds.) (1977), *Seminar Papers on Tribal Coins of Ancient India (C.200 BC to 400 AD)*, Varanasi.

Singh, S.B. (1977), *Brahmanical Icons in Northern India*, New Delhi.

Sinha, Kanchan (1979), *Kārttikeya in Indian Art & Literature*, Delhi.

Sircar, D.C. (1957), *Inscriptions of Aśoka*, Publication Division, Delhi.

——. (1965), *Select Inscriptions*, Vol. I, Calcutta.

——. (1968), *Studies in Indian Coins*, Delhi.

——. (1971), *Studies in the Religious Life of Ancient and Medieval India*, Delhi.

Sivaramamurti, C. (1975), *Naṭarāja in Art, Thought and Literature*, New Delhi.

Smith, H. Daniel (1975 & 1980), *A Descriptive Bibliography of the Pāñcharātrāgama*, 2 Vols., GOS Nos. 25 and 168 respectively, Baroda.

Smith, Vincent A. (1901), *Jaina Stupa of Mathura*, Allahabad.

——. (1906), *Coins of Ancient India: Catalogue of the Coins in the Indian Museum Calcutta*, Vol. I, Oxford (reprint, Delhi-Varanasi, 1972).

Srivastava, A.L. (2004), *Umā-Maheśvara: An Iconographic Study of the Divine Couple*, Kasganj (U.P.).

Srivastava, Sanjeev P. and Srivastava, R.P. (2001), *Studies in Punjab Sculpture*, A.P.H. Publishing Corporation, New Delhi.

Srivastava, V.C. (1971), *Sun-Worship in Ancient India*, Delhi.

Srivastava, V.S (1960-61), *Catalogue & Guide to Ganga Golden Jubilee Museum, Bikaner*, Jaipur.

Stein, M.A. (1937), *Archaeological Reconnaissances in North-Western India and South-Eastern Iran*, London.

Tarn, W.W. (1951), *The Greeks in Bactria and India*, Cambridge.

Thaplyal, K.K. (1971), *Studies in Ancient Indian Seals*, Lucknow.

Tiwari, M.N.P. (1981), *Jaina Pratimā-vijñāna* (Hindi), Varanasi.

Trivedi, R.D. (1981), *Iconography of Pārvatī*, Delhi.

Vaidya, C.V. (1921-26), *History of Medieval Hindu India*, 3 volumes, Pune.

Vaidya, P.L. (Ed) (1959), *Divyāvadāna*, Mithila Institute, Darbhanga.

Vogel, J.Ph. (1910), *Catalogue of the Archaeological Museum of Mathura*, Allahabad.

——. (1930), *La Sculptre de Mathura*, Paris and Bruxelles.

Vyas, R.T. (Chief Editor) (1995), *Śilpasaṃvit; Consciousness Manifest – Studies in Jaina Art and Iconography and Allied Subjects in Honour of Dr. U.P. Shah*, Oriental Institute, Vadodara – Abhinav Publications, New Delhi.

Watters, Thomas (1961), *On Yuan Chwang's Travels in India*, First Indian Edition, Delhi.

Westropp and Wake, C.S. (1979), *Symbol Worship: Influence of the Phallic Ideas in the Religions of Antiquity*, New Delhi.

Whitehead, R.B. (1914), *Catalogue of Coins in the Punjab Museum, Lahore*, Vol. I, Oxford.

## ARTICLES

Agrawal, Ashvini (March 1993), "Jaina Bronzes at Ropar", *Newsletter, INTACH (Chandigarh Pinjore Kalka Regional Chapter*, pp. 24-28.

Agrawala, R.C. (1955), "Dramma in Ancient Indian Epigraphs and Literature", *JNSI*, XVII (2), pp. 64-82.

——. (1955), "Some Sculptures of Durga Mahishasuramardini from Rajasthan", *Brahma Vidya*, New Series, Adyar, Vol.19, Nos. 1-2, pp. 37-46.

——. (1955-56), "A Terracotta plaque of Mahishamardini from Nagar", *Lalit Kala*, Nos. 1-2, p. 73.

——. (March, 1962), Krishna-Balarāma as Attendant Figures", *The Indian Historical Quarterly*, Calcutta, Vol. 38, No. 1, pp. 86-87.

——. (1964), "Khajuraho of Rajasthan: The Temple of Ambikā at Jagat", *Artibus Asiae*, X, pp. 43-65 and plates.

——. (1967), "A Rare Bronze of Skanda Kumāra from the Punjab Hills", *Vishveshvaranand Indological Journal*, Hoshiarpur, Vol. V, pp. 206-08.

——. (Dec. 1969), "Goddess Shaṣṭhī in Mathura Sculpture", *Bulletin of Museums & Archaeology in U.P.*, Lucknow, No. 4, pp.1-6.

——. (1969), "Śuṅga Pillars from Amin, near Kurukshetra", *Lalit Kalā*, No. 14, pp. 50-52.

——. (1975), "The Goddess Mahisasuramardini in Early Indian Art", *Artibus Asiae*, Vol. XXI, no. 2, pp. 124-27, Figs. 1-2.

——. (1989), "Mahisamardini Plaque in the Gurukul Museum at Jhajjar, Haryana" in *Ajaya-Śrī: Recent Studies in Indology (Prof. Ajay Mitra Shastri Felicitation Volume)*, Vol. II, Delhi, pp. 397-98, Pl. 52.

Agrawala, V.S. (1947-48), "Terracotta Figurines of Ahichchhatrā, District Bareilly, U.P.", *Ancient India*, Bulletin of the Archaeological Survey of India, New Delhi, No. 4, pp. 104-79.

——. (1936), "Mathura Terracottas", *The Journal of the United Provinces Historical Society*, Lucknow, Vol. IX, Part II.

——. (1949), "A Catalogue of the Brahmanical Images in Mathura Art", *Ibid.*, Vol. XXII.

——. (1951-52), "A New Yakshī Image from Mehrauli", *Ibid.*, Vols. XXIV-XXV, pp. 191-92 and plate (Reprinted in V.S. Agrawala, *Studies in Indian Art*, Varanasi, 1965, pp. 102-03).

——. (1964), "The Devī-Māhātmya", *Journal of Indian History*, Vol. 43, No. 3, pp. 823-32.

Ahuja, Naman P. (September 2002), "Moulded Terracottas from the Indo-Gangetic Divide with Special Reference to Sugh" in P. Pal (ed.), *Indian Terracotta Sculpture – The Early Period, Marg*, Vol. 54, no. 1.

Asthana, Shashi (1985), "The Kushāṇa Art of Mathura", in S.P. Gupta (ed.), pp. 33-44.

——. (1990), "The Kushana Art of Sanghol", *Lalit Kala*, Vol. 24, pp. 9-13.

Banerjee, P. (1970), "Hindu Deities in Central Asia", in *India's Contribution to World Thought and Culture*, Madras, pp. 281-88.

Banerjee, R. (1987), "The Mahaummaga Jataka in Kushan Sculpture from Sanghol", *Roopa-Lekha*, Vol. LIX, pp. 90-92.

Banerji, R.D. (1909-10), "Three Sculptures in the Lucknow Museum", *ARASI, 1909-10*, pp. 147-48, Pl. LIV, Figs. C, D, and E.

Bautze-Picron, Claudine (2001), "Between Śākyamuni and Vairocana: Mārīcī, Goddess of Light and Victory", *Silk Road Art and Archaeology*, Kamakura, Vol. 7, pp. 263-310.

Bopearachchi, Osmund (1989), "Was Sagala Menander's Capital?", *South Asian Archaeology 1989*, Monographs in World Archaeology, No. 14 (edited by Catherine Jarrige), Paris, pp. 327-37.

——. (1990), "King Milinda's conversion to Buddhism, fact or fiction?" *Ancient Ceylon, Journal of the Archaeological Survey Department of Sri Lanka*, No. 7, pp. 1-15.

——. (March 2005), "Recent Archaeological Discoveries from Afghanistan and Pakistan", *Bulletin of Miho Museum*, Vol. V, pp. 19-30.

——. (1997), "Some Observations on the Chronology of the Early Kushans", Des Indo-Grecs aux Sassanides: donnees pour l'histoire et la geographie historique, *Res Orientales*, Vol. XVII, pp. 41-56.

Chandra, Moti (1954), "Presidential Address", *Journal of the Numismatic Society of India*, XVI.

Chatterjee, B. (1970), "Antiquity of the Concept of Lakṣmī", in *Foreigners in Ancient India and Lakṣmī and Sarasvatī in Art and Literature* (Ed. D.C. Sircar), Calcutta, pp. 152-57.

Chaturvedi, S.N. (1984-85), "The Vaikuṇṭha Images and the Khajuraho Inscription of Yaśovarmmadeva", *Journal of the Indian Society of Oriental Art*, New Series, Calcutta, Vol. XIV, pp. 47ff.

De, Gourishankar (1981), "The Earliest Mahishamardini Image of India", paper presented at the 42nd Annual Session of the Indian History Congress, Bodh Gaya.

Deva, K. (1968), "Iconography of Pārvatī as Tapasvinī", *Bharati*, Varanasi, N.S., No. 1.

Dhavalikar, M.K. (1970), "Gaṇeśa Beyond the Indian Frontiers", in *India's Contribution to World Thought and Culture*, Madras, pp. 1-16.

Diskalkar, D.B. (Jan. 1932), "Some Brahmanical Sculptures in the Mathura Museum", *Journal of the U.P. Historical Society*, Lucknow, Vol. V, Part-I.

Fabri, Charles (March 1957), "Archaeology in the Punjab", *Marg*, X (2).

Goetz, H. (1960), "Sūrya as the Supreme Godhead", in *Professor P.K. Gode Commemoration Volume*, Poona.

Handa, Devendra (Dec. 1978), "Archaeological Remains from Sunam", *Panjab University, Research Bulletin (Arts)*, XVIII (2), pp. 1-30 and figs.

——. (April-October, 1981), "Sculptures from Punjab", *Punjab University, Research Bulletin (Arts)*, Chandigarh, Vol. XII, Nos. 1-2, pp. 67-76 & Figs. 1-22.

——. (January 1982), "Pokaraṇa ke kuchh Aprakāśita Abhilekha", *Maru-Bhāratī*, Pilani, Year 29, No. 4, pp. 33-37.

——. (March 1983), "Medieval Brahmanical Stone Sculpture from Punjab", *Roopa-Lekha*, Vol. LIV, Nos. 1-2, pp. 20-32, Figs. 1-18.

——. (1984-85), "Two Vishṇu Sculptures from Janer", *The Researcher*, Jaipur, Vols. XIV-XV, pp. 51-53 and plates.

——. (June-Sept. 1989), "A Sarvatobhadrika Pratima from Punjab", *Arhat Vacana*, Indore, Year 1, Nos. 3-4, pp. 55-56 & plate.

——. (1992), "Anna's Northern Expedition", in D.W. Macdowal, Savita Sharma and Sanjay Garg (Eds.), *Indian Numismatics, History, Art & Culture: Essays in Honour of Dr. Parameshwari Lal Gupta*, 2 vols., Delhi, II, pp. 297-99.

——. (1996), "Kada Coins from Sugh", *Numismatic Digest*, Vol. 20, pp. 25-32.

——. (Oct. – Dec. 2007), "A Terracotta Seal from Ahrwan (District Palwal, Haryana)", *Indian Coin Society Newsletter*, No. 45, pp. 107-109.

Hultzsch, E. (1925), "Delhi-Topra Pillar Edicts", *Corpus Inscriptionum Indicarum*, Vol. I, London, pp. 119-37.

Huntington, Ronald M. (Jan. 1964), "Avatāras and Yugas: An Essay in Puranic Cosmology", *Purāṇam*, Vol. VI, No. 1, pp. 33-37.

Jain, Mul Raj (1946), "A Jain Pilgrimage to Nagarkot in Saṃ. 1484", *Proceedings and Transactions of All India Oriental Conference*, Thirteenth Session, Nagpur, pp. 398-403.

Joshi, M.C. and Margabandhu, C. (1976-77), "Some Terracottas from Excavations at Mathura – A Study", *Journal of the Indian Society of Oriental Art*, No. 8, pp. 16-32.

Joshi, N.P. (1989), "Sasthi in Literature and Art", in Devendra Handa (ed.), *Ajaya-Śrī: Recent Studies in Indology (Prof. Ajay Mitra Shastri Felicitation Volume)*, Delhi, Vol. 2, pp. 391-95.

Kielhorn, F. (1890), "Delhi Siwalik Pillar Inscription of Vīsaladeva, the Vikrama Year 1220", *Indian Antiquary*, XIX, pp. 210-19, Third Inscription.

Krishna, Brajesh (1983), "The Development of Vaishnavism in Ancient Punjab", *Proceedings, Punjab History Conference, 17th Session*, Patiala, pp. 48ff.

Lalman (October 1989), "Sculptural Remains from Burail (Chandigarh)", *Panjab University Research Bulletin (Arts)*, Vol. XX, No. 2, pp. 177-79, Figs. 1-5.

Kumar, Manmohan (1981), "Some Brahmanical Sculptures From Dholbaha", *Roopa-Lekha*, Vol. L, pp. 49-51.

Marshall, John (1914-15), "Excavations at Taxila", *ARASI*, pp. 1-35.

Meister, Michael W. (2009), "Mapping Masrur's Iconography", in Gerd J.R. Mevissen and Arundhati Banerji (eds.), *Prajñādhara: Essays on Asian Art History, Epigraphy and Culture in Honour of Gouriswar Bhattacharya*, Vol. 1, New Delhi, pp. 89-94 & Pls.

Mishra, P.K. (1999), "A Unique Sealing from Ropar", in Devendra Handa (Ed.), *Oriental Numismatic Studies*, Vol. 2, New Delhi, pp. 51-52, Pls. IV-V.

Mitra, Debala (1975), "Vishṇu Chaturmūrti Images in Hari Rai Temple at Chamba", in *Arts of Himachal Pradesh* (Ed. V.C. Ohri), State Museum, Simla, pp. 2-3.

Mitterwallner, Gritli Von, "The Kusana Type of the Goddess Mahisasuramardini as Compared to the Gupta and Medieval Types", in *German Scholars on India*, Vol. II.

Mukherjee, B.N. (1983), "Foreign Elements in Iconography of Mahishasuramardini – The War Goddess of India", *Zeitschrift der Deutschen Morgenlandischen Gesellschaft*, Supplement VI, Vom. 21, Bis 25, Marz 1983.

Narain, A.K. (1973), "The Two Hindu Divinities on the Coins of Agathocles from Ai-Khanum", *Journal of the Numismatic Society of India*, Vol. XXXV, pp. 73-77, Pl. VII.

Nath, Amarendra (1974-75), "Gaṇeśa in Central Asian Art: An identification", *Journal of the Indian Society of Oriental Art*, New Series, Calcutta, Vol. VI, pp. 1-4.

Pathak, V.S. (1959), "Vaikuṇṭha kā Vikāsa", in *Rāshṭrakavi Maithilīśaraṇa Gupta Abhinandana Grantha*, Calcutta, pp. 532ff.

——. (1960), "Vaikuṇṭha at Khajuraho and Kāśmīrāgama School", *Journal of the Madhya Pradesh Itihāsa Parishad*, Bhopal, No. 2, pp. 9ff.

Pereira, Jose (1955), "The Naṭarāja Theme, a new interpretation", *Journal of the Royal Asiatic Society of Bombay*, vol. XXX (1), pp. 71-86.

Prakash, Buddha (1970), "Kashmir and Haryana in Eleventh Century", *Journal of Haryana Studies*, Kurukshetra, Vol. II, pp. 13-17.

Ram, Sadhu (March, 1977), "Two Unpublished Sculptures: Hari Hara and Narasiṃha", *Vishveshvaranand Indological Journal*, Hoshiarpur, Vol. XV, Part I, pp. 123-24, Pl. I.

Rhys Davids, T.W. (1881), "Mahā-parinibbāna-Suttanta", in *Buddhist Sūtras*, Oxford.

Sen Gupta, R. (1960), "The Panels of Kalyāṇasundaramūrti at Ellora", *Lalit Kala*, No. 7.

Seshadri, M. (1963), "Mahishasuramardini", *Half-Yearly Journal of the Mysore University*, Mysore, Section A - Art, Vol. XXII, no. 2, pp. 1-28 & Pls. 1-43.

Shah, Umakant P. (June 1987), "Beginnings of Jaina Iconography", *Bulletin of Museums & Archaeology in U.P.*, Lucknow, No. 9, pp. 8-9 & pp. 41-46, Fig. 38.

——. (1995-96), "Some Interesting Images of Pārśvanātha", *Indologica Taurinensia*, Vol. XXI-XXII, Torino (Italy), pp. 285-90, Figs. 1-18.

Sharma, B.N. (Jan. 1971), "Puranic Message of Religious Tolerance and its Limitations", *Purāṇa*, Varanasi, Vol. XIII, No. 1, pp. 1ff.

Sharma, G.B. (-), "A Summary of Archaeological Excavations in Punjab", *Archaeology and Sculpture Exhibition*, Chandigarh, no date.

Sharma, R.C. (1993), "Interaction Between Mathura and Gandhara", *National Museum Bulletin*, Nos. 7-8, pp. 7-17.

Sharma, Y.D. (1953), "Exploration of Historical Sites", in *Ancient India*, Bulletin of the Archaeological Survey of India, No. 9, Special Jubilee Number, p. 123, Pl. XLVIII B.

——. (April 1955-March 1956), "Past Pattern in Living as Unfolded by Excavation at Ropar", *Lalit Kala*, Nos. 1-2, pp. 122ff.

——. (1961), "Remains of Early Historical Cities", in *Archaeological Remains: Monuments and Museums*, Part I, Archaeological Survey of India, New Delhi, p. 48, Pl. XVI B.

Shastri, Ajay Mitra (1964), "Herakles in Front of the Infantry of Porus", *Journal of Indian History*, Vol. XLII, pp. 119-26.

——. (1977), "Symbols on Tribal Coins: An Interpretative Study", in *Seminar Papers on the Tribal Coins of Ancient India (C.200 BC to 400 AD)*, Eds. Jai Prakash Singh & Nisar Ahmad, Varanasi.

Shukla, S.P. (1993), "Sanghol: Kushāṇa Buddhist Stupa and Ṣculptures" in *Buddhist Art and Thought* (edited by Kewal Krishan Mittal and Ashvini Agrawal), New Delhi, pp. 131-36.

——. (1993), "Kāmuka Female Figures in the Kushana Art and their Bearing on the Buddhist Ideology", *National Museum Bulletin*, New Delhi, Nos. 7 & 8, pp. 19-28.

Sivaramamurti, C. (1950), "Geographical and Chronological Factors in Indian Iconography", *Ancient India*, No. 6, pp. 21-63.

Soundara Rajan, K.V. (March 1963), "A Devī Cult Nucleus at Jagat, Rajasthan", *Vishveshvaranand Indological Journal*, Hoshiarpur, Vol. I, Part 1, pp. 136-37.

Talwar, S.S. (-), *A Glimpse of Punjab Archaeology at Sanghol & Dholbaha*, Souvenir: Punjab History Conference (7th Session), Punjabi University, Patiala (no date).

Viennot, Odette (1956), "The Goddess Mahishasuramardini in Kushana Art", *Artibus Asiae*, Vol. XIX, nos. 3-4, pp. 368-73, Fig. 1.

## JOURNALS

*Ancient Ceylon*, Journal of the Archaeological Survey Department of Sri Lanka
*Ancient India*, Bulletin of the Archaeological Survey of India, New Delhi
*Annual Report of the Archaeological Survey of India*
*Artibus Asiae*, Paris
*Bhāratī*, Varanasi
*Brahma Vidya*, New Series, Adyar
*Bulletin of Miho Museum*
*Bulletin of Museums & Archaeology in U.P.*, Lucknow
*Epigraphia Indica*
*Indian Antiquary*
*Indian Historical Quarterly*, Calcutta
*Indologica Taurinensia*, Torino (Italy)
*Journal of Indian History*
*Journal of the Indian Society of Oriental Art*, New Series, Calcutta
*Journal of the Madhya Pradesh Itihāsa Parishad*, Bhopal
*Journal of the Mysore University*, Mysore
*Journal of the Numismatic Society of India*
*Journal of the Oriental Institute*, Baroda (now Vadodara)
*Journal of the United Provinces Historical Society*, Lucknow
*Journal of the Royal Asiatic Society of Bombay*
*Lalit Kala*
*Marg*
*National Museum Bulletin*
*Numismatic Digest*
*Panjab University Research Bulletin* (*Arts*), Chandigarh
*Purāṇa*
*Researcher*, Jaipur
*Roopa-Lekha*
*Silk Road Art and Archaeology*, Kamakura
*South Asian Archaeology*
*Times of Chandigarh*
*Tribune*, Chandigarh
*Vishveshvaranand Indological Journal*, Hoshiarpur
*Zeitschrift der Deutschen Morgenlandischen Gesellschaft*

# Index

[The following abbreviations have been used: *a* – author; *b* – book or ancient text; *c* – city, town; *d* – deity; *dyn* – dynasty; *i* – image; *jy* – Jaina yaksha/yakshī; *jt* – Jaina Tīrthaṅkara; *k* – king, chief, ruler; *p* – place-name; *q* – queen; *r* – river or rivulet. Important references have been underlined.]